A GUIDE BOOK OF

SHOTGUN VALUES

© 2015 Whitman Publishing, LLC
3101 Clairmont Road • Suite G • Atlanta, GA 30329

ISBN: 0794842615   EAN: 9780794842611
Printed in the United States of America.

Editors' Letter v
Benefits of Red Book of Rifle Values vi
Our Consumer Friendly Pricing Model vii
Our Firearm Condition Grading Scale viii
Safety, Storage, and Cleaning xvi
Disclaimer xvi
Arrieta & Cia 1
AyA (Aquirre y Aranzabal) 2
Baikal. 3
Baker Gun & Forging. 5
Benelli USA 7
Beretta USA 24
Bernardelli, Vincenzo 57
Breda Meccanica Bresciana 63
Browning Arms Company. 64
Century International Arms, Inc.. 87
Charles Daly. 88
Chiappa Firearms. 93
Churchill, E.J. 97
Connecticut Shotgun Manufacturing Company 100
CZ-USA 100
David McKay Brown Ltd. 110
Escort Shotguns. 111
Fabarm USA, Inc.. 115
Fausti USA, Inc.. 117
FNH USA 122
Franchi. 124
Gamba, Renato 134
Garbi, Armas 135
Grulla Armas, S.L. 137
Guerini, Caesar 140
H&R 1871, LLC. 147
Holland & Holland 152
Huglu. 154
Ithaca Gun Company. 160
Iver Johnson Arms, Inc. 168
Kel-Tec CNC Industries, Inc. 170
Krieghoff International, Inc.. 171
Lanber Armas. 173
Lebeau-Courally 175
LeFever. 176
Marocchi. 177
Mossberg, O.F. & Sons, Inc. 179
New England Firearms. 197
Noble Manufacturing Company 199
Omega Firearms Company 204
Parker Brothers 206
Parker-Hale 209
Parker Reproductions 210
Pedersen Custom Guns 211
Perazzi 214
Remington Arms Company, LLC. 225
Rizzini USA 250
Rock Island Armory (Armscor USA). 254
Rossi USA 254
Sauer & Sohn, J.P. 256
Savage Arms. 258
SKB Arms Company 260
Smith, L.C.. 263
Squires Bingham Company, Inc. 268
Stevens Arms Company, J. 270
Stoeger Industries. 273
Sturm, Ruger & Company 279
Thompson/Center Arms 279
TriStar Sporting Arms, Ltd. 280
Ugartechea, Armas 286
Weatherby, Inc. 289
Webley & Scott, USA 299
Winchester Repeating Arms. 302
Zbrojovka Brno 321
Zoli International 322
Appendix A: Manufacturers 325
Appendix B: Organizations 326
Bibliography and Works Referenced 328
Photography Credits 329

CONTENTS

John Moses Browning—the Father of Modern Firearms.

EDITORS' LETTER

Dear Reader,

One of the greatest liberties afforded Americans is the right to bear arms. Not only are firearms great fun to own and shoot for hunting or for sport, but they are also wise investments, as they tend to hold and even increase in value. More importantly, a firearm can mean the difference between life and death in dangerous situations. Though firearms can be inherently dangerous, with training and responsible handling, any risk is vastly diminished. That risk is far overshadowed by the fact that in circumstances that require self-defense, firearms ensure that anyone, regardless of physical abilities, can effectively defend himself or herself against any assailant. Thus, there is great truth in the famous saying, "God made man, but Samuel Colt made them equal."

Our right as Americans to own firearms is outlined in the Second Amendment of the Constitution. It is here that our forefathers guaranteed that the government could never impose upon an individual's right to defend themselves and their loved ones. The founders understood that a properly functioning government is solely empowered by its people, as opposed to a privileged few who control all weapons and supplies. Personal firearm ownership is essential to the framework of our nation, as it grants us the ability to discourage and deter political tyranny.

While U.S. citizens enjoy their Second Amendment rights, we, the editors of this book, highly encourage the exercise of extreme caution before purchasing, carrying, and utilizing a firearm. Owning a firearm is a great responsibility. It is our hope that upon reviewing this book and purchasing a firearm, all gun owners would operate their weapons with care, with discretion, and within the confines of the law. Presently, we are faced with heated political debate over the issue of firearms. While one group is heavily in favor of relaxing gun laws, the other is just as eager to ban firearms altogether. Because of these shifting political tides, we encourage those in favor of gun rights to handle their weapons with the utmost care and responsibility, so as not to give credence to anti-gun rhetoric.

We hope this book paints a clear picture of the current market and equips readers with the ability to make an informed decision about which firearm best suits their needs. Furthermore, we would like to thank our readers and encourage them to exercise one of the most cherished rights U.S. citizens are privileged to enjoy.

-THE EDITORS

THE BENEFITS OF THE RED BOOK OF SHOTGUN VALUES

In creating the Red Book of Shotgun Values, we, the editors and contributors, sought to compile a book that best reflects the current values of popular shotguns in today's market. We hope that you, the prospective shotgun buyer, can make a well-informed purchase after consulting this book. The editors have no allegiance to any particular company and have remained true to the market when estimating the values of each gun. Many enthusiasts find objectivity difficult when assessing the values of their most beloved firearms, but we've done our best to remain unbiased and to use actual historical sales to guide us as to pricing. We've evaluated the sales history of each model represented in this guide to arrive at real-life estimates, not hypotheticals or ideals. To create an accurate book, we've adhered to the economic principle that a product is worth what a buyer is willing to pay, not what a given expert thinks should be paid.

Along with providing accurate price estimates, we hope this book gives readers an accurate look into the noteworthy specifications of a firearm, and other information of value. While a firearm's price is certainly important, its specifications determine which particular model would suit a gun owner's individual needs. Differences among shooters ranging from the extent of firearm experience to a shooter's height or physical strength can significantly influence which gun best meets that shooter's needs. A gun's specs—ranging from its caliber/gauge options, barrel length, and capacity—often determine whether or not it would be optimal for a particular buyer. That's why we've included additional specifications of each gun to help educate our readers to make good purchase decisions.

In short, we want you to have a clear picture of the firearm you wish to buy before trying to purchase it through a gun shop, auction house, or individual seller. We want readers to walk away from a purchase feeling secure they've reached a fair deal. To aid our readers in the buying process, in this—the first—edition of The Red Book: A Guide Book of Shotgun Values, we utilize our Redbook Code™. The Redbook Code is a universal system of organizing all firearms on the secondary market. Many firearms being bought and sold currently pre-date the UPC system that now allows buyers to differentiate between manufacturers and models. Even newer models that do have UPC numbers are more easily organized with our coding system once they arrive on the secondary market, when UPC numbers become irrelevant.

SHOTGUN SPECIFICATIONS

The shotguns we've featured include a wide range of popular and collectible models. We wanted to provide readers with a broad spectrum of the shotgun market. Among the thousands of models available today, we could not include every make and model, but rather we chose specific models based on current market trends. The specifications given for each gun will help the reader choose wisely for his or her purposes. Our hope is to inform readers so they can feel comfortable and confident about purchasing the right firearm for the right price.

When creating and editing this book, we diligently mined several sources to ensure we included accurate specifications for each model. We consulted manufacturers' records for much of the information as well as a host of online retailers, brick-and-mortar gun shops, auction houses, gun critics and experts, and our panel of contributors. Providing accurate specifications for each model was of the utmost importance to us so that we could provide readers with a clear understanding of any gun they consider for purchase. Given the wide array of shotguns covered in this book, information for some models remains somewhat obscure or vague. We both welcome and appreciate your feedback if you find an error or oversight within this text. Please help us improve by emailing your comments to contact@RedBookofGuns.com.

HOW WE ESTIMATED VALUES

When creating and editing this book, we consulted many sources to construct our value estimates. We've listed many of these resources in the bibliography. While it would be easy to price a firearm based on our own beliefs about its value, we've refused to ignore the current market and estimated the value of each gun based on actual recent sales. Given the shifting tastes within the gun world, estimates based on recent sales provide the best view of how much one could expect to pay for a particular model.

OUR CONSUMER-FRIENDLY PRICING MODEL

We established our pricing model based on market research, considering market conditions like current gun shop prices, online pricing, and auction sale prices. These values reflect our best efforts to establish average pricing for firearms in the current economy. Bear in mind, however, that the firearms market is volatile, given our country's political climate and changes within the landscape of the firearms industry. Prices are thus subject to change as laws, regulations, media coverage, and manufacturing circumstances influence market values. Our pricing reflects U.S. values only. Pricing does not include any VAT if importing from foreign companies.

Our pricing model provides values for multiple buying and selling scenarios. We include prices for the following:

Dealer-to-Consumer (D2C)

Consumer-to-Consumer (C2C)

Consumer-to-Dealer (Trade-In)

Last Manufacturer's Price (LMP)

Our Dealer-to-Consumer prices will naturally tend to be higher than ones associated with private sales, as "brick and mortar" gun shops must compensate for overhead expenses. Our Consumer-to-Consumer prices reflect fair prices one could typically expect to pay from an individual either locally or from an online auction house like gunbroker.com or rockislandauction.com. Our Trade-In values indicate fair prices that a local gun shop may offer to pay for your firearm. Keep in mind that pricing for a firearm will typically be lower for trade-in than for private sales, as gun dealers who receive trades must factor in a margin for profit that doesn't allow them to offer full value for a firearm. The lower price a seller receives trading in a gun is often considered to be offset by avoiding the hassle of trying to sell locally or the expense of delivering a weapon to a Federal Firearms Licensed dealer for legal delivery to its purchaser.

VARIABLES

The prices we present typically account for the base model of a specific firearm. Upgrades, add-ons, limited editions, modifications, and/or other accessories may bring higher, or even lower, values. Any uncertainty about any aspect of a particular firearm should be addressed by a local firearms expert. In addition, for highly collectible firearms, we recommend potential buyers consult an expert before purchase, as miniscule variations can drastically alter a firearm's value. Be aware that certain firearms used in military conflicts, ones owned by famous individuals, or ones used in Hollywood films, etc., should have proper documentation or provenance before purchase.

Also, note that you may encounter differences in pricing between states or regions for particular firearms. Certain areas may have a higher demand for particular types of firearms compared to other areas.

Additionally, be aware of a fairly recent market trend triggered by modernizations in manufacturing. Gun manufacturers have utilized mass production of parts more and more as demand for their products has increased. Some individuals believe this trend towards mass production has resulted in lower quality control standards. These lower standards have given rise to a corresponding fear that the finished product is compromised, thereby driving up the prices of firearms that pre-date such extensive use of mass manufacturing for their perceived higher quality and workmanship.

EXACT MODELS

Before buying or selling a weapon, buyers should be certain of the exact make, model, and details of the firearm. Small nuances, such as serial number ranges, manufacturer seals or stamps, etc. may significantly impact a firearm's value. If unsure of these factors, one should consult an expert. In addition, many manufacturers maintain useful information related to specific models that one can obtain by providing a gun's specific serial number. Manufacturers may charge a fee for this documentation, but providing this information to potential buyers will typically increase the firearm's value.

OUR FIREARM CONDITION GRADING SCALE

Aside from fundamental aspects like the manufacturer and the model of a firearm, the grade and condition of a gun drastically influences its value. We developed our grading scale based on NRA firearms grades and other industry standards.

Our grading scale is as follows:

NIB (New in Box)—New from the factory condition. Unused, unfired, includes box and all paperwork and accessories. Must never have been sold before and, if applicable, must have the factory warranty intact.

Mint—Same condition as new, but may have been sold from a dealer. Unused, but may have been handled. Includes box, paperwork, and accessories.

Ex (Excellent)—Lightly used and may have very slight signs of wear around the end of the barrel or on the edges of the receiver. Minimal to no scratches or dings on wood, polymer, or metal. Mechanically perfect working condition. No rust or corrosion. May or may not include box, paperwork, and accessories. Exposed metal and stock will only show 2% to 5% of surface wear.

VG+ (Very Good Plus)—Used with minor scratches or dings in the wood, polymer, or metal. Must have factory original finish but may show some wear. Mechanically perfect working condition. No rust or corrosion. Exposed metal or grip material will show between 10% and 20% of surface wear.

Good—Used with moderate signs of wear and scratches. May contain some replacement parts or may have been refinished. Mechanically safe working condition. Exposed metal and grip material may show up to 45% of surface wear.

Fair—Used with significant signs of wear and moderate scratches or dings on wood, polymer, or metal. Mechanically safe working condition, but may need minor repairs or parts soon. May have slight rust or pitting that does not interfere with its mechanics. Half or more of metal and grip material finish may be gone. In some models, only 20% of original finish may be present.

Poor—Used with heavy signs of wear. May need full restoration. Needs refinishing and parts replacement. Mechanically inoperable working condition and not safe to fire. May still have 10% of original finish remaining in protected areas.

HIGH-WEAR AREAS

Wear is a huge factor in determining a firearm's value. Internally, as the number of shells fired grows, evidence of wear becomes apparent, and that wear devalues the gun. A qualified gunsmith knows how to determine internal wear, but few gun owners are capable of judging this aspect. The average consumer is left with judging external finish wear in order to discern a gun's value. Unblemished, original factory finish degrades by handling, use, degree of care, and maintenance over time. Through normal use, metal, synthetic, and wood surfaces will show evidence of marring. A simple way to grade finish wear on a firearm is to determine the ratio of blemished area to non-blemished area.

Some firearms may contain upgraded or replacement parts. For newer manufactured firearms, this may increase the value. With older, collectible firearms, adding these upgrades or replacement parts may decrease the value.

With shotguns, external wear will vary depending on the type of surface coating or treatment applied to the metal. Some of the modern coatings may hold up to wear better than traditional blue or parkerized finishes. In this case, you will need to focus more on the wear of the internal parts and surfaces. Focus on high wear areas to determine the condition.

See the following pages for examples of high-wear areas:

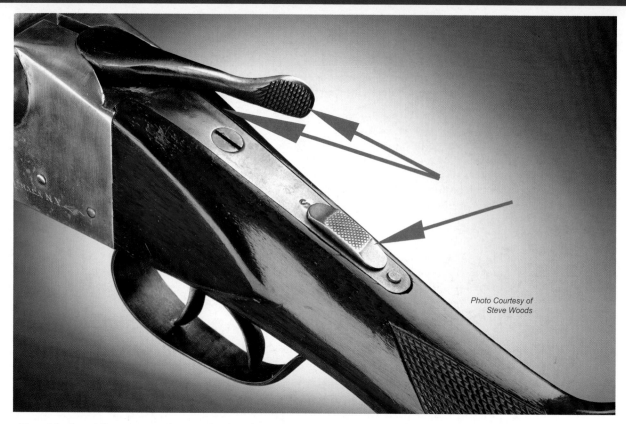

Photo Courtesy of
Steve Woods

For side-by-side, over/under, and other break-action shotguns, check for wear on the top opening lever and under the lever where metal-to-metal contact occurs. Also, look for wear on the safety lever, indicating use.

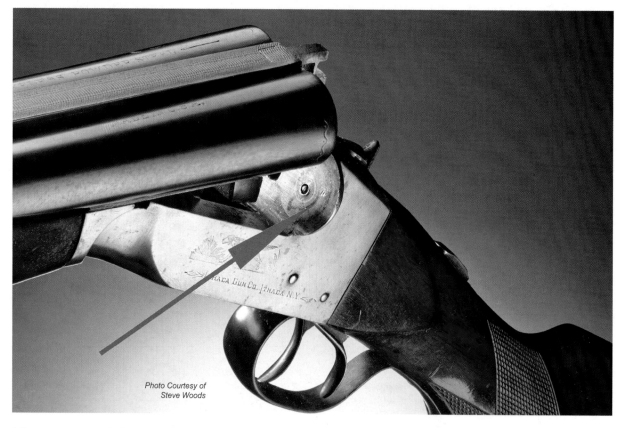

Photo Courtesy of
Steve Woods

The area around the firing pins will typically show wear from shells firing.

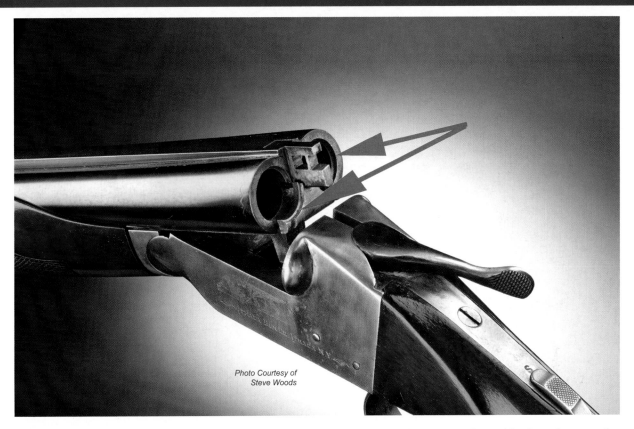

*Photo Courtesy of
Steve Woods*

Check inside the action for wear at the bite points, including the hinge pins, barrel locking lugs, and ejectors/extractors. Look closely around each chamber for wear caused by shells.

*Photo Courtesy of
Steve Woods*

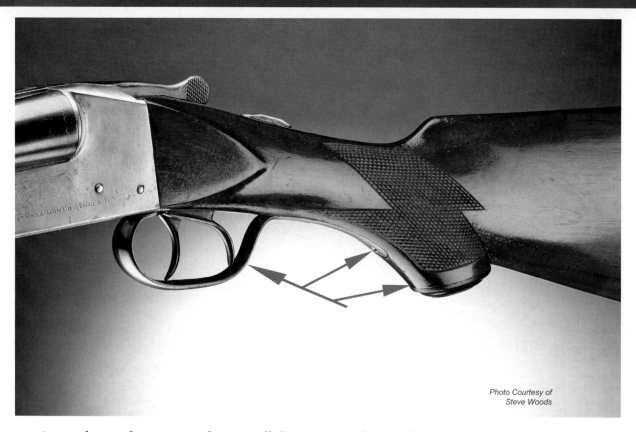

*Photo Courtesy of
Steve Woods*

*Areas where a shooter grips the gun will show increased wear. Check around and under the
pistol grip area and around the trigger guard*

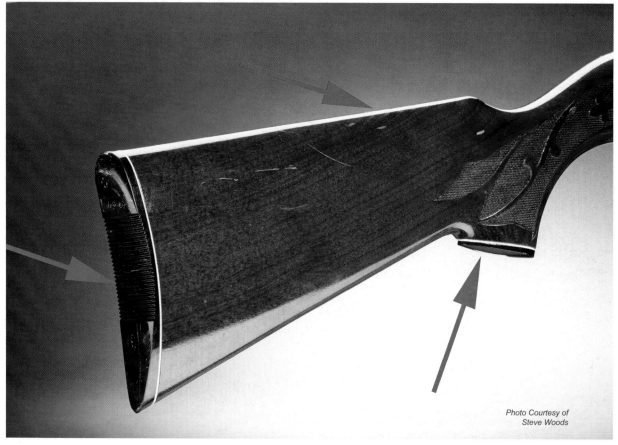

*Photo Courtesy of
Steve Woods*

*High-wear areas include the comb of the stock, the buttplate/buttpad, and the bottom of the
pistol grip.*

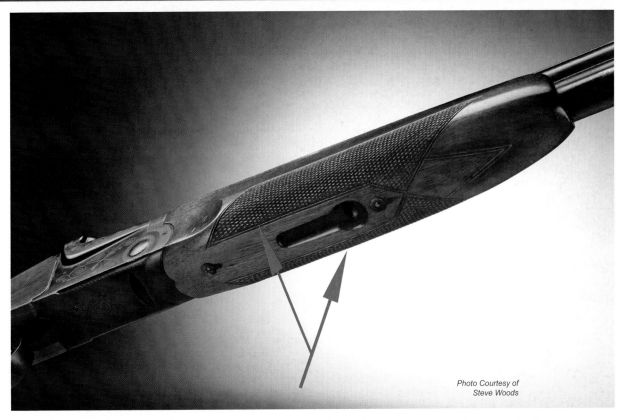

*Photo Courtesy of
Steve Woods*

Wooden forearms may show signs of wear especially in checkered areas. Wear on a high-grade wood stock will dramatically affect the value.

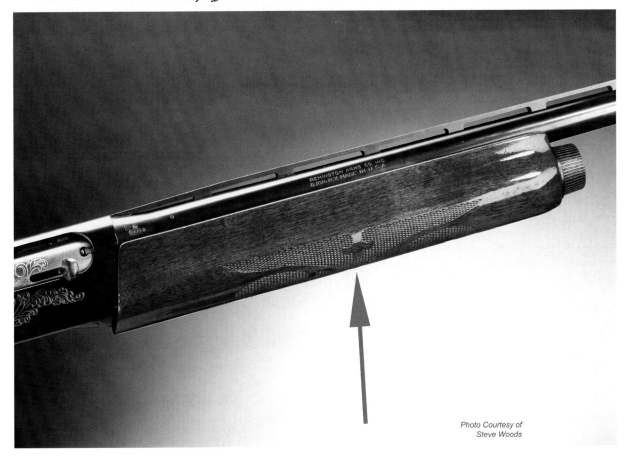

*Photo Courtesy of
Steve Woods*

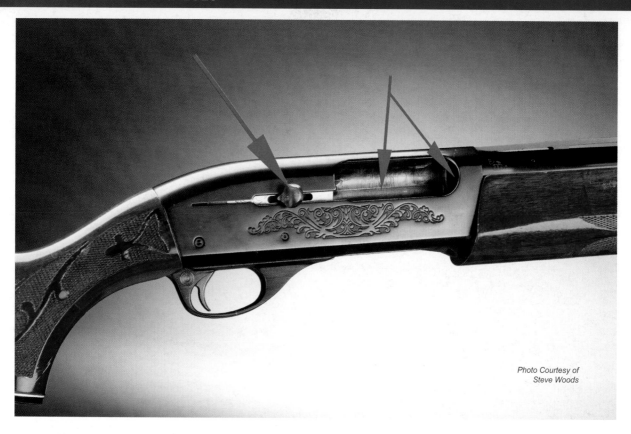

*Photo Courtesy of
Steve Woods*

For semi-automatics, lock the bolt to the rear and check for internal wear inside the receiver and chamber. Also check the bolt face and charging handle.

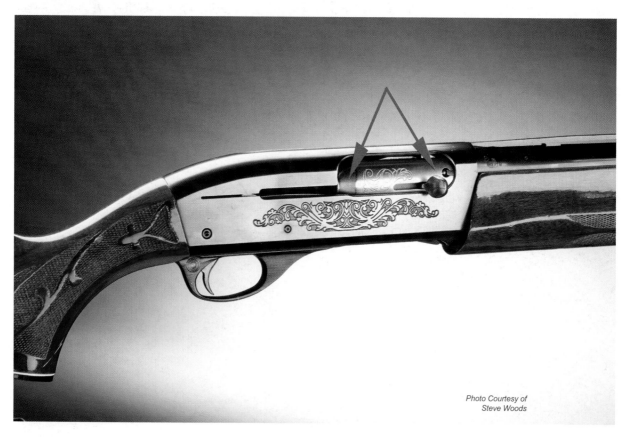

*Photo Courtesy of
Steve Woods*

With the bolt closed, check for wear on the outside of the bolt carrier and around the ejection port.

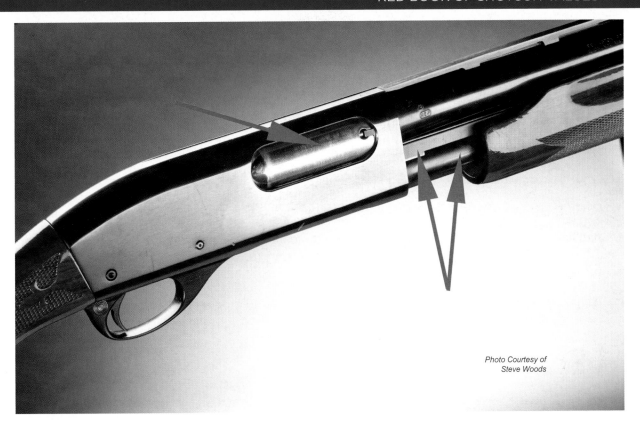

*Photo Courtesy of
Steve Woods*

*For pump-action shotguns, look for wear on the action bars caused by extended use. Also check
along the magazine tube for wear marks.*

*Photo Courtesy of
Steve Woods*

*Check the end of the barrel as this will show wear from shooting as well as wear from attaching
or detaching choke tubes.*

SAFETY

Firearms safety is of the utmost importance. The following safety rules should always be followed:

1. Treat every weapon as if it were loaded.

2. Never point your weapon at anything you don't intend to shoot.

3. Keep your finger straight and off the trigger until you're ready to fire.

4. Keep your weapon on safe until you intend to fire (if applicable).

5. Know your target and what is beyond/behind your target.

First, when handling any firearm, always check to see if it's loaded. To check a firearm, keep the firearm pointed in a safe direction, keep your finger off the trigger, keep the safety on, remove the magazine (if applicable), open the chamber and visually inspect for loaded ammunition.

When using a firearm, make sure to use the proper ammunition for your specific model. Also, make sure the firearm is in operating condition. If there's any uncertainty, consult a professional. Always wear ear and eye protection. Know your local laws and regulations.

STORAGE

When storing a firearm, make sure to keep it in a safe and dry location. Use quality gun safes if possible. Keep all firearms away from small children and anyone who is unfamiliar with proper use and care of them. Many firearms may require dehumidifiers or other humidity absorbing products to keep them from rusting. As the saying goes, "Guns have two enemies—rust and politicians."

CLEANING

Before cleaning, go through the previously mentioned safety and handling procedures to make sure the firearm is unloaded. Any firearm you intend to fire must be properly maintained. All firearms have some type of metal parts that are susceptible to rust or corrosion, so properly clean and lubricate any metal or moving part on the firearm. Any type of dirt, debris, or corrosion on a firearm can cause serious malfunctions and potential harm to the shooter. Always use quality cleaners and lubricants specific to firearms. If soaking a firearm without modern coatings or treatments, never use water based cleaners for extended periods of time, as this can cause rust and corrosion.

Use extreme caution with collectible firearms. Many collectible firearms should NOT be cleaned at all. You may drastically reduce the value of a collectible firearm by cleaning or removing any rust or patina. If you are unsure, consult an expert.

DISCLAIMER

Given the legal restrictions of selling and purchasing firearms, the editors, publishers, writers, and contributors of this book cannot be held responsible for any legal issues a reader may confront while undertaking the commercial, private, or unlawful sale of firearms. We relinquish all responsibility regarding the purchase, sale, safety, and usage of firearms, and we encourage readers to consult their local law enforcement agency or even professional legal counsel before dealing in firearms in any capacity. This book provides value estimates on firearms only and in no way purports to provide legal guidance of any type or for any purpose.

The editors of this book have researched the firearm prices and specifications with great attention to detail, but cannot assume liability for any misinformation within this text. Given the convoluted history and myriad details inherent in the sales of many of these guns, we have tried to ensure the information is as accurate as possible. However, minor discrepancies may exist for which we cannot be held responsible. Also, some figures in this book were rounded or approximated, but these differences are nominal.

Also by 2nd Amendment Media:

RED BOOK OF RIFLE VALUES

RED BOOK OF CARRY GUN VALUES

GRID-DOWN SURVIVAL GUIDE SERIES

CARRY GUN COMPANION

ARMED & SMART

ARMED & SMARTER

LEGALLY ARMED

Arrieta & Cia

Arrieta & Cia was founded by Avelino Arrieta and is still being run by his family four generations later. His grandchildren, Juan Carlos and Asier, have recently reorganized the company. Considered one of Spain's premier gunmakers, Arrieta holds with tradition; every shotgun is hand-made by in-house gunsmiths, many of whom are second-generation employees of the company. Located in the town of Elgoibar, the company is known for its quality craftsmanship and attention to detail. Arrieta firearms are distributed in the U.S. by a handful of companies, but Griffin & Howe is primarily responsible for ones sold here. Collectors treasure the intricate engraving work and high polished wood featured on these firearms, and competition shooters value their renowned accuracy. The company is best known for sidelock action shotguns.

801   REDBOOK CODE: RB-AE-S-ASL801

Chrome-lined chopper-lump Bellota steel barrels in blue finish, level file cut rib, Churchill-style engraving, choice of choke tubes, hand detachable locks (12, 16, and 20 gauge only), slotted lock screws, H&H assisted opening, automatic ejectors, articulated front trigger, and gas escape valves. Custom options (at additional cost) include English concave rib, Churchill rib, semi-pistol grip stock, semi-beavertail for-end, and case-hardened finish.

Production: *current* **Gauge/Bore:** *12 ga., 16 ga., 20 ga., 28 ga., .410*

Action: *SxS*

Barrel Length: any custom length **Wt.:** *N/A*	D2C:	NIB $11,500	Ex $8,750	VG+ $6,325	Good $5,750	
Sights: *bead front*	C2C:	Mint $11,040	Ex $7,950	VG+ $5,750	Good $5,175	Fair $2,645
Capacity: *2*	Trade-In:	Mint $8,170	Ex $6,450	VG+ $4,490	Good $4,025	Poor $1,170

Stock: *straight English stock with checkered butt*

578   REDBOOK CODE: RB-AE-S-ASL578

Chrome-lined chopper-lump Bellota steel barrels in blue finish, level file cut rib, splinter for-end, English-style bouquet and scroll engraving, choice of choke tubes, hand detachable locks (12, 16, and 20 gauge only), H&H assisted opening, automatic ejectors, articulated front trigger, and gas escape valves. Custom options (at additional cost) include English concave rib, Churchill rib, semi-pistol grip stock, and case-hardened or coin finish.

Production: *current* **Gauge/Bore:** *12 ga., 16 ga., 20 ga., 28 ga., .410*

Action: *SxS*

Barrel Length: any custom length **Wt.:** *N/A*	D2C:	NIB $5,449	Ex $4,150	VG+ $3,000	Good $2,725	
Sights: *bead front*	C2C:	Mint $5,240	Ex $3,775	VG+ $2,730	Good $2,455	Fair $1,255
Capacity: *2*	Trade-In:	Mint $3,870	Ex $3,075	VG+ $2,130	Good $1,910	Poor $570

Stock: *straight English stock with checkered butt*

803   REDBOOK CODE: RB-AE-S-ASL803

Chrome-lined chopper-lump Bellota steel barrels in blue finish, Purdey-style rose-and-scroll engraving, level file cut rib, intercepting safety sears, choice of choke tubes, hand detachable locks (12, 16, and 20 gauge only), H&H assisted opening, automatic ejectors, articulated front trigger, and gas escape valves. Custom options (at additional cost) include English concave rib, Churchill rib, semi-pistol grip stock, and case-hardened or coin finish.

Production: *current* **Gauge/Bore:** *12 ga., 16 ga., 20 ga., 28 ga., .410*

Action: *SxS*

Barrel Length: any custom length **Wt.:** *N/A*	D2C:	NIB $8,225	Ex $6,275	VG+ $4,525	Good $4,115	
Sights: *bead front*	C2C:	Mint $7,900	Ex $5,700	VG+ $4,120	Good $3,705	Fair $1,895
Capacity: *2*	Trade-In:	Mint $5,840	Ex $4,625	VG+ $3,210	Good $2,880	Poor $840

Stock: *straight English stock with checkered butt*

ARRIETA

AYA

873 REDBOOK CODE: RB-AE-S-ASL873

Chrome-lined chopper-lump Bellota steel barrels in blue finish,
photo-realistic engraved game scene, level file cut rib, choice of choke tubes, hand detachable locks (12, 16, and
20 gauge only), H&H assisted opening, automatic ejectors, articulated front trigger, and gas
escape valves. Custom options (at additional cost) include English concave rib, Churchill rib, semi-pistol grip stock, and case-hardened or coin finish.

Production: *current* **Gauge/Bore:** *12 ga., 16 ga., 20 ga., 28 ga., .410*					
Action: *SxS*					
Barrel Length: *any custom length* **Wt.:** *N/A*	D2C:	NIB $5,630	Ex $4,300	VG+ $3,100	Good $2,815	
Sights: *bead front*	C2C:	Mint $5,410	Ex $3,900	VG+ $2,820	Good $2,535	Fair $1,295
Capacity: *2*	Trade-In:	Mint $4,000	Ex $3,175	VG+ $2,200	Good $1,975	Poor $570
Stock: *straight English stock with checkered butt*					

(AyA) Aguirre y Aranzabal

The founders of Aguirre y Aranzabal, commonly referred to as AyA, were two gunmakers who lived in the Basque region of Spain, an area known as a haven for gunsmiths. Miguel Aguirre and Nicolas Aranzabal went into business together in 1915 building components for larger, more established companies, but their popularity and reputation for quality propelled them to begin making complete guns in 1938. In the mid-1950s, Andrew and Peter King, two brothers from England, visited Spain and ultimately negotiated with AyA for the company to begin building a series of English range guns. Tapping the British market with the Kings galvanized the company's move to international status in the firearms industry. Using two English guns as patterns, AyA developed the models that would become the company's mainstays: No. 1, No. 2, No. 4, and No. 4 Deluxe. The company's later introduction to the U.S. market came through Sears Roebuck. In the 1980s, AyA merged with about 20 other firearms companies in the Basque region to form Diarm S.A., but the joint venture ultimately failed after only a few years. The AyA name was reintroduced in 1989 when Imanol Aranzabal, a descendant of the Aranzabal founder, bought its remaining stock and set up shop again in Eibar. The reinvented company began with formerly produced models but subsequently added more to production and is now on the rise to achieving its former reknown.

NO. 1 RA   REDBOOK CODE: RB-AY-S-NBR1RA

Chopper-lump barrels, concave rib, rose-and-scroll hand engraving, color-hardened or old silver
finish, forged steel rounded action, double locking mechanism, gas vents, automatic safety, detachable
locks, articulated front trigger, Purdey-style double underlugs. Customizable features include caliber,
barrel length, finish, engraving, wood quality, stock and forend styles, and optional self-opener. Pricing varies with custom options.

Production: *current* **Gauge/Bore:** *12 ga., 16 ga., 20 ga., 28 ga., .410*					
Action: *SxS*					
Barrel Length: 28" **Wt.:** *6.75 lbs.*	D2C:	NIB $11,800	Ex $8,975	VG+ $6,490	Good $5,900	
Sights: *bead front*	C2C:	Mint $11,330	Ex $8,150	VG+ $5,900	Good $5,310	Fair $2,715
Capacity: *2*	Trade-In:	Mint $8,380	Ex $6,625	VG+ $4,610	Good $4,130	Poor $1,200
Stock: *cut-checkered walnut*					

NO. 2   REDBOOK CODE: RB-AY-S-NBRTWO

Chopper-lump steel barrels, concave rib, English scroll engraving, color-hardened or old
silver finish, forged steel standard action, double locking mechanism, gas vents, automatic
safety, hardened steel intercepting safety sears. Customizable features include caliber, barrel
length, finish, engraving, wood quality, stock, forend styles, and self-opening actions. Pricing varies with custom options.

Production: *current* **Gauge/Bore:** *12 ga., 16 ga., 20 ga., 28 ga., .410*					
Action: *SxS*					
Barrel Length: 28" **Wt.:** *6.75 lbs.*	D2C:	NIB $5,330	Ex $4,075	VG+ $2,935	Good $2,665	
Sights: *bead front*	C2C:	Mint $5,120	Ex $3,700	VG+ $2,670	Good $2,400	Fair $1,230
Capacity: *2*	Trade-In:	Mint $3,790	Ex $3,000	VG+ $2,080	Good $1,870	Poor $540
Stock: *standard walnut*					

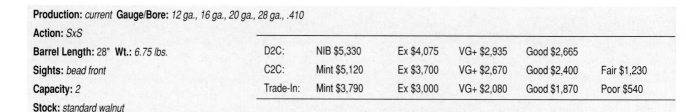

NO. 2 RA REDBOOK CODE: RB-AY-S-NBR2RA

Chopper-lump steel barrels, English scroll engraving, color-hardened or old silver finish, forged steel rounded action, double locking mechanism, gas vents, automatic safety, hardened steel intercepting safety sears, concave rib. Customizable features include caliber, barrel length, finish, engraving, wood quality, stock, forend styles, and self-opening actions. Pricing varies with custom options.

Production: *current* **Gauge/Bore:** *12 ga., 16 ga., 20 ga., 28 ga., .410*
Action: *SxS*
Barrel Length: 28" **Wt.:** *6.75 lbs.*
Sights: *bead front*
Capacity: *2*
Stock: *Grade 2 walnut*

D2C:	NIB $5,700	Ex $4,350	VG+ $3,135	Good $2,850	
C2C:	Mint $5,700	Ex $3,950	VG+ $2,850	Good $2,565	Fair $1,315
Trade-In:	Mint $4,050	Ex $3,200	VG+ $2,230	Good $1,995	Poor $570

Baikal

Baikal was named after a lake in Siberia, although the Russian firearms company was actually founded in Izhevsk. Beginning in 1942 as part of Russia's national defense industry, the company made Tokarev TT pistols. After World War II, the company expanded to include other firearms and now shotguns, rifles, and combination guns are all included in the company's yearly output of 680,000 units per year. The company is known primarily for the IJ-70 model and its variants and the Baikal-442, a sporting model. Products made by Baikal were not imported into the U.S. until 1993 when Russia's export restrictions loosened; since then, they have been imported here at different times by distributors such as U.S. Sporting Goods, Inc., European American Armory Corp., and Big Bear. The company has also marketed guns in the U.S. under the name "Spartan" in partnership with Remington.

MP220 REDBOOK CODE: RB-BI-S-MP220X

Hammerless cowboy action, double triggers, extractors, hammer forged barrels. Plastic butt pad, cast off. Blue finish and 4 screw chokes included with 26" and 28" barrel models. Cylinder choke included with 20" barrel models. 14" length of pull, 1.5" drop at comb, 2" drop at heel.

Production: *current* **Gauge/Bore:** *12 ga., 20 ga.*
Action: *SxS*
Barrel Length: 20", 26", 28" **Wt.:** *6.5 lbs., 7.2 lbs.*
Sights: *bead front*
Capacity: *2*
Stock: *walnut*

D2C:	NIB $360	Ex $275	VG+ $200	Good $180	**LMP:** $382
C2C:	Mint $350	Ex $250	VG+ $180	Good $165	Fair $85
Trade-In:	Mint $260	Ex $225	VG+ $150	Good $130	Poor $60

MP220F REDBOOK CODE: RB-BI-S-MP220F

Formerly known as the IZH43KH from EAA. External hammers, internal hammer block, auto tang safety, walnut stock and forend, steel buttpad, hammer-forged chrome-lined barrels. 4 screw chokes, double trigger, extractor, blue finish, cast off.

Production: *current* **Gauge/Bore:** *12 ga.*
Action: *SxS*
Barrel Length: 20" **Wt.:** *6.5 lbs.*
Sights: *bead front*
Capacity: *2*
Stock: *walnut*

D2C:	NIB $460	Ex $350	VG+ $255	Good $230	**LMP:** $580
C2C:	Mint $450	Ex $325	VG+ $230	Good $210	Fair $110
Trade-In:	Mint $330	Ex $275	VG+ $180	Good $165	Poor $60

MP210   REDBOOK CODE: RB-BI-S-MP210X

Nickel finish, 4 screw chokes (cylinder, improved cylinder, modified, and full) with all calibers but .410, which comes with 2. Single selective trigger, auto selector ejector, rubber butt pad, cast off. .410 model is $40 more.

Production: *current* **Gauge/Bore:** *12 ga., 20 ga., .410*
Action: *SxS*
Barrel Length: 26", 28" **Wt.:** *6.5 lbs., 7.2 lbs.*
Sights: *bead front*
Capacity: *2*
Stock: *walnut*

D2C:	NIB $420	Ex $325	VG+ $235	Good $210	LMP: $541
C2C:	Mint $410	Ex $300	VG+ $210	Good $190	Fair $100
Trade-In:	Mint $300	Ex $250	VG+ $170	Good $150	Poor $60

MP310   REDBOOK CODE: RB-BI-S-MP310X

Hammer forged barrels, machined steel receiver and monoblock, checkered walnut stock and forend, double-dip bluing, hard chrome-lined barrels, ventilated rib, auto selective ejectors, auto tang safety, single selective trigger, screw-in choke tubes, rubber butt pad. "Sport" model available for $100 more.

Production: *current* **Gauge/Bore:** *12 ga., 20 ga., .410*
Action: *O/U*
Barrel Length: 26", 28", 30" **Wt.:** *7.4 lbs., 7.9 lbs.*
Sights: *bead front*
Capacity: *2*
Stock: *walnut*

D2C:	NIB $490	Ex $375	VG+ $270	Good $245	LMP: $655
C2C:	Mint $480	Ex $350	VG+ $250	Good $225	Fair $115
Trade-In:	Mint $350	Ex $275	VG+ $200	Good $175	Poor $60

MP94 CENTERFIRE COMBO   REDBOOK CODE: RB-BI-S-MP94CF

Shotgun over rifle barrel, 3" chamber, boxlock action, fixed or screw-in chokes, checkering on stock.

Production: *current* **Gauge/Bore:** *12 ga./.223 Rem., .30-06 Spfld, .308 Win., 7.62x39mm*
Action: *O/U*
Barrel Length: 19.7" **Wt.:** *8.5 lbs.*
Sights: *express sights*
Capacity: *2*
Stock: *walnut*

D2C:	NIB $580	Ex $450	VG+ $320	Good $290	LMP: $704
C2C:	Mint $560	Ex $425	VG+ $290	Good $265	Fair $135
Trade-In:	Mint $420	Ex $325	VG+ $230	Good $205	Poor $60

MP153   REDBOOK CODE: RB-BI-S-MP153X

Choke tubes, 3" chamber, vented rib.

Production: *current* **Gauge/Bore:** *12 ga.*
Action: *semi-auto*
Barrel Length: 26", 28" **Wt.:** *~8 lbs.*
Sights: *none*
Capacity: *4*
Stock: *walnut or black synthetic*

D2C:	NIB $375	Ex $300	VG+ $210	Good $190	
C2C:	Mint $360	Ex $275	VG+ $190	Good $170	Fair $90
Trade-In:	Mint $270	Ex $225	VG+ $150	Good $135	Poor $60

MP18 SINGLE BARREL REDBOOK CODE: RB-BI-S-MP18SB
Fixed or multichokes, blue or nickel finishes, cocking indicator, trigger block safety.

Production: *current* **Gauge/Bore:** *12 ga., 16 ga., 20 ga., .410*
Action: *single-shot*
Barrel Length: *26", 28", 29.5"* **Wt.:** *5.5 lbs.*
Sights: *none*
Capacity: *1*
Stock: *hardwood or walnut*

D2C:	NIB $140	Ex $125	VG+ $80	Good $70	
C2C:	Mint $140	Ex $100	VG+ $70	Good $65	Fair $35
Trade-In:	Mint $100	Ex $100	VG+ $60	Good $50	Poor $30

Baker Gun & Forging Company

Baker Gun & Forging Company was founded in 1860 by brothers, William H. and Ellis Baker. Firearms associated with the company were introduced or produced by one or both brothers or by H. & D. Folsom, the entity that bought their company and continued to market guns marked "Baker Gun Co." from 1919 to 1930. William H. began gunsmithing in New York, and several of his muzzle loaders, conversions, and two and three-barreled breechloaders were marked "W.H. Baker" until 1877. He went into business with his brother, Ellis, in 1887 following a brief partnership with L.C. Smith and his subsequent formation of Ithaca Gun Co. with several others. The brothers' venture was known as Syracuse Forging & Gun Co. for a year but then was redubbed "Baker Gun & Forging Co." William H. died in 1889, but patents that had just been assigned to the company kept production and business alive beyond his death. The company's firearms were graded in systems that changed repeatedly over the years, and values are largely a function of respective grades and markings.

A GRADE REDBOOK CODE: RB-BG-S-AGRDXX
Hammerless, "London Damascus twist" barrels, matted rib, frame guard and lock plates are line and scroll engraved with hunting scenery, varies on each gun, safety blocks, draw lug, checkered forend, in 1908 new B Grade replaced original, later replaced by S Grade.

Production: *1897–1908* **Gauge/Bore:** *10 ga., 12 ga., 16 ga.*
Action: *SxS*
Barrel Length: *28", 30", 32"* **Wt.:** *6.5–10.5 lbs.*
Sights: *none*
Capacity: *2*
Stock: *imported walnut, fine grain, checkering*

D2C:	NIB $2,300	Ex $1,750	VG+ $1,265	Good $1,150	
C2C:	Mint $2,210	Ex $1,600	VG+ $1,150	Good $1,035	Fair $530
Trade-In:	Mint $1,640	Ex $1,300	VG+ $900	Good $805	Poor $240

B GRADE REDBOOK CODE: RB-BG-S-BGRDXX
Sidelock, nicely engraved with Whitworth fluid steel barrels.

Production: *1897–1909* **Gauge/Bore:** *10 ga., 12 ga., 16 ga.*
Action: *SxS*
Barrel Length: *28", 30", 32"* **Wt.:** *6.5–10.5 lbs.*
Sights: *none*
Capacity: *2*
Stock: *imported walnut, nicely checkered*

D2C:	NIB $1,200	Ex $925	VG+ $660	Good $600	
C2C:	Mint $1,160	Ex $850	VG+ $600	Good $540	Fair $280
Trade-In:	Mint $860	Ex $675	VG+ $470	Good $420	Poor $120

BAKER

PARAGON GRADE   REDBOOK CODE: RB-BG-S-PARGRD
Sidelock with solid black finished Krupp barrels, case hardened frame, scroll work engravings
featuring animal scenes as requested by owner, either full or half pistol grip, hard rubber fancy design cap,
highly polished, customized by customer, add premium for automatic ejector, single trigger adds premium, became Krupp(N Grade) in 1904.

Production: *1898–1919* **Gauge/Bore:** *10 ga., 12 ga., 16 ga.*

Action: *SxS*

Barrel Length: *28", 30", 32"* **Wt.:** *6.5–10.5 lbs.*

Sights: *none*

Capacity: *2*

D2C:	NIB $2,895	Ex $2,225	VG+ $1,595	Good $1,450	
C2C:	Mint $2,780	Ex $2,000	VG+ $1,450	Good $1,305	Fair $670
Trade-In:	Mint $2,060	Ex $1,625	VG+ $1,130	Good $1,015	Poor $300

Stock: *imported select European walnut, rich, dark, fine grain and checkering*

R GRADE   REDBOOK CODE: RB-BG-S-RGRDXX
"London twist" barrels, hammerless with blue finish, extra heavy breech, full or modified choke,
drop forged steel frame, hand fitted action, case hardened steel frame and trigger plate, half pistol grip,
hard rubber butt plate, double triggers, self-compensating forend, polished ebony tip, top safety, later models
with steel barrels, automatic ejector costs extra, add premium for Damascus barrels.

Production: *1915–1933* **Gauge/Bore:** *12 ga., 16 ga., 20 ga.*

Action: *SxS*

Barrel Length: *26", 28", 30", 32"* **Wt.:** *6.5–9 lbs.*

Sights: *none*

Capacity: *2*

D2C:	NIB $2,000	Ex $1,525	VG+ $1,100	Good $1,000	
C2C:	Mint $1,920	Ex $1,400	VG+ $1,000	Good $900	Fair $460
Trade-In:	Mint $1,420	Ex $1,125	VG+ $780	Good $700	Poor $210

Stock: *fancy European walnut, finely checkered*

BATAVIA DAMASCUS   REDBOOK CODE: RB-BG-S-BATDAM
Similar to Batavia Ejector model, blue finished steel barrels, drop-forged case-hardened steel receiver, automatic ejectors, double triggers.

Production: *1906–1916* **Gauge/Bore:** *12 ga., 16 ga., 20 ga.*

Action: *SxS*

Barrel Length: *26", 28", 30", 32"* **Wt.:** *7.3–8 lbs.*

Sights: *none*

Capacity: *2*

D2C:	NIB $1,200	Ex $925	VG+ $660	Good $600	
C2C:	Mint $1,160	Ex $850	VG+ $600	Good $540	Fair $280
Trade-In:	Mint $860	Ex $675	VG+ $470	Good $420	Poor $120

Stock: *imported walnut, plain, oil finished*

BATAVIA SPECIAL   REDBOOK CODE: RB-BG-S-BATSPC
Sidelock with twist or Damascus short barrels, blue finished, case hardened steel receiver, sling rings and swivels available for addition cost.

Production: *1916–1930* **Gauge/Bore:** *12 ga., 16 ga.*

Action: *SxS*

Barrel Length: *28", 30", 32"* **Wt.:** *8.3 lbs.*

Sights: *none*

Capacity: *2*

Stock: *walnut*

D2C:	NIB $900	Ex $700	VG+ $495	Good $450	
C2C:	Mint $870	Ex $625	VG+ $450	Good $405	Fair $210
Trade-In:	Mint $640	Ex $525	VG+ $360	Good $315	Poor $90

STERLING GRADE SINGLE BARREL TRAP REDBOOK CODE: RB-BG-S-SGRSBT

Elaborate line border and scroll engraving, soft rubber recoil pad option extra, 24" and 36" barrel length option affects cost, first series octagon receiver guns made from 1909–1914 with serial numbers 1–300, introduced floating ribs and forend-mounted ejectors with serial numbers 48,500-48,999 from 1915–1919, Folsom Arms Company produced from 1920–1924 with serial numbers 51,000-51,300.

Production: *1909–1923* **Gauge/Bore:** *12 ga.*
Action: *Single-shot*
Barrel Length: 30", 32" **Wt.:** *N/A*
Sights: *none*
Capacity: *1*
Stock: *semi-fancy, dark walnut, neatly checkered*

D2C:	NIB $1,820	Ex $1,400	VG+ $1,005	Good $910	
C2C:	Mint $1,750	Ex $1,275	VG+ $910	Good $820	Fair $420
Trade-In:	Mint $1,300	Ex $1,025	VG+ $710	Good $640	Poor $210

ELITE GRADE SINGLE BARREL TRAP REDBOOK CODE: RB-BG-S-EGRSBT

Ornate scroll and game scene engraving, firing pin safety block, automatic ejectors, extra charge for 34" and 36" barrels, add premium for soft rubber recoil pad, first series octagon receiver guns made from 1909–1914 with serial numbers 1-300, introduced floating ribs and forend-mounted ejectors with serial numbers 48,500-48,999 from 1915–1919.

Production: *1909–1923* **Gauge/Bore:** *12 ga.*
Action: *Single-shot*
Barrel Length: 30", 32", 34", 36" **Wt.:** *N/A*
Sights: *none*
Capacity: *1*
Stock: *fancy dark, select walnut, fancy checkering*

D2C:	NIB $2,750	Ex $2,100	VG+ $1,515	Good $1,375	
C2C:	Mint $2,640	Ex $1,900	VG+ $1,380	Good $1,240	Fair $635
Trade-In:	Mint $1,960	Ex $1,550	VG+ $1,080	Good $965	Poor $300

BLACK BEAUTY REDBOOK CODE: RB-BG-S-BLKBTY

Special steel barrels, straight, full or half pistol grip, top of frame matted, engraved guard and lock plates, add premium for automatic ejectors.

Production: *1914–1919* **Gauge/Bore:** *12 ga., 16 ga., 20 ga.*
Action: *SxS*
Barrel Length: 26", 28", 30", 32" **Wt.:** *N/A*
Sights: *none*
Capacity: *2*
Stock: *upgraded walnut, checkering and finish*

D2C:	NIB $1,100	Ex $850	VG+ $605	Good $550	
C2C:	Mint $1,060	Ex $775	VG+ $550	Good $495	Fair $255
Trade-In:	Mint $790	Ex $625	VG+ $430	Good $385	Poor $120

Benelli

Benelli was formed in 1967 by the Benelli brothers, a family team that had previously owned a motorcycle company. The Benellis' arms company pioneered the development of semi-automatic firearms when they adopted the design ideas of Bruno Civolani, a Bolognese designer who used a simple inertia-driven mechanism in place of a conventional gas system to create the fastest reloading action in existence at that time. Incorporating this invention, the Benelli company produced a cutting edge hunting shotgun capable of firing 5-rounds in less than a second. The company continued to add innovative products and new technologies, and it grew and prospered until it was ultimately purchased by Beretta in 1983. In 2007, Benelli celebrated having manufactured two million shotguns in 40 years of production by releasing the Bimillionaire model shotgun.

BENELLI

ETHOS REDBOOK CODE: RB-BN-S-ETHOSX

Cryogenically treated barrel and choke tubes, Progressive Comfort recoil system, two-part carrier latch, anti-seize magazine cap, rotating bolt-head, removable trigger assembly, shim kit, custom hard case, add $200 for engraved nickel-plated receiver.

Production: *current* **Gauge/Bore:** *12 ga.*
Action: *semi-auto*
Barrel Length: 26", 28" **Wt.:** *6.5 lbs.*
Sights: *fiber optic system*
Capacity: *4*
Stock: *AA-Grade satin walnut*

D2C:	NIB $1,870	Ex $1,425	VG+ $1,030	Good $935	LMP: $1,999
C2C:	Mint $1,800	Ex $1,300	VG+ $940	Good $845	Fair $435
Trade-In:	Mint $1,330	Ex $1,050	VG+ $730	Good $655	Poor $210

CORDOBA REDBOOK CODE: RB-BN-S-CORDOB

Ported Crio barrel with extended chokes, 2 2/4" or 3" chamber, bolt-lock lever, rotating bolt head, removable trigger assembly, shim kit, weatherproof GripTight stock over-coating.

Production: *current* **Gauge/Bore:** *12 ga., 20 ga.*
Action: *semi-auto*
Barrel Length: 28", 30" **Wt.:** *6.3–7.3 lbs.*
Sights: *mid-bead and red bar front*
Capacity: *4*
Stock: *synthetic, black*

D2C:	NIB $2,040	Ex $1,575	VG+ $1,125	Good $1,020	LMP: $2,099
C2C:	Mint $1,960	Ex $1,425	VG+ $1,020	Good $920	Fair $470
Trade-In:	Mint $1,450	Ex $1,150	VG+ $800	Good $715	Poor $210

VINCI CORDOBA REDBOOK CODE: RB-BN-S-VINCOR

Ported Crio barrel with extended chokes, 2 3/4" or 3" chamber, bolt-lock lever, rotating bolt head, removable trigger assembly, shim kit, weatherproof GripTight stock over-coating, ComforTech Plus recoil reduction management system.

Production: *current* **Gauge/Bore:** *12 ga.*
Action: *semi-auto*
Barrel Length: 28", 30" **Wt.:** *7 lbs.*
Sights: *mid-bead and red bar front*
Capacity: *9*
Stock: *synthetic, black*

D2C:	NIB $1,875	Ex $1,425	VG+ $1,035	Good $940	LMP: $2,069
C2C:	Mint $1,800	Ex $1,300	VG+ $940	Good $845	Fair $435
Trade-In:	Mint $1,340	Ex $1,050	VG+ $740	Good $660	Poor $210

VINCI REDBOOK CODE: RB-BN-S-VINCIX

Crio barrel and choke tubes, Inertia-Driven operating system, ComforTech Plus recoil management system, 2 3/4" and 3" chamber, bolt-lock lever, rotating bolt head, drilled and tapped receiver, dual purpose release lever, removable trigger assembly, hard case, add $110 for Realtree camouflage pattern, add $240 for Speedbolt option, add $270 for SteadyGrip.

Production: *current* **Gauge/Bore:** *12 ga.*
Action: *semi-auto*
Barrel Length: 24", 26", 28" **Wt.:** *6.7–6.9 lbs.*
Sights: *mid-bead and red bar front*
Capacity: *4*
Stock: *black synthetic, Realtree Max5, Realtree APG, Speedbolt*

D2C:	NIB $1,400	Ex $1,075	VG+ $770	Good $700	LMP: $1,359
C2C:	Mint $1,350	Ex $975	VG+ $700	Good $630	Fair $325
Trade-In:	Mint $1,000	Ex $800	VG+ $550	Good $490	Poor $150

SUPER VINCI
REDBOOK CODE: RB-BN-S-SUPVIN

Crio barrel with choke tubes, ComforTech recoil management system with replaceable comb inserts, shock-absorbing chevrons and gel recoil pads, 2 3/4", 3", or 3" chamber, drilled and tapped receiver, In-Line Inertia Driven operating system, rotating bolt head, removable trigger assembly, dual purpose release lever, hard case, add $100 for Realtree pattern or Gore Optifade Concealment camouflage pattern.

Production: *current* **Gauge/Bore:** *12 ga.*
Action: *semi-auto*
Barrel Length: 26", 28", 30" **Wt.:** *6.9–7.1 lbs.*
Sights: *mid-bead and red bar front*
Capacity: *94*
Stock: *synthetic, black*

D2C:	NIB $1,770	Ex $1,350	VG+ $975	Good $885	LMP: $1,799
C2C:	Mint $1,700	Ex $1,225	VG+ $890	Good $800	Fair $410
Trade-In:	Mint $1,260	Ex $1,000	VG+ $700	Good $620	Poor $180

VINCI TACTICAL
REDBOOK CODE: RB-BN-S-VINTAC

Cryogenically treated barrel and choke tubes, In-Line Inertia-Driven operating system, Picatinny rail, beveled magazine loading port, bolt-lock lever, rotating bolt-head, dual-purpose release lever, pistol grip, modular stock system, V-grip checkering, adjustable QuadraFit buttstock, add $200 ComforTech Plus recoil system.

Production: *current* **Gauge/Bore:** *12 ga.*
Action: *semi-auto*
Barrel Length: 18.5" **Wt.:** *6.7 lbs.*
Sights: *Ghost Ring*
Capacity: *4*
Stock: *synthetic, black*

D2C:	NIB $1,400	Ex $1,075	VG+ $770	Good $700	LMP: $1,499
C2C:	Mint $1,350	Ex $975	VG+ $700	Good $630	Fair $325
Trade-In:	Mint $1,000	Ex $800	VG+ $550	Good $490	Poor $150

SUPER BLACK EAGLE II
REDBOOK CODE: RB-BN-S-SBEIIX

Crio barrel and choke tubes, Inertia-Driven system, ComforTech recoil management system, 2 3/4", 3" or 3 1/2" chamber, bolt-lock lever, rotating bolt head, drilled and tapped receiver, hard case, add $100 for Realtree camouflage pattern, add $100 for LH configuration, add $100 for Rifled Slug model, deduct $230 for satin walnut option.

Production: *current* **Gauge/Bore:** *12 ga.*
Action: *semi-auto*
Barrel Length: 24", 26", 28" **Wt.:** *7.1–7.4 lbs.*
Sights: *mid-bead and red bar front*
Capacity: *4*
Stock: *synthetic, black*

D2C:	NIB $1,725	Ex $1,325	VG+ $950	Good $865	LMP: $1,799
C2C:	Mint $1,660	Ex $1,200	VG+ $870	Good $780	Fair $400
Trade-In:	Mint $1,230	Ex $975	VG+ $680	Good $605	Poor $180

MONTEFELTRO
REDBOOK CODE: RB-BN-S-MONFEL

Cryogenically treated barrel and choke tubes, Inertia-Driven operating system, bolt-lock lever, rotating bolt head, removable trigger assembly, Compact model option at no added cost, add $90 for LH model, add $160 for Combo model with both Compact and Standard configurations.

Production: *current* **Gauge/Bore:** *12 ga., 20 ga.*
Action: *semi-auto*
Barrel Length: 24", 26", 28" **Wt.:** *5.3–7.1 lbs.*
Sights: *red bar front*
Capacity: *5*
Stock: *synthetic, black or satin walnut*

D2C:	NIB $1,040	Ex $800	VG+ $575	Good $520	LMP: $1,139
C2C:	Mint $1,000	Ex $725	VG+ $520	Good $470	Fair $240
Trade-In:	Mint $740	Ex $600	VG+ $410	Good $365	Poor $120

BENELLI

MONTEFELTRO SILVER   REDBOOK CODE: RB-BN-S-MONSIL
Engraved nickel-plated alloy receiver, Inertia-driven system, slim forend, low-profile vent rib.

Production: *current* **Gauge/Bore:** *12 ga., 20 ga.*
Action: *semi-auto*
Barrel Length: 26", 28" **Wt.:** *5.6 lbs., 7.1 lbs.*
Sights: *mid-bead and red bar front*
Capacity: *5*
Stock: *AA-Grade satin walnut*

D2C:	NIB $1,700	Ex $1,300	VG+ $935	Good $850	**LMP: $1,779**
C2C:	Mint $1,640	Ex $1,175	VG+ $850	Good $765	Fair $395
Trade-In:	Mint $1,210	Ex $975	VG+ $670	Good $595	Poor $180

SUPERNOVA PUMP RIFLED SLUG   REDBOOK CODE: RB-BN-S-SNPRSX
Chambered for 3.5" magnum shells, ComforTech recoil reduction system, steel skeletal framework overmolded with polymer, enlarged trigger guard. Available in Realtree model for $120 premium.

Production: *current* **Gauge/Bore:** *12 ga.*
Action: *pump-action*
Barrel Length: 24" **Wt.:** *8 lbs.*
Sights: *adjustable rifle*
Capacity: *4*
Stock: *synthetic*

D2C:	NIB $800	Ex $625	VG+ $440	Good $400	**LMP: $829**
C2C:	Mint $770	Ex $575	VG+ $400	Good $360	Fair $185
Trade-In:	Mint $570	Ex $450	VG+ $320	Good $280	Poor $90

SUPERNOVA PUMP   REDBOOK CODE: RB-BN-S-SNPXXX
Steel skeletal framework over-molded with polymer, enlarged trigger guard.

Production: *current* **Gauge/Bore:** *12 ga.*
Action: *pump-action*
Barrel Length: 24", 26", 28" **Wt.:** *7.8–8 lbs.*
Sights: *red-bar front, metal mid-bead*
Capacity: *5*
Stock: *synthetic*

D2C:	NIB $520	Ex $400	VG+ $290	Good $260	**LMP: $549**
C2C:	Mint $500	Ex $375	VG+ $260	Good $235	Fair $120
Trade-In:	Mint $370	Ex $300	VG+ $210	Good $185	Poor $60

SUPERNOVA TACTICAL PUMP   REDBOOK CODE: RB-BN-S-SNTACP
ComforTech recoil reduction system or pistol grip stock, steel skeletal framework over-molded with polymer, forend shell-stop button.

Production: *current* **Gauge/Bore:** *12 ga.*
Action: *pump-action*
Barrel Length: 18" **Wt.:** *7.6 lbs.*
Sights: *open rifle or ghost ring*
Capacity: *5*
Stock: *synthetic*

D2C:	NIB $480	Ex $375	VG+ $265	Good $240	**LMP: $499**
C2C:	Mint $470	Ex $350	VG+ $240	Good $220	Fair $115
Trade-In:	Mint $350	Ex $275	VG+ $190	Good $170	Poor $60

ULTRA LIGHT REDBOOK CODE: RB-BN-S-ULTLIT

Featherweight alloy receiver, lightweight magazine tube, cryogenically treated barrel and choke tubes, Inertia-Driven operating system, rotating bolt-head, bolt-lock lever, removable trigger assembly, gold-plated trigger, carbon-fiber rib, hard case, add $130 for 28 gauge.

Production: *current* **Gauge/Bore:** *12 ga., 20 ga., 28 ga.*
Action: *semi-auto*
Barrel Length: 24", 26" **Wt.:** *5–6 lbs.*
Sights: *mid-bead and red bar front*
Capacity: *4*
Stock: *satin walnut*

D2C:	NIB $1,600	Ex $1,225	VG+$880	Good $800	**LMP:** $1,669
C2C:	Mint $1,540	Ex $1,125	VG+ $800	Good $720	Fair $370
Trade-In:	Mint $1,140	Ex $900	VG+ $630	Good $560	Poor $180

LEGACY REDBOOK CODE: RB-BN-S-LEGACY

Cryogenically treated barrel and choke tubes, Inertia-Driven operating system, 2-tone with nickel-plated lower receiver, bolt-lock lever, rotating bolt-head, game scene etchings and engraving, removable trigger assembly, gold-plated trigger, carbon fiber rib, includes hard case, satin walnut stock on 28 gauge, add $240 for 28 gauge option.

Production: *current* **Gauge/Bore:** *12 ga., 20 ga., 28 ga.*
Action: *semi-auto*
Barrel Length: 24", 26", 28" **Wt.:** *5–7.4 lbs.*
Sights: *mid-bead and red bar front*
Capacity: *4*
Stock: *select AA-Grade walnut, satin finish*

D2C:	NIB $1,680	Ex $1,300	VG+ $925	Good $840	**LMP:** $1,799
C2C:	Mint $1,620	Ex $1,175	VG+ $840	Good $760	Fair $390
Trade-In:	Mint $1,200	Ex $950	VG+ $660	Good $590	Poor $180

LEGACY SPORT REDBOOK CODE: RB-BN-S-LEGSPT

Cryogenically treated barrel and extended chrome choke tubes, Inertia-Driven operating system, engraved receiver.

Production: *current* **Gauge/Bore:** *12 ga.*
Action: *semi-auto*
Barrel Length: 28", 30" **Wt.:** *7.5 lbs.*
Sights: *mid-bead and red bar front*
Capacity: *4*
Stock: *AA-Grade satin walnut*

D2C:	NIB $2,199	Ex $1,675	VG+ $1,210	Good $1,100	**LMP:** $2,439
C2C:	Mint $2,120	Ex $1,525	VG+ $1,100	Good $990	Fair $510
Trade-In:	Mint $1,570	Ex $1,250	VG+ $860	Good $770	Poor $240

SUPERSPORT REDBOOK CODE: RB-BN-S-SUPSPT

Carbon fiber finish, Inertia Driven system, ComforTech recoil reduction system, ported Crio barrle with extended Crio chokes, SpeedBolt configuration optional.

Production: *current* **Gauge/Bore:** *12 ga., 20 ga.*
Action: *semi-auto*
Barrel Length: 28", 30" **Wt.:** *6.3–7.3 lbs.*
Sights: *mid-bead and red bar front*
Capacity: *4*
Stock: *synthetic, carbon fiber finish*

D2C:	NIB $2,095	Ex $1,600	VG+ $1,155	Good $1,050	**LMP:** $2,199
C2C:	Mint $2,020	Ex $1,450	VG+ $1,050	Good $945	Fair $485
Trade-In:	Mint $1,490	Ex $1,175	VG+ $820	Good $735	Poor $210

BENELLI

SPORT II REDBOOK CODE: RB-BN-S-SPORT2

Similar to the Legacy Sport model, but with A-Grade walnut stock. Inertia Driven system, ported Crio barrel and extended Crio chokes.

Production: *current* **Gauge/Bore:** *12 ga., 20 ga.*
Action: *semi-auto*
Barrel Length: *28", 30"* **Wt.:** *6.3–7.3 lbs.*
Sights: *mid-bead and red bar*
Capacity: *4*
Stock: *A-Grade walnut*

D2C:	NIB $1,790	Ex $1,375	VG+ $985	Good $895	LMP: $1,899
C2C:	Mint $1,720	Ex $1,250	VG+ $900	Good $810	Fair $415
Trade-In:	Mint $1,280	Ex $1,025	VG+ $700	Good $630	Poor $180

M2 FIELD REDBOOK CODE: RB-BN-S-M2FILD

Lightweight, Cryogenically treated barrel and choke tubes, Inertia-Driven operating system, ComforTech recoil reduction system, GripTight slip-proof coating, AirTouch checkering pattern, bolt-lock lever, rotating bolt-head, removable trigger assembly, includes hard case, add $50 for 20 gauge model and Rifled Slug model, add $100 for LH configuration, add $100 for Realtree camouflage pattern.

Production: *current* **Gauge/Bore:** *12 ga., 20 ga.*
Action: *semi-auto*
Barrel Length: *21", 24", 26", 28"* **Wt.:** *5.6–7.3 lbs.*
Sights: *mid-bead and red bar front*
Capacity: *4*
Stock: *black synthetic, Realtree Max5 or Realtree APG*

D2C:	NIB $1,350	Ex $1,050	VG+ $745	Good $675	LMP: $1,449
C2C:	Mint $1,300	Ex $950	VG+ $680	Good $610	Fair $315
Trade-In:	Mint $960	Ex $775	VG+ $530	Good $475	Poor $150

M2 TACTICAL REDBOOK CODE: RB-BN-S-M2TACT

Inertia Driven system, available in three stock configurations. Add $110 for ghost-ring sight or tactical stock model. Add $220 for ComforTech model with ghost ring sights.

Production: *current* **Gauge/Bore:** *12 ga.*
Action: *semi-auto*
Barrel Length: *18.5"* **Wt.:** *6.7 lbs.*
Sights: *ghost-ring or open rifle*
Capacity: *6*
Stock: *synthetic black*

D2C:	NIB $1,250	Ex $950	VG+ $690	Good $625	LMP: $1,249
C2C:	Mint $1,200	Ex $875	VG+ $630	Good $565	Fair $290
Trade-In:	Mint $890	Ex $700	VG+ $490	Good $440	Poor $150

M2 AMERICAN SERIES REDBOOK CODE: RB-BN-S-M2AMSE

Inertia-driven action, receiver drilled & tapped for scope mounts, multi-chokes (full, improved cylinder, modified), 14.375 length of pull, fires 2.75" and 3" shells.

Production: *discontinued* **Gauge/Bore:** *12 ga.*
Action: *semi-auto*
Barrel Length: *26", 28"* **Wt.:** *~7 lbs.*
Sights: *red bar front, mid-bead*
Capacity: *4*
Stock: *black synthetic, Realtree Max-4 camouflage option*

D2C:	NIB $1,190	Ex $925	VG+ $655	Good $595	
C2C:	Mint $1,150	Ex $825	VG+ $600	Good $540	Fair $275
Trade-In:	Mint $850	Ex $675	VG+ $470	Good $420	Poor $120

BENELLI

M2 PRACTICAL REDBOOK CODE: RB-BN-S-M2PRAC
Universal scope mount, matte black finish, ported barrel with magnum chambering, ComforTech recoil system.

Production: *discontinued* **Gauge/Bore:** *12 ga.*
Action: *semi-auto*
Barrel Length: *18.5", 20", 24", 26"* **Wt.:** *~7 lbs.*
Sights: *ghost-ring*
Capacity: *10*
Stock: *black synthetic*

D2C:	NIB $1,400	Ex $1,075	VG+ $770	Good $700	
C2C:	Mint $1,350	Ex $975	VG+ $700	Good $630	Fair $325
Trade-In:	Mint $1,000	Ex $800	VG+ $550	Good $490	Poor $150

M2 3-GUN EDITION REDBOOK CODE: RB-BN-S-M23GUN
Performance Shop edition, Inertia Driven System, oversized bolt release, extended tactical bolt handle, enlarged loading port.

Production: *current* **Gauge/Bore:** *12 ga.*
Action: *semi-auto*
Barrel Length: *21"* **Wt.:** *7.3 lbs.*
Sights: *HiVIZ Comp front, metal mid-bead*
Capacity: *4*
Stock: *black synthetic ComforTech*

D2C:	NIB $2,250	Ex $1,725	VG+ $1,240	Good $1,125	**LMP:** $2,499
C2C:	Mint $2,160	Ex $1,575	VG+ $1,130	Good $1,015	Fair $520
Trade-In:	Mint $1,600	Ex $1,275	VG+ $880	Good $790	Poor $240

M3 CONVERTIBLE SEMI-AUTO PUMP REDBOOK CODE: RB-BN-S-M3CSAP
Standard chokes, auto-regulating gas-operated, bolt-lock lever, drilled and tapped receiver with Picatinny rail, rotating bolt-head, removable trigger assembly, available with pistol grip, for optional H20 model with nickel plating on metal surfaces add $500.

Production: *current* **Gauge/Bore:** *12 ga.*
Action: *semi-auto/pump-action*
Barrel Length: *19.75"* **Wt.:** *7.2 lbs.*
Sights: *ghost-ring*
Capacity: *2*
Stock: *synthetic*

D2C:	NIB $1,425	Ex $1,100	VG+ $785	Good $715	**LMP:** $1,589
C2C:	Mint $1,370	Ex $1,000	VG+ $720	Good $645	Fair $330
Trade-In:	Mint $1,020	Ex $800	VG+ $560	Good $500	Poor $150

M4 TACTICAL REDBOOK CODE: RB-BN-S-M4TACT
A.R.G.O. (Auto-Regulating Gas-Operated), Picatinny rail, designed for the U.S. Marine Corps as the M1014, available with pistol grip, for optional H20 model with nickel plating on metal surfaces add $500.

Production: *current* **Gauge/Bore:** *12 ga.*
Action: *semi-auto*
Barrel Length: *18.5 "* **Wt.:** *7.8 lbs.*
Sights: *adjustable front, ghost-ring rear*
Capacity: *6*
Stock: *synthetic, black*

D2C:	NIB $1,850	Ex $1,425	VG+ $1,020	Good $925	**LMP:** $1,899
C2C:	Mint $1,780	Ex $1,300	VG+ $930	Good $835	Fair $430
Trade-In:	Mint $1,320	Ex $1,050	VG+ $730	Good $650	Poor $210

BENELLI

NOVA PUMP FIELD REDBOOK CODE: RB-BN-S-NVPMFD

Lightweight with steel skeletal framework over-molded with high-tech polymer, fore-end shell-stop button, stock and receiver are formed as one solid unit. IC, M, and F chokes, red-bar front and metal bead mid-sight. Recoil reducer fits 12 gauge stocks only. Realtree finish models available for about $100 more. Compact configuration available in 20 gauge for $20 more.

Production: *1999–current* **Gauge/Bore:** *12 ga., 20 ga.*
Action: *pump-action*
Barrel Length: *24", 26", 28"* **Wt.:** *6.4–8 lbs.*
Sights: *red-bar front*
Capacity: *5*
Stock: *synthetic*

D2C:	NIB $460	Ex $350	VG+ $255	Good $230	**LMP:** $449
C2C:	Mint $450	Ex $325	VG+ $230	Good $210	Fair $110
Trade-In:	Mint $330	Ex $275	VG+ $180	Good $165	Poor $60

NOVA TACTICAL REDBOOK CODE: RB-BN-S-NOVTAC

Lightweight with corrosion-resistant 1-piece stock and receiver design, steel skeletal framework over-molded with high-tech polymer, dual-action bars, fore-end shell-stop button, fixed cylinder choke. 14.25" length of pull, 2.25" drop at heel, and 1.25" drop at comb, Ghost Ring sight version available for $40 more.

Production: *current* **Gauge/Bore:** *12 ga.*
Action: *pump-action*
Barrel Length: *18.5"* **Wt.:** *7.2 lbs.*
Sights: *open rifle*
Capacity: *5*
Stock: *synthetic*

D2C:	NIB $450	Ex $350	VG+ $250	Good $225	**LMP:** $419
C2C:	Mint $440	Ex $325	VG+ $230	Good $205	Fair $105
Trade-In:	Mint $320	Ex $275	VG+ $180	Good $160	Poor $60

NOVA TACTICAL H2O REDBOOK CODE: RB-BN-S-NOVH2O

Lightweight with corrosion-resistant 1-piece synthetic stock and receiver design. Steel skeletal framework over-molded with high-tech polymer. Dual-action bars, fore-end shell-stop button. Fixed cylinder choke. 14.25" length of pull, 2.25" drop at heel, and 1.25" drop at comb. Matte nickel-plated barrel, magazine tube and cap, trigger group, and all other inner metal parts.

Production: *current* **Gauge/Bore:** *12 ga.*
Action: *pump-action*
Barrel Length: *18.5"* **Wt.:** *7.2 lbs.*
Sights: *open rifle*
Capacity: *5*
Stock: *synthetic*

D2C:	NIB $625	Ex $475	VG+ $345	Good $315	**LMP:** $669
C2C:	Mint $600	Ex $450	VG+ $320	Good $285	Fair $145
Trade-In:	Mint $450	Ex $350	VG+ $250	Good $220	Poor $90

PERFORMANCE SHOP SUPERSPORT REDBOOK CODE: RB-BN-S-PERSSS

Competition gun designed for trap, skeet, or sporting clays. Inertia Driven system, recoil reduction system, ported Crio barrel with extended Crio chokes, Briley Spectrum extended choke, lengthened forcing cone, Briley EZ bolt release and enlarged bolt handle, Briley weighted fore-end cap, polished actions. Red-bar front and metal bead mid-sight. 20 gauge model sells for $110 less.

Production: *current* **Gauge/Bore:** *12 ga., 20 ga.*
Action: *semi-auto*
Barrel Length: *28", 30"* **Wt.:** *6.7 lbs., 7.8 lbs.*
Sights: *red-bar front*
Capacity: *4*
Stock: *carbon fiber*

D2C:	NIB $2,799	Ex $2,150	VG+ $1,540	Good $1,400	**LMP:** $2,949
C2C:	Mint $2,690	Ex $1,950	VG+ $1,400	Good $1,260	Fair $645
Trade-In:	Mint $1,990	Ex $1,575	VG+ $1,100	Good $980	Poor $300

PERFORMANCE SHOP CORDOBA
REDBOOK CODE: RB-BN-S-PERSCD

Ported Crio barrel with extended Crio chokes, Briley spectrum extended choke also included, ComforTech recoil management system with replaceable comb inserts, shock absorbing chevrons, and gel recoil pads, 2" or 3" chamber, GripTight finish, Briley EZ bolt release, enlarged bolt handle, weighted for-end cap, polished actions, add $110 for 12 gauge model.

Production: *current* **Gauge/Bore:** *12 ga., 20 ga.*
Action: *semi-auto*
Barrel Length: 28" **Wt.:** *6.7 lbs., 7.7 lbs.*
Sights: *mid-bead, red bar front*
Capacity: *4*
Stock: *synthetic black*

D2C:	NIB $2,500	Ex $1,900	VG+ $1,375	Good $1,250	LMP: $2,719
C2C:	Mint $2,400	Ex $1,725	VG+ $1,250	Good $1,125	Fair $575
Trade-In:	Mint $1,780	Ex $1,400	VG+ $980	Good $875	Poor $270

PERFORMANCE SHOP M2 3-GUN EDITION
REDBOOK CODE: RB-BN-S-PERSM2

Cryogenically treated barrel and chokes, Inertia-Driven operating system, over-sized bolt release, extended tactical-style bolt handle, modified carrier, enlarged loading port, rotating bolt-head, removable trigger assembly, ComforTech recoil reduction management system, AirTouch secure grip coating.

Production: *current* **Gauge/Bore:** *12 ga.*
Action: *semi-auto*
Barrel Length: 21" **Wt.:** *7.3 lbs.*
Sights: *HiVIZ Comp multi-color inserts*
Capacity: *7*
Stock: *synthetic, black*

D2C:	NIB $2,460	Ex $1,875	VG+ $1,355	Good $1,230	LMP: $2,499
C2C:	Mint $2,370	Ex $1,700	VG+ $1,230	Good $1,110	Fair $570
Trade-In:	Mint $1,750	Ex $1,400	VG+ $960	Good $865	Poor $270

PERFORMANCE SHOP SBE II TURKEY
REDBOOK CODE: RB-BN-S-PSSBE2T

Cryogenically treated barrel, extra-full turkey (XFT) choke tubes, Inertia-Driven operating system, large bolt handle, polished action, paddle bolt release, rotating bolt-head, drilled and tapped receiver, removable trigger assembly, pistol grip included, ComforTech recoil reduction management system, gel comb pads included, AirTouch secure grip coating, hard case.

Production: *current* **Gauge/Bore:** *12 ga.*
Action: *semi-auto*
Barrel Length: 24" **Wt.:** *7.1 lbs.*
Sights: *mid-bead and red bar front*
Capacity: *2, 3*
Stock: *synthetic, Realtree APG*

D2C:	NIB $2,750	Ex $2,100	VG+ $1,515	Good $1,375	LMP: $2,949
C2C:	Mint $2,640	Ex $1,900	VG+ $1,380	Good $1,240	Fair $635
Trade-In:	Mint $1,960	Ex $1,550	VG+ $1,080	Good $965	Poor $300

PERFORMANCE SHOP SBE II WATERFOWL
REDBOOK CODE: RB-BN-S-PSSBEW

Custom-built waterfowl gun, ported Crio barrel with Triple Threat choke tube system, ComforTech recoil management system with replaceable comb inserts, shock-absorbing chevrons and gel recoil pads, 3" chamber, polished actions, drilled and tapped receiver, removable trigger assembly, GripTight finish, Paddle bolt release, large bolt handle.

Production: *current* **Gauge/Bore:** *12 ga.*
Action: *semi-auto*
Barrel Length: 28" **Wt.:** *7.3 lbs.*
Sights: *HiVIZ Comp multi-color inserts*
Capacity: *2, 3*
Stock: *synthetic, Realtree Max5*

D2C:	NIB $2,500	Ex $1,900	VG+ $1,375	Good $1,250	LMP: $2,669
C2C:	Mint $2,400	Ex $1,725	VG+ $1,250	Good $1,125	Fair $575
Trade-In:	Mint $1,780	Ex $1,400	VG+ $980	Good $875	Poor $270

BIMILLIONAIRE REDBOOK CODE: RB-BN-S-BIMAIR

Limited production, two-tone receiver with blue top and coin finish engraved bottom, engraved in Ceasare Giovanelli's workshop, gold inlays and gold trigger.

Production: *2010–2012* **Gauge/Bore:** *12ga., 20ga.*
Action: *semi-auto*
Barrel Length: 26" **Wt.:** *6–7.3 lbs.*
Sights: *red bar front, mid-bead*
Capacity: *5*
Stock: *AAA Grade walnut*

D2C:	NIB $2,225	Ex $1,700	VG+ $1,225	Good $1,115	**LMP: $2,900**
C2C:	Mint $2,140	Ex $1,550	VG+ $1,120	Good $1,005	Fair $515
Trade-In:	Mint $1,580	Ex $1,250	VG+ $870	Good $780	Poor $240

BLACK EAGLE (1 OF 1,000) 1994 LIMITED EDITION REDBOOK CODE: RB-BN-S-BE1994

Limited 1 of 1,000 produciton, gold inlays on engraved receiver, extra fancy grade stock, Inertia Driven system, polished blue upper receiver and barrel.

Production: *1994–1995* **Gauge/Bore:** *12ga.*
Action: *semi-auto*
Barrel Length: 26" **Wt.:** *N/A*
Sights: *N/A*
Capacity: *N/A*
Stock: *wood*

D2C:	NIB $1,900	Ex $1,450	VG+ $1,045	Good $950	**LMP: $2,000**
C2C:	Mint $1,830	Ex $1,325	VG+ $950	Good $855	Fair $440
Trade-In:	Mint $1,350	Ex $1,075	VG+ $750	Good $665	Poor $210

BLACK EAGLE COMPETITION REDBOOK CODE: RB-BN-S-BECOMP

Blue upper receiver and barrel, etched silver lower receiver, 3" chamber, includes five screw-in choke tubes. Imported by Heckler & Koch, Inc., Sterling, VA.

Production: *1983–1997* **Gauge/Bore:** *12 ga.*
Action: *semi-auto*
Barrel Length: 26", 28" **Wt.:** *7.3 lbs.*
Sights: *bead front*
Capacity: *5*
Stock: *walnut*

D2C:	NIB $1,100	Ex $850	VG+ $605	Good $550	
C2C:	Mint $1,060	Ex $775	VG+ $550	Good $495	Fair $255
Trade-In:	Mint $790	Ex $625	VG+ $430	Good $385	Poor $120

BLACK EAGLE SLUG GUN REDBOOK CODE: RB-BN-S-BESLGN

Rifled barrel, integral scope-mounting bases.

Production: *discontinued* **Gauge/Bore:** *12 ga.*
Action: *semi-auto*
Barrel Length: 24" **Wt.:** *~7 lbs.*
Sights: *rifle sights*
Capacity: *N/A*
Stock: *walnut*

D2C:	NIB $830	Ex $650	VG+ $460	Good $415	
C2C:	Mint $800	Ex $575	VG+ $420	Good $375	Fair $195
Trade-In:	Mint $590	Ex $475	VG+ $330	Good $295	Poor $90

ELITE TWO-GUN SET   REDBOOK CODE: RB-BN-S-ELTTGS

Receivers are engraved with landscapes inset with gold cartouches, part of the Benelli World
Class Collection, high-polished blue upper receiver, gold trigger, 2-set in hard case.

Production: *discontinued* **Gauge/Bore:** *12 ga., 20 ga.*

Action: *semi-auto*

Barrel Length: 26" **Wt.:** *5.8–7.4 lbs.*

Sights: *red bar front, metal bead mid*

Capacity: *5*

Stock: *AAA-Grade walnut*

D2C:	NIB $5,000	Ex $3,800	VG+ $2,750	Good $2,500	
C2C:	Mint $4,800	Ex $3,450	VG+ $2,500	Good $2,250	Fair $1,150
Trade-In:	Mint $3,550	Ex $2,800	VG+ $1,950	Good $1,750	Poor $510

SPECIAL 80   REDBOOK CODE: RB-BN-S-M80SST

Vent rib, modified choke, lower receiver in nickel finish, buttpad.

Production: *discontinued* **Gauge/Bore:** *12 ga.*

Action: *semi-auto*

Barrel Length: 26" **Wt.:** *7.6 lbs*

Sights: *phosphorescent bead front*

Capacity: *5*

Stock: *hardwood Monte Carlo*

D2C:	NIB $850	Ex $650	VG+ $470	Good $425	
C2C:	Mint $820	Ex $600	VG+ $430	Good $385	Fair $200
Trade-In:	Mint $610	Ex $500	VG+ $340	Good $300	Poor $90

NOVA SLUG   REDBOOK CODE: RB-BN-S-NOVASL

Rifled barrel is drilled and tapped, fires 3" shells. Add $90 to value with Advantage Max-4 camouflage finish.

Production: *discontinued* **Gauge/Bore:** *12 ga., 20 ga.*

Action: *pump-action*

Barrel Length: 24" **Wt.:** *8.1 lbs.*

Sights: *open rifle-type*

Capacity: *5*

Stock: *black synthetic, Advantage Timber HD camouflage option*

D2C:	NIB $480	Ex $375	VG+ $265	Good $240	
C2C:	Mint $470	Ex $350	VG+ $240	Good $220	Fair $115
Trade-In:	Mint $350	Ex $275	VG+ $190	Good $170	Poor $60

CRIO 28   REDBOOK CODE: RB-BN-S-RAFC28

Inertia-driven action, rotating bolt, multi-chokes, chrome-lined vented 7mm barrel, anodized receiver, combination matte/high-polish finish.

Production: *discontinued* **Gauge/Bore:** *28 ga.*

Action: *semi-auto*

Barrel Length: 24", 26" **Wt.:** *5.25 lbs.*

Sights: *red fiber optic front, mid-bead*

Capacity: *4*

Stock: *select cut-checkered walnut*

D2C:	NIB $1,915	Ex $1,475	VG+ $1,055	Good $960	
C2C:	Mint $1,840	Ex $1,325	VG+ $960	Good $865	Fair $445
Trade-In:	Mint $1,360	Ex $1,075	VG+ $750	Good $675	Poor $210

DE LUXE   REDBOOK CODE: RB-BN-S-RAFDLX

Inertia-driven, vent rib, Ergal white nickel-plated aluminum alloy receiver with scroll-engraved game scenes, Bakelite recoil pad, fires 3" Magnum shells.

Production: *discontinued* **Gauge/Bore:** *12 ga.*
Action: *semi-auto*
Barrel Length: 26" **Wt.:** *7.4 lbs*
Sights: *fluorescent red*
Capacity: *5*
Stock: *checkered deluxe walnut*

D2C:	NIB $2,000	Ex $1,525	VG+ $1,100	Good $1,000	
C2C:	Mint $1,920	Ex $1,400	VG+ $1,000	Good $900	Fair $460
Trade-In:	Mint $1,420	Ex $1,125	VG+ $780	Good $700	Poor $210

STANDARD   REDBOOK CODE: RB-BN-S-RAFSTD

Vent rib, Ergal aluminum alloy receiver in polished black finish, Bakelite recoil pad, fires 3" Magnum shells.

Production: *discontinued* **Gauge/Bore:** *12 ga.*
Action: *semi-auto*
Barrel Length: 26" **Wt.:** *7.4 lbs*
Sights: *fluorescent red*
Capacity: *5*
Stock: *checkered high-quality walnut*

D2C:	NIB $1,650	Ex $1,275	VG+ $910	Good $825	
C2C:	Mint $1,590	Ex $1,150	VG+ $830	Good $745	Fair $380
Trade-In:	Mint $1,180	Ex $925	VG+ $650	Good $580	Poor $180

SL-201 FIELD (SL-80 SERIES)   REDBOOK CODE: RB-BN-S-SL201F

Vent rib, modified choke, lower receiver in black anodized finish.

Production: *discontinued* **Gauge/Bore:** *20 ga.*
Action: *semi-auto*
Barrel Length: 26" **Wt.:** *~5.6 lbs.*
Sights: *N/A*
Capacity: *4*
Stock: *walnut*

D2C:	NIB $550	Ex $425	VG+ $305	Good $275	
C2C:	Mint $530	Ex $400	VG+ $280	Good $250	Fair $130
Trade-In:	Mint $400	Ex $325	VG+ $220	Good $195	Poor $60

SL-121 M1 POLICE/MILITARY (SL-80 SERIES)   REDBOOK CODE: RB-BN-S-121M1P

Inertia recoil system, fixed choke, aluminum alloy receiver, matte finish, fires 3" shells.

Production: *discontinued 1985* **Gauge/Bore:** *12 ga.*
Action: *semi-auto*
Barrel Length: 18.75" **Wt.:** *N/A*
Sights: *post front, fixed rear*
Capacity: *8*
Stock: *hardwood Monte Carlo*

D2C:	NIB $625	Ex $475	VG+ $345	Good $315	
C2C:	Mint $600	Ex $450	VG+ $320	Good $285	Fair $145
Trade-In:	Mint $450	Ex $350	VG+ $250	Good $220	Poor $90

SL-123 SLUG (SL-80 SERIES) REDBOOK CODE: RB-BN-S-123SLG
Drilled and tapped rifled barrel, various barrel lengths and chokes, photo-engraved aluminum alloy receiver, fires 3" shells, very rare.

Production: *discontinued 1985* **Gauge/Bore:** *12 ga.*

Action: *semi-auto*

Barrel Length: *N/A* **Wt.:** *N/A*

Sights: *rifle-type*

Capacity: *5*

Stock: *hardwood Monte Carlo*

D2C:	NIB $1,800	Ex $1,375	VG+ $990	Good $900	
C2C:	Mint $1,730	Ex $1,250	VG+ $900	Good $810	Fair $415
Trade-In:	Mint $1,280	Ex $1,025	VG+ $710	Good $630	Poor $180

SL-121/122 SLUG (SL-80 SERIES) REDBOOK CODE: RB-BN-S-SL121S
Rifled slug barrel, anodized semi-gloss black finish, buttpad.

Production: *discontinued 1985* **Gauge/Bore:** *12 ga.*

Action: *semi-auto*

Barrel Length: *21"* **Wt.:** *~7.2 lbs.*

Sights: *rifle-type*

Capacity: *5*

Stock: *hardwood Monte Carlo*

D2C:	NIB $700	Ex $550	VG+ $385	Good $350	
C2C:	Mint $680	Ex $500	VG+ $350	Good $315	Fair $165
Trade-In:	Mint $500	Ex $400	VG+ $280	Good $245	Poor $90

SL-121V (SL-80 SERIES) REDBOOK CODE: RB-BN-S-SL121V
Field grade, inertia recoil system, vent rib, various choke combinations, anodized lower receiver in black semi-gloss finish.

Production: *discontinued 1985* **Gauge/Bore:** *12 ga.*

Action: *semi-auto*

Barrel Length: *26", 28"* **Wt.:** *N/A*

Sights: *N/A*

Capacity: *5*

Stock: *straight walnut*

D2C:	NIB $700	Ex $550	VG+ $385	Good $350	
C2C:	Mint $680	Ex $500	VG+ $350	Good $315	Fair $165
Trade-In:	Mint $500	Ex $400	VG+ $280	Good $245	Poor $90

SL-123V (SL-80 SERIES) REDBOOK CODE: RB-BN-S-SL123V
Field grade, photo-engraved Ergal aluminum alloy receiver, vent rib, various chokes.

Production: *discontinued 1985* **Gauge/Bore:** *12 ga.*

Action: *semi-auto*

Barrel Length: *26", 28", 30"* **Wt.:** *~6.75 lbs.*

Sights: *N/A*

Capacity: *N/A*

Stock: *walnut*

D2C:	NIB $725	Ex $575	VG+ $400	Good $365	
C2C:	Mint $700	Ex $525	VG+ $370	Good $330	Fair $170
Trade-In:	Mint $520	Ex $425	VG+ $290	Good $255	Poor $90

BENELLI

SPORT REDBOOK CODE: RB-BN-S-SPORTX

Interchangeable carbon fiber vent ribs, set of five chokes, one-piece aluminum alloy receiver in blue finish, buttpad, fires 3" shells.

Production: *imported 1997–2002* **Gauge/Bore:** *12 ga.*

Action: *semi-auto*

Barrel Length: 26", 28" **Wt.:** *~7.1 lbs.*

Sights: *N/A*

Capacity: *5*

Stock: *checkered select walnut with satin finish*

D2C:	NIB $1,215	Ex $925	VG+ $670	Good $610	
C2C:	Mint $1,170	Ex $850	VG+ $610	Good $550	Fair $280
Trade-In:	Mint $870	Ex $700	VG+ $480	Good $430	Poor $150

SPORT II REDBOOK CODE: RB-BN-S-SPORT2

Inertia-driven bolt mechanism, set of five chokes, ported barrel.

Production: *current* **Gauge/Bore:** *12 ga., 20 ga.*

Action: *semi-auto*

Barrel Length: 28", 30" **Wt.:** *~7.9 lbs.*

Sights: *twin bead*

Capacity: *5*

Stock: *AA Grade walnut*

D2C:	NIB $1,660	Ex $1,275	VG+ $915	Good $830	
C2C:	Mint $1,600	Ex $1,150	VG+ $830	Good $750	Fair $385
Trade-In:	Mint $1,180	Ex $950	VG+ $650	Good $585	Poor $180

M1 SUPER 90 DEFENSE REDBOOK CODE: RB-BN-S-S90M1D

Inertia recoil system, aluminum alloy receiver, integral pistol-grip stock, fires 3" shells. Add $41 to value with ghost ring sights.

Production: *imported through 1998* **Gauge/Bore:** *12 ga.*

Action: *semi-auto*

Barrel Length: 18.5," 20" **Wt.:** *7.1 lbs.*

Sights: *rifle-type, optional ghost ring*

Capacity: *8*

Stock: *black synthetic with pistol grip*

D2C:	NIB $750	Ex $575	VG+ $415	Good $375	
C2C:	Mint $720	Ex $525	VG+ $380	Good $340	Fair $175
Trade-In:	Mint $540	Ex $425	VG+ $300	Good $265	Poor $90

M1 SUPER 90 FIELD REDBOOK CODE: RB-BN-S-S90M1F

Inertia recoil system, vent rib, set of five screw-in chokes, aluminum alloy receiver, matte finish, fires 3" shells. Value varies according to finish and stock type.

Production: *imported through 2006* **Gauge/Bore:** *12 ga., 20 ga.*

Action: *semi-auto*

Barrel Length: 21", 24", 26", 28" **Wt.:** *5.8 lbs., 7.2 lbs.*

Sights: *bead front*

Capacity: *4*

Stock: *satin walnut or synthetic in matte black, Realtree Xtra Brown or Advantage Timber HD camouflage*

D2C:	NIB $915	Ex $700	VG+ $505	Good $460	
C2C:	Mint $880	Ex $650	VG+ $460	Good $415	Fair $215
Trade-In:	Mint $650	Ex $525	VG+ $360	Good $325	Poor $120

M1 SUPER 90 SLUG REDBOOK CODE: RB-BN-S-90M1SG

Rotating Montefeltro bolt system, changed from 12 ga. to 20 ga. in 2004, models made after 1997 have drilled and tapped rifled 24" barrel. Add $100 for camouflage finish.

Production: *discontinued* **Gauge/Bore:** *12 ga., 20 ga.*

Action: *semi-auto*

Barrel Length: 19.75", 24" **Wt.:** *6.5 lbs.*

Sights: *rifle-type*

Capacity: *8*

D2C:	NIB $925	Ex $725	VG+ $510	Good $465	
C2C:	Mint $890	Ex $650	VG+ $470	Good $420	Fair $215
Trade-In:	Mint $660	Ex $525	VG+ $370	Good $325	Poor $120

Stock: *synthetic in matte black, Realtree Xtra Brown or Advantage Timber HD camouflage*

M1 SUPER 90 PRACTICAL REDBOOK CODE: RB-BN-S-S90M1P

Plain barrel with muzzle brake, Picatinny rail, set of three chokes, matte metal finish, oversized safety and bolt handle.

Production: *discontinued* **Gauge/Bore:** *12 ga.*

Action: *semi-auto*

Barrel Length: 26" **Wt.:** *7.6 lbs.*

Sights: *mil spec adjustable ghost ring*

Capacity: *9*

D2C:	NIB $1,080	Ex $825	VG+ $595	Good $540	
C2C:	Mint $1,040	Ex $750	VG+ $540	Good $490	Fair $250
Trade-In:	Mint $770	Ex $625	VG+ $430	Good $380	Poor $120

Stock: *black synthetic*

M1 SUPER 90 SPORTING SPECIAL REDBOOK CODE: RB-BN-S-90M1SS

Matte black finish, set of three chokes (improved cylinder, modified, full), buttpad.

Production: *discontinued* **Gauge/Bore:** *12 ga.*

Action: *semi-auto*

Barrel Length: 18.5" **Wt.:** *6.5 lbs.*

Sights: *ghost ring*

Capacity: *8*

D2C:	NIB $725	Ex $575	VG+ $400	Good $365	
C2C:	Mint $700	Ex $525	VG+ $370	Good $330	Fair $170
Trade-In:	Mint $520	Ex $425	VG+ $290	Good $255	Poor $90

Stock: *synthetic*

M1 SUPER 90 TACTICAL REDBOOK CODE: RB-BN-S-S90M1T

Inertia recoil system, set of three chokes, fires 3" Magnum shells.

Production: *discontinued* **Gauge/Bore:** *12 ga.*

Action: *semi-auto*

Barrel Length: 18.5" **Wt.:** *6.5 lbs.*

Sights: *fixed rifle-type or ghost ring*

Capacity: *6*

D2C:	NIB $770	Ex $600	VG+ $425	Good $385	
C2C:	Mint $740	Ex $550	VG+ $390	Good $350	Fair $180
Trade-In:	Mint $550	Ex $450	VG+ $310	Good $270	Poor $90

Stock: *synthetic pistol grip or standard stock*

SUPER 90 MONTEFELTRO REDBOOK CODE: RB-BN-S-S90MFT

Vent rib, inertia-driven, set of five screw-in chokes, matte blue metal finish, fires 3" shells. Add $50 for left-handed model. Additional value for models with Realtree camouflage finish.

Production: *discontinued* **Gauge/Bore:** *12 ga.*

Action: *semi-auto*

Barrel Length: 21", 24", 26", 28" **Wt.:** *5.3–7.5 lbs.*

Sights: *N/A*

Capacity: *5*

Stock: *high-gloss walnut or Realtree camouflage finish*

D2C:	NIB $915	Ex $700	VG+ $505	Good $460	
C2C:	Mint $880	Ex $650	VG+ $460	Good $415	Fair $215
Trade-In:	Mint $650	Ex $525	VG+ $360	Good $325	Poor $120

SUPER 90 MONTEFELTRO LIMITED EDITION REDBOOK CODE: RB-BN-S-S90MLE

Vent rib, inertia-driven, engraved gold-inlaid nickel-plated receiver, matte blue finish, fires 3" shells. Add approximately 50% to value compared to base model.

Production: *1995–1996* **Gauge/Bore:** *20 ga.*

Action: *semi-auto*

Barrel Length: 26" **Wt.:** *5.75 lbs.*

Sights: *N/A*

Capacity: *5*

Stock: *European walnut with satin finish*

D2C:	NIB $1,760	Ex $1,350	VG+ $970	Good $880	
C2C:	Mint $1,690	Ex $1,225	VG+ $880	Good $795	Fair $405
Trade-In:	Mint $1,250	Ex $1,000	VG+ $690	Good $620	Poor $180

SUPER 90 MONTEFELTRO SILVER REDBOOK CODE: RB-BN-S-S90MSL

Inertia-driven, low-profile vent rib, set of five choke tubes, engraved nickel-plated alloy receiver, game scenes etched on stock, matte blue finish, fires 3" shells.

Production: *discontinued* **Gauge/Bore:** *20 ga.*

Action: *semi-auto*

Barrel Length: 26" **Wt.:** *5.6 lbs.*

Sights: *red bar front, metal bead mid*

Capacity: *5*

Stock: *AA-Grade satin walnut*

D2C:	NIB $1,550	Ex $1,200	VG+ $855	Good $775	
C2C:	Mint $1,490	Ex $1,075	VG+ $780	Good $700	Fair $360
Trade-In:	Mint $1,110	Ex $875	VG+ $610	Good $545	Poor $180

SUPER 90 MONTEFELTRO SLUG GUN REDBOOK CODE: RB-BN-S-S90MSG

Rifled slug barrel, stock with adjustable drop, set of five choke tubes, aluminum alloy receiver, matte blue metal finish, fires 3" shells.

Production: *discontinued 1992* **Gauge/Bore:** *12 ga.*

Action: *semi-auto*

Barrel Length: 24" **Wt.:** *7 lbs.*

Sights: *N/A*

Capacity: *5*

Stock: *European walnut with satin finish*

D2C:	NIB $635	Ex $500	VG+ $350	Good $320	
C2C:	Mint $610	Ex $450	VG+ $320	Good $290	Fair $150
Trade-In:	Mint $460	Ex $375	VG+ $250	Good $225	Poor $90

SUPER 90 MONTEFELTRO STANDARD HUNTER REDBOOK CODE: RB-BN-S-S90MSH

Inertia-driven, vent rib, rotary bolt, set of five choke tubes, aluminum alloy receiver, fires 3" shells.

Production: *discontinued* **Gauge/Bore:** *12 ga., 20 ga.*

Action: *semi-auto*

Barrel Length: 24", 26", 28" **Wt.:** *5.5 lbs., 7.1 lbs.*

Sights: *bead front*

Capacity: *5*

D2C:	NIB $1,200	Ex $925	VG+ $660	Good $600	
C2C:	Mint $1,160	Ex $850	VG+ $600	Good $540	Fair $280
Trade-In:	Mint $860	Ex $675	VG+ $470	Good $420	Poor $120

Stock: *walnut with high-gloss and satin-finish options, or synthetic with matte-black metal and Realtree full-camouflage options.*

SUPER 90 MONTEFELTRO TURKEY GUN REDBOOK CODE: RB-BN-S-S90MTG

Vent rib, inertia-driven, set of five choke tubes, aluminum alloy receiver, fires 3" shells.

Production: *discontinued* **Gauge/Bore:** *12 ga., 20 ga.*

Action: *semi-auto*

Barrel Length: 24" **Wt.:** *7 lbs.*

Sights: *bead front*

Capacity: *5*

D2C:	NIB $640	Ex $500	VG+ $355	Good $320	
C2C:	Mint $620	Ex $450	VG+ $320	Good $290	Fair $150
Trade-In:	Mint $460	Ex $375	VG+ $250	Good $225	Poor $90

Stock: *walnut with satin finish*

SUPER 90 MONTEFELTRO UPLANDER REDBOOK CODE: RB-BN-S-S90MUP

Inertia-driven, vent rib, set of five choke tubes, aluminum alloy receiver, matte blue metal finish, fires 3" shells.

Production: *discontinued 1992* **Gauge/Bore:** *12 ga.*

Action: *semi-auto*

Barrel Length: 21", 24" **Wt.:** *7 lbs.*

Sights: *N/A*

Capacity: *5*

D2C:	NIB $625	Ex $475	VG+ $345	Good $315	
C2C:	Mint $600	Ex $450	VG+ $320	Good $285	Fair $145
Trade-In:	Mint $450	Ex $350	VG+ $250	Good $220	Poor $90

Stock: *walnut with satin finish*

SUPER BLACK EAGLE REDBOOK CODE: RB-BN-S-SPRBLE

Montefeltro inertia recoil system, vent rib, set of five choke tubes, stock with adjustable drop, matte or blue finish, fires 2.75", 3", and 3.5" shells. Add $85 for Advantage Timber HD camouflage. Add $50 for left-handed model.

Production: *1991–2005* **Gauge/Bore:** *12 ga.*

Action: *semi-auto*

Barrel Length: 24", 26", 28" **Wt.:** *7.4 lbs.*

Sights: *red bar front*

Capacity: *3, 4*

D2C:	NIB $1,275	Ex $975	VG+ $705	Good $640	
C2C:	Mint $1,230	Ex $900	VG+ $640	Good $575	Fair $295
Trade-In:	Mint $910	Ex $725	VG+ $500	Good $450	Poor $150

Stock: *walnut with high-gloss and satin-finish options, or synthetic with Realtree Xtra Brown and Advantage Timber HD camouflage options.*

BENELLI

SUPER BLACK EAGLE II TURKEY   REDBOOK CODE: RB-BN-S-SBE2TK

Drilled & tapped, vent rib barrel, inertia recoil system, Realtree APG HD full camouflage, large trigger
guard, chambers 3.5" shells. Add $100 for left-hand action with ComforTech stock. Add $100 for SteadyGrip pistol-grip stock.

Production: *discontinued* **Gauge/Bore:** *12 ga.*

Action: *semi-auto*

Barrel Length: 24" **Wt.:** *7.1 lbs.*

Sights: *red bar front*

Capacity: 4

D2C:	NIB $2,650	Ex $2,025	VG+ $1,460	Good $1,325	
C2C:	Mint $2,550	Ex $1,850	VG+ $1,330	Good $1,195	Fair $610
Trade-In:	Mint $1,890	Ex $1,500	VG+ $1,040	Good $930	Poor $270

Stock: *synthetic ComforTech or SteadyGrip pistol-grip, Realtree APG HD camouflage finish*

SUPER BLACK EAGLE SLUG   REDBOOK CODE: RB-BN-S-SBESLG

Drilled & tapped for scope mount, rifled slug barrel, inertia recoil system, Realtree APG HD
full camouflage, large trigger guard, fires 3" shells. Add $100 for full camouflage finish. Subtract approximately $100 for walnut stock model.

Production: *discontinued* **Gauge/Bore:** *12 ga.*

Action: *semi-auto*

Barrel Length: 24" **Wt.:** *7.6 lbs.*

Sights: *adjustable rifle-type*

Capacity: 4

D2C:	NIB $1,525	Ex $1,175	VG+ $840	Good $765	
C2C:	Mint $1,470	Ex $1,075	VG+ $770	Good $690	Fair $355
Trade-In:	Mint $1,090	Ex $875	VG+ $600	Good $535	Poor $180

Stock: *walnut with satin finish or synthetic ComforTech with choice of Advantage Timber HD or Realtree APG HD camouflage*

Beretta USA

BERETTA

Fabbrica d'Armi Pietro Beretta, or simply Beretta, has manufactured guns and weaponry since 1526, making it the oldest firearms manufacturer in the world, as well as one of the best known. The company has a rich history of manufacturing submachine guns, rifles, and pistols for military and police forces worldwide. In 1977, Beretta USA was created as an American subsidiary of the Italian-based Beretta. Currently, Beretta produces a number of different types of rifles, pistols, and machine guns, and shotgun offerings include semi-automatic, over/under, and side-by-side product lines. Beretta USA was originally based in Accokeek, Maryland. However, in 2014, after several disputes with the state of Maryland prompted by changes in the state's gun laws, Beretta USA announced that all of its operations would be relocated to Gallatin, Tennessee.

TX4 STORM   REDBOOK CODE: RB-BR-S-TX4STM

Ventilated rib Steelium barrel, Unico system allows hunter to shoot lead or steel shells, from 2 3/4"-3"
Mag., Optima-Bore HP choke tubes, Blink gas operating system, rotating bolt head, add $100 for Kick-off recoil reduction system.

Production: *current* **Gauge/Bore:** *12 ga.*

Action: *semi-auto*

Barrel Length: 18.5" **Wt.:** *6.4 lbs.*

Sights: *ghost ring front, removable rear*

Capacity: 5

Stock: *synthetic, black*

D2C:	NIB $1,450	Ex $1,125	VG+ $800	Good $725	
C2C:	Mint $1,400	Ex $1,025	VG+ $730	Good $655	Fair $335
Trade-In:	Mint $1,030	Ex $825	VG+ $570	Good $510	Poor $150

A400 XPLOR UNICO REDBOOK CODE: RB-BR-S-A400XU
Lightweight Steelium barrel with OptimaBore HP, Blink technology, low-profile receiver, Kick-Off 3 advanced recoil-reducing device, MicroCore buttpad, stock with internally mounted shock-absorber, tool-free disassembly.

Production: *current* **Gauge/Bore:** *12 ga.*
Action: *semi-auto*
Barrel Length: 24", 26", 28", 30" **Wt.:** *7.1 lbs.*
Sights: *bead*
Capacity: *5*
Stock: *walnut*

D2C:	NIB $1,590	Ex $1,225	VG+ $875	Good $795	**LMP: $1,745**
C2C:	Mint $1,530	Ex $1,100	VG+ $800	Good $720	Fair $370
Trade-In:	Mint $1,130	Ex $900	VG+ $630	Good $560	Poor $180

A400 XPLOR LIGHT REDBOOK CODE: RB-BR-S-A400XL
Vent ribbed tri-alloy Steelium barrel, Optima-Bore HP choke tubes, bronze receiver, Blink gas operating system, rotating bolt head and new feeding system, Gun POD digital display in stock, add $105 for Kick-off recoil reduction system.

Production: *current* **Gauge/Bore:** *12 ga.*
Action: *semi-auto*
Barrel Length: 24", 26", 28", 30" **Wt.:** *6.1 lbs.*
Sights: *bead*
Capacity: *5*
Stock: *select walnut*

D2C:	NIB $1,430	Ex $1,100	VG+ $790	Good $715	
C2C:	Mint $1,380	Ex $1,000	VG+ $720	Good $645	Fair $330
Trade-In:	Mint $1,020	Ex $825	VG+ $560	Good $505	Poor $150

A400 XPLOR ACTION REDBOOK CODE: RB-BR-S-A400XA
Low-profile action, gas-operated action, 3" chamber, multiple recoil-reducers, bronze colored receiver, fine checkering.

Production: *current* **Gauge/Bore:** *12 ga., 20 ga., 28 ga.*
Action: *semi-auto*
Barrel Length: 24", 26", 28", 30" **Wt.:** *N/A*
Sights: *fiber optic*
Capacity: *5*
Stock: *Xtra grain walnut*

D2C:	NIB $1,480	Ex $1,125	VG+ $815	Good $740	**LMP: $1,550**
C2C:	Mint $1,430	Ex $1,025	VG+ $740	Good $670	Fair $345
Trade-In:	Mint $1,060	Ex $850	VG+ $580	Good $520	Poor $150

A400 XPLOR NOVATOR REDBOOK CODE: RB-BR-S-A400SN
Vent ribbed tri-alloy Steelium barrel with chrome-plated bore, anodized aluminum receiver, corrosion resistant finish, Blink gas operating system, rotating bolt head, new feeding system, B-lock forend cap, anti-glare on slide, carrier and trigger, Kick-off recoil reduction system.

Production: *current* **Gauge/Bore:** *12 ga.*
Action: *semi-auto*
Barrel Length: 28", 30" **Wt.:** *N/A*
Sights: *fiber optic*
Capacity: *5*
Stock: *select walnut*

D2C:	NIB $1,500	Ex $1,150	VG+ $825	Good $750	
C2C:	Mint $1,440	Ex $1,050	VG+ $750	Good $675	Fair $345
Trade-In:	Mint $1,070	Ex $850	VG+ $590	Good $525	Poor $150

A400 XTREME UNICO CAMOUFLAGE-MAX5 REDBOOK CODE: RB-BR-S-A400C5

Vent ribbed tri-alloy Steelium barrel, 3.5" chamber, Optima Bore HP choke tubes, Unico system allowing varying loads, corrosion and weather resistant finish, Blink gas operating system rotating bolt head and new feeding system, B-lock forend cap, Kick-off recoil reduction system.

Production: *current* **Gauge/Bore:** *12 ga.*
Action: *semi-auto*
Barrel Length: 26", 28", 30" **Wt.:** *N/A*
Sights: *fiber optic*
Capacity: *5*
Stock: *synthetic, Max5 camouflage*

D2C:	NIB $1,850	Ex $1,425	VG+ $1,020	Good $925	**LMP:** $1,895
C2C:	Mint $1,780	Ex $1,300	VG+ $930	Good $835	Fair $430
Trade-In:	Mint $1,320	Ex $1,050	VG+ $730	Good $650	Poor $210

A400 XTREME UNICO CAMOUFLAGE-MAX4 REDBOOK CODE: RB-BR-S-A400C4

Vent ribbed tri-alloy Steelium barrel, 3.5" chamber, Optima Bore HP choke tubes, Unico system allowing varying loads, corrosion and weather resistant finish, Blink gas operating system, rotating bolt head, new feeding system, B-lock forend cap, Kick-off recoil reduction system.

Production: *current* **Gauge/Bore:** *12 ga.*
Action: *semi-auto*
Barrel Length: 26", 28", 30" **Wt.:** *N/A*
Sights: *fiber optic*
Capacity: *5*
Stock: *synthetic, RealTree Max4 camouflage*

D2C:	NIB $1,875	Ex $1,425	VG+ $1,035	Good $940	**LMP:** $1,895
C2C:	Mint $1,800	Ex $1,300	VG+ $940	Good $845	Fair $435
Trade-In:	Mint $1,340	Ex $1,050	VG+ $740	Good $660	Poor $210

A400 XTREME UNICO CAMOUFLAGE-OPTIFADE REDBOOK CODE: RB-BR-S-A400CO

Vent ribbed tri-alloy Steelium barrel, 3.5" chamber, Optima Bore HP choke tubes, Unico system allowing varying loads, corrosion resistant finish, Blink gas operating system rotating bolt head and new feeding system, B-lock for-end cap, Kick-off recoil reduction system, adjustable shim system at buttpad, Micro Core polymer recoil pad.

Production: *current* **Gauge/Bore:** *12 ga.*
Action: *semi-auto*
Barrel Length: 26", 28" **Wt.:** *N/A*
Sights: *fiber optic*
Capacity: *5*
Stock: *synthetic, Optifade camouflage*

D2C:	NIB $1,895	Ex $1,450	VG+ $1,045	Good $950	**LMP:** $1,895
C2C:	Mint $1,820	Ex $1,325	VG+ $950	Good $855	Fair $440
Trade-In:	Mint $1,350	Ex $1,075	VG+ $740	Good $665	Poor $210

A400 XTREME UNICO CAMOUFLAGE-SYNTHETIC REDBOOK CODE: RB-BR-S-A400CS

Gas operated, satin nickel-phosphate receiver, self-cleaning piston action, low-profile action, soft rubber recoil pad, also available in black finish.

Production: *current* **Gauge/Bore:** *12 ga.*
Action: *semi-auto*
Barrel Length: 26", 28", 30" **Wt.:** *N/A*
Sights: *fiber optic*
Capacity: *5*
Stock: *synthetic, black*

D2C:	NIB $1,745	Ex $1,350	VG+ $960	Good $875	**LMP:** $1,745
C2C:	Mint $1,680	Ex $1,225	VG+ $880	Good $790	Fair $405
Trade-In:	Mint $1,240	Ex $1,000	VG+ $690	Good $615	Poor $180

A300 OUTLANDER REDBOOK CODE: RB-BR-S-A300OL

Vent ribbed tri-alloy Steelium barrel and self-cleaning piston, Mobile Choke interchangeable tubes, 3" chamber, B-Lok forend cap, reversible safety, includes spacers for adjustable stock, sling attachments, also available in woodland camouflage pattern as A300 Outlander camouflage Max5.

Production: *current* **Gauge/Bore:** *12 ga.*
Action: *semi-auto*
Barrel Length: 24", 26", 28" **Wt.:** *7.3 lbs.*
Sights: *bead front*
Capacity: *3*
Stock: *walnut*

D2C:	NIB $875	Ex $675	VG+ $485	Good $440	**LMP: $875**
C2C:	Mint $840	Ex $625	VG+ $440	Good $395	Fair $205
Trade-In:	Mint $630	Ex $500	VG+ $350	Good $310	Poor $90

A300 OUTLANDER CAMOUFLAGE MAX4 REDBOOK CODE: RB-BR-S-A300C4

Vent ribbed tri-alloy Steelium black finished barrel, grooved receiver, Mobile Choke interchangeable tubes, 3" chamber, reversible safety, pistol grip, includes spacers for LOP and drop and cast, sling attachments, A300 available in other camouflage patterns, such as Outlander camouflage Max4, Outlander camouflage Max5 and blue finished Outlander with walnut stock.

Production: *current* **Gauge/Bore:** *12 ga.*
Action: *semi-auto*
Barrel Length: 28" **Wt.:** *N/A*
Sights: *bead front*
Capacity: *3*
Stock: *synthetic, Max4 camouflage*

D2C:	NIB $845	Ex $650	VG+ $465	Good $425	**LMP: $845**
C2C:	Mint $820	Ex $600	VG+ $430	Good $385	Fair $195
Trade-In:	Mint $600	Ex $475	VG+ $330	Good $300	Poor $90

A300 OUTLANDER SYNTHETIC REDBOOK CODE: RB-BR-S-A300OS

Cold hammer forged ventilated rib barrel with chrome-plated bore, Optima Bore HP choke tubes, "Beretta blue" receiver, three interchangeable weighted balance caps, Blink gas-operating system, self-cleaning piston, Micro Core polymer buttpad, add $100 for Kick-Off option, add $150 for optional Gun Pod digital display.

Production: *current* **Gauge/Bore:** *12 ga.*
Action: *semi-auto*
Barrel Length: 24", 26", 28", 30" **Wt.:** *7.3 lbs.*
Sights: *bead front*
Capacity: *3*
Stock: *synthetic, black*

D2C:	NIB $775	Ex $600	VG+ $430	Good $390	**LMP: $775**
C2C:	Mint $750	Ex $550	VG+ $390	Good $350	Fair $180
Trade-In:	Mint $560	Ex $450	VG+ $310	Good $275	Poor $90

A400 XCEL REDBOOK CODE: RB-BR-S-A400XC

Steelium alloy barrels, flat ventilated rib, Optima HP choke tubes, double top receiver and shoulder design, adjustable extractor or ejector, single selective trigger, rounded forend, 2.4" drop, pistol grip, Micro Core polymer recoil pad.

Production: *current* **Gauge/Bore:** *12 ga.*
Action: *semi-auto*
Barrel Length: 28", 30", 32" **Wt.:** *N/A*
Sights: *bead front*
Capacity: *3*
Stock: *hardwood*

D2C:	NIB $1,745	Ex $1,350	VG+ $960	Good $875	**LMP: $1,745**
C2C:	Mint $1,680	Ex $1,225	VG+ $880	Good $790	Fair $405
Trade-In:	Mint $1,240	Ex $1,000	VG+ $690	Good $615	Poor $180

686 SILVER PIGEON I REDBOOK CODE: RB-BR-S-686SPI

Cold hammer-forged steel barrels with ventilated rib, 3" chamber, Mobil Choked interchangeable tubes, Schnabel forend, low profile floral engraved Monoblock receiver, dual conical locking lugs, tang safety and barrel selector, only 2 3/4" chamber on 28 gauge, other barrel lengths available on 12 gauge only.

Production: *current* **Gauge/Bore:** *12 ga., 20 ga., 28 ga., .410*
Action: *O/U*
Barrel Length: 26", 28", 30" **Wt.:** *N/A*
Sights: *bead front*
Capacity: *2*
Stock: *select walnut, pistol grip*

D2C:	NIB $2,100	Ex $1,600	VG+ $1,155	Good $1,050	LMP: $2,245
C2C:	Mint $2,020	Ex $1,450	VG+ $1,050	Good $945	Fair $485
Trade-In:	Mint $1,500	Ex $1,200	VG+ $820	Good $735	Poor $210

686 SILVER PIGEON I SPORTING REDBOOK CODE: RB-BR-S-686SPS

Lightweight, tri-alloy steel chrome lined barrels, Mobilchoke system, ventilated rib, 2" chamber, dual conical self-adjusting locking lugs, gold-plated trigger, also available in Classic SR with a rifled MC choke, and Ultralight Gold.

Production: *current* **Gauge/Bore:** *12 ga., 20 ga., 28 ga., .410*
Action: *O/U*
Barrel Length: 30" **Wt.:** *N/A*
Sights: *bead front*
Capacity: *2*
Stock: *select walnut, pistol grip*

D2C:	NIB $2,245	Ex $1,725	VG+ $1,235	Good $1,125	LMP: $2,245
C2C:	Mint $2,160	Ex $1,550	VG+ $1,130	Good $1,015	Fair $520
Trade-In:	Mint $1,600	Ex $1,275	VG+ $880	Good $790	Poor $240

686 ULTRALIGHT REDBOOK CODE: RB-BR-S-686ULT

Cold-hammer forged tri-alloy steel chrome lined barrels, with Optimabore/Optimachoke system, ventilated rib, 2" chamber, dual conical self-adjusting locking lugs, gold-plated trigger, available in Sporting model.

Production: *current* **Gauge/Bore:** *12 ga.*
Action: *O/U*
Barrel Length: 24", 26", 28" **Wt.:** *5.9 lbs.*
Sights: *bead front*
Capacity: *2*
Stock: *walnut*

D2C:	NIB $1,250	Ex $950	VG+ $690	Good $625	
C2C:	Mint $1,200	Ex $875	VG+ $630	Good $565	Fair $290
Trade-In:	Mint $890	Ex $700	VG+ $490	Good $440	Poor $150

686 WHITE ONYX REDBOOK CODE: RB-BR-S-686WOX

Cold hammer-forged steel barrels with vented rib, 3" chamber, Mobile Choke interchangeable tubes, Schnabel forend, low profile Monoblock receiver engraved with scroll work and game scenes, dual conical locking lugs, tang safety and barrel selector, only 2" chamber on 28 gauge, 30" barrel length not available on 28 gauge and .410 gauge.

Production: *current* **Gauge/Bore:** *12 ga., 20 ga., 28 ga.*
Action: *O/U*
Barrel Length: 26", 28" **Wt.:** *6.7 lbs.*
Sights: *bead front*
Capacity: *2*
Stock: *gloss finish walnut*

D2C:	NIB $1,980	Ex $1,525	VG+ $1,090	Good $990	
C2C:	Mint $1,910	Ex $1,375	VG+ $990	Good $895	Fair $460
Trade-In:	Mint $1,410	Ex $1,125	VG+ $780	Good $695	Poor $210

BERETTA

687 SILVER PIGEON III   REDBOOK CODE: RB-BR-S-687SP3

Cold hammer-forged steel barrels with ventilated rib, 3" chamber, Mobil Choke interchangeable tubes, Schnabel forend, low profile Monoblock color-case finished receiver engraved with gold game scenes and a Beretta gold medallion, dual conical locking lugs, tang safety and barrel selector, only 2" chamber on 28 gauge, 30" barrel length not available on 28 gauge and .410 gauge, available with English straight stock.

Production: *current* **Gauge/Bore:** *12 ga., 20 ga., 28 ga., .410*
Action: *O/U*
Barrel Length: 26", 28", 30" **Wt.:** *7 lbs.*
Sights: *bead front*
Capacity: *2*
Stock: *select walnut, crisp checkering*

D2C:	NIB $3,400	Ex $2,600	VG+ $1,870	Good $1,700	**LMP: $3,425**
C2C:	Mint $3,270	Ex $2,350	VG+ $1,700	Good $1,530	Fair $785
Trade-In:	Mint $2,420	Ex $1,925	VG+ $1,330	Good $1,190	Poor $360

687 SILVER PIGEON V   REDBOOK CODE: RB-BR-S-687SP5

Cold-hammer forged Optima Bore barrels, flat ventilated rib, 3" chamber, low-profile action, self-adjusting forend, detachable trigger group, pistol grip, for optional Kick-Off recoil reducer add $400.

Production: *current* **Gauge/Bore:** *12 ga., 20 ga., 28 ga., .410*
Action: *O/U*
Barrel Length: 26", 28" **Wt.:** *N/A*
Sights: *bead front*
Capacity: *2*
Stock: *figured select walnut, pistol grip*

D2C:	NIB $4,075	Ex $3,100	VG+ $2,245	Good $2,040	**LMP: $4,075**
C2C:	Mint $3,920	Ex $2,825	VG+ $2,040	Good $1,835	Fair $940
Trade-In:	Mint $2,900	Ex $2,300	VG+ $1,590	Good $1,430	Poor $420

687 EELL CLASSIC   REDBOOK CODE: RB-BR-S-687ELC

Top of the 687 line, tri-blend alloy Steelium blue finished barrel with ventilated rib, low profile receiver, side-plates with lavishly hand-chased engraving extending to the trigger plate, trigger guard and forend lever, tang safety and barrel selector in one control, oval brass shield inlaid in the stock for engraving, carry case, receiver scaled down on smaller gauges, optional Combo model in 20/28 ga. available for an additional $1720.

Production: *current* **Gauge/Bore:** *12 ga., 20 ga., 28 ga., .410*
Action: *O/U*
Barrel Length: 26", 28", 30" **Wt.:** *7 lbs.*
Sights: *bead front*
Capacity: *2*
Stock: *European walnut, semi-beavertail, fine-line checkering*

D2C:	NIB $8,000	Ex $6,100	VG+ $4,400	Good $4,000	**LMP: $7,995**
C2C:	Mint $7,680	Ex $5,525	VG+ $4,000	Good $3,600	Fair $1,840
Trade-In:	Mint $5,680	Ex $4,500	VG+ $3,120	Good $2,800	Poor $810

687 EELL DIAMOND PIGEON   REDBOOK CODE: RB-BR-S-687ELD

Cold-hammer forged Boehler Antinit steel barrels with file-cut ventilated rib, sophisticated hand engraved action with no visible screws, safety/barrel selector in one control switch also activates side-opening side-locks, Mobile Choke interchangeable tubes, replaceable locking shoulders, Monobloc lugs cross-bolt locking system, pistol grip or straight English classic stock, hand-cut diamond checkered buttstock and forend, leather carry case with accessories.

Production: *current* **Gauge/Bore:** *12 ga., 20 ga., 28 ga., .410*
Action: *O/U*
Barrel Length: 26", 28" **Wt.:** *7 lbs.*
Sights: *bead front*
Capacity: *2*
Stock: *European walnut, semi-beavertail, fine-line checkering*

D2C:	NIB $7,825	Ex $5,950	VG+ $4,305	Good $3,915	**LMP: $7,825**
C2C:	Mint $7,520	Ex $5,400	VG+ $3,920	Good $3,525	Fair $1,800
Trade-In:	Mint $5,560	Ex $4,400	VG+ $3,060	Good $2,740	Poor $810

BERETTA

690 FIELD III   REDBOOK CODE: RB-BR-S-690FD3

Cold hammer-forged steel barrels with vented rib, 3" chamber, Mobile Choke interchangeable tubes, Schnabel and other forends, low profile scroll engraved receiver, tang safety and barrel selector, 2 3/4" chamber on 28 gauge, case, 30" barrel not offered on .410 gauge.

Production: *current* **Gauge/Bore:** *12 ga.*
Action: *O/U*
Barrel Length: 26", 28", 30" **Wt.:** *7.4 lbs.*
Sights: *bead front*
Capacity: *2*
Stock: *high-grade hardwood*

D2C:	NIB $3,495	Ex $2,675	VG+ $1,925	Good $1,750	LMP: $3,495
C2C:	Mint $3,360	Ex $2,425	VG+ $1,750	Good $1,575	Fair $805
Trade-In:	Mint $2,490	Ex $1,975	VG+ $1,370	Good $1,225	Poor $360

692 TRAP   REDBOOK CODE: RB-BR-S-692TRP

Tri-alloy blend Steelium barrels with a ventilated rib, 3" chamber, OBSK-HP chokes, replaceable locking shoulders, wide receiver, adjustable single selective trigger and ejector/extractor, teardrop polymer opening lever, safety/barrel selector, optional B-Fast adjustable comb system, weight adjustable buttstock, Micro Core polymer recoil pad.

Production: *current* **Gauge/Bore:** *12 ga.*
Action: *O/U*
Barrel Length: 30", 32" **Wt.:** *N/A*
Sights: *bead front*
Capacity: *2*
Stock: *select walnut, checkering, pistol grip*

D2C:	NIB $5,200	Ex $3,975	VG+ $2,860	Good $2,600	LMP: $5,225
C2C:	Mint $5,000	Ex $3,600	VG+ $2,600	Good $2,340	Fair $1,200
Trade-In:	Mint $3,700	Ex $2,925	VG+ $2,030	Good $1,820	Poor $540

692 SPORTING   REDBOOK CODE: RB-BR-S-692STG

Premium-grade tri-alloy blend Steelium-Pro barrels, vault-like crossbolt action, wide receiver, detachable "drop" trigger group, HP choke tubes, priced for "headed" option, add $349 for formed stock, optional B-Fast comb adjustment system available for additional cost.

Production: *current* **Gauge/Bore:** *12 ga.*
Action: *O/U*
Barrel Length: 28", 30", 32" **Wt.:** *N/A*
Sights: *bead front*
Capacity: *2*
Stock: *select walnut, checkering, pistol grip*

D2C:	NIB $4,200	Ex $3,200	VG+ $2,310	Good $2,100	LMP: $4,755
C2C:	Mint $4,040	Ex $2,900	VG+ $2,100	Good $1,890	Fair $970
Trade-In:	Mint $2,990	Ex $2,375	VG+ $1,640	Good $1,470	Poor $420

SV10 PERENNIA I   REDBOOK CODE: RB-BR-S-SVXPA1

Cold-hammer forged Optima Bore aluminum alloy barrels, OCHP chokes, flat ventilated rib, 3" chamber, low-profile action, engraved with hunting scenes, self-adjusting forend, detachable trigger group, for optional Kick-Off recoil reducing device add $325.

Production: *current* **Gauge/Bore:** *12 ga., 20 ga.*
Action: *O/U*
Barrel Length: 26", 28", 30" **Wt.:** *N/A*
Sights: *bead front*
Capacity: *2*
Stock: *select hardwood, checkering*

D2C:	NIB $2,895	Ex $2,225	VG+ $1,595	Good $1,450	LMP: $2,895
C2C:	Mint $2,780	Ex $2,000	VG+ $1,450	Good $1,305	Fair $670
Trade-In:	Mint $2,060	Ex $1,625	VG+ $1,130	Good $1,015	Poor $300

SV10 PERENNIA III REDBOOK CODE: RB-BR-S-SVXPA3

Cold-hammer forged Optima Bore aluminum alloy barrels, flat ventilated rib, chrome-lined 3" chamber, low-profile action, engraved with hunting scenes, self-adjusting forend, detachable trigger group, optional Kick-Off recoil reducing device, optional scroll engraving, offered in Trap or Sporting models with various options.

Production: *current* **Gauge/Bore:** *12 ga., 20 ga.*
Action: *O/U*
Barrel Length: 26", 28", 30" **Wt.:** *N/A*
Sights: *bead front*
Capacity: *2*
Stock: *select walnut, checkering, pistol grip*

D2C:	NIB $3,295	Ex $2,525	VG+ $1,815	Good $1,650	**LMP:** $3,295
C2C:	Mint $3,170	Ex $2,275	VG+ $1,650	Good $1,485	Fair $760
Trade-In:	Mint $2,340	Ex $1,850	VG+ $1,290	Good $1,155	Poor $330

SV10 PREVAIL I REDBOOK CODE: RB-BR-S-SVXPR1

Cold-hammer forged Optima Bore aluminum alloy barrels, flat ventilated rib, chrome-lined 2 3/4" chamber, low-profile action, self-adjusting forend, detachable trigger group, optional Kick-Off recoil reducing device on select models.

Production: *current* **Gauge/Bore:** *12 ga.*
Action: *O/U*
Barrel Length: 30" **Wt.:** *N/A*
Sights: *bead front*
Capacity: *2*
Stock: *select walnut, checkering, pistol grip*

D2C:	NIB $3,000	Ex $2,300	VG+ $1,650	Good $1,500	
C2C:	Mint $2,880	Ex $2,075	VG+ $1,500	Good $1,350	Fair $690
Trade-In:	Mint $2,130	Ex $1,700	VG+ $1,170	Good $1,050	Poor $300

SV10 PREVAIL III REDBOOK CODE: RB-BR-S-SVXPR3

Tri-alloy blend Steelium barrels with a ventilated rib, 3" chamber, replaceable locking shoulders, wide receiver, adjustable single selective trigger and ejector/extractor, teardrop polymer opening lever, safety/barrel selector, optional B-Fast adjustable comb system, weight adjustable buttstock, Micro Core polymer recoil pad.

Production: *current* **Gauge/Bore:** *12 ga.*
Action: *O/U*
Barrel Length: 28", 30", 32" **Wt.:** *N/A*
Sights: *bead front*
Capacity: *2*
Stock: *select walnut, checkering, pistol grip*

D2C:	NIB $2,798	Ex $2,150	VG+ $1,540	Good $1,400	
C2C:	Mint $2,690	Ex $1,950	VG+ $1,400	Good $1,260	Fair $645
Trade-In:	Mint $1,990	Ex $1,575	VG+ $1,100	Good $980	Poor $300

DT11 - SPORTING REDBOOK CODE: RB-BR-S-DT11SP

Premium-grade tri-alloy blend Steelium-Pro barrels, vault-like crossbolt action, wider receiver, detachable "drop" trigger group, OptimaBore HP choke tubes, optional B-Fast comb adjustment system available at additional cost, priced "headed", add $349 for International Skeet model, add $670 for Skeet USA model.

Production: *current* **Gauge/Bore:** *12 ga.*
Action: *O/U*
Barrel Length: 28", 30", 32" **Wt.:** *N/A*
Sights: *bead front*
Capacity: *2*
Stock: *high grade walnut, checkered, pistol grip*

D2C:	NIB $8,575	Ex $6,525	VG+ $4,720	Good $4,290	**LMP:** $12,500
C2C:	Mint $8,240	Ex $5,925	VG+ $4,290	Good $3,860	Fair $1,975
Trade-In:	Mint $6,090	Ex $4,825	VG+ $3,350	Good $3,005	Poor $870

DT11 - SKEET REDBOOK CODE: RB-BR-S-DT11SK

Premium-grade tri-alloy blend Steelium-Pro barrels, vault-like crossbolt action, wider receiver, detachable
"drop" trigger group, OptimaBore HP choke tubes, optional B-Fast comb adjustment system available at additional cost.

Production: *current* **Gauge/Bore:** *12 ga.*
Action: *O/U*
Barrel Length: 28", 28.7" **Wt.:** *N/A*
Sights: *bead front*
Capacity: 2
Stock: *high grade walnut, checkered, pistol grip*

D2C:	NIB $10,705	Ex $8,150	VG+ $5,890	Good $5,355	LMP: $8,650
C2C:	Mint $10,280	Ex $7,400	VG+ $5,360	Good $4,820	Fair $2,465
Trade-In:	Mint $7,610	Ex $6,000	VG+ $4,180	Good $3,750	Poor $1,080

DT11 - TRAP REDBOOK CODE: RB-BR-S-DT11TP

Premium-grade tri-alloy blend Steelium-Pro barrels, vault-like crossbolt action, wider receiver,
detachable "drop" trigger group, OptimaBore HP choke tubes, with B-Fast comb adjustment system,
available in optional XTrap Combo with Unsingle 32"/34" barrel with adjustable rib for additional $4,130. For LH XTrap Combo add $4,130.

Production: *current* **Gauge/Bore:** *12 ga.*
Action: *O/U*
Barrel Length: 29.5", 30", 32" **Wt.:** *N/A*
Sights: *bead front*
Capacity: 2
Stock: *high grade walnut, checkered, pistol grip*

D2C:	NIB $9,591	Ex $7,300	VG+ $5,280	Good $4,800	LMP: $8,699
C2C:	Mint $9,210	Ex $6,625	VG+ $4,800	Good $4,320	Fair $2,210
Trade-In:	Mint $6,810	Ex $5,375	VG+ $3,750	Good $3,360	Poor $960

DT11 - X-TRAP REDBOOK CODE: RB-BR-S-DT11XT

Cold-hammer forged, tri-alloy Steelium Pro barrels, Optimabore tubes, nickel-based finish on
wide receiver, matte finished side walls, mirror polished ribbon borders, jeweled satin finished
top lever, hand engraved, adjustable/removable trigger group, open-cell techno-polymer Micro-Core
recoil pad, checkered pistol grip and forend, silver polymer case with Beretta logo.

Production: *current* **Gauge/Bore:** *12 ga.*
Action: *O/U*
Barrel Length: 30", 32" **Wt.:** *N/A*
Sights: *bead front*
Capacity: 2
Stock: *high grade walnut, checkered, pistol grip*

D2C:	NIB $9,872	Ex $7,525	VG+ $5,430	Good $4,940	LMP: $9,320
C2C:	Mint $9,480	Ex $6,825	VG+ $4,940	Good $4,445	Fair $2,275
Trade-In:	Mint $7,010	Ex $5,550	VG+ $3,860	Good $3,460	Poor $990

DT11 ACS REDBOOK CODE: RB-BR-S-DT11AC

Steelium technology barrel, cold hammer-forged, reduced perceived muzzle rise, increase in
shooting stability, increased penetration and target breakage, quicker first shot and second target
acquisition, cross-bolt locking system, increase of the receiver side wall thickness, interchangeable barrel locking shoulders, nickel-based surface finish.

Production: *current* **Gauge/Bore:** *12 ga.*
Action: *O/U*
Barrel Length: 30", 32" **Wt.:** *N/A*
Sights: *bead front*
Capacity: 2
Stock: *high quality walnut, hand-checkered, custom fitted*

D2C:	NIB $9,260	Ex $7,050	VG+ $5,095	Good $4,630	
C2C:	Mint $8,890	Ex $6,400	VG+ $4,630	Good $4,170	Fair $2,130
Trade-In:	Mint $6,580	Ex $5,200	VG+ $3,620	Good $3,245	Poor $930

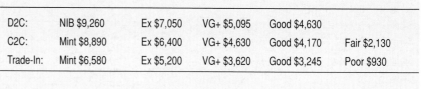

DT11 L REDBOOK CODE: RB-BR-S-DT11LX

Tri-blend alloy Steelium blue-finished barrel with ventilated rib, low profile receiver, sideplates engraved with super-fine classic game scene with details of branches, leaves, and flowers extending to the trigger plate, trigger guard and forend lever, oval brass shield inlaid in the stock, carry case, optional Combo model available with either 28/.410 or 20/28 ga. for an additional $1700.

Production: *current* **Gauge/Bore:** *12 ga.*

Action: *O/U*

Barrel Length: *28", 30", 32"* **Wt.:** *N/A*

Sights: *bead front*

Capacity: *2*

Stock: *high quality walnut*

D2C:	NIB $11,868	Ex $9,025	VG+ $6,530	Good $5,935	
C2C:	Mint $11,400	Ex $8,200	VG+ $5,940	Good $5,345	Fair $2,730
Trade-In:	Mint $8,430	Ex $6,650	VG+ $4,630	Good $4,155	Poor $1,200

SO SPARVIERE REDBOOK CODE: RB-BR-S-SOSPAR

Trapezoidal locking shoulders, high-resistance tri-alloy solid steel machined receiver, screw and pin-free, receiver exterior and interior hand-polished and engraved, hand-detachable engraved sidelocks, either 2 3/4" or 3" chamber, two additional lower receiver locking lugs, noiseless locking system, full tapered rib, action available in four sizes, custom engraving. Pricing varies heavily. Though currently in production, these models tend to be rare. Pricing, at this time, is inconclusive.

Production: *current* **Gauge/Bore:** *12 ga.*

Action: *O/U*

Barrel Length: *26", 28", 30", 32"* **Wt.:** *N/A*

Sights: *bead front*

Capacity: *2*

Stock: *finest walnut briarwood, customized to preference*

SO4 REDBOOK CODE: RB-BR-S-MODSO4

Sidelock action, auto ejectors, elaborate artisan engraving, various choke combinations, vent rib Bohler steel barrels, chrome-nickel receiver, chromed internal parts. Available in field, skeet and trap models.

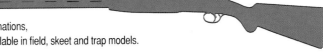

Production: *discontinued* **Gauge/Bore:** *12 ga.*

Action: *O/U*

Barrel Length: *26", 28", 29", 30"* **Wt.:** *N/A*

Sights: *N/A*

Capacity: *2*

Stock: *European walnut with straight or pistol grip*

D2C:	NIB $9,100	Ex $6,925	VG+ $5,005	Good $4,550	
C2C:	Mint $8,740	Ex $6,300	VG+ $4,550	Good $4,095	Fair $2,095
Trade-In:	Mint $6,470	Ex $5,100	VG+ $3,550	Good $3,185	Poor $930

SO5 (NEWER PRODUCTION) REDBOOK CODE: RB-BR-S-SO5XXX

Break-open Optima-Bore barrel with lengthened forcing cone, Extended Optimachoke tubes, removable aluminum alloy top rib, 2 3/4" chamber, light alloy streamlined receiver, polished sides, matte finished top surface, extended checkered forend, Gel-Tek recoil pad.

Production: *current* **Gauge/Bore:** *12 ga.*

Action: *O/U*

Barrel Length: *26", 28", 30", 32"* **Wt.:** *N/A*

Sights: *bead front*

Capacity: *2*

Stock: *highly figured walnut, diamond checkering*

D2C:	NIB $27,583	Ex $20,975	VG+ $15,175	Good $13,795	**LMP:** $27,500
C2C:	Mint $26,480	Ex $19,050	VG+ $13,800	Good $12,415	Fair $6,345
Trade-In:	Mint $19,590	Ex $15,450	VG+ $10,760	Good $9,655	Poor $2,760

S06 EELL   REDBOOK CODE: RB-BR-S-SO6ELL

Tri-alloy blend Steelium barrels, ventilated rib, hand-chased floral scroll engraved receiver, shoulders, trigger guard, safety and top lever, Renaissance-style Beretta shield underneath, no visible screws, diamond checkered pistol grip and forend, scaled down receivers for smaller gauges, for SportingModel add $623, available in Field Combo 12/20, 20/28, or 28/410 for $1,500 more, for Sporting Combo in 12/20 or 20/28 add $2,124, Matched Pairs model available in any configuration for additional $4,076 by special order.

Production: *current* **Gauge/Bore:** *12 ga.*

Action: *O/U*

Barrel Length: 26", 28", 30", 32" **Wt.:** *N/A*

Sights: *bead front*

Capacity: 2

Stock: *finest walnut briarwood, hand-cut deep diamond checkering*

D2C:	NIB $45,275	Ex $34,425	VG+ $24,905	Good $22,640	LMP: $46,800
C2C:	Mint $43,470	Ex $31,250	VG+ $22,640	Good $20,375	Fair $10,415
Trade-In:	Mint $32,150	Ex $25,375	VG+ $17,660	Good $15,850	Poor $4,530

S07   REDBOOK CODE: RB-BR-S-MODSO7

Sidelock action, vent rib Bohler steel barrels, various choke combinations, chrome-silver receiver, chromed internal parts, elaborate artisan engraving. Market research provides no conclusive pricing suggestion(s) for this particular model. The model is either too rare or contains too many custom options, which drastically affects pricing.

Production: *discontinued* **Gauge/Bore:** *12 ga.*

Action: *O/U*

Barrel Length: 26", 28" **Wt.:** *N/A*

Sights: *N/A*

Capacity: 2

Stock: *European walnut with straight or pistol grip*

S09   REDBOOK CODE: RB-BR-S-MODSO9

Engraving, sidelock, cold hammer-forged barrel, solid matte rib, 3" chamber, blue barrel, coin-finished receiver, round panel, walnut forearm, straight grip stock, fine hand checkering.

Production: *discontinued* **Gauge/Bore:** *12 ga., 20 ga., 28 ga., .410*

Action: *O/U*

Barrel Length: 26", 28", 30", 32" **Wt.:** *N/A*

Sights: *bead front*

Capacity: 2

Stock: *walnut*

D2C:	NIB $33,200	Ex $25,250	VG+ $18,260	Good $16,600	
C2C:	Mint $31,880	Ex $22,925	VG+ $16,600	Good $14,940	Fair $7,640
Trade-In:	Mint $23,580	Ex $18,600	VG+ $12,950	Good $11,620	Poor $3,330

S010   REDBOOK CODE: RB-BR-S-SO10XX

Receiver machined from solid block of high-resistance tri-alloy steel, no visible screws or pins, exterior and interior hand-polished and engraved, hand-detachable engraved sidelocks, either 2 3/4" or 3" chamber, two additional lower receiver locking lugs, noiseless locking system, customizable engraving, offered with full tapered rib, action available in four sizes, for optional .410 gauge add $4,020.

Production: *current* **Gauge/Bore:** *12 ga., 20 ga., 28 ga., .410*

Action: *O/U*

Barrel Length: 26", 28", 30", 32" **Wt.:** *N/A*

Sights: *bead front*

Capacity: 2

Stock: *premium wood, individually customized*

D2C:	NIB $94,998	Ex $72,200	VG+ $52,250	Good $47,500	LMP: $85,800
C2C:	Mint $91,200	Ex $65,550	VG+ $47,500	Good $42,750	Fair $21,850
Trade-In:	Mint $67,450	Ex $53,200	VG+ $37,050	Good $33,250	Poor $9,510

SO10 EELL REDBOOK CODE: RB-BR-S-SO10EL

Cold hammer-forged Boehler Antinit steel barrels with file-cut ventilated rib, low profile sidelock receiver, Monobloc lug crossbolt, replaceable locking shoulders, hand-engraved and signed action, choice of traditional or customized engravings, selective or non-selective trigger available, removable sidelock option, either pistol grip or straight English stock, diamond checkered forend, leather carry case with accessories, for optional Sporting Model add $600.

Production: *current* **Gauge/Bore:** *12 ga., 20 ga., 28 ga., .410*

Action: *O/U*

Barrel Length: 26", 28", 30" **Wt.:** *N/A*

Sights: *bead front*

Capacity: 2

Stock: *premium wood, individually customized*

D2C:	NIB $129,996	Ex $98,800	VG+ $71,500	Good $65,000	**LMP: $95,880**
C2C:	Mint $124,800	Ex $89,700	VG+ $65,000	Good $58,500	Fair $29,900
Trade-In:	Mint $92,300	Ex $72,800	VG+ $50,700	Good $45,500	Poor $13,020

GIUBILEO REDBOOK CODE: RB-BR-S-GUBLEO

Cold hammer-forged Boehler Antinit steel barrels, low-profile sidelock action with hand-engraved side plates, option of fitted stock blank and/or removable sidelocks, Trap model features special rubber recoil pad, heavy beavertail competition forend, single non-selective trigger, International or Monte Carlo stock, Skeet model has short barrels, competition stock, diamond checkering on forend, either checkered buttplate or rubber recoil pad, available with Skeet chokes or interchangeable Mobilchoke tubes, Sporting model features single selective trigger, anti-recoil rubber pad, Schnabel forend, medium-weight barrels with Mobilchoke choke tubes, option of Optima-Bore barrels with Extended Optimachoke tubes, for option of hand-detachable sidelock add $1,250.

Production: *current* **Gauge/Bore:** *12 ga., 20 ga., 28 ga., .410*

Action: *O/U*

Barrel Length: 26", 28", 30", 32" **Wt.:** *N/A*

Sights: *bead front*

Capacity: 2

Stock: *highly select walnut, checkered, TruOil finish*

D2C:	NIB $14,398	Ex $10,950	VG+ $7,920	Good $7,200	**LMP: $16,875**
C2C:	Mint $13,830	Ex $9,950	VG+ $7,200	Good $6,480	Fair $3,315
Trade-In:	Mint $10,230	Ex $8,075	VG+ $5,620	Good $5,040	Poor $1,440

UGB25 XCEL REDBOOK CODE: RB-BR-S-UGB25X

Cold hammer-forged Optima Choke barrels, 3" chamber, round action with English-style scroll engraving extending to top lever and trigger guard, action with new leaf springs, 30" barrel length available with fixed choke only.

Production: *current* **Gauge/Bore:** *12 ga.*

Action: *semi-auto*

Barrel Length: 28", 30" **Wt.:** *N/A*

Sights: *bead front*

Capacity: 5

Stock: *select walnut*

D2C:	NIB $2,399	Ex $1,825	VG+ $1,320	Good $1,200	
C2C:	Mint $2,310	Ex $1,675	VG+ $1,200	Good $1,080	Fair $555
Trade-In:	Mint $1,710	Ex $1,350	VG+ $940	Good $840	Poor $240

486 PARALLELO REDBOOK CODE: RB-BR-S-486PRL

Top of Beretta's line, deep-blue Demibloc barrels with glossy black finish, compact receiver with fine ribbon border engraving, cut from solid steel ingot and hand-finished, extensively engraved per client design, rebounding hammer-fired mechanism, manual extractors, internal parts mirror finished or jeweled as requested, either double trigger with articulated front trigger or single selective trigger, classic English straight or swan-style stock, hand-checkered full or half pistol grip, either classic or splinter beavertail forend, gold inlaid crown of laurels, barrels also available in red damask finish.

Production: *current* **Gauge/Bore:** *12 ga.*

Action: *SxS*

Barrel Length: 26", 28", 28.7", 30", 32" **Wt.:** *7 lbs.*

Sights: *bead front*

Capacity: 2

Stock: *select walnut, straight grip*

D2C:	NIB $5,030	Ex $3,825	VG+ $2,770	Good $2,515	**LMP: $5,350**
C2C:	Mint $4,830	Ex $3,475	VG+ $2,520	Good $2,265	Fair $1,160
Trade-In:	Mint $3,580	Ex $2,825	VG+ $1,970	Good $1,765	Poor $510

BERETTA

IMPERIALE MONTECARLO REDBOOK CODE: RB-BR-S-IMPMON

Top of Beretta's line, very small quantities produced, deep-blue Demibloc barrels with glossy black finish, compact receiver, fine ribbon border engraving, receiver cut from solid steel ingot and hand-finished, extensively engraved per client design, rebounding exposed hammers, manual extractors, internal parts mirror finished or jeweled as requested, either double trigger with articulated front trigger or single selective trigger, classic English straight or swan-style stock, hand-checkered full or half pistol grip, either classic or splinter beavertail forend, gold inlaid crown of laurels, barrels also available in red damask finish. Model too rare or customizable to price.

Production: *current* **Gauge/Bore:** *12 ga., 20 ga., 28 ga.*

Action: *SxS*

Barrel Length: 26", 28" **Wt.:** *N/A*

Sights: *none*

Capacity: *2*

Stock: *highest quality walnut briar, custom dimensions*

DIANA REDBOOK CODE: RB-BR-S-DIANAX

Top of the line engraving, fully handmade, external hammer action, fine ribbon border, engraved floor plates, triple compass-turn lug, double trigger with articulated front or single-selective trigger, gold inlays, fine checkering on forend and stock. Model too rare or customizable to price.

Production: *current* **Gauge/Bore:** *12 ga., 20 ga.*

Action: *SxS*

Barrel Length: any custom length **Wt.:** *N/A*

Sights: *none*

Capacity: *2*

Stock: *highest quality walnut briar, custom dimensions*

A391 XTREMA 2 REDBOOK CODE: RB-BR-S-A391X2

Aqua Technology treated, stainless steel parts, crossbolt safety, rubber inlays in stock, 3.5" chamber. Available in black, AP camouflage, or Max-4 HD camouflage. Slight premium for optional Kick-Off recoil reduction system.

Production: *current* **Gauge/Bore:** *12 ga.*

Action: *semi-auto*

Barrel Length: 26", 28" **Wt.:** *7.8 lbs.*

Sights: *bead front*

Capacity: *5*

Stock: *synthetic*

D2C:	NIB $1,150	Ex $875	VG+ $635	Good $575	
C2C:	Mint $1,110	Ex $800	VG+ $580	Good $520	Fair $265
Trade-In:	Mint $820	Ex $650	VG+ $450	Good $405	Poor $120

AL 391 LIGHT REDBOOK CODE: RB-BR-S-AL391L

Vent ribbed tri-alloy Steelium barrel and self-cleaning piston, Mobile Choke interchangeable tubes, 3" chamber, corrosion resistant finish, Kick-Off recoil reduction system, reversible safety, wood spacers for adjustable stock, sling attachments.

Production: *current* **Gauge/Bore:** *20 ga.*

Action: *semi-auto*

Barrel Length: 24", 26", 28" **Wt.:** *6.1 lbs.*

Sights: *bead front*

Capacity: *3*

Stock: *California walnut*

D2C:	NIB $1,290	Ex $1,000	VG+ $710	Good $645	
C2C:	Mint $1,240	Ex $900	VG+ $650	Good $585	Fair $300
Trade-In:	Mint $920	Ex $725	VG+ $510	Good $455	Poor $150

AL 391 URIKA   REDBOOK CODE: RB-BR-S-AL391U
Cold hammer-forged barrel, black anodized metal finish, aluminum alloy receiver, self-compensating gas valve, set of five interchangeable chokes.

Production: *imported 2001–2006* **Gauge/Bore:** *12 ga., 20 ga.*
Action: *semi-auto*
Barrel Length: 28", 30", 32" **Wt.:** *6.6–7.7 lbs.*
Sights: *N/A*
Capacity: *5*
Stock: *adjustable walnut and synthetic*

D2C:	NIB $900	Ex $700	VG+ $495	Good $450	
C2C:	Mint $870	Ex $625	VG+ $450	Good $405	Fair $210
Trade-In:	Mint $640	Ex $525	VG+ $360	Good $315	Poor $90

AL 391 URIKA 2 (X-TRA GRAIN)   REDBOOK CODE: RB-BR-S-A391U2
Gas-driven recoil system, vent rib with choice of OptimaChokes or MobilChokes, fine scroll engraved receiver, self-cleaning action.

Production: *discontinued* **Gauge/Bore:** *12 ga., 20 ga.*
Action: *semi-auto*
Barrel Length: 26", 28" **Wt.:** *~6–7.3 lbs.*
Sights: *bead front*
Capacity: *5*
Stock: *X-Tra grain wood-enhanced*

D2C:	NIB $1,250	Ex $950	VG+ $690	Good $625	
C2C:	Mint $1,200	Ex $875	VG+ $630	Good $565	Fair $290
Trade-In:	Mint $890	Ex $700	VG+ $490	Good $440	Poor $150

DT10 TRIDENT TRAP   REDBOOK CODE: RB-BR-S-D10TTR
Target vent rib, crossbolt locking system, OptimaBore barrels, OptimaChoke competition tubes, fires 3" shells.

Production: *discontinued* **Gauge/Bore:** *12 ga., 20 ga.*
Action: *O/U*
Barrel Length: 30", 32" **Wt.:** *8.8 lbs.*
Sights: *N/A*
Capacity: *2*
Stock: *highly select adjustable walnut*

D2C:	NIB $6,500	Ex $4,950	VG+ $3,575	Good $3,250	
C2C:	Mint $6,240	Ex $4,500	VG+ $3,250	Good $2,925	Fair $1,495
Trade-In:	Mint $4,620	Ex $3,650	VG+ $2,540	Good $2,275	Poor $660

DT10 TRIDENT SKEET   REDBOOK CODE: RB-BR-S-D10TSK
Target vent rib, crossbolt locking system, OptimaBore barrels, OptimaChoke competition tubes, fires 3" shells.

Production: *discontinued* **Gauge/Bore:** *12 ga.*
Action: *O/U*
Barrel Length: 28", 30" **Wt.:** *7.9 lbs.*
Sights: *N/A*
Capacity: *2*
Stock: *adjustable walnut*

D2C:	NIB $5,700	Ex $4,350	VG+ $3,135	Good $2,850	
C2C:	Mint $5,480	Ex $3,950	VG+ $2,850	Good $2,565	Fair $1,315
Trade-In:	Mint $4,050	Ex $3,200	VG+ $2,230	Good $1,995	Poor $570

DT10 TRIDENT L SPORTING REDBOOK CODE: RB-BR-S-D10TSP
Vent rib, set of five OptimaChoke extended tubes, modified crossbolt locking system, receiver and trigger guard engraved with floral scroll pattern, adjustable trigger.

Production: *discontinued* **Gauge/Bore:** *12 ga.*
Action: *O/U*
Barrel Length: 30", 32" **Wt.:** ~6 lbs.
Sights: *N/A*
Capacity: 2
Stock: *American walnut with Weathercoat finish*

D2C:	NIB $7,300	Ex $5,550	VG+ $4,015	Good $3,650	
C2C:	Mint $7,010	Ex $5,050	VG+ $3,650	Good $3,285	Fair $1,680
Trade-In:	Mint $5,190	Ex $4,100	VG+ $2,850	Good $2,555	Poor $750

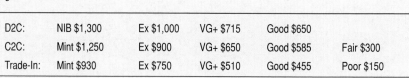

GR-2 REDBOOK CODE: RB-BR-S-GXRX2X
Boxlock action, various choke/barrel combinations, plain extractors, double triggers. Add 50% for 20 gauge model.

Production: *imported 1968–1976* **Gauge/Bore:** *12 ga., 20 ga.*
Action: *SxS*
Barrel Length: 26", 28", 30" **Wt.:** *6.5–7.5 lbs.*
Sights: *N/A*
Capacity: 2
Stock: *checkered pistol grip*

D2C:	NIB $1,150	Ex $875	VG+ $635	Good $575	
C2C:	Mint $1,110	Ex $800	VG+ $580	Good $520	Fair $265
Trade-In:	Mint $820	Ex $650	VG+ $450	Good $405	Poor $120

GR-3 REDBOOK CODE: RB-BR-S-GXRX3X
Boxlock action, plain extractors, various choke combinations, fires 3" shells. Magnum model comes with 30" barrel and modified/full choke tubes. Add 50% for 20 gauge model.

Production: *imported 1968–1976* **Gauge/Bore:** *12 ga., 20 ga.*
Action: *SxS*
Barrel Length: 26", 28", 30" **Wt.:** ~8 lbs.
Sights: *N/A*
Capacity: 2
Stock: *checkered high-grade hardwood with pistol grip*

D2C:	NIB $1,300	Ex $1,000	VG+ $715	Good $650	
C2C:	Mint $1,250	Ex $900	VG+ $650	Good $585	Fair $300
Trade-In:	Mint $930	Ex $750	VG+ $510	Good $455	Poor $150

MARK II TRAP REDBOOK CODE: RB-BR-S-MARK2X
Vent rib, full choke, boxlock action, 14.25" length of pull.

Production: *discontinued* **Gauge/Bore:** *12 ga.*
Action: *single-shot*
Barrel Length: 34" **Wt.:** *N/A*
Sights: *white bead front, mid-bead*
Capacity: 4
Stock: *high-gloss Monte Carlo*

D2C:	NIB $1,150	Ex $875	VG+ $635	Good $575	
C2C:	Mint $1,110	Ex $800	VG+ $580	Good $520	Fair $265
Trade-In:	Mint $820	Ex $650	VG+ $450	Good $405	Poor $120

3901 STANDARD   REDBOOK CODE: RB-BR-S-3901ST
Gas operated system, vent rib, MobilChokes, reversible crossbolt system, steel alloy hammer-forged barrel, blue finish.

Production: *discontinued* **Gauge/Bore:** *12 ga.*

Action: *semi-auto*

Barrel Length: *26", 28"* **Wt.:** *7.5 lbs.*

Sights: *steel bead front*

Capacity: *5*

Stock: *black synthetic*

D2C:	NIB $750	Ex $575	VG+ $415	Good $375	
C2C:	Mint $720	Ex $525	VG+ $380	Good $340	Fair $175
Trade-In:	Mint $540	Ex $425	VG+ $300	Good $265	Poor $90

409PB HAMMERLESS DOUBLE   REDBOOK CODE: RB-BR-S-409PBH
Boxlock action, improved cylinder/modified or modified/full chokes, plain extractors, double triggers, blue finish. Add 50% for 20 gauge. Add 100% for 28 gauge.

Production: *1934–1964* **Gauge/Bore:** *12 ga., 16 ga., 20 ga., 28 ga.*

Action: *SxS*

Barrel Length: *27", 28", 30"* **Wt.:** *5.5–7.75 lbs.*

Sights: *N/A*

Capacity: *2*

Stock: *checkered walnut*

D2C:	NIB --	Ex $725	VG+ $525	Good $475	
C2C:	Mint --	Ex $675	VG+ $480	Good $430	Fair $220
Trade-In:	Mint --	Ex $550	VG+ $380	Good $335	Poor $120

410   REDBOOK CODE: RB-BR-S-MD410X
Boxlock action, full chokes, plain extractors, double triggers, engraving, blue finish, chambers 3.5 shells.
Market research provides no conclusive pricing suggestion(s) for this particular model. The model is either too rare or contains too many custom options, which drastically affects pricing.

Production: *1934-1981* **Gauge/Bore:** *10 ga. Magnum*

Action: *SxS*

Barrel Length: *32"* **Wt.:** *~10 lbs.*

Sights: *N/A*

Capacity: *2*

Stock: *checkered pistol grip*

410E   REDBOOK CODE: RB-BR-S-MD410E
Boxlock action, improved cylinder/modified or modified/full chokes, automatic ejectors, double triggers, blue finish. Slightly higher value for 20 gauge and roughly double the value for 28 gauge model.

Production: *1934–1964* **Gauge/Bore:** *12 ga., 16 ga., 20 ga., 28 ga.*

Action: *SxS*

Barrel Length: *27", 28", 30"* **Wt.:** *5.5–7.75 lbs.*

Sights: *N/A*

Capacity: *2*

Stock: *finely finished checkered walnut*

D2C:	NIB $3,400	Ex $2,600	VG+ $1,870	Good $1,700	
C2C:	Mint $3,270	Ex $2,350	VG+ $1,700	Good $1,530	Fair $785
Trade-In:	Mint $2,420	Ex $1,925	VG+ $1,330	Good $1,190	Poor $360

411E REDBOOK CODE: RB-BR-S-MD411E

Boxlock action, improved cylinder/modified or modified/full chokes, plain extractors, double triggers, false sideplates, heavy engraving, blue finish.

Production: *1934–1964* **Gauge/Bore:** *12 ga., 16 ga., 20 ga., 28 ga.*
Action: *SxS*
Barrel Length: 27", 28", 30" **Wt.:** *5.5–7.75 lbs.*
Sights: *N/A*
Capacity: *2*
Stock: *finely finished checkered walnut*

D2C:	NIB $2,600	Ex $2,000	VG+ $1,430	Good $1,300	
C2C:	Mint $2,500	Ex $1,800	VG+ $1,300	Good $1,170	Fair $600
Trade-In:	Mint $1,850	Ex $1,475	VG+ $1,020	Good $910	Poor $270

424 REDBOOK CODE: RB-BR-S-424HLD

Boxlock action, extractors, various chokes, double triggers, engraving. 12 gauge model fires 2.75" shells, 20 gauge model fires 3" shells.

Production: *discontinued* **Gauge/Bore:** *12 ga., 20 ga.*
Action: *SxS*
Barrel Length: 26", 28", 30" **Wt.:** *5.8–6.6 lbs.*
Sights: *bead front*
Capacity: *2*
Stock: *checkered walnut with straight grip*

D2C:	NIB $1,800	Ex $1,375	VG+ $990	Good $900	
C2C:	Mint $1,730	Ex $1,250	VG+ $900	Good $810	Fair $415
Trade-In:	Mint $1,280	Ex $1,025	VG+ $710	Good $630	Poor $180

426E REDBOOK CODE: RB-BR-S-MD426E

Boxlock action, various chokes, double triggers, receiver in coin-silver finish, silver pigeon inlay on top lever.

Production: *imported through 1984* **Gauge/Bore:** *12 ga., 20 ga.*
Action: *SxS*
Barrel Length: 26", 28" **Wt.:** *N/A*
Sights: *bead front*
Capacity: *2*
Stock: *select European walnut*

D2C:	NIB $1,850	Ex $1,425	VG+ $1,020	Good $925	
C2C:	Mint $1,780	Ex $1,300	VG+ $930	Good $835	Fair $430
Trade-In:	Mint $1,320	Ex $1,050	VG+ $730	Good $650	Poor $210

450 SERIES REDBOOK CODE: RB-BR-S-MD450X

English-style sidelock action, selective automatic ejectors, double triggers, receiver in coin-silver finish, silver pigeon inlay on top lever. Customized to customer specs with various chokes, degree of engraving and other features. These are made-to-order and pricing varies drastically with options. Prices may range from $7,000 to over $20,000.

Production: *discontinued* **Gauge/Bore:** *12 ga.*
Action: *SxS*
Barrel Length: 26", 28", 30" **Wt.:** *~7 lbs.*
Sights: *N/A*
Capacity: *2*
Stock: *high-grade walnut*

451 REDBOOK CODE: RB-BR-S-MD451X

Sidelock action, ejectors, scroll engraving. Market research provides no conclusive pricing
suggestion(s) for this particular model. The model is either too rare or contains too many custom options, which drastically affects pricing.

Production: *discontinued* **Gauge/Bore:** *12 ga.*

Action: *SxS*

Barrel Length: custom made-to-order **Wt.:** *N/A*

Sights: *N/A*

Capacity: *2*

Stock: *various grades/styles to order*

451 E REDBOOK CODE: RB-BR-S-MD451E

Sidelock action, ejectors, double triggers, scroll engraving. Add approximately 12% for
model with selective single trigger. Add approximately 40% for additional set of barrels. Market research
provides no conclusive pricing suggestion(s) for this particular model. The model is either too rare or
contains too many custom options, which drastically affects pricing.

Production: *discontinued* **Gauge/Bore:** *12 ga.*

Action: *SxS*

Barrel Length: custom made-to-order **Wt.:** *N/A*

Sights: *N/A*

Capacity: *2*

Stock: *various grades/styles to order*

SILVER HAWK REDBOOK CODE: RB-BR-S-SLVRHK

Boxlock action, extractors, double triggers, blue finish, silver-finished receiver. Available with 3" and 3.5" chambers. Add approximately 20% for 10 gauge model.

Production: *discontinued 1967* **Gauge/Bore:** *10 ga. Magnum, 12 ga. Magnum*

Action: *SxS*

Barrel Length: 30" **Wt.:** *N/A*

Sights: *N/A*

Capacity: *2*

Stock: *checkered walnut*

D2C:	NIB $1,560	Ex $1,200	VG+ $860	Good $780	
C2C:	Mint $1,500	Ex $1,100	VG+ $780	Good $705	Fair $360
Trade-In:	Mint $1,110	Ex $875	VG+ $610	Good $550	Poor $180

470 SILVER HAWK REDBOOK CODE: RB-BR-S-470SHK

Selectable auto ejection or mechanical extraction, fixed or multi-choke tubes, engraved steel alloy
receiver in silver-chrome finish, checkered top lever with hawks head in gold inlay, fires 3" shells. Add 15% for 20 gauge model. Add $130 for MobilChokes

Production: *1997–discontinued* **Gauge/Bore:** *12 ga., 20 ga.*

Action: *SxS*

Barrel Length: 26", 28" **Wt.:** *~6 lbs., ~6.5 lbs.*

Sights: *N/A*

Capacity: *2*

Stock: *select walnut with oil finish*

D2C:	NIB $2,300	Ex $1,750	VG+ $1,265	Good $1,150	
C2C:	Mint $2,210	Ex $1,600	VG+ $1,150	Good $1,035	Fair $530
Trade-In:	Mint $1,640	Ex $1,300	VG+ $900	Good $805	Poor $240

BERETTA

470 EL SILVER HAWK REDBOOK CODE: RB-BR-S-470ELH

Case-colored boxlock action, MC3 chokes or OptimaBore barrels with OptimaChokes, selectable auto ejection or mechanical extraction, hard silver-chrome finish, side plates with game birds in gold inlay, fires 3" shells.

Production: *discontinued* **Gauge/Bore:** *12 ga., 20 ga.*

Action: *SxS*

Barrel Length: *26", 28"* **Wt.:** *5.9 lbs., 6.5 lbs.*

Sights: *N/A*

Capacity: *2*

Stock: *select walnut with oil finish*

D2C:	NIB $4,200	Ex $3,200	VG+ $2,310	Good $2,100	
C2C:	Mint $4,040	Ex $2,900	VG+ $2,100	Good $1,890	Fair $970
Trade-In:	Mint $2,990	Ex $2,375	VG+ $1,640	Good $1,470	Poor $420

471 SILVER HAWK REDBOOK CODE: RB-BR-S-471SHK

Cold hammer-forged barrels, chrome-lined chambers, fixed chokes or OptimaChokes, blue finish, selectable auto ejectors or mechanical extractors, blue finish, scroll-engraved receiver. Add $625 for color case-hardened frame with straight-grip stock/splinter forearm.

Production: *discontinued* **Gauge/Bore:** *12 ga., 20 ga.*

Action: *SxS*

Barrel Length: *26", 28"* **Wt.:** *5.9 lbs., 6.5 lbs.*

Sights: *bead front*

Capacity: *2*

Stock: *European walnut with straight or pistol grip*

D2C:	NIB $3,540	Ex $2,700	VG+ $1,950	Good $1,770	
C2C:	Mint $3,400	Ex $2,450	VG+ $1,770	Good $1,595	Fair $815
Trade-In:	Mint $2,520	Ex $2,000	VG+ $1,390	Good $1,240	Poor $360

S 57E REDBOOK CODE: RB-BR-S-MOD57E

Boxlock action, auto ejectors, vent rib, modified/full chokes, fires 2.75" shells.

Production: *imported 1955–1967* **Gauge/Bore:** *12 ga., 20 ga.*

Action: *O/U*

Barrel Length: *26", 28", 30"* **Wt.:** *6–8.5 lbs.*

Sights: *N/A*

Capacity: *2*

Stock: *checkered pistol grip walnut*

D2C:	NIB $2,580	Ex $1,975	VG+ $1,420	Good $1,290	
C2C:	Mint $2,480	Ex $1,800	VG+ $1,290	Good $1,165	Fair $595
Trade-In:	Mint $1,840	Ex $1,450	VG+ $1,010	Good $905	Poor $270

625 REDBOOK CODE: RB-BR-S-MOD625

Boxlock action, extractors, various choke combinations, moderate engraving. Add 50% for 20 gauge model. Add 15% for selective single trigger.

Production: *imported 1984–1986* **Gauge/Bore:** *12 ga., 20 ga.*

Action: *SxS*

Barrel Length: *26", 28", 30"* **Wt.:** *N/A*

Sights: *bead front*

Capacity: *2*

Stock: *checkered walnut straight grip*

D2C:	NIB $2,100	Ex $1,600	VG+ $1,155	Good $1,050	
C2C:	Mint $2,020	Ex $1,450	VG+ $1,050	Good $945	Fair $485
Trade-In:	Mint $1,500	Ex $1,200	VG+ $820	Good $735	Poor $210

626 FIELD REDBOOK CODE: RB-BR-S-MD626F
Boxlock action, various chokes, extractors or auto ejectors, moderate engraving, blue finish, fires 2.75" shells.

Production: *discontinued* **Gauge/Bore:** *12 ga., 20 ga.*
Action: *SxS*
Barrel Length: 26", 28" **Wt.:** *6.75 lbs.*
Sights: *bead front*
Capacity: *2*
Stock: *pistol grip or checkered straight*

D2C:	NIB $1,740	Ex $1,325	VG+ $960	Good $870	
C2C:	Mint $1,680	Ex $1,225	VG+ $870	Good $785	Fair $405
Trade-In:	Mint $1,240	Ex $975	VG+ $680	Good $610	Poor $180

626 ONYX REDBOOK CODE: RB-BR-S-MD626O
Boxlock action, vent rib barrels with MobilChokes, matte finish, 14.375" length of pull, fires 3" shells. Also available in a 12 gauge, 3.5" Magnum model.

Production: *discontinued* **Gauge/Bore:** *12 ga., 20 ga.*
Action: *SxS*
Barrel Length: 26", 28" **Wt.:** *6.75 lbs.*
Sights: *bead front*
Capacity: *2*
Stock: *checkered select walnut*

D2C:	NIB $2,490	Ex $1,900	VG+ $1,370	Good $1,245	
C2C:	Mint $2,400	Ex $1,725	VG+ $1,250	Good $1,125	Fair $575
Trade-In:	Mint $1,770	Ex $1,400	VG+ $980	Good $875	Poor $270

627 EELL REDBOOK CODE: RB-BR-S-627ELL
Boxlock action with sideplates and elaborately engraved game scene, ejectors, various chokes, single trigger, 2.75" or 3" chamber (latter in 12 gauge only). Add 10% for 20 gauge model. Add 25% for 28" barrels. Subtract 10% for fixed chokes only.

Production: *discontinued* **Gauge/Bore:** *12 ga., 20 ga.*
Action: *SxS*
Barrel Length: 26", 28" **Wt.:** *7 lbs.*
Sights: *bead front*
Capacity: *2*
Stock: *fancy walnut pistol or straight English grip*

D2C:	NIB $5,200	Ex $3,975	VG+ $2,860	Good $2,600	
C2C:	Mint $5,000	Ex $3,600	VG+ $2,600	Good $2,340	Fair $1,200
Trade-In:	Mint $3,700	Ex $2,925	VG+ $2,030	Good $1,820	Poor $540

627 EL REDBOOK CODE: RB-BR-S-627ELF
Boxlock action, various chokes, ejectors, single trigger, extensive engraving, 2.75" or 3" chamber. Add 25% to value for 20 gauge model. Subtract 10% from value for fixed chokes/2.75" chambers.

Production: *discontinued* **Gauge/Bore:** *12 ga., 20 ga.*
Action: *SxS*
Barrel Length: 26", 28" **Wt.:** *N/A*
Sights: *bead front*
Capacity: *2*
Stock: *pistol grip or checkered straight*

D2C:	NIB $3,900	Ex $2,975	VG+ $2,145	Good $1,950	
C2C:	Mint $3,750	Ex $2,700	VG+ $1,950	Good $1,755	Fair $900
Trade-In:	Mint $2,770	Ex $2,200	VG+ $1,530	Good $1,365	Poor $390

BERETTA

682 TRAP REDBOOK CODE: RB-BR-S-MD682T

Blue or silver finish, vent rib barrel, adjustable length of pull, adjustable trigger, buttpad, available with fixed or screw-in choke tubes.

Production: *discontinued* **Gauge/Bore:** *12 ga.*
Action: *O/U*
Barrel Length: *28", 30", 32"* **Wt.:** *N/A*
Sights: *N/A*
Capacity: *2*
Stock: *checkered walnut with Monte Carlo option*

D2C:	NIB $2,100	Ex $1,600	VG+ $1,155	Good $1,050	
C2C:	Mint $2,020	Ex $1,450	VG+ $1,050	Good $945	Fair $485
Trade-In:	Mint $1,500	Ex $1,200	VG+ $820	Good $735	Poor $210

682 SKEET REDBOOK CODE: RB-BR-S-MD682S

Vent rib skeet-choked barrels, special skeet rubber buttpad.

Production: *discontinued* **Gauge/Bore:** *12 ga.*
Action: *O/U*
Barrel Length: *26", 28"* **Wt.:** *7.5 lbs.*
Sights: *N/A*
Capacity: *2*
Stock: *walnut*

D2C:	NIB $2,800	Ex $2,150	VG+ $1,540	Good $1,400	
C2C:	Mint $2,690	Ex $1,950	VG+ $1,400	Good $1,260	Fair $645
Trade-In:	Mint $1,990	Ex $1,575	VG+ $1,100	Good $980	Poor $300

682 SUPER SKEET REDBOOK CODE: RB-BR-S-M682SS

Ported vent rib barrels with skeet chokes, single trigger, auto ejectors, adjustable drop and length of pull.

Production: *discontinued* **Gauge/Bore:** *12 ga.*
Action: *O/U*
Barrel Length: *28"* **Wt.:** *7.5 lbs.*
Sights: *N/A*
Capacity: *2*
Stock: *walnut*

D2C:	NIB $2,200	Ex $1,675	VG+ $1,210	Good $1,100	
C2C:	Mint $2,120	Ex $1,525	VG+ $1,100	Good $990	Fair $510
Trade-In:	Mint $1,570	Ex $1,250	VG+ $860	Good $770	Poor $240

682 SUPER TRAP REDBOOK CODE: RB-BR-S-M682ST

Ported vent rib barrels with fixed or screw-in chokes, single trigger, auto ejectors, adjustable drop and length of pull.

Production: *discontinued* **Gauge/Bore:** *12 ga.*
Action: *O/U*
Barrel Length: *30", 32"* **Wt.:** *~6.3 lbs.*
Sights: *N/A*
Capacity: *2*
Stock: *checkered walnut with Monte Carlo option*

D2C:	NIB $2,400	Ex $1,825	VG+ $1,320	Good $1,200	
C2C:	Mint $2,310	Ex $1,675	VG+ $1,200	Good $1,080	Fair $555
Trade-In:	Mint $1,710	Ex $1,350	VG+ $940	Good $840	Poor $240

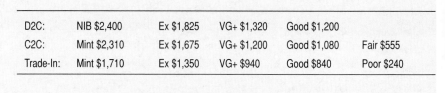

682/682 GOLD   REDBOOK CODE: RB-BR-S-MD682X

Vent rib, various fixed & screw-in choke combinations, silver frame. Market research provides no conclusive pricing suggestion(s) for this particular model. The model is either too rare or contains too many custom options, which drastically affects pricing.

Production: *discontinued* **Gauge/Bore:** *12 ga., 20 ga. (select models in 28 ga., .410)*

Action: *O/U*

Barrel Length: *26", 28", 30", 32", 34"* **Wt.:** *N/A*

Sights: *N/A*

Capacity: *2*

Stock: *checkered European walnut*

682 GOLD SPORTING   REDBOOK CODE: RB-BR-S-M682GS

Ported or unported vent rib barrels, MobilChokes, hand-engraved receiver with silver or titanium nitrate finish, 14.7" length of pull, fires 3" shells. Subtract 10% of value for 28" barrel.

Production: *discontinued* **Gauge/Bore:** *12 ga., 20 ga.*

Action: *O/U*

Barrel Length: *28", 30", 31"* **Wt.:** *7.6 lbs.*

Sights: *bead front*

Capacity: *2*

Stock: *checkered European walnut*

D2C:	NIB $1,735	Ex $1,325	VG+ $955	Good $870	
C2C:	Mint $1,670	Ex $1,200	VG+ $870	Good $785	Fair $400
Trade-In:	Mint $1,240	Ex $975	VG+ $680	Good $610	Poor $180

682 GOLD "LIVE BIRD"   REDBOOK CODE: RB-BR-S-M682GB

Vent rib, MobilChokes, sliding trigger, adjustable length of pull, matte black or titanium nitrate finish, light scroll engraving.

Production: *discontinued* **Gauge/Bore:** *12 ga.*

Action: *O/U*

Barrel Length: *30"* **Wt.:** *8.8 lbs.*

Sights: *mid-rib and front bead*

Capacity: *2*

Stock: *semi-gloss American walnut*

D2C:	NIB $2,600	Ex $2,000	VG+ $1,430	Good $1,300	
C2C:	Mint $2,500	Ex $1,800	VG+ $1,300	Good $1,170	Fair $600
Trade-In:	Mint $1,850	Ex $1,475	VG+ $1,020	Good $910	Poor $270

682 GOLD TRAP   REDBOOK CODE: RB-BR-S-M682GT

Vent rib, fixed or screw-in chokes, three-position sliding trigger, 14.7" length of pull, fires 2.75" shells. Also available with fully adjustable stock.

Production: *discontinued* **Gauge/Bore:** *12 ga.*

Action: *O/U*

Barrel Length: *28", 30", 32"* **Wt.:** *8.8 lbs.*

Sights: *bead front*

Capacity: *2*

Stock: *checkered walnut*

D2C:	NIB $2,700	Ex $2,075	VG+ $1,485	Good $1,350	
C2C:	Mint $2,600	Ex $1,875	VG+ $1,350	Good $1,215	Fair $625
Trade-In:	Mint $1,920	Ex $1,525	VG+ $1,060	Good $945	Poor $270

BERETTA

682 GOLD SKEET REDBOOK CODE: RB-BR-S-682GSK
Boxlock action, skeet chokes, hand-engraved receiver with silver or titanium nitrate finish, 14.7" length of pull, fires 2.75" shells. Also available with fully adjustable stock.

Production: *discontinued* **Gauge/Bore:** *12 ga.*
Action: *O/U*
Barrel Length: *28"* **Wt.:** *7.5 lbs.*
Sights: *N/A*
Capacity: *2*
Stock: *premium walnut*

D2C:	NIB $2,920	Ex $2,225	VG+ $1,610	Good $1,460	
C2C:	Mint $2,810	Ex $2,025	VG+ $1,460	Good $1,315	Fair $675
Trade-In:	Mint $2,080	Ex $1,650	VG+ $1,140	Good $1,025	Poor $300

1200 FIELD REDBOOK CODE: RB-BR-S-1200FD
Vent rib, MobilChokes, inertia recoil system, screw-in chokes, matte blue finish, fires 3" shells. Magnum option has similar value.

Production: *discontinued* **Gauge/Bore:** *12 ga.*
Action: *semi-auto*
Barrel Length: *28"* **Wt.:** *8 lbs.*
Sights: *N/A*
Capacity: *5, 7*
Stock: *walnut or black synthetic*

D2C:	NIB $500	Ex $400	VG+ $275	Good $250	
C2C:	Mint $480	Ex $350	VG+ $250	Good $225	Fair $115
Trade-In:	Mint $360	Ex $300	VG+ $200	Good $175	Poor $60

1201 FIELD REDBOOK CODE: RB-BR-S-M1201F
Lightweight alloy receiver, short recoil system.

Production: *discontinued* **Gauge/Bore:** *12 ga.*
Action: *semi-auto*
Barrel Length: *24", 26", 28"* **Wt.:** *6.75 lbs.*
Sights: *N/A*
Capacity: *5*
Stock: *black synthetic*

D2C:	NIB $525	Ex $400	VG+ $290	Good $265	
C2C:	Mint $510	Ex $375	VG+ $270	Good $240	Fair $125
Trade-In:	Mint $380	Ex $300	VG+ $210	Good $185	Poor $60

1301 COMP REDBOOK CODE: RB-BR-S-1301CP
Black finished Steelium barrel, 3" chamber, Picatinny rail, aggressive grip checkering on pistol grip and forend, oversized safety at trigger guard, sling attachment, adjustable LOP, oversize bolt release and handle, Blink self-cleaning piston, Optimabore HP choke.

Production: *current* **Gauge/Bore:** *12 ga.*
Action: *semi-auto*
Barrel Length: *21", 24"* **Wt.:** *6.7 lbs.*
Sights: *fiber optic*
Capacity: *6*
Stock: *synthetic, black*

D2C:	NIB $1,140	Ex $875	VG+ $630	Good $570	**LMP:** $1,255
C2C:	Mint $1,100	Ex $800	VG+ $570	Good $515	Fair $265
Trade-In:	Mint $810	Ex $650	VG+ $450	Good $400	Poor $120

1301 TACTICAL   REDBOOK CODE: RB-BR-S-1301TC

Designed as a home defense or law enforcement weapon, threaded barrel, ready for choke tubes, self-regulating gas-operating system, elongated forend with soft rubber grip inlay, Picatinny rail, shims included for adjustable LOP.

BERETTA

Production: *current* **Gauge/Bore:** *12 ga.*
Action: *semi-auto*
Barrel Length: *18.5"* **Wt.:** *6.7 lbs.*
Sights: *interchangeable blade front, Ghost Ring rear*
Capacity: *6*
Stock: *synthetic, black*

D2C:	NIB $1,040	Ex $800	VG+ $575	Good $520	LMP: $1,059
C2C:	Mint $1,000	Ex $725	VG+ $520	Good $470	Fair $240
Trade-In:	Mint $740	Ex $600	VG+ $410	Good $365	Poor $120

A-301 FIELD   REDBOOK CODE: RB-BR-S-MA301F

Gas operated, various choke/barrel combinations, vent rib, receiver with scroll decoration.

Production: *discontinued* **Gauge/Bore:** *12 ga., 20 ga.*
Action: *semi-auto*
Barrel Length: *26", 28"* **Wt.:** *~6.25–6.8 lbs.*
Sights: *N/A*
Capacity: *4*
Stock: *checkered pistol grip*

D2C:	NIB $600	Ex $475	VG+ $330	Good $300	
C2C:	Mint $580	Ex $425	VG+ $300	Good $270	Fair $140
Trade-In:	Mint $430	Ex $350	VG+ $240	Good $210	Poor $60

A-301 SLUG   REDBOOK CODE: RB-BR-S-MA301S

Gas operated, slug barrel, vent rib, receiver with scroll decoration.

Production: *discontinued* **Gauge/Bore:** *12 ga., 20 ga.*
Action: *semi-auto*
Barrel Length: *22"* **Wt.:** *~6.8 lbs.*
Sights: *rifle-type*
Capacity: *4*
Stock: *checkered pistol grip*

D2C:	NIB $600	Ex $475	VG+ $330	Good $300	
C2C:	Mint $580	Ex $425	VG+ $300	Good $270	Fair $140
Trade-In:	Mint $430	Ex $350	VG+ $240	Good $210	Poor $60

A-301 TRAP   REDBOOK CODE: RB-BR-S-MA301T

Gas operated, vent rib barrel with full choke, receiver with scroll decoration, gold-plated trigger, blue finish.

Production: *discontinued* **Gauge/Bore:** *12ga., 20 ga.*
Action: *semi-auto*
Barrel Length: *30"* **Wt.:** *~7.6 lbs.*
Sights: *N/A*
Capacity: *4*
Stock: *checkered Monte Carlo stock*

D2C:	NIB $820	Ex $625	VG+ $455	Good $410	
C2C:	Mint $790	Ex $575	VG+ $410	Good $370	Fair $190
Trade-In:	Mint $590	Ex $475	VG+ $320	Good $290	Poor $90

BERETTA

A-302 REDBOOK CODE: RB-BR-S-MDA302

Gas operated, hammerless, interchangeable chokes in various barrel/gauge combinations, vent rib, scroll work, chambers both 2.75" and 3" Magnum shells. Add $30 to value for multi-choke set.

Production: *discontinued 1987* **Gauge/Bore:** *12 ga., 20 ga.*
Action: *semi-auto*
Barrel Length: *26", 28", 30"* **Wt.:** *6.5–7.25 lbs.*
Sights: *N/A*
Capacity: *4*
Stock: *checkered European walnut with pistol grip*

D2C:	NIB $650	Ex $500	VG+ $360	Good $325	
C2C:	Mint $630	Ex $450	VG+ $330	Good $295	Fair $150
Trade-In:	Mint $470	Ex $375	VG+ $260	Good $230	Poor $90

A-302 SUPER LUSSO REDBOOK CODE: RB-BR-S-A302SL

Gas operated, hammerless, interchangeable chokes in various barrel/gauge combinations, vent rib, receiver with hand-cut engraving, chambers both 2.75" and 3" Magnum shells.

Production: *discontinued* **Gauge/Bore:** *12 ga., 20 ga.*
Action: *semi-auto*
Barrel Length: *26", 28", 30"* **Wt.:** *6.5–7.25 lbs.*
Sights: *N/A*
Capacity: *4*
Stock: *presentation-grade walnut*

D2C:	NIB $2,300	Ex $1,750	VG+ $1,265	Good $1,150	
C2C:	Mint $2,210	Ex $1,600	VG+ $1,150	Good $1,035	Fair $530
Trade-In:	Mint $1,640	Ex $1,300	VG+ $900	Good $805	Poor $240

A-303 FIELD REDBOOK CODE: RB-BR-S-MA303F

Gas operated, vent rib, alloy receiver, 2.75" or 3" chamber. Models without MobilChokes are valued approximately 20% lower. Subtract $20 from value for straight-grip model.

Production: *imported through 1996* **Gauge/Bore:** *12 ga., 20 ga.*
Action: *semi-auto*
Barrel Length: *26", 28"* **Wt.:** *N/A*
Sights: *N/A*
Capacity: *4*
Stock: *walnut with straight or pistol grip*

D2C:	NIB $850	Ex $650	VG+ $470	Good $425	
C2C:	Mint $820	Ex $600	VG+ $430	Good $385	Fair $200
Trade-In:	Mint $610	Ex $500	VG+ $340	Good $300	Poor $90

A-303 UPLAND REDBOOK CODE: RB-BR-S-MA303U

Vent rib barrel with MobilChokes, gas operated, fires 3" shells.

Production: *imported through 1996* **Gauge/Bore:** *12 ga., 20 ga.*
Action: *semi-auto*
Barrel Length: *24"* **Wt.:** *~7 lbs.*
Sights: *N/A*
Capacity: *4*
Stock: *English-style straight*

D2C:	NIB $700	Ex $550	VG+ $385	Good $350	
C2C:	Mint $680	Ex $500	VG+ $350	Good $315	Fair $165
Trade-In:	Mint $500	Ex $400	VG+ $280	Good $245	Poor $90

A-303 SLUG REDBOOK CODE: RB-BR-S-MA303S
Cylinder bore barrel.

Production: *discontinued* **Gauge/Bore:** *12 ga., 20 ga.*

Action: *semi-auto*

Barrel Length: 22" **Wt.:** *N/A*

Sights: *rifle-type*

Capacity: *4*

Stock: *walnut with pistol grip*

D2C:	NIB $690	Ex $525	VG+ $380	Good $345	
C2C:	Mint $670	Ex $500	VG+ $350	Good $315	Fair $160
Trade-In:	Mint $490	Ex $400	VG+ $270	Good $245	Poor $90

AL390 REDBOOK CODE: RB-BR-S-AL390X
Self-compensating gas operation, vent rib, fixed chokes or MobilChokes , one-piece receiver machined
from aluminum alloy, adjustable comb, accepts loads up to 3" Magnum.

Production: *discontinued* **Gauge/Bore:** *12 ga., 20 ga.*

Action: *semi-auto*

Barrel Length: 24", 26", 28", 30" **Wt.:** *7.5 lbs.*

Sights: *N/A*

Capacity: *4*

Stock: *checkered walnut*

D2C:	NIB $900	Ex $700	VG+ $495	Good $450	
C2C:	Mint $870	Ex $625	VG+ $450	Good $405	Fair $210
Trade-In:	Mint $640	Ex $525	VG+ $360	Good $315	Poor $90

AL390 FIELD REDBOOK CODE: RB-BR-S-AL390F
Self-compensating gas operation, vent rib, fixed chokes or MobilChokes , one-piece receiver
machined from aluminum alloy, adjustable comb, accepts loads up to 3" Magnum.

Production: *imported 1992–1999* **Gauge/Bore:** *12 ga., 20 ga.*

Action: *semi-auto*

Barrel Length: 22", 24", 26", 28", 30" **Wt.:** *6.4–7.5 lbs.*

Sights: *N/A*

Capacity: *4*

Stock: *checkered walnut*

D2C:	NIB $775	Ex $600	VG+ $430	Good $390	
C2C:	Mint $750	Ex $550	VG+ $390	Good $350	Fair $180
Trade-In:	Mint $560	Ex $450	VG+ $310	Good $275	Poor $90

AL390 DELUXE/GOLD MALLARD REDBOOK CODE: RB-BR-S-AL390D
Self-compensating gas operation, vent rib, fixed chokes or MobilChokes , one-piece aluminum alloy receiver with
gold inlaid snipe and other accents, accepts loads up to 3" Magnum. Add approximately 20% to value compared to base model.

Production: *discontinued* **Gauge/Bore:** *12 ga., 20 ga.*

Action: *semi-auto*

Barrel Length: 22", 24", 26", 28", 30" **Wt.:** *7.2 lbs.*

Sights: *N/A*

Capacity: *4*

Stock: *checkered walnut*

D2C:	NIB $825	Ex $650	VG+ $455	Good $415	
C2C:	Mint $800	Ex $575	VG+ $420	Good $375	Fair $190
Trade-In:	Mint $590	Ex $475	VG+ $330	Good $290	Poor $90

AL390 TARGET   REDBOOK CODE: RB-BR-S-AL390T

Self-compensating gas operation, vent rib, fixed chokes or MobilChokes, one-piece receiver machined from aluminum alloy, adjustable buttstock, accepts loads up to 3" Magnum. Skeet model features 28" ported barrel with wide vent rib and fixed choke. Trap model features 30" or 32" barrel with MobilChokes.

Production: *discontinued* **Gauge/Bore:** *12 ga., 20 ga.*
Action: *semi-auto*
Barrel Length: 22", 24", 26", 28", 30" **Wt.:** *7.5 lbs.*
Sights: *N/A*
Capacity: *2*
Stock: *checkered walnut*

D2C:	NIB $825	Ex $650	VG+ $455	Good $415	
C2C:	Mint $800	Ex $575	VG+ $420	Good $375	Fair $190
Trade-In:	Mint $590	Ex $475	VG+ $330	Good $290	Poor $90

AL-1 FIELD   REDBOOK CODE: RB-BR-S-AL1XFX

Gas operated, vent rib, various choke/barrel combinations, fires 2.75" shells.

Production: *imported 1971–1973* **Gauge/Bore:** *12 ga., 20 ga.*
Action: *semi-auto*
Barrel Length: 26", 28", 30" **Wt.:** *N/A*
Sights: *N/A*
Capacity: *4*
Stock: *checkered pistol grip*

D2C:	NIB $610	Ex $475	VG+ $340	Good $305	
C2C:	Mint $590	Ex $425	VG+ $310	Good $275	Fair $145
Trade-In:	Mint $440	Ex $350	VG+ $240	Good $215	Poor $90

AL-2   REDBOOK CODE: RB-BR-S-MODAL2

Gas operated, vent rib, various choke/barrel combinations, engraved receiver, fires 2.75" shells.

Production: *discontinued* **Gauge/Bore:** *12 ga., 20 ga.*
Action: *semi-auto*
Barrel Length: 26", 28", 30" **Wt.:** *6.5–7.25 lbs.*
Sights: *N/A*
Capacity: *4*
Stock: *checkered pistol grip*

D2C:	NIB $550	Ex $425	VG+ $305	Good $275	
C2C:	Mint $530	Ex $400	VG+ $280	Good $250	Fair $130
Trade-In:	Mint $400	Ex $325	VG+ $220	Good $195	Poor $60

AL-2 MAGNUM   REDBOOK CODE: RB-BR-S-AL2MAG

Gas operated, vent rib, full or modified choke, heavy action bar, chambers 3" Magnum shells.

Production: *1973–1975* **Gauge/Bore:** *12 ga.*
Action: *semi-auto*
Barrel Length: 28", 30" **Wt.:** *~8 lbs.*
Sights: *N/A*
Capacity: *4*
Stock: *checkered pistol grip*

D2C:	NIB $630	Ex $500	VG+ $350	Good $315	
C2C:	Mint $610	Ex $450	VG+ $320	Good $285	Fair $145
Trade-In:	Mint $450	Ex $375	VG+ $250	Good $225	Poor $90

AL-2 SKEET   REDBOOK CODE: RB-BR-S-AL2SKT
Gas operated, vent rib, skeet choke, engraved receiver, fires 2.75" shells.

Production: *1973–1975* **Gauge/Bore:** *12 ga., 20 ga.*

Action: *semi-auto*

Barrel Length: 26" **Wt.:** *~7 lbs.*

Sights: *N/A*

Capacity: *4*

Stock: *checkered pistol grip*

D2C:	NIB $795	Ex $625	VG+ $440	Good $400	
C2C:	Mint $770	Ex $550	VG+ $400	Good $360	Fair $185
Trade-In:	Mint $570	Ex $450	VG+ $320	Good $280	Poor $90

AL-2 TRAP   REDBOOK CODE: RB-BR-S-AL2TRP
Gas operated, wide vent rib barrel, full choke, fully engraved receiver, fires 2.75" shells.

Production: *1973–1975* **Gauge/Bore:** *12 ga., 20 ga.*

Action: *semi-auto*

Barrel Length: 30" **Wt.:** *7.75 lbs.*

Sights: *N/A*

Capacity: *4*

Stock: *Monte Carlo*

D2C:	NIB $750	Ex $575	VG+ $415	Good $375	
C2C:	Mint $720	Ex $525	VG+ $380	Good $340	Fair $175
Trade-In:	Mint $540	Ex $425	VG+ $300	Good $265	Poor $90

AL-3   REDBOOK CODE: RB-BR-S-MODAL3
AL-3 is a continuation of the AL-2 series, with the same general specs.

Production: *discontinued 1987* **Gauge/Bore:** *12 ga., 20 ga.*

Action: *semi-auto*

Barrel Length: 26", 28", 30" **Wt.:** *7 lbs.*

Sights: *N/A*

Capacity: *4*

Stock: *checkered walnut*

D2C:	NIB $725	Ex $575	VG+ $400	Good $365	
C2C:	Mint $700	Ex $525	VG+ $370	Good $330	Fair $170
Trade-In:	Mint $520	Ex $425	VG+ $290	Good $255	Poor $90

ASEL   REDBOOK CODE: RB-BR-S-MDASEL
Vent rib, various chokes, single trigger, auto ejectors, engraved receiver.

Production: *1947–1964* **Gauge/Bore:** *12 ga., 20 ga.*

Action: *O/U*

Barrel Length: 26", 28", 30" **Wt.:** *N/A*

Sights: *N/A*

Capacity: *2*

Stock: *checkered pistol grip*

D2C:	NIB $7,000	Ex $5,325	VG+ $3,850	Good $3,500	
C2C:	Mint $6,720	Ex $4,850	VG+ $3,500	Good $3,150	Fair $1,610
Trade-In:	Mint $4,970	Ex $3,925	VG+ $2,730	Good $2,450	Poor $720

BERETTA

ASE 90 DELUXE REDBOOK CODE: RB-BR-S-ASE90D

Specifications fully customizable, deep scroll engraving. Available in sporting and field models.

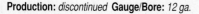

Production: *discontinued* **Gauge/Bore:** *12 ga.*

Action: *O/U*

Barrel Length: any custom length **Wt.:** *~8.5 lbs.*

Sights: *N/A*

Capacity: *2*

Stock: *checkered high-grade walnut*

D2C:	NIB $7,000	Ex $5,325	VG+ $3,850	Good $3,500	
C2C:	Mint $6,720	Ex $4,850	VG+ $3,500	Good $3,150	Fair $1,610
Trade-In:	Mint $4,970	Ex $3,925	VG+ $2,730	Good $2,450	Poor $720

ASE 90 PIGEON REDBOOK CODE: RB-BR-S-ASE90P

Cold hammer-forged barrel with vent rib, improved modified/full chokes, receiver in blue or coin-silver finish and gold etching, single trigger with optional barrel selector. Available with 2.75" or 3" chambers.

Production: *imported 1992–1994* **Gauge/Bore:** *12 ga.*

Action: *O/U*

Barrel Length: 28" **Wt.:** *7.8 lbs.*

Sights: *N/A*

Capacity: *2*

Stock: *high-grade checkered walnut*

D2C:	NIB $7,000	Ex $5,325	VG+ $3,850	Good $3,500	
C2C:	Mint $6,720	Ex $4,850	VG+ $3,500	Good $3,150	Fair $1,610
Trade-In:	Mint $4,970	Ex $3,925	VG+ $2,730	Good $2,450	Poor $720

ASE 90 SKEET REDBOOK CODE: RB-BR-S-ASE90S

Cold hammer-forged ventilated barrel with vent rib, specs similar to ASE 90 Pigeon but with skeet choke and more extensive engraving.

Production: *discontinued* **Gauge/Bore:** *12 ga.*

Action: *O/U*

Barrel Length: 28" **Wt.:** *~7.2 lbs.*

Sights: *N/A*

Capacity: *2*

Stock: *extra-high-grade walnut*

D2C:	NIB $6,250	Ex $4,750	VG+ $3,440	Good $3,125	
C2C:	Mint $6,000	Ex $4,325	VG+ $3,130	Good $2,815	Fair $1,440
Trade-In:	Mint $4,440	Ex $3,500	VG+ $2,440	Good $2,190	Poor $630

ASE 90 TRAP REDBOOK CODE: RB-BR-S-ASE90T

Specs similar to ASE 90 Pigeon with extra trigger group.

Production: *discontinued* **Gauge/Bore:** *12 ga.*

Action: *O/U*

Barrel Length: 30" **Wt.:** *8.2 lbs.*

Sights: *N/A*

Capacity: *2*

Stock: *high-grade walnut*

D2C:	NIB $4,800	Ex $3,650	VG+ $2,640	Good $2,400	
C2C:	Mint $4,610	Ex $3,325	VG+ $2,400	Good $2,160	Fair $1,105
Trade-In:	Mint $3,410	Ex $2,700	VG+ $1,880	Good $1,680	Poor $480

BL-1   REDBOOK CODE: RB-BR-S-MODBL1
Boxlock action, extractors, various choke/barrel combinations, blue finish, double triggers, fires 2.75" shells.

Production: *imported 1968–1973* **Gauge/Bore:** *12 ga.*

Action: *O/U*

Barrel Length: *26", 28", 30"* **Wt.:** *~6.75 lbs.*

Sights: *N/A*

Capacity: *2*

Stock: *checkered pistol grip*

D2C:	NIB $700	Ex $550	VG+ $385	Good $350	
C2C:	Mint $680	Ex $500	VG+ $350	Good $315	Fair $165
Trade-In:	Mint $500	Ex $400	VG+ $280	Good $245	Poor $90

BL-2   REDBOOK CODE: RB-BR-S-MODBL2
Specs similar to BL-1 but with single trigger, additional engraving. Also available with speed trigger (BL-2/S) and in riot configuration with 18" barrel.

Production: *imported 1968–1973* **Gauge/Bore:** *12 ga.*

Action: *O/U*

Barrel Length: *26", 28", 30"* **Wt.:** *~6.75 lbs.*

Sights: *N/A*

Capacity: *2*

Stock: *checkered pistol grip*

D2C:	NIB $650	Ex $500	VG+ $360	Good $325	
C2C:	Mint $630	Ex $450	VG+ $330	Good $295	Fair $150
Trade-In:	Mint $470	Ex $375	VG+ $260	Good $230	Poor $90

BL-3   REDBOOK CODE: RB-BR-S-MODBL3
Specs similar to BL-1 but with single trigger, vent rib barrels, additional engraving. Fires 3" shells
(12 ga. model is also available with 2.75" chambers). Add $100 for 28 gauge model in excellent condition.

Production: *imported 1968–1976* **Gauge/Bore:** *12 ga., 20 ga., 28 ga.*

Action: *O/U*

Barrel Length: *26", 28", 30"* **Wt.:** *6–7.25 lbs.*

Sights: *N/A*

Capacity: *2*

Stock: *checkered pistol grip*

D2C:	NIB $900	Ex $700	VG+ $495	Good $450	
C2C:	Mint $870	Ex $625	VG+ $450	Good $405	Fair $210
Trade-In:	Mint $640	Ex $525	VG+ $360	Good $315	Poor $90

BL-4   REDBOOK CODE: RB-BR-S-MODBL4
Improved version of BL-3 with similar specs plus auto ejectors, more extensive engraving and
higher-quality wood. Add 50% for 20 gauge model. Add $100 for 28 gauge model.

Production: *discontinued* **Gauge/Bore:** *12 ga., 20 ga., 28 ga.*

Action: *O/U*

Barrel Length: *26", 28", 30"* **Wt.:** *6–7.25 lbs.*

Sights: *N/A*

Capacity: *2*

Stock: *high-quality checkered walnut pistol grip*

D2C:	NIB $1,100	Ex $850	VG+ $605	Good $550	
C2C:	Mint $1,060	Ex $775	VG+ $550	Good $495	Fair $255
Trade-In:	Mint $790	Ex $625	VG+ $430	Good $385	Poor $120

BERETTA

BL-5 REDBOOK CODE: RB-BR-S-MODBL5
Improved version of BL-3 and BL-4 with similar specs plus auto ejectors, more extensive engraving and higher-quality wood.

Production: *discontinued* **Gauge/Bore:** *12 ga., 20 ga., 28 ga.*
Action: *O/U*
Barrel Length: 26", 28", 30" **Wt.:** *6–7.25 lbs.*
Sights: *N/A*
Capacity: *2*
Stock: *high-quality checkered walnut with full pistol grip*

D2C:	NIB $1,160	Ex $900	VG+ $640	Good $580	
C2C:	Mint $1,120	Ex $825	VG+ $580	Good $525	Fair $270
Trade-In:	Mint $830	Ex $650	VG+ $460	Good $410	Poor $120

BL-6 REDBOOK CODE: RB-BR-S-MODBL6
Boxlock action, sideplates with coin finish and engraving, ejectors, single trigger.

Production: *discontinued* **Gauge/Bore:** *12 ga., 20 ga., 28 ga.*
Action: *O/U*
Barrel Length: 26", 28", 30" **Wt.:** *N/A*
Sights: *N/A*
Capacity: *2*
Stock: *deluxe checkered walnut with full pistol grip*

D2C:	NIB $4,500	Ex $3,425	VG+ $2,475	Good $2,250	
C2C:	Mint $4,320	Ex $3,125	VG+ $2,250	Good $2,025	Fair $1,035
Trade-In:	Mint $3,200	Ex $2,525	VG+ $1,760	Good $1,575	Poor $450

FS-1 REDBOOK CODE: RB-BR-S-MODFS1
Boxlock action, under lever break open, solid rib barrel with full choke, blue finish.

Production: *discontinued* **Gauge/Bore:** *12 ga., 16 ga., 20 ga., 28 ga., .410*
Action: *single-shot*
Barrel Length: 26", 28" **Wt.:** *N/A*
Sights: *N/A*
Capacity: *1*
Stock: *checkered walnut with pistol or straight grip*

D2C:	NIB $450	Ex $350	VG+ $250	Good $225	
C2C:	Mint $440	Ex $325	VG+ $230	Good $205	Fair $105
Trade-In:	Mint $320	Ex $275	VG+ $180	Good $160	Poor $60

S55B REDBOOK CODE: RB-BR-S-MDS55B
Boxlock action, single trigger, extractors.

Production: *discontinued* **Gauge/Bore:** *12 ga., 20 ga.*
Action: *O/U*
Barrel Length: 26", 28", 30" **Wt.:** *6.5–7.5 lbs.*
Sights: *N/A*
Capacity: *2*
Stock: *checkered pistol grip*

D2C:	NIB $650	Ex $500	VG+ $360	Good $325	
C2C:	Mint $630	Ex $450	VG+ $330	Good $295	Fair $150
Trade-In:	Mint $470	Ex $375	VG+ $260	Good $230	Poor $90

S56E REDBOOK CODE: RB-BR-S-MDS56E
Same general specs as S55B model plus auto ejectors and scroll-engraved receiver

Production: *discontinued* **Gauge/Bore:** *12 ga., 20 ga.*
Action: *O/U*
Barrel Length: 26", 28", 30" **Wt.:** *6.5–7.5 lbs.*
Sights: *N/A*
Capacity: 2
Stock: *checkered pistol grip*

D2C:	NIB $900	Ex $700	VG+ $495	Good $450	
C2C:	Mint $870	Ex $625	VG+ $450	Good $405	Fair $210
Trade-In:	Mint $640	Ex $525	VG+ $360	Good $315	Poor $90

S58 SKEET REDBOOK CODE: RB-BR-S-MS58SK
Specs similar to svm but with skeet-choked Bohler steel barrel with wide vent rib.

Production: *discontinued* **Gauge/Bore:** *12 ga., 20 ga.*
Action: *O/U*
Barrel Length: 26" **Wt.:** *N/A*
Sights: *N/A*
Capacity: 2
Stock: *checkered pistol grip*

D2C:	NIB $1,000	Ex $775	VG+ $550	Good $500	
C2C:	Mint $960	Ex $700	VG+ $500	Good $450	Fair $230
Trade-In:	Mint $710	Ex $575	VG+ $390	Good $350	Poor $120

TR-1 TRAP REDBOOK CODE: RB-BR-S-MDTR1T
Hammerless, vent rib barrel with full choke, blue finish, under lever break open, buttpad

Production: *1968–1971* **Gauge/Bore:** *12 ga.*
Action: *single-shot*
Barrel Length: 32" **Wt.:** *~8.25 lbs.*
Sights: *N/A*
Capacity: 1
Stock: *Monte Carlo pistol grip*

D2C:	NIB $775	Ex $600	VG+ $430	Good $390	
C2C:	Mint $750	Ex $550	VG+ $390	Good $350	Fair $180
Trade-In:	Mint $560	Ex $450	VG+ $310	Good $275	Poor $90

TR-2 TRAP REDBOOK CODE: RB-BR-S-MDTR2T
Same specs as TR-1 but with extended vent rib.

Production: *1969–1973* **Gauge/Bore:** *12 ga.*
Action: *single-shot*
Barrel Length: 32" **Wt.:** *~8.25 lbs.*
Sights: *N/A*
Capacity: 1
Stock: *Monte Carlo pistol grip*

D2C:	NIB $550	Ex $425	VG+ $305	Good $275	
C2C:	Mint $530	Ex $400	VG+ $280	Good $250	Fair $130
Trade-In:	Mint $400	Ex $325	VG+ $220	Good $195	Poor $60

BERETTA

ONYX PRO REDBOOK CODE: RB-BR-S-ONXPRX
Vent rib barrels with set of five choke tubes, matte blue finish, receiver in Dura-Jewel finish, buttpad, fires 3" shells.

Production: *discontinued* **Gauge/Bore:** *12 ga., 20 ga., 28 ga.*
Action: *O/U*
Barrel Length: 26", 28" **Wt.:** *~6.8 lbs.*
Sights: *N/A*
Capacity: *2*
Stock: *checkered X-Tra Wood finish*

D2C:	NIB $1,850	Ex $1,425	VG+ $1,020	Good $925	
C2C:	Mint $1,780	Ex $1,300	VG+ $930	Good $835	Fair $430
Trade-In:	Mint $1,320	Ex $1,050	VG+ $730	Good $650	Poor $210

ONYX PRO 3.5 REDBOOK CODE: RB-BR-S-ONXPR3
Same general specs as Onyx Pro but with 3.5" chamber.

Production: *discontinued* **Gauge/Bore:** *12 ga.*
Action: *O/U*
Barrel Length: 26", 28" **Wt.:** *6.9 lbs.*
Sights: *N/A*
Capacity: *2*
Stock: *checkered X-Tra Wood finish*

D2C:	NIB $1,335	Ex $1,025	VG+ $735	Good $670	
C2C:	Mint $1,290	Ex $925	VG+ $670	Good $605	Fair $310
Trade-In:	Mint $950	Ex $750	VG+ $530	Good $470	Poor $150

SILVER SNIPE REDBOOK CODE: RB-BR-S-SLVSNP
Boxlock action, extractors, double triggers, blue finish. Single trigger model with vent rib and auto ejectors increases value by approximately 50%. Add 50% for 20 gauge model. Add 100% for 28 gauge model.

Production: *1955–1967* **Gauge/Bore:** *12 ga., 20 ga., 28 ga.*
Action: *O/U*
Barrel Length: 26", 28", 30" **Wt.:** *6–8.5 lbs.*
Sights: *N/A*
Capacity: *2*
Stock: *checkered pistol grip*

D2C:	NIB $825	Ex $650	VG+ $455	Good $415	
C2C:	Mint $800	Ex $575	VG+ $420	Good $375	Fair $190
Trade-In:	Mint $590	Ex $475	VG+ $330	Good $290	Poor $90

GOLDEN SNIPE REDBOOK CODE: RB-BR-S-GLDSNP
Same general specs as Silver Snipe but with vent rib and auto ejectors. Add 10% for single trigger model.

Production: *discontinued* **Gauge/Bore:** *12 ga., 20 ga., 28 ga.*
Action: *O/U*
Barrel Length: 26", 28", 30" **Wt.:** *N/A*
Sights: *N/A*
Capacity: *2*
Stock: *checkered pistol grip*

D2C:	NIB $1,000	Ex $775	VG+ $550	Good $500	
C2C:	Mint $960	Ex $700	VG+ $500	Good $450	Fair $230
Trade-In:	Mint $710	Ex $575	VG+ $390	Good $350	Poor $120

SV10 PERENNIA III REDBOOK CODE: RB-BR-S-SV10P3

Vent rib OptimaBore barrels, OptimaChokes, alloy receiver with laser engraving, reduced recoil system.

BERETTA

Production: *current* **Gauge/Bore:** *12 ga., 20 ga.*

Action: *O/U*

Barrel Length: *26", 28", 30"* **Wt.:** *7.3 lbs.*

Sights: *N/A*

Capacity: *2*

D2C:	NIB $3,550	Ex $2,700	VG+ $1,955	Good $1,775	
C2C:	Mint $3,410	Ex $2,450	VG+ $1,780	Good $1,600	Fair $820
Trade-In:	Mint $2,530	Ex $2,000	VG+ $1,390	Good $1,245	Poor $360

Stock: *checkered select walnut with matte finish and pistol grip*

GRADE 100 REDBOOK CODE: RB-BR-S-GDE100

Sidelock action, any common choke, automatic ejectors, double triggers.

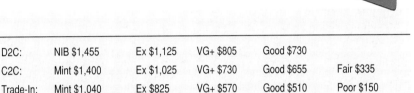

Production: *discontinued* **Gauge/Bore:** *12 ga.*

Action: *O/U*

Barrel Length: *26", 28", 30"* **Wt.:** *~7.5 lbs.*

Sights: *N/A*

Capacity: *2*

D2C:	NIB $1,455	Ex $1,125	VG+ $805	Good $730	
C2C:	Mint $1,400	Ex $1,025	VG+ $730	Good $655	Fair $335
Trade-In:	Mint $1,040	Ex $825	VG+ $570	Good $510	Poor $150

Stock: *checkered walnut, straight or pistol grip*

GRADE 200 REDBOOK CODE: RB-BR-S-GDE200

Sidelock action, choice of high-quality choke, chrome-plated action parts, automatic ejectors, double triggers. .

Production: *discontinued* **Gauge/Bore:** *12 ga.*

Action: *O/U*

Barrel Length: *26", 28", 30"* **Wt.:** *~7.5 lbs.*

Sights: *N/A*

Capacity: *2*

D2C:	NIB $1,800	Ex $1,375	VG+ $990	Good $900	
C2C:	Mint $1,730	Ex $1,250	VG+ $900	Good $810	Fair $415
Trade-In:	Mint $1,280	Ex $1,025	VG+ $710	Good $630	Poor $180

Stock: *checkered walnut, straight or pistol grip*

Bernardelli, Vincenzo

BERNARDELLI

Bernardelli, Vincenzo, headquartered in Brescia, Italy, began manufacturing handguns in 1865 and has remained a fixture in the firearms industry ever since. While the company no longer manufactures handguns, SAR Arms (Sarsilmaz), Bernardelli's parent company, produces a vest-pocket model reminiscent of the Bernardelli design. Bernardelli still manufactures and is best known for its line of quality, ornate shotguns. In 1947, the company was the first Italian shotgun maker to introduce a semi-automatic model, and the brand first gained its international notoriety for its side-by-side hunting models. The company has also manufactured military shotguns like the Galil. Various companies have bought and sold the Bernardelli, Vincenzo trademark over the years, but the standards for Benardelli guns have never faltered.

BERNARDELLI

MEGA REDBOOK CODE: RB-BV-S-MEGAXX

Sand-blasted black anodized receiver, mirror polished sides, gold engraved logo, oil polished stock and forend, 3-inch chamber, cylinder choke.

Production: *current* **Gauge/Bore:** *12 ga.*
Action: *semi-auto*
Barrel Length: 24", 26", 28", 30" **Wt.:** *6.8 lbs.*
Sights: *brass*
Capacity: *4*
Stock: *select walnut*

D2C:	NIB $1,315	Ex $1,000	VG+ $725	Good $660	
C2C:	Mint $1,270	Ex $925	VG+ $660	Good $595	Fair $305
Trade-In:	Mint $940	Ex $750	VG+ $520	Good $465	Poor $150

MEGA SILVER REDBOOK CODE: RB-BV-S-MEGASL

Nickel-plated over sand-blasted black anodized receiver, mirror polished sides, gold engraved logo, oil polished stock and forend, 3-inch chamber, cylinder choke.

Production: *current* **Gauge/Bore:** *12 ga.*
Action: *semi-auto*
Barrel Length: 24", 26", 28", 30" **Wt.:** *6.8 lbs.*
Sights: *brass*
Capacity: *4*
Stock: *select walnut*

D2C:	NIB $1,460	Ex $1,125	VG+ $805	Good $730	
C2C:	Mint $1,410	Ex $1,025	VG+ $730	Good $660	Fair $340
Trade-In:	Mint $1,040	Ex $825	VG+ $570	Good $515	Poor $150

MEGA SPORTING REDBOOK CODE: RB-BV-S-MEGASP

Developed for sporting clay, carbon-fiber finished barrel and receiver, adjustable stock, professional sporting choke tubes, red drive inside the muzzle, comes with plastic case.

Production: *current* **Gauge/Bore:** *12 ga.*
Action: *semi-auto*
Barrel Length: 28", 30" **Wt.:** *6.8 lbs.*
Sights: *brass*
Capacity: *4*
Stock: *select walnut*

D2C:	NIB $1,620	Ex $1,250	VG+ $895	Good $810	
C2C:	Mint $1,560	Ex $1,125	VG+ $810	Good $730	Fair $375
Trade-In:	Mint $1,160	Ex $925	VG+ $640	Good $570	Poor $180

MEGA SYNTHETIC REDBOOK CODE: RB-BV-S-SYNTHC

Sand-blasted and anodized Ergal 55/aluminum receiver, pistol grip with Soft-Touch finish on
stock and forend, rubber recoil pad, comes with ABS carry case, ABS case for two barrels available, optional slug barrel for additional cost.

Production: *current* **Gauge/Bore:** *12 ga.*
Action: *semi-auto*
Barrel Length: 24", 26", 28", 30" **Wt.:** *6.8 lbs.*
Sights: *brass*
Capacity: *4*
Stock: *black synthetic*

D2C:	NIB $1,350	Ex $1,050	VG+ $745	Good $675	
C2C:	Mint $1,300	Ex $950	VG+ $680	Good $610	Fair $315
Trade-In:	Mint $960	Ex $775	VG+ $530	Good $475	Poor $150

MEGA CAMOUFLAGE REDBOOK CODE: RB-BV-S-CAMOUFLAGEFL

Fully covered in camouflage, Ergal 55/aluminum receiver, Rubber recoil pad, pistol grip, slug barrel optional at added cost, comes with ABS carry case, optional carry case for two barrels at added cost, in two versions, Api Brown and Max 4.

Production: *current* **Gauge/Bore:** *12 ga.*
Action: *semi-auto*
Barrel Length: *24", 26", 28", 30"* **Wt.:** *6.8 lbs.*
Sights: *brass*
Capacity: *4*
Stock: *camouflage synthetic*

D2C:	NIB $1,340	Ex $1,025	VG+ $740	Good $670	
C2C:	Mint $1,290	Ex $925	VG+ $670	Good $605	Fair $310
Trade-In:	Mint $960	Ex $775	VG+ $530	Good $470	Poor $150

CIGNO REDBOOK CODE: RB-BV-S-CIGNOX

Black anodized sand-blasted Ergal 55/aluminum receiver, sides highly polished and engraved, pistol grip, rubber butt pad, forend and stock oil polished, optional slug barrel available, comes with ABS carry case, optional two barrel carry case available for added cost.

Production: *current* **Gauge/Bore:** *12 ga.*
Action: *semi-auto*
Barrel Length: *24", 26", 28", 30"* **Wt.:** *6.8 lbs.*
Sights: *optical fiber*
Capacity: *4*
Stock: *select walnut*

D2C:	NIB $1,560	Ex $1,200	VG+ $860	Good $780	
C2C:	Mint $1,500	Ex $1,100	VG+ $780	Good $705	Fair $360
Trade-In:	Mint $1,110	Ex $875	VG+ $610	Good $550	Poor $180

REGINA REDBOOK CODE: RB-BV-S-REGINA

Black anodized sand-blasted Ergal 55/aluminum receiver, polished and engraved, 3" chamber, pistol grip, rubber recoil pad, optional slug barrel, ABS carry case or optional two barrel carry case for additional cost.

Production: *current* **Gauge/Bore:** *12 ga.*
Action: *semi-auto*
Barrel Length: *24", 26", 28", 30"* **Wt.:** *6.8 lbs.*
Sights: *optical fiber*
Capacity: *4*
Stock: *select walnut*

D2C:	NIB $1,615	Ex $1,250	VG+ $890	Good $810	
C2C:	Mint $1,560	Ex $1,125	VG+ $810	Good $730	Fair $375
Trade-In:	Mint $1,150	Ex $925	VG+ $630	Good $570	Poor $180

NIBBIO REDBOOK CODE: RB-BV-S-NIBBIO

Highly polished black anodized Ergal 55/aluminum receiver, game scene engravings, rubber recoil pad, pistol grip, ABS carry case, optional slug barrel, optional ABS carry case for two barrels, available as Nibbio Gold with game scene engravings finished in gold.

Production: *current* **Gauge/Bore:** *12 ga.*
Action: *semi-auto*
Barrel Length: *24", 26", 28", 30"* **Wt.:** *6.8 lbs.*
Sights: *optical fiber*
Capacity: *4*
Stock: *highly selected walnut*

D2C:	NIB $1,830	Ex $1,400	VG+ $1,010	Good $915	
C2C:	Mint $1,760	Ex $1,275	VG+ $920	Good $825	Fair $425
Trade-In:	Mint $1,300	Ex $1,025	VG+ $720	Good $645	Poor $210

HEMINGWAY REDBOOK CODE: RB-BV-S-HEMWAY

Light, small receiver and barrels, forged steel frame, 2.8" chamber, Anson & Deeley action, double trigger/single trigger with selector, fixed chokes, simple or automatic extractors, long beavertail forend, comes with ABS carry case, 3" chamber option available, interchangeable chokes on request, Hemingway De Luxe model features lighter weight, fine engraved side plates, and best wood selection.

Production: *current* **Gauge/Bore:** *12 ga., 20 ga.*

Action: *SxS*

Barrel Length: 24", 26", 27", 28", 29" **Wt.:** *6.1–6.2 lbs.*

Sights: *bead*

Capacity: *2*

Stock: *English walnut straight grip*

D2C:	NIB $1,900	Ex $1,450	VG+ $1,045	Good $950	
C2C:	Mint $1,830	Ex $1,325	VG+ $950	Good $855	Fair $440
Trade-In:	Mint $1,350	Ex $1,075	VG+ $750	Good $665	Poor $210

ROMA 6 REDBOOK CODE: RB-BV-S-ROMAXX

Forged steel frame with side plates, frame reinforcement, extra fine engraving, 2.8" chamber, Anson & Deeley action, fixed chokes, double trigger/single trigger with selector, simple or automatic extractors, long beavertail forend, ABS carry case, 3" chamber available on request, interchangeable chokes optional.

Production: *current* **Gauge/Bore:** *12 ga., 20 ga.*

Action: *SxS*

Barrel Length: 24", 26", 27", 28", 29"

Wt.: *6.2 lbs., 6.8 lbs.*

Sights: *bead*

Capacity: *2*

Stock: *select fancy English walnut, pistol grip*

D2C:	NIB $2,115	Ex $1,625	VG+ $1,165	Good $1,060	
C2C:	Mint $2,040	Ex $1,475	VG+ $1,060	Good $955	Fair $490
Trade-In:	Mint $1,510	Ex $1,200	VG+ $830	Good $745	Poor $240

BECCACCIA REDBOOK CODE: RB-BV-S-BECCIA

Variation of Roma model with forged steel frame and frame reinforcement, extra fine engraving, fences with refined border, 2.8" chamber, Anson & Deeley action, fixed chokes, double trigger/single trigger with selector, simple or automatic extractors, long beavertail forend, ABS carry case, 3" chamber available on request, interchangeable chokes optional, also offered in Beccaccia Oro or "Gold" with gold game scenes on the side plates, higher grade walnut.

Production: *current* **Gauge/Bore:** *12 ga.*

Action: *SxS*

Barrel Length: 24", 26", 27", 28", 29" **Wt.:** *6.8 lbs.*

Sights: *bead*

Capacity: *2*

Stock: *English walnut pistol grip*

D2C:	NIB $2,137	Ex $1,625	VG+ $1,180	Good $1,070	
C2C:	Mint $2,060	Ex $1,475	VG+ $1,070	Good $965	Fair $495
Trade-In:	Mint $1,520	Ex $1,200	VG+ $840	Good $750	Poor $240

V.B. HOLLAND REDBOOK CODE: RB-BV-S-HOLAND

Hand-fitted Holland-type locks, engraved according to customer request, custom stock and forend dimensions and shapes, side lock with safety double sear, articulated single or double trigger, Triplice Purdey type breech locking system, chopper lump barrel, fixed chokes, extended length forend tip or optional beavertail with inlaid golden shield, leather carry case included.

Production: *current* **Gauge/Bore:** *12 ga.*

Action: *SxS*

Barrel Length: 26", 27", 28" **Wt.:** *7 lbs.*

Sights: *bead*

Capacity: *2*

Stock: *English walnut with shield, straight*

D2C:	NIB $2,731	Ex $2,100	VG+ $1,505	Good $1,370	
C2C:	Mint $2,630	Ex $1,900	VG+ $1,370	Good $1,230	Fair $630
Trade-In:	Mint $1,940	Ex $1,550	VG+ $1,070	Good $960	Poor $300

ANNIVERSARY REDBOOK CODE: RB-BV-S-ANNSRY

Nickel-plated Ergal 55/aluminum receiver with floral themes and game scene engraving with gold inlays, designed as Bernardelli's 60th Anniversary gun, 3" chamber, rubber recoil pad, ABS carry case included, optional slug barrel, optional ABS two barrel case available for additional cost. Market research provides no conclusive pricing suggestion(s) for this particular model. The model is either too rare or contains too many custom options, which drastically affects pricing.

Production: *current* **Gauge/Bore:** *12 ga.*
Action: *semi-auto*
Barrel Length: 24", 26", 28", 30" **Wt.:** *6.8 lbs.*
Sights: *brass*
Capacity: *4*
Stock: *select walnut, checkering, Optowood finish*

ANNIVERSARY CERAMICA REDBOOK CODE: RB-BV-S-ANNSRC

"Top of the line" gun designed to celebrate the 60th Anniversary of the first semi-automatic Bernardelli Shotgun, nickel-plated Ergal 55/aluminum receiver with floral themes and game scene engraving with gold inlays, ceramic inlaid names and logo, 3" chamber, rubber recoil pad, pistol grip stock, ABS carry case included, optional slug barrel, optional two barrel ABS carry case. Market research provides no conclusive pricing suggestion(s) for this particular model. The model is either too rare or contains too many custom options, which drastically affects pricing.

Production: *current* **Gauge/Bore:** *12 ga.*
Action: *semi-auto*
Barrel Length: 24", 26", 28", 30" **Wt.:** *6.8 lbs.*
Sights: *optical fiber*
Capacity: *4*
Stock: *very highly selected walnut, checkering*

LEVRIERO REDBOOK CODE: RB-BV-S-LEVIRO

Nickel-plated with gold inlaid game scenes on the sides of the Ergal 55/aluminum engraved receiver, 3" chamber, pistol grip stock, rubber recoil pad, ABS carry case, optional ABS carry case for two barrels, optional slug barrel available. The model is either too rare or contains too many custom options, which drastically affects pricing.

Production: *current* **Gauge/Bore:** *12 ga.*
Action: *semi-auto*
Barrel Length: 24", 26", 28", 30" **Wt.:** *6.8 lbs.*
Sights: *optical fiber*
Capacity: *4*
Stock: *very highly selected walnut, checkering*

MEGA 20 REDBOOK CODE: RB-BV-S-MEGA20

Carbon-finished barrel and receiver, 3" chamber, Teflon-protected main spring, "auto-compensator" gas system, four shims to adjust stock, 5 sporting choke tubes, Mega Synthetic model is the synthetic version with soft-touch polymer stock, Karbon-fiber finished receiver and silicium protection on breech bolt, trigger and lever button. Market research provides no conclusive pricing suggestion(s) for this particular model. The model is either too rare or contains too many custom options, which drastically affects pricing.

Production: *current* **Gauge/Bore:** *20 ga.*
Action: *semi-auto*
Barrel Length: 24", 26", 28", 30" **Wt.:** *4.4 lbs.*
Sights: *optical fiber*
Capacity: *5*
Stock: *select walnut, checkering*

BERNARDELLI

RISERVA REDBOOK CODE: RB-BV-S-RISRVA

Forged steel frame, engraved shell shaped fences, 2.8 chamber, Anson & Deeley action, fixed chokes, double trigger/single trigger selector, simple or automatic extractors, long beavertail for-end, comes with ABS carry case, 3" chamber option available, interchangeable chokes on request. Market research provides no conclusive pricing suggestion(s) for this particular model. The model is either too rare or contains too many custom options, which drastically affects pricing.

Production: *current* **Gauge/Bore:** *12 ga.*

Action: *SxS*

Barrel Length: *24", 26", 27", 28", 29"* **Wt.:** *6.8 lbs.*

Sights: *bead*

Capacity: *2*

Stock: *English, pistol grip*

MIRA ONYX REDBOOK CODE: RB-BV-S-MIRAON

Lightweight forged steel frame, 2.8" chamber, Anson & Deeley action, fixed chokes, double trigger/single trigger with selector, simple or automatic extractors, beavertail for-end, ABS carry case, 3" chamber on 20 gauge, optional for other gauges, interchangeable chokes on request, three other Mira models available: Mira Silver without side plates, Mira Adamas an entry model with side plates, Mira Exclusive with fancy walnut and engraved, and top-of-the-line Mira Gold with gold engraved game scenes. Market research provides no conclusive pricing suggestion(s) for this particular model. The model is either too rare or contains too many custom options, which drastically affects pricing.

Production: *current* **Gauge/Bore:** *12 ga., 20 ga., 28 ga.*

Action: *SxS*

Barrel Length: *24", 26", 27", 28", 29"* **Wt.:** *6–6.2 lbs.*

Sights: *bead*

Capacity: *2*

Stock: *English, straight grip*

PA 12 REDBOOK CODE: RB-BV-S-PA12XX

Black anodized finish on Ergal 55/aluminum receiver, 3" chamber, "steel proof" tested, optional magazines in either 5 or 8 round capacities, option of different stocks. Market research suggests pricing for this model is inconclusive at this time.

Production: *current* **Gauge/Bore:** *12 ga.*

Action: *pump-action*

Barrel Length: *20"* **Wt.:** *6 lbs.*

Sights: *bead*

Capacity: *6*

Stock: *synthetic, black*

PA 12 TELESCOPIC REDBOOK CODE: RB-BV-S-PA12TL

Black anodized finish on Ergal 55/aluminum receiver, 3" chamber, "steel proof" tested, Picatinny rail, long forearm, optional magazines in either 5 or 8 round capacities, optional Ghost Ring sights. Market research suggests pricing for this model is inconclusive at this time.

Production: *current* **Gauge/Bore:** *12 ga.*

Action: *pump-action*

Barrel Length: *20"* **Wt.:** *6 lbs.*

Sights: *bead*

Capacity: *8*

Stock: *synthetic, black telescopic*

PA 12 COMPACT REDBOOK CODE: RB-BV-S-PA12CP

Black anodized finish, 3" chamber, "steel proof" tested, long forearm, optional magazines in either 5 or 8 round capacities, different stocks available. Market research suggests pricing for this model is inconclusive at this time.

Production: *current* **Gauge/Bore:** *12 ga.*

Action: *pump-action*

Barrel Length: 20" **Wt.:** *N/A*

Sights: *bead*

Capacity: *8*

Stock: *synthetic, black folding*

PA 12 DEFENSE REDBOOK CODE: RB-BV-S-PA12DF

Black anodized finish, 3" chamber, Picatinny rail, pistol grip, long for-end, "steel proof" tested, muzzle thread for accessories, optional magazines in either 5 or 8 round capacities, different stocks available. Market research suggests pricing for this model is inconclusive at this time.

Production: *current* **Gauge/Bore:** *12 ga.*

Action: *pump-action*

Barrel Length: 18" **Wt.:** *N/A*

Sights: *bead*

Capacity: *5*

Stock: *synthetic, black folding*

Breda Meccanica Bresciana

Headquartered in Brescia, Breda Meccanica Bresciana, commonly known as simply "Breda," is the portion of a monolithic Italian conglomerate that is devoted to the manufacture of firearms. The company was founded just before World War II and became known for contributing weapons, artillery, and aircraft for the Italian military, including the Breda machine guns that were standard issue for Italian forces during that conflict. In 1994, Breda merged with another Italian military arms company called Otomelara, and today, Breda produces a wide range of shotguns for game and competitive shooting, specializing in semi-automatic and over/under models.

XANTHOS REDBOOK CODE: RB-BD-S-XANTHS

Inertia system, superior block locking system, steel receiver, special rubber cover over stock, laser checkering, Breda steel barrel.

Production: *current* **Gauge/Bore:** *12 ga.*

Action: *semi-auto*

Barrel Length: 24"–30" **Wt.:** *6.4 lbs.*

Sights: *fiber-optic front*

Capacity: *4*

Stock: *oiled walnut (regular, select, semi-fancy, or fancy)*

D2C:	NIB $1,190	Ex $925	VG+ $655	Good $595
C2C:	Mint $1,150	Ex $825	VG+ $600	Good $540	Fair $275
Trade-In:	Mint $850	Ex $675	VG+ $470	Good $420	Poor $120

BREDA

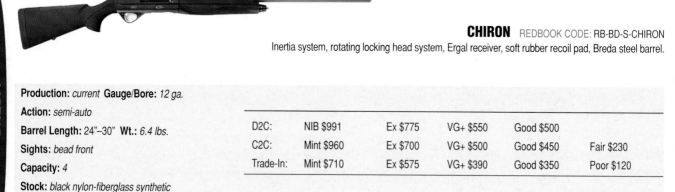

CHIRON   REDBOOK CODE: RB-BD-S-CHIRON

Inertia system, rotating locking head system, Ergal receiver, soft rubber recoil pad, Breda steel barrel.

Production: *current* **Gauge/Bore:** *12 ga.*
Action: *semi-auto*
Barrel Length: 24"–30" **Wt.:** *6.4 lbs.*
Sights: *bead front*
Capacity: *4*
Stock: *black nylon-fiberglass synthetic*

D2C:	NIB $991	Ex $775	VG+ $550	Good $500	
C2C:	Mint $960	Ex $700	VG+ $500	Good $450	Fair $230
Trade-In:	Mint $710	Ex $575	VG+ $390	Good $350	Poor $120

ECHO   REDBOOK CODE: RB-BD-S-ECHOXX

Inertia system, rotating locking head system, set of 5 choke tubes, soft rubber recoil pad, Breda steel barrel. Available in choice of nickel, black, or Breda Hard Coating finish.

Production: *current* **Gauge/Bore:** *12 ga.*
Action: *semi-auto*
Barrel Length: 24"–30" **Wt.:** *6.3 lbs.*
Sights: *bead front*
Capacity: *4*
Stock: *hardwood*

D2C:	NIB $1,032	Ex $800	VG+ $570	Good $520	
C2C:	Mint $1,000	Ex $725	VG+ $520	Good $465	Fair $240
Trade-In:	Mint $740	Ex $600	VG+ $410	Good $365	Poor $120

ECHO 20   REDBOOK CODE: RB-BD-S-ECHO20

Inertia system, rotating locking head system, Ergal aluminum alloy receiver in weather-resistant blue finish, soft rubber recoil pad, Breda steel barrel. Available in choice of nickel, black, or grey finish.

Production: *current* **Gauge/Bore:** *20 ga.*
Action: *semi-auto*
Barrel Length: 24"–30" **Wt.:** *5.8 lbs.*
Sights: *bead front*
Capacity: *4*
Stock: *walnut*

D2C:	NIB $1,110	Ex $850	VG+ $615	Good $555	
C2C:	Mint $1,070	Ex $775	VG+ $560	Good $500	Fair $260
Trade-In:	Mint $790	Ex $625	VG+ $440	Good $390	Poor $120

BROWNING

Browning

John Moses Browning, one of the most prolific firearm designers of all time, founded Browning Firearms in Ogden, Utah, in 1878, and it has since become one of the most influential firearm manufacturers in history. John Moses Browning's designs have been utilized by nearly every rifle manufacturer from Colt to Winchester. From the development of the "Potato Digger" to the first semi-automatic shotgun, the company has continuously changed the face of the firearms industry with their constant innovations and improvements. In terms of shotguns, Browning is most widely known for the Citori series, a series of over/under shotguns with many variants spanning several years right up to current production, all known for their accuracy and durability. Today, Browning holds influence over many areas of the hunting industry. Along with their quality rifles, shotguns, and handguns, Browning produces fishing equipment, knives, clothing, gun accessories, media, etc. Currently, Browning is headquartered in Morgan, Utah.

MAXUS, ALL-PURPOSE REDBOOK CODE: RB-BW-S-MAXUSX

Dura-Touch camouflage finish, aluminum alloy receiver, Lightning trigger, speed lock forearm. 14.5" length of pull, Mossy Oak Break-Up Infinity finish on both barrel and stock, Invector-Plus flush choke system and several chokes included. Steel barrel, aluminum alloy receiver, Inflex 1 recoil pad with hard heel insert, textured grip panels. Maxus Hunter is a similar model for $40 cheaper with polished blue barrel and Turkish walnut stock.

Production: *current* **Gauge/Bore:** *12 ga.*

Action: *semi-auto*

Barrel Length: 26" **Wt.:** *7 lbs.*

Sights: *HiViz Magnetic Combo*

Capacity: *5*

Stock: *composite*

D2C:	NIB $1,512	Ex $1,150	VG+ $835	Good $760	**LMP:** $1,680
C2C:	Mint $1,460	Ex $1,050	VG+ $760	Good $685	Fair $350
Trade-In:	Mint $1,080	Ex $850	VG+ $590	Good $530	Poor $180

MAXUS RIFLED DEER STALKER REDBOOK CODE: RB-BW-S-MAXRDS

Dura-Touch armor coating, twist rate of 1:28, chrome-plated chamber, Inflex 1 recoil pad with hard heel insert, textured grip panels, aluminum alloy receiver, matte black trigger guard finish, brushed nickel bolt slide finish, tubular magazine, alloy trigger, thick-walled steel barrel that is fully rifled for slug ammunition. Maxus Rifled Deer model comes with Mossy Oak Break-Up Infinity finish for about $100 less.

Production: *current* **Gauge/Bore:** *12 ga.*

Action: *semi-auto*

Barrel Length: 22" **Wt.:** *7.2 lbs.*

Sights: *none*

Capacity: *5*

Stock: *composite*

D2C:	NIB $1,282	Ex $975	VG+ $710	Good $645	**LMP:** $1,700
C2C:	Mint $1,240	Ex $900	VG+ $650	Good $580	Fair $295
Trade-In:	Mint $920	Ex $725	VG+ $500	Good $450	Poor $150

MAXUS SPORTING REDBOOK CODE: RB-BW-S-MAXSPG

Lightweight aluminum alloy receiver with nickel finish. Flat barrel with ventilated rib and lightweight profile. Close radius pistol grip, speed lock forearm, adjustable shim for length of pull, cast, and drop. Vector Pro lengthened forcing cone, 5 Invector-Plus choke tubes, Inflex recoil pad. Also offered in Maxus Sporting Carbon Fiber model with carbon fiber finish on top and bottom and offered at $200 less.

Production: *current* **Gauge/Bore:** *12 ga.*

Action: *semi-auto*

Barrel Length: 28", 30" **Wt.:** *7 lbs.*

Sights: *HiViz TriComp*

Capacity: *5*

Stock: *Turkish walnut*

D2C:	NIB $1,477	Ex $1,125	VG+ $815	Good $740	**LMP:** $1,700
C2C:	Mint $1,420	Ex $1,025	VG+ $740	Good $665	Fair $340
Trade-In:	Mint $1,050	Ex $850	VG+ $580	Good $520	Poor $150

MAXUS SPORTING GOLDEN CLAYS REDBOOK CODE: RB-BW-S-MAXSGC

Lightweight aluminum alloy receiver and barrel with flat ventilated rib and lightweight profile. Close radius pistol grip, speed lock forearm, adjustable shim for length of pull, cast, and drop. Dura-Touch armor coating, Vector Pro lengthened forcing cone, 3 Invector-Plus choke tubes, Inflex recoil pad, magazine cut-off. Matte blue finish on barrel, matte black receiver finish, chrome plated chamber, brushed nickel bolt slide finish.

Production: *current* **Gauge/Bore:** *12 ga.*

Action: *semi-auto*

Barrel Length: 28", 30" **Wt.:** *7.2 lbs., 7.3 lbs.*

Sights: *HiViz TriComp*

Capacity: *5*

Stock: *Turkish walnut*

D2C:	NIB $1,624	Ex $1,250	VG+ $895	Good $815	**LMP:** $2,000
C2C:	Mint $1,560	Ex $1,125	VG+ $820	Good $735	Fair $375
Trade-In:	Mint $1,160	Ex $925	VG+ $640	Good $570	Poor $180

MAXUS STALKER REDBOOK CODE: RB-BW-S-MAXSTK

Lightweight aluminum alloy with satin nickel finish and barrel with flat ventilated rib and lightweight profile. Close radius pistol grip, sharp 22 lines-per-inch checkering on the stock, speed lock forearm, adjustable shim for length of pull, cast, and drop. Vector Pro lengthened forcing cone, 3 Invector-Plus choke tubes, Inflex recoil pad with hard heel insert, magazine cut-off. Chrome plated chamber, polished blue barrel finish, jeweled bolt slide finish.

Production: *current* **Gauge/Bore:** *12 ga.*
Action: *semi-auto*
Barrel Length: *26", 28"* **Wt.:** *6.9 lbs., 7.1 lbs.*
Sights: *fiber optic*
Capacity: *5*
Stock: *composite*

D2C:	NIB $1,158	Ex $900	VG+ $640	Good $580	**LMP:** $1,500
C2C:	Mint $1,120	Ex $800	VG+ $580	Good $525	Fair $270
Trade-In:	Mint $830	Ex $650	VG+ $460	Good $410	Poor $120

MAXUS ULTIMATE REDBOOK CODE: RB-BW-S-MAXULT

Lightweight aluminum alloy receiver with black anodized bi-tone finish, barrel with flat ventilated rib and lightweight profile. Offered in 3" or 3.5" chambering with 3.5" at a bit of a premium. Close radius pistol grip, sharp 22 lines-per-inch checkering, chrome-plated chamber. Vector Pro lengthened forcing cone, speed load plus, 3 Invector-DS choke tubes, Inflex recoil pad. Several synthetic models offered with camouflage finishes.

Production: *current* **Gauge/Bore:** *12 ga.*
Action: *semi-auto*
Barrel Length: *26", 28", 30"* **Wt.:** *7.1–7.3 lbs.*
Sights: *brass bead*
Capacity: *5*
Stock: *Turkish walnut*

D2C:	NIB $1,517	Ex $1,175	VG+ $835	Good $760	**LMP:** $1,870
C2C:	Mint $1,460	Ex $1,050	VG+ $760	Good $685	Fair $350
Trade-In:	Mint $1,080	Ex $850	VG+ $600	Good $535	Poor $180

A5 HUNTER REDBOOK CODE: RB-BW-S-A5HUNT

Lightweight aluminum alloy receiver and barrel with lightweight profile and flat ventilated rib. Recoil operated Kinematic Drive, close radius pistol grip, textured gripping surfaces, adjustable shim for cast and drop, Dura-Touch armor coating, Vector Pro lengthened forcing cone, Speed Load Plus, 3 Invector-DS choke tubes, Inflex II recoil pad, chrome–plated chamber, brushed nickel bolt slide finish, tubular magazine type.

Production: *current* **Gauge/Bore:** *12 ga.*
Action: *semi-auto*
Barrel Length: *26", 28", 30"* **Wt.:** *6.8 lbs., 6.9 lbs.*
Sights: *fiber optic*
Capacity: *5*
Stock: *Turkish walnut*

D2C:	NIB $1,340	Ex $1,025	VG+ $740	Good $670	**LMP:** $1,580
C2C:	Mint $1,290	Ex $925	VG+ $670	Good $605	Fair $310
Trade-In:	Mint $960	Ex $775	VG+ $530	Good $470	Poor $150

A5 STALKER REDBOOK CODE: RB-BW-S-A5STLK

Lightweight aluminum alloy receiver with satin finish with brushed sides. Lightweight profile barrel with flat ventilated rib and gloss blue finish. 3" chamber with recoil operated Kinematic Drive, close radius pistol grip, sharp 22 lines-per-inch checkering, adjustable shim for length of pull, cast, and drop. Vector Pro lengthened forcing cone, 3 Invector-DS choke tubes, Inflex II recoil pad, chrome plated chamber, tubular magazine.

Production: *current* **Gauge/Bore:** *12 ga.*
Action: *semi-auto*
Barrel Length: *26", 28", 30"* **Wt.:** *7.2 lbs., 7.4 lbs.*
Sights: *fiber optic*
Capacity: *5*
Stock: *Dura-Touch Armor coating*

D2C:	NIB $1,299	Ex $1,000	VG+ $715	Good $650	**LMP:** $1,420
C2C:	Mint $1,250	Ex $900	VG+ $650	Good $585	Fair $300
Trade-In:	Mint $930	Ex $750	VG+ $510	Good $455	Poor $150

A5 ULTIMATE REDBOOK CODE: RB-BW-S-A5ULTM

Low profile receiver of lightweight alloy with steel breech face and hinge pin and silver nitride finish. Ventilated top rib barrel, Fire Lite mechanical trigger system, hammer ejectors, top-tang barrel selector/safety. Close radius pistol grip, Vector Pro lengthened forcing cones, 3 Invector-DS choke tubes, ivory mid-bead sights. Polished blue barrel finish, chrome plated chamber, Inflex 2 recoil pad, cut 20 LPI checkering.

Production: *current* **Gauge/Bore:** *12 ga.*
Action: *semi-auto*
Barrel Length: *26", 28"* **Wt.:** *6.7 lbs., 6.8 lbs.*
Sights: *fiber optic*
Capacity: *5*
Stock: *walnut*

D2C:	NIB $1,702	Ex $1,300	VG+ $940	Good $855	**LMP: $1,920**
C2C:	Mint $1,640	Ex $1,175	VG+ $860	Good $770	Fair $395
Trade-In:	Mint $1,210	Ex $975	VG+ $670	Good $600	Poor $180

CITORI 725 FEATHER REDBOOK CODE: RB-BW-S-C725FR

Engraved low profile steel receiver, mechanical trigger, Inflex recoil pad, Investor DS chokes. Polished blue barrel finish, gloss oil stock finish, silver nitride receiver finish, chrome plated chamber, steel barrel, solid side ribs, Inflex 2 recoil pad, cut 20 LPI checkering, gold plated trigger finish, silver nitride trigger guard finish, alloy trigger, steel trigger guard, gold Buck Mark engraved on trigger guard.

Production: *current* **Gauge/Bore:** *12 ga.*
Action: *O/U*
Barrel Length: *26", 28"* **Wt.:** *6.4 lbs., 6.6 lbs.*
Sights: *ivory bead*
Capacity: *2*
Stock: *black walnut*

D2C:	NIB $2,002	Ex $1,525	VG+ $1,105	Good $1,005	**LMP: $2,550**
C2C:	Mint $1,930	Ex $1,400	VG+ $1,010	Good $905	Fair $465
Trade-In:	Mint $1,430	Ex $1,125	VG+ $790	Good $705	Poor $210

CITORI 725 FIELD REDBOOK CODE: RB-BW-S-C725FD

Low profile steel receiver with silver nitride finish. Ventilated top and side rib. Victor Pro lengthened forcing cones, Invector-DS choke tubes, Fire Lite mechanical trigger system, hammer ejectors, top-tang barrel selector/safety. Semi-beavertail forearm with finger groove, Inflex II recoil pad. Polished blue barrel finish, chrome plated chamber, cut 20 LPI checkering, alloy trigger with gold plated finish. Adjustable comb model available for about $90 more.

Production: *current* **Gauge/Bore:** *12 ga.*
Action: *O/U*
Barrel Length: *26", 28", 30"* **Wt.:** *6.3–7.5 lbs.*
Sights: *ivory bead*
Capacity: *2*
Stock: *black walnut*

D2C:	NIB $1,993	Ex $1,525	VG+ $1,100	Good $1,000	**LMP: $2,470**
C2C:	Mint $1,920	Ex $1,400	VG+ $1,000	Good $900	Fair $460
Trade-In:	Mint $1,420	Ex $1,125	VG+ $780	Good $700	Poor $210

CITORI 725 SKEET REDBOOK CODE: RB-BW-S-C725SK

Low profile steel receiver with silver nitride finish. Signature 725 rounded forearm, ventilated top and side rib, Vector Pro lengthened forcing cones, Invector-DS choke tubes, Fire Lite mechanical trigger system, hammer ejectors, top-tang barrel selector-safety, close radius pistol grip and palm swell with detailed cut 20 LPI checkering, Inflex II recoil pad, chrome plated chamber. Left hand model and one with adjustable comb available for same price.

Production: *current* **Gauge/Bore:** *12 ga.*
Action: *O/U*
Barrel Length: *28", 30"* **Wt.:** *7.6 lbs., 7.7 lbs.*
Sights: *HiViz Pro-Comp*
Capacity: *2*
Stock: *black walnut*

D2C:	NIB $2,849	Ex $2,175	VG+ $1,570	Good $1,425	**LMP: $3,140**
C2C:	Mint $2,740	Ex $1,975	VG+ $1,430	Good $1,285	Fair $660
Trade-In:	Mint $2,030	Ex $1,600	VG+ $1,120	Good $1,000	Poor $300

CITORI 725 SPORTING REDBOOK CODE: RB-BW-S-C725SP

Low profile receiver, Invector-DS choke system with 5 choke tubes included, Fire Lite mechanical triggers, Ergo balanced fit, polished blue barrel finish, silver nitride receiver finish, chrome plated chamber finish, steel ported barrels. Large Inflex 2 recoil pad, cut 20 LPI checkering, steel receiver, gold plated trigger, silver nitride trigger guard finish, alloy trigger, steel trigger guard, Buck Mark laser engraved in gold.

Production: *current* **Gauge/Bore:** *12 ga.*
Action: *O/U*
Barrel Length: 28", 30", 32" **Wt.:** *6.3–7.6 lbs.*
Sights: *HiViz Pro-Comp*
Capacity: *2*
Stock: *black walnut*

D2C:	NIB $2,617	Ex $2,000	VG+ $1,440	Good $1,310	**LMP:** $3,140
C2C:	Mint $2,520	Ex $1,825	VG+ $1,310	Good $1,180	Fair $605
Trade-In:	Mint $1,860	Ex $1,475	VG+ $1,030	Good $920	Poor $270

CITORI 725 SPORTING GRADE V REDBOOK CODE: RB-BW-S-C725S5

Steel receiver with low profile and silver nitride finish. Ported barrel with ventilated top and side ribs and gloss blue finish. Close radius pistol grip, right-hand palm swell, Vector Pro lengthened forcing cones, Invector-DS choke tubes, Fire Lite mechanical trigger system, hammer ejectors, semi-beavertail forearm with finger groove, Inflex II recoil pad. Also offered in an adjustable comb model and in left-handed versions for about $300 more.

Production: *current* **Gauge/Bore:** *12 ga.*
Action: *O/U*
Barrel Length: 30", 32" **Wt.:** *7.5 lbs.*
Sights: *HiViz Pro-Comp*
Capacity: *2*
Stock: *black walnut*

D2C:	NIB $4,499	Ex $3,425	VG+ $2,475	Good $2,250	**LMP:** $5,340
C2C:	Mint $4,320	Ex $3,125	VG+ $2,250	Good $2,025	Fair $1,035
Trade-In:	Mint $3,200	Ex $2,525	VG+ $1,760	Good $1,575	Poor $450

CITORI 725 TRAP REDBOOK CODE: RB-BW-S-C725TP

Steel receiver with silver nitride finish and gold engraving. Ported barrels with ventilated top and side rib, tapered floating top rib, chrome plated chamber, polished blue finish. Vector Pro lengthened forcing cones, 5 Invector-Plus choke tubes, sporting recoil pad, Triple Trigger system, close radius pistol grip, right-hand palm swell, Schnabel forearm. Also available in an adjustable comb model and a left-handed model for the same price.

Production: *current* **Gauge/Bore:** *12 ga.*
Action: *O/U*
Barrel Length: 30", 32" **Wt.:** *8.4 lbs., 8.6 lbs.*
Sights: *HiViz Pro-Comp*
Capacity: *2*
Stock: *black walnut*

D2C:	NIB $2,121	Ex $1,625	VG+ $1,170	Good $1,065	**LMP:** $3,340
C2C:	Mint $2,040	Ex $1,475	VG+ $1,070	Good $955	Fair $490
Trade-In:	Mint $1,510	Ex $1,200	VG+ $830	Good $745	Poor $240

CITORI 625 SPORTING GOLDEN CLAYS REDBOOK CODE: RB-BW-S-C625SG

Steel receiver with silver nitride finish and high-relief engraving. Lightweight profile barrel with ventilated rib and polished blue finish. Single selective trigger, hammer ejectors, top tang barrel selector safety, close radius pistol grip, jeweled receiver block, Schnabel forearm, 5 Invector-Plus choke tubes. Chrome plated chamber, alloy trigger with gold plated finish and steel guard.

Production: *current* **Gauge/Bore:** *12 ga.*
Action: *O/U*
Barrel Length: 30", 32" **Wt.:** *7.1–8.2 lbs.*
Sights: *HiViz Pro-Comp*
Capacity: *2*
Stock: *black walnut*

D2C:	NIB $3,931	Ex $3,000	VG+ $2,165	Good $1,970	**LMP:** $4,800
C2C:	Mint $3,780	Ex $2,725	VG+ $1,970	Good $1,770	Fair $905
Trade-In:	Mint $2,800	Ex $2,225	VG+ $1,540	Good $1,380	Poor $420

CITORI BLACK GOLD COMBO   REDBOOK CODE: RB-BW-S-CBGCOM

Steel receiver engraved with "Citori Crossover Target" on side. Lightweight profile barrel with blue high polish, high post rib, and vented side rib. 60/40 point of impact suitable for all target disciplines. 3 Midas grade extended Invector Plus choke tubes, Triple Trigger system with one trigger supplied, ivory front and mid bead sights, polymer recoil pad. Cut 18 LPI checkering, alloy trigger with steel guard.

Production: *current* **Gauge/Bore:** *12 ga.*
Action: *O/U*
Barrel Length: *30", 32"* **Wt.:** *7.1 lbs., 7.3 lbs.*
Sights: *HiViz Pro-Comp*
Capacity: *2*
Stock: *black walnut*

D2C:	NIB $6,199	Ex $4,725	VG+ $3,410	Good $3,100	**LMP: $6,400**
C2C:	Mint $5,960	Ex $4,300	VG+ $3,100	Good $2,790	Fair $1,430
Trade-In:	Mint $4,410	Ex $3,475	VG+ $2,420	Good $2,170	Poor $630

CITORI CROSSOVER TARGET   REDBOOK CODE: RB-BW-S-CROSTG

Steel receiver with blue finish and high-relief engraving. Barrel with ventilated rib. Hammer ejectors, chrome plated chamber, plastic buttplate, solid side ribs, allow trigger with gold plated finish, top-tang barrel selector/safety, lightning-style stock and forearm, Vector Pro lengthened forcing cones and 3 Invector-Plus choke tubes on 12 and 20 gauge. 3 standard Invector choke tubes on 28 gauge and .410. Recoil pad on 12 gauge.

Production: *current* **Gauge/Bore:** *12 ga.*
Action: *O/U*
Barrel Length: *30", 32"* **Wt.:** *8.2 lbs., 8.3 lbs.*
Sights: *ivory bead*
Capacity: *2*
Stock: *black walnut*

D2C:	NIB $1,765	Ex $1,350	VG+ $975	Good $885	**LMP: $2,000**
C2C:	Mint $1,700	Ex $1,225	VG+ $890	Good $795	Fair $410
Trade-In:	Mint $1,260	Ex $1,000	VG+ $690	Good $620	Poor $180

CITORI LIGHTNING   REDBOOK CODE: RB-BW-S-CLIGHT

Lightweight alloy receiver with steel breech face and hinge pin and high relief engraving. Barrel with ventilated rib and polished blue finish, chrome plated chamber, cut 18 LPI checkering. Hammer ejectors, top tang barrel selector/safety, lightning-style stock and forearm, Vector Pro lengthened forcing cones, three Invector-Plus choke tubes, recoil pad on 12 gauge model. Alloy trigger with gold plated trigger and silver nitride finish on the guard.

Production: *current* **Gauge/Bore:** *12 ga.*
Action: *O/U*
Barrel Length: *26", 28"* **Wt.:** *6.4–8.1 lbs.*
Sights: *silver bead*
Capacity: *2*
Stock: *black walnut*

D2C:	NIB $1,655	Ex $1,275	VG+ $915	Good $830	**LMP: $1,990**
C2C:	Mint $1,590	Ex $1,150	VG+ $830	Good $745	Fair $385
Trade-In:	Mint $1,180	Ex $950	VG+ $650	Good $580	Poor $180

CITORI FEATHER LIGHTNING   REDBOOK CODE: RB-BW-S-FLIGHT

High grade marbled grain walnut stock with extended side plates. Case colored receiver embellished with quality engraving. Polished blue barrel, 4 choke tubes, chrome plated chamber, Invector-Plus flush choke system, black ventilated recoil pad, cut 22 LPI checkering, alloy trigger with gold plated finish, hammer ejectors. Steel trigger guard with color case finish. Buck Mark engraved in gold on trigger guard.

Production: *current* **Gauge/Bore:** *12 ga., 20 ga.*
Action: *O/U*
Barrel Length: *26", 28"* **Wt.:** *5.9–7 lbs.*
Sights: *silver bead*
Capacity: *2*
Stock: *black walnut*

D2C:	NIB $1,708	Ex $1,300	VG+ $940	Good $855	**LMP: $2,180**
C2C:	Mint $1,640	Ex $1,200	VG+ $860	Good $770	Fair $395
Trade-In:	Mint $1,220	Ex $975	VG+ $670	Good $600	Poor $180

BROWNING

CITORI GRADE III REDBOOK CODE: RB-BW-S-CGRAD3

Case colored steel receiver, extended side plates, hammer ejectors, polished blue barrel finish. Invector-Plus flush choke system with 4 choke tubes included, chrome plated chamber. Steel barrel, solid side ribs, black ventilated recoil pad, cut 22 LPI checkering. Alloy trigger with gold plated finish and steel trigger guard with color case finish. Buck Mark engraved in gold on trigger guard.

Production: *current* **Gauge/Bore:** *12 ga.*
Action: *O/U*
Barrel Length: 28" **Wt.:** *8.2 lbs.*
Sights: *ivory bead*
Capacity: *2*
Stock: *black walnut*

D2C:	NIB $3,042	Ex $2,325	VG+ $1,675	Good $1,525	**LMP:** $4,670
C2C:	Mint $2,930	Ex $2,100	VG+ $1,530	Good $1,370	Fair $700
Trade-In:	Mint $2,160	Ex $1,725	VG+ $1,190	Good $1,065	Poor $330

CITORI GRADE VI REDBOOK CODE: RB-BW-S-CGRAD4

Lightweight alloy receiver with steel breech face and hinge pin and high relief engraving. Ventilated rib in steel barrel with polished blue finish. Hammer ejectors, top-tang barrel selector/safety, single selective trigger, English-style straight grip stock, Schnabel forearm. Vector Pro lengthened forcing cones, 3 Invector-Plus choke tubes, chrome plated chamber, cut 18 LPI checking. Alloy trigger with gold plated finish and steel trigger guard with silver nitride finish.

Production: *current* **Gauge/Bore:** *12 ga.*
Action: *O/U*
Barrel Length: 28" **Wt.:** *8.2 lbs.*
Sights: *ivory bead*
Capacity: *2*
Stock: *black walnut*

D2C:	NIB $3,248	Ex $2,475	VG+ $1,790	Good $1,625	**LMP:** $7,340
C2C:	Mint $3,120	Ex $2,250	VG+ $1,630	Good $1,465	Fair $750
Trade-In:	Mint $2,310	Ex $1,825	VG+ $1,270	Good $1,140	Poor $330

CITORI SUPERLIGHT FEATHER REDBOOK CODE: RB-BW-S-SFEATH

Steel receiver with silver nitride finish and high-relief engraving. Steel barrel with ventilated rib and high polished blue finish. Single selective trigger, hammer ejectors, top-tang barrel selector/safety. Lightning-style stock and forearm. Vector Pro lengthened forcing cones and 3 Invector-Plus choke tubes on 12 and 20 gauge. 3 standard Invector tubes on the 28 gauge and .410. Recoil pad on 12 gauge model. Chrome plated chamber.

Production: *current* **Gauge/Bore:** *12 ga., 20 ga.*
Action: *O/U*
Barrel Length: 26" **Wt.:** *5.7 lbs., 6.8 lbs.*
Sights: *silver bead*
Capacity: *2*
Stock: *black walnut*

D2C:	NIB $1,949	Ex $1,500	VG+ $1,075	Good $975	**LMP:** $2,390
C2C:	Mint $1,880	Ex $1,350	VG+ $980	Good $880	Fair $450
Trade-In:	Mint $1,390	Ex $1,100	VG+ $770	Good $685	Poor $210

CITORI WHITE LIGHTNING REDBOOK CODE: RB-BW-S-CWLITE

Steel receiver with high polish blued finish, gold enhanced engraving. Unsingle ported barrel with high gloss blue finish and adjustable rib. Single selective trigger, hammer ejector, top tang safety. Monte Carlo style buttstock and forearm, trap style recoil pad. 2 Invector Plus choke tubes, ivory mid bead, chrome plated chamber, alloy trigger with gold plated finish. Also available in adjustable comb model for $540 more.

Production: *current* **Gauge/Bore:** *12 ga., 20 ga., 28 ga., .410*
Action: *O/U*
Barrel Length: 26", 28" **Wt.:** *6.4–8.1 lbs.*
Sights: *silver bead*
Capacity: *2*
Stock: *black walnut*

D2C:	NIB $1,704	Ex $1,300	VG+ $940	Good $855	**LMP:** $2,070
C2C:	Mint $1,640	Ex $1,200	VG+ $860	Good $770	Fair $395
Trade-In:	Mint $1,210	Ex $975	VG+ $670	Good $600	Poor $180

CITORI XT TRAP UNSINGLE GRADE I REDBOOK CODE: RB-BW-S-XTTUG1

Built for competition, adjustable cheek rest, semi-beavertail forearm with finger grooves, gold accented blue steel engraved receiver, ported barrels. 2 full, improved modified chokes included, chrome plated chamber, Invector-Plus flush choke system. Brown trap recoil pad, vented side ribs, cut 20 LPI checkering, adjustable comb, alloy trigger with gold plated finish and steel trigger guard with polished steel finish and gold Buck Mark engraving.

Production: *current* **Gauge/Bore:** *12 ga.*
Action: *single-shot*
Barrel Length: *32", 34"* **Wt.:** *8.1 lbs.*
Sights: *HiViz Pro-Comp*
Capacity: *1*
Stock: *black walnut*

D2C:	NIB $2,295	Ex $1,750	VG+ $1,265	Good $1,150	LMP: $2,999
C2C:	Mint $2,210	Ex $1,600	VG+ $1,150	Good $1,035	Fair $530
Trade-In:	Mint $1,630	Ex $1,300	VG+ $900	Good $805	Poor $240

CITORI XT TRAP WITH ADJUSTABLE COMB, GRADE I REDBOOK CODE: RB-BW-S-XTTAD1

Built for competition, raised cheek rest, semi-beavertail forearm with finger grooves, gold accented blue steel engraved receiver, ported barrels. 2 full, improved modified chokes included, chrome plated chamber, Invector-Plus flush choke system. Brown trap recoil pad, vented side ribs, cut 20 LPI checkering, alloy trigger with gold plated finish and steel trigger guard with polished steel finish and gold Buck Mark engraving.

Production: *current* **Gauge/Bore:** *12 ga.*
Action: *O/U*
Barrel Length: *30", 32"* **Wt.:** *8.7 lbs., 8.8 lbs.*
Sights: *HiViz Pro-Comp*
Capacity: *2*
Stock: *black walnut*

D2C:	NIB $2,529	Ex $1,925	VG+ $1,395	Good $1,265	LMP: $3,000
C2C:	Mint $2,430	Ex $1,750	VG+ $1,270	Good $1,140	Fair $585
Trade-In:	Mint $1,800	Ex $1,425	VG+ $990	Good $890	Poor $270

CITORI XT TRAP, GRADE I REDBOOK CODE: RB-BW-S-CXTTG1

Coin-finished receiver with engraving pattern featuring pheasant, duck, and quail. Palm swell on 12 gauge only. Steel barrel with polished blue finish. Satin oil stock finish. Chrome plated chamber. Alloy trigger with steel trigger guard. Chamber length of 3" in .410 gauge and 2.75" in all others. 2.2" drop at heel, 1.6" drop at comb. Also available in a left-handed model.

Production: *current* **Gauge/Bore:** *12 ga.*
Action: *O/U*
Barrel Length: *30", 32"* **Wt.:** *8.4 lbs., 8.5 lbs.*
Sights: *HiViz Pro-Comp*
Capacity: *2*
Stock: *black walnut*

D2C:	NIB $2,129	Ex $1,625	VG+ $1,175	Good $1,065	LMP: $2,650
C2C:	Mint $2,050	Ex $1,475	VG+ $1,070	Good $960	Fair $490
Trade-In:	Mint $1,520	Ex $1,200	VG+ $840	Good $750	Poor $240

CITORI, 425 AMERICAN SPORTER REDBOOK CODE: RB-BW-S-C425AS

Coin finish receiver with engraving pattern featuring pheasant, duck, and quail. Palm swell on 12 gauge only. Steel barrel with polished blue finish. Satin oil stock finish. Chrome plated chamber. Alloy trigger with steel trigger guard. Chamber length of 3" in .410 gauge and 2.75" in all others. 2.2" drop at heel, 1.6" drop at comb. Also available in a left-handed model.

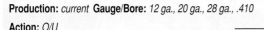

Production: *current* **Gauge/Bore:** *12 ga., 20 ga., 28 ga., .410*
Action: *O/U*
Barrel Length: *28", 30", 32"* **Wt.:** *6.5–8 lbs.*
Sights: *none*
Capacity: *2*
Stock: *black walnut*

D2C:	NIB $2,064	Ex $1,575	VG+ $1,140	Good $1,035	LMP: $2,899
C2C:	Mint $1,990	Ex $1,425	VG+ $1,040	Good $930	Fair $475
Trade-In:	Mint $1,470	Ex $1,175	VG+ $810	Good $725	Poor $210

BROWNING

CITORI, 425 AMERICAN SPORTER GOLD REDBOOK CODE: RB-BW-S-425ASG

Fully adjustable rib, under barrel is ported and aligned directly to recoil on a straight plane into the shoulder.
Factory choke tubes. Monte Carlo stock model also available. Steel barrels have polished blue finish and
chrome plated chamber. Receiver with silver nitride finish. adjustable comb. Alloy trigger with gold plated finish and steel trigger guard.

Production: *current* **Gauge/Bore:** *12 ga., 20 ga., 28 ga., .410*
Action: *O/U*
Barrel Length: 30", 32" **Wt.:** *6.5–8 lbs.*
Sights: *none*
Capacity: *2*
Stock: *black walnut*

D2C:	NIB $2,710	Ex $2,075	VG+ $1,495	Good $1,355	**LMP:** $3,179
C2C:	Mint $2,610	Ex $1,875	VG+ $1,360	Good $1,220	Fair $625
Trade-In:	Mint $1,930	Ex $1,525	VG+ $1,060	Good $950	Poor $300

*Photo Courtesy of
Rock Island Auction Company*

CITORI GRADE I REDBOOK CODE: RB-BW-S-CITGD1

Ventilated rib barrels, straight-grip stock, ejectors, varying degrees of checkering
and engraving.

Production: *discontinued* **Gauge/Bore:** *12 ga., 16 ga., 20 ga.*
Action: *O/U*
Barrel Length: 24" **Wt.:** *6.9 lbs.*
Sights: *none*
Capacity: *2*
Stock: *hardwood*

D2C:	NIB $1,437	Ex $1,100	VG+ $795	Good $720
C2C:	Mint $1,380	Ex $1,000	VG+ $720	Good $650	Fair $335
Trade-In:	Mint $1,030	Ex $825	VG+ $570	Good $505	Poor $150

*Photo Courtesy of
Rock Island Auction Company*

CITORI GRADE V REDBOOK CODE: RB-BW-S-CITGD5

Steel low-profile receiver, silver-nitride receiver finish, full coverage engraving, gold inlays on receiver,
ventilated top rib barrel, Fire Lite mechanical trigger, hammer ejectors, top-tang safety, gloss finished wood,
close radius pistol grip, 22 LPI checkering, Vector Pro lengthened forcing cones, leather case included.

Production: *discontinued 2013* **Gauge/Bore:** *12 ga.*
Action: *O/U*
Barrel Length: 26", 28" **Wt.:** *7.2–7.4 lbs.*
Sights: *ivory front, mid-bead*
Capacity: *2*
Stock: *Grade V/VI walnut*

D2C:	NIB $3,506	Ex $2,675	VG+ $1,930	Good $1,755	**LMP:** $5,599
C2C:	Mint $3,370	Ex $2,425	VG+ $1,760	Good $1,580	Fair $810
Trade-In:	Mint $2,490	Ex $1,975	VG+ $1,370	Good $1,230	Poor $360

CITORI SATIN HUNTER REDBOOK CODE: RB-BW-S-CITSPH

Steel blue finished receiver, scroll engraving, matte blue barrel, ventilated
top rib, solid side rib, single-selective trigger, hammer ejectors, top-tang
barrel selector, satin finish on stock, Vector Pro lengthened forcing cones,
F/M/IC chokes included, 1" black ventilated recoil pad, 3.5" chamber.

*Photo Courtesy of
Rock Island Auction Company*

Production: *discontinued 2013* **Gauge/Bore:** *12 ga.*
Action: *O/U*
Barrel Length: 26", 28" **Wt.:** *~8 lbs.*
Sights: *ivory bead front*
Capacity: *2*
Stock: *Grade I walnut*

D2C:	NIB $1,282	Ex $975	VG+ $710	Good $645	**LMP:** $1,599
C2C:	Mint $1,240	Ex $900	VG+ $650	Good $580	Fair $295
Trade-In:	Mint $920	Ex $725	VG+ $500	Good $450	Poor $150

CYNERGY CLASSIC TRAP REDBOOK CODE: RB-BW-S-CYNCTX

Steel receiver with silver nitride finish and ultra-low profile, jeweled monobloc and MonoLock hinge, ported double and single barrel sets included; over/under barrel set is lightweight profile and single barrel set has adjustable unsingle rib. Reverse striker ignition system, impact ejectors, top-tang barrel selector/safety, right-hand palm swell, modified semi-beavertail forearm with finger grooves, Vector Pro lengthened forcing cones, 4 Invector-Plus Midas grade choke tubes.

Production: *current* **Gauge/Bore:** *12 ga.*
Action: *O/U*
Barrel Length: *30", 32"* **Wt.:** *8.6 lbs., 8.8 lbs.*
Sights: *fiber optic*
Capacity: *2*
Stock: *black walnut*

D2C:	NIB $2,484	Ex $1,900	VG+ $1,370	Good $1,245	**LMP:** $3,880
C2C:	Mint $2,390	Ex $1,725	VG+ $1,250	Good $1,120	Fair $575
Trade-In:	Mint $1,770	Ex $1,400	VG+ $970	Good $870	Poor $270

CYNERGY CLASSIC TRAP UNSINGLE COMBO WITH ADJUSTABLE COMB REDBOOK CODE: RB-BW-S-CCTUCA

Black rubber over molded grip panels on stock, low profile receiver, Inflex recoil pad, reverse striker mechanical trigger, Vector Pro lengthened forcing cones, chrome plated chambers, Invector-Plus flush choke system with 3 choke tubes, steel barrel with satin blue finish and vented side ribs, alloy trigger with gold plated finish, steel trigger guard with silver nitride finish with Buck Mark engraved in gold.

Production: *current* **Gauge/Bore:** *12 ga.*
Action: *O/U*
Barrel Length: *30", 32"* **Wt.:** *8.8 lbs., 8.9 lbs.*
Sights: *HiViz Pro-Comp*
Capacity: *2*
Stock: *black walnut*

D2C:	NIB $5,023	Ex $3,825	VG+ $2,765	Good $2,515	**LMP:** $6,000
C2C:	Mint $4,830	Ex $3,475	VG+ $2,520	Good $2,265	Fair $1,160
Trade-In:	Mint $3,570	Ex $2,825	VG+ $1,960	Good $1,760	Poor $510

CYNERGY DESERT TAN REDBOOK CODE: RB-BW-S-CYNDTX

Lightweight alloy receiver with steel breech face, gold enhanced grayed finish, ultra-low profile, MonoLock hinge, jeweled monobloc, lightweight profile barrel with ventilated top and side ribs, reverse striker ignition system, impact ejectors, top-tang barrel selector/safety, Vector Pro lengthened forcing cones and 3 Invector-Plus choke tubes on 12 and 20 gauges, 3 standard Invector choke tubes with 28 and .410 gauges, Inflex technology recoil pad system.

Production: *current* **Gauge/Bore:** *12 ga.*
Action: *O/U*
Barrel Length: *28", 30"* **Wt.:** *7.5 lbs., 7.6 lbs.*
Sights: *ivory bead*
Capacity: *2*
Stock: *desert tan composite*

D2C:	NIB $1,218	Ex $950	VG+ $670	Good $610	**LMP:** $1,600
C2C:	Mint $1,170	Ex $850	VG+ $610	Good $550	Fair $285
Trade-In:	Mint $870	Ex $700	VG+ $480	Good $430	Poor $150

CYNERGY FEATHER REDBOOK CODE: RB-BW-S-CYNFEA

Lightweight alloy receiver with steel breech face, gold enhanced grayed finish, ultra-low profile, MonoLock hinge, jeweled monobloc, lightweight profile barrel with ventilated top and side ribs, reverse striker ignition system, impact ejectors, top-tang barrel selector/safety, black composite stock with rubber over moldings in grip areas, Dura-Touch armor coating, adjustable comb, 3 Invector-Plus choke tubes, Inflex technology recoil pad system, .25" stock spacer.

Production: *current* **Gauge/Bore:** *12 ga., 20 ga., 28 ga., .410*
Action: *O/U*
Barrel Length: *26", 28"* **Wt.:** *5.5–6 lbs.*
Sights: *ivory bead*
Capacity: *2*
Stock: *black walnut*

D2C:	NIB $2,349	Ex $1,800	VG+ $1,295	Good $1,175	**LMP:** $2,930
C2C:	Mint $2,260	Ex $1,625	VG+ $1,180	Good $1,060	Fair $545
Trade-In:	Mint $1,670	Ex $1,325	VG+ $920	Good $825	Poor $240

CYNERGY FEATHER COMPOSITE WITH ADJUSTABLE COMB REDBOOK CODE: RB-BW-S-CYNFCA

Steel receiver with silver nitride finish and ultra-low profile, MonoLock hinge, jeweled monobloc, high-relief engraving on the receiver, forearm iron and top lever, lightweight profile barrel with ventilated top and side ribs, reverse striker ignition system, impact ejectors, top-tang barrel selector/safety, Vector Pro lengthened forcing cones and 3 Invector-Plus choke tubes with 12 and 20 gauges, 3 standard Invector choke tubes with 28 and .410.

Production: *current* **Gauge/Bore:** *12 ga.*
Action: *O/U*
Barrel Length: *26", 28"* **Wt.:** *6.4 lbs., 6.6 lbs.*
Sights: *ivory bead*
Capacity: *2*
Stock: *composite*

D2C:	NIB $2,263	Ex $1,725	VG+ $1,245	Good $1,135	LMP: $2,800
C2C:	Mint $2,180	Ex $1,575	VG+ $1,140	Good $1,020	Fair $525
Trade-In:	Mint $1,610	Ex $1,275	VG+ $890	Good $795	Poor $240

CYNERGY FIELD REDBOOK CODE: RB-BW-S-CYNFLD

Reverse striker mechanical trigger, Inflex recoil pad, Vector Pro lengthened forcing cones, chrome plated chambers, satin blue finish on barrel with vented side ribs, 3 choke tubes included and Invector-Plus flush choke system, cut 18 LPI checkering. Steel receiver, alloy trigger with gold plated finish, steel trigger guard with silver nitride finish and Buck Mark engraved in gold.

Production: *current* **Gauge/Bore:** *12 ga., 20 ga., 28 ga., .410*
Action: *O/U*
Barrel Length: *26", 28"* **Wt.:** *5.9–7.7 lbs.*
Sights: *ivory bead*
Capacity: *2*
Stock: *black walnut*

D2C:	NIB $1,880	Ex $1,875	VG+ $1,350	Good $1,225	LMP: $2,450
C2C:	Mint $2,360	Ex $1,700	VG+ $1,230	Good $1,105	Fair $565
Trade-In:	Mint $1,740	Ex $1,375	VG+ $960	Good $860	Poor $270

CYNERGY SATIN FIELD REDBOOK CODE: RB-BW-S-CYNSFD

Steel receiver with silver nitride finish and ultra-low profile, monoLock hinge, jeweled monobloc. High-relief scroll engraving on the receiver, forearm iron, and top lever. Lightweight profile ported barrel with ventilated top and side ribs, reverse striker ignition system, top-tang barrel selector/safety, Vector Pro lengthened forcing cones, 3 Invector-Plus choke tubes, Inflex technology recoil pad system, triple trigger system. Adjustable comb model available for $500 more.

Production: *current* **Gauge/Bore:** *12 ga.*
Action: *O/U*
Barrel Length: *26", 28"* **Wt.:** *7.1 lbs., 7.7 lbs.*
Sights: *ivory bead*
Capacity: *2*
Stock: *black walnut*

D2C:	NIB $1,740	Ex $1,325	VG+ $960	Good $870	LMP: $1,740
C2C:	Mint $1,680	Ex $1,225	VG+ $870	Good $785	Fair $405
Trade-In:	Mint $1,240	Ex $975	VG+ $680	Good $610	Poor $180

CYNERGY SPORTING REDBOOK CODE: RB-BW-S-CYNSPT

Black Dura-Touch armor finish, bottom ejection, forged and machined steel receiver, brass bead sight, 3 standard Invector choke tubes, steel barrel with ventilated rib, dual steel action bars, top-tang safety, satin blue barrel finish, matte black stock finish, chrome plated chamber, polymer recoil pad, molded checkering, alloy trigger and guard with matte black finishes and Buck Mark engraving in black.

Production: *current* **Gauge/Bore:** *12 ga., 20 ga.*
Action: *O/U*
Barrel Length: *28", 30", 32"* **Wt.:** *6.3–8.1 lbs.*
Sights: *HiViz Pro-Comp*
Capacity: *2*
Stock: *black walnut*

D2C:	NIB $2,494	Ex $1,900	VG+ $1,375	Good $1,250	LMP: $4,000
C2C:	Mint $2,400	Ex $1,725	VG+ $1,250	Good $1,125	Fair $575
Trade-In:	Mint $1,780	Ex $1,400	VG+ $980	Good $875	Poor $270

BPS 10 GAUGE STALKER REDBOOK CODE: RB-BW-S-BPS10S

Receiver of forged and machined steel with matte blue finish, fixed cylinder choke on barrel with matte blue finish, bottom ejection, dual steel action bars, top-tang safety, two-toned silver/carbon fiber finish stock and forearm, chrome plated chamber, plastic buttplate, cut 18 LPI checkering, alloy trigger and guard with matte black finishes and Buck Mark engraved in black on the guard.

Production: *current* **Gauge/Bore:** *10 ga.*

Action: *pump-action*

Barrel Length: 26", 28" **Wt.:** *10.4 lbs, 10.6 lbs.*

Sights: *silver bead*

Capacity: *4*

Stock: *composite*

D2C:	NIB $597	Ex $475	VG+ $330	Good $300	**LMP:** $800
C2C:	Mint $580	Ex $425	VG+ $300	Good $270	Fair $140
Trade-In:	Mint $430	Ex $350	VG+ $240	Good $210	Poor $60

BPS CARBON FIBER HIGH CAPACITY REDBOOK CODE: RB-BW-S-BPSCFH

Forged/machined steel receiver, bottom ejection, barrel with ventilated rib, dual steel action bars, top-tang safety. 3 Invector-Plus choke tubes with 12 and 20 gauges. 3 standard Invector choke tubes with 16, 28, and .410 gauges. Recoil pad on 12 gauge model. Cut 18 LPI checkering. Alloy trigger and trigger guard with gold plating on trigger and high gloss finish on guard.

Production: *current* **Gauge/Bore:** *0.41*

Action: *pump-action*

Barrel Length: 20" **Wt.:** *6.8 lbs.*

Sights: *silver bead*

Capacity: *5*

Stock: *black walnut*

D2C:	NIB $713	Ex $550	VG+ $395	Good $360	**LMP:** $800
C2C:	Mint $690	Ex $500	VG+ $360	Good $325	Fair $165
Trade-In:	Mint $510	Ex $400	VG+ $280	Good $250	Poor $90

BPS HUNTER REDBOOK CODE: RB-BW-S-BPSHUN

Gloss blue finish barrel with ventilated rib and forged/machined steel receiver with scroll engraving. Bottom ejection, dual steel action bars, top-tang safety. 3 Invector Plus choke tubes with 12 and 20 gauges and 3 standard Invector choke tubes with 16, 28, and .410 gauges. Cut 18 LPI checkering. Alloy trigger and guard with gold plated finish on the trigger and high gloss finish on the guard.

Production: *current* **Gauge/Bore:** *12 ga., 16 ga., 20 ga., 28 ga., .410*

Action: *pump-action*

Barrel Length: 26", 28" **Wt.:** *6.9–7.7 lbs.*

Sights: *silver bead*

Capacity: *4*

Stock: *satin finish walnut*

D2C:	NIB $587	Ex $450	VG+ $325	Good $295	**LMP:** $700
C2C:	Mint $570	Ex $425	VG+ $300	Good $265	Fair $140
Trade-In:	Mint $420	Ex $350	VG+ $230	Good $210	Poor $60

BPS MEDALLION REDBOOK CODE: RB-BW-S-BPSMED

Compact design, blue steel receiver and barrel, bottom ejection, dual action bars. Forged and machined steel receiver, barrel with ventilated rib, top-tang safety. Compact 13" lengthof pull, 3 Invector-Plus choke tubes with 12 and 20 gauges, 3 standard Invector choke tubes with 28 and .410 gauges, Inflex technology recoil pad on 12 gauge, cut 18 LPI checkering, 2 .25" stock spacers.

Production: *current* **Gauge/Bore:** *12 ga., 16 ga., 20 ga., 28 ga., .410*

Action: *pump-action*

Barrel Length: 26", 28" **Wt.:** *6.9–7.7 lbs.*

Sights: *silver bead*

Capacity: *4*

Stock: *black walnut*

D2C:	NIB $730	Ex $575	VG+ $405	Good $365	**LMP:** $830
C2C:	Mint $710	Ex $525	VG+ $370	Good $330	Fair $170
Trade-In:	Mint $520	Ex $425	VG+ $290	Good $260	Poor $90

BPS MICRO MIDAS REDBOOK CODE: RB-BW-S-BPSMMS

Smaller dimension in the length of pull and barrel for beginner shooters. Raised cheek piece, premium brown tap recoil pad. Forged and machined steel receiver with highly polished blue finish. Ventilated rib on barrel with bottom ejection, dual steel action bars, and top-tang safety. Raised comb, compact stock dimensions. Magazine cut-off, 3 Invector-Plus choke tubes, cut 18 LPI checkering, alloy trigger and guard.

Production: *current* **Gauge/Bore:** *12 ga., 20 ga., 28 ga., .410*
Action: *pump-action*
Barrel Length: 22", 24", 26" **Wt.:** *6.9–7.9 lbs.*
Sights: *silver bead*
Capacity: *4*
Stock: *black walnut*

D2C:	NIB $571	Ex $450	VG+ $315	Good $290	**LMP: $700**
C2C:	Mint $550	Ex $400	VG+ $290	Good $260	Fair $135
Trade-In:	Mint $410	Ex $325	VG+ $230	Good $200	Poor $60

BPS MICRO TRAP REDBOOK CODE: RB-BW-S-BPSMTP

Forged and machined steel receiver with chrome plated chamber. Ventilated rib barrel with Mossy Oak Break-Up Infinity finish on barrel and stock and Dura-Touch armor coating. Bottom ejection, dual steel action bars, top-tang safety. Invector-Plus flush choke system with 3 chokes tubes included. Polymer recoil pad, molded checkering, alloy trigger and guard with matte black finishes. Trigger guard engraved with Buck Mark in black.

Production: *current* **Gauge/Bore:** *12 ga.*
Action: *pump-action*
Barrel Length: 28" **Wt.:** *8.1 lbs.*
Sights: *HiViz Pro-Comp*
Capacity: *4*
Stock: *black walnut*

D2C:	NIB $702	Ex $550	VG+ $390	Good $355	**LMP: $840**
C2C:	Mint $680	Ex $500	VG+ $360	Good $320	Fair $165
Trade-In:	Mint $500	Ex $400	VG+ $280	Good $250	Poor $90

BPS MOSSY OAK BREAK-UP INFINITY REDBOOK CODE: RB-BW-S-BPSMBI

Dura-Touch coating on composite black stock, forged/machined steel receiver with matte blue finish and chrome plated chamber. Bottom ejection, dual steel action bars, top-tang safety, 3 Invector Plus choke tubes, Williams "Ace in the Hole" rear peep sight and Picatinny scope base, polymer recoil pad, molded checkering. Alloy trigger and guard with matte black finishes. Also available in Mossy Oak Brush for $70 more.

Production: *current* **Gauge/Bore:** *12 ga.*
Action: *pump-action*
Barrel Length: 26", 28" **Wt.:** *8–8.3 lbs.*
Sights: *silver bead*
Capacity: *4*
Stock: *composite*

D2C:	NIB $512	Ex $400	VG+ $285	Good $260	**LMP: $820**
C2C:	Mint $500	Ex $375	VG+ $260	Good $235	Fair $120
Trade-In:	Mint $370	Ex $300	VG+ $200	Good $180	Poor $60

BPS PREDATOR HUNTER REDBOOK CODE: RB-BW-S-BPSPHT

Realtree Max-5 finish, forged and machined steel receiver, bottom ejection, dual action steel bars. Ventilated rib, top-tang safety, Dura-Touch coating on the stock, chromeplated chamber, molded checkering. Invector-Plus flush choke system with 3 choke tubes. Steel barrel, polymer recoil pad, alloy trigger and guard with matte black finishes. Buck Mark engraved in black on the trigger guard.

Production: *current* **Gauge/Bore:** *12 ga.*
Action: *pump-action*
Barrel Length: 20.5" **Wt.:** *7.6 lbs.*
Sights: *fiber optic*
Capacity: *6*
Stock: *composite*

D2C:	NIB $702	Ex $550	VG+ $390	Good $355	**LMP: $800**
C2C:	Mint $680	Ex $500	VG+ $360	Good $320	Fair $165
Trade-In:	Mint $500	Ex $400	VG+ $280	Good $250	Poor $90

BPS REALTREE MAX-5 REDBOOK CODE: RB-BW-S-BPSRM5

Rifled barrel with twist rate of 1:28 in 12 gauge and 1:35 in 20 gauge. Matte blue barrel and receiver finish. Forged and machined steel receiver. Thick-walled steel barrel for slug and sabot ammunition only. Chrome plated chamber, bottom ejection, dual steel action bars, top-tang safety, cut 18 LPI checkering. Cantilever scope mount. 1.75" drop at comb and 1.75" drop at heel.

Production: *current* **Gauge/Bore:** *12 ga.*
Action: *pump-action*
Barrel Length: 26", 28" **Wt.:** *8.3 lbs.*
Sights: *silver bead*
Capacity: *4*
Stock: *composite*

D2C:	NIB $866	Ex $675	VG+ $480	Good $435	LMP: $950
C2C:	Mint $840	Ex $600	VG+ $440	Good $390	Fair $200
Trade-In:	Mint $620	Ex $500	VG+ $340	Good $305	Poor $90

BPS RIFLED DEER HUNTER REDBOOK CODE: RB-BW-S-BPSRDH

Forged and machined steel receiver. Thick-walled steel barrel for slug and sabot ammunition. Rifled with a twist rate of 1:28 in 12 gauge and 1:35 in 20 gauge. Bottom ejection, dual steel action bars, top-tang safety. Composite stock on 12 gauge only (wood stock in 20 gauge); both have Mossy Oak Break-Up Infinity finish. Dura-Touch Armor coating. Cantilever scope mount, polymer recoil pad, molded checkering.

Production: *current* **Gauge/Bore:** *12 ga., 20 ga.*
Action: *pump-action*
Barrel Length: 22" **Wt.:** *7.3 lbs., 7.6 lbs.*
Sights: *none*
Capacity: *4*
Stock: *satin finish walnut*

D2C:	NIB $606	Ex $475	VG+ $335	Good $305	LMP: $830
C2C:	Mint $590	Ex $425	VG+ $310	Good $275	Fair $140
Trade-In:	Mint $440	Ex $350	VG+ $240	Good $215	Poor $90

BPS RIFLED DEER, MOSSY OAK BREAK-UP INFINITY REDBOOK CODE: RB-BW-S-BPSRDM

Forged and machined steel receiver and steel barrel with ventilated rib and satin blue finish. Bottom ejection, dual steel action bars, top-tang safety, chrome plated chamber. Stock has matte black finish. Invector-Plus flush choke system with 3 choke tubes. Polymer recoil pad, molded checkering, alloy trigger and guard with matte black finishes. 1.5" drop at comb and 2.5" drop at heel.

Production: *current* **Gauge/Bore:** *12 ga., 20 ga.*
Action: *pump-action*
Barrel Length: 22" **Wt.:** *7.3 lbs., 7.6 lbs.*
Sights: *none*
Capacity: *4*
Stock: *composite*

D2C:	NIB $742	Ex $575	VG+ $410	Good $375	LMP: $870
C2C:	Mint $720	Ex $525	VG+ $380	Good $335	Fair $175
Trade-In:	Mint $530	Ex $425	VG+ $290	Good $260	Poor $90

BPS STALKER REDBOOK CODE: RB-BW-S-BPSSTK

Forged and machined engraved steel receiver with highly polished blue finish and steel barrel with ventilated rib and polished blue finish. Chrome plated chamber, cut 18 LPI checkering, brown trap recoil pad. Bottom ejection, dual steel action bars, top-tang safety, raised comb, magazine cut-off, Invector-Plus flush choking system with 3 choke tubes, fiber-optic sight with mid-bead. Alloy trigger and guard with gold plated trigger finish.

Production: *current* **Gauge/Bore:** *12 ga.*
Action: *pump-action*
Barrel Length: 26", 28", 30" **Wt.:** *8–8.3 lbs.*
Sights: *silver bead*
Capacity: *4*
Stock: *composite*

D2C:	NIB $610	Ex $475	VG+ $340	Good $305	LMP: $700
C2C:	Mint $590	Ex $425	VG+ $310	Good $275	Fair $145
Trade-In:	Mint $440	Ex $350	VG+ $240	Good $215	Poor $90

BROWNING

BPS TRAP REDBOOK CODE: RB-BW-S-BPSTRP

Forged and machined steel receiver and barrel with ventilated rib. Bottom ejection, dual steel action bars, top-tang safety. English-style straight grip. Invector-Plus flush choke system with 3 Invector-Plus choke tubes with 12 and 20 gauge and 3 standard Invector tubes with 16 gauge. Cut 18 LPI checkering, alloy trigger and guard with gold plated trigger finish and high gloss trigger guard finish.

Production: *current* Gauge/Bore: *12 ga.*
Action: *pump-action*
Barrel Length: *30"* Wt.: *8.1 lbs.*
Sights: *HiViz Pro-Comp*
Capacity: *5*
Stock: *black walnut*

D2C:	NIB $706	Ex $550	VG+ $390	Good $355	**LMP: $840**
C2C:	Mint $680	Ex $500	VG+ $360	Good $320	Fair $165
Trade-In:	Mint $510	Ex $400	VG+ $280	Good $250	Poor $90

BPS UPLAND SPECIAL REDBOOK CODE: RB-BW-S-BPSUPL

Exclusive engraved receiver with polished blue finish, bottom loading and ejecting, tang safety. Polished blue finish on steel barrel, chrome plated chamber. Standard Invector flush choke system with 3 choke tubes. Cut 18 LPI checkering, plastic buttplate. Alloy trigger and guard with gold plated trigger finish and high gloss trigger guard finish. Buck Mark engraved in gold on trigger guard.

Production: *current* Gauge/Bore: *12 ga., 16 ga., 20 ga.*
Action: *pump-action*
Barrel Length: *22", 24", 26"* Wt.: *6.8–7.5 lbs.*
Sights: *silver bead*
Capacity: *4*
Stock: *black walnut*

D2C:	NIB $557	Ex $425	VG+ $310	Good $280	**LMP: $700**
C2C:	Mint $540	Ex $400	VG+ $280	Good $255	Fair $130
Trade-In:	Mint $400	Ex $325	VG+ $220	Good $195	Poor $60

BPS WITH ENGRAVED RECEIVER REDBOOK CODE: RB-BW-S-BPSENR

Forged and machined steel receiver with matte blue finish. Bottom ejection, dual steel bars, top-tang safety. Chrome plated chamber, steel barrel with satin blue finish, polymer recoil pad. Alloy trigger with matte black finish. Fixed choke system with cylinder choke included. Cut 18 LPI checkering. Buck Mark engraved in black on the trigger guard. 1.6" drop at comb and 1.9" drop at heel.

Production: *current* Gauge/Bore: *12 ga., 20 ga., 28 ga., .410*
Action: *pump-action*
Barrel Length: *26", 28"* Wt.: *6.9–8 lbs.*
Sights: *silver bead*
Capacity: *4*
Stock: *black walnut*

D2C:	NIB $546	Ex $425	VG+ $305	Good $275	**LMP: $640**
C2C:	Mint $530	Ex $400	VG+ $280	Good $250	Fair $130
Trade-In:	Mint $390	Ex $325	VG+ $220	Good $195	Poor $60

BPS WOOD HIGH CAPACITY REDBOOK CODE: RB-BW-S-BPSWHC

Aluminum alloy receiver and barrel with ventilated rib. Gas-operated autoloader, Dura-Touch armor coating in Mossy Oak Break-Up Infinity. Also available in same finish with National Wild Turkey Federation stamp on the stock for $130 more and in Mossy Oak Shadow Grass Blades finish for same price. Standard Invector flush choke system with 3 choke tubes. Molded checkering, chrome plated chamber, black ventilated recoil pad.

Production: *current* Gauge/Bore: *.410*
Action: *pump-action*
Barrel Length: *20"* Wt.: *6.6 lbs.*
Sights: *silver bead*
Capacity: *6*
Stock: *black walnut*

D2C:	NIB $556	Ex $425	VG+ $310	Good $280	**LMP: $730**
C2C:	Mint $540	Ex $400	VG+ $280	Good $255	Fair $130
Trade-In:	Mint $400	Ex $325	VG+ $220	Good $195	Poor $60

BPS GAME GUN DEER SPECIAL REDBOOK CODE: RB-BW-S-BPSGGD
5" rifled barrel or fully rifled barrel, cantilever mounting system.

Production: *discontinued* **Gauge/Bore:** *12 ga.*
Action: *pump-action*
Barrel Length: 20.5" **Wt.:** *N/A*
Sights: *iron*
Capacity: *4, 5*
Stock: *hardwood*

D2C:	NIB $390	Ex $300	VG+ $215	Good $195	
C2C:	Mint $380	Ex $275	VG+ $200	Good $180	Fair $90
Trade-In:	Mint $280	Ex $225	VG+ $160	Good $140	Poor $60

BPS GAME GUN TURKEY SPECIAL REDBOOK CODE: RB-BW-S-BPSGGT
Fixed extra-full choke, drilled and tapped for scope mounts.

Production: *discontinued* **Gauge/Bore:** *12 ga.*
Action: *pump-action*
Barrel Length: 20.5" **Wt.:** *N/A*
Sights: *iron*
Capacity: *4, 5*
Stock: *hardwood*

D2C:	NIB $400	Ex $325	VG+ $220	Good $200	
C2C:	Mint $390	Ex $300	VG+ $200	Good $180	Fair $95
Trade-In:	Mint $290	Ex $225	VG+ $160	Good $140	Poor $60

BPS PIGEON GRADE REDBOOK CODE: RB-BW-S-BPSPNG
3" chamber, gold trimmed receiver, ventilated rib barrel.

Production: *discontinued* **Gauge/Bore:** *12 ga.*
Action: *pump-action*
Barrel Length: 26", 28" **Wt.:** *7.8 lbs.*
Sights: *bead front*
Capacity: *4, 5*
Stock: *high grade walnut*

D2C:	NIB $633	Ex $500	VG+ $350	Good $320	
C2C:	Mint $610	Ex $450	VG+ $320	Good $285	Fair $150
Trade-In:	Mint $450	Ex $375	VG+ $250	Good $225	Poor $90

GOLD LIGHT 10 GAUGE, MOSSY OAK BREAK-UP INFINITY REDBOOK CODE: RB-BW-S-BPSGLB
Lightweight aluminum alloy receiver with semi-humpback design and gloss black finish. Lightweight profile barrel with ventilated rib and gloss blue finish. Gas operated, lightning-style stock, pistol grip. Invector-Plus flush choke system with 3 choke tubes. Cut 18 LPI checkering. Alloy trigger and guard with gold plated trigger finish and matte black trigger guard finish. Buck Mark engraved in gold on trigger guard.

Production: *current* **Gauge/Bore:** *10 ga.*
Action: *semi-auto*
Barrel Length: 26", 28" **Wt.:** *9.6 lbs.*
Sights: *bead front*
Capacity: *4*
Stock: *composite*

D2C:	NIB $1,227	Ex $950	VG+ $675	Good $615	**LMP:** $1,740
C2C:	Mint $1,180	Ex $850	VG+ $620	Good $555	Fair $285
Trade-In:	Mint $880	Ex $700	VG+ $480	Good $430	Poor $150

BROWNING

SILVER BLACK LIGHTNING REDBOOK CODE: RB-BW-S-SVRBLG

Lightweight aluminum alloy receiver with semi-humpback design and silver finish. Lightweight profile barrel with ventilated rib. Invector-Plus flush choke system with 3 Invector-Plus choke tubes. 1.75" drop at comb and 2" drop at heel. Brown ventilated recoil pad, cut 18 LPI checkering. Alloy trigger and guard with gold plated trigger finish and matte black trigger guard finish. Buck Mark engraved in gold on trigger guard.

Production: *current* **Gauge/Bore:** *12 ga.*
Action: *semi-auto*
Barrel Length: 26", 28" **Wt.:** *7.3 lbs., 7.4 lbs.*
Sights: *brass bead*
Capacity: *4*
Stock: *Turkish walnut*

D2C:	NIB $1,048	Ex $800	VG+ $580	Good $525	**LMP:** $1,190
C2C:	Mint $1,010	Ex $725	VG+ $530	Good $475	Fair $245
Trade-In:	Mint $750	Ex $600	VG+ $410	Good $370	Poor $120

SILVER HUNTER REDBOOK CODE: RB-BW-S-SLVHUN

Aluminum alloy receiver with semi-humpback design and lightweight profile barrel with ventilated rib. Composite stock and forearm, Dura-Touch armor coating, Mossy Oak Break-Up Infinity finish. Invector-Plus flush choke system and 3 Invector-Plus choke tubes. Chrome plated chamber, steel barrel, black ventilated recoil pad, molded checkering, alloy trigger with gold plated finish. Also available in Mossy Oak Shadow Grass Blades finish for the same price.

Production: *current* **Gauge/Bore:** *12 ga., 20 ga.*
Action: *semi-auto*
Barrel Length: 26", 28", 30" **Wt.:** *6.3–7.6 lbs.*
Sights: *brass bead*
Capacity: *4*
Stock: *Turkish walnut*

D2C:	NIB $990	Ex $775	VG+ $545	Good $495	**LMP:** $1,340
C2C:	Mint $960	Ex $700	VG+ $500	Good $450	Fair $230
Trade-In:	Mint $710	Ex $575	VG+ $390	Good $350	Poor $120

SILVER MOSSY OAK BREAK-UP INFINITY REDBOOK CODE: RB-BW-S-SLVMBI

Aluminum alloy receiver with semi-humpback design and thick-walled steel barrel fully rifled for slug ammunition. Dura-Touch armor coating, Mossy Oak Break-Up Infinity finish. Chrome plated chamber, black ventilated recoil pad, alloy trigger and guard, gold plated trigger finish, matte black finish on trigger guard and bolt slide, molded checkering, Cantilever scope mount. Twist rate of 1:28. Also available in matte black finish for $140 less.

Production: *current* **Gauge/Bore:** *12 ga.*
Action: *semi-auto*
Barrel Length: 26" **Wt.:** *7.5 lbs.*
Sights: *brass bead*
Capacity: *4*
Stock: *composite*

D2C:	NIB $1,109	Ex $850	VG+ $610	Good $555	**LMP:** $1,340
C2C:	Mint $1,070	Ex $775	VG+ $560	Good $500	Fair $260
Trade-In:	Mint $790	Ex $625	VG+ $440	Good $390	Poor $120

SILVER RIFLED DEER MOSSY OAK BREAK-UP INFINITY REDBOOK CODE: RB-BW-S-SLVRDM

Aluminum alloy receiver with semi-humpback design and thick-walled steel barrel fully rifled for slug ammunition. Dura-Touch armor coating, matte black finish. Chrome plated chamber, black ventilated recoil pad, alloy trigger and guard, gold plated trigger finish, matte blue barrel finish, molded checkering, Cantilever scope mount. Also available in Silver Rifled Deer Satin model with wood stock and foregrip for $60 more.

Production: *current* **Gauge/Bore:** *12 ga., 20 ga.*
Action: *semi-auto*
Barrel Length: 22" **Wt.:** *6.8 lbs., 7.8 lbs.*
Sights: *brass bead*
Capacity: *4*
Stock: *composite*

D2C:	NIB $1,113	Ex $850	VG+ $615	Good $560	**LMP:** $1,420
C2C:	Mint $1,070	Ex $775	VG+ $560	Good $505	Fair $260
Trade-In:	Mint $800	Ex $625	VG+ $440	Good $390	Poor $120

SILVER RIFLED DEER STALKER REDBOOK CODE: RB-BW-S-SLVRDS

Lightweight aluminum alloy with semi-humpback design and silver finish. Ported steel barrel with lightweight profile, ventilated rib, and polished blue finish. Stock features .75" length of pull adjustment in .25" increments with 3 included spacers. Invector-Plus flush choke system with 3 Invector-Plus choke tubes. Mid-bead sight, chrome plated chamber, Pachmayr decelerator with hard heel insert, cut 19 LPI checkering. Available in "Micro" youth model.

Production: *current* **Gauge/Bore:** *12 ga.*
Action: *semi-auto*
Barrel Length: 22" **Wt.:** *7.8 lbs.*
Sights: *brass bead*
Capacity: 4
Stock: *composite*

D2C:	NIB $1,024	Ex $800	VG+ $565	Good $515	**LMP:** $1,280
C2C:	Mint $990	Ex $725	VG+ $520	Good $465	Fair $240
Trade-In:	Mint $730	Ex $575	VG+ $400	Good $360	Poor $120

SILVER SPORTING REDBOOK CODE: RB-BW-S-SLVSPT

Aluminum alloy receiver with semi-humpback design. Steel barrel with lightweight profile and ventilated rib. Matte black stock with Dura-Touch armor coating. Invector-Plus flush choke system with 3 Invector-Plus choke tubes. Molded checkering, black ventilated recoil pad, alloy trigger and guard with gold plated trigger finish and matte black finish on trigger guard and bolt slide. Buck Mark engraved in gold on trigger guard.

Production: *current* **Gauge/Bore:** *12 ga.*
Action: *semi-auto*
Barrel Length: 28", 30" **Wt.:** *7.5 lbs., 7.6 lbs.*
Sights: *brass bead*
Capacity: 4
Stock: *Turkish walnut*

D2C:	NIB $1,108	Ex $850	VG+ $610	Good $555	**LMP:** $1,300
C2C:	Mint $1,070	Ex $775	VG+ $560	Good $500	Fair $255
Trade-In:	Mint $790	Ex $625	VG+ $440	Good $390	Poor $120

SILVER STALKER REDBOOK CODE: RB-BW-S-SLVSTK

Steel receiver with blue finish. Steel barrel with high-post ventilated rib and satin blue finish. Beavertail on satin finished stock, Invector-Plus flush choke system with full choke included, chrome plated chamber, cut 18 LPI checkering, brown trap recoil pad. Gold plated trigger and satin blue finish on trigger guard. Also available in adjustable comb model for $250 more and in youth "Micro" model for same price.

Production: *current* **Gauge/Bore:** *12 ga.*
Action: *semi-auto*
Barrel Length: 26", 28" **Wt.:** *7.5 lbs., 7.6 lbs.*
Sights: *brass bead*
Capacity: 4
Stock: *composite*

D2C:	NIB $1,041	Ex $800	VG+ $575	Good $525	**LMP:** $1,200
C2C:	Mint $1,000	Ex $725	VG+ $530	Good $470	Fair $240
Trade-In:	Mint $740	Ex $600	VG+ $410	Good $365	Poor $120

BT-99 REDBOOK CODE: RB-BW-S-BT99XX

Steel receiver with silver nitride finish and gold accented high-relief engraving. Ported barrel with high-post ventilated rib and polished blue finish. Invector-Plus flush choke system with 3 Invector-Plus choke tubes. Vector-Pro lengthened forcing cone, beavertail forearm, ivory front and mid-bead sights, adjustable GraCoil recoil reduction system, cut 18 LPI checkering, brown trap recoil trap. Gold plated trigger finish and silver nitride trigger guard finish.

Production: *current* **Gauge/Bore:** *12 ga.*
Action: *single-shot*
Barrel Length: 32", 34" **Wt.:** *8.2 lbs., 8.3 lbs.*
Sights: *ivory bead*
Capacity: 1
Stock: *black walnut*

D2C:	NIB $1,230	Ex $950	VG+ $680	Good $615	**LMP:** $1,430
C2C:	Mint $1,190	Ex $850	VG+ $620	Good $555	Fair $285
Trade-In:	Mint $880	Ex $700	VG+ $480	Good $435	Poor $150

BROWNING

BT-99 GOLDEN CLAYS WITH ADJUSTABLE COMB REDBOOK CODE: RB-BW-S-BT99GA

Steel receiver with silver nitride finish and gold accented high-relief engraving. Ported steel barrel with high-post ventilated rib. Beavertail forearm, gloss finish Monte Carlo stock. Vector-Pro lengthened forcing cone, ivory front and mid-bead sights. Invector-Plus flush choke system with 3 Invector-Plus choke tubes. Brown trap recoil pad, cut 18 LPI checkering. Also available in adjustable comb model for $290 more.

Production: *current* Gauge/Bore: *12 ga.*					
Action: *single-shot*					
Barrel Length: 32", 34" **Wt.:** *8.9 lbs., 9 lbs.*	D2C:	NIB $3,197	Ex $2,450	VG+ $1,760	Good $1,600	**LMP: $4,340**
Sights: *ivory bead*	C2C:	Mint $3,070	Ex $2,225	VG+ $1,600	Good $1,440	Fair $740
Capacity: *1*	Trade-In:	Mint $2,270	Ex $1,800	VG+ $1,250	Good $1,120	Poor $330
Stock: *black walnut*					

BT-99 GRADE III REDBOOK CODE: RB-BW-S-BT99G3

Steel receiver with silver nitride finish and high-relief chemical etch engraving. Steel ported barrel with high post, ventilated rib, and polished blue finish. Tight radius pistol grip, finger-grooved forearm, Vector Pro lengthened forcing cone, 1 extended Invector Plus choke tube, ivory front and mid sights, Pachmayr Decelerator XLT Ultra Soft Magnum Trap recoil pad, cut 18 LPI checkering, chrome plated chamber.

Production: *current* Gauge/Bore: *12 ga.*					
Action: *single-shot*					
Barrel Length: 32", 34" **Wt.:** *8.3 lbs., 8.4 lbs.*	D2C:	NIB $2,483	Ex $1,900	VG+ $1,370	Good $1,245	**LMP: $2,540**
Sights: *ivory bead*	C2C:	Mint $2,390	Ex $1,725	VG+ $1,250	Good $1,120	Fair $575
Capacity: *1*	Trade-In:	Mint $1,770	Ex $1,400	VG+ $970	Good $870	Poor $270
Stock: *black walnut*					

BT-99 PLUS REDBOOK CODE: RB-BW-S-BT99PL

Steel receiver with low-luster blue finish, drilled and tapped for scope mounts. Thick-walled steel barrel with low-luster blue finish, fully rifled for slug and sabot ammunition. Top-tang safety, rear sight adjustable for windage and elevation, black ventilated recoil pad, 60 degree bolt lift, cut 18 LPI checkering. Alloy trigger and guard with matte black finishes on both and on bolt slide. Twist rate of 1:28.

Production: *current* Gauge/Bore: *12 ga.*					
Action: *single-shot*					
Barrel Length: 32", 34" **Wt.:** *8.6 lbs.*	D2C:	NIB $1,684	Ex $1,300	VG+ $930	Good $845	**LMP: $2,670**
Sights: *ivory bead*	C2C:	Mint $1,620	Ex $1,175	VG+ $850	Good $760	Fair $390
Capacity: *1*	Trade-In:	Mint $1,200	Ex $950	VG+ $660	Good $590	Poor $180
Stock: *black walnut*					

*Photo Courtesy of
Rock Island Auction Company*

BT-99 TRAP REDBOOK CODE: RB-BW-S-BT99CT

Ventilated rib barrel, M/IM/F choke, boxlock action, automatic ejector, checkering on pistol grip, Monte Carlo style stock, beavertail forearm.

Production: *discontinued* Gauge/Bore: *12 ga.*					
Action: *single-shot*					
Barrel Length: 32", 34" **Wt.:** *N/A*	D2C:	NIB $853	Ex $650	VG+ $470	Good $430	
Sights: *bead front*	C2C:	Mint $820	Ex $600	VG+ $430	Good $385	Fair $200
Capacity: *1*	Trade-In:	Mint $610	Ex $500	VG+ $340	Good $300	Poor $90
Stock: *walnut*					

BT-99 PLUS GRADE I REDBOOK CODE: RB-BW-S-BT99G1
Adjustable rib, recoil-reduction system, back-bored barrel, Invector chokes.

Production: *discontinued* **Gauge/Bore:** *12 ga.*
Action: *single-shot*
Barrel Length: *32", 34"* **Wt.:** *8.7 lbs.*
Sights: *bead front*
Capacity: *1*
Stock: *walnut*

D2C:	NIB $1,409	Ex $1,075	VG+ $775	Good $705	
C2C:	Mint $1,360	Ex $975	VG+ $710	Good $635	Fair $325
Trade-In:	Mint $1,010	Ex $800	VG+ $550	Good $495	Poor $150

BT-99 MAX REDBOOK CODE: RB-BW-S-BT99MX
Blue steel, engraving on stainless steel receiver, stainless steel trigger guard, ventilated rib barrel, thin forearm with finger grooves, high gloss finish on walnut, ejector/extractor selector, no safety.

Production: *discontinued* **Gauge/Bore:** *12 ga.*
Action: *single-shot*
Barrel Length: *32", 34"* **Wt.:** *8.8 lbs.*
Sights: *bead front*
Capacity: *1*
Stock: *select walnut pistol grip in regular or Monte Carlo style*

D2C:	NIB $1,527	Ex $1,175	VG+ $840	Good $765	
C2C:	Mint $1,470	Ex $1,075	VG+ $770	Good $690	Fair $355
Trade-In:	Mint $1,090	Ex $875	VG+ $600	Good $535	Poor $180

BT-99 PLUS MICRO REDBOOK CODE: RB-BW-S-BT99PM
High post ventilated rib barrel, shortened length of pull, same as the BT-99 but with reduced dimensions.

Production: *discontinued* **Gauge/Bore:** *12 ga.*
Action: *single-shot*
Barrel Length: *24"–34"* **Wt.:** *7.7 lbs.*
Sights: *bead fornt*
Capacity: *1*
Stock: *select walnut*

D2C:	NIB $1,435	Ex $1,100	VG+ $790	Good $720	
C2C:	Mint $1,380	Ex $1,000	VG+ $720	Good $650	Fair $335
Trade-In:	Mint $1,020	Ex $825	VG+ $560	Good $505	Poor $150

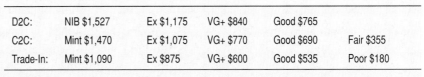

A-BOLT SHOTGUN HUNTER REDBOOK CODE: RB-BW-S-ABOLTH
Steel receiver with low-luster blue finish, drilled and tapped for scope mounts. Thick-walled steel barrel with low-luster blue finish, fully rifled for slug and sabot ammunition. Top-tang safety, rear sight adjustable for windage and elevation, black ventilated recoil pad, 60 degree bolt lift, molded checkering. Alloy trigger and guard with gold plated finish on trigger and matte black finishes on guard and bolt slide. Twist rate of 1:28.

Production: *current* **Gauge/Bore:** *12 ga.*
Action: *bolt-action*
Barrel Length: *22"* **Wt.:** *7.1 lbs.*
Sights: *TruGlo fiber optic*
Capacity: *2*
Stock: *black walnut*

D2C:	NIB $790	Ex $625	VG+ $435	Good $395	**LMP:** $1,280
C2C:	Mint $760	Ex $550	VG+ $400	Good $360	Fair $185
Trade-In:	Mint $570	Ex $450	VG+ $310	Good $280	Poor $90

A-BOLT SHOTGUN STALKER REDBOOK CODE: RB-BW-S-ABOLTS

Steel receiver with low-luster blue finish, drilled and tapped for scope mounts. Thick-walled steel barrel with low-luster blue finish, fully rifled for slug and sabot ammunition. Top-tang safety, rear sight adjustable for windage and elevation, black ventilated recoil pad, 60 degree bolt lift, molded checkering. Alloy trigger with gold plating and alloy guard with matte black finish. Matte black bolt slide. Twist rate of 1:28.

Production: *current* **Gauge/Bore:** *12 ga.*
Action: *bolt-action*
Barrel Length: 22" **Wt.:** *7 lbs.*
Sights: *TruGlo fiber optic*
Capacity: *2*
Stock: *composite*

D2C:	NIB $852	Ex $650	VG+ $470	Good $430	**LMP:** $1,150
C2C:	Mint $820	Ex $600	VG+ $430	Good $385	Fair $200
Trade-In:	Mint $610	Ex $500	VG+ $340	Good $300	Poor $90

A-BOLT SHOTGUN, MOSSY OAK BREAK-UP INFINITY REDBOOK CODE: RB-BW-S-ABOLTM

Steel receiver, blue finished receiver and barrel, drilled and tapped for scope mounts, low-luster finish on barrel, thick-walled fully rifled slug barrel, 3" chamber, top-tang safety, detachable 2 round magazine, checkering on gripping surfaces on stock and forearm, sling-swivel studs.

Production: *current* **Gauge/Bore:** *12 ga.*
Action: *bolt-action*
Barrel Length: 22" **Wt.:** *7 lbs.*
Sights: *TruGlo fiber optic*
Capacity: *2*
Stock: *composite*

D2C:	NIB $983	Ex $750	VG+ $545	Good $495	**LMP:** $1,300
C2C:	Mint $950	Ex $700	VG+ $500	Good $445	Fair $230
Trade-In:	Mint $700	Ex $575	VG+ $390	Good $345	Poor $120

Photo Courtesy of Rock Island Auction Company

A-500G REDBOOK CODE: RB-BW-S-A500GX

Gas operated, gold accents on receiver, 2.75" or 3" chamber, blue barrel finish, checkering on stock, recoil pad, light engraving.

Production: *1990–1993* **Gauge/Bore:** *12 ga.*
Action: *semi-auto*
Barrel Length: 26", 28", 30" **Wt.:** *8 lbs.*
Sights: *bead front*
Capacity: *5*
Stock: *walnut*

D2C:	NIB $564	Ex $450	VG+ $315	Good $285	
C2C:	Mint $550	Ex $400	VG+ $290	Good $255	Fair $130
Trade-In:	Mint $410	Ex $325	VG+ $220	Good $200	Poor $60

Photo Courtesy of Rock Island Auction Company

A-500R REDBOOK CODE: RB-BW-S-A500RX

3" chamber, short recoil system, four-lug rotary bolt, ventilated rib barrel, high-polished blue finish, red accents on receiver, gold trigger, semi-pistol grip, ventilated recoil pad.

Production: *1987–1983* **Gauge/Bore:** *12 ga.*
Action: *semi-auto*
Barrel Length: 26"–30" **Wt.:** *7.7–8 lbs.*
Sights: *bead front*
Capacity: *5*
Stock: *walnut*

D2C:	NIB $497	Ex $400	VG+ $275	Good $250	
C2C:	Mint $480	Ex $350	VG+ $250	Good $225	Fair $115
Trade-In:	Mint $360	Ex $300	VG+ $200	Good $175	Poor $60

BROWNING

AMERICAN BROWNING AUTO-5 REDBOOK CODE: RB-BW-S-AMERBR
Engraved receiver, recoil-operated, Browning logo engraved on receiver.

Production: *1940–discontinued* **Gauge/Bore:** *12 ga., 16 ga., 20 ga.*
Action: *semi-auto*
Barrel Length: 26"–32" **Wt.:** *N/A*
Sights: *bead front*
Capacity: *4, 5*
Stock: *walnut*

D2C:	NIB $376	Ex $300	VG+ $210	Good $190	
C2C:	Mint $370	Ex $275	VG+ $190	Good $170	Fair $90
Trade-In:	Mint $270	Ex $225	VG+ $150	Good $135	Poor $60

B-SS REDBOOK CODE: RB-BW-S-BSSXXX
Various choke combinations offered, boxlock action, automatic ejectors, non-selective single trigger or selective trigger, blue finished barrel and receiver, checkering on walnut, beavertail forearm.

Photo Courtesy of Rock Island Auction Company

Production: *discontinued* **Gauge/Bore:** *12 ga., 20 ga.*
Action: *SxS*
Barrel Length: 26", 28", 30" **Wt.:** *7–7.5 lbs.*
Sights: *none*
Capacity: *2*
Stock: *walnut*

D2C:	NIB $1,422	Ex $1,100	VG+ $785	Good $715	
C2C:	Mint $1,370	Ex $1,000	VG+ $720	Good $640	Fair $330
Trade-In:	Mint $1,010	Ex $800	VG+ $560	Good $500	Poor $150

B-SS 20 GAUGE SPORTER REDBOOK CODE: RB-BW-S-BSSSPO
Various choke combinations offered, boxlock action, automatic ejectors, English style straight-grip stock, oil-finished walnut, longer lower tang, slimmed down beavertail forearm.

Photo Courtesy of Rock Island Auction Company

Production: *discontinued* **Gauge/Bore:** *20 ga.*
Action: *SxS*
Barrel Length: 26", 28" **Wt.:** *7–7.5 lbs.*
Sights: *none*
Capacity: *2*
Stock: *walnut*

D2C:	NIB $2,122	Ex $1,625	VG+ $1,170	Good $1,065	
C2C:	Mint $2,040	Ex $1,475	VG+ $1,070	Good $955	Fair $490
Trade-In:	Mint $1,510	Ex $1,200	VG+ $830	Good $745	Poor $240

GOLD DEER HUNTER REDBOOK CODE: RB-BW-S-GOLDDH
3" chamber, fully rifled or smooth bore barrel, checkering on satin finished stock and forearm, cantilever scope mount, sling swivel studs, cantilever scope mount.

Photo Courtesy of Rock Island Auction Company

Production: *discontinued* **Gauge/Bore:** *12 ga., 20 ga.*
Action: *semi-auto*
Barrel Length: 22" **Wt.:** *7.7 lbs.*
Sights: *none*
Capacity: *4, 5*
Stock: *walnut*

D2C:	NIB $845	Ex $650	VG+ $465	Good $425	
C2C:	Mint $820	Ex $600	VG+ $430	Good $385	Fair $195
Trade-In:	Mint $600	Ex $475	VG+ $330	Good $300	Poor $90

BROWNING

MODEL 12 REDBOOK CODE: RB-BW-S-MODE12

Modified choke, ventilated rib barrel, tubular magazine, floating high-post rib, takedown style, blue metal, checkering on stock and forend, Monte Carlo style stock.

Photo Courtesy of Rock Island Auction Company

Production: *discontinued* **Gauge/Bore:** *20 ga., 28 ga.*
Action: *pump-action*
Barrel Length: 26" **Wt.:** *N/A*
Sights: *bead front*
Capacity: 5
Stock: *walnut*

D2C:	NIB $1,243	Ex $950	VG+ $685	Good $625	
C2C:	Mint $1,200	Ex $875	VG+ $630	Good $560	Fair $290
Trade-In:	Mint $890	Ex $700	VG+ $490	Good $440	Poor $150

MODEL 42 LIMITED EDITION REDBOOK CODE: RB-BW-S-MO42LE

3" chamber, ventilated rib full choke barrel, 5 digit serial number, plain blue receiver.

Photo Courtesy of Rock Island Auction Company

Production: *discontinued* **Gauge/Bore:** *0.41*
Action: *pump-action*
Barrel Length: 26" **Wt.:** *6.8 lbs.*
Sights: *bead front*
Capacity: 5
Stock: *walnut*

D2C:	NIB $879	Ex $675	VG+ $485	Good $440	
C2C:	Mint $850	Ex $625	VG+ $440	Good $400	Fair $205
Trade-In:	Mint $630	Ex $500	VG+ $350	Good $310	Poor $90

MODEL B-80 REDBOOK CODE: RB-BW-S-MODB80

2.75" or 3" chamber, capable of barrel change, gas-operated, steel or aluminum receiver, invector chokes became an option after production started.

Production: *discontinued* **Gauge/Bore:** *12 ga., 20 ga.*
Action: *semi-auto*
Barrel Length: various barrel lengths available
Wt.: *6–8 lbs.*
Sights: *bead front*
Capacity: 4
Stock: *walnut*

Photo Courtesy of Rock Island Auction Company

D2C:	NIB $478	Ex $375	VG+ $265	Good $240	
C2C:	Mint $460	Ex $350	VG+ $240	Good $220	Fair $110
Trade-In:	Mint $340	Ex $275	VG+ $190	Good $170	Poor $60

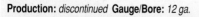

RECOILLESS TRAP SHOTGUN REDBOOK CODE: RB-BW-S-RETRAP

Recoil eliminating bolt-action, high-post ventilated rib, Invector Plus choked back-bored barrel, adjustable 3-points of impact, adjustable pull stock, anodized receiver.

Production: *discontinued* **Gauge/Bore:** *12 ga.*
Action: *single-shot*
Barrel Length: 27", 30" **Wt.:** *8.5 lbs.*
Sights: *bead front*
Capacity: 1
Stock: *walnut*

D2C:	NIB $925	Ex $725	VG+ $510	Good $465	
C2C:	Mint $890	Ex $650	VG+ $470	Good $420	Fair $215
Trade-In:	Mint $660	Ex $525	VG+ $370	Good $325	Poor $120

Century International Arms, Inc.

Century International Arms, Inc. is an importer of surplus foreign firearms into the United States. Many of the factory-imported firearms they distribute must be modified to meet the standard regulations imposed by United States firearms laws. The company also carries newly manufactured firearms, knives, swords, ammunition, scopes, and related accessories.

JW-2000 COACH   REDBOOK CODE: RB-CA-S-JS2000
Rabbit ear hammer, double trigger, rubber buttpad, sling swivels, chambered for 3", checkering on forearm and grip.

Production: *current* **Gauge/Bore:** *12 ga., 20 ga.*					
Action: *SxS*	D2C:	NIB $300	Ex $250	VG+ $165	Good $150	
Barrel Length: 20" **Wt.:** *7.8 lbs.*	C2C:	Mint $290	Ex $225	VG+ $150	Good $135	Fair $70
Sights: *brass bead front*	Trade-In:	Mint $220	Ex $175	VG+ $120	Good $105	Poor $30
Capacity: *2*						
Stock: *stained walnut*						

PW87   REDBOOK CODE: RB-CA-S-PW87XX
Cylinder bore choke, 2 3/4" chamber, blue finished metal.

Production: *current* **Gauge/Bore:** *12 ga.*					
Action: *lever-action*	D2C:	NIB $400	Ex $325	VG+ $220	Good $200	
Barrel Length: 19" **Wt.:** *7.9 lbs.*	C2C:	Mint $390	Ex $300	VG+ $200	Good $180	Fair $95
Sights: *brass bead front*	Trade-In:	Mint $290	Ex $225	VG+ $160	Good $140	Poor $60
Capacity: *5*						
Stock: *hardwood*						

SPM COACH   REDBOOK CODE: RB-CA-S-SPMCOA
Fully functional rabbit ear hammer, double trigger, steel construction, rubber buttpad, sling swivel, chambered for 3", checkering on forearm and grip.

Production: *current* **Gauge/Bore:** *.410*					
Action: *SxS*	D2C:	NIB $350	Ex $275	VG+ $195	Good $175	
Barrel Length: 20" **Wt.:** *7.8 lbs.*	C2C:	Mint $340	Ex $250	VG+ $180	Good $160	Fair $85
Sights: *brass bead front*	Trade-In:	Mint $250	Ex $200	VG+ $140	Good $125	Poor $60
Capacity: *2*						
Stock: *walnut stained hardwood*						

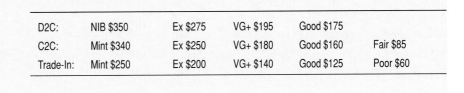

Charles Daly

Charles Daly, located in Harrisburg, Pennsylvania, began operations when Charles Daly and August Shoverling contracted with several foreign manufacturers to import firearms into the U.S. Later, Joseph Gales joined the business as a partner, and the company was called "Shoverling, Daly, and Gales" for a while before it was finally shortened to simply Charles Daly. After Charles Daly's death, his son continued operations for about twenty years before selling the company to Henry Modell, who later sold it to the Walzer family, a family who already owned a large sporting goods company. Under the new ownership, Charles Daly guns were produced by several major manufacturers. The brand changed hands several more times, and by 2008, an AR-15 rifle line was added to production and became the first product the company manufactured domestically. In 2010, the company announced that it was closing its doors but then resumed operations in 2012. At present, Charles Daly only produces shotguns.

206S SPORTING REDBOOK CODE: RB-C5-S-206SSC

3" chamber, steel frame with silver finish and top tang button safety. Chrome-moly steel barrels are ported and deep-hole drilled, steel shot compatible, and have a high polish blue finish. Features single-selective trigger and auto selective ejectors. Includes MC-5 (SK, IC, M, IM, F) extended target chokes with REM choke pattern, 13.875" length of pull.

Production: current Gauge/Bore: 12 ga.					
Action: O/U					
Barrel Length: 28", 30", 32" Wt.: ~7.3 lbs.	D2C:	NIB $915	Ex $700	VG+ $505	Good $460	LMP: $1,185
Sights: brass bead front	C2C:	Mint $880	Ex $650	VG+ $460	Good $415	Fair $215
Capacity: 2	Trade-In:	Mint $650	Ex $525	VG+ $360	Good $325	Poor $120
Stock: oil finish semi-fancy walnut					

206SL MID-SPORT REDBOOK CODE: RB-C5-S-206SLM

13.5" length of pull, 3" drop at heel, and 1.5" drop at comb for mid-sized stature, 2 3/4" and 3" chamber, steel frame, top tang button safety. Chrome-moly steel barrels are deep-hole drilled, and steel shot compatible. Single-selective trigger, auto selective ejectors, REM choke thread pattern on MC-5 (SK, IC, M, IM, F) extended chokes.

Production: current Gauge/Bore: 12 ga.					
Action: O/U					
Barrel Length: 28", 30" Wt.: ~7.3 lbs.	D2C:	NIB $900	Ex $700	VG+ $495	Good $450	LMP: $1,185
Sights: twin beads front fiber optic	C2C:	Mint $870	Ex $625	VG+ $450	Good $405	Fair $210
Capacity: 2	Trade-In:	Mint $640	Ex $525	VG+ $360	Good $315	Poor $90
Stock: oil finish semi-fancy walnut					

206T TRAP REDBOOK CODE: RB-C5-S-206TTP

2 3/4" and 3" chamber, steel frame with silver finish and top tang button safety. Chrome-moly steel barrels are deep-hole drilled, ported, steel shot compatible, and have a high polish blue finish. Features single-selective trigger and auto selective ejectors. REM choke thread pattern on MC-T3 (M, IM, F) extended chokes, 13.875" length of pull, 45.3" overall length on 28", Monte Carlo trap stock.

Production: current Gauge/Bore: 12 ga.					
Action: O/U					
Barrel Length: 28", 30", 32" Wt.: ~7.3 lbs.	D2C:	NIB $1,050	Ex $800	VG+ $580	Good $525	LMP: $1,199
Sights: twin beads front fiber optic	C2C:	Mint $1,010	Ex $725	VG+ $530	Good $475	Fair $245
Capacity: 2	Trade-In:	Mint $750	Ex $600	VG+ $410	Good $370	Poor $120
Stock: oil finish semi-fancy walnut					

206 FIELD   REDBOOK CODE: RB-C5-S-206FLD

2 3/4" and 3" chamber, steel frame with silver finish and automatic safety. Chrome-moly steel barrels are deep-hole drilled, steel shot compatible, and have a matte blue finish. Features single-selective trigger and auto selective ejectors. REM choke thread pattern on MC-3 (IC, M, F) chokes, 13.875" length of pull, 45.3" overall length on 28".

Production: *current* **Gauge/Bore:** *12 ga.*

Action: *O/U*

Barrel Length: 26", 28" **Wt.:** *~7.3 lbs.*

Sights: *brass bead front*

Capacity: *2*

Stock: *oil finish standard walnut*

D2C:	NIB $1,000	Ex $775	VG+ $550	Good $500	**LMP:** $1,013
C2C:	Mint $960	Ex $700	VG+ $500	Good $450	Fair $230
Trade-In:	Mint $710	Ex $575	VG+ $390	Good $350	Poor $120

600S SPORTING CLAYS   REDBOOK CODE: RB-C5-S-600SSC

Features recoil-reducing gas operating system and aluminum alloy receiver, vent rib, chambered for 2 3/4" and 3". Includes MC-5 external fit choke tubes (SK, IC, M, IM, F), blue finish.

Production: *current* **Gauge/Bore:** *12 ga., 20 ga., 28 ga.*

Action: *semi-auto*

Barrel Length: 28", 30" **Wt.:** *N/A*

Sights: *brass bead front*

Capacity: *6*

Stock: *oil finish walnut*

D2C:	NIB $739	Ex $575	VG+ $410	Good $370	**LMP:** $739
C2C:	Mint $710	Ex $525	VG+ $370	Good $335	Fair $170
Trade-In:	Mint $530	Ex $425	VG+ $290	Good $260	Poor $90

600T TRAP   REDBOOK CODE: RB-C5-S-600TTP

Features recoil-reducing gas operating system and aluminum alloy receiver, blue finish, raised comb on stock, vent rib, chambered for 2 3/4" and 3". Includes MC-3 extended choke tubes (M, IM, F), blue finish.

Production: *current* **Gauge/Bore:** *12 ga.*

Action: *semi-auto*

Barrel Length: 28", 30", 32" **Wt.:** *N/A*

Sights: *brass bead front*

Capacity: *6*

Stock: *oil finish walnut*

D2C:	NIB $700	Ex $550	VG+ $385	Good $350	**LMP:** $741
C2C:	Mint $680	Ex $500	VG+ $350	Good $315	Fair $165
Trade-In:	Mint $500	Ex $400	VG+ $280	Good $245	Poor $90

600SL MID-SPORT   REDBOOK CODE: RB-C5-S-600SLM

Mid-sized stature, vent rib, 2 3/4" and 3" chamber, includes MC-5 (SK, IC, M, IM, F) extended chokes.

Production: *current* **Gauge/Bore:** *12 ga.*

Action: *semi-auto*

Barrel Length: 28", 30" **Wt.:** *N/A*

Sights: *brass bead front*

Capacity: *6*

Stock: *walnut*

D2C:	NIB $736	Ex $575	VG+ $405	Good $370	**LMP:** $736
C2C:	Mint $710	Ex $525	VG+ $370	Good $335	Fair $170
Trade-In:	Mint $530	Ex $425	VG+ $290	Good $260	Poor $90

335 MASTER-MAG REDBOOK CODE: RB-C5-S-335MMG

Features anti-binding twin action bars and aluminum alloy receiver.
Chrome-moly steel barrels deep-hole drilled, ported, and steel shot compatible,
vent rib, four stock adjustment shims. Chambered for 2 3/4", 3", and 3 1/2". Includes one flush fit choke tube,
featuring REM choke thread patterns. Available in black synthetic or camouflage synthetic.

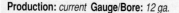

Production: *current* **Gauge/Bore:** *12 ga.*

Action: *pump-action*

Barrel Length: 24", 26", 28" **Wt.:** *~8 lbs.*

Sights: *brass bead front*

Capacity: 6

Stock: *synthetic black or camo*

D2C:	NIB $412	Ex $325	VG+ $230	Good $210	LMP: $397
C2C:	Mint $400	Ex $300	VG+ $210	Good $190	Fair $95
Trade-In:	Mint $300	Ex $250	VG+ $170	Good $145	Poor $60

335 MASTER-MAG WATERFOWL REDBOOK CODE: RB-C5-S-335MMW

Features anti-binding twin action bars and aluminum alloy receiver.
Chrome-moly steel barrels deep-hole drilled, ported, and steel shot compatible. Vent rib, four stock
adjustment shims, 2 3/4", 3", and 3 1/2" magnum chamber. Includes one flush fit choke tube with REM choke
thread patterns, rifle style 13.75" length of pull, full camouflage finish.

Production: *current* **Gauge/Bore:** *12 ga.*

Action: *pump-action*

Barrel Length: 24", 26", 28" **Wt.:** *N/A*

Sights: *brass bead front*

Capacity: 6

Stock: *synthetic*

D2C:	NIB $450	Ex $350	VG+ $250	Good $225	
C2C:	Mint $440	Ex $325	VG+ $230	Good $205	Fair $105
Trade-In:	Mint $320	Ex $275	VG+ $180	Good $160	Poor $60

335 MASTER-MAG TURKEY REDBOOK CODE: RB-C5-S-335MMT

Anti-binding twin action bars and aluminum alloy receiver. Chrome-moly
steel barrels deep-hole drilled and steel shot compatible. Vent rib, 3 1/2" magnum
chamber, sling swivel studs, Mil-Spec Picatinny accessory rail for mounting optics. Includes Extra Full, ported,
removable choke tube, with a REM Choke thread pattern MC-1XF. Rifle style 13.75" length of pull, full camouflage finish, optional pistol grip stock.

Production: *current* **Gauge/Bore:** *12 ga.*

Action: *pump-action*

Barrel Length: 24" **Wt.:** *N/A*

Sights: *fiber optic front bead*

Capacity: 6

Stock: *synthetic*

D2C:	NIB $450	Ex $350	VG+ $250	Good $225	LMP: $547
C2C:	Mint $440	Ex $325	VG+ $230	Good $205	Fair $105
Trade-In:	Mint $320	Ex $275	VG+ $180	Good $160	Poor $60

635 MASTER-MAG REDBOOK CODE: RB-C5-S-635MMG

Aluminum alloy receiver, chrome-moly steel barrel, gas-assisted recoil operation, push-button
safety, flush mount choke tube, black oxide blue finished metal, 3 1/2" chamber.

Production: *current* **Gauge/Bore:** *12 ga.*

Action: *semi-auto*

Barrel Length: 24", 26", 28" **Wt.:** *~8 lbs.*

Sights: *brass bead front*

Capacity: 6

Stock: *synthetic*

D2C:	NIB $525	Ex $400	VG+ $290	Good $265	LMP: $556
C2C:	Mint $510	Ex $375	VG+ $270	Good $240	Fair $125
Trade-In:	Mint $380	Ex $300	VG+ $210	Good $185	Poor $60

635 MASTER-MAG WATERFOWL REDBOOK CODE: RB-C5-S-635MMW

Features recoil-reducing gas operating system and aluminum alloy receiver.
Chrome-moly steel barrels deep-hole drilled, ported, and steel shot compatible.
Removable choke tube with REM choke thread pattern,
vent rib, four stock adjustment shims, 3 1/2" magnum chamber, rifle style 13.75" length of pull, camo finish.

Production: *current* **Gauge/Bore:** *12 ga.*
Action: *semi-auto*
Barrel Length: 24", 26", 28" **Wt.:** *N/A*
Sights: *brass front bead*
Capacity: *6*
Stock: *synthetic camo*

D2C:	NIB $575	Ex $450	VG+ $320	Good $290	
C2C:	Mint $560	Ex $400	VG+ $290	Good $260	Fair $135
Trade-In:	Mint $410	Ex $325	VG+ $230	Good $205	Poor $60

635 MASTER-MAG TURKEY REDBOOK CODE: RB-C5-S-635MMT

Recoil-reducing gas operating system and aluminum alloy receiver.
Chrome-moly steel barrels deep-hole drilled and steel shot compatible, vent rib, 3 1/2"
magnum chamber, sling swivel studs, Mil-Spec Picatinny accessory rail for mounting optics. Includes Extra Full, ported, removable choke
tube with a REM Choke thread pattern (MC-1XF), 13.75" length of pull, full camouflage finish, optional pistol grip stock.

Production: *current* **Gauge/Bore:** *12 ga.*
Action: *semi-auto*
Barrel Length: 24" **Wt.:** *N/A*
Sights: *fiber optic front bead*
Capacity: *6*
Stock: *synthetic*

D2C:	NIB $508	Ex $400	VG+ $280	Good $255	LMP: $699
C2C:	Mint $490	Ex $375	VG+ $260	Good $230	Fair $120
Trade-In:	Mint $370	Ex $300	VG+ $200	Good $180	Poor $60

600 SUPERIOR REDBOOK CODE: RB-C5-S-600SUP

Recoil reducing gas operating system and aluminum alloy receiver.
Chrome-moly steel barrels deep-hole drilled and steel shot compatible, vent rib,
chambered for 2.75" and 3", REM choke pattern thread on 12 and 20 gauge and mobile choke thread
pattern on 28 gauge, 13.87" length of pull. Available in black synthetic, camouflage synthetic, or walnut stock.

Production: *current* **Gauge/Bore:** *12 ga., 20 ga., 28 ga.*
Action: *semi-auto*
Barrel Length: 26", 28" **Wt.:** *8 lbs.*
Sights: *brass front bead*
Capacity: *6*
Stock: *synthetic, walnut*

D2C:	NIB $500	Ex $400	VG+ $275	Good $250	LMP: $571
C2C:	Mint $480	Ex $350	VG+ $250	Good $225	Fair $115
Trade-In:	Mint $360	Ex $300	VG+ $200	Good $175	Poor $60

600 FIELD REDBOOK CODE: RB-C5-S-600FLD

Aluminum alloy receiver, chrome-moly steel barrel, gas-assisted recoil operation,
push-button safety, flush mount choke tube, black oxide blue finished metal, 3" chamber.

Production: *current* **Gauge/Bore:** *12 ga., 20 ga., 28 ga.*
Action: *semi-auto*
Barrel Length: 24", 26", 28", 30" **Wt.:** *8 lbs.*
Sights: *brass bead front*
Capacity: *6*
Stock: *synthetic*

D2C:	NIB $452	Ex $350	VG+ $250	Good $230	LMP: $523
C2C:	Mint $440	Ex $325	VG+ $230	Good $205	Fair $105
Trade-In:	Mint $330	Ex $275	VG+ $180	Good $160	Poor $60

CHARLES DALY

CHARLES DALY

300 FIELD   REDBOOK CODE: RB-C5-S-300FLD

Anti-binding twin action bars and aluminum alloy receiver. Chrome-moly steel barrels deep-hole drilled and steel shot compatible, vent rib, chambered for 2 3/4" and 3", REM choke pattern thread on 12 and 20 gauge and mobile choke thread pattern on 28 gauge. 13.87" length of pull.

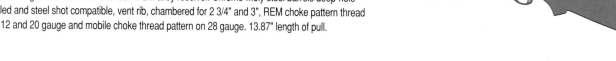

Production: *current* **Gauge/Bore:** *12 ga., 20 ga., 28 ga.*

Action: *pump-action*

Barrel Length: 24", 26", 28", 30" **Wt.:** *N/A*

Sights: *brass front bead*

Capacity: *6*

Stock: *walnut*

D2C:	NIB $359	Ex $275	VG+ $200	Good $180	**LMP:** $359
C2C:	Mint $350	Ex $250	VG+ $180	Good $165	Fair $85
Trade-In:	Mint $260	Ex $225	VG+ $150	Good $130	Poor $60

300 SUPERIOR   REDBOOK CODE: RB-C5-S-300SUP

Anti-binding twin action bars and aluminum alloy receiver. Chrome-moly steel barrels deep-hole drilled and steel shot compatible, vent rib, chambered for 2 3/4" and 3", REM choke pattern thread on 12 and 20 gauge and mobile choke thread pattern on 28 gauge, 13.87" length of pull.

Production: *current* **Gauge/Bore:** *12 ga., 20 ga., 28 ga.*

Action: *pump-action*

Barrel Length: 26", 28" **Wt.:** *N/A*

Sights: *brass front bead*

Capacity: *6*

Stock: *walnut*

D2C:	NIB $373	Ex $300	VG+ $210	Good $190	**LMP:** $403
C2C:	Mint $360	Ex $275	VG+ $190	Good $170	Fair $90
Trade-In:	Mint $270	Ex $225	VG+ $150	Good $135	Poor $60

600THD SP-TACTICAL   REDBOOK CODE: RB-C5-S-600THD

Recoil reducing gas operating system and aluminum alloy receiver, pistol grip black synthetic stock, aluminum alloy receiver, MC-1c choke, Picatinny scope rail for mounting optics.

Production: *current* **Gauge/Bore:** *12 ga.*

Action: *semi-auto*

Barrel Length: 18.5" **Wt.:** *N/A*

Sights: *ghost ring sights*

Capacity: *6*

Stock: *synthetic*

D2C:	NIB $480	Ex $375	VG+ $265	Good $240	**LMP:** $599
C2C:	Mint $470	Ex $350	VG+ $240	Good $220	Fair $115
Trade-In:	Mint $350	Ex $275	VG+ $190	Good $170	Poor $60

600HD HOME DEFENSE   REDBOOK CODE: RB-C5-S-600HDD

Recoil reducing gas operating system and aluminum alloy receiver, cylinder choke, cross bolt safety button at trigger guard rear. Also available in left hand model 600HD-LH.

Production: *current* **Gauge/Bore:** *12 ga.*

Action: *semi-auto*

Barrel Length: 18.5" **Wt.:** *N/A*

Sights: *front bead*

Capacity: *6*

Stock: *synthetic*

D2C:	NIB $420	Ex $325	VG+ $235	Good $210	**LMP:** $499
C2C:	Mint $410	Ex $300	VG+ $210	Good $190	Fair $100
Trade-In:	Mint $300	Ex $250	VG+ $170	Good $150	Poor $60

CHARLES DALY

300HD HOME DEFENSE REDBOOK CODE: RB-C5-S-300HDD

Extended sure-grip pump handle forends with limited slip gripping serrations, aluminum alloy receiver, deep hole drilled chrome-moly steel barrels with cylinder bore chokes and/or MC-1c choke tubes, cross bolt safety button at trigger guard rear, black or nickel finish options. Also available in left hand model 300HD-LH.

Production: *current* **Gauge/Bore:** *12 ga., 20 ga., 28 ga.*
Action: *pump-action*
Barrel Length: 18.5" **Wt.:** *N/A*
Sights: *front bead*
Capacity: *6*
Stock: *synthetic*

D2C:	NIB $299	Ex $250	VG+ $165	Good $150	**LMP: $333**
C2C:	Mint $290	Ex $225	VG+ $150	Good $135	Fair $70
Trade-In:	Mint $220	Ex $175	VG+ $120	Good $105	Poor $30

300THD SP-TACTICAL REDBOOK CODE: RB-C5-S-300THD

Extended sure-grip pump handle forends with limited slip gripping serrations, pistol grip black synthetic stock, aluminum alloy receiver, deep hole drilled chrome-moly steel barrel, cross bolt safety button at trigger guard rear, MC-1c choke, Picatinny scope rail for mounting optics.

Production: *current* **Gauge/Bore:** *12 ga., 20 ga., 28 ga.*
Action: *pump-action*
Barrel Length: 18.5" **Wt.:** *N/A*
Sights: *ghost ring sights*
Capacity: *6*
Stock: *synthetic*

D2C:	NIB $287	Ex $225	VG+ $160	Good $145	**LMP: $409**
C2C:	Mint $280	Ex $200	VG+ $150	Good $130	Fair $70
Trade-In:	Mint $210	Ex $175	VG+ $120	Good $105	Poor $30

Chiappa

CHIAPPA

Ezechiele Chiappa founded Armi Sport in 1958 in his basement; the company would later evolve into the Chiappa Group and Chiappa Firearms. The company began small with only one pistol model but another was added four years later, and a year after that, a line of rifles was produced. Chiappa's son, Rino, became involved with the company in the 1980s and updated manufacturing in ways that greatly increased production. While perhaps best known for replica firearms, the Dayton, Ohio, company produces handguns— including tactical pistols, rifles, shotguns, percussion arms, blank-firing arms, and air guns. To this day, the company remains under the control and leadership of the original Chiappa family.

1887 LEVER-ACTION REDBOOK CODE: RB-CI-S-1887LA

Reproduction of Winchester 1887, steel receiver, hardwood forearm, 2 3/4" chamber.

Production: *current* **Gauge/Bore:** *12 ga.*
Action: *lever-action*
Barrel Length: 22", 24", 28" **Wt.:** *9.3 lbs.*
Sights: *bead front*
Capacity: *7*
Stock: *hardwood*

D2C:	NIB $996	Ex $775	VG+ $550	Good $500	
C2C:	Mint $960	Ex $700	VG+ $500	Good $450	Fair $230
Trade-In:	Mint $710	Ex $575	VG+ $390	Good $350	Poor $120

CHIAPPA

1887 LEVER-ACTION CHROME REDBOOK CODE: RB-CI-S-1887CH

Reproduction of Winchester Model 1887 Lever-Action, 2 3/4" chamber, chrome receiver, chrome barrel, chrome lever, internal safety design.

Production: *current* **Gauge/Bore:** *12 ga.*
Action: *lever-action*
Barrel Length: *22", 24", 28"* **Wt.:** *9 lbs.*
Sights: *bead front*
Capacity: *2, 7*
Stock: *hardwood*

D2C:	NIB $1,106	Ex $850	VG+ $610	Good $555	
C2C:	Mint $1,070	Ex $775	VG+ $560	Good $500	Fair $255
Trade-In:	Mint $790	Ex $625	VG+ $440	Good $390	Poor $120

1887 MARE'S LEG REDBOOK CODE: RB-CI-S-1887ML

Color case-hardened receiver finish, walnut grip and forearm, reproduction of a Winchester 1887 Lever-Action Mare's Leg.

Production: *current* **Gauge/Bore:** *12 ga.*
Action: *lever-action*
Barrel Length: *18.5"* **Wt.:** *7.8 lbs.*
Sights: *bead front*
Capacity: *6*
Stock: *walnut grip*

D2C:	NIB $1,075	Ex $825	VG+ $595	Good $540	
C2C:	Mint $1,040	Ex $750	VG+ $540	Good $485	Fair $250
Trade-In:	Mint $770	Ex $625	VG+ $420	Good $380	Poor $120

1887 T-SERIES REDBOOK CODE: RB-CI-S-1887TS

"T-Series" reproduction, matte black barrel finish, wood forearm, "Soft Touch" black rubber coating on pistol grip.

Production: *current* **Gauge/Bore:** *12 ga.*
Action: *lever-action*
Barrel Length: *18.5"* **Wt.:** *7.9 lbs.*
Sights: *none*
Capacity: *6*
Stock: *black synthetic*

D2C:	NIB $900	Ex $700	VG+ $495	Good $450	
C2C:	Mint $870	Ex $625	VG+ $450	Good $405	Fair $210
Trade-In:	Mint $640	Ex $525	VG+ $360	Good $315	Poor $90

1887 TROPHY HUNTER REDBOOK CODE: RB-CI-S-1887TH

Rifled-slug barrel, walnut forend, rubber buttplate, matte blue finish on metal.

Production: *current* **Gauge/Bore:** *12 ga.*
Action: *lever-action*
Barrel Length: *22"* **Wt.:** *9 lbs.*
Sights: *Skinner rear, fiber optic front*
Capacity: *6*
Stock: *walnut*

D2C:	NIB $1,146	Ex $875	VG+ $635	Good $575	
C2C:	Mint $1,110	Ex $800	VG+ $580	Good $520	Fair $265
Trade-In:	Mint $820	Ex $650	VG+ $450	Good $405	Poor $120

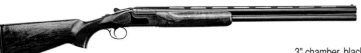

204-X REDBOOK CODE: RB-CI-S-204XXX
3" chamber, black receiver and barrel, walnut forearm, five chokes included, ejector system.

Production: *current* **Gauge/Bore:** *12 ga., 20 ga.*
Action: *O/U*
Barrel Length: *26", 28"* **Wt.:** *6.4–6.8 lbs.*
Sights: *bead front*
Capacity: *2*
Stock: *walnut*

D2C:	NIB $719	Ex $550	VG+ $400	Good $360	
C2C:	Mint $700	Ex $500	VG+ $360	Good $325	Fair $170
Trade-In:	Mint $520	Ex $425	VG+ $290	Good $255	Poor $90

214-E REDBOOK CODE: RB-CI-S-214EXX
3" chamber, black receiver and barrel, walnut forearm, five chokes included, ejector system.

Production: *current* **Gauge/Bore:** *12 ga., 20 ga.*
Action: *O/U*
Barrel Length: *26", 28"* **Wt.:** *6.6–7.3 lbs.*
Sights: *bead front*
Capacity: *2*
Stock: *walnut*

D2C:	NIB $810	Ex $625	VG+ $450	Good $405	
C2C:	Mint $780	Ex $575	VG+ $410	Good $365	Fair $190
Trade-In:	Mint $580	Ex $475	VG+ $320	Good $285	Poor $90

C6-12 REDBOOK CODE: RB-CI-S-C612XX
Drilled and tapped for Picatinny rail, polymer pistol grip, polymer forearm with ridges.

Production: *current* **Gauge/Bore:** *12 ga., 20 ga.*
Action: *pump-action*
Barrel Length: *18.5", 22"* **Wt.:** *5–7 lbs.*
Sights: *ghost ring front*
Capacity: *6, 9*
Stock: *black polymer, available as fixed or adjustable*

D2C:	NIB $265	Ex $225	VG+ $150	Good $135	
C2C:	Mint $260	Ex $200	VG+ $140	Good $120	Fair $65
Trade-In:	Mint $190	Ex $150	VG+ $110	Good $95	Poor $30

C9-12 REDBOOK CODE: RB-CI-S-C912XX
Drilled and tapped for Picatinny rail, polymer pistol grip, polymer forearm with ridges, "Rem-Choke" barrel.

Production: *current* **Gauge/Bore:** *12 ga.*
Action: *pump-action*
Barrel Length: *22"* **Wt.:** *6.5 lbs.*
Sights: *ghost ring front*
Capacity: *9*
Stock: *black polymer*

D2C:	NIB $300	Ex $250	VG+ $165	Good $150	
C2C:	Mint $290	Ex $225	VG+ $150	Good $135	Fair $70
Trade-In:	Mint $220	Ex $175	VG+ $120	Good $105	Poor $30

CHIAPPA

C9-12 GHOST   REDBOOK CODE: RB-CI-S-C912GH
Polymer pistol grip, polymer forearm, "Rem-Choke" barrel.

Production: *current* **Gauge/Bore:** *12 ga.*
Action: *pump-action*
Barrel Length: 22" **Wt.:** *7.5 lbs.*
Sights: *ghost ring rear, fiber-optic front*
Capacity: *9*
Stock: *black polymer*

D2C:	NIB $335	Ex $275	VG+ $185	Good $170	
C2C:	Mint $330	Ex $250	VG+ $170	Good $155	Fair $80
Trade-In:	Mint $240	Ex $200	VG+ $140	Good $120	Poor $60

CA612 FIELD   REDBOOK CODE: RB-CI-S-CA612F
3" chamber, five chokes included, ejector system, inertia driven action. Available in black, Realtree Field camouflage, or Realtree XTRA camouflage, and with pistol grip.

Production: *current* **Gauge/Bore:** *12 ga.*
Action: *semi-auto*
Barrel Length: 28" **Wt.:** *7 lbs.*
Sights: *fiber-optic front*
Capacity: *5*
Stock: *black polymer*

D2C:	NIB $489	Ex $375	VG+ $270	Good $245	
C2C:	Mint $470	Ex $350	VG+ $250	Good $225	Fair $115
Trade-In:	Mint $350	Ex $275	VG+ $200	Good $175	Poor $60

TRIPLE CROWN   REDBOOK CODE: RB-CI-S-TRICRO
"Rem-Choke" on all 3 barrels, 3" magnum chamber, sling loop in front, rubber buttpad.

Production: *current* **Gauge/Bore:** *12 ga., 20 ga.*
Action: *triple-barrel*
Barrel Length: 26", 28" **Wt.:** *7.6–8.7 lbs.*
Sights: *bead front*
Capacity: *3*
Stock: *walnut*

D2C:	NIB $1,365	Ex $1,050	VG+ $755	Good $685	
C2C:	Mint $1,320	Ex $950	VG+ $690	Good $615	Fair $315
Trade-In:	Mint $970	Ex $775	VG+ $540	Good $480	Poor $150

TRIPLE MAGNUM   REDBOOK CODE: RB-CI-S-TRIMAG
"Rem-Choke" on barrel, five chokes included, 3" magnum chamber, black receiver, available in Realtree MAX-5.

Production: *current* **Gauge/Bore:** *12 ga.*
Action: *triple-barrel*
Barrel Length: 28" **Wt.:** *8.6 lbs.*
Sights: *bead front*
Capacity: *3*
Stock: *black synthetic*

D2C:	NIB $1,400	Ex $1,075	VG+ $770	Good $700	
C2C:	Mint $1,350	Ex $975	VG+ $700	Good $630	Fair $325
Trade-In:	Mint $1,000	Ex $800	VG+ $550	Good $490	Poor $150

TRIPLE THREAT   REDBOOK CODE: RB-CI-S-TRITHR

"Rem-Choke" on all 3 barrels, 3" magnum chamber, stock can be partly disassembled, sling loop in front, gold ring around stock, rubber buttpad.

Production: *current* **Gauge/Bore:** *12 ga.*
Action: *triple-barrel*
Barrel Length: *18.5", 26", 28"* **Wt.:** *7.6–8.6 lbs.*
Sights: *fiber-optic front*
Capacity: *3*
Stock: *hardwood*

D2C:	NIB $1,535	Ex $1,175	VG+ $845	Good $770	
C2C:	Mint $1,480	Ex $1,075	VG+ $770	Good $695	Fair $355
Trade-In:	Mint $1,090	Ex $875	VG+ $600	Good $540	Poor $180

TRIPLE TOM   REDBOOK CODE: RB-CI-S-TRITOM

"Rem-Choke" on all three barrels, five included chokes, 3.5" chamber, Realtree extra green camouflage.

Production: *current* **Gauge/Bore:** *12 ga.*
Action: *triple-barrel*
Barrel Length: *24"* **Wt.:** *8.3 lbs.*
Sights: *fiber-optic front*
Capacity: *3*
Stock: *synthetic*

D2C:	NIB $1,395	Ex $1,075	VG+ $770	Good $700	
C2C:	Mint $1,340	Ex $975	VG+ $700	Good $630	Fair $325
Trade-In:	Mint $1,000	Ex $800	VG+ $550	Good $490	Poor $150

X-CALIBER (COMBO GUN)   REDBOOK CODE: RB-CI-S-XCALIB

Eight caliber adapters included, folding/break-open action, steel barrel, double trigger, top-tang manual safety, matte black finish, entire rifle will fold in half.

Production: *current* **Gauge/Bore:** *12 ga./.22 LR*
Action: *O/U*
Barrel Length: *18.5"* **Wt.:** *5.8 lbs.*
Sights: *fiber-optic front, M1 style adjustable*
Capacity: *2*
Stock: *pre-formed polypropylene foam*

D2C:	NIB $653	Ex $500	VG+ $360	Good $330	
C2C:	Mint $630	Ex $475	VG+ $330	Good $295	Fair $155
Trade-In:	Mint $470	Ex $375	VG+ $260	Good $230	Poor $90

Churchill, E.J.

Edwin John Churchill opened his gun shop in London in 1891, and he grew it into the company that is currently the largest British-owned gunmaker, E.J. Churchill. The company is also the only shooting business that includes its own gunmaking facility, range, corporate entertainment company, and sporting agency. The company currently offers a proprietary line of rifles and lines of over/under and side-by-side shotguns, and at the company facility, new and used guns of those proprietary models are sold alongside shotguns made by Benelli, Berretta, Browning, and Perazzi—all companies for which E.J. Churchill is a dealer.

CHURCHILL, E.J.

CORONET OVER AND UNDER REDBOOK CODE: RB-EJ-S-CNETOU

Made-to-measure stocks, 2 3/4" chamber, silver action with scroll engraving, single-selective detachable trigger, rounded forend.
LMP pricing converted to US dollars.

Production: *current* **Gauge/Bore:** *12 ga., 20 ga.*					
Action: *O/U*					
Barrel Length: 30", 32" **Wt.:** *N/A*	D2C:	NIB $10,200	Ex $7,775	VG+ $5,610	Good $5,100	**LMP:** $10,447
Sights: *none*	C2C:	Mint $9,800	Ex $7,050	VG+ $5,100	Good $4,590	Fair $2,350
Capacity: *2*	Trade-In:	Mint $7,250	Ex $5,725	VG+ $3,980	Good $3,570	Poor $1,020
Stock: *semi pistol-grip stock*					

CROWN SIDE BY SIDE REDBOOK CODE: RB-EJ-S-CRWNSS

2 3/4" chamber, silver engraving, square bodied action, double trigger, southgate ejector work, English splinter forend,
choice of choke.

Production: *current* **Gauge/Bore:** *12 ga., 20 ga., 28 ga., .410*					
Action: *SxS*					
Barrel Length: 28", 30" **Wt.:** *N/A*	D2C:	NIB $8,000	Ex $6,100	VG+ $4,400	Good $4,000	**LMP:** $9,390
Sights: *bead front*	C2C:	Mint $7,680	Ex $5,525	VG+ $4,000	Good $3,600	Fair $1,840
Capacity: *2*	Trade-In:	Mint $5,680	Ex $4,500	VG+ $3,120	Good $2,800	Poor $810
Stock: *straight grip walnut*					

CROWN OVER AND UNDER REDBOOK CODE: RB-EJ-S-CRWNOU

2 3/4" chamber, silver action with scroll engraving, trigger plate action, single selective trigger, rounded forend, choice of choke.

Production: *current* **Gauge/Bore:** *12 ga., 20 ga., 28 ga.*					
Action: *O/U*					
Barrel Length: 28", 30" **Wt.:** *N/A*	D2C:	NIB $20,000	Ex $15,200	VG+ $11,000	Good $10,000	**LMP:** $20,151
Sights: *bead front*	C2C:	Mint $19,200	Ex $13,800	VG+ $10,000	Good $9,000	Fair $4,600
Capacity: *2*	Trade-In:	Mint $14,200	Ex $11,200	VG+ $7,800	Good $7,000	Poor $2,010
Stock: *semi pistol-grip stock*					

REGAL SIDE BY SIDE REDBOOK CODE: RB-EJ-S-REGLSS

2 3/4" chamber, silver engraving, round bodied action, english splinter forend, double trigger, southgate ejector work, choice of choke,
fitted leather cases.

Production: *current* **Gauge/Bore:** *12 ga., 20 ga., 28 ga., .410*					
Action: *SxS*					
Barrel Length: 28", 30" **Wt.:** *N/A*	D2C:	NIB $11,000	Ex $8,375	VG+ $6,050	Good $5,500	**LMP:** $11,738
Sights: *bead front*	C2C:	Mint $10,560	Ex $7,600	VG+ $5,500	Good $4,950	Fair $2,530
Capacity: *2*	Trade-In:	Mint $7,810	Ex $6,175	VG+ $4,290	Good $3,850	Poor $1,110
Stock: *straight grip*					

REGAL OVER AND UNDER REDBOOK CODE: RB-EJ-S-REGLOU

2 3/4" chamber, fine engraving, trigger plate action, rounded forend, single selective trigger, choice of choke.

Production: *current* **Gauge/Bore:** *12 ga., 20 ga., 28 ga.*
Action: *O/U*
Barrel Length: 28", 30" **Wt.:** *N/A*
Sights: *bead front*
Capacity: *2*
Stock: *semi pistol-grip hardwood*

D2C:	NIB $23,477	Ex $17,850	VG+ $12,915	Good $11,740	LMP: $23,477
C2C:	Mint $22,540	Ex $16,200	VG+ $11,740	Good $10,565	Fair $5,400
Trade-In:	Mint $16,670	Ex $13,150	VG+ $9,160	Good $8,220	Poor $2,370

HERCULES SIDE BY SIDE REDBOOK CODE: RB-EJ-S-HERCSS

2 3/4" chamber, English splinter forend, square bodied action, Churchill silver scroll engraving, double trigger, choice of choke.

Production: *current* **Gauge/Bore:** *12 ga., 20 ga., 28 ga., .410*
Action: *SxS*
Barrel Length: 28", 30" **Wt.:** *N/A*
Sights: *bead front*
Capacity: *2*
Stock: *straight grip hardwood*

D2C:	NIB $21,129	Ex $16,075	VG+ $11,625	Good $10,565	LMP: $21,129
C2C:	Mint $20,290	Ex $14,600	VG+ $10,570	Good $9,510	Fair $4,860
Trade-In:	Mint $15,010	Ex $11,850	VG+ $8,250	Good $7,400	Poor $2,130

HERCULES OVER AND UNDER REDBOOK CODE: RB-EJ-S-HERCOU

2 3/4" chamber, rounded forend, trigger plate action, single selective trigger, choice of choke.

Production: *current* **Gauge/Bore:** *12 ga., 20 ga., 28 ga.*
Action: *O/U*
Barrel Length: 28", 30" **Wt.:** *N/A*
Sights: *bead front*
Capacity: *2*
Stock: *semi pistol-grip hardwood*

D2C:	NIB $32,868	Ex $25,000	VG+ $18,080	Good $16,435	LMP: $32,868
C2C:	Mint $31,560	Ex $22,700	VG+ $16,440	Good $14,795	Fair $7,560
Trade-In:	Mint $23,340	Ex $18,425	VG+ $12,820	Good $11,505	Poor $3,300

IMPERIAL OVER AND UNDER REDBOOK CODE: RB-EJ-S-IMPLOU

3" magnum chamber, tapering flat game rib, choke's built to requirements, auto-safe trigger-plate mechanism, single trigger, auto-ejector, bolstered action, brushed bright finish, English rose and scroll, Prince of Wales grip, hand checkering, wooden buttplate.

Production: *current* **Gauge/Bore:** *12 ga., 20 ga.*
Action: *O/U*
Barrel Length: 28", 30" **Wt.:** *N/A*
Sights: *brass bead front*
Capacity: *2*
Stock: *walnut*

D2C:	NIB $65,736	Ex $49,975	VG+ $36,155	Good $32,870	LMP: $65,736
C2C:	Mint $63,110	Ex $45,375	VG+ $32,870	Good $29,585	Fair $15,120
Trade-In:	Mint $46,680	Ex $36,825	VG+ $25,640	Good $23,010	Poor $6,600

Connecticut Shotgun Manufacturing Company

Interestingly, Connecticut Shotgun Manufacturing Company began when its founder, Antony Galazan, was visited by the ATF in 1975 and told that the large number of guns in his possession mandated a federal dealer's license. Galazan complied and started his business selling used shotguns and parts and accessories that the company still manufactures today. Through the years, the company began manufacturing complete firearms as well, and product lines now include side-by-side, sidelock over/under, Parker, limited edition, and large bore models. The company still buys and sells used shotguns and also offers repair work in-house, but the focus lies in manufacturing proprietary arms from start to finish, with the company even making its own tooling, fixturing, and prototypes. Since all construction is done on-site, CSMC stands by its products with extensive warranties for craftsmanship and superior quality.

A-10 AMERICAN   REDBOOK CODE: RB-CN-S-A10AME

Detachable sidelock, coin finished receiver, rose and scroll engraving, hand-rubbed oil stock finish, 24 LPI checkering, 2 3/4" chamber, ventilated top rib, solid center rib, standard forcing cones, five Tru-Lock chokes, single-selective trigger, automatic safety.

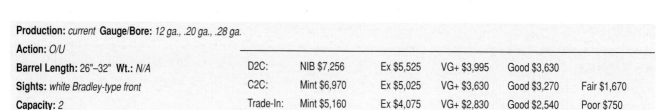

Production: *current* Gauge/Bore: *12 ga., .20 ga., .28 ga.*				
Action: *O/U*				
Barrel Length: *26"–32"* Wt.: *N/A*	D2C:	NIB $7,256	Ex $5,525	VG+ $3,995	Good $3,630
Sights: *white Bradley-type front*	C2C:	Mint $6,970	Ex $5,025	VG+ $3,630	Good $3,270	Fair $1,670
Capacity: *2*	Trade-In:	Mint $5,160	Ex $4,075	VG+ $2,830	Good $2,540	Poor $750
Stock: *hardwood*				

A-10 AMERICAN DELUXE   REDBOOK CODE: RB-CN-S-A10DEL

Detachable sidelock, coin finished receiver, game scene engraving, hand-rubbed oil stock finish, 24 LPI checkering, 2 3/4" chamber, ventilated top rib, solid center rib, standard forcing cones, five Tru-Lock chokes, game or sporting forend, single-selective trigger, automatic safety. Much higher premium can be brought by models with engraving and platinum receiver/barrel.

Production: *current* Gauge/Bore: *12 ga., .20 ga., .28 ga.*				
Action: *O/U*				
Barrel Length: *26"–32"* Wt.: *N/A*	D2C:	NIB $9,950	Ex $7,575	VG+ $5,475	Good $4,975
Sights: *white Bradley-type front*	C2C:	Mint $9,560	Ex $6,875	VG+ $4,980	Good $4,480	Fair $2,290
Capacity: *2*	Trade-In:	Mint $7,070	Ex $5,575	VG+ $3,890	Good $3,485	Poor $1,020
Stock: *hardwood*				

CZ-USA

Ceska zbrojobka Uhersky Brod began producing firearms in Czechoslovakia in 1936. Due to National Defense Council mandates, the company began manufacturing military and civilian firearms. They also produced aircraft machine guns, military pistols, and small-bore rifles until the Nazi occupation began, at which point the plant was commandeered to build and repair Nazi firearms. In 1945, the plant returned to original production until the 1980's when they merged with Agrozet Brno and began producing gears and driveshafts for airplanes and hydraulic powered attachments for tractors. CZ rifles were first imported into the United States through various distributors in 1991, and in 1997, the company took control of their market share here by creating an American subsidiary, CZ-USA, in Oakhurst, California. In 2005, CZ-USA acquired Dan Wesson Firearms, and that brand, long esteemed for innovation, near-indestructibility, and accuracy, is currently being developed further.

612 FIELD REDBOOK CODE: RB-CZ-S-612FLD

Chambered for 2 3/4" and 3" shells and includes three chokes. Single set trigger, 14.5" length of pull, 1.56" drop at comb, and 2.5" drop at heel.

Production: *current* **Gauge/Bore:** *12 ga.*
Action: *pump-action*
Barrel Length: 28" **Wt.:** *6.2 lbs.*
Sights: *front bead*
Capacity: *5*
Stock: *walnut*

D2C:	NIB $360	Ex $275	VG+ $200	Good $180	**LMP: $389**
C2C:	Mint $350	Ex $250	VG+ $180	Good $165	Fair $85
Trade-In:	Mint $260	Ex $225	VG+ $150	Good $130	Poor $60

612 HOME DEFENSE REDBOOK CODE: RB-CZ-S-612HDC

Chambered for 2 3/4" and 3" shells and includes fixed cylinder choke. Single trigger, 14.5" length of pull, 1.625" drop at comb, and 2.25" drop at heel. Also available in 612 Home Defense Combo, with additional 26" vent-rib field barrel and M choke. Add $105 for combo.

Production: *current* **Gauge/Bore:** *12 ga.*
Action: *pump-action*
Barrel Length: 18.5", 26" **Wt.:** *6 lbs.*
Sights: *front post*
Capacity: *5*
Stock: *synthetic*

D2C:	NIB $310	Ex $250	VG+ $175	Good $155	**LMP: $304**
C2C:	Mint $300	Ex $225	VG+ $160	Good $140	Fair $75
Trade-In:	Mint $230	Ex $175	VG+ $130	Good $110	Poor $60

612 WILDFOWL MAGNUM REDBOOK CODE: RB-CZ-S-612MAG

2 3/4", 3", and 3 1/2" chambers with modified and extra full turkey chokes. Camo finish, single trigger, 14.5" length of pull, 1.625" drop at comb, and 2.25" drop at heel.

Production: *current* **Gauge/Bore:** *12 ga.*
Action: *pump-action*
Barrel Length: 26" **Wt.:** *6.8 lbs.*
Sights: *front bead*
Capacity: *5*
Stock: *synthetic*

D2C:	NIB $440	Ex $350	VG+ $245	Good $220	**LMP: $428**
C2C:	Mint $430	Ex $325	VG+ $220	Good $200	Fair $105
Trade-In:	Mint $320	Ex $250	VG+ $180	Good $155	Poor $60

612 HC-P REDBOOK CODE: RB-CZ-S-612HCP

Full-length pump forend and pistol grip stock, chambered for 2 3/4" and 3" shells, accepts CZ choke tubes and ships with one cylinder choke, single trigger, 14.5" length of pull, 1.625" drop at comb, and 2.25" drop at heel.

Production: *current* **Gauge/Bore:** *12 ga.*
Action: *pump-action*
Barrel Length: 20" **Wt.:** *6.5 lbs.*
Sights: *ghost ring sights*
Capacity: *5*
Stock: *synthetic*

D2C:	NIB $350	Ex $275	VG+ $195	Good $175	**LMP: $366**
C2C:	Mint $340	Ex $250	VG+ $180	Good $160	Fair $85
Trade-In:	Mint $250	Ex $200	VG+ $140	Good $125	Poor $60

CZ-USA

620 BIG GAME REDBOOK CODE: RB-CZ-S-620BIG

Smooth bore barrel fitted with cantilever Weaver-style rail for mounting low-power scope or red-dot optics. Rifled choke, single trigger, 13.875" length of pull, 1.56" drop at comb, and 2.24" drop at heel.

Production: *current* **Gauge/Bore:** *20 ga.*
Action: *pump-action*
Barrel Length: 22" **Wt.:** *5.2 lbs.*
Sights: *none*
Capacity: *5*
Stock: *synthetic*

D2C:	NIB $390	Ex $300	VG+ $215	Good $195	**LMP:** $399
C2C:	Mint $380	Ex $275	VG+ $200	Good $180	Fair $90
Trade-In:	Mint $280	Ex $225	VG+ $160	Good $140	Poor $60

912 SEMI-AUTO REDBOOK CODE: RB-CZ-S-912SMA

Modern-style, snag-free recoil paid with long recoil spring in butt of stock, chambered for 2 3/4" and 3" shells, includes three choke tubes, single trigger, 14.5" length of pull, 1.44" drop at comb, and 2.25" drop at heel.

Production: *current* **Gauge/Bore:** *12 ga.*
Action: *semi-auto*
Barrel Length: 28" **Wt.:** *7.3 lbs.*
Sights: *none*
Capacity: *4*
Stock: *walnut*

D2C:	NIB $530	Ex $425	VG+ $295	Good $265	**LMP:** $544
C2C:	Mint $510	Ex $375	VG+ $270	Good $240	Fair $125
Trade-In:	Mint $380	Ex $300	VG+ $210	Good $190	Poor $60

920 SEMI-AUTO REDBOOK CODE: RB-CZ-S-920SMA

Similar to the 912 model, snag-free recoil paid with long recoil spring in butt of stock, chambered for 2 3/4" and 3" shells, includes three choke tubes, single trigger, 14.5" length of pull, 1.44" drop at comb, and 2.25" drop at heel.

Production: *current* **Gauge/Bore:** *20 ga.*
Action: *semi-auto*
Barrel Length: 28" **Wt.:** *6.4 lbs.*
Sights: *bead front*
Capacity: *4*
Stock: *walnut*

D2C:	NIB $550	Ex $425	VG+ $305	Good $275	**LMP:** $557
C2C:	Mint $530	Ex $400	VG+ $280	Good $250	Fair $130
Trade-In:	Mint $400	Ex $325	VG+ $220	Good $195	Poor $60

712 UTILITY REDBOOK CODE: RB-CZ-S-712UTL

Shorter barrel, chambered for 2 3/4" and 3" shells, includes three chokes, single trigger, 14.5" length of pull, 1.44" drop at comb, and 2.25" drop at heel.

Production: *current* **Gauge/Bore:** *12 ga.*
Action: *semi-auto*
Barrel Length: 20" **Wt.:** *6.6 lbs.*
Sights: *bead front*
Capacity: *4*
Stock: *synthetic*

D2C:	NIB $450	Ex $350	VG+ $250	Good $225	**LMP:** $499
C2C:	Mint $440	Ex $325	VG+ $230	Good $205	Fair $105
Trade-In:	Mint $320	Ex $275	VG+ $180	Good $160	Poor $60

712 TARGET REDBOOK CODE: RB-CZ-S-712TGT

10mm stepped rib patterns high for rising trap targets, gas-operated system and full-size target stock minimize recoil, includes three choke tubes, single trigger, chambered for 2 3/4" and 3" shells, 14.75" length of pull, 1.44" drop at comb, and 2.5" drop at heel.

Production: *current* **Gauge/Bore:** *12 ga.*
Action: *semi-auto*
Barrel Length: 30" **Wt.:** *7.6 lbs.*
Sights: *front*
Capacity: *4*
Stock: *walnut*

D2C:	NIB $655	Ex $500	VG+ $365	Good $330	LMP: $680
C2C:	Mint $630	Ex $475	VG+ $330	Good $295	Fair $155
Trade-In:	Mint $470	Ex $375	VG+ $260	Good $230	Poor $90

712 PRACTICAL REDBOOK CODE: RB-CZ-S-712PRC

ATI fluted magazine extension, includes five flush choke tubes, chambered for 2 3/4" and 3" shells, single trigger, 11.25"–15" length of pull, 1.25" drop at comb, and 1.63" drop at heel.

Production: *current* **Gauge/Bore:** *12 ga.*
Action: *semi-auto*
Barrel Length: 22" **Wt.:** *8.1 lbs.*
Sights: *bead front*
Capacity: *10*
Stock: *adjustable 6-position polymer*

D2C:	NIB $670	Ex $525	VG+ $370	Good $335	LMP: $699
C2C:	Mint $650	Ex $475	VG+ $340	Good $305	Fair $155
Trade-In:	Mint $480	Ex $400	VG+ $270	Good $235	Poor $90

712 REDBOOK CODE: RB-CZ-S-712SMA

Gas-operated action and lightweight alloy receiver, chambered for 2 3/4" and 3" shells, chrome-lined bore and black hard chrome exterior finish, three choke tubes and magazine tube plug, 14.5" length of pull, 1.44" drop at comb, 2.25" drop at heel.

Production: *current* **Gauge/Bore:** *12 ga.*
Action: *semi-auto*
Barrel Length: 26", 28" **Wt.:** *7.3 lbs., 7.4 lbs.*
Sights: *front bead*
Capacity: *4*
Stock: *Turkish walnut*

D2C:	NIB $465	Ex $375	VG+ $260	Good $235	LMP: $499
C2C:	Mint $450	Ex $325	VG+ $240	Good $210	Fair $110
Trade-In:	Mint $340	Ex $275	VG+ $190	Good $165	Poor $60

720 REDBOOK CODE: RB-CZ-S-720SMA

Similar to 712 model, gas-operated action and lightweight alloy receiver, chambered for 2 3/4" and 3" shells, chrome-lined bore and black hard chrome exterior finish, three choke tubes and magazine tube plug, 14.5" length of pull, 1.44" drop at comb, 2.25" drop at heel.

Production: *current* **Gauge/Bore:** *20 ga.*
Action: *semi-auto*
Barrel Length: 26", 28" **Wt.:** *6.3 lbs.*
Sights: *front bead*
Capacity: *4*
Stock: *Turkish walnut*

D2C:	NIB $495	Ex $400	VG+ $275	Good $250	LMP: $516
C2C:	Mint $480	Ex $350	VG+ $250	Good $225	Fair $115
Trade-In:	Mint $360	Ex $300	VG+ $200	Good $175	Poor $60

CZ-USA

712 ALS REDBOOK CODE: RB-CZ-S-712ALS
ATI adjustable stock and gas-operated action, chambered for 2 3/4" and 3" shells, single trigger, 12"–14" length of pull, 1.75" drop at comb, and 2.63"–3" drop at heel, includes five chokes.

Production: *current* **Gauge/Bore:** *12 ga.*
Action: *semi-auto*
Barrel Length: 26", 28" **Wt.:** *7.8 lbs.*
Sights: *front bead*
Capacity: *4*
Stock: *synthetic*

D2C:	NIB $550	Ex $425	VG+ $305	Good $275	LMP: $579
C2C:	Mint $530	Ex $400	VG+ $280	Good $250	Fair $130
Trade-In:	Mint $400	Ex $325	VG+ $220	Good $195	Poor $60

720 ALS REDBOOK CODE: RB-CZ-S-720ALS
ATI adjustable stock and gas-operated action, chambered for 2 3/4" and 3" shells, single trigger, 12"–14" length of pull, 1.75" drop at comb, and 2.63"–3" drop at heel, includes five chokes.

Production: *discontinued* **Gauge/Bore:** *20 ga.*
Action: *semi-auto*
Barrel Length: 24" **Wt.:** *6.6 lbs.*
Sights: *front bead*
Capacity: *4*
Stock: *synthetic*

D2C:	NIB $560	Ex $450	VG+ $310	Good $280	LMP: $544
C2C:	Mint $540	Ex $400	VG+ $280	Good $255	Fair $130
Trade-In:	Mint $400	Ex $325	VG+ $220	Good $200	Poor $60

SPORTER STANDARD GRADE REDBOOK CODE: RB-CZ-S-SPRTSG
Single set trigger, adjustable comb, six stainless steel extended choke tubes, 14.75" length of pull.

Production: *current* **Gauge/Bore:** *12 ga.*
Action: *O/U*
Barrel Length: 30", 32" **Wt.:** *8.5 lbs., 8.7 lbs.*
Sights: *front bead*
Capacity: *2*
Stock: *II Grade Monte Carlo*

D2C:	NIB $1,920	Ex $1,475	VG+ $1,060	Good $960	LMP: $1,899
C2C:	Mint $1,850	Ex $1,325	VG+ $960	Good $865	Fair $445
Trade-In:	Mint $1,370	Ex $1,100	VG+ $750	Good $675	Poor $210

SPORTER REDBOOK CODE: RB-CZ-S-SPRT01
Single-set trigger, adjustable comb, deep black chrome finish with hand engraving, six stainless steel extended choke tubes, 14.75" length of pull.

Production: *current* **Gauge/Bore:** *12 ga.*
Action: *O/U*
Barrel Length: 30", 32" **Wt.:** *8.5 lbs., 8.7 lbs.*
Sights: *front bead*
Capacity: *2*
Stock: *III Grade walnut*

D2C:	NIB $2,415	Ex $1,850	VG+ $1,330	Good $1,210	LMP: $2,497
C2C:	Mint $2,320	Ex $1,675	VG+ $1,210	Good $1,090	Fair $560
Trade-In:	Mint $1,720	Ex $1,375	VG+ $950	Good $850	Poor $270

CZ-USA

SPORTER STANDARD GRADE WITH ADJUSTABLE RIB REDBOOK CODE: RB-CZ-S-SPRTAR

Six Kick's stainless steel extended chokes, pistol grip, palm swell, chokes designed by Tom Mack, black chrome receiver, flat vent rib, mechanical trigger, manual tang safety.

Production: *current* **Gauge/Bore:** *12 ga.*

Action: *O/U*

Barrel Length: *30", 32"* **Wt.:** *8.5 lbs., 8.7 lbs.*

Sights: *bead front*

Capacity: *2*

Stock: *Turkish walnut*

D2C:	NIB $2,950	Ex $2,250	VG+ $1,625	Good $1,475	**LMP:** $3,122
C2C:	Mint $2,840	Ex $2,050	VG+ $1,480	Good $1,330	Fair $680
Trade-In:	Mint $2,100	Ex $1,675	VG+ $1,160	Good $1,035	Poor $300

SUPER SCROLL COMBO SET REDBOOK CODE: RB-CZ-S-SCROLL

Ornate hand-engraved scrollwork on receiver, faux sideplates, trigger guard, and monobloc. Both barrel sets equipped with ejectors. Comes standard with five chokes per gauge and a full grip. Ships in a custom-fit aluminum case from Americase. Chambered for 2 3/4" and 3", with 14.5" length of pull, 1.375" drop at comb, and 2.25" drop at heel.

Production: *current* **Gauge/Bore:** *20 ga., 28 ga.*

Action: *O/U*

Barrel Length: *30"* **Wt.:** *6.7 lbs.*

Sights: *none*

Capacity: *2*

Stock: *walnut*

D2C:	NIB $3,560	Ex $2,725	VG+ $1,960	Good $1,780	**LMP:** $3,899
C2C:	Mint $3,420	Ex $2,475	VG+ $1,780	Good $1,605	Fair $820
Trade-In:	Mint $2,530	Ex $2,000	VG+ $1,390	Good $1,250	Poor $360

REDHEAD REDUCED LENGTH REDBOOK CODE: RB-CZ-S-REDREL

Single selective trigger and auto ejectors, chrome-lined barrels with a durable satin chrome finish that is also corrosion-resistant, five chokes, chambered for 2 3/4" and 3", with 13" length of pull, 1.375" drop at comb, and 2.125" drop at heel.

Production: *current* **Gauge/Bore:** *20 ga.*

Action: *O/U*

Barrel Length: *24"* **Wt.:** *6 lbs.*

Sights: *bead front*

Capacity: *2*

Stock: *Turkish walnut*

D2C:	NIB $880	Ex $675	VG+ $485	Good $440	**LMP:** $873
C2C:	Mint $850	Ex $625	VG+ $440	Good $400	Fair $205
Trade-In:	Mint $630	Ex $500	VG+ $350	Good $310	Poor $90

REDHEAD DELUXE REDBOOK CODE: RB-CZ-S-REDDLX

Single selective trigger and auto ejectors, chrome-lined barrels with a durable satin chrome finish that is also corrosion-resistant, five chokes, chambered for 2 3/4" and 3", with 14.5" length of pull, 1.375" drop at comb, and 2.25" drop at heel.

Production: *current* **Gauge/Bore:** *12 ga., 20 ga.*

Action: *O/U*

Barrel Length: *26", 28"* **Wt.:** *6.7 lbs.–7.9 lbs.*

Sights: *bead front*

Capacity: *2*

Stock: *Turkish walnut*

D2C:	NIB $850	Ex $650	VG+ $470	Good $425	**LMP:** $953
C2C:	Mint $820	Ex $600	VG+ $430	Good $385	Fair $200
Trade-In:	Mint $610	Ex $500	VG+ $340	Good $300	Poor $90

CZ-USA

REDHEAD TARGET REDBOOK CODE: RB-CZ-S-REDTGT

Right-hand palm swell and a 10mm stepped rib, set of six Kicks stainless steel extended choke tubes: two Skeet, two LM and two IM; designed by competition shooter Tom Mack. Single trigger, ejector, chambered for 2 3/4" and 3", with 14.75" length of pull, 1.5" drop at comb, and 2.5" drop at heel.

Production: *current* **Gauge/Bore:** *12 ga.*
Action: *O/U*
Barrel Length: 30" **Wt.:** *8 lbs.*
Sights: *bead front*
Capacity: 2
Stock: *Monte Carlo*

D2C:	NIB $1,310	Ex $1,000	VG+ $725	Good $655	**LMP:** $1,389
C2C:	Mint $1,260	Ex $925	VG+ $660	Good $590	Fair $305
Trade-In:	Mint $940	Ex $750	VG+ $520	Good $460	Poor $150

RINGNECK TARGET REDBOOK CODE: RB-CZ-S-RNGTGT

Full-size target stock, Greener top-cross bolt, bottom locking lug, six extended chokes, 3" chamber, 14.75" length of pull.

Production: *current* **Gauge/Bore:** *12 ga.*
Action: *SxS*
Barrel Length: 30" **Wt.:** *7.5 lbs.*
Sights: *bead front*
Capacity: 2
Stock: *Turkish walnut*

D2C:	NIB $1,299	Ex $1,000	VG+ $715	Good $650	**LMP:** $1,298
C2C:	Mint $1,250	Ex $900	VG+ $650	Good $585	Fair $300
Trade-In:	Mint $930	Ex $750	VG+ $510	Good $455	Poor $150

WINGSHOOTER REDBOOK CODE: RB-CZ-S-WINGSH

Elegant and hand-engraved, single selective trigger and auto ejectors, five chokes, chambered for 2 3/4" and 3", with 14.5" length of pull, 1.437" drop at comb, and 2.25" drop at heel.

Production: *current* **Gauge/Bore:** *12 ga., 20 ga.*
Action: *O/U*
Barrel Length: 28" **Wt.:** *6.9 lbs., 7.4 lbs.*
Sights: *bead front*
Capacity: 2
Stock: *Turkish walnut*

D2C:	NIB $985	Ex $750	VG+ $545	Good $495	**LMP:** $999
C2C:	Mint $950	Ex $700	VG+ $500	Good $445	Fair $230
Trade-In:	Mint $700	Ex $575	VG+ $390	Good $345	Poor $120

CANVASBACK GOLD REDBOOK CODE: RB-CZ-S-CBGOLD

Black-chrome receiver engraved with two gold birds, barrels have solid mid-ribs, single-set trigger, pistol grip, flat vent rib, manual tang safety.

Production: *current* **Gauge/Bore:** *12 ga., 20 ga., 28 ga., .410*
Action: *O/U*
Barrel Length: 26", 28" **Wt.:** *6 lbs.–7.5 lbs.*
Sights: *bead front*
Capacity: *2*
Stock: *Turkish walnut*

D2C:	NIB $765	Ex $600	VG+ $425	Good $385	**LMP:** $827
C2C:	Mint $740	Ex $550	VG+ $390	Good $345	Fair $180
Trade-In:	Mint $550	Ex $450	VG+ $300	Good $270	Poor $90

MALLARD REDBOOK CODE: RB-CZ-S-MALLAR

Features the standard box-lock frame with the same hinge system used in the more detailed models, but employs a dual trigger system with double extractors. Includes five chokes, chambered for 2 3/4" and 3", with 14.5" length of pull, 1.375" drop at comb, and 2.25" drop at heel.

CZ-USA

Production: *current* **Gauge/Bore:** *12 ga., 20 ga.*
Action: *O/U*
Barrel Length: 28" **Wt.:** *6.5 lbs., 7.4 lbs.*
Sights: *bead front*
Capacity: *2*
Stock: *Turkish walnut*

D2C:	NIB $550	Ex $425	VG+ $305	Good $275	**LMP:** $583
C2C:	Mint $530	Ex $400	VG+ $280	Good $250	Fair $130
Trade-In:	Mint $400	Ex $325	VG+ $220	Good $195	Poor $60

UPLAND STERLING REDBOOK CODE: RB-CZ-S-UPSTER

CNC-milled steel receiver, stippled grip area on the wrist and forend rather than traditional checkering, includes five chokes, chambered for 2 3/4" and 3", with 14.5" length of pull, 1.375" drop at comb, and 2.25" drop at heel.

Production: *current* **Gauge/Bore:** *12 ga.*
Action: *O/U*
Barrel Length: 28" **Wt.:** *7.5 lbs.*
Sights: *bead front*
Capacity: *2*
Stock: *Turkish walnut*

D2C:	NIB $940	Ex $725	VG+ $520	Good $470	**LMP:** $999
C2C:	Mint $910	Ex $650	VG+ $470	Good $425	Fair $220
Trade-In:	Mint $670	Ex $550	VG+ $370	Good $330	Poor $120

LADY STERLING REDBOOK CODE: RB-CZ-S-LADYST

Special stock dimensions fit for women, 14" length of pull, 1.25" drop at comb, 3.25" drop at heel, single extractor. Handles both 2 3/4" and 3" shells. Five interchangeable flush mount chokes.

Production: *current* **Gauge/Bore:** *12 ga.*
Action: *O/U*
Barrel Length: 28" **Wt.:** *7.5 lbs.*
Sights: *bead front*
Capacity: *2*
Stock: *Turkish walnut*

D2C:	NIB $1,281	Ex $975	VG+ $705	Good $645	**LMP:** $1,281
C2C:	Mint $1,230	Ex $900	VG+ $650	Good $580	Fair $295
Trade-In:	Mint $910	Ex $725	VG+ $500	Good $450	Poor $150

UPLAND ULTRALIGHT REDBOOK CODE: RB-CZ-S-UPULTR

CNC-cut lightweight aluminum alloy frame. Metal coated with a non-reflective, weather-resistant matte finish. Sport-styled stock, no mid-rib between barrels, includes five chokes, chambered for 2 3/4" and 3", with 14.5" length of pull, 1.375" drop at comb, and 2.25" drop at heel.

Production: *current* **Gauge/Bore:** *12 ga.*
Action: *O/U*
Barrel Length: 26", 28" **Wt.:** *5.9 lbs., 6 lbs.*
Sights: *bead front*
Capacity: *2*
Stock: *Turkish walnut*

D2C:	NIB $730	Ex $575	VG+ $405	Good $365	**LMP:** $762
C2C:	Mint $710	Ex $525	VG+ $370	Good $330	Fair $170
Trade-In:	Mint $520	Ex $425	VG+ $290	Good $260	Poor $90

CZ-USA

RINGNECK REDBOOK CODE: RB-CZ-S-RINGNK

Each gauge has its own specific frame size, Greener Top Cross Bolt and bottom locking lug. Includes five chokes, except for 16 gauge and .410, which have Fixed IC and Mod chokes. Chambered for 2 3/4" and 3", with 14.5" length of pull, 1.5" drop at comb, and 2.25" drop at heel. Add $207 for .410 and 16 gauge with fixed chokes.

Production: *current* **Gauge/Bore:** *12 ga., 16 ga., 20 ga., 28 ga., .410*
Action: *SxS*
Barrel Length: 28" **Wt.:** *5.9 lbs., 6.3 lbs., 6.8 lbs.*
Sights: *bead front*
Capacity: *2*
Stock: *Turkish walnut*

D2C:	NIB $1,030	Ex $800	VG+ $570	Good $515	LMP: $1,022
C2C:	Mint $990	Ex $725	VG+ $520	Good $465	Fair $240
Trade-In:	Mint $740	Ex $600	VG+ $410	Good $365	Poor $120

BOBWHITE REDBOOK CODE: RB-CZ-S-BOBWHT

Dual trigger system with straight grip, hand-engraved and case-hardened sideplates. Five chokes, except for 16 gauge and .410, which have Fixed IC and Mod chokes. Chambered for 2 3/4" and/or 3", with 14.5" length of pull, 1.5" drop at comb, and 2.25" drop at heel. Add $196 for .410 and 16 gauge with fixed chokes.

Production: *current* **Gauge/Bore:** *12 ga., 16 ga., 20 ga., 28 ga., .410*
Action: *SxS*
Barrel Length: 26" **Wt.:** *5.2 lbs., 7 lbs.*
Sights: *bead front*
Capacity: *2*
Stock: *Turkish walnut*

D2C:	NIB $690	Ex $525	VG+ $380	Good $345	LMP: $778
C2C:	Mint $670	Ex $500	VG+ $350	Good $315	Fair $160
Trade-In:	Mint $490	Ex $400	VG+ $270	Good $245	Poor $90

HAMMER COACH REDBOOK CODE: RB-CZ-S-HAMCCH

Features double triggers, 19th century color case-hardening, fully functional external hammers, fixed Cylinder bore, chambered for 2 3/4" and 3", 14.5" length of pull, 1.437" drop at comb, and 2.25" drop at heel.

Production: *current* **Gauge/Bore:** *12 ga.*
Action: *SxS*
Barrel Length: 20" **Wt.:** *6.7 lbs.*
Sights: *bead front*
Capacity: *2*
Stock: *Turkish walnut*

D2C:	NIB $890	Ex $700	VG+ $490	Good $445	LMP: $922
C2C:	Mint $860	Ex $625	VG+ $450	Good $405	Fair $205
Trade-In:	Mint $640	Ex $500	VG+ $350	Good $315	Poor $90

HAMMER CLASSIC REDBOOK CODE: RB-CZ-S-HAMCLS

Case-hardened sidelock receiver and fully functional external hammers, includes five chokes, chambered for 2 3/4" and 3", with 14.5" length of pull, 1.437" drop at comb, and 2.25" drop at heel.

Production: *current* **Gauge/Bore:** *12 ga.*
Action: *SxS*
Barrel Length: 30" **Wt.:** *7.5 lbs.*
Sights: *bead front*
Capacity: *2*
Stock: *Turkish walnut*

D2C:	NIB $920	Ex $700	VG+ $510	Good $460	LMP: $963
C2C:	Mint $890	Ex $650	VG+ $460	Good $415	Fair $215
Trade-In:	Mint $660	Ex $525	VG+ $360	Good $325	Poor $120

BRNO 801.1 REDBOOK CODE: RB-CZ-S-BRNO81
Engraved silver receiver, barrel selector, includes three screw-in choke tubes.

Production: *discontinued* **Gauge/Bore:** *12 ga.*
Action: *O/U*
Barrel Length: 30" **Wt.:** *N/A*
Sights: *bead front*
Capacity: *2*
Stock: *Turkish walnut*

D2C:	NIB $2,040	Ex $1,575	VG+ $1,125	Good $1,020	
C2C:	Mint $1,960	Ex $1,425	VG+ $1,020	Good $920	Fair $470
Trade-In:	Mint $1,450	Ex $1,150	VG+ $800	Good $715	Poor $210

BRNO 801.1 MAGNUM REDBOOK CODE: RB-CZ-S-BRNO8M
3 1/2" chamber, fixed choke.

Production: *discontinued* **Gauge/Bore:** *12 ga.*
Action: *O/U*
Barrel Length: 30" **Wt.:** *N/A*
Sights: *bead front*
Capacity: *2*
Stock: *Turkish walnut*

D2C:	NIB $2,800	Ex $2,150	VG+ $1,540	Good $1,400	
C2C:	Mint $2,690	Ex $1,950	VG+ $1,400	Good $1,260	Fair $645
Trade-In:	Mint $1,990	Ex $1,575	VG+ $1,100	Good $980	Poor $300

BRNO COMBO RIFLE/SHOTGUN REDBOOK CODE: RB-CZ-S-BRNOCB
Pairs a 12 gauge shotgun with one of several popular rifle cartridges: .243 Win., .30-06, .308 Win.

Production: *discontinued* **Gauge/Bore:** *12 ga./.243 Win., 30-06 Spfld, .308 Win.*
Action: *O/U*
Barrel Length: 30" **Wt.:** *N/A*
Sights: *ramp front*
Capacity: *2*
Stock: *Turkish walnut*

D2C:	NIB $2,020	Ex $1,550	VG+ $1,115	Good $1,010	
C2C:	Mint $1,940	Ex $1,400	VG+ $1,010	Good $910	Fair $465
Trade-In:	Mint $1,440	Ex $1,150	VG+ $790	Good $710	Poor $210

COMPETITION RINGNECK REDBOOK CODE: RB-CZ-S-CMPRNG
Choke tubes included, single-selective trigger, checkering on stock and pistol grip.

Production: *discontinued* **Gauge/Bore:** *12 ga., 16 ga., 20 ga., 28 ga., .410*
Action: *SxS*
Barrel Length: 26", 28" **Wt.:** *N/A*
Sights: *center bead, front fiber optics*
Capacity: *2*
Stock: *walnut*

D2C:	NIB $2,910	Ex $2,225	VG+ $1,605	Good $1,455	
C2C:	Mint $2,800	Ex $2,025	VG+ $1,460	Good $1,310	Fair $670
Trade-In:	Mint $2,070	Ex $1,650	VG+ $1,140	Good $1,020	Poor $300

REDHEAD MINI REDBOOK CODE: RB-CZ-S-REDMIN

Single selective trigger and extractors, checkering on stock and pistol grip, silver receiver finish.

Production: *discontinued 2011, 2013* **Gauge/Bore:** *12 ga., 20 ga., 28 ga., .410*
Action: *O/U*
Barrel Length: 26", 28" **Wt.:** *6–8 lbs.*
Sights: *none*
Capacity: *2*
Stock: *walnut*

D2C:	NIB $910	Ex $700	VG+ $505	Good $455	
C2C:	Mint $880	Ex $650	VG+ $460	Good $410	Fair $210
Trade-In:	Mint $650	Ex $525	VG+ $360	Good $320	Poor $120

RINGNECK CUSTOM GRADE REDBOOK CODE: RB-CZ-S-RINGCG

Custom grade (case hardened), wood upgrade.

Production: *discontinued 2013* **Gauge/Bore:** *20 ga.*
Action: *SxS*
Barrel Length: 28" **Wt.:** *6.3 lbs.*
Sights: *none*
Capacity: *2*
Stock: *Grade IV walnut*

D2C:	NIB $2,020	Ex $1,550	VG+ $1,115	Good $1,010	
C2C:	Mint $1,940	Ex $1,400	VG+ $1,010	Good $910	Fair $465
Trade-In:	Mint $1,440	Ex $1,150	VG+ $790	Good $710	Poor $210

David McKay Brown

David McKay Brown began gunsmithing in 1957, and his skills culminated in his formation of the company that is his namesake in 1967. He did work for established companies in the firearms industry until 1974 when he produced his own guns with round actions, a type of action that has been made since 1887 but that is almost completely unknown outside of Brown's native Scotland. David McKay Brown separates operations between three facilities, all located in or very near the village of Bothwell, which is just 8 miles out of Glasgow. At present, the company is still an extremely small enterprise with only four employees dedicated to production and only about 30 units produced each year, mostly side-by-side or over/under gaming models. Most models imported to the U.S. are small bore offerings chambered in .410 or 20 gauge.

ROUND ACTION SIDE BY SIDE REDBOOK CODE: RB-DM-S-MBRASS

Chopper lump barrel tubes forged from alloy steel, British specification EN19, coil spring assisted ejectors, precision chokes can be fitted for greater versatility. Price varies with custom specifications.

Production: *current* **Gauge/Bore:** *12 ga., 16 ga., 20 ga., 28 ga., .410*
Action: *SxS*
Barrel Length: 28" or custom **Wt.:** *~5.25–6.5 lbs.*
Sights: *none*
Capacity: *2*
Stock: *Turkish walnut*

D2C:	NIB $44,000	Ex $33,450	VG+ $24,200	Good $22,000	LMP: $68,848
C2C:	Mint $42,240	Ex $30,375	VG+ $22,000	Good $19,800	Fair $10,120
Trade-In:	Mint $31,240	Ex $24,650	VG+ $17,160	Good $15,400	Poor $4,410

ROUND ACTION OVER AND UNDER REDBOOK CODE: RB-DM-S-MBRAOU

Single stable unit with safety work and both locks, with either double or non-selective single trigger mechanism. Demi-block barrels from black annealed EN19 steel with British specification. Thicker action walls, supporting joint pins and buttresses, optional Prince of Wales pistol grip, precision screw-in chokes can be fitted. Price varies with custom specifications.

DAVID MCKAY BROWN

Production: *1992-current* Gauge/Bore: *12 ga., 16 ga., 20 ga., 28 ga.*					
Action: *O/U*	D2C:	NIB $48,000	Ex $36,500	VG+ $26,400	Good $24,000	LMP: $75,107
Barrel Length: *31", 32", or custom* Wt.: *6.1–7.5 lbs.*	C2C:	Mint $46,080	Ex $33,125	VG+ $24,000	Good $21,600	Fair $11,040
Sights: *none*	Trade-In:	Mint $34,080	Ex $26,900	VG+ $18,720	Good $16,800	Poor $4,800
Capacity: *2*					
Stock: *Turkish walnut*					

Escort Shotguns

ESCORT

Escort is a trademark for shotguns that have been imported and distributed by Legacy Sports International out of Reno, Nevada, since 2002. The "Escort" name is actually the name for a product line of shotguns manufactured in Izmir, Turkey, by a company called Hatsan Arms Co. that makes a wide array of shotguns and air guns. The manufacturer machines, heat treats, finishes, molds, welds, engraves, coats, and assembles all parts and then tests all complete firearms in-house. The company prides itself on outsourcing only the raw materials that are used to produce the finished firearms on-site and on being the only Turkish manufacturer licensed to use Mossy Oak camouflage patterns. Escort models imported to the U.S. are of the over/under, semi-automatic, and pump action varieties.

EXTREME REDBOOK CODE: RB-ES-S-EXTREM

3" chamber, 14" length of pull, 5 chokes included, non-slip grip pads on forend and pistol grip, available with Realtree camo patterns, comes with extended waterfowl choke tube.

Production: *current* Gauge/Bore: *12 ga., 20 ga.*					
Action: *semi-auto*					
Barrel Length: *26", 28"* Wt.: *7–7.4 lbs.*	D2C:	NIB $495	Ex $400	VG+ $275	Good $250	LMP: $551
Sights: *HiVis MagniSight fiber optic magnetic sight*	C2C:	Mint $480	Ex $350	VG+ $250	Good $225	Fair $115
Capacity: *6*	Trade-In:	Mint $360	Ex $300	VG+ $200	Good $175	Poor $60
Stock: *black synthetic*					

EXTREME MAGNUM REDBOOK CODE: RB-ES-S-EXTMAG

3 1/2" chamber, 14" length of pull, multichokes, SMART valve gas pistons, available with Realtree camo patterns, extended waterfowl choke tubes.

Production: *current* Gauge/Bore: *12 ga.*					
Action: *semi-auto*					
Barrel Length: *28"* Wt.: *7.7 lbs.*	D2C:	NIB $585	Ex $450	VG+ $325	Good $295	LMP: $649
Sights: *HiVis MagniSight fiber optic magnetic sight*	C2C:	Mint $570	Ex $425	VG+ $300	Good $265	Fair $135
Capacity: *6*	Trade-In:	Mint $420	Ex $350	VG+ $230	Good $205	Poor $60
Stock: *black synthetic*					

ESCORT

SUPREME MAGNUM REDBOOK CODE: RB-ES-S-SUPMAG
Blue barrel, 14" length of pull, SMART valve system, 3" magnum chamber, aluminum alloy receiver, 5 chokes included, chrome-moly barrel, sling swivel studs, two stock adjustment shims.

Production: *current* **Gauge/Bore:** *12 ga., 20 ga.*
Action: *semi-auto*
Barrel Length: 26", 28" **Wt.:** *6.5–7.4 lbs.*
Sights: *fiber-optic front*
Capacity: 6
Stock: *Turkish walnut*

D2C:	NIB $580	Ex $450	VG+ $320	Good $290	LMP: $623
C2C:	Mint $560	Ex $425	VG+ $290	Good $265	Fair $135
Trade-In:	Mint $420	Ex $325	VG+ $230	Good $205	Poor $60

STANDARD MAGNUM REDBOOK CODE: RB-ES-S-STAMAG
Top of receiver milled with 3/8" dovetail, ventilated sight rib, nickel chrome-moly lined barrel, SMART Valve self-regulating gas piston, chokes included are: IC, M, and F.

Production: *current* **Gauge/Bore:** *12 ga., 20 ga.*
Action: *semi-auto*
Barrel Length: 26", 28" **Wt.:** *5.8–7 lbs.*
Sights: *fiber-optic front*
Capacity: 6
Stock: *black polymer*

D2C:	NIB $440	Ex $350	VG+ $245	Good $220	LMP: $489
C2C:	Mint $430	Ex $325	VG+ $220	Good $200	Fair $105
Trade-In:	Mint $320	Ex $250	VG+ $180	Good $155	Poor $60

YOTE REDBOOK CODE: RB-ES-S-YOTEXX
14" length of pull, multichokes, rubber gripping surfaces on stock and forearm.

Production: *current* **Gauge/Bore:** *12 ga.*
Action: *semi-auto*
Barrel Length: 22", 28" **Wt.:** *6.4–7.7 lbs.*
Sights: *fiber-optic front*
Capacity: 6
Stock: *camo synthetic*

D2C:	NIB $430	Ex $350	VG+ $240	Good $215	LMP: $475
C2C:	Mint $420	Ex $300	VG+ $220	Good $195	Fair $100
Trade-In:	Mint $310	Ex $250	VG+ $170	Good $155	Poor $60

PUMP-ACTION REDBOOK CODE: RB-ES-S-PUMPAC
14" length of pull, multichokes, two stock-adjustment shims, sling swivel studs, positive trigger guard safety, large button slide release, dovetail for accessory sights, raised ventilated sight rib, nickel chrome-moly lined barrel.

Production: *current* **Gauge/Bore:** *12 ga., 20 ga.*
Action: *pump-action*
Barrel Length: 26" **Wt.:** *6–7.4 lbs.*
Sights: *fiber-optic front*
Capacity: 3
Stock: *black synthetic*

D2C:	NIB $330	Ex $275	VG+ $185	Good $165	LMP: $379
C2C:	Mint $320	Ex $250	VG+ $170	Good $150	Fair $80
Trade-In:	Mint $240	Ex $200	VG+ $130	Good $120	Poor $60

TURKEY/COYOTE TACTICAL REDBOOK CODE: RB-ES-S-TURCOY

14.5" length of pull, extended pistol grip, extra shell storage in stock, chrome-moly lined barrel, low-density recoil pad, sling swivel studs, Picatinny rail, SMART valve self-regulating system, extra full turkey/coyote choke.

Production: *current* **Gauge/Bore:** *12 ga.*
Action: *semi-auto*
Barrel Length: 24" **Wt.:** *7.4 lbs.*
Sights: *fiber optic ghost ring rear, fiber optic front*
Capacity: 6
Stock: *Realtree camouflage synthetic*

D2C:	NIB $620	Ex $475	VG+ $345	Good $310	**LMP:** $659
C2C:	Mint $600	Ex $450	VG+ $310	Good $280	Fair $145
Trade-In:	Mint $450	Ex $350	VG+ $250	Good $220	Poor $90

OVER/UNDER REDBOOK CODE: RB-ES-S-OVEUND

14" length of pull, multichokes, blue tang lever, adjustable comb, Trio recoil pad, blue barrel, cobblestone grip inserts in stock, nickel plated receiver.

Production: *current* **Gauge/Bore:** *12 ga.*
Action: *O/U*
Barrel Length: 28" **Wt.:** *7.7–8.2 lbs.*
Sights: *fiber optic front*
Capacity: 2
Stock: *wood or synthetic*

D2C:	NIB $595	Ex $475	VG+ $330	Good $300	**LMP:** $641
C2C:	Mint $580	Ex $425	VG+ $300	Good $270	Fair $140
Trade-In:	Mint $430	Ex $350	VG+ $240	Good $210	Poor $60

HOME DEFENSE AIMGUARD REDBOOK CODE: RB-ES-S-HOMDEF

14" length of pull, sling swivel studs, dovetail, large slide release button, matte black receiver finish.

Production: *current* **Gauge/Bore:** *12 ga.*
Action: *pump-action*
Barrel Length: 18" **Wt.:** *6.3 lbs.*
Sights: *rifle-style front*
Capacity: 6
Stock: *black synthetic*

D2C:	NIB $290	Ex $225	VG+ $160	Good $145	**LMP:** $312
C2C:	Mint $280	Ex $225	VG+ $150	Good $135	Fair $70
Trade-In:	Mint $210	Ex $175	VG+ $120	Good $105	Poor $30

HOME DEFENSE MARINEGUARD REDBOOK CODE: RB-ES-S-HODEMG

14" length of pull, sling swivel studs, dovetail, large slide release button, water resistant nickel finish on receiver.

Production: *current* **Gauge/Bore:** *12 ga.*
Action: *pump-action*
Barrel Length: 18" **Wt.:** *6.3 lbs.*
Sights: *rifle-style front*
Capacity: 6
Stock: *black synthetic*

D2C:	NIB $350	Ex $275	VG+ $195	Good $175	**LMP:** $379
C2C:	Mint $340	Ex $250	VG+ $180	Good $160	Fair $85
Trade-In:	Mint $250	Ex $200	VG+ $140	Good $125	Poor $60

ESCORT

HOME DEFENSE TACTICAL SEMI-AUTO   REDBOOK CODE: RB-ES-S-HDTACT

14.5" length of pull, low-density recoil pad, holder for two shells in stock, cushioned pistol grip, upper Picatinny rail, aluminum alloy machined receiver, extended length forend, sling swivel studs, muzzle brake.

Production: *current* **Gauge/Bore:** *12 ga.*
Action: *semi-auto*
Barrel Length: *18"* **Wt.:** *6.9 lbs.*
Sights: *fiber-optic front, ghost ring rear*
Capacity: *6*
Stock: *black TacStock2*

D2C:	NIB $485	Ex $375	VG+ $270	Good $245	LMP: $529
C2C:	Mint $470	Ex $350	VG+ $250	Good $220	Fair $115
Trade-In:	Mint $350	Ex $275	VG+ $190	Good $170	Poor $60

HOME DEFENSE TACTICAL PUMP-ACTION   REDBOOK CODE: RB-ES-S-HDTACP

14.5" length of pull, low-density recoil pad, holder for two shells in stock, cushioned pistol grip, upper Picatinny rail, aluminum alloy machined receiver, extended length forend, sling swivel studs, muzzle brake.

Production: *current* **Gauge/Bore:** *12 ga.*
Action: *pump-action*
Barrel Length: *18"* **Wt.:** *6.9 lbs.*
Sights: *fiber-optic front, ghost ring rear*
Capacity: *6*
Stock: *black TacStock2*

D2C:	NIB $380	Ex $300	VG+ $210	Good $190	LMP: $393
C2C:	Mint $370	Ex $275	VG+ $190	Good $175	Fair $90
Trade-In:	Mint $270	Ex $225	VG+ $150	Good $135	Poor $60

GLADIUS HOME DEFENSE (SEMI-AUTO)   REDBOOK CODE: RB-ES-S-GLADIU

Picatinny rail, cylinder bore barrel, muzzle brake, extended length forend, forend pistol grip, aluminum alloy receiver, cushioned pistol grip, sling swivel studs, low-density recoil pad, built-in holder in stock for 2 shells, adjustable cheek pad. Add $27 for 12 gauge model.

Production: *current* **Gauge/Bore:** *12 ga., 20 ga.*
Action: *semi-auto*
Barrel Length: *18"* **Wt.:** *6.8 lbs.*
Sights: *fiber-optic front, ghost ring rear*
Capacity: *6*
Stock: *black TacStock2 or TacStock3*

D2C:	NIB $550	Ex $425	VG+ $305	Good $275	LMP: $579
C2C:	Mint $530	Ex $400	VG+ $280	Good $250	Fair $130
Trade-In:	Mint $400	Ex $325	VG+ $220	Good $195	Poor $60

GLADIUS HOME DEFENSE (PUMP-ACTION)   REDBOOK CODE: RB-ES-S-GLADPA

Picatinny rail, cylinder bore barrel, muzzle brake, extended length forend, forend pistol grip, aluminum alloy receiver, cushioned pistol grip, sling swivel studs, low-density recoil pad, built-in holder in stock for 2 shells, adjustable cheek pad.

Production: *current* **Gauge/Bore:** *20 ga.*
Action: *pump-action*
Barrel Length: *18"* **Wt.:** *6.8 lbs.*
Sights: *fiber-optic front, ghost ring rear*
Capacity: *6*
Stock: *black TacStock3*

D2C:	NIB $435	Ex $350	VG+ $240	Good $220	LMP: $485
C2C:	Mint $420	Ex $325	VG+ $220	Good $200	Fair $105
Trade-In:	Mint $310	Ex $250	VG+ $170	Good $155	Poor $60

ESCORT

MUDDY GIRL   REDBOOK CODE: RB-ES-S-MUDGIR
14" length of pull, SMART valve gas pistons, 3" magnum chamber, FAST loading system.

Production: *current* **Gauge/Bore:** *20 ga.*
Action: *semi-auto*
Barrel Length: *26"* **Wt.:** *6.5 lbs.*
Sights: *fiber-optic front*
Capacity: *6*
Stock: *Muddy Girl camouflage synthetic*

D2C:	NIB $530	Ex $425	VG+ $295	Good $265	**LMP: $552**
C2C:	Mint $510	Ex $375	VG+ $270	Good $240	Fair $125
Trade-In:	Mint $380	Ex $300	VG+ $210	Good $190	Poor $60

Fabarm USA

FABARM

The Galesi family of Brescia, Italy, started Luciano Galesi, now referred to as Fabarm S.p.A., in 1900. Production began with mainly side-by-side shotguns and pistols, but after World War II, over/under, break-action, pump, and semi-automatic shotgun models were added, along with air rifles. In 1979, the company was purchased and moved to Travagliato, and at that time, focus was placed on the manufacture of semi-automatic, pump, and break-action shotguns. In 2010, the company merged with Caesar Guerini Srl, making the combo the second largest shotgun manufacturing group in Italy. At present, the company produces almost 20,000 weapons per year, and Fabarm firearms are distributed in over 50 countries. The original Italian headquarters is supplemented by a subsidiary in France and one in the U.S. in Cambridge, Maryland.

AXIS RS 12 SPORTING   REDBOOK CODE: RB-FB-S-AXSPRT
Tribore HP barrel, Exis HP competition chokes, steel frame with titanium finish, matte oiled finish on stock, 14.75" length of pull, monolithic locking lug, adjustable trigger, Fabarm Kinetik recoil reducer, optional adjustable comb.

Production: *current* **Gauge/Bore:** *12 ga.*
Action: *O/U*
Barrel Length: *30"–32"* **Wt.:** *8.4 lbs.*
Sights: *none*
Capacity: *2*
Stock: *semi-deluxe Turkish walnut*

D2C:	NIB $2,820	Ex $2,150	VG+ $1,555	Good $1,410	**LMP: $3,085**
C2C:	Mint $2,710	Ex $1,950	VG+ $1,410	Good $1,270	Fair $650
Trade-In:	Mint $2,010	Ex $1,600	VG+ $1,100	Good $990	Poor $300

AXIS RS 12 TRAP O/U   REDBOOK CODE: RB-FB-S-AXTRP1
Exis HP competition chokes, steel frame, titanium frame finish, adjustable comb, hand-oiled matte stock finish, tapered barrel bores, optional recoil reducer, Kinetik recoil reducer, automatic ejectors.

Production: *current* **Gauge/Bore:** *12 ga.*
Action: *O/U*
Barrel Length: *32"* **Wt.:** *8.6 lbs.*
Sights: *none*
Capacity: *2*
Stock: *semi-deluxe Turkish walnut*

D2C:	NIB $3,950	Ex $3,025	VG+ $2,175	Good $1,975	**LMP: $4,115**
C2C:	Mint $3,800	Ex $2,750	VG+ $1,980	Good $1,780	Fair $910
Trade-In:	Mint $2,810	Ex $2,225	VG+ $1,550	Good $1,385	Poor $420

FABARM

AXIS RS 12 TRAP UNSINGLE REDBOOK CODE: RB-FB-S-AXTRP2

Exis HP competition chokes, steel frame, titanium frame finish, adjustable comb, hand-oiled matte stock finish, tapered barrel bores, optional recoil reducer, Kinetik recoil reducer, automatic ejectors.

Production: *current* **Gauge/Bore:** *12 ga.*
Action: *O/U, unsingle*
Barrel Length: 34" **Wt.:** *8.6 lbs.*
Sights: *none*
Capacity: *1*
Stock: *semi-deluxe Turkish walnut*

D2C:	NIB $3,950	Ex $3,025	VG+ $2,175	Good $1,975	**LMP:** $4,115
C2C:	Mint $3,800	Ex $2,750	VG+ $1,980	Good $1,780	Fair $910
Trade-In:	Mint $2,810	Ex $2,225	VG+ $1,550	Good $1,385	Poor $420

ELOS B REDBOOK CODE: RB-FB-S-ELOSBA

Tribore HP barrel, steel or aluminum alloy frame, hand-oiled matte stock finish, round action, Inner HP chokes.

Production: *current* **Gauge/Bore:** *20 ga., 28 ga.*
Action: *O/U*
Barrel Length: 28" **Wt.:** *6.6 lbs.*
Sights: *bead front*
Capacity: *2*
Stock: *semi-deluxe Turkish walnut*

D2C:	NIB $2,260	Ex $1,725	VG+ $1,245	Good $1,130	**LMP:** $2,420
C2C:	Mint $2,170	Ex $1,575	VG+ $1,130	Good $1,020	Fair $520
Trade-In:	Mint $1,610	Ex $1,275	VG+ $890	Good $795	Poor $240

ELOS DELUXE REDBOOK CODE: RB-FB-S-ELOSDX

Tribore HP barrel, Inner HP choke tubes, steel or aluminum alloy frame, round action engraved with contemporary game scene, pistol grip style stock, semi-Schnabel forend with satin oil finish.

Production: *current* **Gauge/Bore:** *20 ga., 28 ga.*
Action: *O/U*
Barrel Length: 28" **Wt.:** *5.9–6.6 lbs.*
Sights: *bead front*
Capacity: *2*
Stock: *European walnut*

D2C:	NIB $2,630	Ex $2,000	VG+ $1,450	Good $1,315	**LMP:** $2,980
C2C:	Mint $2,530	Ex $1,825	VG+ $1,320	Good $1,185	Fair $605
Trade-In:	Mint $1,870	Ex $1,475	VG+ $1,030	Good $925	Poor $270

XLR5 VELOCITY FR REDBOOK CODE: RB-FB-S-XVFLAT

Stainless steel piston gas operated, Tribore HP barrel, Exis HP competition chokes, black anodized frame finish, Triwood wood finish, 14.75" length of pull, flat rib, oversized bolt handle, 3 magazine cap weights, adjustable trigger, Fabarm shim system.

Production: *current* **Gauge/Bore:** *12 ga.*
Action: *semi-auto*
Barrel Length: 30", 32" **Wt.:** *7.6 lbs., 7.8 lbs.*
Sights: *bead front*
Capacity: *4*
Stock: *European walnut*

D2C:	NIB $1,830	Ex $1,400	VG+ $1,010	Good $915	**LMP:** $1,950
C2C:	Mint $1,760	Ex $1,275	VG+ $920	Good $825	Fair $425
Trade-In:	Mint $1,300	Ex $1,025	VG+ $720	Good $645	Poor $210

XLR5 VELOCITY LR REDBOOK CODE: RB-FB-S-XVLONG
Stainless steel piston gas operated, Tribore HP, Exis HP competition chokes, adjustable comb, black anodized or titanium silver frame finish, ramp style fixed rib. Add $300 for titanium receiver.

Production: *current* **Gauge/Bore:** *12 ga.*

Action: *semi-auto*

Barrel Length: 30"–32" **Wt.:** *8.3 lbs.*

Sights: *bead front*

Capacity: *4*

Stock: *European walnut*

D2C:	NIB $2,100	Ex $1,600	VG+ $1,155	Good $1,050	LMP: $2,215
C2C:	Mint $2,020	Ex $1,450	VG+ $1,050	Good $945	Fair $485
Trade-In:	Mint $1,500	Ex $1,200	VG+ $820	Good $735	Poor $210

XLR5 VELOCITY REDBOOK CODE: RB-FB-S-XVNORM
Pulse Piston gas operating system, Tribore HP barrel, 2.75" chamber, Exis HP competition chokes, black anodized or titanium silver frame finish, adjustable comb, hand-oiled matte stock finish, 14.75" length of pull, weight adjustable magazine cap, integrated recoil reducer. Add $300 for titanium silver receiver finish.

Production: *current* **Gauge/Bore:** *12 ga.*

Action: *semi-auto*

Barrel Length: 30"–32" **Wt.:** *8.3 lbs.*

Sights: *bead front*

Capacity: *4*

Stock: *Turkish walnut*

D2C:	NIB $2,590	Ex $1,975	VG+ $1,425	Good $1,295	LMP: $2,700
C2C:	Mint $2,490	Ex $1,800	VG+ $1,300	Good $1,170	Fair $600
Trade-In:	Mint $1,840	Ex $1,475	VG+ $1,020	Good $910	Poor $270

Fausti USA Inc.

Fausti Stefano Ltd. was founded by Cavalier Stefano Fausti in 1948 in Brescia, Italy, and the company is now run by his three daughters, Elena, Giovanna, and Barbara—all of whom are avid hunters who are directly involved in the design and development of current product lines. The company specializes in side-by-side and over/under shotguns, and the staff at Fausti still assembles, stocks, and finishes all shotguns by hand, although the components themselves are produced by CNC machinery. The company's high end products are featured in the Fausti Boutique line that is designed with exquisite quality and aesthetics as its focus. Fausti offers base models, but a variety of shotgun models are highly customizable with varying wood grades, engravings, etc. The company opened an American subsidiary in Fredericksburg, Virginia, in 2009.

BRIXIAN LX FUTURO ANTICO REDBOOK CODE: RB-FS-S-BLXFAN
Fixed or multichokes, high-polished barrel flats, box lock, scaled frame, round forend, steel grip cap, oil finished stock, long tang trigger guard. Market research provides no conclusive pricing suggestion(s) for this particular model.

Production: *current* **Gauge/Bore:** *12 ga., 16 ga., 20 ga., 28 ga., .410*

Action: *SxS*

Barrel Length: 26", 28", 29" **Wt.:** *N/A*

Sights: *brass bead front*

Capacity: *2*

Stock: *5A Turkish walnut*

FAUSTI

CLASS REDBOOK CODE: RB-FS-S-CLASSX

Laser engraved with gold inlays, 3" chamber, 14 3/8" length of pull, automatic ejector. Includes C, IC, M, IM, and F chokes.
Add $550 for 16 ga., 28 ga., or .410 models.

Production: *current* Gauge/Bore: *12 ga., 16 ga., 20 ga., 28 ga., .410*					
Action: *O/U*					
Barrel Length: *26"–30"* Wt.: *5.8–7.3 lbs.*	D2C:	NIB $2,116	Ex $1,625	VG+ $1,165	Good $1,060	**LMP: $2,449**
Sights: *metallic bead front*	C2C:	Mint $2,040	Ex $1,475	VG+ $1,060	Good $955	Fair $490
Capacity: *2*	Trade-In:	Mint $1,510	Ex $1,200	VG+ $830	Good $745	Poor $240
Stock: *AA walnut*					

CLASS ROUND (THEME 1-2) REDBOOK CODE: RB-FS-S-CLAR12

Fixed or multichokes, jewel barrel flats, box lock, single selective trigger, auto ejector, round forend,
Prince of Wales grip, oil finished wood, long tang trigger guard. Pricing this particular model is difficult; the range projected here reveals the best estimation.

Production: *current* Gauge/Bore: *16 ga., 20 ga., 28 ga., .410*					
Action: *O/U*					
Barrel Length: *26", 28", 29"* Wt.: *N/A*	D2C:	NIB $10,557	Ex $8,025	VG+ $5,810	Good $5,280	
Sights: *brass bead front*	C2C:	Mint $10,140	Ex $7,300	VG+ $5,280	Good $4,755	Fair $2,430
Capacity: *2*	Trade-In:	Mint $7,500	Ex $5,925	VG+ $4,120	Good $3,695	Poor $1,080
Stock: *4A Turkish walnut*					

CLASS ROUND REDBOOK CODE: RB-FS-S-CLAROU

Hand rounded receiver, coin or color case finishing, pierced top lever, round pistol grip, Scottish checkering,
hand finished engraving, 3" chamber, 14 3/8" length of pull, single selectable trigger, automatic ejector. Includes C, IC, M, IM, and F chokes.

Production: *current* Gauge/Bore: *16 ga., 20 ga., .410*					
Action: *O/U*					
Barrel Length: *28", 30"* Wt.: *5.8–6.3 lbs.*	D2C:	NIB $4,350	Ex $3,325	VG+ $2,395	Good $2,175	**LMP: $4,789**
Sights: *metallic bead front*	C2C:	Mint $4,180	Ex $3,025	VG+ $2,180	Good $1,960	Fair $1,005
Capacity: *2*	Trade-In:	Mint $3,090	Ex $2,450	VG+ $1,700	Good $1,525	Poor $450
Stock: *AAA walnut*					

CLASS SL REDBOOK CODE: RB-FS-S-CLASSL

Pierced top lever, laser engraved, 3" chamber, 14 3/8" length of pull, single selectable trigger,
automatic ejector. Chokes included: C, IC, M, IM, and F. Add $588 for 16 ga., 28 ga., or .410 models.

Production: *current* Gauge/Bore: *12 ga., 16 ga., 20 ga., 28 ga., .410*					
Action: *O/U*					
Barrel Length: *26"–30"* Wt.: *5.8–7.3 lbs.*	D2C:	NIB $2,650	Ex $2,025	VG+ $1,460	Good $1,325	**LMP: $3,206**
Sights: *metallic bead front*	C2C:	Mint $2,550	Ex $1,850	VG+ $1,330	Good $1,195	Fair $610
Capacity: *2*	Trade-In:	Mint $1,890	Ex $1,500	VG+ $1,040	Good $930	Poor $270
Stock: *AA walnut*					

CLASS SL DE LUXE   REDBOOK CODE: RB-FS-S-SLDELU

Fixed or multichokes, single selective trigger, auto ejection, round forend, straight English stock, oil finished wood.

FAUSTI

Production: *current* **Gauge/Bore:** *12 ga., 16 ga., 20 ga., 28 ga., .410*
Action: *O/U*
Barrel Length: *26", 28", 29"* **Wt.:** *N/A*
Sights: *brass bead front*
Capacity: *2*
Stock: *4A Turkish walnut*

D2C:	NIB $7,137	Ex $5,425	VG+ $3,930	Good $3,570	
C2C:	Mint $6,860	Ex $4,925	VG+ $3,570	Good $3,215	Fair $1,645
Trade-In:	Mint $5,070	Ex $4,000	VG+ $2,790	Good $2,500	Poor $720

CLASS SL "WOODCOCK DEDICATED"   REDBOOK CODE: RB-FS-S-CLSLWD

Fixed or multichokes, box lock, jewel barrel flats, side plates, single selective trigger, automatic ejection, round forend, Prince of Wales grip, long tang trigger guard.

Production: *current* **Gauge/Bore:** *12 ga., 16 ga., 20 ga., 28 ga., .410*
Action: *O/U*
Barrel Length: *26", 28", 29"* **Wt.:** *N/A*
Sights: *brass bead front*
Capacity: *2*
Stock: *3A Turkish walnut*

D2C:	NIB $6,990	Ex $5,325	VG+ $3,845	Good $3,495	
C2C:	Mint $6,720	Ex $4,825	VG+ $3,500	Good $3,150	Fair $1,610
Trade-In:	Mint $4,970	Ex $3,925	VG+ $2,730	Good $2,450	Poor $720

CALEDON   REDBOOK CODE: RB-FS-S-CALEDO

Laser engraving on chrome plating, single oversize block, double lugs, internally-chromed bore, oil finished stock, 14.5" length of pull, single selectable trigger, automatic ejector. Add $570 for 16 ga., 28 ga., or .410 models.

Production: *current* **Gauge/Bore:** *12 ga., 16 ga., 20 ga., 28 ga.*
Action: *O/U*
Barrel Length: *26"–30"* **Wt.:** *5.8–7.3 lbs.*
Sights: *metallic bead front*
Capacity: *2*
Stock: *A+ walnut*

D2C:	NIB $1,840	Ex $1,400	VG+ $1,015	Good $920	**LMP:** $1,999
C2C:	Mint $1,770	Ex $1,275	VG+ $920	Good $830	Fair $425
Trade-In:	Mint $1,310	Ex $1,050	VG+ $720	Good $645	Poor $210

CALEDON SL   REDBOOK CODE: RB-FS-S-CALESL

Coin finishing on receiver, single oversize block or double lugs, 3" chamber, oil finished stock, 14.5" length of pull, round pistol grip, single selectable trigger, automatic ejector. Includes C, IC, M, IM, and F chokes.

Production: *current* **Gauge/Bore:** *12 ga., 20 ga., 28 ga., .410*
Action: *O/U*
Barrel Length: *26"–30"* **Wt.:** *5.8–7.3 lbs.*
Sights: *metallic bead front*
Capacity: *2*
Stock: *AA+ walnut*

D2C:	NIB $2,630	Ex $2,000	VG+ $1,450	Good $1,315	**LMP:** $2,749
C2C:	Mint $2,530	Ex $1,825	VG+ $1,320	Good $1,185	Fair $605
Trade-In:	Mint $1,870	Ex $1,475	VG+ $1,030	Good $925	Poor $270

DEA REDBOOK CODE: RB-FS-S-DEAXXX

3" chamber, oil finished stock, 14 3/8" length of pull, single-set trigger, automatic ejector. Includes C, IC, M, IM, and F chokes. Add $640 for 16 ga., 28 ga., and .410 models.

Production: *current* Gauge/Bore: *12 ga., 16 ga., 20 ga., 28 ga., .410*				
Action: *SxS*				
Barrel Length: 26", 28", 30" **Wt.:** *4.9–6.8 lbs.*	D2C:	NIB $2,765	Ex $2,125	VG+ $1,525	Good $1,385	**LMP: $3,350**
Sights: *metallic bead front*	C2C:	Mint $2,660	Ex $1,925	VG+ $1,390	Good $1,245	Fair $640
Capacity: 2	Trade-In:	Mint $1,970	Ex $1,550	VG+ $1,080	Good $970	Poor $300
Stock: *AAA walnut*				

DEA DUETTO REDBOOK CODE: RB-FS-S-DEADUE

Color case or coin finish, 3" chamber, oil-finished stock, 14 3/8" length of pull, single-set trigger, automatic ejector. Includes C, IC, M, IM, and F chokes.

Production: *current* Gauge/Bore: *28 ga., .410*				
Action: *SxS*				
Barrel Length: 28" **Wt.:** *5 lbs.*	D2C:	NIB $4,597	Ex $3,500	VG+ $2,530	Good $2,300	**LMP: $5,300**
Sights: *metallic bead front*	C2C:	Mint $4,420	Ex $3,175	VG+ $2,300	Good $2,070	Fair $1,060
Capacity: 2	Trade-In:	Mint $3,270	Ex $2,575	VG+ $1,800	Good $1,610	Poor $480
Stock: *AAA walnut*				

DEA BRITISH SL (THEME 7-8) REDBOOK CODE: RB-FS-S-DEABSL

Fixed or multichokes, high-polished barrel flats, box lick, scaled frame, side plates, single trigger, auto ejector, semi-beavertail forend, straight English style stock.

Production: *current* Gauge/Bore: *12 ga., 16 ga., 20 ga., 28 ga., .410*				
Action: *SxS*				
Barrel Length: 26", 28", 29" **Wt.:** *N/A*	D2C:	NIB $20,950	Ex $15,925	VG+ $11,525	Good $10,475	
Sights: *brass bead front*	C2C:	Mint $20,120	Ex $14,475	VG+ $10,480	Good $9,430	Fair $4,820
Capacity: 2	Trade-In:	Mint $14,880	Ex $11,750	VG+ $8,180	Good $7,335	Poor $2,100
Stock: *4A Turkish walnut*				

DEA SL "WOODCOCK DEDICATED" REDBOOK CODE: RB-FS-S-DEASLW

Silver engraving inlay in case colored receiver, jewel barrel flats, box lock, side plates, scaled frame, single trigger, auto ejection, semi-beavertail forend, oil finished stock, long tang trigger guard.

Production: *current* Gauge/Bore: *12 ga., 16 ga., 20 ga., 28 ga., .410*				
Action: *SxS*				
Barrel Length: 26", 28", 29" **Wt.:** *N/A*	D2C:	NIB $6,990	Ex $5,325	VG+ $3,845	Good $3,495	
Sights: *bead front*	C2C:	Mint $6,720	Ex $4,825	VG+ $3,500	Good $3,150	Fair $1,610
Capacity: 2	Trade-In:	Mint $4,970	Ex $3,925	VG+ $2,730	Good $2,450	Poor $720
Stock: *3A Turkish walnut*				

DEA SL REDBOOK CODE: RB-FS-S-DEASLX

Fixed or multichokes, jewel barrel flats, box lock, side plates, single trigger, auto ejector, semi-beavertail forend, straight English style stock, oil finished wood, rubber recoil pad, long tang trigger guard.

Production: *current* **Gauge/Bore:** *12 ga., 16 ga., 20 ga., 28 ga., .410*
Action: *SxS*
Barrel Length: 26", 28", 29" **Wt.:** *N/A*
Sights: *brass bead front*
Capacity: 2
Stock: *3A Turkish walnut*

D2C:	NIB $4,295	Ex $3,275	VG+ $2,365	Good $2,150	
C2C:	Mint $4,130	Ex $2,975	VG+ $2,150	Good $1,935	Fair $990
Trade-In:	Mint $3,050	Ex $2,425	VG+ $1,680	Good $1,505	Poor $450

DEA BRITISH REDBOOK CODE: RB-FS-S-DEABRI

Fixed or multichokes, high-polished barrel flats, box lock, side plates, scaled frame, single trigger, auto ejector, semi-beavertail forend, long tang trigger guard.

Production: *current* **Gauge/Bore:** *16 ga., 20 ga., 28 ga., .410*
Action: *SxS*
Barrel Length: 26", 28", 29" **Wt.:** *N/A*
Sights: *brass bead front*
Capacity: 2
Stock: *4A Turkish walnut*

D2C:	NIB $13,557	Ex $10,325	VG+ $7,460	Good $6,780	
C2C:	Mint $13,020	Ex $9,375	VG+ $6,780	Good $6,105	Fair $3,120
Trade-In:	Mint $9,630	Ex $7,600	VG+ $5,290	Good $4,745	Poor $1,380

MAGNIFICENT FIELD REDBOOK CODE: RB-FS-S-MAGFIE

Tri-dimensional laser engraving, 3" chamber, oil finished stock, 14 3/8" length of pull, round pistol grip style, single selectable trigger, automatic ejector. Includes C, IC, M, IM, and F chokes.

Production: *current* **Gauge/Bore:** *12 ga., 16 ga., 20 ga., 28 ga., .410*
Action: *O/U*
Barrel Length: 26"–30" **Wt.:** *5.9–7.4 lbs.*
Sights: *metallic bead front*
Capacity: 2
Stock: *AAA+ walnut*

D2C:	NIB $3,875	Ex $2,950	VG+ $2,135	Good $1,940	
C2C:	Mint $3,720	Ex $2,675	VG+ $1,940	Good $1,745	Fair $895
Trade-In:	Mint $2,760	Ex $2,175	VG+ $1,520	Good $1,360	Poor $390

MAGNIFICENT SPORTING REDBOOK CODE: RB-FS-S-MAGSPO

Long forcing cones, oversized bore, 10mm top rib, 5 high-performance Fausti chokes, rubber recoil pad, adjustable comb available, 3" chamber, 14 3/8" length of pull, single selectable trigger, automatic ejector. Chokes included: C, IC, M, IM, F

Production: *current* **Gauge/Bore:** *12 ga., 20 ga., 28 ga., .410*
Action: *O/U*
Barrel Length: 28", 30", 32" **Wt.:** *5.9–7.4 lbs.*
Sights: *competition bead*
Capacity: 2
Stock: *AAA+ walnut*

D2C:	NIB $4,651	Ex $3,550	VG+ $2,560	Good $2,330	
C2C:	Mint $4,470	Ex $3,225	VG+ $2,330	Good $2,095	Fair $1,070
Trade-In:	Mint $3,310	Ex $2,625	VG+ $1,820	Good $1,630	Poor $480

FAUSTI

NOBLESSE REDBOOK CODE: RB-FS-S-NOBLES
Gold and silver engraving on case-colored receiver, choice of two engraving themes, high polished barrel flats, side lock, color-case hardened, double trigger, splinter forend, straight English stock, long tang trigger guard.

Production: *current* Gauge/Bore: *12 ga., 16 ga., 20 ga., 28 ga.*
Action: *SxS*
Barrel Length: 26", 28", 29" Wt.: *N/A*
Sights: *bead front*
Capacity: 2
Stock: *4A Turkish walnut*

D2C:	NIB $12,595	Ex $9,575	VG+ $6,930	Good $6,300	
C2C:	Mint $12,100	Ex $8,700	VG+ $6,300	Good $5,670	Fair $2,900
Trade-In:	Mint $8,950	Ex $7,075	VG+ $4,920	Good $4,410	Poor $1,260

FNH USA

Belgium firearm manufacturer Fabrique Nationale d'Herstal, or FN Herstal, began operations in the late 1880s and has remained a significant force in the firearms industry ever since. Now a subsidiary of the Herstal Group, the entity that also controls Browning and Winchester, FNH became a dominate force in the firearms industry after teaming with John Moses Browning in 1897 to develop and manufacture an array of significant weapons, such as the Browning Hi-Power and the M2 Machine Gun. It's well known within the firearms industry that the Herstal Group manufactures all Browning firearms, making the two companies essentially one and the same. In 1998, the Herstal Group formed FN USA, its American marketing and distribution subsidiary, in McLean, Virginia. The company also manufactures some weapons at the plant in Columbia, South Carolina, dubbed FN Manufacturing. FNH and Browning together stand as two of the most recognizable and influential names in the history of modern firearms.

FN SLP REDBOOK CODE: RB-FN-S-FNSLPX
3" chamber, active valve gas system, Standard Invector choke tube system, 14" length of pull, matte black finish, two-piece bolt, aluminum alloy receiver, hard chromed bore, interchangeable choke tubes, non-slip recoil pad, steel sling-swivel studs, crossbolt safety on rear trigger guard, extended tube.

Production: *current* Gauge/Bore: *12 ga.*
Action: *semi-auto*
Barrel Length: 18" Wt.: *7.7 lbs.*
Sights: *high profile, adjustable rear*
Capacity: 7
Stock: *black synthetic*

D2C:	NIB $1,375	Ex $1,050	VG+ $760	Good $690	
C2C:	Mint $1,320	Ex $950	VG+ $690	Good $620	Fair $320
Trade-In:	Mint $980	Ex $775	VG+ $540	Good $485	Poor $150

FN SLP TACTICAL REDBOOK CODE: RB-FN-S-SLPTAC
Active valve gas system, 3" magnum chamber, interchangeable recoil pads, aluminum alloy receiver, hard-chromed bore barrel, Standard Invector interchangeable choke tubes, checkered gripping panels on forearm and pistol grip, steel sling-swivel studs, curved-bolt operating handle, extended magazine tube.

Production: *current* Gauge/Bore: *12 ga.*
Action: *semi-auto*
Barrel Length: 18" Wt.: *7.4 lbs.*
Sights: *high profile adjustable ghost-ring front and rear*
Capacity: 7
Stock: *matte black synthetic*

D2C:	NIB $1,600	Ex $1,225	VG+ $880	Good $800	
C2C:	Mint $1,540	Ex $1,125	VG+ $800	Good $720	Fair $370
Trade-In:	Mint $1,140	Ex $900	VG+ $630	Good $560	Poor $180

FN SLP MK 1 REDBOOK CODE: RB-FN-S-SLPMK1

Active valve gas system, two-piece bolt, aluminum alloy receiver, top-mounted cantilever Weaver-pattern accessory rail, 3" chamber, Standard Vector interchangeable choke tubes, checkered gripping panels on forearm and grip, non-slip recoil pad, steel sling swivel studs, receiver-mounted bolt release, crossbolt safety on rear of trigger guard, extended tube magazine.

Production: *current* **Gauge/Bore:** *12 ga.*
Action: *semi-auto*
Barrel Length: 22" **Wt.:** *7.9 lbs.*
Sights: *low-profile adjustable folding rear blade and red fiber-optic front*
Capacity: *9*
Stock: *matte black synthetic*

D2C:	NIB $1,300	Ex $1,000	VG+ $715	Good $650	
C2C:	Mint $1,250	Ex $900	VG+ $650	Good $585	Fair $300
Trade-In:	Mint $930	Ex $750	VG+ $510	Good $455	Poor $150

FN SLP MK 1 TACTICAL REDBOOK CODE: RB-FN-S-MK1TAC

Active valve gas system, 3" magnum chamber, two-piece bolt, interchangeable recoil pads, aluminum alloy receiver, top-mounted cantilever Weaver-pattern accessory rail, hard-chromed bore barrel, Standard Invector interchangeable choke rubes, checkered gripping panels on forearm and grip, interchangeable comb inserts, steel-sling swivel studs, receiver-mounted bolt release button, crossbolt safety on trigger guard, extended tube magazine.

Production: *current* **Gauge/Bore:** *12 ga.*
Action: *semi-auto*
Barrel Length: 18" **Wt.:** *7.9 lbs.*
Sights: *low-profile adjustable folding rear blade and red fiber-optic front*
Capacity: *7*
Stock: *matte black synthetic*

D2C:	NIB $1,475	Ex $1,125	VG+ $815	Good $740	
C2C:	Mint $1,420	Ex $1,025	VG+ $740	Good $665	Fair $340
Trade-In:	Mint $1,050	Ex $850	VG+ $580	Good $520	Poor $150

FN SC1 OVER/UNDER REDBOOK CODE: RB-FN-S-SC1OVU

Invector-Plus choke, ventilated top rib, ported vent rib with Invector-Plus choke threads, adjustable for comb height and length of pull, recoil-activated single-stage trigger, tang safety doubles as barrel selector.

Production: *current* **Gauge/Bore:** *12 ga.*
Action: *O/U*
Barrel Length: 30" **Wt.:** *8.2 lbs.*
Sights: *ventilated top rib with white mid-bead, fiber optic front*
Capacity: *2*
Stock: *blue, black, or green checkered laminated wood*

D2C:	NIB $2,550	Ex $1,950	VG+ $1,405	Good $1,275	
C2C:	Mint $2,450	Ex $1,775	VG+ $1,280	Good $1,150	Fair $590
Trade-In:	Mint $1,820	Ex $1,450	VG+ $1,000	Good $895	Poor $270

FN P-12 REDBOOK CODE: RB-FN-S-FNP12X

3" chamber, matte black metal finish, aluminum alloy receiver, cantilever barrel, chrome-lined chamber and bore, Standard Invector interchangeable choke tubes, Weaver rail pattern, non-slip recoil pad, sling-swivel studs, speed pump design, curved operating handle, extended tube magazine.

Production: *current* **Gauge/Bore:** *12 ga.*
Action: *pump-action*
Barrel Length: 18" **Wt.:** *7.4 lbs.*
Sights: *flip-up iron rear, fiber-optic front*
Capacity: *6*
Stock: *matte black synthetic*

D2C:	NIB $765	Ex $600	VG+ $425	Good $385	
C2C:	Mint $740	Ex $550	VG+ $390	Good $345	Fair $180
Trade-In:	Mint $550	Ex $450	VG+ $300	Good $270	Poor $90

Franchi USA

In 1868, Luigi Franchi S.p.A. opened its doors in Brescia, Italy. The company specializes in side-by-side and over/under double-barrel models and semi-automatics. The company was still operated by the founding family until 1987 when it was acquired by Milan-based Socimi. Following Socimi's bankruptcy in 1993, the brand was purchased by the Beretta Group, but it was later acquired by its current owner, Benelli USA, in 1998. Franchi USA was established as the American headquarters for the company in Pocomoke, Maryland.

48 AL FIELD DELUXE REDBOOK CODE: RB-FR-S-48ALDX

Long-recoiling sub-gauge, 14 1/4" length of pull, 1.5" drop at comb, 2 3/4" chamber. Comes with IC, M, and F chokes.

Production: *current* **Gauge/Bore:** *20 ga., 28 ga.*
Action: *semi-auto*
Barrel Length: 26" **Wt.:** *~5.5 lbs.*
Sights: *bead*
Capacity: *5*
Stock: *satin walnut*

D2C:	NIB $1,199	Ex $925	VG+ $660	Good $600	**LMP:** $1,199
C2C:	Mint $1,160	Ex $850	VG+ $600	Good $540	Fair $280
Trade-In:	Mint $860	Ex $675	VG+ $470	Good $420	Poor $120

48 AL FIELD REDBOOK CODE: RB-FR-S-48ALFI

Long-recoiling sub-gauge, 14 1/4" length of pull, 1.5" drop at comb, 2 3/4" chamber. Comes with IC, M, and F chokes.

Production: *current* **Gauge/Bore:** *20 ga., 28 ga.*
Action: *semi-auto*
Barrel Length: 24", 26", 28" **Wt.:** *5.4–5.7 lbs.*
Sights: *bead*
Capacity: *5*
Stock: *satin walnut*

D2C:	NIB $899	Ex $700	VG+ $495	Good $450	**LMP:** $899
C2C:	Mint $870	Ex $625	VG+ $450	Good $405	Fair $210
Trade-In:	Mint $640	Ex $525	VG+ $360	Good $315	Poor $90

48 AL HUNTER REDBOOK CODE: RB-FR-S-48HNTR

Recoil-operated autoloader, chrome-lined barrel with vent rib, etched alloy receiver, multi-choke set (improved, modified, full). Franchokes (set of three) became standard in 1989. Additional cost for Franchoke-equipped model.

Production: *1950–1990* **Gauge/Bore:** *12 ga., 20 ga.*
Action: *semi-auto*
Barrel Length: 24", 26", 28", 30" **Wt.:** *~5.8 lbs.*
Sights: *bead*
Capacity: *N/A*
Stock: *hand-checkered European walnut pistol grip*

D2C:	NIB $500	Ex $400	VG+ $275	Good $250	
C2C:	Mint $480	Ex $350	VG+ $250	Good $225	Fair $115
Trade-In:	Mint $360	Ex $300	VG+ $200	Good $175	Poor $60

AFFINITY COMPACT   REDBOOK CODE: RB-FR-S-AFFCMP

Adjustable length of pull 12.375-13.375", 3" chamber, included spacers adjust length of pull, can be fitted with full-size buttstock. Comes with IC and M chokes.

Production: *current* **Gauge/Bore:** *12 ga., 20 ga.*

Action: *semi-auto*

Barrel Length: 24", 26" **Wt.:** *5.5–6.3 lbs.*

Sights: *fiber optic red-bar front sight*

Capacity: *5*

Stock: *black synthetic*

D2C:	NIB $850	Ex $650	VG+ $470	Good $425	**LMP: $899**
C2C:	Mint $820	Ex $600	VG+ $430	Good $385	Fair $200
Trade-In:	Mint $610	Ex $500	VG+ $340	Good $300	Poor $90

AFFINITY   REDBOOK CODE: RB-FR-S-AFFNTY

Slim forend, 14 3/8" length of pull. Comes with IC, M, and F chokes. 3" chamber.

Production: *current* **Gauge/Bore:** *12 ga., 20 ga.*

Action: *semi-auto*

Barrel Length: 26", 28" **Wt.:** *5.6–6.4 lbs.*

Sights: *fiber optic red-bar front sight*

Capacity: *5*

Stock: *black synthetic*

D2C:	NIB $849	Ex $650	VG+ $470	Good $425	**LMP: $849**
C2C:	Mint $820	Ex $600	VG+ $430	Good $385	Fair $200
Trade-In:	Mint $610	Ex $500	VG+ $340	Good $300	Poor $90

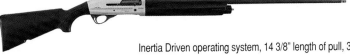

AFFINITY SPORTING   REDBOOK CODE: RB-FR-S-AFFSPT

Inertia Driven operating system, 14 3/8" length of pull, 3" chamber. Comes with extended IC, extended M, and extended F chokes.

Production: *current* **Gauge/Bore:** *12 ga., 20 ga.*

Action: *semi-auto*

Barrel Length: 28", 30" **Wt.:** *5.8 lbs., 6.8 lbs.*

Sights: *raised target rib with red-bar front sight*

Capacity: *5*

Stock: *black synthetic*

D2C:	NIB $1,159	Ex $900	VG+ $640	Good $580	**LMP: $1,159**
C2C:	Mint $1,120	Ex $800	VG+ $580	Good $525	Fair $270
Trade-In:	Mint $830	Ex $650	VG+ $460	Good $410	Poor $120

ASPIRE   REDBOOK CODE: RB-FR-S-ASPIRE

14.5" length of pull, 1 3/8" drop at comb. Comes with IC, M, and F chokes.

Production: *current* **Gauge/Bore:** *28 ga., .410 ga.*

Action: *O/U*

Barrel Length: 28" **Wt.:** *5.9 lbs.*

Sights: *red fiber optic front bead*

Capacity: *2*

Stock: *AA-Grade walnut*

D2C:	NIB $2,100	Ex $1,600	VG+ $1,155	Good $1,050	**LMP: $2,299**
C2C:	Mint $2,020	Ex $1,450	VG+ $1,050	Good $945	Fair $485
Trade-In:	Mint $1,500	Ex $1,200	VG+ $820	Good $735	Poor $210

FRANCHI

FENICE   REDBOOK CODE: RB-FR-S-FENICE

Chambered for 2 3/4", nickel-plated lightweight alloy receiver, oil-finished stock, chrome-plated bolt, 14 1/4" length of pull.
Comes with C, IC, M, IM, and F chokes.

Production: *current* **Gauge/Bore:** *20 ga., 28 ga.*
Action: *semi-auto*
Barrel Length: *26", 28"* **Wt.:** *5.4–5.7 lbs.*
Sights: *front/mid*
Capacity: *4*
Stock: *AA-Grade walnut*

D2C:	NIB $1,359	Ex $1,050	VG+ $750	Good $680	LMP: $1,359
C2C:	Mint $1,310	Ex $950	VG+ $680	Good $615	Fair $315
Trade-In:	Mint $970	Ex $775	VG+ $540	Good $480	Poor $150

INSTINCT L OVER AND UNDER   REDBOOK CODE: RB-FR-S-INSTLO

Chambered for 2 3/4", 14 1/4" length of pull, 1.5" drop at come, casehardened receiver. Comes with IC, M, and F chokes.

Production: *current* **Gauge/Bore:** *12 ga., 20 ga.*
Action: *O/U*
Barrel Length: *26", 28"* **Wt.:** *6.1–6.9 lbs.*
Sights: *red fiber optic front bead*
Capacity: *2*
Stock: *A-Grade walnut*

D2C:	NIB $1,149	Ex $875	VG+ $635	Good $575	LMP: $1,149
C2C:	Mint $1,110	Ex $800	VG+ $580	Good $520	Fair $265
Trade-In:	Mint $820	Ex $650	VG+ $450	Good $405	Poor $120

INSTINCT SL OVER AND UNDER   REDBOOK CODE: RB-FR-S-INSTSL

Chambered for 2.75" and 3". Offers IC, M, and F chokes. Overall length 42.25" or 44.25". Length of pull 14.25".
Drop at heel 2" with 1.5" drop at comb. Aluminum alloy receiver.

Production: *current* **Gauge/Bore:** *12 ga., 20 ga.*
Action: *O/U*
Barrel Length: *26", 28"* **Wt.:** *5.3 lbs.–5.8 lbs.*
Sights: *red fiber optic front bead*
Capacity: *2*
Stock: *AA-Grade walnut*

D2C:	NIB $1,400	Ex $1,075	VG+ $770	Good $700	LMP: $1,449
C2C:	Mint $1,350	Ex $975	VG+ $700	Good $630	Fair $325
Trade-In:	Mint $1,000	Ex $800	VG+ $550	Good $490	Poor $150

INSTINCT SPORT   REDBOOK CODE: RB-FR-S-INSTSP

Chambered for 2.75" and 3". Offers Extended IC, Extended M, and Extended F chokes. Overall
length 48.125" or 44.25". Length of pull 14.5". Drop at heel 2" with 1.5" drop at comb. Aluminum alloy receiver.

Production: *current* **Gauge/Bore:** *12 ga.*
Action: *O/U*
Barrel Length: *30"* **Wt.:** *7.5 lbs.*
Sights: *red fiber optic front bead*
Capacity: *2*
Stock: *A-Grade walnut*

D2C:	NIB $1,799	Ex $1,375	VG+ $990	Good $900	LMP: $1,899
C2C:	Mint $1,730	Ex $1,250	VG+ $900	Good $810	Fair $415
Trade-In:	Mint $1,280	Ex $1,025	VG+ $710	Good $630	Poor $180

INTENSITY   REDBOOK CODE: RB-FR-S-INTENS
14.375" length of pull, Inertia Driven operating system, 3.5" chamber. Comes with IC, M, and F chokes.

Production: current **Gauge/Bore:** 12 ga.					
Action: semi-auto					
Barrel Length: 26", 28", 30" **Wt.:** 6.7–6.9 lbs.	D2C:	NIB $1,000	Ex $775	VG+ $550	Good $500	**LMP:** $1,099
Sights: fiber optic red-bar front sight	C2C:	Mint $960	Ex $700	VG+ $500	Good $450	Fair $230
Capacity: 5	Trade-In:	Mint $710	Ex $575	VG+ $390	Good $350	Poor $120
Stock: black synthetic					

CONDOR   REDBOOK CODE: RB-FR-S-CONDOR
Sidelock, self-opening action, automatic ejectors, optional single trigger, various engraving options, stocks in custom lengths and wood grades, pistol grip option.

Production: discontinued **Gauge/Bore:** 12 ga., 16 ga., 20 ga.					
Action: SxS					
Barrel Length: 27.5" and other various lengths	D2C:	NIB $4,897	Ex $3,725	VG+ $2,695	Good $2,450	
Wt.: ~6.7 lbs. **Sights:** N/A	C2C:	Mint $4,710	Ex $3,400	VG+ $2,450	Good $2,205	Fair $1,130
Capacity: 2	Trade-In:	Mint $3,480	Ex $2,750	VG+ $1,910	Good $1,715	Poor $510
Stock: walnut					

*Photo Courtesy of
Rock Island Auction Company*

HIGHLANDER (ORIGINAL PRODUCTION)   REDBOOK CODE: RB-FR-S-HLNDRO
Boxlock action, steel receiver with coin finish, fixed chokes, extractors. Additional cost for 28 gauge model.

Production: 2003–2004 **Gauge/Bore:** 12 ga., 20 ga., 28 ga.					
Action: SxS					
Barrel Length: 26" **Wt.:** 5.7–6.4 lbs.	D2C:	NIB $1,300	Ex $1,000	VG+ $715	Good $650	
Sights: bead front	C2C:	Mint $1,250	Ex $900	VG+ $650	Good $585	Fair $300
Capacity: 2	Trade-In:	Mint $930	Ex $750	VG+ $510	Good $455	Poor $150
Stock: walnut					

MODEL 612 VARIOPRESS AUTOLOADING 12 GA.   REDBOOK CODE: RB-FR-S-612VPS
VarioSystem/Variomax gas-operation, advanced safety system, fires 3" shells. Available in blue, matte or Advantage camouflage finish.

Production: 2000–2004 **Gauge/Bore:** 12 ga.					
Action: semi-auto, pump-action					
Barrel Length: 24", 26", 28" **Wt.:** 6.8–7 lbs.	D2C:	NIB $450	Ex $350	VG+ $250	Good $225	
Sights: bead	C2C:	Mint $440	Ex $325	VG+ $230	Good $205	Fair $105
Capacity: 6	Trade-In:	Mint $320	Ex $275	VG+ $180	Good $160	Poor $60
Stock: cut-checkered satin-finish walnut or synthetic, Advantage camouflage option.					

RED BOOK OF SHOTGUN VALUES

FRANCHI

MODEL 620 VARIOPRESS AUTOLOADING 20 GA. REDBOOK CODE: RB-FR-S-620VPS

VarioSystem/Variomax gas-operation, advanced safety system, fires 3" shells. Available in blue, matte or Advantage camouflage finish. Additional cost for camouflage finish.

Production: *2000–2004* **Gauge/Bore:** *20 ga.*
Action: *semi-auto, pump-action*
Barrel Length: *24", 26", 28"* **Wt.:** *5.9–6.1 lbs.*
Sights: *bead*
Capacity: *6*

D2C:	NIB $445	Ex $350	VG+ $245	Good $225	
C2C:	Mint $430	Ex $325	VG+ $230	Good $205	Fair $105
Trade-In:	Mint $320	Ex $250	VG+ $180	Good $160	Poor $60

Stock: *cut-checkered satin-finish walnut or synthetic, Advantage camouflage option.*

Photo Courtesy of
Rock Island Auction Company

ALCIONE O/U REDBOOK CODE: RB-FR-S-ALCNOU

Single trigger, improved cylinder/modified or modified/full chokes, ejectors, engraved receiver, fires 3" shells.

Production: *1982–1989* **Gauge/Bore:** *12 ga.*
Action: *O/U*
Barrel Length: *26", 28"* **Wt.:** *6.75 lbs.*
Sights: *N/A*
Capacity: *2*

D2C:	NIB $1,150	Ex $875	VG+ $635	Good $575	
C2C:	Mint $1,110	Ex $800	VG+ $580	Good $520	Fair $265
Trade-In:	Mint $820	Ex $650	VG+ $450	Good $405	Poor $120

Stock: *cut-checkered French walnut*

Photo Courtesy of
Rock Island Auction Company

ALCIONE FIELD REDBOOK CODE: RB-FR-S-ALCNFD

Single trigger, ejectors, engraved nickel-finished receiver, Franchoke tubes, fires 3" shells.

Production: *1998–2005* **Gauge/Bore:** *12 ga.*
Action: *O/U*
Barrel Length: *26", 28"* **Wt.:** *7.5 lbs.*
Sights: *N/A*
Capacity: *2*

D2C:	NIB $1,000	Ex $775	VG+ $550	Good $500	
C2C:	Mint $960	Ex $700	VG+ $500	Good $450	Fair $230
Trade-In:	Mint $710	Ex $575	VG+ $390	Good $350	Poor $120

Stock: *cut-checkered French walnut*

ARISTOCRAT FIELD REDBOOK CODE: RB-FR-S-ASCTFD

Boxlock action, vent rib, improved cylinder/modified or modified/full chokes, single trigger, automatic ejectors.

Production: *1960–1969* **Gauge/Bore:** *12 ga.*
Action: *O/U*
Barrel Length: *26", 28", 30"* **Wt.:** *7 lbs.*
Sights: *N/A*
Capacity: *2*

D2C:	NIB $665	Ex $525	VG+ $370	Good $335	
C2C:	Mint $640	Ex $475	VG+ $340	Good $300	Fair $155
Trade-In:	Mint $480	Ex $375	VG+ $260	Good $235	Poor $90

Stock: *cut-checkered pistol grip stock*

PAGE 128

redbookofguns.com

FALCONET O/U REDBOOK CODE: RB-FR-S-FLCNFD

Boxlock action, vent rib, automatic ejectors, engraved alloy receiver, various chokes, choice of blue, light-colored or pickled silver finish. Receiver available in tan, ebony or silver finish. Add 10% for silver finish; add 25% for 28 gauge and .410 bore models.

Production: *1968–1975* **Gauge/Bore:** *12 ga., 16 ga., 20 ga., 28 ga., .410*

Action: *O/U*

Barrel Length: 24", 26", 28", 30" **Wt.:** *~6 lbs.*

Sights: *N/A*

Capacity: *2*

Stock: *cut-checkered walnut*

D2C:	NIB $600	Ex $475	VG+ $330	Good $300	
C2C:	Mint $580	Ex $425	VG+ $300	Good $270	Fair $140
Trade-In:	Mint $430	Ex $350	VG+ $240	Good $210	Poor $60

FALCONET SKEET REDBOOK CODE: RB-FR-S-FLCNSK

Boxlock action, wide vent rib, no. 1 & no. 2 skeet chokes, color case-hardened receiver.

Production: *1970–1974* **Gauge/Bore:** *12 ga., 16 ga., 20 ga., 28 ga., .410*

Action: *O/U*

Barrel Length: 26" **Wt.:** *~6 lbs.*

Sights: *N/A*

Capacity: *2*

Stock: *cut-checkered walnut*

D2C:	NIB $800	Ex $625	VG+ $440	Good $400	
C2C:	Mint $770	Ex $575	VG+ $400	Good $360	Fair $185
Trade-In:	Mint $570	Ex $450	VG+ $320	Good $280	Poor $90

SPORTING 2000 REDBOOK CODE: RB-FR-S-SP2000

Boxlock action, automatic ejectors, vent rib barrel, chambers 2.75" shells, solid plastic buttpad, hard case. Ported barrel model available.

Production: *discontinued 1998* **Gauge/Bore:** *12 ga.*

Action: *O/U*

Barrel Length: 28" **Wt.:** *7.75 lbs.*

Sights: *bead front*

Capacity: *2*

Stock: *cut-checkered walnut*

D2C:	NIB $1,049	Ex $800	VG+ $580	Good $525	
C2C:	Mint $1,010	Ex $725	VG+ $530	Good $475	Fair $245
Trade-In:	Mint $750	Ex $600	VG+ $410	Good $370	Poor $120

SPAS-12 REDBOOK CODE: RB-FR-S-SPAS12

Tactical shotgun, selective operating system switches from gas-operated semi-auto to pump-action, alloy receiver, matte finish, chambers 2.75" shells. Models are available with folding or fixed metal stock in addition to standard pistol grip model.

Production: *discontinued 1994* **Gauge/Bore:** *12 ga.*

Action: *semi-auto, pump-action*

Barrel Length: 21.5" **Wt.:** *8.75 lbs.*

Sights: *blade front, aperture rear*

Capacity: *8*

Stock: *black synthetic with pistol grip*

D2C:	NIB $1,800	Ex $1,375	VG+ $990	Good $900	
C2C:	Mint $1,730	Ex $1,250	VG+ $900	Good $810	Fair $415
Trade-In:	Mint $1,280	Ex $1,025	VG+ $710	Good $630	Poor $180

AIRONE REDBOOK CODE: RB-FR-S-AIRONE
Boxlock action, double triggers, automatic ejectors, highly engraved receiver, blue finish.

Production: *1940-1950* **Gauge/Bore:** *12 ga.*
Action: *SxS*
Barrel Length: various lengths **Wt.:** *N/A*
Sights: *N/A*
Capacity: *2*
Stock: *walnut*

D2C:	NIB $1,290	Ex $1,000	VG+ $710	Good $645	
C2C:	Mint $1,240	Ex $900	VG+ $650	Good $585	Fair $300
Trade-In:	Mint $920	Ex $725	VG+ $510	Good $455	Poor $150

ASTORE REDBOOK CODE: RB-FR-S-ASTORE
Boxlock action, automatic ejectors, double triggers, blue finish, cut-checkered straight stock.

Production: *1937-1960* **Gauge/Bore:** *12 ga.*
Action: *SxS*
Barrel Length: various lengths **Wt.:** *N/A*
Sights: *N/A*
Capacity: *2*
Stock: *walnut*

D2C:	NIB $900	Ex $700	VG+ $495	Good $450	
C2C:	Mint $870	Ex $625	VG+ $450	Good $405	Fair $210
Trade-In:	Mint $640	Ex $525	VG+ $360	Good $315	Poor $90

ASTORE II REDBOOK CODE: RB-FR-S-ASTOR2
Boxlock action, improved cylinder/improved modified or modified/full chokes, automatic ejectors or plain extractors, double triggers, blue finish.

Production: *current* **Gauge/Bore:** *12 ga.*
Action: *SxS*
Barrel Length: 27", 28" **Wt.:** *N/A*
Sights: *N/A*
Capacity: *2*
Stock: *walnut*

D2C:	NIB $1,110	Ex $850	VG+ $615	Good $555	
C2C:	Mint $1,070	Ex $775	VG+ $560	Good $500	Fair $260
Trade-In:	Mint $790	Ex $625	VG+ $440	Good $390	Poor $120

ASTORE 5 REDBOOK CODE: RB-FR-S-ASTOR5
Boxlock action, modified/full or improved modified/full chokes, single trigger, automatic ejectors, engraved receiver.

Production: *discontinued* **Gauge/Bore:** *12 ga.*
Action: *SxS*
Barrel Length: 28" **Wt.:** *N/A*
Sights: *N/A*
Capacity: *2*
Stock: *walnut*

D2C:	NIB $1,995	Ex $1,525	VG+ $1,100	Good $1,000	
C2C:	Mint $1,920	Ex $1,400	VG+ $1,000	Good $900	Fair $460
Trade-In:	Mint $1,420	Ex $1,125	VG+ $780	Good $700	Poor $210

IMPERIAL   REDBOOK CODE: RB-FR-S-IMPRL1

Sidelock, self-opening action, automatic ejectors, optional single trigger, various engraving options, stocks in custom lengths and wood grades, pistol grip option.

Production: *discontinued* **Gauge/Bore:** *12 ga., 16 ga., 20 ga.*

Action: *SxS*

Barrel Length: various lengths **Wt.:** *N/A*

Sights: *N/A*

Capacity: *2*

Stock: *walnut*

D2C:	NIB $10,400	Ex $7,925	VG+ $5,720	Good $5,200	
C2C:	Mint $9,990	Ex $7,200	VG+ $5,200	Good $4,680	Fair $2,395
Trade-In:	Mint $7,390	Ex $5,825	VG+ $4,060	Good $3,640	Poor $1,050

IMPERIALES   REDBOOK CODE: RB-FR-S-IMPRLS

Sidelock, self-opening action, automatic ejectors, optional single trigger, various engraving options, stocks in custom lengths and wood grades, pistol grip option.

Production: *discontinued* **Gauge/Bore:** *12 ga., 16 ga., 20 ga.*

Action: *SxS*

Barrel Length: various lengths **Wt.:** *N/A*

Sights: *N/A*

Capacity: *2*

Stock: *walnut*

D2C:	NIB $9,970	Ex $7,600	VG+ $5,485	Good $4,985	
C2C:	Mint $9,580	Ex $6,900	VG+ $4,990	Good $4,490	Fair $2,995
Trade-In:	Mint $7,080	Ex $5,600	VG+ $3,890	Good $3,490	Poor $1,020

NO. 5 IMPERIAL MONTE CARLO   REDBOOK CODE: RB-FR-S-IMPMC5

Sidelock, self-opening action, automatic ejectors, optional single trigger, various engraving options, stocks in custom lengths and wood grades, pistol grip option. Pricing research for this model proves inconclusive at this time. There have not been any recent sales on the secondary market to suggest a price range.

Production: *discontinued* **Gauge/Bore:** *12 ga., 16 ga., 20 ga.*

Action: *SxS*

Barrel Length: various lengths **Wt.:** *N/A*

Sights: *N/A*

Capacity: *2*

Stock: *walnut*

D2C:	NIB $27,000	Ex $20,525	VG+ $14,850	Good $13,500	
C2C:	Mint $25,920	Ex $18,650	VG+ $13,500	Good $12,150	Fair $6,210
Trade-In:	Mint $19,170	Ex $15,125	VG+ $10,530	Good $9,450	Poor $2,700

NO. 11 IMPERIAL MONTE CARLO   REDBOOK CODE: RB-FR-S-IMMC11

Sidelock, self-opening action, automatic ejectors, optional single trigger, various engraving options, stocks in custom lengths and wood grades, pistol grip option. Pricing research for this model proves inconclusive at this time. There have not been any recent sales on the secondary market to suggest a price range.

Production: *discontinued* **Gauge/Bore:** *12 ga., 16 ga., 20 ga.*

Action: *SxS*

Barrel Length: various lengths **Wt.:** *N/A*

Sights: *N/A*

Capacity: *2*

Stock: *walnut*

D2C:	NIB $34,500	Ex $26,225	VG+ $18,975	Good $17,250	
C2C:	Mint $33,120	Ex $23,825	VG+ $17,250	Good $15,525	Fair $7,935
Trade-In:	Mint $24,500	Ex $19,325	VG+ $13,460	Good $12,075	Poor $3,450

IMPERIAL MONTE CARLO EXTRA REDBOOK CODE: RB-FR-S-IMMCEX

Sidelock, self-opening action, automatic ejectors, optional single trigger, various engraving options, stocks in custom lengths and wood grades, pistol grip option. Pricing research for this model proves inconclusive at this time. There have not been any recent sales on the secondary market to suggest a price range.

Production: *discontinued* **Gauge/Bore:** *12 ga., 16 ga., 20 ga.*

Action: *SxS*

Barrel Length: *various lengths* **Wt.:** *N/A*

Sights: *N/A*

Capacity: *2*

Stock: *walnut*

D2C:	NIB $14,520	Ex $11,050	VG+ $7,990	Good $7,260	
C2C:	Mint $13,940	Ex $10,025	VG+ $7,260	Good $6,535	Fair $3,340
Trade-In:	Mint $10,310	Ex $8,150	VG+ $5,670	Good $5,085	Poor $1,470

ARISTOCRAT DELUXE REDBOOK CODE: RB-FR-S-ASCTDX

Vent rib, automatic ejectors, various choke combinations, engraving on receiver, trigger guard, and tang. Pricing research for this model proves inconclusive at this time. There have not been any recent sales on the secondary market to suggest a price range.

Production: *1960-1966* **Gauge/Bore:** *12 ga.*

Action: *O/U*

Barrel Length: *26", 28", 30"* **Wt.:** *N/A*

Sights: *N/A*

Capacity: *2*

Stock: *select walnut*

D2C:	NIB $890	Ex $700	VG+ $490	Good $445	
C2C:	Mint $860	Ex $625	VG+ $450	Good $405	Fair $205
Trade-In:	Mint $640	Ex $500	VG+ $350	Good $315	Poor $90

ARISTOCRAT SUPREME REDBOOK CODE: RB-FR-S-ASCTSP

Vent rib, automatic ejectors, various choke combinations, game birds in gold inlay, engraving on receiver, trigger guard, and tang. Pricing research for this model proves inconclusive at this time. There have not been any recent sales on the secondary market to suggest a price range.

Production: *1960–1966* **Gauge/Bore:** *12 ga.*

Action: *O/U*

Barrel Length: *26", 28", 30"* **Wt.:** *N/A*

Sights: *N/A*

Capacity: *2*

Stock: *select walnut*

D2C:	NIB $1,365	Ex $1,050	VG+ $755	Good $685	
C2C:	Mint $1,320	Ex $950	VG+ $690	Good $615	Fair $315
Trade-In:	Mint $970	Ex $775	VG+ $540	Good $480	Poor $150

ARISTOCRAT IMPERIAL REDBOOK CODE: RB-FR-S-ASCTIP

Vent rib, automatic ejectors, scroll engraving on receiver. Pricing research for this model proves inconclusive at this time. There have not been any recent sales on the secondary market to suggest a price range.

Production: *1967-1969* **Gauge/Bore:** *12 ga.*

Action: *O/U*

Barrel Length: *26", 28", 30"* **Wt.:** *N/A*

Sights: *N/A*

Capacity: *2*

Stock: *high-quality European walnut*

D2C:	NIB $2,440	Ex $1,875	VG+ $1,345	Good $1,220	
C2C:	Mint $2,350	Ex $1,700	VG+ $1,220	Good $1,100	Fair $565
Trade-In:	Mint $1,740	Ex $1,375	VG+ $960	Good $855	Poor $270

ARISTOCRAT MONTE CARLO   REDBOOK CODE: RB-FR-S-ASCTMC

Vent rib, automatic ejectors, extra-fine engraving and inlay. Pricing research for this model proves inconclusive at this time. There have not been any recent sales on the secondary market to suggest a price range.

Production: *1967-1969* **Gauge/Bore:** *12 ga.*

Action: *O/U*

Barrel Length: *26", 28", 30"* **Wt.:** *N/A*

Sights: *N/A*

Capacity: *2*

Stock: *high-quality European walnut*

D2C:	NIB $3,250	Ex $2,475	VG+ $1,790	Good $1,625	
C2C:	Mint $3,120	Ex $2,250	VG+ $1,630	Good $1,465	Fair $750
Trade-In:	Mint $2,310	Ex $1,825	VG+ $1,270	Good $1,140	Poor $330

FALCONET INTERNATIONAL SKEET   REDBOOK CODE: RB-FR-S-FLCNIS

Boxlock action, wide vent rib, no. 1 & no. 2 skeet chokes, engraved color case-hardened receiver. Pricing research for this model proves inconclusive at this time. There have not been any recent sales on the secondary market to suggest a price range.

Production: *1970-1974* **Gauge/Bore:** *12 ga., 16 ga., 20 ga., 28 ga., .410*

Action: *O/U*

Barrel Length: *26"* **Wt.:** *~6 lbs.*

Sights: *N/A*

Capacity: *2*

Stock: *walnut*

D2C:	NIB $945	Ex $725	VG+ $520	Good $475	
C2C:	Mint $910	Ex $675	VG+ $480	Good $430	Fair $220
Trade-In:	Mint $680	Ex $550	VG+ $370	Good $335	Poor $120

FALCONET INTERNATIONAL TRAP   REDBOOK CODE: RB-FR-S-FLCNIT

Boxlock action, wide vent rib, modified/full chokes, automatic ejectors, buttpad. Pricing research for this model proves inconclusive at this time. There have not been any recent sales on the secondary market to suggest a price range.

Production: *1970-1974* **Gauge/Bore:** *12 ga.*

Action: *O/U*

Barrel Length: *30"* **Wt.:** *~8 lbs.*

Sights: *N/A*

Capacity: *2*

Stock: *walnut, straight or Monte Carlo comb option*

D2C:	NIB $945	Ex $725	VG+ $520	Good $475	
C2C:	Mint $910	Ex $675	VG+ $480	Good $430	Fair $220
Trade-In:	Mint $680	Ex $550	VG+ $370	Good $335	Poor $120

PEREGRINE MODEL 400   REDBOOK CODE: RB-FR-S-PGN400

Boxlock action, vent rib, alloy receiver, automatic ejectors, various chokes. Pricing research for this model proves inconclusive at this time. There have not been any recent sales on the secondary market to suggest a price range.

Production: *1975-1978* **Gauge/Bore:** *12 ga.*

Action: *O/U*

Barrel Length: *26", 28"* **Wt.:** *~7 lbs.*

Sights: *N/A*

Capacity: *2*

Stock: *cut-checkered walnut with pistol grip*

D2C:	NIB $645	Ex $500	VG+ $355	Good $325	
C2C:	Mint $620	Ex $450	VG+ $330	Good $295	Fair $150
Trade-In:	Mint $460	Ex $375	VG+ $260	Good $230	Poor $90

Gamba, Renato

In the area of Garbone in Italy, a rich history of gunsmithing dates back to the first half of the 18th century. Part of that history was made when the Gamba family moved to Val Trompia and through marriage, became intertwined with other famous gunmaking families of the region. For generations, the Gambas were involved in the industry, and in 1967, Renato Gamba bought equipment from his brother that the pair had previously used in gunmaking in a venture known as Filli Gamba, or Gamba Brothers in English, since 1946. Using the tooling to create his own company in Val Trompia, Renato steadily grew his business and acquired several others to add to its footprint in the marketplace in 1989, including Gambarmi and Stefano Zanotti. Renato, along with his son Enrico, is still involved in the operations of the company today in order to keep his family's traditions alive, but shotguns bearing the Gamba name have been manufactured by Bremec, Ltd. since 2007.

CONCORDE HUNTING/SKEET ROUND BODY   REDBOOK CODE: RB-RG-S-CONSKE
Non-detachable trigger group, boss-style locking system, heat-treated steel receiver CNC machined and hand finished, automatic ejectors, Schnabel forend, single-selective or non-selective trigger, low-profile receiver.

Production: *current* **Gauge/Bore:** *12 ga., 20 ga.*
Action: *O/U*
Barrel Length: 26"–32" **Wt.:** *N/A*
Sights: *bead front*
Capacity: 2
Stock: *pistol grip or English style, selective walnut*

D2C:	NIB $4,800	Ex $3,650	VG+ $2,640	Good $2,400	
C2C:	Mint $4,610	Ex $3,325	VG+ $2,400	Good $2,160	Fair $1,105
Trade-In:	Mint $3,410	Ex $2,700	VG+ $1,880	Good $1,680	Poor $480

DAYTONA   REDBOOK CODE: RB-RG-S-DAYTON
Monobloc barrel, chokes can be requested. Double, single, or single-selective trigger. Trigger with sideplates, English or pistol-grip style stock, hand checkering, high-gloss finish done by hand, Schnabel forend.

Production: *current* **Gauge/Bore:** *12 ga., 16 ga., 20 ga.*
Action: *O/U*
Barrel Length: 27.5" **Wt.:** *N/A*
Sights: *bead front*
Capacity: 2
Stock: *hardwood*

D2C:	NIB $5,500	Ex $4,200	VG+ $3,025	Good $2,750	
C2C:	Mint $5,280	Ex $3,800	VG+ $2,750	Good $2,475	Fair $1,265
Trade-In:	Mint $3,910	Ex $3,100	VG+ $2,150	Good $1,925	Poor $570

DAYTONA SL   REDBOOK CODE: RB-RG-S-DAYTSL
Monobloc barrel, chokes can be requested. Flat, knurled, or ventilated rib. Double, single, or single-selective trigger, trigger with sideplates, boss type locking system, English or pistol-grip style stock, high-gloss hand finished stock, Schnabel forend.

Production: *current* **Gauge/Bore:** *12 ga., 16 ga., 20 ga.*
Action: *O/U*
Barrel Length: 27.5" **Wt.:** *N/A*
Sights: *bead front*
Capacity: 2
Stock: *root wood*

D2C:	NIB $24,900	Ex $18,925	VG+ $13,695	Good $12,450	
C2C:	Mint $23,910	Ex $17,200	VG+ $12,450	Good $11,205	Fair $5,730
Trade-In:	Mint $17,680	Ex $13,950	VG+ $9,720	Good $8,715	Poor $2,490

DAYTONA SLHH   REDBOOK CODE: RB-RG-S-DASLHH

Monobloc or demibloc barrel, chokes can be requested. Flat, knurled, or ventilated rib. Double, single, or single-selective trigger. Sidelocks on leg plates, boss type locking system, English or pistol-grip style stock, hand checkering, hand finished high-gloss wood, Schnabel forend. Market research provides no conclusive pricing suggestion(s) for this particular model.

Production: *current* **Gauge/Bore:** *12 ga., 16 ga., 20 ga.*

Action: *O/U*

Barrel Length: 27.5" **Wt.:** *N/A*

Sights: *bead front*

Capacity: *2*

Stock: *root wood*

GAMBA

LONDON   REDBOOK CODE: RB-RG-S-LONDON

Demibloc barrel, double or single trigger, flat or knurled rib, H&H sidelocks type, three bite double Purdey locking system, English style stock, hand checkering and matte finish on walnut root, standard forend.

Production: *current* **Gauge/Bore:** *12 ga., 16 ga., 20 ga.*

Action: *O/U*

Barrel Length: 27"–28" **Wt.:** *6.8 lbs.*

Sights: *bead front*

Capacity: *2*

Stock: *walnut root*

D2C:	NIB $4,180	Ex $3,200	VG+ $2,300	Good $2,090	
C2C:	Mint $4,020	Ex $2,900	VG+ $2,090	Good $1,885	Fair $965
Trade-In:	Mint $2,970	Ex $2,350	VG+ $1,640	Good $1,465	Poor $420

AMBASSADOR   REDBOOK CODE: RB-RG-S-AMBASS

Demibloc barrel, chokes can be requested, flat or knurled rib, double or single trigger, patented Leg sidelocks linear movement hammer, three bite double Purdey locking system, English or pistol-grip style stock, hand-checkered oil-finished walnut root, standard forend.

Production: *current* **Gauge/Bore:** *12 ga., 16 ga., 20 ga.*

Action: *O/U*

Barrel Length: 27"–28" **Wt.:** *6.8 lbs.*

Sights: *bead front*

Capacity: *2*

Stock: *walnut root*

D2C:	NIB $23,450	Ex $17,825	VG+ $12,900	Good $11,725	
C2C:	Mint $22,520	Ex $16,200	VG+ $11,730	Good $10,555	Fair $5,395
Trade-In:	Mint $16,650	Ex $13,150	VG+ $9,150	Good $8,210	Poor $2,370

Garbi, Armas

GARBI, ARMAS

Located in the Basque region of Northern Spain, Armas Garbi's name is an acronym composed of the initials of each of its founders' names. "G"uerrena Barrena's responsibility within the company lies in scale adjustments, Juan "A"lday supervises engraving, "R"amon Churruca is charged with assembly and final finishing, Pedro "B"arrenechea serves as general manager, and "I"rondo oversees adjustments and finishing of stocks. The Spanish company is known for producing English sidelock action shotguns much akin to the Holland & Holland type, and with superlative quality standards, the company only produces between 60 and 70 units per year. Manufacturing is headquartered in Eibar, Spain, and Garbi shotguns imported to the U.S. are distributed exclusively by William Larkin Moore & Co. in Scottsdale, Arizona.

GARBI, ARMAS

MODEL 100 SIDELOCK REDBOOK CODE: RB-GB-S-M100SL

H&H pattern sidelock, automatic ejectors, double trigger, English-style straight grip, fine-line hand checkering, classic forend, drop-forged steel action frame, gas escape valves, chopper lump barrels, double safety sears, hand rubbed oil finish, rose and scroll engraving done partially by machine.

Production: *1985–current* **Gauge/Bore:** *12 ga., 16 ga., 20 ga., 28 ga.*
Action: *SxS*
Barrel Length: 25", 28", 30" **Wt.:** *5 –7 lbs.*
Sights: *bead front*
Capacity: *2*
Stock: *walnut*

D2C:	NIB $4,886	Ex $3,725	VG+ $2,690	Good $2,445	
C2C:	Mint $4,700	Ex $3,375	VG+ $2,450	Good $2,200	Fair $1,125
Trade-In:	Mint $3,470	Ex $2,750	VG+ $1,910	Good $1,715	Poor $510

MODEL 101 SIDELOCK REDBOOK CODE: RB-GB-S-M101SL

Handcrafted sidelocks, hand-engraved receiver, straight grip walnut stock, drop-forged action frame, gas escape valves, chopper lump barrels, Bellota steel barrel, 5-pin sidelock mechanism, double safety sears, automatic selective ejectors, double triggers, articulated front blade, hand rubbed oil finish, large scroll engraving, case-hardened or coin finish.

Production: *1985–current* **Gauge/Bore:** *12 ga., 16 ga., 20 ga., 28 ga.*
Action: *SxS*
Barrel Length: 25", 28", 30" **Wt.:** *N/A*
Sights: *bead front*
Capacity: *2*
Stock: *walnut*

D2C:	NIB $7,448	Ex $5,675	VG+ $4,100	Good $3,725	
C2C:	Mint $7,160	Ex $5,150	VG+ $3,730	Good $3,355	Fair $1,715
Trade-In:	Mint $5,290	Ex $4,175	VG+ $2,910	Good $2,610	Poor $750

MODEL 102 SIDELOCK REDBOOK CODE: RB-GB-S-M102SL

H&H pattern sidelock, automatic ejectors, double trigger, English-style straight grip, fine-line hand checkering, classic forend, drop-forged steel action frame, gas escape valves, chopper lump barrels, double safety sears, hand rubbed oil finish, large scroll engraving. Market research provides no conclusive pricing suggestion(s) for this particular model.

Production: *1985–discontinued* **Gauge/Bore:** *12 ga., 16 ga., 20 ga., 28 ga.*
Action: *SxS*
Barrel Length: 25", 28", 30" **Wt.:** *N/A*
Sights: *bead front*
Capacity: *2*
Stock: *walnut*

MODEL 103 HAMMERLESS DOUBLE REDBOOK CODE: RB-GB-S-M103HD

Drop forged steel action, gas escape valves, chopper lump barrels, Bellota steel barrels, 5-pin sidelock mechanism, double safety sears, automatic selective ejectors, double triggers, articulated front blade, walnut hand rubbed finish, rose and scroll engraving, case-hardened or coin finish.

Production: *current* **Gauge/Bore:** *12 ga., 16 ga., 20 ga., 28 ga.*
Action: *SxS*
Barrel Length: 25", 28", 30" **Wt.:** *N/A*
Sights: *bead front*
Capacity: *2*
Stock: *walnut*

D2C:	NIB $17,970	Ex $13,675	VG+ $9,885	Good $8,985	
C2C:	Mint $17,260	Ex $12,400	VG+ $8,990	Good $8,090	Fair $4,135
Trade-In:	Mint $12,760	Ex $10,075	VG+ $7,010	Good $6,290	Poor $1,800

MODEL 200 HAMMERLESS DOUBLE REDBOOK CODE: RB-GB-S-M200HD

Drop forged steel action frame, gas escape valves, chopper lump barrels, Bellota steel barrel, 5-pin sidelock, double safety sears, automatic selective ejectors, double trigger with articulated front blade, walnut with hand-checkering, full-coverage continental style engraving.

Production: *current* **Gauge/Bore:** *12 ga., 16 ga., 20 ga., 28 ga.*

Action: *SxS*

Barrel Length: *25", 28", 30"* **Wt.:** *N/A*

Sights: *bead front*

Capacity: *2*

Stock: *walnut*

D2C:	NIB $10,750	Ex $8,175	VG+ $5,915	Good $5,375		
C2C:	Mint $10,320	Ex $7,425	VG+ $5,380	Good $4,840	Fair $2,475	
Trade-In:	Mint $7,640	Ex $6,025	VG+ $4,200	Good $3,765	Poor $1,080	

Grulla Armas

Grulla Armas is located in Eibar, Spain, a town so steeped with history in firearms manufacturing that it has been nicknamed "Gunsmith City." The company was started in 1932 by five master gunsmiths from the area who wanted to build a prestigious brand of 100% handmade shotguns and rifles. All aspects of the models produced can be customized and personalized, making Grulla arms unique. The company specialty is typically said to be side-by-side model shotguns, but all firearms offered are of the utmost quality. Two generations later, the company still enjoys a reputation for luxury firearms and still uses methods passed down from generation to generation to create them. Grulla firearms are coveted all over the world, and they are distributed in the U.S. through a handful of importers.

MODEL 215 REDBOOK CODE: RB-GR-S-215XXX

Drop-forged steel frame, rose & scroll hand-engraving, old-silver or case hardened finishing, drop-forged demibloc, automatic ejector, double trigger, articulated front, double safety sears, hand rubbed oil finished walnut, silver oval for initials.

Production: *current* **Gauge/Bore:** *12 ga., 16 ga., 20 ga., 28 ga., .410*

Action: *O/U*

Barrel Length: *26"–30"* **Wt.:** *N/A*

Sights: *front bead*

Capacity: *2*

Stock: *walnut*

D2C:	NIB $5,400	Ex $4,125	VG+ $2,970	Good $2,700		
C2C:	Mint $5,190	Ex $3,750	VG+ $2,700	Good $2,430	Fair $1,245	
Trade-In:	Mint $3,840	Ex $3,025	VG+ $2,110	Good $1,890	Poor $540	

MODEL 216 REDBOOK CODE: RB-GR-S-216XXX

Drop-forged steel frame, gas-escape valves, rose and scroll hand-engraved action, round or tradition bodied action, drop-forged demibloc, chopper lump barrels, automatic-selective ejectors, double trigger w/ articulated front, double safety sears, custom stock measurements available, silver oval for initials. Market research suggests pricing for this model is inconclusive at this time.

Production: *current* **Gauge/Bore:** *12 ga., 16 ga., 20 ga., 28 ga., .410*

Action: *SxS*

Barrel Length: *26"–30"* **Wt.:** *N/A*

Sights: *front bead*

Capacity: *2*

Stock: *walnut*

MODEL 209 H REDBOOK CODE: RB-GR-S-209HXX

Drop-forged steel frame, gas-escape valves, rose and scroll hand-engraved action, round or tradition bodied action, old-silver or case-hardened finishing, drop-forged demibloc, chopper lump barrels, automatic-selective ejectors, double trigger w/ articulated front, double safety sears, hand-rubbed oil finish, custom stock measurements available, silver oval for initials. Prices vary with options.

Production: *current* **Gauge/Bore:** *12 ga., 16 ga., 20 ga., 28 ga., .410*

Action: *SxS*

Barrel Length: 26"–30" **Wt.:** *N/A*

Sights: *front bead*

Capacity: *2*

Stock: *walnut*

D2C:	NIB $7,500	Ex $5,700	VG+ $4,125	Good $3,750	
C2C:	Mint $7,200	Ex $5,175	VG+ $3,750	Good $3,375	Fair $1,725
Trade-In:	Mint $5,330	Ex $4,200	VG+ $2,930	Good $2,625	Poor $750

MODEL 216 RB REDBOOK CODE: RB-GR-S-216RBX

Drop-forged steel frame, gas-escape valves, rose and scroll hand-engraved action, round or tradition bodied action, old-silver or case-hardened finishing, drop-forged demibloc, chopper lump barrels, automatic-selective ejectors, double trigger with articulated front, double safety sears, hand-rubbed oil stock finish, silver oval for initials.

Production: *current* **Gauge/Bore:** *12 ga., 16 ga., 20 ga., 28 ga., .410*

Action: *SxS*

Barrel Length: 26"–30" **Wt.:** *N/A*

Sights: *front bead*

Capacity: *2*

Stock: *walnut*

D2C:	NIB $8,195	Ex $6,250	VG+ $4,510	Good $4,100	**LMP:** $9,995
C2C:	Mint $7,870	Ex $5,675	VG+ $4,100	Good $3,690	Fair $1,885
Trade-In:	Mint $5,820	Ex $4,600	VG+ $3,200	Good $2,870	Poor $840

CELTIC REDBOOK CODE: RB-GR-S-CELTIC

Old silver finishing, drop-forged steel action, round body style action, H&H assisted opening action, hand engraved game scene, drop-forged chopper, disc set strikers, automatic selective ejectors, hand-rubbed oil finish. Market research suggests pricing for this model is inconclusive at this time.

Production: *current* **Gauge/Bore:** *12 ga., 16 ga., 20 ga., 28 ga., .410*

Action: *SxS*

Barrel Length: 26"–30" **Wt.:** *N/A*

Sights: *front bead*

Capacity: *2*

Stock: *walnut*

CONSORT REDBOOK CODE: RB-GR-S-CONSOR

Drop-forged steel action, completely hand engraved, old silver or case-hardened finishing, drop-forged demibloc, H&H style assisted opening action, automatic-selective ejectors, double-trigger with articulated front, double safety sears, walnut forearm, hand-rubbed oil finished wood, silver oval for initials. Market research suggests pricing for this model is inconclusive at this time.

Production: *current* **Gauge/Bore:** *12 ga., 16 ga., 20 ga., 28 ga., .410*

Action: *SxS*

Barrel Length: 26"–30" **Wt.:** *N/A*

Sights: *front bead*

Capacity: *2*

Stock: *walnut*

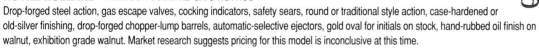

ROYAL CHURCHILL   REDBOOK CODE: RB-GR-S-ROYCHU
Drop-forged steel action, gas escape valves, safety sears, cocking indicator, traditional or round body action style, hand engraved, case-hardened or old-silver finishing, drop-forged chopper-lump barrels, disc set strikers, automatic-selective ejectors, exhibition-grade walnut, walnut forearm, hand-rubbed oil finished wood, gold oval for initials. Market research suggests pricing for this model is inconclusive at this time.

Production: *current* **Gauge/Bore:** *12 ga., 16 ga., 20 ga., 28 ga., .410*
Action: *SxS*
Barrel Length: 26"–30" **Wt.:** *N/A*
Sights: *front bead*
Capacity: *2*
Stock: *walnut*

GRULLA

ROYAL HOLLAND   REDBOOK CODE: RB-GR-S-ROYHOL
Drop-forged steel action, gas escape valves, cocking indicators, safety sears, round or traditional style action, case-hardened or old-silver finishing, drop-forged chopper-lump barrels, automatic-selective ejectors, gold oval for initials on stock, hand-rubbed oil finish on walnut, exhibition grade walnut. Market research suggests pricing for this model is inconclusive at this time.

Production: *current* **Gauge/Bore:** *12 ga., 16 ga., 20 ga., 28 ga., .410*
Action: *SxS*
Barrel Length: 26"–30" **Wt.:** *N/A*
Sights: *front bead*
Capacity: *2*
Stock: *walnut*

ROYAL PURDEY   REDBOOK CODE: RB-GR-S-ROYPUR
Drop-forged steel action, gas escape valves, safety sears, cocking indicators, traditional or round body action, hand engraved, case-hardened or old-silver finishing, drop-forged chopper-lump barrels, nickel-chromium steel, disc set strikers, automatic-selective ejectors, exhibition grade walnut on stock and forearm, hand-rubbed oil finish, gold oval for initials. Market research suggests pricing for this model is inconclusive at this time.

Production: *current* **Gauge/Bore:** *12 ga., 16 ga., 20 ga., 28 ga., .410*
Action: *SxS*
Barrel Length: 26"–30" **Wt.:** *N/A*
Sights: *front bead*
Capacity: *2*
Stock: *walnut*

SUPREME   REDBOOK CODE: RB-GR-S-SUPREM
Case-hardened finishing, drop-forged steel action, gas escape valves, safety sears, cocking indicators, round body action style, H&H style assisted opening action, hand engraved, drop-forged chopper, disc set strikers, automatic selective ejectors, drop-forged chopper, disc set strikers, exhibition grade walnut stock and forearm, hand-rubbed oil measurements, gold oval for initials. Market research suggests pricing for this model is inconclusive at this time.

Production: *current* **Gauge/Bore:** *12 ga., 16 ga., 20 ga., 28 ga., .410*
Action: *SxS*
Barrel Length: 26"–30" **Wt.:** *N/A*
Sights: *front bead*
Capacity: *2*
Stock: *walnut*

GRULLA

WINDSOR REDBOOK CODE: RB-GR-S-WINDSO

Drop-forged steel action frame, gas-escape valves, hand engraving, old silver or case-hardened finishing, drop-forged demibloc, chopper lump barrels, H&H style opening action, double-triggers with articulated front, double safety sears, stock and forearm made of selected walnut, hand-rubbed oil finished walnut, silver oval for initials.

Production: *current* **Gauge/Bore:** *12 ga., 16 ga., 20 ga., 28 ga., .410*
Action: *SxS*
Barrel Length: 26"–30" **Wt.:** *N/A*
Sights: *front bead*
Capacity: *2*
Stock: *walnut*

D2C:	NIB $6,300	Ex $4,800	VG+ $3,465	Good $3,150	
C2C:	Mint $6,050	Ex $4,350	VG+ $3,150	Good $2,835	Fair $1,450
Trade-In:	Mint $4,480	Ex $3,550	VG+ $2,460	Good $2,205	Poor $630

GUERINI

Guerini, Caesar

Caesar Guerini was founded in 2002 by two nephews, and former employees, of Battista Rizzini, the founder of another esteemed shotgun maker in Italy, Rizzini. Guerini is located in Marcheno, Italy, but products are distributed internationally, with over/under models distributed in the U.S. through Caesar Guerini USA, an American subsidiary in Cambridge, Maryland . In 2010, the company merged with Fabarm S.p.A., making the combo the second largest shotgun manufacturing group in Italy.

APEX REDBOOK CODE: RB-GU-S-APEXXX

Hand-polished coin finish on receiver, stock with hand rubbed oil, 26 lines per inch checkering, wooden butt plate, 3" chamber, non-ventilated center rib, standard forcing cone, chrome-lined barrel, nickel-plated flush-fitting chokes, Schnabel forend, single-selective trigger, manual safety.

Production: *current* **Gauge/Bore:** *12 ga., 20 ga., 28 ga.*
Action: *O/U*
Barrel Length: 28" **Wt.:** *6.3–7 lbs.*
Sights: *silver front bead*
Capacity: *2*
Stock: *hardwood*

D2C:	NIB $6,806	Ex $5,175	VG+ $3,745	Good $3,405	**LMP:** $7,995
C2C:	Mint $6,540	Ex $4,700	VG+ $3,410	Good $3,065	Fair $1,570
Trade-In:	Mint $4,840	Ex $3,825	VG+ $2,660	Good $2,385	Poor $690

APEX SPORTING REDBOOK CODE: RB-GU-S-APEXSP

Hand-polished coin finish on receiver, hand rubbed oil stock finish, black rubber recoil pad, 26 lines per inch checkering, 2 3/4" chamber, ventilated center rib, 5" DuoCon forcing cone, chrome lined barrel, DTS trigger system, rounded forend.

Production: *current* **Gauge/Bore:** *12 ga.*
Action: *O/U*
Barrel Length: 30", 32" **Wt.:** *7.9 lbs.*
Sights: *white Bradley style front, silver center bead*
Capacity: *2*
Stock: *hardwood*

D2C:	NIB $8,000	Ex $6,100	VG+ $4,400	Good $4,000	**LMP:** $8,495
C2C:	Mint $7,680	Ex $5,525	VG+ $4,000	Good $3,600	Fair $1,840
Trade-In:	Mint $5,680	Ex $4,500	VG+ $3,120	Good $2,800	Poor $810

CHALLENGER ASCENT REDBOOK CODE: RB-GU-S-CHASCE

Hand-polished coin finish on receiver, 26 LPI checkering, black rubber recoil pad, 2 3/4" chamber, 8mm tapered top rib, ventilated center rib, 5" DuoCon forcing cones, MAXIS competition chokes, rounded forend, DTS trigger system, manual safety.

Production: *current* **Gauge/Bore:** *12 ga.*
Action: *O/U*
Barrel Length: 30", 32" **Wt.:** *8.3 lbs.*
Sights: *white Bradley style front, silver center bead*
Capacity: *2*
Stock: *hardwood*

D2C:	NIB $4,693	Ex $3,575	VG+ $2,585	Good $2,350	**LMP:** $6,175
C2C:	Mint $4,510	Ex $3,250	VG+ $2,350	Good $2,115	Fair $1,080
Trade-In:	Mint $3,340	Ex $2,650	VG+ $1,840	Good $1,645	Poor $480

CHALLENGER IMPACT REDBOOK CODE: RB-GU-S-CHIMPA

Hand-polished coin finish on receiver, 26 LPI checkering, black rubber recoil pad, 2 3/4" chamber, ventilated center rib, 5" DuoCon forcing cones, MAXIS competition chokes, rounded forend, DTS trigger system, manual safety.

Production: *current* **Gauge/Bore:** *12 ga.*
Action: *O/U*
Barrel Length: 30", 32" **Wt.:** *8.2–9.4 lbs.*
Sights: *white Bradley style front, silver center bead*
Capacity: *2*
Stock: *hardwood*

D2C:	NIB $5,665	Ex $4,325	VG+ $3,120	Good $2,835	**LMP:** $7,200
C2C:	Mint $5,440	Ex $3,925	VG+ $2,840	Good $2,550	Fair $1,305
Trade-In:	Mint $4,030	Ex $3,175	VG+ $2,210	Good $1,985	Poor $570

CHALLENGER SPORTING REDBOOK CODE: RB-GU-S-CHSPOR

Hand-polished coin finish on receiver, hand rubbed oil stock finish, 26 LPI checkering, black rubber recoil pad, 2 3/4" chamber, ventilated center rib, 5" DuoCon forcing cones, chrome lined barrel, MAXIS competition chokes, Schnabel forend, DTS trigger system, manual safety.

Production: *current* **Gauge/Bore:** *12 ga.*
Action: *O/U*
Barrel Length: 30", 32" **Wt.:** *7.7–8 lbs.*
Sights: *white Bradley style front, silver center bead*
Capacity: *2*
Stock: *hardwood*

D2C:	NIB $5,150	Ex $3,925	VG+ $2,835	Good $2,575	**LMP:** $5,150
C2C:	Mint $4,950	Ex $3,575	VG+ $2,580	Good $2,320	Fair $1,185
Trade-In:	Mint $3,660	Ex $2,900	VG+ $2,010	Good $1,805	Poor $540

ELLIPSE REDBOOK CODE: RB-GU-S-ELLIPS

Hand-polished coin finish on receiver, hand rubbed oil stock finish, 26 LPI, wooden buttplate, 3" chamber, non-ventilated center rib, chrome lined barrel, nickel-plated flush fitting chokes, ellipse rounded forend, single selective trigger.

Production: *current* **Gauge/Bore:** *20 ga., 28 ga.*
Action: *O/U*
Barrel Length: 28" **Wt.:** *6.3–6.6 lbs.*
Sights: *silver front bead*
Capacity: *2*
Stock: *hardwood*

D2C:	NIB $4,224	Ex $3,225	VG+ $2,325	Good $2,115	**LMP:** $4,325
C2C:	Mint $4,060	Ex $2,925	VG+ $2,120	Good $1,905	Fair $975
Trade-In:	Mint $3,000	Ex $2,375	VG+ $1,650	Good $1,480	Poor $450

GUERINI

ELLIPSE CURVE REDBOOK CODE: RB-GU-S-ELLCUR

Hand-polished coin finish on receiver, hand rubbed oil stock finish, 26 LPI checkering, wooden buttplate, 3" chamber, non-ventilated center rib, standard forcing cones, chrome lined barrel, nickel-plated flush-fitting chokes, ellipse rounded forend, manual safety.

Production: *current* **Gauge/Bore:** *20 ga, 28 ga.*
Action: *O/U*
Barrel Length: 28" **Wt.:** *6.3–6.6 lbs.*
Sights: *silver front bead*
Capacity: *2*
Stock: *hardwood*

D2C:	NIB $5,973	Ex $4,550	VG+ $3,290	Good $2,990	**LMP: $6,795**
C2C:	Mint $5,740	Ex $4,125	VG+ $2,990	Good $2,690	Fair $1,375
Trade-In:	Mint $4,250	Ex $3,350	VG+ $2,330	Good $2,095	Poor $600

ELLIPSE EVO REDBOOK CODE: RB-GU-S-ELLEVO

Hand-polished coin finish, hand rubbed oil stock finish, 3" chamber, non-ventilated center rib, standard forcing cones, chrome-lined barrel, nickel-plated flush-fitting chokes, ellipse rounded forend, single selective trigger.

Production: *current* **Gauge/Bore:** *12 ga., 20 ga., 28 ga.*
Action: *O/U*
Barrel Length: 28" **Wt.:** *6.3–7 lbs.*
Sights: *silver front bead*
Capacity: *2*
Stock: *hardwood*

D2C:	NIB $5,300	Ex $4,050	VG+ $2,915	Good $2,650	**LMP: $6,150**
C2C:	Mint $5,090	Ex $3,675	VG+ $2,650	Good $2,385	Fair $1,220
Trade-In:	Mint $3,770	Ex $2,975	VG+ $2,070	Good $1,855	Poor $540

ELLIPSE EVO LIGHT REDBOOK CODE: RB-GU-S-ELLEVL

Nickel alloy finish, hand rubbed oil stock finish, wood buttplate, 3" chamber, non-ventilated center rib, standard forcing cone, chrome lined barrel, nickel-plated flush-fitting chokes, single selective trigger, manual safety.

Production: *current* **Gauge/Bore:** *20 ga., 28 ga.*
Action: *O/U*
Barrel Length: 28" **Wt.:** *5.3 lbs.*
Sights: *silver front bead*
Capacity: *2*
Stock: *hardwood*

D2C:	NIB $5,605	Ex $4,275	VG+ $3,085	Good $2,805	**LMP: $6,150**
C2C:	Mint $5,390	Ex $3,875	VG+ $2,810	Good $2,525	Fair $1,290
Trade-In:	Mint $3,980	Ex $3,150	VG+ $2,190	Good $1,965	Poor $570

ELLIPSE EVO SPORTING REDBOOK CODE: RB-GU-S-ELLEVS

Hand-polished coin finish, hand rubbed oil stock finish, 26 LPI checkering, black rubber recoil pad, 2 3/4" chamber, ventilated center rib, 5" DuoCon forcing cones, chrome lined barrel, MAXIS competition chokes, ellipse rounded forend, DTS trigger system, manual safety.

Production: *current* **Gauge/Bore:** *12 ga.*
Action: *O/U*
Barrel Length: 30", 32" **Wt.:** *7.8–8 lbs.*
Sights: *white Bradley style front, silver center bead*
Capacity: *2*
Stock: *hardwood*

D2C:	NIB $5,732	Ex $4,375	VG+ $3,155	Good $2,870	**LMP: $6,695**
C2C:	Mint $5,510	Ex $3,975	VG+ $2,870	Good $2,580	Fair $1,320
Trade-In:	Mint $4,070	Ex $3,225	VG+ $2,240	Good $2,010	Poor $600

ELLIPSE EVOLUTION REDBOOK CODE: RB-GU-S-ELEVOL

Hand-polished coin finish on receiver, hand rubbed oil stock finish, 26 LPI checkering, 2 3/4" chamber, ventilated center rib, 5" DuoCon, chrome-lined barrel, ellipse rounded forend, DTS trigger system, manual safety.

Production: *current* **Gauge/Bore:** *12 ga.*
Action: *O/U*
Barrel Length: *32"* **Wt.:** *8.7 lbs.*
Sights: *white Bradley style front, silver center bead*
Capacity: *2*
Stock: *hardwood*

D2C:	NIB $7,416	Ex $5,650	VG+ $4,080	Good $3,710	**LMP: $8,450**
C2C:	Mint $7,120	Ex $5,125	VG+ $3,710	Good $3,340	Fair $1,710
Trade-In:	Mint $5,270	Ex $4,175	VG+ $2,900	Good $2,600	Poor $750

FORUM REDBOOK CODE: RB-GU-S-FORUMX

Hand-polished coin finish on receiver, 26 LPI checkering, black rubber recoil pad, 2 3/4" chamber, ventilated center rib, standard forcing cones, chrome lined barrel, rounded forend, DTS trigger system, manual safety.

Production: *current* **Gauge/Bore:** *12 ga., 20 ga., 28 ga.*
Action: *O/U*
Barrel Length: *28"* **Wt.:** *6.3–7 lbs.*
Sights: *silver front bead*
Capacity: *2*
Stock: *hardwood*

D2C:	NIB $9,650	Ex $7,350	VG+ $5,310	Good $4,825	**LMP: $10,300**
C2C:	Mint $9,270	Ex $6,675	VG+ $4,830	Good $4,345	Fair $2,220
Trade-In:	Mint $6,860	Ex $5,425	VG+ $3,770	Good $3,380	Poor $990

FORUM SPORTING REDBOOK CODE: RB-GU-S-FORUMS

Hand-polished coin finish on receiver, 26 LPI checkering, black rubber recoil pad, 2 3/4" chamber, ventilated center rib, 5" DuoCon forcing cones, chrome lined barrel, rounded forend, DTS trigger system, manual safety.

Production: *current* **Gauge/Bore:** *12 ga.*
Action: *O/U*
Barrel Length: *30", 32"* **Wt.:** *7.8–8 lbs.*
Sights: *white Bradley style, silver center bead*
Capacity: *2*
Stock: *hardwood*

D2C:	NIB $8,295	Ex $6,325	VG+ $4,565	Good $4,150	**LMP: $10,600**
C2C:	Mint $7,970	Ex $5,725	VG+ $4,150	Good $3,735	Fair $1,910
Trade-In:	Mint $5,890	Ex $4,650	VG+ $3,240	Good $2,905	Poor $840

INVICTUS I SPORTING REDBOOK CODE: RB-GU-S-INVICT

Hand-polished coin finish, hand rubbed oil stock finish, 26 LPI checkering, black rubber recoil pad, 2 3/4" chamber, 5" DuoCon forcing cones, chrome lined barrel, MAXIS competition chokes, white Bradley style front, silver center bead, rounded forend, DPS trigger system, manual safety.

Production: *current* **Gauge/Bore:** *12 ga.*
Action: *O/U*
Barrel Length: *30", 32"* **Wt.:** *~8 lbs.*
Sights: *white Bradley style front, silver center bead*
Capacity: *2*
Stock: *hardwood*

D2C:	NIB $6,750	Ex $5,150	VG+ $3,715	Good $3,375	**LMP: $6,750**
C2C:	Mint $6,480	Ex $4,675	VG+ $3,380	Good $3,040	Fair $1,555
Trade-In:	Mint $4,800	Ex $3,800	VG+ $2,640	Good $2,365	Poor $690

GUERINI

MAGNUS   REDBOOK CODE: RB-GU-S-MAGNUS

Case colored with Invisalloy protective finish, hand rubbed oil stock finish, 26 LPI checkering, 3" chamber, non-ventilated center rib, standard forcing cones, chrome lined barrel, Schnabel forend, single selective trigger, manual safety.

Production: *current* **Gauge/Bore:** *12 ga., 20 ga., 28 ga.*
Action: *O/U*
Barrel Length: 28" **Wt.:** *6–7.6 lbs.*
Sights: *silver front bead*
Capacity: *2*
Stock: *hardwood*

D2C:	NIB $3,845	Ex $2,925	VG+ $2,115	Good $1,925	LMP: $4,530
C2C:	Mint $3,700	Ex $2,675	VG+ $1,930	Good $1,735	Fair $885
Trade-In:	Mint $2,730	Ex $2,175	VG+ $1,500	Good $1,350	Poor $390

MAGNUS LIGHT   REDBOOK CODE: RB-GU-S-MAGLIG

Nickel alloy finish on receiver, hand-rubbed oil finish on stock, 26 LPI checkering, 3" chamber, wooden buttplate, non-ventilated center rib, standard forcing cones, chrome lined barrel, nickel-plated flush fitting chokes, Schnabel forend, single selective trigger, manual safety.

Production: *current* **Gauge/Bore:** *12 ga., 20 ga., 28 ga.*
Action: *O/U*
Barrel Length: 26" **Wt.:** *5.7–6 lbs.*
Sights: *silver front bead*
Capacity: *2*
Stock: *hardwood*

D2C:	NIB $3,462	Ex $2,650	VG+ $1,905	Good $1,735	LMP: $4,530
C2C:	Mint $3,330	Ex $2,400	VG+ $1,740	Good $1,560	Fair $800
Trade-In:	Mint $2,460	Ex $1,950	VG+ $1,360	Good $1,215	Poor $360

MAGNUS SPORTING   REDBOOK CODE: RB-GU-S-MAGSPO

Hand-polished coin finish on receiver, hand rubbed oil stock finish, 26 LPI checkering on wood, black rubber recoil pad, ventilated center rib, 5" DuoCon forcing cones, chrome line barrel, MAXIS competition chokes, DTS trigger system, manual safety.

Production: *current* **Gauge/Bore:** *12 ga., 20 ga., 28 ga.*
Action: *O/U*
Barrel Length: 30", 32" **Wt.:** *7.4–8 lbs.*
Sights: *white Bradley style front, silver center bead*
Capacity: *2*
Stock: *hardwood*

D2C:	NIB $4,289	Ex $3,275	VG+ $2,360	Good $2,145	LMP: $5,150
C2C:	Mint $4,120	Ex $2,975	VG+ $2,150	Good $1,935	Fair $990
Trade-In:	Mint $3,050	Ex $2,425	VG+ $1,680	Good $1,505	Poor $450

MAXUM   REDBOOK CODE: RB-GU-S-MAXUMX

Hand-polished coin finish on receiver, hand-rubbed oil stock finish, 26 LPI checkering, wooden buttplate, 2" chamber, non-ventilated center rib, standard forcing cones, chrome lined barrel, nickel-plated flush-fitting chokes, Schnabel forend, single selective trigger, manual safety.

Production: *current* **Gauge/Bore:** *12 ga., 20 ga., 28 ga.*
Action: *O/U*
Barrel Length: 28" **Wt.:** *6.8–7 lbs.*
Sights: *silver front bead*
Capacity: *2*
Stock: *hardwood*

D2C:	NIB $4,897	Ex $3,725	VG+ $2,695	Good $2,450	LMP: $6,175
C2C:	Mint $4,710	Ex $3,400	VG+ $2,450	Good $2,205	Fair $1,130
Trade-In:	Mint $3,480	Ex $2,750	VG+ $1,910	Good $1,715	Poor $510

MAXUM IMPACT REDBOOK CODE: RB-GU-S-MAXIMP

Hand-polished coin finish on receiver, hand-rubbed oil stock finish, 26 LPI checkering, black rubber recoil pad, ventilated center rib, 5" DuoCon forcing cones, chrome lined barrel, MAXIS competition chokes, rounded forend, DTS trigger system, manual safety.

Production: *current* **Gauge/Bore:** *12 ga., 20 ga., 28 ga.*
Action: *O/U*
Barrel Length: *30", 32", 34"* **Wt.:** *7.8–9.2 lbs.*
Sights: *white Bradley style front, silver center bead*
Capacity: *2*
Stock: *hardwood*

D2C:	NIB $7,450	Ex $5,675	VG+ $4,100	Good $3,725	LMP: $8,450
C2C:	Mint $7,160	Ex $5,150	VG+ $3,730	Good $3,355	Fair $1,715
Trade-In:	Mint $5,290	Ex $4,175	VG+ $2,910	Good $2,610	Poor $750

MAXUM SPORTING REDBOOK CODE: RB-GU-S-MAXSPO

Hand-polished coin finish, hand rubbed oil stock finish, 26 LPI checkering, black rubber recoil pad, ventilated center rib, 5" DuoCon forcing cones, MAXIS competition chokes, Schnabel forend, DTS trigger system, manual safety.

Production: *current* **Gauge/Bore:** *12 ga., 20 ga., 28 ga.*
Action: *O/U*
Barrel Length: *30", 32"* **Wt.:** *7.4–8.1 lbs.*
Sights: *white Bradley style front, silver center bead*
Capacity: *2*
Stock: *hardwood*

D2C:	NIB $5,346	Ex $4,075	VG+ $2,945	Good $2,675	LMP: $6,750
C2C:	Mint $5,140	Ex $3,700	VG+ $2,680	Good $2,410	Fair $1,230
Trade-In:	Mint $3,800	Ex $3,000	VG+ $2,090	Good $1,875	Poor $540

SUMMIT ASCENT REDBOOK CODE: RB-GU-S-SUMASC

Satin blue receiver finish, hand-rubbed oil stock finish, 26 LPI checkering, black rubber recoil pad, ventilated center rib, 5" DuoCon forcing cones, MAXIS competition chokes, rounded forend, DTS trigger system, manual safety.

Production: *current* **Gauge/Bore:** *12 ga.*
Action: *O/U*
Barrel Length: *30", 32"* **Wt.:** *~8.5 lbs.*
Sights: *white Bradley style front, silver center bead*
Capacity: *2*
Stock: *hardwood*

D2C:	NIB $4,287	Ex $3,275	VG+ $2,360	Good $2,145	LMP: $4,650
C2C:	Mint $4,120	Ex $2,975	VG+ $2,150	Good $1,930	Fair $990
Trade-In:	Mint $3,050	Ex $2,425	VG+ $1,680	Good $1,505	Poor $450

SUMMIT IMPACT REDBOOK CODE: RB-GU-S-SUMIMP

Satin blue receiver finish, hand-rubbed oil stock finish, 26 LPI checkering, black rubber recoil pad, 2 3/4" chamber, ventilated center rib, 5" DuoCon forcing cones, chrome-lined barrel, MAXIS competition chokes, rounded forend, DTS trigger system, manual safety.

Production: *current* **Gauge/Bore:** *12 ga., 20 ga.*
Action: *O/U*
Barrel Length: *30", 32", 34"* **Wt.:** *8.4–9.2 lbs.*
Sights: *white Bradley style front, silver center bead*
Capacity: *2*
Stock: *hardwood*

D2C:	NIB $4,778	Ex $3,650	VG+ $2,630	Good $2,390	LMP: $5,495
C2C:	Mint $4,590	Ex $3,300	VG+ $2,390	Good $2,155	Fair $1,100
Trade-In:	Mint $3,400	Ex $2,700	VG+ $1,870	Good $1,675	Poor $480

GUERINI

SUMMIT LIMITED   REDBOOK CODE: RB-GU-S-SUMLIM

Case colored with Invisalloy protective finish, hand rubbed oil stock finish, 26 LPI checkering, 2 3/4" chamber, ventilated center rib, 5" DuoCon forcing cones, chrome-lined barrel, MAXIS competition chokes, Schnabel forend, manual safety.

Production: *current* **Gauge/Bore:** *12 ga., 20 ga., 28 ga., .410*
Action: *O/U*
Barrel Length: 30", 32" **Wt.:** *7.8–8 lbs.*
Sights: *white Bradley style front, silver center bead*
Capacity: *2*
Stock: *hardwood*

D2C:	NIB $3,855	Ex $2,950	VG+ $2,125	Good $1,930	**LMP: $4,495**
C2C:	Mint $3,710	Ex $2,675	VG+ $1,930	Good $1,735	Fair $890
Trade-In:	Mint $2,740	Ex $2,175	VG+ $1,510	Good $1,350	Poor $390

SUMMIT SPORTING   REDBOOK CODE: RB-GU-S-SUMSPO

Hand-polished coin finish, hand-rubbed oil stock finish, 26 LPI checkering, black rubber recoil pad, ventilated top and center rib, chrome lined barrel, MAXIS competition chokes, Schnabel forend, DTS trigger system, manual safety.

Production: *current* **Gauge/Bore:** *12 ga.*
Action: *O/U*
Barrel Length: 30", 32", 34" **Wt.:** *7.8–8.1 lbs.*
Sights: *white Bradley style front, silver center bead*
Capacity: *2*
Stock: *hardwood*

D2C:	NIB $3,299	Ex $2,525	VG+ $1,815	Good $1,650	**LMP: $3,700**
C2C:	Mint $3,170	Ex $2,300	VG+ $1,650	Good $1,485	Fair $760
Trade-In:	Mint $2,350	Ex $1,850	VG+ $1,290	Good $1,155	Poor $330

TEMPIO   REDBOOK CODE: RB-GU-S-TEMPIO

Hand-polished coin finish on receiver, hand-rubbed oil stock finish, 26 LPI checkering, wooden buttplate, 3" chamber, ventilated top rib, non-ventilated center rib, standard forcing cones, chrome lined barrel, nickel-plated flush fitting cones, Schnabel forend, single selective trigger, manual safety.

Production: *current* **Gauge/Bore:** *12 ga., 20 ga., 28 ga., .410*
Action: *O/U*
Barrel Length: 26", 28", 30" **Wt.:** *6.5–7 lbs.*
Sights: *silver front bead*
Capacity: *2*
Stock: *hardwood*

D2C:	NIB $3,184	Ex $2,425	VG+ $1,755	Good $1,595	**LMP: $3,950**
C2C:	Mint $3,060	Ex $2,200	VG+ $1,600	Good $1,435	Fair $735
Trade-In:	Mint $2,270	Ex $1,800	VG+ $1,250	Good $1,115	Poor $330

TEMPIO LIGHT   REDBOOK CODE: RB-GU-S-TEMLIG

Nickel alloy receiver finish, hand rubbed oil stock finish, wooden buttplate, 3" chamber, ventilated top rib, non-ventilated center rib, standard forcing cones, chrome lined barrel, nickel-plated flush-fitting chokes, Schnabel forend, single-selective trigger, manual safety.

Production: *current* **Gauge/Bore:** *12 ga., 20 ga., 28 ga.*
Action: *O/U*
Barrel Length: 26", 28" **Wt.:** *5.8–6 lbs.*
Sights: *silver front bead*
Capacity: *2*
Stock: *hardwood*

D2C:	NIB $3,231	Ex $2,475	VG+ $1,780	Good $1,620	**LMP: $3,950**
C2C:	Mint $3,110	Ex $2,250	VG+ $1,620	Good $1,455	Fair $745
Trade-In:	Mint $2,300	Ex $1,825	VG+ $1,270	Good $1,135	Poor $330

WOODLANDER REDBOOK CODE: RB-GU-S-WOODLA

Case colored with Invisalloy protective finish, hand rubbed oil stock finish, 26 LPI checkering, 3" chamber, wooden buttplate, non-ventilated center rib, ventilated top rib, nickel-plated flush-fitting chokes, Schnabel forend, single selective trigger, manual safety.

Production: *current* **Gauge/Bore:** *12 ga., 20 ga., 28 ga.*
Action: *O/U*
Barrel Length: 26", 28" **Wt.:** *6.3–6.8 lbs.*
Sights: *silver front bead*
Capacity: *2*
Stock: *hardwood*

D2C:	NIB $2,822	Ex $2,150	VG+ $1,555	Good $1,415	LMP: $3,350
C2C:	Mint $2,710	Ex $1,950	VG+ $1,420	Good $1,270	Fair $650
Trade-In:	Mint $2,010	Ex $1,600	VG+ $1,110	Good $990	Poor $300

Harrington & Richardson, Inc. (H&R 1871)

In 1871, Gilbert H. Harrington produced the first top-breaking, shell-ejecting revolver; he and William A. Richardson began the original company that is now known as H&R 1871. In less than ten years, the company's superlative reputation for quality garnered it the opportunity to be named the sole North American licensee to manufacture Anson & Deely's double-barrel hammerless shotgun—a great honor because the gun was widely considered to be the finest shotgun available at that time. By 1893, they began building a new factory in Worcester, Massachusetts, a space that had to expand again to meet production demands within only a few years. The company continued to increase its product offerings, adding what became a mainstay with a single-barrel shotgun that featured automatic shell ejection. The company also got involved with defense initiatives, producing shoulder flare guns during World War I and enough military firearms during World War II to make it the most prolific producer of M14s at that time. In 2000, Marlin Firearms purchased the company, and doing business as H&R 1871, the company in its current form is the largest manufacturer of single-shot shotguns and rifles in the world.

EXCELL AUTO SYNTHETIC REDBOOK CODE: RB-HR-S-EXCATO

Black finished barrel with vented-rib, molded-in checkering, ventilated recoil pad, four screw-in choke tubes, 3" chamber, steel shot compatible.

Production: *current* **Gauge/Bore:** *12 ga.*
Action: *semi-auto*
Barrel Length: 28" **Wt.:** *7 lbs.*
Sights: *bead*
Capacity: *5*
Stock: *synthetic black or walnut*

D2C:	NIB $460	Ex $350	VG+ $255	Good $230	LMP: $499
C2C:	Mint $450	Ex $325	VG+ $230	Good $210	Fair $110
Trade-In:	Mint $330	Ex $275	VG+ $180	Good $165	Poor $60

EXCELL AUTO WATERFOWL REDBOOK CODE: RB-HR-S-EXCATW

Complete camo-dip finish. Four steel-shot compatible choke tubes (IC, M, IM, F). Up to 3" chamber, 3 shot plug furnished.

Production: *current* **Gauge/Bore:** *12 ga.*
Action: *semi-auto*
Barrel Length: 28" **Wt.:** *7 lbs.*
Sights: *bead*
Capacity: *5*
Stock: *synthetic Realtree camo*

D2C:	NIB $510	Ex $400	VG+ $285	Good $255	LMP: $579
C2C:	Mint $490	Ex $375	VG+ $260	Good $230	Fair $120
Trade-In:	Mint $370	Ex $300	VG+ $200	Good $180	Poor $60

H&R 1871

EXCELL AUTO TURKEY REDBOOK CODE: RB-HR-S-EXCATT
Full camo finish with vent-rib barrel. Four screw-in choke tubes (IC, M, F, Extra Full Turkey). Up to 3" chamber, 3 shot plug furnished.

Production: *current* **Gauge/Bore:** *12 ga.*
Action: *semi-auto*
Barrel Length: 22" **Wt.:** *7 lbs.*
Sights: *fiber-optic*
Capacity: *5*
Stock: *synthetic Realtree camo*

D2C:	NIB $470	Ex $375	VG+ $260	Good $235	**LMP:** $579
C2C:	Mint $460	Ex $325	VG+ $240	Good $215	Fair $110
Trade-In:	Mint $340	Ex $275	VG+ $190	Good $165	Poor $60

EXCELL AUTO TACTICAL REDBOOK CODE: RB-HR-S-EXATTL
Black finished barrel with vented rib, heavy black oxide finish, ventilated recoil pad, four screw-in choke tubes, 3" chamber.

Production: *current* **Gauge/Bore:** *12 ga.*
Action: *semi-auto*
Barrel Length: 18.5" **Wt.:** *6.5 lbs.*
Sights: *bead*
Capacity: *5*
Stock: *synthetic black oxide*

D2C:	NIB $410	Ex $325	VG+ $230	Good $205	**LMP:** $499
C2C:	Mint $400	Ex $300	VG+ $210	Good $185	Fair $95
Trade-In:	Mint $300	Ex $250	VG+ $160	Good $145	Poor $60

EXCELL AUTO COMBO REDBOOK CODE: RB-HR-S-EXCATC
Black finished barrel with vented-rib, comes with additional 24" fully rifled slug barrel, molded-in checkering, ventilated recoil pad, four screw-in choke tubes, up to 3" chamber, steel-shot compatible.

Production: *current* **Gauge/Bore:** *12 ga.*
Action: *semi-auto*
Barrel Length: 28", 24" **Wt.:** *7 lbs.*
Sights: *bead front or fiber optic front and rear*
Capacity: *5*
Stock: *synthetic black*

D2C:	NIB $480	Ex $375	VG+ $265	Good $240	
C2C:	Mint $470	Ex $350	VG+ $240	Good $220	Fair $115
Trade-In:	Mint $350	Ex $275	VG+ $190	Good $170	Poor $60

TOPPER REDBOOK CODE: RB-HR-S-TPPRXX
Black finished hardwood stock, nickel-finished receiver and fixed choke, automatic ejection, transfer bar system, automatic ejectors, pistol grip.

Production: *current* **Gauge/Bore:** *12 ga., 20 ga., .410*
Action: *single-shot*
Barrel Length: 26", 28" **Wt.:** *5–6 lbs.*
Sights: *bead*
Capacity: *1*
Stock: *American hardwood, black finish*

D2C:	NIB $150	Ex $125	VG+ $85	Good $75	
C2C:	Mint $150	Ex $125	VG+ $80	Good $70	Fair $35
Trade-In:	Mint $110	Ex $100	VG+ $60	Good $55	Poor $30

TOPPER DELUXE CLASSIC REDBOOK CODE: RB-HR-S-TPPRDC

Black finished barrel with ventilated rib, nickel-finished receiver and screw-in modified choke, transfer bar system, automatic ejectors, checkered pistol grip, ventilated recoil pad.

Production: *current* **Gauge/Bore:** *12 ga., 20 ga.*
Action: *single-shot*
Barrel Length: 28" **Wt.:** *6–7 lbs.*
Sights: *bead*
Capacity: *1*
Stock: *American black walnut*

D2C:	NIB $220	Ex $175	VG+ $125	Good $110	
C2C:	Mint $220	Ex $175	VG+ $110	Good $100	Fair $55
Trade-In:	Mint $160	Ex $125	VG+ $90	Good $80	Poor $30

TOPPER JR REDBOOK CODE: RB-HR-S-TPPRJR

Black finished barrel, full and modified choke, transfer bar system, automatic ejectors, full pistol grip, ventilated recoil pad.

Production: *current* **Gauge/Bore:** *20 ga., .410*
Action: *single-shot*
Barrel Length: 22" **Wt.:** *5–6 lbs.*
Sights: *bead*
Capacity: *1*
Stock: *American hardwood, black finish*

D2C:	NIB $160	Ex $125	VG+ $90	Good $80	
C2C:	Mint $160	Ex $125	VG+ $80	Good $75	Fair $40
Trade-In:	Mint $120	Ex $100	VG+ $70	Good $60	Poor $30

TOPPER JR CLASSIC REDBOOK CODE: RB-HR-S-TPPJRC

Black finished barrel and receiver, modified/full choke, side lever release, transfer bar system, automatic ejectors, checkered pistol grip, ventilated recoil pad.

Production: *current* **Gauge/Bore:** *20 ga., .410*
Action: *single-shot*
Barrel Length: 22" **Wt.:** *5–6 lbs.*
Sights: *bead*
Capacity: *1*
Stock: *American black walnut*

D2C:	NIB $190	Ex $150	VG+ $105	Good $95	
C2C:	Mint $190	Ex $150	VG+ $100	Good $90	Fair $45
Trade-In:	Mint $140	Ex $125	VG+ $80	Good $70	Poor $30

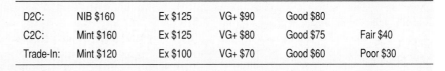

TOPPER TRAP GUN REDBOOK CODE: RB-HR-S-TPPRTG

Electroless nickel-coated frame, vented rib, screw-in IM extended choke, transfer bar safety, fluted comb, pistol grip, cut checkering, trap buttstock, Pachmayr trap recoil pad.

Production: *current* **Gauge/Bore:** *12 ga.*
Action: *single-shot*
Barrel Length: 30" **Wt.:** *7 lbs.*
Sights: *two white trap beads*
Capacity: *1*
Stock: *Select Grade walnut*

D2C:	NIB $360	Ex $275	VG+ $200	Good $180	
C2C:	Mint $350	Ex $250	VG+ $180	Good $165	Fair $85
Trade-In:	Mint $260	Ex $225	VG+ $150	Good $130	Poor $60

H&R 1871

PARDNER REDBOOK CODE: RB-HR-S-PRDNRX

Blue finished barrel and receiver, modified or full fixed choke depending on gauge, 2 3/4" chamber for 28 gauge with 3" chamber otherwise, transfer bar safety system, automatic ejection.

Production: *current* **Gauge/Bore:** *12 ga., 20 ga., 28 ga., .410*
Action: *single-shot*
Barrel Length: *26", 28", 32"* **Wt.:** *5–6 lbs.*
Sights: *bead*
Capacity: *1*
Stock: *American hardwood*

D2C:	NIB $200	Ex $175	VG+ $110	Good $100	LMP: $206
C2C:	Mint $200	Ex $150	VG+ $100	Good $90	Fair $50
Trade-In:	Mint $150	Ex $125	VG+ $80	Good $70	Poor $30

PARDNER TURKEY REDBOOK CODE: RB-HR-S-PRDNRT

Blue-finished barrel and receiver, fixed full chokes or screw-in turkey chokes, side lever release, 3.5" chamber, 10 gauge is drilled and tapped for scope and Extra-full screw-in choke, automatic ejection, pistol grip, ventilated rubber recoil pad, sling swivel studs and sling, 22" barrel on 20 gauge Compact model.

Production: *current* **Gauge/Bore:** *10 ga., 12 ga.*
Action: *single-shot*
Barrel Length: *24", 22"* **Wt.:** *9 lbs., 6 lbs.*
Sights: *bead*
Capacity: *1*
Stock: *American hardwood, camo pattern*

D2C:	NIB $250	Ex $200	VG+ $140	Good $125	LMP: $322
C2C:	Mint $240	Ex $175	VG+ $130	Good $115	Fair $60
Trade-In:	Mint $180	Ex $150	VG+ $100	Good $90	Poor $30

PARDNER COMPACT REDBOOK CODE: RB-HR-S-PRDCMP

Youth model with blue-finished barrel and receiver, modified choke in 20 gauge and full choke in .410, 3" chamber, transfer bar safety system, automatic ejection, butt plate recoil pad, proportioned for small frame.

Production: *current* **Gauge/Bore:** *20 ga., .410*
Action: *single-shot*
Barrel Length: *22"* **Wt.:** *5–5.5 lbs.*
Sights: *bead*
Capacity: *1*
Stock: *American hardwood*

D2C:	NIB $210	Ex $175	VG+ $120	Good $105	LMP: $225
C2C:	Mint $210	Ex $150	VG+ $110	Good $95	Fair $50
Trade-In:	Mint $150	Ex $125	VG+ $90	Good $75	Poor $30

PARDNER PUMP COMPACT REDBOOK CODE: RB-HR-S-PRDPCP

Youth model with screw-in modified choke, vent rib, drilled and tapped for scope base, available with a rugged black synthetic stock or full camo/synthetic, reduced 13" length of pull.

Production: *current* **Gauge/Bore:** *20 ga.*
Action: *pump-action*
Barrel Length: *21"* **Wt.:** *6.5 lbs.*
Sights: *bead*
Capacity: *5*
Stock: *American walnut*

D2C:	NIB $210	Ex $175	VG+ $120	Good $105	
C2C:	Mint $210	Ex $150	VG+ $110	Good $95	Fair $50
Trade-In:	Mint $150	Ex $125	VG+ $90	Good $75	Poor $30

PARDNER PUMP SYNTHETIC REDBOOK CODE: RB-HR-S-PRDNRP

Basic features of Pardner Pump Walnut model but with black synthetic stock for rougher conditions. Molded-in checkering and ventilated recoil pad. Grooved forend, barrel drilled and tapped for scope base. Screw-in modified choke.

Production: *current* **Gauge/Bore:** *12 ga., 20 ga.*
Action: *pump-action*
Barrel Length: 26", 28" **Wt.:** *7.5 lbs.*
Sights: *bead*
Capacity: *5*
Stock: *synthetic black*

D2C:	NIB $210	Ex $175	VG+ $120	Good $105	LMP: $231
C2C:	Mint $210	Ex $150	VG+ $110	Good $95	Fair $50
Trade-In:	Mint $150	Ex $125	VG+ $90	Good $75	Poor $30

PARDNER PUMP PROTECTOR REDBOOK CODE: RB-HR-S-PRDPTR

Home defense model, grooved forend with sling swivel studs installed, ventilated recoil pad, drilled and tapped for scope base, 3" chamber, black finish, 14.25" length of pull.

Production: *current* **Gauge/Bore:** *12 ga.*
Action: *pump-action*
Barrel Length: 18.5" **Wt.:** *7.5 lbs.*
Sights: *bead front*
Capacity: *5*
Stock: *black synthetic*

D2C:	NIB $180	Ex $150	VG+ $100	Good $90	LMP: $231
C2C:	Mint $180	Ex $125	VG+ $90	Good $85	Fair $45
Trade-In:	Mint $130	Ex $125	VG+ $80	Good $65	Poor $30

PARDNER TURKEY REDBOOK CODE: RB-HR-S-PRDNRT

Blue-finished barrel and receiver, camo pattern finish on stock and forend, extra full screw-in choke on 10 gauge, fixed full or screw-in turkey chokes on 12 gauge, 3 1/2" chamber, 10 gauge is drilled and tapped for scope and extra-full screw-in choke, automatic ejection, pistol grip, ventilated rubber recoil pad, sling swivel studs and sling, 22" barrel on 20 gauge Compact model.

Production: *current* **Gauge/Bore:** *10 ga., 12 ga., 20 ga.*
Action: *single-shot*
Barrel Length: 24", 22" **Wt.:** *9 lbs., 6 lbs.*
Sights: *bead*
Capacity: *1*
Stock: *American hardwood*

D2C:	NIB $250	Ex $200	VG+ $140	Good $125	LMP: $322
C2C:	Mint $240	Ex $175	VG+ $130	Good $115	Fair $60
Trade-In:	Mint $180	Ex $150	VG+ $100	Good $90	Poor $30

ULTRA SLUG HUNTER REDBOOK CODE: RB-HR-S-USHNTR

Fully rifled Ultragon barrel of heavy steel for long range accuracy with high-velocity slugs. Monte Carlo comb, scope mounts included. 12 gauge available with factory-mounted and bore-sighted 3-9x scope. Compact 20 gauge has 22" barrel. Deluxe version has added weather resistance and laminated stock.

Production: *current* **Gauge/Bore:** *12 ga., 20 ga.*
Action: *single-shot*
Barrel Length: 24" **Wt.:** *8–9 lbs.*
Sights: *none*
Capacity: *1*
Stock: *American hardwood*

D2C:	NIB $300	Ex $250	VG+ $165	Good $150	LMP: $290
C2C:	Mint $290	Ex $225	VG+ $150	Good $135	Fair $70
Trade-In:	Mint $220	Ex $175	VG+ $120	Good $105	Poor $30

H&R 1871

TRACKER LL SLUG REDBOOK CODE: RB-HR-S-TRKR2S
Lightweight, blue-finished barrel and receiver, fully Ultragon rifled with six oval lands and grooves and no sharp corners, pistol grip, sling swivel studs, recoil pad.

Production: *current* **Gauge/Bore:** *12 ga., 20 ga.*
Action: *single-shot*
Barrel Length: 24" **Wt.:** *5.25 lbs.*
Sights: *adjustable rifle*
Capacity: *1*
Stock: *American hardwood*

D2C:	NIB $220	Ex $175	VG+ $125	Good $110	LMP: $290
C2C:	Mint $220	Ex $175	VG+ $110	Good $100	Fair $55
Trade-In:	Mint $160	Ex $125	VG+ $90	Good $80	Poor $30

SURVIVOR .410/.45 LC REDBOOK CODE: RB-HR-S-SURVVR
Shotgun/rifle combo, screw-in Modified choke, buttstock storage compartment, swivel studs and sling, add $20 more for nickel-finish.

Production: *current* **Gauge/Bore:** *.410/.45 LC*
Action: *single-shot*
Barrel Length: 20" **Wt.:** *7 lbs.*
Sights: *bead*
Capacity: *1*
Stock: *black polymer thumbhole*

D2C:	NIB $300	Ex $250	VG+ $165	Good $150	LMP: $326
C2C:	Mint $290	Ex $225	VG+ $150	Good $135	Fair $70
Trade-In:	Mint $220	Ex $175	VG+ $120	Good $105	Poor $30

TAMER REDBOOK CODE: RB-HR-S-TAMERX
Matte nickel-finished receiver and compact barrel with fixed full choke, 3" chamber, automatic ejection, thumbhole/pistol grip, storage in stock.

Production: *current* **Gauge/Bore:** *20 ga., .410*
Action: *single-shot*
Barrel Length: 20" **Wt.:** *6 lbs.*
Sights: *bead*
Capacity: *1*
Stock: *black polymer thumbhole*

D2C:	NIB $210	Ex $175	VG+ $120	Good $105	LMP: $223
C2C:	Mint $210	Ex $150	VG+ $110	Good $95	Fair $50
Trade-In:	Mint $150	Ex $125	VG+ $90	Good $75	Poor $30

HOLLAND & HOLLAND

Holland & Holland

Holland & Holland Ltd. is one of the most esteemed makers in the rifle and shotgun industry, and the brand's handmade firearms are associated with luxury and quality. Company history dates back to 1835 when Harris Holland founded the company in London. In 1860, Harris hired his nephew, Henry, a man who would not only become his partner in 1876 but would also come to be known as one of the most prolific gun inventors in history. Holland & Holland has registered fifty-one patents, more than any other British firearms manufacturer. The first of those came in 1861 for a bolt action rifle and slide and drop action, and many innovations followed, with one of the biggest coming in 1908 with the detachable lock. Ever ahead of the competition, in 1985, Holland & Holland was the first British firearms manufacturer to acquire and implement the CNC technology that is still used in gunmaking today. The company introduced the Round Action sidelock shotgun and double barrel rifle in 2002, in keeping with the company's history of variants of the sidelock design.

'ROYAL' SIDE-BY-SIDE   REDBOOK CODE: RB-HH-S-ROYSBS

Self-opening system sidelock ejector, two triggers, manual or automatic safety, 2 3/4" chamber, polished and oiled wood, hand checkering, 'Royal' scroll engraving pattern, option oval engraved or inlaid with gold with initials or crest. Prices reflect recent production. Slightly higher value for 28 gauge and .410 models.

Production: *current* **Gauge/Bore:** *12 ga., 16 ga., 20 ga., 28 ga., .410*

Action: *SxS*

Barrel Length: *25"–32"* **Wt.:** *5–6.8 lbs.*

Sights: *none*

Capacity: *2*

Stock: *straight or semi-pistol walnut*

D2C:	NIB $91,000	Ex $69,175	VG+ $50,050	Good $45,500	LMP: $111,269
C2C:	Mint $87,360	Ex $62,800	VG+ $45,500	Good $40,950	Fair $20,930
Trade-In:	Mint $64,610	Ex $50,975	VG+ $35,490	Good $31,850	Poor $9,120

'ROYAL' OVER-AND-UNDER   REDBOOK CODE: RB-HH-S-ROYOVU

Sidelock ejector with hand-detachable locks, single trigger, manual or automatic safety, game or ventilated top rib, 3" chamber, polished and oiled stock, hand checkering, 'Royal' scroll engraving pattern. Prices reflect recent production. Slightly higher value for 28 gauge and .410 models.

Production: *current* **Gauge/Bore:** *12 ga., 16 ga., 20 ga., 28 ga., .410*

Action: *O/U*

Barrel Length: *25"–32"* **Wt.:** *5.6–7.4 lbs.*

Sights: *none*

Capacity: *2*

Stock: *walnut w/ choice of grip styles*

D2C:	NIB $104,600	Ex $79,500	VG+ $57,530	Good $52,300	LMP: $128,508
C2C:	Mint $100,420	Ex $72,175	VG+ $52,300	Good $47,070	Fair $24,060
Trade-In:	Mint $74,270	Ex $58,600	VG+ $40,800	Good $36,610	Poor $10,470

'SPORTING' OVER-AND-UNDER   REDBOOK CODE: RB-HH-S-SPORTX

Quick-detachable single trigger-lock, top-lever opening, non-automatic thumbpiece safety, integral breech barrel construction, game or ventilated top rib, optional interchangeable chokes, 3" chamber, polished and oil finished hardwood, hand checkering, recoil pad or buttplate. Prices reflect recent production.

Production: *current* **Gauge/Bore:** *12 ga., 20 ga., 28 ga.*

Action: *O/U*

Barrel Length: *25"–32"* **Wt.:** *6–7.2 lbs.*

Sights: *none*

Capacity: *2*

Stock: *walnut w/ choice of grip styles*

D2C:	NIB $65,100	Ex $49,500	VG+ $35,805	Good $32,550	LMP: $70,523
C2C:	Mint $62,500	Ex $44,925	VG+ $32,550	Good $29,295	Fair $14,975
Trade-In:	Mint $46,230	Ex $36,475	VG+ $25,390	Good $22,785	Poor $6,510

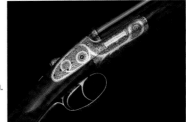

'ROUND ACTION SIDELOCK'   REDBOOK CODE: RB-HH-S-ROUNDA

Pronounced rounded back-action, two triggers, manual or automatic safety, 2 3/4" chamber, game rib, polished and oiled straight grip, recoil pad or heelplate. Prices reflect recent production.

Production: *current* **Gauge/Bore:** *12 ga., 20 ga.*

Action: *SxS*

Barrel Length: *25"–32"* **Wt.:** *6–6.8 lbs.*

Sights: *none*

Capacity: *2*

Stock: *straight grip walnut*

D2C:	NIB $44,000	Ex $33,450	VG+ $24,200	Good $22,000	LMP: $78,359
C2C:	Mint $42,240	Ex $30,375	VG+ $22,000	Good $19,800	Fair $10,120
Trade-In:	Mint $31,240	Ex $24,650	VG+ $17,160	Good $15,400	Poor $4,410

'BADMINTON' SIDELOCK   REDBOOK CODE: RB-HH-S-BADMIN

Traditional rose and scroll engraving, does not have self-opening action, double trigger, side-ejection, 15" length of pull, 2 3/4" chamber.

Production: *discontinued* **Gauge/Bore:** *12 ga., 16 ga., 20 ga.*
Action: *SxS*
Barrel Length: 25"–32" **Wt.:** *6.2 lbs.*
Sights: *none*
Capacity: *2*
Stock: *pistol grip walnut*

D2C:	NIB $23,000	Ex $17,500	VG+ $12,650	Good $11,500	
C2C:	Mint $22,080	Ex $15,875	VG+ $11,500	Good $10,350	Fair $5,290
Trade-In:	Mint $16,330	Ex $12,900	VG+ $8,970	Good $8,050	Poor $2,310

'CAVALIER' BOXLOCK SIDELOCK   REDBOOK CODE: RB-HH-S-CAVALI

Scalloped frame, double trigger, case colored receiver, hand checkering, double trigger, case-hardened receiver.

Production: *discontinued* **Gauge/Bore:** *12 ga., 20 ga., 28 ga.*
Action: *SxS*
Barrel Length: 28", 30" **Wt.:** *N/A*
Sights: *none*
Capacity: *2*
Stock: *straight grip*

D2C:	NIB $15,000	Ex $11,400	VG+ $8,250	Good $7,500	
C2C:	Mint $14,400	Ex $10,350	VG+ $7,500	Good $6,750	Fair $3,450
Trade-In:	Mint $10,650	Ex $8,400	VG+ $5,850	Good $5,250	Poor $1,500

Huglu

Established in 1962 in Huglu, Turkey, Huglu Hunting Firearms Cooperative produces over/under, side-by-side, pump, and semi-automatic shotgun models in all gauges. Eighty percent of the products produced by the company are distributed to other countries, chiefly to the U.S. American distribution has been handled by several different companies and dates back to the 1990s. For a time, Huglu models were distributed in the U.S. through Huglu USA, but that company was reorganized in January 2003 and renamed H-Legacy Shotguns Ltd. Co. now serves only as a dealer of Huglu products. CZ-USA has distributed Huglu firearms to the U.S. since 2005.

101-BE   REDBOOK CODE: RB-HL-S-101BEX

Single trigger, manual or automatic safety, silver scroll engraving, white or black chrome options, barrel interior is white chromed.

Production: *current* **Gauge/Bore:** *12 ga.*
Action: *O/U*
Barrel Length: 30" **Wt.:** *7.6 lbs.*
Sights: *bead front*
Capacity: *2*
Stock: *walnut*

D2C:	NIB $1,660	Ex $1,275	VG+ $915	Good $830	
C2C:	Mint $1,600	Ex $1,150	VG+ $830	Good $750	Fair $385
Trade-In:	Mint $1,180	Ex $950	VG+ $650	Good $585	Poor $180

101-SE REDBOOK CODE: RB-HL-S-101SXX

Single trigger, 3" chamber, manual or automatic safety, silver scroll engraving, white or black chrome options, white chrome barrel interior.

Production: *current* **Gauge/Bore:** *12 ga.*

Action: *O/U*

Barrel Length: *28"* **Wt.:** *7.6 lbs.*

Sights: *bead front*

Capacity: *2*

Stock: *walnut*

D2C:	NIB $1,850	Ex $1,425	VG+ $1,020	Good $925	
C2C:	Mint $1,780	Ex $1,300	VG+ $930	Good $835	Fair $430
Trade-In:	Mint $1,320	Ex $1,050	VG+ $730	Good $650	Poor $210

103-C REDBOOK CODE: RB-HL-S-103CXX

Single trigger, 3" chamber, manual or automatic safety, choice of engraving, white or black chrome, silver chrome barrel interior.

Production: *current* **Gauge/Bore:** *12 ga., 16 ga., 20 ga., 28 ga., 36 ga.*

Action: *O/U*

Barrel Length: *24"–30"* **Wt.:** *7.2 lbs.*

Sights: *bead front*

Capacity: *2*

Stock: *walnut*

D2C:	NIB $790	Ex $625	VG+ $435	Good $395	
C2C:	Mint $760	Ex $550	VG+ $400	Good $360	Fair $185
Trade-In:	Mint $570	Ex $450	VG+ $310	Good $280	Poor $90

103-CE REDBOOK CODE: RB-HL-S-103CEX

Single trigger, 3" chamber, manual or automatic safety, choice of engraving, white or black chrome, white chrome barrel interior.

Production: *current* **Gauge/Bore:** *12 ga., 20 ga.*

Action: *O/U*

Barrel Length: *24"–30"* **Wt.:** *7.3 lbs.*

Sights: *bead front*

Capacity: *2*

Stock: *walnut*

D2C:	NIB $949	Ex $725	VG+ $525	Good $475	
C2C:	Mint $920	Ex $675	VG+ $480	Good $430	Fair $220
Trade-In:	Mint $680	Ex $550	VG+ $380	Good $335	Poor $120

103-D REDBOOK CODE: RB-HL-S-103DXX

Single trigger, manual or optional safety, silver or black engraving, white or black chrome options, white chromed barrel interior.

Production: *current* **Gauge/Bore:** *12 ga., 16 ga., 20 ga., 28 ga., 36 ga.*

Action: *O/U*

Barrel Length: *24"–30"* **Wt.:** *7.2 lbs.*

Sights: *bead front*

Capacity: *2*

Stock: *walnut*

D2C:	NIB $679	Ex $525	VG+ $375	Good $340	
C2C:	Mint $660	Ex $475	VG+ $340	Good $310	Fair $160
Trade-In:	Mint $490	Ex $400	VG+ $270	Good $240	Poor $90

103-DE REDBOOK CODE: RB-HL-S-103DEX

Single trigger, 3" chamber, manual or automatic safety, choice of engraving, white or black chrome, white chrome barrel interior.

Production: *current* **Gauge/Bore:** *12 ga., 20 ga.*
Action: *O/U*
Barrel Length: 24"–30" **Wt.:** *7.3 lbs.*
Sights: *bead front*
Capacity: 2
Stock: *walnut*

D2C:	NIB $755	Ex $575	VG+ $420	Good $380	
C2C:	Mint $730	Ex $525	VG+ $380	Good $340	Fair $175
Trade-In:	Mint $540	Ex $425	VG+ $300	Good $265	Poor $90

103-F REDBOOK CODE: RB-HL-S-103FXX

Single trigger, manual or automatic safety, choice of engraving, black or white chrome options, 8mm rib, 3" chamber, barrel interior is white chrome.

Production: *current* **Gauge/Bore:** *12 ga., 16 ga., 20 ga., 28 ga., 36 ga.*
Action: *O/U*
Barrel Length: 24"–30" **Wt.:** *7.2 lbs.*
Sights: *bead front*
Capacity: 2
Stock: *walnut*

D2C:	NIB $925	Ex $725	VG+ $510	Good $465	
C2C:	Mint $890	Ex $650	VG+ $470	Good $420	Fair $215
Trade-In:	Mint $660	Ex $525	VG+ $370	Good $325	Poor $120

103-FE REDBOOK CODE: RB-HL-S-103FEX

Single trigger, manual or automatic safety with selector, choice of engraving, black or white chrome options, 8mm rib, interior of barrel is white chromed.

Production: *current* **Gauge/Bore:** *12 ga., 20 ga.*
Action: *O/U*
Barrel Length: 24"–30" **Wt.:** *7.3 lbs.*
Sights: *bead front*
Capacity: 2
Stock: *walnut*

D2C:	NIB $950	Ex $725	VG+ $525	Good $475	
C2C:	Mint $920	Ex $675	VG+ $480	Good $430	Fair $220
Trade-In:	Mint $680	Ex $550	VG+ $380	Good $335	Poor $120

104-A REDBOOK CODE: RB-HL-S-104AXX

Double trigger, manual safety, silver or black engraving, 8mm rib, barrel interior is white chrome.

Production: *current* **Gauge/Bore:** *12 ga., 16 ga., 20 ga., 28 ga., 36 ga.*
Action: *O/U*
Barrel Length: 24"–30" **Wt.:** *7.3 lbs.*
Sights: *bead front*
Capacity: 2
Stock: *walnut*

D2C:	NIB $525	Ex $400	VG+ $290	Good $265	
C2C:	Mint $510	Ex $375	VG+ $270	Good $240	Fair $125
Trade-In:	Mint $380	Ex $300	VG+ $210	Good $185	Poor $60

200-A REDBOOK CODE: RB-HL-S-200AXX

Single trigger, manual or automatic safety, optional engraving, white or black chrome options, sunken top rib, barrel interior is white chrome.

Production: *current* **Gauge/Bore:** *12 ga., 16 ga., 20 ga., 28 ga., 36 ga.*
Action: *SxS*
Barrel Length: *24"–30"* **Wt.:** *7.2 lbs.*
Sights: *none*
Capacity: *2*
Stock: *walnut*

D2C:	NIB $975	Ex $750	VG+ $540	Good $490	
C2C:	Mint $940	Ex $675	VG+ $490	Good $440	Fair $225
Trade-In:	Mint $700	Ex $550	VG+ $390	Good $345	Poor $120

200-AC REDBOOK CODE: RB-HL-S-200ACX

Single trigger, 3" chamber, manual or automatic safety, choice of engraving, white or black chrome, silver chrome barrel interior.

Production: *current* **Gauge/Bore:** *12 ga., 16 ga., 20 ga., 28 ga., 36 ga.*
Action: *SxS*
Barrel Length: *24"–30"* **Wt.:** *7.2 lbs.*
Sights: *none*
Capacity: *2*
Stock: *walnut*

D2C:	NIB $890	Ex $700	VG+ $490	Good $445	
C2C:	Mint $860	Ex $625	VG+ $450	Good $405	Fair $205
Trade-In:	Mint $640	Ex $500	VG+ $350	Good $315	Poor $90

201-A REDBOOK CODE: RB-HL-S-201AXX

Double trigger, 3" chamber, manual or automatic safety, choice of engraving, white or black chrome, white chrome barrel interior.

Production: *current* **Gauge/Bore:** *12 ga., 16 ga., 20 ga., 28 ga., 36 ga.*
Action: *SxS*
Barrel Length: *24"–30"* **Wt.:** *7.1 lbs.*
Sights: *none*
Capacity: *2*
Stock: *walnut*

D2C:	NIB $945	Ex $725	VG+ $520	Good $475	
C2C:	Mint $910	Ex $675	VG+ $480	Good $430	Fair $220
Trade-In:	Mint $680	Ex $550	VG+ $370	Good $335	Poor $120

201-HRZ REDBOOK CODE: RB-HL-S-201HRZ

Double trigger, manual safety, silver or black engraving, sunken top rib, interior of barrel is white chromed.

Production: *current* **Gauge/Bore:** *12 ga.*
Action: *SxS*
Barrel Length: *24"–30"* **Wt.:** *7.1 lbs.*
Sights: *bead front*
Capacity: *2*
Stock: *walnut*

D2C:	NIB $700	Ex $550	VG+ $385	Good $350	
C2C:	Mint $680	Ex $500	VG+ $350	Good $315	Fair $165
Trade-In:	Mint $500	Ex $400	VG+ $280	Good $245	Poor $90

HUGLU

202-B   REDBOOK CODE: RB-HL-S-202BXX
Double trigger, 3" chamber, manual safety, white or black chrome receiver, sunken top rib, interior white chrome lined.

Production: *current* **Gauge/Bore:** *12 ga., 16 ga., 20 ga., 28 ga., 36 ga.*
Action: *SxS*
Barrel Length: 24"–30" **Wt.:** *7.2 LBS.*
Sights: *none*
Capacity: *2*
Stock: *walnut*

D2C:	NIB $575	Ex $450	VG+ $320	Good $290	
C2C:	Mint $560	Ex $400	VG+ $290	Good $260	Fair $135
Trade-In:	Mint $410	Ex $325	VG+ $230	Good $205	Poor $60

301-A   REDBOOK CODE: RB-HL-S-301AXX
Single trigger, 3" chamber, manual safety, silver engraving, white or black chrome options, barrel interior is white chrome.

Production: *current* **Gauge/Bore:** *12 ga., 16 ga., 20 ga., 28 ga., 36 ga.*
Action: *single-shot*
Barrel Length: 24" **Wt.:** *4.6 lbs.*
Sights: *bead front*
Capacity: *1*
Stock: *walnut*

D2C:	NIB $295	Ex $225	VG+ $165	Good $150	
C2C:	Mint $290	Ex $225	VG+ $150	Good $135	Fair $70
Trade-In:	Mint $210	Ex $175	VG+ $120	Good $105	Poor $30

401 KINETIC   REDBOOK CODE: RB-HL-S-401KIN
Single trigger, black engraving, barrel interior is white chrome, mobile choke.

Production: *current* **Gauge/Bore:** *12 ga.*
Action: *semi-auto*
Barrel Length: 20"–30" **Wt.:** *7.1 lbs.*
Sights: *bead front*
Capacity: *4*
Stock: *walnut*

D2C:	NIB $300	Ex $250	VG+ $165	Good $150	
C2C:	Mint $290	Ex $225	VG+ $150	Good $135	Fair $70
Trade-In:	Mint $220	Ex $175	VG+ $120	Good $105	Poor $30

601-G GAMO   REDBOOK CODE: RB-HL-S-601GAM
Manual safety, engraving, aluminum receiver, 8mm ventilated rib, barrel interior is white chromed, mobile choke.

Production: *current* **Gauge/Bore:** *12 ga.*
Action: *semi-auto*
Barrel Length: 20"–30" **Wt.:** *7.2 lbs.*
Sights: *none*
Capacity: *4*
Stock: *walnut or synthetic*

D2C:	NIB $500	Ex $400	VG+ $275	Good $250	
C2C:	Mint $480	Ex $350	VG+ $250	Good $225	Fair $115
Trade-In:	Mint $360	Ex $300	VG+ $200	Good $175	Poor $60

901-G REDBOOK CODE: RB-HL-S-901GXX

Action spring in stock, 3" chamber, white or black receiver, 8mm vented rib, barrel interior is white chromed, mobile choke.

Production: *current* **Gauge/Bore:** *12 ga.*
Action: *semi-auto*
Barrel Length: 20"–30" **Wt.:** *7.2 lbs.*
Sights: *bead front*
Capacity: *4*
Stock: *walnut*

D2C:	NIB $490	Ex $375	VG+ $270	Good $245	
C2C:	Mint $480	Ex $350	VG+ $250	Good $225	Fair $115
Trade-In:	Mint $350	Ex $275	VG+ $200	Good $175	Poor $60

920-G REDBOOK CODE: RB-HL-S-920GXX

Action spring in stock, 3" chamber, white or black receiver, 8mm vented rib, barrel interior is white chromed, mobile choke.

Production: *current* **Gauge/Bore:** *20 ga.*
Action: *semi-auto*
Barrel Length: 20"–30" **Wt.:** *7.2 lbs.*
Sights: *bead front*
Capacity: *4*
Stock: *walnut*

D2C:	NIB $500	Ex $400	VG+ $275	Good $250	
C2C:	Mint $480	Ex $350	VG+ $250	Good $225	Fair $115
Trade-In:	Mint $360	Ex $300	VG+ $200	Good $175	Poor $60

GX-512 REDBOOK CODE: RB-HL-S-GX512X

3.5" chamber, manual safety, white or black eloxal options, 8mm vented rib, inside barrel white chromed, mobile chokes, aluminum receiver.

Production: *current* **Gauge/Bore:** *12 ga.*
Action: *semi-auto*
Barrel Length: 20"–30" **Wt.:** *7.2 lbs.*
Sights: *bead front*
Capacity: *4*
Stock: *walnut*

D2C:	NIB $460	Ex $350	VG+ $255	Good $230	
C2C:	Mint $450	Ex $325	VG+ $230	Good $210	Fair $110
Trade-In:	Mint $330	Ex $275	VG+ $180	Good $165	Poor $60

GX-520 REDBOOK CODE: RB-HL-S-GX520X

3" chamber, manual safety, white or black eloxal options, 8mm vented rib, barrel interior is white chrome, mobile chokes.

Production: *current* **Gauge/Bore:** *20 ga.*
Action: *semi-auto*
Barrel Length: 20"–30" **Wt.:** *5.9 lbs.*
Sights: *bead front*
Capacity: *4*
Stock: *walnut*

D2C:	NIB $490	Ex $375	VG+ $270	Good $245	
C2C:	Mint $480	Ex $350	VG+ $250	Good $225	Fair $115
Trade-In:	Mint $350	Ex $275	VG+ $200	Good $175	Poor $60

HUGLU EAGLE   REDBOOK CODE: RB-HL-S-HUGLUE

Single trigger, manual safety, choice of engraving, aluminum block receiver, silver or black receiver.

Production: *current* **Gauge/Bore:** *12 ga.*
Action: *O/U*
Barrel Length: *24"–30"* **Wt.:** *2.5 lbs.*
Sights: *bead front*
Capacity: *2*
Stock: *walnut*

D2C:	NIB $700	Ex $550	VG+ $385	Good $350	
C2C:	Mint $680	Ex $500	VG+ $350	Good $315	Fair $165
Trade-In:	Mint $500	Ex $400	VG+ $280	Good $245	Poor $90

NITRO BEAST   REDBOOK CODE: RB-HL-S-NITROB

3" chamber, manual safety, barrel interior is white chromed, aluminum receiver.

Production: *current* **Gauge/Bore:** *12 ga.*
Action: *semi-auto*
Barrel Length: *20"–30"* **Wt.:** *6.6 lbs.*
Sights: *bead*
Capacity: *4*
Stock: *walnut*

D2C:	NIB $500	Ex $400	VG+ $275	Good $250	
C2C:	Mint $480	Ex $350	VG+ $250	Good $225	Fair $115
Trade-In:	Mint $360	Ex $300	VG+ $200	Good $175	Poor $60

S12E   REDBOOK CODE: RB-HL-S-S12EXX

3" chamber, single trigger, vent rib, MobilChokes, manual safety, monobloc receiver, white chrome-plated receiver and interior barrels, optional side rib.

Production: *current* **Gauge/Bore:** *12 ga.*
Action: *O/U*
Barrel Length: *~28"* **Wt.:** *~7 lbs.*
Sights: *bead*
Capacity: *2*
Stock: *walnut*

D2C:	NIB $700	Ex $550	VG+ $385	Good $350	
C2C:	Mint $680	Ex $500	VG+ $350	Good $315	Fair $165
Trade-In:	Mint $500	Ex $400	VG+ $280	Good $245	Poor $90

Ithaca Guns

In 1883, William Henry Baker and some partners started a business called Ithaca Gun Company and began producing side-by-side shotguns. The company's flagship model, the Model 37, was put into production in 1937 after being designed by John Browning. The model name changed to Model 87 in 1987, but the original name was restored in 1996. The company itself changed names a few times as it was bought and sold, but the word "Ithaca" remained a part of each version. Its current moniker mirrors the original, and today's Ithaca Gun Company does business out of Upper Sandusky, Ohio, making pump action shotguns and a 1911 style pistol. Interestingly, because the designers at Ithaca believe that solder joints are prone to failure and the high temperatures necessary for soldering compromise barrel materials, the company makes barrels with a solderless system. To enhance the integrity of Ithaca barrels, all peripheral components are held in place by lugs machined of the parent material of the barrel itself, instead of by soldered seams.

HUGLU

ITHACA

DEERSLAYER II (NEW MODEL) REDBOOK CODE: RB-IG-S-DEERII

Receiver machined from a solid block of steel, 3" chamber, rifled barrel with 1:28 or 1:24 twist rate, deluxe-checkered forend, Pachmayr Decelerator recoil pad, gold-plated trigger.

Production: *current* **Gauge/Bore:** *12 ga., 20 ga.*
Action: *pump-action*
Barrel Length: *24"* **Wt.:** *6.8–8.4 lbs.*
Sights: *fiber-optic Marble Arms front*
Capacity: *5*
Stock: *fancy black walnut Monte Carlo style or laminated thumbhole*

D2C:	NIB $887	Ex $675	VG+ $490	Good $445	
C2C:	Mint $860	Ex $625	VG+ $450	Good $400	Fair $205
Trade-In:	Mint $630	Ex $500	VG+ $350	Good $315	Poor $90

DEERSLAYER III REDBOOK CODE: RB-IG-S-DSLIII

3" chamber, heavy-walled fluted barrel, rifled barrel with 1:28 or 1:24 twist rate, Weaver #62 rail, flat bottomed forend, sling swivel studs, matte blue finish, gold plated trigger, 14.3" length of pull.

Production: *current* **Gauge/Bore:** *12 ga., 20 ga.*
Action: *pump-action*
Barrel Length: *26"* **Wt.:** *8.1–9.5 lbs.*
Sights: *none*
Capacity: *5*
Stock: *A-Grade fancy walnut Monte Carlo*

D2C:	NIB $1,271	Ex $975	VG+ $700	Good $640	
C2C:	Mint $1,230	Ex $900	VG+ $640	Good $575	Fair $295
Trade-In:	Mint $910	Ex $725	VG+ $500	Good $445	Poor $150

MODEL 37 DEFENSE GUN REDBOOK CODE: RB-IG-S-MOD37D

3" chamber, Pachmayr decelerator recoil pad, receiver machined from solid block of steel, 4-6 lb. trigger pull.

Production: *current* **Gauge/Bore:** *12 ga., 20 ga.*
Action: *pump-action*
Barrel Length: *18.5", 20"* **Wt.:** *6.6–7.1 lbs.*
Sights: *brass bead front*
Capacity: *5, 8*
Stock: *walnut or black synthetic*

D2C:	NIB $805	Ex $625	VG+ $445	Good $405	
C2C:	Mint $780	Ex $575	VG+ $410	Good $365	Fair $190
Trade-In:	Mint $580	Ex $475	VG+ $320	Good $285	Poor $90

MODEL 37 FEATHERLIGHT REDBOOK CODE: RB-IG-S-MOD37F

3" chamber, Briley choke tubes, matte blue receiver, gold-plated trigger, slim-grip checkered forend.

Production: *current* **Gauge/Bore:** *12 ga., 16 ga., 20 ga., 28 ga.*
Action: *pump-action*
Barrel Length: *28", 30"* **Wt.:** *6.1–7.4 lbs.*
Sights: *TruGlo high-visibility red fiber-optic front*
Capacity: *5*
Stock: *fancy black walnut semi-pistol*

D2C:	NIB $375	Ex $300	VG+ $210	Good $190	
C2C:	Mint $360	Ex $275	VG+ $190	Good $170	Fair $90
Trade-In:	Mint $270	Ex $225	VG+ $150	Good $135	Poor $60

MODEL 37 LADIES STOCK REDBOOK CODE: RB-IG-S-MOD37L

3" chamber, lengthened forcing cone, Briley choke tubes, matte blue receiver, gold-plated trigger, slim-grip checkered forend, Pachmayr 752 Decelerator recoil pad, duck plug included.

Production: *current* **Gauge/Bore:** *20 ga.*
Action: *pump-action*
Barrel Length: *26", 28"* **Wt.:** *6.8 lbs.*
Sights: *TruGlo high-visibility red fiber-optic front*
Capacity: *5*
Stock: *fancy black walnut semi-pistol*

D2C:	NIB $827	Ex $650	VG+ $455	Good $415	
C2C:	Mint $800	Ex $575	VG+ $420	Good $375	Fair $195
Trade-In:	Mint $590	Ex $475	VG+ $330	Good $290	Poor $90

MODEL 37 TRAP MODEL REDBOOK CODE: RB-IG-S-MOD37T

3" chamber, bottom ejection, Briley choke tubes, classic game scene engraving, gold plated trigger, 4–6 lb. trigger pull, duck plug included.

Production: *current* **Gauge/Bore:** *12 ga.*
Action: *pump-action*
Barrel Length: *30"* **Wt.:** *7.8 lbs.*
Sights: *bead front*
Capacity: *5*
Stock: *standard walnut Monte Carlo*

D2C:	NIB $1,247	Ex $950	VG+ $690	Good $625	
C2C:	Mint $1,200	Ex $875	VG+ $630	Good $565	Fair $290
Trade-In:	Mint $890	Ex $700	VG+ $490	Good $440	Poor $150

MODEL 37 TURKEY SLAYER REDBOOK CODE: RB-IG-S-MD37TS

3" chamber, fixed barrel, Briley extended extra-full choke tubes, Pachmayr 752 Decelerator recoil pad, lengthened forcing cone.

Production: *current* **Gauge/Bore:** *12 ga., 20 ga.*
Action: *pump-action*
Barrel Length: *24"* **Wt.:** *7.2–8.2 lbs.*
Sights: *TruGlo high-visibility red fiber-optic front*
Capacity: *5*
Stock: *camouflage, synthetic, or thumbhole laminate*

D2C:	NIB $504	Ex $400	VG+ $280	Good $255	
C2C:	Mint $490	Ex $350	VG+ $260	Good $230	Fair $120
Trade-In:	Mint $360	Ex $300	VG+ $200	Good $180	Poor $60

MODEL 37 WATERFOWL REDBOOK CODE: RB-IG-S-MOD37W

Bottom ejector, 3" chamber, Briley choke tubes, gold-plated trigger, 4–6 lb. trigger pull, duck plug included.

Production: *current* **Gauge/Bore:** *12 ga., 20 ga.*
Action: *pump-action*
Barrel Length: *30"* **Wt.:** *7.3 lbs.*
Sights: *bead front*
Capacity: *5*
Stock: *synthetic*

D2C:	NIB $416	Ex $325	VG+ $230	Good $210	
C2C:	Mint $400	Ex $300	VG+ $210	Good $190	Fair $100
Trade-In:	Mint $300	Ex $250	VG+ $170	Good $150	Poor $60

MODEL 37 (28 GAUGE) REDBOOK CODE: RB-IG-S-MD3728

Receiver machined from single block of steel, solderless barrel system, lengthened forcing cone, 4-6 lb. trigger, fancy black walnut forend, 2 3/4" chamber, three Briley choke tubes, Pachmayr Decelerator recoil pad, trim available in Fancy A, Fancy AA, or Fancy AAA. Pricing for base model starts at $1,149 and additional features and details will increase pricing dramatically.

Production: *current* **Gauge/Bore:** *28 ga.*

Action: *pump-action*

Barrel Length: 26", 28" **Wt.:** *6.1 lbs.*

Sights: *brass bead front*

Capacity: *5*

Stock: *fancy black walnut field*

D2C:	NIB $1,149	Ex $875	VG+ $635	Good $575	**LMP:** $1,149
C2C:	Mint $1,110	Ex $800	VG+ $580	Good $520	Fair $265
Trade-In:	Mint $820	Ex $650	VG+ $450	Good $405	Poor $120

MODEL 37 ULTRALIGHT REDBOOK CODE: RB-IG-S-MOD37U

Aluminum receiver, vent rib, standard chokes, gold trigger, sleek forend, Sid Bell grip cap. Models with choke tubes command a higher price.

Production: *discontinued* **Gauge/Bore:** *12 ga., 16 ga., 20 ga.*

Action: *pump-action*

Barrel Length: 26", 28", 30" **Wt.:** *5–5.75 lbs.*

Sights: *TruGlo fiber optic*

Capacity: *5*

Stock: *cut-checkered walnut with pistol grip*

D2C:	NIB $468	Ex $375	VG+ $260	Good $235	
C2C:	Mint $450	Ex $325	VG+ $240	Good $215	Fair $110
Trade-In:	Mint $340	Ex $275	VG+ $190	Good $165	Poor $60

MODEL 37 CLASSIC REDBOOK CODE: RB-IG-S-MOD37C

Knuckle-cut receiver, vent rib, chokes tubes, buttpad.

Production: *1998–2005* **Gauge/Bore:** *12 ga., 16 ga., 20 ga.*

Action: *pump-action*

Barrel Length: 26", 28" **Wt.:** *6.5–7 lbs.*

Sights: *bead front*

Capacity: *5*

Stock: *cut-checkered walnut with pistol grip or straight English stock*

D2C:	NIB $472	Ex $375	VG+ $260	Good $240	
C2C:	Mint $460	Ex $350	VG+ $240	Good $215	Fair $110
Trade-In:	Mint $340	Ex $275	VG+ $190	Good $170	Poor $60

MODEL 37 $1000 GRADE (ALSO NAMED $2000, $2500, $3000) REDBOOK CODE: RB-IG-S-MOD37G

Inlay in gold, ornately engraved. $3,000 Grade model commands approximately 20% lower price. Market research provides no conclusive pricing suggestion(s) for this particular model. The model is either too rare or contains too many custom options, which drastically affects pricing.

Production: *discontinued 1967* **Gauge/Bore:** *12 ga., 16 ga., 20 ga.*

Action: *pump-action*

Barrel Length: *various lengths* **Wt.:** *N/A*

Sights: *N/A*

Capacity: *5*

Stock: *highly figured walnut*

ITHACA

MODEL 37R SOLID RIB GRADE REDBOOK CODE: RB-IG-S-MOD37R
Raised solid rib, blue finish, fires 2 3/4" shells. May have grooved forend. Model with checkered stock commands higher price.

Photo Courtesy of
Rock Island Auction Company

Production: *discontinued 1967* **Gauge/Bore:** *12 ga., 16 ga.*
Action: *pump-action*
Barrel Length: 26", 28", 30" **Wt.:** *6–7.75 lbs.*
Sights: *bead front*
Capacity: 5
Stock: *plain or cut-checkered walnut*

D2C:	NIB $386	Ex $300	VG+ $215	Good $195	
C2C:	Mint $380	Ex $275	VG+ $200	Good $175	Fair $90
Trade-In:	Mint $280	Ex $225	VG+ $160	Good $140	Poor $60

MODEL 37S SKEET GRADE REDBOOK CODE: RB-IG-S-MOD37S
Knicker vent rib, extra-large forend with fleur-de-lis checkering pattern, blue finish. Pre-WWII models command approximately 50% higher price.

Production: *1937–1955* **Gauge/Bore:** *12 ga., 16 ga.*
Action: *pump-action*
Barrel Length: 26", 28" **Wt.:** *6–7.75 lbs.*
Sights: *bead front*
Capacity: 5
Stock: *highly figured walnut*

D2C:	NIB $513	Ex $400	VG+ $285	Good $260	
C2C:	Mint $500	Ex $375	VG+ $260	Good $235	Fair $120
Trade-In:	Mint $370	Ex $300	VG+ $210	Good $180	Poor $60

MODEL 37T TARGET GRADE REDBOOK CODE: RB-IG-S-MD37TG
Vent rib, ambidextrous, fires 2 3/4" shells.

Production: *1955–1961* **Gauge/Bore:** *12 ga., 20 ga.*
Action: *pump-action*
Barrel Length: 24", 26", 28", 30" **Wt.:** *N/A*
Sights: *bead front, mid-bead*
Capacity: 5
Stock: *cut-checkered walnut in skeet or trap-style*

D2C:	NIB $493	Ex $375	VG+ $275	Good $250	
C2C:	Mint $480	Ex $350	VG+ $250	Good $225	Fair $115
Trade-In:	Mint $360	Ex $300	VG+ $200	Good $175	Poor $60

MODEL 51A FEATHERLIGHT REDBOOK CODE: RB-IG-S-MD51FL
Gas-operated, plain or vent rib barrel (plain barrel discontinued in later production), various choke options (full, modified, improved cylinder). Models with vent rib command higher price; models with checkered stock command approximately 50% higher price.

Production: *1970–1985* **Gauge/Bore:** *12 ga., 20 ga.*
Action: *semi-auto*
Barrel Length: 26", 28", 30" **Wt.:** *7.25–7.75 lbs.*
Sights: *Raybar front*
Capacity: 4
Stock: *cut-checkered pistol grip stock*

D2C:	NIB $304	Ex $250	VG+ $170	Good $155	
C2C:	Mint $300	Ex $225	VG+ $160	Good $140	Fair $70
Trade-In:	Mint $220	Ex $175	VG+ $120	Good $110	Poor $60

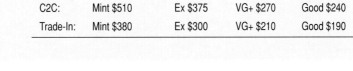

MODEL 51A DEERSLAYER REDBOOK CODE: RB-IG-S-MD51DS
Rifled slug barrel, gas-operated, reversible safety, engraved receiver, fires 2 3/4" shells.

Production: *discontinued 1984* **Gauge/Bore:** *12 ga., 20 ga.*

Action: *semi-auto*

Barrel Length: 24" **Wt.:** *N/A*

Sights: *Raybar front, open adjustable rear*

Capacity: *4*

Stock: *walnut or black synthetic*

D2C:	NIB $531	Ex $425	VG+ $295	Good $270	
C2C:	Mint $510	Ex $375	VG+ $270	Good $240	Fair $125
Trade-In:	Mint $380	Ex $300	VG+ $210	Good $190	Poor $60

MODEL 51A SUPREME SKEET REDBOOK CODE: RB-IG-S-MD51SS
Gas-operated, reversible safety, skeet choke, engraved receiver, fires 2 3/4" shells.

Production: *discontinued 1987* **Gauge/Bore:** *12 ga., 20 ga.*

Action: *semi-auto*

Barrel Length: 26", 28" **Wt.:** *~8 lbs.*

Sights: *Raybar front*

Capacity: *4*

Stock: *hand-checkered walnut*

D2C:	NIB $525	Ex $400	VG+ $290	Good $265	
C2C:	Mint $510	Ex $375	VG+ $270	Good $240	Fair $125
Trade-In:	Mint $380	Ex $300	VG+ $210	Good $185	Poor $60

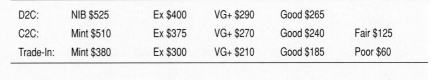

MODEL 51A SUPREME TRAP REDBOOK CODE: RB-IG-S-MD51ST
Gas-operated, reversible safety, full choke, engraved receiver, fires 2 3/4" shells.

Production: *discontinued 1987* **Gauge/Bore:** *12 ga.*

Action: *semi-auto*

Barrel Length: 30" **Wt.:** *~8 lbs.*

Sights: *Raybar front*

Capacity: *4*

Stock: *trap-style with straight or Monte Carlo comb*

D2C:	NIB $456	Ex $350	VG+ $255	Good $230	
C2C:	Mint $440	Ex $325	VG+ $230	Good $210	Fair $105
Trade-In:	Mint $330	Ex $275	VG+ $180	Good $160	Poor $60

MODEL 51A STANDARD MAGNUM REDBOOK CODE: RB-IG-S-MD51SM
Gas-operated, plain or vent rib barrel, full or modified choke, blue finish, fires 3" Magnum shells. Models with vent rib command approximately 10% higher price; camo-finish models command higher price.

Production: *discontinued 1985* **Gauge/Bore:** *12 ga., 20 ga.*

Action: *semi-auto*

Barrel Length: 28", 30" **Wt.:** *7.75–8 lbs.*

Sights: *Raybar front*

Capacity: *4*

Stock: *walnut pistol grip stock*

D2C:	NIB $390	Ex $300	VG+ $215	Good $195	
C2C:	Mint $380	Ex $275	VG+ $200	Good $180	Fair $90
Trade-In:	Mint $280	Ex $225	VG+ $160	Good $140	Poor $60

MODEL 51A TURKEY GUN REDBOOK CODE: RB-IG-S-MD51TK
Gas-operated, Magnum model, vent rib, matte finish, sling swivels.

Production: *discontinued 1986* **Gauge/Bore:** *12 ga.*
Action: *semi-auto*
Barrel Length: 26" **Wt.:** ~8 lbs.
Sights: *Raybar front*
Capacity: 4
Stock: *walnut pistol grip stock*

D2C:	NIB $5,812	Ex $4,425	VG+ $3,200	Good $2,910	
C2C:	Mint $5,580	Ex $4,025	VG+ $2,910	Good $2,620	Fair $1,340
Trade-In:	Mint $4,130	Ex $3,275	VG+ $2,270	Good $2,035	Poor $600

MODEL 66 LONG TOM REDBOOK CODE: RB-IG-S-MD66LT
Full choke, hand-cocked hammer, buttpad, fires 3" shells.

Production: *discontinued 1986* **Gauge/Bore:** *12 ga.*
Action: *single-shot*
Barrel Length: 36" **Wt.:** ~7 lbs.
Sights: *bead front*
Capacity: 1
Stock: *cut-checkered walnut*

D2C:	NIB $275	Ex $225	VG+ $155	Good $140	
C2C:	Mint $270	Ex $200	VG+ $140	Good $125	Fair $65
Trade-In:	Mint $200	Ex $175	VG+ $110	Good $100	Poor $30

Photo Courtesy of Rock Island Auction Company

MODEL 66 SUPER SINGLE REDBOOK CODE: RB-IG-S-MD66SS
Lever action, hand-cocked hammer, blue finish. Models in 20 gauge and .410 bore command approximately 50% higher price.

Production: *discontinued 1978* **Gauge/Bore:** *12 ga., 20 ga., .410*
Action: *single-shot*
Barrel Length: 26", 28", 30" **Wt.:** ~7 lbs.
Sights: *bead front*
Capacity: 1
Stock: *plain or cut-checkered walnut*

D2C:	NIB $195	Ex $150	VG+ $110	Good $100	
C2C:	Mint $190	Ex $150	VG+ $100	Good $90	Fair $45
Trade-In:	Mint $140	Ex $125	VG+ $80	Good $70	Poor $30

Photo Courtesy of Rock Island Auction Company

MODEL 66RS BUCK BUSTER REDBOOK CODE: RB-IG-S-MD66BB
Lever action, blue finish, buttpad, 3" chamber.

Production: *discontinued 1978* **Gauge/Bore:** *12 ga., 20 ga.*
Action: *single-shot*
Barrel Length: 22", 28" **Wt.:** *N/A*
Sights: *rifle-type sights*
Capacity: 1
Stock: *walnut*

D2C:	NIB $173	Ex $150	VG+ $100	Good $90	
C2C:	Mint $170	Ex $125	VG+ $90	Good $80	Fair $40
Trade-In:	Mint $130	Ex $100	VG+ $70	Good $65	Poor $30

MODEL 87 DEERSLAYER REDBOOK CODE: RB-IG-S-MD87DS
Special or rifled bore, receiver grooved for scope, fires 3" shells.

Production: *1989–1996* **Gauge/Bore:** *12 ga., 20 ga.*
Action: *pump-action*
Barrel Length: *18.5", 20", 25"* **Wt.:** *6–6.75 lbs.*
Sights: *ramp blade front, adjustable rear*
Capacity: *5*
Stock: *cut-checkered walnut pistol grip stock*

D2C:	NIB $385	Ex $300	VG+ $215	Good $195	
C2C:	Mint $370	Ex $275	VG+ $200	Good $175	Fair $90
Trade-In:	Mint $280	Ex $225	VG+ $160	Good $135	Poor $60

MODEL 87 DEERSLAYER II REDBOOK CODE: RB-IG-S-MD87D2
Rifled barrel, receiver drilled and tapped for scope mounting, solid-frame construction, fires 3" shells.

Production: *discontinued 1996* **Gauge/Bore:** *12 ga.*
Action: *pump-action*
Barrel Length: *20", 25"* **Wt.:** *7 lbs.*
Sights: *ramp blade front, adjustable rear*
Capacity: *5*
Stock: *cut-checkered Monte Carlo stock*

D2C:	NIB $450	Ex $350	VG+ $250	Good $225	
C2C:	Mint $440	Ex $325	VG+ $230	Good $205	Fair $105
Trade-In:	Mint $320	Ex $275	VG+ $180	Good $160	Poor $60

MODEL 87 ULTRALIGHT FIELD PUMP REDBOOK CODE: RB-IG-S-MD87UF
Aluminum receiver, multi-chokes, fires 3" shells.

Production: *discontinued 1990* **Gauge/Bore:** *12 ga., 20 ga.*
Action: *pump-action*
Barrel Length: *20", 24", 25", 26"* **Wt.:** *5 lbs., 5.75 lbs.*
Sights: *bead front*
Capacity: *5*
Stock: *walnut*

D2C:	NIB $364	Ex $300	VG+ $205	Good $185	
C2C:	Mint $350	Ex $275	VG+ $190	Good $165	Fair $85
Trade-In:	Mint $260	Ex $225	VG+ $150	Good $130	Poor $60

MODEL 87 FIELD GRADE REDBOOK CODE: RB-IG-S-MD87FD
Vent rib barrel, fixed or screw-in chokes, fires 3" shells. Camo model commands approximately 10% higher price.

Production: *discontinued 1996* **Gauge/Bore:** *12 ga., 20 ga.*
Action: *pump-action*
Barrel Length: *26", 28", 30"* **Wt.:** *5–7lbs.*
Sights: *bead front*
Capacity: *5*
Stock: *walnut*

D2C:	NIB $372	Ex $300	VG+ $205	Good $190	
C2C:	Mint $360	Ex $275	VG+ $190	Good $170	Fair $90
Trade-In:	Mint $270	Ex $225	VG+ $150	Good $135	Poor $60

ITHACA

FIELD GRADE HAMMERLESS DOUBLE REDBOOK CODE: RB-IG-S-FGHLDB

Boxlock, automatic ejectors, plain extractors, double triggers, all common chokes, fluid steel or Damascus barrels. Values vary with production year and gauge. Value is higher for models with selective single trigger.

Production: *discontinued 1948* **Gauge/Bore:** *10 ga., 12 ga., 16 ga., 20 ga., 28 ga., .410*

Action: *SxS*

Barrel Length: *any common length, 26"–32"*

Wt.: *5.75–10.5 lbs.* **Sights:** *bead front*

Capacity: *2*

Stock: *cut-checkered walnut pistol grip*

D2C:	NIB $578	Ex $450	VG+ $320	Good $290	
C2C:	Mint $560	Ex $400	VG+ $290	Good $265	Fair $135
Trade-In:	Mint $420	Ex $325	VG+ $230	Good $205	Poor $60

LSA-55 TURKEY GUN REDBOOK CODE: RB-IG-S-LSA55T

Boxlock, plain extractors, exposed hammer, single trigger, solid serrated-rib shotgun barrel, rifle barrel with muzzle brake.

Production: *discontinued 1981* **Gauge/Bore:** *12 ga., .222 Rem.*

Action: *O/U*

Barrel Length: *24.5"* **Wt.:** *~7 lbs.*

Sights: *bead front, folding leaf rear*

Capacity: *2*

Stock: *cut-checkered Monte Carlo stock*

D2C:	NIB $546	Ex $425	VG+ $305	Good $275	
C2C:	Mint $530	Ex $400	VG+ $280	Good $250	Fair $130
Trade-In:	Mint $390	Ex $325	VG+ $220	Good $195	Poor $60

Photo Courtesy of
Rock Island Auction Company

MAG-10 AUTOMATIC REDBOOK CODE: RB-IG-S-MAG10A

Gas-operated, plain or vent rib barrel, full choke, matte finish, chambers 3.5" shells. Models with vent rib are valued approximately $100 higher. Add $60 to value for vent rib camo model. Available in Roadblocker model with ribless parkerized 22" barrel (valued higher than standard, plain-barrel model). Also available in Deluxe and Supreme models with cut-checkering, higher-quality wood, and sling swivels. For Deluxe model, value increases by approximately $150; for Supreme, value increases by approximately $200.

Production: *1977–1986* **Gauge/Bore:** *10 ga.*

Action: *semi-auto*

Barrel Length: *32"* **Wt.:** *11 lbs., 11.5 lbs.*

Sights: *bead front*

Capacity: *4*

Stock: *walnut*

D2C:	NIB $672	Ex $525	VG+ $370	Good $340	
C2C:	Mint $650	Ex $475	VG+ $340	Good $305	Fair $155
Trade-In:	Mint $480	Ex $400	VG+ $270	Good $240	Poor $90

IVER JOHNSON ARMS

Iver Johnson Arms, Inc.

The Iver Johnson name traces its origins in the firearms industry back to the 1880s, during which time a company known as Iver Johnson Arms & Cycle Works manufactured a host of different derringers, single-shot revolvers, double-action revolvers, and shotguns. However, that incarnation of Iver Johnson folded in the early 1990s. Established around 2006, Iver Johnson Arms, Inc., located in Rockledge, Florida, bears no connection to the original Iver Johnson aside from the name. The current namesake, affiliated at its inception with Squires Bingham International, Inc., manufactures 1911-style pistols with some parts and labor contracted out to foreign manufacturers. The company also imports a line of pump action shotguns manufactured by Armed Guns of Turkey.

PAS12 REDBOOK CODE: RB-IJ-S-PAS12X

3" chamber, polished black receiver, matte black barrel, with or without ventilated muzzle brake, lightweight alloy receiver, medium length forend with deep grooves.

Production: *current* **Gauge/Bore:** *12 ga.*

Action: *pump-action*

Barrel Length: 18" **Wt.:** *6 lbs.*

Sights: *blade front*

Capacity: *5*

Stock: *synthetic black fixed*

D2C:	NIB $275	Ex $225	VG+ $155	Good $140	**LMP: $294**
C2C:	Mint $270	Ex $200	VG+ $140	Good $125	Fair $65
Trade-In:	Mint $200	Ex $175	VG+ $110	Good $100	Poor $30

PAS12 18/28 OR 18/30 REDBOOK CODE: RB-IJ-S-182818

28" and 30" models come with ventilated rib and bead sight, 3 internally threaded chokes, polished black receiver, matte black barrels.

Production: *current* **Gauge/Bore:** *12 ga.*

Action: *pump-action*

Barrel Length: 18", 28", 30" **Wt.:** *6–6.8 lbs.*

Sights: *blade front or brass bead front depending on barrel being used*

Capacity: *5*

Stock: *synthetic black fixed*

D2C:	NIB $377	Ex $300	VG+ $210	Good $190	**LMP: $397**
C2C:	Mint $370	Ex $275	VG+ $190	Good $170	Fair $90
Trade-In:	Mint $270	Ex $225	VG+ $150	Good $135	Poor $60

PAS12 A/C REDBOOK CODE: RB-IJ-S-AS12AC

Polished black receiver, matte black barrel, with or without ventilated muzzle brake, lightweight alloy receiver, medium length forend with deep grooves, sure-grip pumping action, dual-action rails, cross-trigger block safety, sling swivel on end of mag tube.

Production: *current* **Gauge/Bore:** *12 ga.*

Action: *pump-action*

Barrel Length: 18" **Wt.:** *6 lbs.*

Sights: *fully adjustable white dot rear, fiber optic front*

Capacity: *5*

Stock: *black synthetic fixed*

D2C:	NIB $300	Ex $250	VG+ $165	Good $150	**LMP: $312**
C2C:	Mint $290	Ex $225	VG+ $150	Good $135	Fair $70
Trade-In:	Mint $220	Ex $175	VG+ $120	Good $105	Poor $30

PAS12 PG REDBOOK CODE: RB-IJ-S-AS12PG

3" chamber, polished black receiver, matte black barrel, lightweight alloy receiver, sure-grip pumping action, dual-action rails, extended bolt-release latch, cross-trigger block safety, sling-swivel cross-trigger block safety, sling swivel.

Production: *current* **Gauge/Bore:** *12 ga.*

Action: *pump-action*

Barrel Length: 18" **Wt.:** *6 lbs.*

Sights: *metal blade front*

Capacity: *5*

Stock: *2-piece pistol grip*

D2C:	NIB $307	Ex $250	VG+ $170	Good $155	**LMP: $327**
C2C:	Mint $300	Ex $225	VG+ $160	Good $140	Fair $75
Trade-In:	Mint $220	Ex $175	VG+ $120	Good $110	Poor $60

 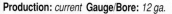

PAS12 PG-R/C REDBOOK CODE: RB-IJ-S-PAPGRC

Thick rubber buttpad, 3" chamber, polished black receiver, matte black barrel, Picatinny rail, muzzle brake, 14.5" length of pull, lightweight alloy receiver, dual-action rails, extended bolt-release latch, cross-trigger block-safety, sling-swivel on end of mag tube.

Production: *current* **Gauge/Bore:** *12 ga.*
Action: *pump-action*
Barrel Length: 18" **Wt.:** *6 lbs.*
Sights: *fiber optic front*
Capacity: *5*
Stock: *2-piece pistol grip*

D2C:	NIB $324	Ex $250	VG+ $180	Good $165	**LMP:** $346
C2C:	Mint $320	Ex $225	VG+ $170	Good $150	Fair $75
Trade-In:	Mint $240	Ex $200	VG+ $130	Good $115	Poor $60

PAS12 RAIL REDBOOK CODE: RB-IJ-S-PARAIL

Picatinny rail, 3" chamber, polished black receiver, matte black barrel, lightweight alloy receiver, sure-grip pumping action, dual-action rails, cross-trigger block safety.

Production: *current* **Gauge/Bore:** *12 ga.*
Action: *pump-action*
Barrel Length: 18" **Wt.:** *6 lbs.*
Sights: *fully adjustable white-dot rear*
Capacity: *5*
Stock: *synthetic black fixed*

D2C:	NIB $250	Ex $200	VG+ $140	Good $125	**LMP:** $310
C2C:	Mint $240	Ex $175	VG+ $130	Good $115	Fair $60
Trade-In:	Mint $180	Ex $150	VG+ $100	Good $90	Poor $30

PAS12 SATIN REDBOOK CODE: RB-IJ-S-PSATIN

Satin nickel receiver, black stock and forend, lightweight alloy receiver, sure-grip pumping action, dual-action rails, cross-trigger block safety, sling swivel, with or without ventilated muzzle brake.

Production: *current* **Gauge/Bore:** *12 ga.*
Action: *pump-action*
Barrel Length: 18" **Wt.:** *6 lbs.*
Sights: *front blade*
Capacity: *5*
Stock: *fixed synthetic*

D2C:	NIB $296	Ex $225	VG+ $165	Good $150	**LMP:** $365
C2C:	Mint $290	Ex $225	VG+ $150	Good $135	Fair $70
Trade-In:	Mint $220	Ex $175	VG+ $120	Good $105	Poor $30

Kel-Tec CNC Industries, Inc.

Kel-Tec CNC Industries, Inc. was founded in Cocoa, Florida, as a CNC machine shop that made firearms components for Grendel, Inc. In 1995, Kel-Tec began producing firearms and specialized in rifle and handgun designs for concealed carry and law enforcement. With growing success, the company has been forced to expand its original space many times. In 2011, the company made its first foray into the shotgun world with the KSG 12 gauge model. Although innovative in many ways, this model stands out most perhaps for its high capacity. The KSG holds two magazines simultaneously. Magazines for original models held 6 shells each, and current model magazines hold up to 7 each. With +1 factored in, the KSG, as it is currently being produced, is a shotgun capable of holding 15 shells at once.

KSG   REDBOOK CODE: RB-KT-S-KSGXXX

Cylinder bore barrel, internal dual tube magazines, 3" chamber, manually selected feed side, Picatinny rail, forward and rear sling loops, soft rubber butt pad.

Production: *current* **Gauge/Bore:** *12 ga.*

Action: *pump-action*

Barrel Length: 18.5" **Wt.:** *6.9 lbs.*

Sights: *none*

Capacity: *13*

Stock: *black synthetic*

D2C:	NIB $850	Ex $650	VG+ $470	Good $425	LMP: $990
C2C:	Mint $820	Ex $600	VG+ $430	Good $385	Fair $200
Trade-In:	Mint $610	Ex $500	VG+ $340	Good $300	Poor $90

Krieghoff International

Founded originally as Sempert & Krieghoff in 1886, the company now known as H. Krieghoff produces rifles and shotguns from its headquarters in Ulm, Germany. The company began with hunting models but then branched out into competition guns. The Model 32, K-80, and K-20 shotguns have taken the U.S. market by storm, but in Europe and the rest of the world, the brand is mainly associated with fine hunting guns like drillings and double rifles. Today, the company is still run by representatives of the fourth and fifth generations of the Krieghoff family, specifically, Dieter and Phil Krieghoff. Dieter founded Krieghoff International, the portion of the conglomerate responsible for all sales in the western hemisphere and the exclusive importer of the brand's firearms to the U.S. The American facilities are located in Bucks County, Pennsylvania.

K-80 PRO SPORTER   REDBOOK CODE: RB-KG-S-K80PRO

3" chamber, adjustable floating rib on barrel, bottom and top choke tubes, case hardened action, nickel-plated steel receiver, single-selective mechanical trigger, top tang push button safety, fine-checkering, satin epoxy finish on wood, classic scroll engraving.

Production: *current* **Gauge/Bore:** *12 ga.*

Action: *O/U*

Barrel Length: 30", 32" **Wt.:** *8.8 lbs.*

Sights: *white-pearl front-bead and metal center bead*

Capacity: *2*

Stock: *Turkish walnut*

D2C:	NIB $9,665	Ex $7,350	VG+ $5,320	Good $4,835	
C2C:	Mint $9,280	Ex $6,675	VG+ $4,840	Good $4,350	Fair $2,225
Trade-In:	Mint $6,870	Ex $5,425	VG+ $3,770	Good $3,385	Poor $990

K-80 SPORTING   REDBOOK CODE: RB-KG-S-K80SPO

3" chamber, standard rib, case-hardened nickel-plated receiver, satin gray finish on receiver, single-selective mechanical trigger, top tang push button safety, fine-checkering, satin epoxy finish on wood, scroll engraving. Includes CT, C, S, IC, LM, M, LIM, IM, F, and SF chokes.

Production: *current* **Gauge/Bore:** *12 ga.*

Action: *O/U*

Barrel Length: 30", 32" **Wt.:** *8.8 lbs.*

Sights: *white pearl front bead, metal center bead*

Capacity: *2*

Stock: *Turkish walnut*

D2C:	NIB $9,374	Ex $7,125	VG+ $5,160	Good $4,690	
C2C:	Mint $9,000	Ex $6,475	VG+ $4,690	Good $4,220	Fair $2,160
Trade-In:	Mint $6,660	Ex $5,250	VG+ $3,660	Good $3,285	Poor $960

K-80 PARCOURS REDBOOK CODE: RB-KG-S-K80PAR

3" chamber, single-selective mechanical trigger, top tang push button safety, parcour forearm, scroll engraving.

Production: *current* **Gauge/Bore:** *12 ga.*

Action: *O/U*

Barrel Length: 32" **Wt.:** *~8 lbs.*

Sights: *white pearl front bead, metal center bead*

Capacity: *2*

Stock: *Turkish walnut*

D2C:	NIB $10,798	Ex $8,225	VG+ $5,940	Good $5,400	
C2C:	Mint $10,370	Ex $7,475	VG+ $5,400	Good $4,860	Fair $2,485
Trade-In:	Mint $7,670	Ex $6,050	VG+ $4,220	Good $3,780	Poor $1,080

K-80 TRAP SPECIAL COMBO REDBOOK CODE: RB-KG-S-K80TSC

3" chamber, fully adjustable high-post ventilated tapered rib,
case-hardened nickel-plated steel receiver with satin grey finish,
single-selective mechanical trigger, top tang push-button safety,
fine-checkering on walnut, scroll engraving.

Production: *current* **Gauge/Bore:** *12 ga.*

Action: *unsingle*

Barrel Length: 30", 32", 34" **Wt.:** *9 lbs.*

Sights: *white pearl front, metal center bead*

Capacity: *1, 2*

Stock: *Turkish walnut*

D2C:	NIB $7,291	Ex $5,550	VG+ $4,015	Good $3,650	
C2C:	Mint $7,000	Ex $5,050	VG+ $3,650	Good $3,285	Fair $1,680
Trade-In:	Mint $5,180	Ex $4,100	VG+ $2,850	Good $2,555	Poor $750

K-80 SKEET REDBOOK CODE: RB-KG-S-K80SKE

3" chamber, case-hardened nickel-plated steel receiver with satin =-gray finish, 5 included chokes,
top tang push button safety, single-selective mechanical trigger, fine checkering, satin epoxy finish on walnut, adjustable comb.

Production: *current* **Gauge/Bore:** *12 ga., 20 ga.*

Action: *O/U*

Barrel Length: 30", 32", 34" **Wt.:** *8.8 lbs.*

Sights: *white pearl front bead, metal center bead*

Capacity: *2*

Stock: *Turkish walnut*

D2C:	NIB $4,850	Ex $3,700	VG+ $2,670	Good $2,425	
C2C:	Mint $4,660	Ex $3,350	VG+ $2,430	Good $2,185	Fair $1,120
Trade-In:	Mint $3,450	Ex $2,725	VG+ $1,900	Good $1,700	Poor $510

K-80 ACS REDBOOK CODE: RB-KG-S-K80ACS

3" chamber, floating rib, 8 factory steel chokes, case-hardened nickel-plated steel receiver,
single-selective mechanical trigger, top tang push button safety, fine checkering. Market
research provides no conclusive pricing suggestion(s) for this particular model.

Production: *current* **Gauge/Bore:** *12 ga.*

Action: *O/U*

Barrel Length: 30", 32", 34" **Wt.:** *8.7 lbs.*

Sights: *white pearl front bead, metal center bead*

Capacity: *2*

Stock: *Turkish walnut*

KX-6 SINGLE SHOT TRAP   REDBOOK CODE: RB-KG-S-KX6SST

3" chamber, single barrel with factory chokes, case-hardened long-lasting black-nitro carbonized receiver finish, position adjustable trigger, top tang push-button safety, Monte Carlo buttstock.

Production: *current* **Gauge/Bore:** *12 ga.*
Action: *single-shot*
Barrel Length: 34" **Wt.:** *8.8 lbs.*
Sights: *white pearl front, metal center bead*
Capacity: *2*
Stock: *European walnut*

D2C:	NIB $4,947	Ex $3,775	VG+ $2,725	Good $2,475	
C2C:	Mint $4,750	Ex $3,425	VG+ $2,480	Good $2,230	Fair $1,140
Trade-In:	Mint $3,520	Ex $2,775	VG+ $1,930	Good $1,735	Poor $510

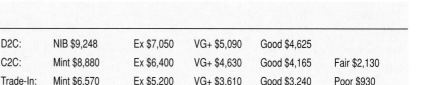

ESSENCIA SIDELOCK   REDBOOK CODE: RB-KG-S-ESSENC

Round-bodied steel receiver, English scroll engraving, gold accented inlays, color case-hardened finish, straight grip or Prince of Wales pistol grip stock.

Production: *current* **Gauge/Bore:** *12 ga.*
Action: *SxS*
Barrel Length: 28", 30" **Wt.:** *6.4 lbs.*
Sights: *bead front*
Capacity: *2*
Stock: *hardwood*

D2C:	NIB $21,266	Ex $16,175	VG+ $11,700	Good $10,635	
C2C:	Mint $20,420	Ex $14,675	VG+ $10,640	Good $9,570	Fair $4,895
Trade-In:	Mint $15,100	Ex $11,925	VG+ $8,300	Good $7,445	Poor $2,130

K-20   REDBOOK CODE: RB-KG-S-K20XXX

3" chamber, tapered-flat rib, 5 included chokes, case-hardened nickel-plated steel receiver with satin gray finish, single-selective mechanical trigger, top tang push button safety, satin epoxy finish on walnut, Schnabel forearm, classic scroll engraving.

Production: *current* **Gauge/Bore:** *20 ga., 28 ga., .410*
Action: *O/U*
Barrel Length: 30", 32" **Wt.:** *7.5 lbs.*
Sights: *white pearl front bead, metal center bead*
Capacity: *2*
Stock: *Turkish walnut*

D2C:	NIB $9,248	Ex $7,050	VG+ $5,090	Good $4,625	
C2C:	Mint $8,880	Ex $6,400	VG+ $4,630	Good $4,165	Fair $2,130
Trade-In:	Mint $6,570	Ex $5,200	VG+ $3,610	Good $3,240	Poor $930

Lanber

Lanber was a trademark used to market over/under and semi-automatic shotguns that were manufactured in Zaldibar, Spain, from 1973-2013 by a company called ComLanber, S.A. A subsidiary known as Lanber USA, located in Westfield, Massachusetts, imported the shotguns to the U.S. from 2006-2011. Prior to those years, the guns had been imported through several other companies unaffiliated with the manufacturer since the early 1990s.

2087 HUNTER REDBOOK CODE: RB-LA-S-2087HU

5 poly chokes included, scroll engraving with gold duck, automatic split ejectors, lightweight alloy receiver.

Production: *current* **Gauge/Bore:** *12 ga.*
Action: *O/U*
Barrel Length: 28", 30" **Wt.:** *7.1 lbs.*
Sights: *fiber optic front*
Capacity: *2*
Stock: *hardwood*

D2C:	NIB $651	Ex $500	VG+ $360	Good $330	
C2C:	Mint $630	Ex $450	VG+ $330	Good $295	Fair $150
Trade-In:	Mint $470	Ex $375	VG+ $260	Good $230	Poor $90

2187 IMPERIAL HUNTER REDBOOK CODE: RB-LA-S-2187IH

High quality wood finish, distinctive gold game scene, oversized receiver, automatic ejectors, rubber buttplate.
Market research suggests pricing for this model is inconclusive at this time.

Production: *current* **Gauge/Bore:** *12 ga.*
Action: *O/U*
Barrel Length: 30" **Wt.:** *7.2 lbs.*
Sights: *fiber optic front*
Capacity: *2*
Stock: *hardwood*

TWENTY REDBOOK CODE: RB-LA-S-TWENTY

Greystone receiver, steel ejector, 5 Lanber chokes included. Market research suggests pricing for this model is inconclusive at this time.

Production: *current* **Gauge/Bore:** *12 ga.*
Action: *O/U*
Barrel Length: 28" **Wt.:** *6 lbs.*
Sights: *fiber optic front*
Capacity: *2*
Stock: *hardwood*

2097 SPORTING REDBOOK CODE: RB-LA-S-2097SP

Pulse-plasma-nitriding technology built receiver, comes with 5 Lanber chokes, checkering on stock and forearm, beaver tailed forearm.

Production: *current* **Gauge/Bore:** *12 ga.*
Action: *O/U*
Barrel Length: 30" **Wt.:** *7.6 lbs.*
Sights: *fiber optic front*
Capacity: *2*
Stock: *hardwood*

D2C:	NIB $751	Ex $575	VG+ $415	Good $380	
C2C:	Mint $730	Ex $525	VG+ $380	Good $340	Fair $175
Trade-In:	Mint $540	Ex $425	VG+ $300	Good $265	Poor $90

LANBER

2097 SPORTING CASE-HARDENED   REDBOOK CODE: RB-LA-S-2097SC
Case-hardened receiver finish, comes with 5 Lanber chokes, checkering on stock and forearm, vented rib.

Production: *current* **Gauge/Bore:** *12 ga.*
Action: *O/U*
Barrel Length: 30" **Wt.:** *7.6 lbs.*
Sights: *fiber optic front*
Capacity: *2*
Stock: *hardwood*

D2C:	NIB $785	Ex $600	VG+ $435	Good $395	
C2C:	Mint $760	Ex $550	VG+ $400	Good $355	Fair $185
Trade-In:	Mint $560	Ex $450	VG+ $310	Good $275	Poor $90

2097 SPORTING LUX   REDBOOK CODE: RB-LA-S-97SPLU
High-quality steel ejector, checkering on stock and forearm, beavertail forearm, ventilated rib.

Production: *current* **Gauge/Bore:** *12 ga.*
Action: *O/U*
Barrel Length: 30" **Wt.:** *7.6 lbs.*
Sights: *fiber optic front*
Capacity: *2*
Stock: *hardwood*

D2C:	NIB $807	Ex $625	VG+ $445	Good $405	
C2C:	Mint $780	Ex $575	VG+ $410	Good $365	Fair $190
Trade-In:	Mint $580	Ex $475	VG+ $320	Good $285	Poor $90

Lebeau-Courally

LEBEAU-COURALLY

Lebeau-Courally is a manufacturer of quality rifles and double-barrel shotguns that was founded in 1865 and is based in Liege, Belgium. Such care is taken with each firearm produced that only about 30 units are produced per year, and each gun requires an estimated 400 to 1,000 hours of hand craftsmanship. Every finished gun is unique and perfectly customized to customers' specifications. Lebeau-Courally shotguns are imported to the U.S. by Griffin & Howe of Bernardsville, New Jersey, and William Larkin Moore of Scottsdale, Arizona, but they were previously imported by Heirloom Armes of Howard Lake, Minnesota.

LE BARON   REDBOOK CODE: RB-LE-S-LEBARO
Sidelock ejector, steel-shot proof, engraving, checkering on stock and forearm. These shotguns are custom made to each buyer's specifications and are too unique to price.

Production: *current* **Gauge/Bore:** *12 ga., 16 ga., 20 ga.*
Action: *O/U*
Barrel Length: made to customer specs **Wt.:** *N/A*
Sights: *N/A*
Capacity: *2*
Stock: *hardwood*

LE PRINCE REDBOOK CODE: RB-LE-S-LEPRIN

Sidelock ejector, steel-shot proof, engraving, double trigger. These shotguns are custom made to each buyer's specifications and are too unique to price.

Production: *current* **Gauge/Bore:** *12 ga., 16 ga., 20 ga., 28 ga., .410*

Action: *SxS*

Barrel Length: *made to customer specs* **Wt.:** *N/A*

Sights: *N/A*

Capacity: *2*

Stock: *hardwood*

LeFever Arms Co.

Dan LeFever started LeFever Arms Company in 1884 in Syracuse, New York, and guns were produced and sold under the brand until 1942. Best known as the inventor of the "hammerless" shotgun, Mr. Lefever developed a new automatic hammerless action that cocked upon opening. This action replaced the previous sidecocker design. These guns are referred to as "Syracuse models" and are the most common Lefever guns collected today. Lefever left the company in 1901 to produce guns under the DM Lefever and Sons label, but that company saw little success and closed in 1906. In the meantime, Lefever's former partners at Lefever Arms Co., Durston and Howell, continued to manufacture Lefever Automatic Hammerless guns. In 1916, Durston and Howell sold Lefever Arms Co. to Ithaca Gun Company, and Ithaca marketed the brand until around 1942.

NITRO SPECIAL REDBOOK CODE: RB-LC-S-NITROS

Various choke combinations available, boxlock action, double trigger, extractors, blue finish, case-colored receiver, checkering on walnut stock. The .410 bore brings the highest premium, pricing for which is shown here.

Production: *discontinued* **Gauge/Bore:** *12 ga., 16 ga., 20 ga., .410*

Action: *SxS*

Barrel Length: *26"–32"* **Wt.:** *N/A*

Sights: *bead front*

Capacity: *2*

Stock: *walnut*

D2C:	NIB $1,821	Ex $1,400	VG+ $1,005	Good $915	
C2C:	Mint $1,750	Ex $1,275	VG+ $920	Good $820	Fair $420
Trade-In:	Mint $1,300	Ex $1,025	VG+ $720	Good $640	Poor $210

EE HAMMERLESS REDBOOK CODE: RB-LC-S-EEHAMM

Various choke combinations available, Damascus or fluid steel barrels, fractional sidelock, hammers mounted in frame, double trigger, checkering on walnut, automatic ejectors on some models. There are some models that are highly engraved with precious metal inlays that should be appraised by an expert.

Production: *discontinued* **Gauge/Bore:** *10 ga., 12 ga., 16 ga., 20 ga.*

Action: *SxS*

Barrel Length: *26"–32"* **Wt.:** *N/A*

Sights: *bead front*

Capacity: *2*

Stock: *walnut*

D2C:	NIB $3,737	Ex $2,850	VG+ $2,060	Good $1,870	
C2C:	Mint $3,590	Ex $2,600	VG+ $1,870	Good $1,685	Fair $860
Trade-In:	Mint $2,660	Ex $2,100	VG+ $1,460	Good $1,310	Poor $390

Marocchi (CD Europe S.R.L.)

Marocchi was founded in 1922 by Stefano Marocchi, and the company continues to be managed by the Marocchi family in Sarezzo, Italy, to this day. Stefano began his career making parts for high end side-by-side shotgun makers, but he branched out to produce his own complete shotguns and ultimately introduced the award-winning Marocchi SM57, the first over/under shotgun in history. The shotgun left an indelible mark on the industry and has been emulated by manufacturers worldwide. The company also produces air rifles and is a distributor of Breda products. Marocchi firearms have been imported to the U.S. through several different companies over the years, but they are now distributed through Whitworth Arms, LLC of May, Texas.

SI12 POLICHASSE REDBOOK CODE: RB-MC-S-SI12PO

5 included chokes, 3" chamber, oil finished walnut forend, barrel extension included, checkering on stock and forend. Current market value suggests this model is valued between $1,000-$1,600 NIB.

Production: *current* **Gauge/Bore:** *12 ga.*

Action: *semi-auto*

Barrel Length: 24"–30" **Wt.:** *6.5 lbs.*

Sights: *bead front*

Capacity: *4, 5*

Stock: *oil finished walnut*

SI12 GRADE 3 REDBOOK CODE: RB-MC-S-SE12G3

5 included chokes, engraving on both sides of the receiver, engraving on bolt, checkering on stock and forearm. Current market value for NIB price ranges from $1,500-$2,000.

Production: *current* **Gauge/Bore:** *12 ga.*

Action: *semi-auto*

Barrel Length: 24"–30" **Wt.:** *6.5 lbs.*

Sights: *bead front*

Capacity: *4, 5*

Stock: *oil finished walnut*

SI12 GRADE 2 REDBOOK CODE: RB-MC-S-SE12G2

5 included chokes, 3" chamber, walnut forearm, LaserTech checkering, woodcock on window side and rear. Research suggests that this model has a NIB value between $1,400-$1,700 in the current market.

Production: *current* **Gauge/Bore:** *12 ga.*

Action: *semi-auto*

Barrel Length: 24"–30" **Wt.:** *6.5 lbs.*

Sights: *bead front*

Capacity: *4, 5*

Stock: *oil finished walnut*

MAROCCHI

SI12 GRADE 1 REDBOOK CODE: RB-MC-S-SE12G1
3" chamber, walnut forearm, 5 chokes included, nickel-plated steel color. As it stands in the current marketplace, a NIB price for this model ranges between $1,000-$1,500.

Production: *current* **Gauge/Bore:** *12 ga.*
Action: *semi-auto*
Barrel Length: *24"–30"* **Wt.:** *6.5 lbs.*
Sights: *bead front*
Capacity: *4, 5*
Stock: *oil finished walnut*

SI12 COMPLUS REDBOOK CODE: RB-MC-S-SE12CO
3" chamber, synthetic complus forearm, 5 chokes included, sandblasted finish on stock and forearm, shock resistant stock. NIB price ranges between $900-$1,300.

Production: *current* **Gauge/Bore:** *12 ga.*
Action: *semi-auto*
Barrel Length: *24"–30"* **Wt.:** *6.5 lbs.*
Sights: *bead front*
Capacity: *4*
Stock: *black synthetic*

SI12 LIGHT REDBOOK CODE: RB-MC-S-SE12LI
3" chamber, black anodized receiver finish, standard stock and forend, 5 included chokes, no rib for reduced weight. Current market research for this gun suggests that it is unable to be priced. Importation to the U.S may have ceased and models have become progressively harder to find, making sales research difficult.

Production: *current* **Gauge/Bore:** *12 ga.*
Action: *semi-auto*
Barrel Length: *24"–30"* **Wt.:** *6.4 lbs.*
Sights: *bead front*
Capacity: *4, 5*
Stock: *walnut*

SI12 REDBOOK CODE: RB-MC-S-SE12XX
3" chamber, walnut forend, 5 included chokes, walnut forearm, walnut checkering. Current market research for this gun suggests that it is unable to be priced. Importation to the U.S may have ceased and models have become progressively harder to find, making sales research difficult.

Production: *current* **Gauge/Bore:** *12 ga.*
Action: *semi-auto*
Barrel Length: *24"–30"* **Wt.:** *6.5 lbs.*
Sights: *bead front*
Capacity: *4, 5*
Stock: *walnut*

O.F. Mossberg & Sons, Inc.

Founded in 1919, O.F. Mossberg & Sons, Inc. is based in North Haven, Connecticut, and is the oldest family-owned and operated firearms manufacturer in America, as well as the largest pump-action shotgun manufacturer in the world. Production began with a .22 caliber handgun, known as the "Brownie," but the company now specializes in shotguns, rifles, scopes, and accessories. The company is credited with being the first ever to offer Monte Carlo style stocks, molded trigger housings, and spring-loaded quick-release swivels as standard features. Mossberg was the first company to develop a 3.5" chambered 12 gauge shotgun. Their best-known models are the Mossberg 500, 500A, 500 Tactical, and the Maverick series of shotguns. In addition to innovative designs and features, the company is also known for quality, with Mossberg shotguns being the only ones purchased by the U.S. government that meet or exceed military specifications.

MOSSBERG

FLEX 500 ALL-PURPOSE, STANDARD
REDBOOK CODE: RB-MS-S-500FST

Ported barrel with vented rib and matte blue finish, Accu-Set choke tubes, fires 3" shells, 14.25" length of pull. The FLEX TLS (Tool-less Locking System) offers interchangeable stocks, forends, and recoil pads.

Production: *current* **Gauge/Bore:** *12 ga.*
Action: *pump-action*
Barrel Length: 28" **Wt.:** *7.5 lbs.*
Sights: *twin bead*
Capacity: *6*
Stock: *black synthetic*

D2C:	NIB $432	Ex $350	VG+ $240	Good $220	**LMP:** $630
C2C:	Mint $420	Ex $300	VG+ $220	Good $195	Fair $100
Trade-In:	Mint $310	Ex $250	VG+ $170	Good $155	Poor $60

FLEX 500 ALL-PURPOSE, ADJUSTABLE TRIGGER
REDBOOK CODE: RB-MS-S-500FAP

Ported and vented rib barrel in matte blue finish, LPA (Lightning Pump Action) adjustable trigger, Accu-Set choke tubes, FLEX TLS (Tool-less Locking System), fires 3" shells, 14.25" length of pull.

Production: *current* **Gauge/Bore:** *12 ga.*
Action: *pump-action*
Barrel Length: 28" **Wt.:** *7.5 lbs.*
Sights: *twin bead*
Capacity: *6*
Stock: *black synthetic*

D2C:	NIB $484	Ex $375	VG+ $270	Good $245	**LMP:** $682
C2C:	Mint $470	Ex $350	VG+ $250	Good $220	Fair $115
Trade-In:	Mint $350	Ex $275	VG+ $190	Good $170	Poor $60

FLEX 500 ALL-PURPOSE, MARINECOTE
REDBOOK CODE: RB-MS-S-500FMC

Ported and vented rib barrel in Marinecote finish, Accu-Set choke tubes, fires 3" shells, 14.25" length of pull. The FLEX Tool-less Locking System offers interchangeable stocks, forends, and recoil pads.

Production: *current* **Gauge/Bore:** *12 ga.*
Action: *pump-action*
Barrel Length: 26" **Wt.:** *7.5 lbs.*
Sights: *twin bead*
Capacity: *6*
Stock: *black synthetic*

D2C:	NIB $489	Ex $375	VG+ $270	Good $245	**LMP:** $687
C2C:	Mint $470	Ex $350	VG+ $250	Good $225	Fair $115
Trade-In:	Mint $350	Ex $275	VG+ $200	Good $175	Poor $60

MOSSBERG

FLEX 500 HUNTING SLUG REDBOOK CODE: RB-MS-S-500FHS

Vented rib barrel in matte finish, fully-rifled Slugster barrel, LPA (Lightning Pump Action) adjustable trigger, cantilever scope mount, FLEX TLS (Tool-less Locking System), fires 3" shells.

Production: *current* **Gauge/Bore:** *12 ga.*
Action: *pump-action*
Barrel Length: 24" **Wt.:** *7.25 lbs.*
Sights: *adjustable fiber optic*
Capacity: 6
Stock: *4-position adjustable with Dual Comb*

D2C:	NIB $578	Ex $450	VG+ $320	Good $290	LMP: $881
C2C:	Mint $560	Ex $400	VG+ $290	Good $265	Fair $135
Trade-In:	Mint $420	Ex $325	VG+ $230	Good $205	Poor $60

FLEX 500 HUNTING TURKEY REDBOOK CODE: RB-MS-S-500FHT

Vented rib barrel in OD Green or Mossy Oak Break-Up Infinity finish, FLEX TLS (Tool-less Locking System), X-Factor ported tube chokes, fires 3" shells, 14.25" length of pull.

Production: *current* **Gauge/Bore:** *12 ga.*
Action: *pump-action*
Barrel Length: 24" **Wt.:** *7.25 lbs.*
Sights: *adjustable fiber optic*
Capacity: 6
Stock: *synthetic with Mossy Oak Break-Up Infinity*

D2C:	NIB $503	Ex $400	VG+ $280	Good $255	LMP: $770
C2C:	Mint $490	Ex $350	VG+ $260	Good $230	Fair $120
Trade-In:	Mint $360	Ex $300	VG+ $200	Good $180	Poor $60

FLEX 500 HUNTING REDBOOK CODE: RB-MS-S-500F20

Vented rib barrel in OD Green or matte blue finish, Accu-Set choke tubes, ambidextrous top-mounted safety, FLEX Tool-less Locking System, fires 2.75" or 3" shells. Add $107 for Mossy Oak Break-Up Infinity stock and X-Factor ported tube chokes.

Production: *current* **Gauge/Bore:** *20 ga.*
Action: *pump-action*
Barrel Length: 24", 26" **Wt.:** *7 lbs.*
Sights: *dual bead or adjustable fiber optic*
Capacity: 6
Stock: *black synthetic, matte blue or Mossy Oak Break-Up Infinity*

D2C:	NIB $441	Ex $350	VG+ $245	Good $225	LMP: $484
C2C:	Mint $430	Ex $325	VG+ $230	Good $200	Fair $105
Trade-In:	Mint $320	Ex $250	VG+ $180	Good $155	Poor $60

FLEX 500 TACTICAL, ADJUSTABLE STOCK REDBOOK CODE: RB-MS-S-500FTA

Vented rib barrel in OD Green or matte blue finish, Accu-Set choke tubes, FLEX TLS (Tool-less Locking System), tactical forend with Picatinny tri-rails, front mag cap, rear swing swivel studs, fires 2.75" shells.

Production: *current* **Gauge/Bore:** *12 ga., 20 ga.*
Action: *pump-action*
Barrel Length: 20" **Wt.:** *6.25 lbs.*
Sights: *bead*
Capacity: 6, 8
Stock: *adjustable synthetic stock*

D2C:	NIB $488	Ex $375	VG+ $270	Good $245	LMP: $643
C2C:	Mint $470	Ex $350	VG+ $250	Good $220	Fair $115
Trade-In:	Mint $350	Ex $275	VG+ $200	Good $175	Poor $60

FLEX 500 TACTICAL CRUISER, PISTOL GRIP   REDBOOK CODE: RB-MS-S-500FTP

Cruiser model (20 ga. only) with stand-off/ breacher barrel in matte blue finish, fires 3" shells, 14.25" length of pull. The FLEX Tool-less Locking System offers interchangeable stocks, forends, and recoil pads. Add $176 for 12 ga. model.

Production: *current* **Gauge/Bore:** *12 ga., 20 ga.*

Action: *pump-action*

Barrel Length: *18.5"* **Wt.:** *5.75 lbs.*

Sights: *white dot*

Capacity: *6*

Stock: *none*

D2C:	NIB $502	Ex $400	VG+ $280	Good $255	**LMP: $577**
C2C:	Mint $490	Ex $350	VG+ $260	Good $230	Fair $120
Trade-In:	Mint $360	Ex $300	VG+ $200	Good $180	Poor $60

FLEX 500 DUCK COMMANDER   REDBOOK CODE: RB-MS-S-500FDC

Vented rib barrel with OD Green finish, Accu-Set choke tubes, drilled and tapped receiver, FLEX Tool-less Locking System, ambidextrous top safety, dual extractors, anti-jam elevator, steel-to-steel lockup, fires 3" shells.

Production: *current* **Gauge/Bore:** *12 ga.*

Action: *pump-action*

Barrel Length: *28"* **Wt.:** *7.5 lbs.*

Sights: *TruGlo Tru-Bead*

Capacity: *6*

Stock: *synthetic with Realtree Max-5*

D2C:	NIB $479	Ex $375	VG+ $265	Good $240	**LMP: $835**
C2C:	Mint $460	Ex $350	VG+ $240	Good $220	Fair $115
Trade-In:	Mint $350	Ex $275	VG+ $190	Good $170	Poor $60

500 DUCK COMMANDER, SIGNATURE (TALO)   REDBOOK CODE: RB-MS-S-500DCS

Vented rib barrel in OD Green, Accu-Mag choke set, drilled and tapped receiver, dual extractors, twin action bars, steel-to-steel lockup, fires 3" shells, 14.5" length of pull.

Production: *current* **Gauge/Bore:** *12 ga.*

Action: *pump-action*

Barrel Length: *28"* **Wt.:** *7.25 lbs.*

Sights: *TruGlo Tru-Bead*

Capacity: *6*

Stock: *synthetic with Realtree Max-5*

D2C:	NIB $379	Ex $300	VG+ $210	Good $190	**LMP: $627**
C2C:	Mint $370	Ex $275	VG+ $190	Good $175	Fair $90
Trade-In:	Mint $270	Ex $225	VG+ $150	Good $135	Poor $60

500 ALL-PURPOSE   REDBOOK CODE: RB-MS-S-500APX

Ported and vented rib barrel in Mossy Oak Break-Up Infinity, matte or high-polish blue finish, Accu-Set or full-fixed choke tube, LPA (Lightning Pump Action) adjustable trigger, fires 3" shells.

Production: *current* **Gauge/Bore:** *12 ga., 20 ga., .410*

Action: *pump-action*

Barrel Length: *24", 26", 28"* **Wt.:** *7.5 lbs.*

Sights: *twin bead*

Capacity: *6*

Stock: *synthetic or high-gloss walnut*

D2C:	NIB $305	Ex $250	VG+ $170	Good $155	**LMP: $414**
C2C:	Mint $300	Ex $225	VG+ $160	Good $140	Fair $75
Trade-In:	Mint $220	Ex $175	VG+ $120	Good $110	Poor $60

MOSSBERG

500 DUCK COMMANDER REDBOOK CODE: RB-MS-S-500DCX

Ported barrel with vented rib in OD Green or Realtree Max-5 finish, Accu-Mag choke set, drilled and tapped receiver, dual extractors, twin action bars, steel-to-steel lockup, fires 3" shells, 14.5" length of pull.

Production: *current* **Gauge/Bore:** *12 ga.*
Action: *pump-action*
Barrel Length: 28" **Wt.:** *7.5 lbs.*
Sights: *TruGlo Tru-Bead*
Capacity: *6*
Stock: *synthetic with Realtree Max-5*

D2C:	NIB $434	Ex $350	VG+ $240	Good $220	LMP: $561
C2C:	Mint $420	Ex $300	VG+ $220	Good $200	Fair $100
Trade-In:	Mint $310	Ex $250	VG+ $170	Good $155	Poor $60

500 TURKEY REDBOOK CODE: RB-MS-S-500TKY

Ported and vented rib barrel in Mossy Oak Break-Up Infinity, Realtree Xtra Green or matte blue finish, standard or LPA (Lightning Pull Action) adjustable trigger, XX-Full or X-Factor ported choke tube, fires 3" shells.

Production: *current* **Gauge/Bore:** *12 ga., 20 ga.*
Action: *pump-action*
Barrel Length: 20", 24" **Wt.:** *7.25 lbs.*
Sights: *adjustable fiber optic*
Capacity: *6*
Stock: *fixed synthetic, adjustable or thumbhole (on standard model only)*

D2C:	NIB $312	Ex $250	VG+ $175	Good $160	LMP: $481
C2C:	Mint $300	Ex $225	VG+ $160	Good $145	Fair $75
Trade-In:	Mint $230	Ex $175	VG+ $130	Good $110	Poor $60

500 TURKEY THUG REDBOOK CODE: RB-MS-S-500TTH

Ported and vented rib barrel in Mossy Oak Obsession or blue finish, XX-Full or X-Factor ported choke tube, fires 3" shells.

Production: *current* **Gauge/Bore:** *12 ga., 20 ga.*
Action: *pump-action*
Barrel Length: 20", 24" **Wt.:** *7.25 lbs.*
Sights: *adjustable fiber optic*
Capacity: *6*
Stock: *black synthetic adjustable*

D2C:	NIB $392	Ex $300	VG+ $220	Good $200	LMP: $451
C2C:	Mint $380	Ex $275	VG+ $200	Good $180	Fair $95
Trade-In:	Mint $280	Ex $225	VG+ $160	Good $140	Poor $60

500 WATERFOWL REDBOOK CODE: RB-MS-S-500WFL

Vented rib barrel (ported or non-ported) in Mossy Oak Shadow Grass Blades or Realtree Max-4 finish, Accu-Set or X-Factor ported choke tube, fires 3" shells, 14.5" length of pull.

Production: *current* **Gauge/Bore:** *12 ga.*
Action: *pump-action*
Barrel Length: 28" **Wt.:** *7.5 lbs.*
Sights: *fiber optic front*
Capacity: *6*
Stock: *synthetic*

D2C:	NIB $374	Ex $300	VG+ $210	Good $190	LMP: $480
C2C:	Mint $360	Ex $275	VG+ $190	Good $170	Fair $90
Trade-In:	Mint $270	Ex $225	VG+ $150	Good $135	Poor $60

500 SLUGSTER REDBOOK CODE: RB-MS-S-500SLG

Ported and fully-rifled Slugster barrel in Mossy Oak Break-Up Infinity, Realtree Xtra or blue finish, fires 3" shells, 13.875" length of pull.

Production: *current* **Gauge/Bore:** *12 ga., 20 ga.*

Action: *pump-action*

Barrel Length: 24" **Wt.:** *7 lbs.*

Sights: *rifle-type sights*

Capacity: *6*

Stock: *synthetic or Dual Comb wood*

D2C:	NIB $345	Ex $275	VG+ $190	Good $175	**LMP:** $447
C2C:	Mint $340	Ex $250	VG+ $180	Good $160	Fair $80
Trade-In:	Mint $250	Ex $200	VG+ $140	Good $125	Poor $60

500 COMBO, STANDARD REDBOOK CODE: RB-MS-S-500CST

Ported and vented rib field barrel plus ported and fully-rifled Slugster barrel in Mossy Oak Break-Up Infinity or blue finish, scope base, available with Dual Comb stock, fires 3" shells, 13.875" length of pull.

Production: *current* **Gauge/Bore:** *12 ga., 20 ga.*

Action: *pump-action*

Barrel Length: 18.5", 24", 26", 28" **Wt.:** *7.5 lbs.*

Sights: *dual bead or adjustable rifle-type*

Capacity: *6*

Stock: *synthetic or Dual Comb wood*

D2C:	NIB $383	Ex $300	VG+ $215	Good $195	**LMP:** $502
C2C:	Mint $370	Ex $275	VG+ $200	Good $175	Fair $90
Trade-In:	Mint $280	Ex $225	VG+ $150	Good $135	Poor $60

500 COMBO, LPA TRIGGER REDBOOK CODE: RB-MS-S-500CLP

THUG ON SLUG Mossy Oak Turkey THUG & Deer THUG Combo includes ported and vented rib field barrel plus ported fully-rifled Slugster barrel in Mossy Oak Break-Up Infinity finish, LPA (Lightning Pump Action) adjustable trigger, engraved receiver, fires 3" shells.

Production: *current* **Gauge/Bore:** *12 ga.*

Action: *pump-action*

Barrel Length: 24" **Wt.:** *7 lbs.*

Sights: *adjustable fiber optic or rifle-type*

Capacity: *6*

Stock: *synthetic*

D2C:	NIB $493	Ex $375	VG+ $275	Good $250	**LMP:** $612
C2C:	Mint $480	Ex $350	VG+ $250	Good $225	Fair $115
Trade-In:	Mint $360	Ex $300	VG+ $200	Good $175	Poor $60

500 MARINER REDBOOK CODE: RB-MS-S-500MAR

All-weather Marinecote-finished barrel, pistol grip conversion kit, fires 3" shells, 13.875" length of pull. Also available with adjustable 6-position stock.

Production: *current* **Gauge/Bore:** *12 ga.*

Action: *pump-action*

Barrel Length: 18.5" **Wt.:** *6.75 lbs.*

Sights: *bead*

Capacity: *6*

Stock: *black synthetic*

D2C:	NIB $485	Ex $375	VG+ $270	Good $245	**LMP:** $630
C2C:	Mint $470	Ex $350	VG+ $250	Good $220	Fair $115
Trade-In:	Mint $350	Ex $275	VG+ $190	Good $170	Poor $60

MOSSBERG

500 TACTICAL 6-SHOT REDBOOK CODE: RB-MS-S-500T6S
Barrel in matte finish, pistol grip, fires 3" shells, 10.75"–14.625" length of pull. Also available in all-weather Marinecote finish.

Production: *current* **Gauge/Bore:** *12 ga.*
Action: *pump-action*
Barrel Length: 18.5" **Wt.:** *6.75 lbs.*
Sights: *bead*
Capacity: 6
Stock: *adjustable synthetic stock with side saddle*

D2C:	NIB $541	Ex $425	VG+ $300	Good $275	**LMP:** $596
C2C:	Mint $520	Ex $375	VG+ $280	Good $245	Fair $125
Trade-In:	Mint $390	Ex $325	VG+ $220	Good $190	Poor $60

500 SPX 6-SHOT REDBOOK CODE: RB-MS-S-500SP6
Barrel in matte finish, M-16-style front sight, Picatinny rail, 6-position adjustable stock, pistol grip, fires 3" shells, 10.75-14.625" length of pull.

Production: *current* **Gauge/Bore:** *12 ga.*
Action: *pump-action*
Barrel Length: 18.5" **Wt.:** *6.75 lbs.*
Sights: *Ghost Ring rear, fiber optic front*
Capacity: 6
Stock: *adjustable synthetic stock with side saddle*

D2C:	NIB $532	Ex $425	VG+ $295	Good $270	**LMP:** $726
C2C:	Mint $520	Ex $375	VG+ $270	Good $240	Fair $125
Trade-In:	Mint $380	Ex $300	VG+ $210	Good $190	Poor $60

500 THUNDER RANCH REDBOOK CODE: RB-MS-S-500THR
Stand-off/breacher barrel in matte finish, fires 3" shells, 13" length of pull. Designed in conjunction with Marine Corps veteran and former SWAT team leader Clint Smith, current president/director of the Thunder Ranch training facility in Lakeview, Oregon.

Production: *current* **Gauge/Bore:** *12 ga.*
Action: *pump-action*
Barrel Length: 18.5" **Wt.:** *6.75 lbs.*
Sights: *white dot*
Capacity: 6
Stock: *black synthetic*

D2C:	NIB $380	Ex $300	VG+ $210	Good $190	**LMP:** $507
C2C:	Mint $370	Ex $275	VG+ $190	Good $175	Fair $90
Trade-In:	Mint $270	Ex $225	VG+ $150	Good $135	Poor $60

500 TACTICAL TRI-RAIL REDBOOK CODE: RB-MS-S-500TTR
Barrel in matte finish, pistol grip, tri-rail forend with full-length bottom rail and two removable side rails, fires 3" shells. Add $38 for 8-shot model.

Production: *current* **Gauge/Bore:** *12 ga.*
Action: *pump-action*
Barrel Length: 18.5", 20" **Wt.:** *6.75 lbs.*
Sights: *bead, Ghost Ring*
Capacity: 6, 8
Stock: *adjustable synthetic stock with side saddle*

D2C:	NIB $441	Ex $350	VG+ $245	Good $225	**LMP:** $612
C2C:	Mint $430	Ex $325	VG+ $230	Good $200	Fair $105
Trade-In:	Mint $320	Ex $250	VG+ $180	Good $155	Poor $60

500 PERSUADER   REDBOOK CODE: RB-MS-S-500PSD
Barrel in matte blue finish, compact stock, fires 3" shells, 13" length of pull.

Production: *current* **Gauge/Bore:** *20 ga.*
Action: *pump-action*
Barrel Length: 20" **Wt.:** *6 lbs.*
Sights: *Ghost Ring*
Capacity: *8*
Stock: *black synthetic*

D2C:	NIB $375	Ex $300	VG+ $210	Good $190	**LMP:** $500
C2C:	Mint $360	Ex $275	VG+ $190	Good $170	Fair $90
Trade-In:	Mint $270	Ex $225	VG+ $150	Good $135	Poor $60

500 HS410   REDBOOK CODE: RB-MS-S-500HS4
Barrel in blue finish, spreader choke, fires 3" shells, 13.875" length of pull.

Production: *current* **Gauge/Bore:** *.410*
Action: *pump-action*
Barrel Length: 18.5" **Wt.:** *5.5 lbs.*
Sights: *bead*
Capacity: *6*
Stock: *black synthetic*

D2C:	NIB $363	Ex $300	VG+ $200	Good $185	**LMP:** $473
C2C:	Mint $350	Ex $275	VG+ $190	Good $165	Fair $85
Trade-In:	Mint $260	Ex $225	VG+ $150	Good $130	Poor $60

500 ZMB   REDBOOK CODE: RB-MS-S-500ZMB
Barrel in matte finish, engraved receiver, fires 3" shells. Add $175 for 6-shot pistol grip version with breacher barrel, tri-rail forend, white dot sight, tactical light/laser combo, sling, and removable top handle.

Production: *current* **Gauge/Bore:** *12 ga.*
Action: *pump-action*
Barrel Length: 18.5", 20" **Wt.:** *7 lbs.*
Sights: *bead*
Capacity: *6, 8*
Stock: *black synthetic*

D2C:	NIB $333	Ex $275	VG+ $185	Good $170	**LMP:** $475
C2C:	Mint $320	Ex $250	VG+ $170	Good $150	Fair $80
Trade-In:	Mint $240	Ex $200	VG+ $130	Good $120	Poor $60

500 BLACKWATER   REDBOOK CODE: RB-MS-S-500BKW
Stand-off/breacher barrel in matte finish, pistol grip, engraved receiver, fires 3" shells, 31" overall length.

Production: *current* **Gauge/Bore:** *12 ga.*
Action: *pump-action*
Barrel Length: 18.5" **Wt.:** *5.75 lbs.*
Sights: *white dot*
Capacity: *6*
Stock: *black synthetic*

D2C:	NIB $361	Ex $275	VG+ $200	Good $185	**LMP:** $493
C2C:	Mint $350	Ex $250	VG+ $190	Good $165	Fair $85
Trade-In:	Mint $260	Ex $225	VG+ $150	Good $130	Poor $60

MOSSBERG

500 BANTAM ALL-PURPOSE   REDBOOK CODE: RB-MS-S-500BAP

Vented rib barrel in blue finish, Accu-Set choke tubes, fires 3" shells, 13" length of pull. Available in field, turkey, slug and multi-barrel combo varieties with 24" ported, fully-rifled Slugster barrel. Add $57 for combo model.

Production: *current* **Gauge/Bore:** *12 ga., 20 ga., .410*
Action: *pump-action*
Barrel Length: *18.5", 20", 22", 24"* **Wt.:** *7.25 lbs.*
Sights: *dual bead*
Capacity: *6*
Stock: *black synthetic or hardwood*

D2C:	NIB $314	Ex $250	VG+ $175	Good $160	**LMP: $414**
C2C:	Mint $310	Ex $225	VG+ $160	Good $145	Fair $75
Trade-In:	Mint $230	Ex $200	VG+ $130	Good $110	Poor $60

500 SUPER BANTAM ALL-PURPOSE   REDBOOK CODE: RB-MS-S-500BSU

Vented rib barrel in pink marble or blue finish, Accu-Set choke tubes, available in ported barrel Slugster option (blue or Realtree Xtra finish). Add $67 for Turkey model with Mossy Oak camo finish options, X-Full chokes. Add $120 for Combo model with Mossy Oak camo finish options and ported, fully-rifled Slugster barrel. Add $142 for Duck Commander model with Realtree Max-5 finish, engraved stock, and spacer system.

Production: *current* **Gauge/Bore:** *12 ga., 20 ga., .410*
Action: *pump-action*
Barrel Length: *18.5", 20", 22", 24"* **Wt.:** *5.25 lbs.*
Sights: *dual bead, TruGlo Tru-Bead, adjustable fiber optic*
Capacity: *6*
Stock: *adjustable synthetic*

D2C:	NIB $395	Ex $325	VG+ $220	Good $200	**LMP: $414**
C2C:	Mint $380	Ex $275	VG+ $200	Good $180	Fair $95
Trade-In:	Mint $290	Ex $225	VG+ $160	Good $140	Poor $60

535 ALL-PURPOSE   REDBOOK CODE: RB-MS-S-535APX

Vented rib barrel with blue finish, Accu-Set choke tubes, 14" length of pull, chambers 3.5" shells.

Production: *current* **Gauge/Bore:** *12 ga.*
Action: *pump-action*
Barrel Length: *28"* **Wt.:** *6.75 lbs.*
Sights: *bead*
Capacity: *6*
Stock: *wood*

D2C:	NIB $371	Ex $300	VG+ $205	Good $190	**LMP: $440**
C2C:	Mint $360	Ex $275	VG+ $190	Good $170	Fair $90
Trade-In:	Mint $270	Ex $225	VG+ $150	Good $130	Poor $60

535 DUCK COMMANDER   REDBOOK CODE: RB-MS-S-535DCX

Ported and vented rib barrel in Realtree Max-5 finish, Accu-Set choke tubes, drilled and tapped receiver, ambidextrous top safety, dual extractors, twin action bars, steel-to-steel lockup, 14" length of pull, chambers 3.5" shells.

Production: *current* **Gauge/Bore:** *12 ga.*
Action: *pump-action*
Barrel Length: *28"* **Wt.:** *7.75 lbs.*
Sights: *TruGlo Tru-Bead*
Capacity: *6*
Stock: *synthetic with Realtree Max-5*

D2C:	NIB $459	Ex $350	VG+ $255	Good $230	**LMP: $597**
C2C:	Mint $450	Ex $325	VG+ $230	Good $210	Fair $110
Trade-In:	Mint $330	Ex $275	VG+ $180	Good $165	Poor $60

535 TURKEY REDBOOK CODE: RB-MS-S-535TKY

Vented rib barrel in matte blue finish, X-Factor ported choke tube, thumbhole (standard model only), 14" length of pull, 40.25" overall length, chambers 3.5" shells. Add $10 for model with 22" barrel, XX-Full chokes, and Mossy Oak Obsession or Break-Up Infinity finish. Add $52 for model with LPA (Lightning Pull Action) adjustable trigger and Mossy Oak Break-Up Infinity finish.

Production: *current* **Gauge/Bore:** *12 ga.*
Action: *pump-action*
Barrel Length: *22"* **Wt.:** *7 lbs.*
Sights: *adjustable fiber optic*
Capacity: *6*
Stock: *fixed synthetic, adjustable, thumbhole*

D2C:	NIB $363	Ex $300	VG+ $200	Good $185	**LMP:** $503
C2C:	Mint $350	Ex $275	VG+ $190	Good $165	Fair $85
Trade-In:	Mint $260	Ex $225	VG+ $150	Good $130	Poor $60

535 TURKEY THUG REDBOOK CODE: RB-MS-S-535TTH

Vented rib barrel in Mossy Oak Break-Up Infinity finish, X-Factor ported tube chokes, LPA (Lightning Pump Action) adjustable trigger, pistol grip, chambers 3.5" shells. Add $63 for TRUGLO red dot sight option.

Production: *current* **Gauge/Bore:** *12 ga.*
Action: *pump-action*
Barrel Length: *20"* **Wt.:** *6.5 lbs.*
Sights: *adjustable fiber optic*
Capacity: *6*
Stock: *synthetic with pistol grip*

D2C:	NIB $446	Ex $350	VG+ $250	Good $225	**LMP:** $677
C2C:	Mint $430	Ex $325	VG+ $230	Good $205	Fair $105
Trade-In:	Mint $320	Ex $250	VG+ $180	Good $160	Poor $60

535 WATERFOWL REDBOOK CODE: RB-MS-S-535WFL

Vented rib barrel in matte blue finish, Accu-Set choke tubes, 14" length of pull, chambers 3.5" shells. Add $73 for Mossy Oak Shadow Grass Blades or Realtree Max-4 finish.

Production: *current* **Gauge/Bore:** *12 ga.*
Action: *pump-action*
Barrel Length: *28"* **Wt.:** *6.75 lbs.*
Sights: *fiber optic front*
Capacity: *6*
Stock: *black synthetic*

D2C:	NIB $346	Ex $275	VG+ $195	Good $175	**LMP:** $440
C2C:	Mint $340	Ex $250	VG+ $180	Good $160	Fair $80
Trade-In:	Mint $250	Ex $200	VG+ $140	Good $125	Poor $60

535 SLUGSTER REDBOOK CODE: RB-MS-S-535SLG

Fully-rifled Slugster barrel in matte blue finish, adjustable sights, 14" length of pull, chambers 3.5" shells. Add $146 for model with LPA (Lightning Pump Action) adjustable trigger, fully-rifled & fluted Slugster barrel, scope base and Realtree Xtra finish.

Production: *current* **Gauge/Bore:** *12 ga.*
Action: *pump-action*
Barrel Length: *24"* **Wt.:** *7 lbs.*
Sights: *adjustable rifle-type sights*
Capacity: *6*
Stock: *black synthetic or Dual Comb*

D2C:	NIB $344	Ex $275	VG+ $190	Good $175	**LMP:** $440
C2C:	Mint $340	Ex $250	VG+ $180	Good $155	Fair $80
Trade-In:	Mint $250	Ex $200	VG+ $140	Good $125	Poor $60

MOSSBERG

535 COMBO REDBOOK CODE: RB-MS-S-535CMB

Vented rib barrel in blue finish, Accu-Set choke tubes, fully-rifled 24" Slugster barrel, 14" length of pull, chambers 3.5" shells. Add $77 for Mossy Oak Break-Up Infinity model with adjustable fiber optic sights. Add $118 for Mossy Oak Break-Up Infinity model with LPA (Lightning Pump Action) adjustable trigger.

Production: *current* **Gauge/Bore:** *12 ga.*
Action: *pump-action*
Barrel Length: *22", 24", 28"* **Wt.:** *6.75 lbs.*
Sights: *dual bead, adjustable fiber optic, adjustable rifle-type sights*
Capacity: *6*
Stock: *synthetic or wood*

D2C:	NIB $428	Ex $350	VG+ $240	Good $215	**LMP:** $488
C2C:	Mint $420	Ex $300	VG+ $220	Good $195	Fair $100
Trade-In:	Mint $310	Ex $250	VG+ $170	Good $150	Poor $60

590 SPECIAL PURPOSE REDBOOK CODE: RB-MS-S-590SPP

Barrel with heat shield and blue finish, 14.5" length of pull. Add $40 for matte finish. Add $43 for Ghost Ring sights. Add $93 for model with matte finish and SpeedFeed stock. Add $134 for model with matte finish, Ghost Ring sights, and SpeedFeed stock. Add $108 to price of base model for Parkerized barrel and SpeedFeed stock with shell storage. (All 410 bore options come with a 2.5" chamber.)

Production: *current* **Gauge/Bore:** *12 ga., 20 ga., .410*
Action: *pump-action*
Barrel Length: *18.5", 20"* **Wt.:** *7.25 lbs.*
Sights: *bead, Ghost Ring*
Capacity: *9*
Stock: *black synthetic or SpeedFeed*

D2C:	NIB $500	Ex $400	VG+ $275	Good $250	**LMP:** $553
C2C:	Mint $480	Ex $350	VG+ $250	Good $225	Fair $115
Trade-In:	Mint $360	Ex $300	VG+ $200	Good $175	Poor $60

590 TACTICAL TRI-RAIL REDBOOK CODE: RB-MS-S-590TTR

Barrel in Parkerized finish, heat shield, tri-rail forend, SpeedFeed shell storage stock, fires 3" shells, 13.875" length of pull.

Production: *current* **Gauge/Bore:** *12 ga.*
Action: *pump-action*
Barrel Length: *20"* **Wt.:** *7.25 lbs.*
Sights: *bead*
Capacity: *9*
Stock: *SpeedFeed black synthetic*

D2C:	NIB $480	Ex $375	VG+ $265	Good $240	**LMP:** $661
C2C:	Mint $470	Ex $350	VG+ $240	Good $220	Fair $115
Trade-In:	Mint $350	Ex $275	VG+ $190	Good $170	Poor $60

590 MAGPUL SERIES REDBOOK CODE: RB-MS-S-590MAG

Barrel in Parkerized finish, MOE forend (fully compatible with MOE rails, mounts, and accessories) with extended length and front/rear hand stops, stock with spacer system, fires 3" shells, 12.25"/14.25" length of pull.

Production: *current* **Gauge/Bore:** *12 ga.*
Action: *pump-action*
Barrel Length: *20"* **Wt.:** *7.25 lbs.*
Sights: *Ghost Ring*
Capacity: *9*
Stock: *Magpul SGA*

D2C:	NIB $594	Ex $475	VG+ $330	Good $300	**LMP:** $773
C2C:	Mint $580	Ex $425	VG+ $300	Good $270	Fair $140
Trade-In:	Mint $430	Ex $350	VG+ $240	Good $210	Poor $60

590A1 MAGPUL SERIES, 6-SHOT REDBOOK CODE: RB-MS-S-590AM6

Heavy-walled barrel in Parkerized finish, metal trigger guard and safety buttons built to Mil-Spec demands. Add $40 for model with Ghost Ring sights. Add $99 for Typhon camo pattern by Kryptek option. Add $159 for model including MOE forend (with extended length front and rear hand stops) and SGA stock with spacer system and buttpad. Add $267 for model with adjustable aluminum stock.

Production: *current* **Gauge/Bore:** *12 ga.*
Action: *pump-action*
Barrel Length: *18.5"* **Wt.:** *7.25 lbs.*
Sights: *bead*
Capacity: *6*
Stock: *black synthetic*

D2C:	NIB $554	Ex $425	VG+ $305	Good $280	**LMP:** $599
C2C:	Mint $540	Ex $400	VG+ $280	Good $250	Fair $130
Trade-In:	Mint $400	Ex $325	VG+ $220	Good $195	Poor $60

590A1 MAGPUL SERIES, 9-SHOT REDBOOK CODE: RB-MS-S-590AM9

Heavy-walled barrel in Parkerized finish, spacer system for LOP adjustment, MOE forends with extended length and front/rear hand stops, rear & front sling mount, fires 3" shells.

Production: *current* **Gauge/Bore:** *12 ga.*
Action: *pump-action*
Barrel Length: *20"* **Wt.:** *7.25 lbs.*
Sights: *XS Ghost Ring*
Capacity: *9*
Stock: *Magpul SGA*

D2C:	NIB $654	Ex $500	VG+ $360	Good $330	**LMP:** $855
C2C:	Mint $630	Ex $475	VG+ $330	Good $295	Fair $155
Trade-In:	Mint $470	Ex $375	VG+ $260	Good $230	Poor $90

590A1 SHELL STORAGE STOCK REDBOOK CODE: RB-MS-S-590ASH

Heavy-walled barrel in Parkerized finish, metal trigger guard and safety buttons built to Mil-Spec demands, fires 3" shells. Add $37 for 3-dot sight or Ghost Ring option. Add $110 for 9-shot model with 20" barrel and Ghost Ring sights.

Production: *current* **Gauge/Bore:** *12 ga.*
Action: *pump-action*
Barrel Length: *18.5", 20"* **Wt.:** *7.25 lbs.*
Sights: *bead, 3-dot, Ghost Ring*
Capacity: *6, 9*
Stock: *SpeedFeed black synthetic*

D2C:	NIB $554	Ex $425	VG+ $305	Good $280	**LMP:** $653
C2C:	Mint $540	Ex $400	VG+ $280	Good $250	Fair $130
Trade-In:	Mint $400	Ex $325	VG+ $220	Good $195	Poor $60

590A1 MARINER REDBOOK CODE: RB-MS-S-590AMR

Heavy-walled barrel in corrosion-resistant Marinecote finish, metal trigger guard and safety buttons built to Mil-Spec demands, fires 3" shells, 14" length of pull.

Production: *current* **Gauge/Bore:** *12 ga.*
Action: *pump-action*
Barrel Length: *18.5"* **Wt.:** *6.75 lbs*
Sights: *bead*
Capacity: *6*
Stock: *black synthetic*

D2C:	NIB $556	Ex $425	VG+ $310	Good $280	**LMP:** $749
C2C:	Mint $540	Ex $400	VG+ $280	Good $255	Fair $130
Trade-In:	Mint $400	Ex $325	VG+ $220	Good $195	Poor $60

MOSSBERG

590A1 SPX REDBOOK CODE: RB-MS-S-590ASP

Heavy-walled barrel in Parkerized finish, M9 bayonet & scabbard, Picatinny rail, metal trigger guard & safety buttons built to Mil-Spec demands, fires 3" shells, 13.875" length of pull.

Production: *current* **Gauge/Bore:** *12 ga.*
Action: *pump-action*
Barrel Length: 20" **Wt.:** *7.25 lbs.*
Sights: *Ghost Ring rear, M16-style front*
Capacity: *9*
Stock: *black synthetic*

D2C:	NIB $642	Ex $500	VG+ $355	Good $325	**LMP:** $894
C2C:	Mint $620	Ex $450	VG+ $330	Good $290	Fair $150
Trade-In:	Mint $460	Ex $375	VG+ $260	Good $225	Poor $90

590A1 TACTICAL TRI-RAIL REDBOOK CODE: RB-MS-S-590ATR

Heavy-walled barrel in Parkerized finish, metal trigger guard & safety buttons built to Mil-Spec demands, fires 3" shells, 10.5"-14.25" length of pull.

Production: *current* **Gauge/Bore:** *12 ga.*
Action: *pump-action*
Barrel Length: 20" **Wt.:** *7.25 lbs.*
Sights: *Ghost Ring*
Capacity: *9*
Stock: *black adjustable aluminum*

D2C:	NIB $633	Ex $500	VG+ $350	Good $320	**LMP:** $872
C2C:	Mint $610	Ex $450	VG+ $320	Good $285	Fair $150
Trade-In:	Mint $450	Ex $375	VG+ $250	Good $225	Poor $90

590A1 U.S. SERVICE MODEL (TALO) REDBOOK CODE: RB-MS-S-590AUS

Heavy-walled barrel in Parkerized finish, receiver serialized with prefix USSM, metal trigger guard & safety buttons built to Mil-Spec demands, fires 3" shells, 14" length of pull.

Production: *current* **Gauge/Bore:** *12 ga.*
Action: *pump-action*
Barrel Length: 20" **Wt.:** *7.25 lbs.*
Sights: *bead*
Capacity: *9*
Stock: *black synthetic*

D2C:	NIB $554	Ex $425	VG+ $305	Good $280	**LMP:** $615
C2C:	Mint $540	Ex $400	VG+ $280	Good $250	Fair $130
Trade-In:	Mint $400	Ex $325	VG+ $220	Good $195	Poor $60

835 ULTI-MAG TURKEY REDBOOK CODE: RB-MS-S-835TKY

Overbored and vented rib barrel in matte blue finish, thumbhole, X-Factor ported choke tube, 14" length of pull, chambers 3.5" shells. Add. $21 for Mossy Oak Obsession model. Add $38 for Mossy Oak Break-Up Infinity model. Add $41 for model with LPA (Lightning Pump Action) adjustable trigger with barrel in matte blue finish and thumbhole stock.

Production: *current* **Gauge/Bore:** *12 ga.*
Action: *pump-action*
Barrel Length: 20" **Wt.:** *7.25 lbs.*
Sights: *adjustable fiber optic"*
Capacity: *6*
Stock: *fixed synthetic, adjustable, thumbhole*

D2C:	NIB $485	Ex $375	VG+ $270	Good $245	**LMP:** $559
C2C:	Mint $470	Ex $350	VG+ $250	Good $220	Fair $115
Trade-In:	Mint $350	Ex $275	VG+ $190	Good $170	Poor $60

MOSSBERG

835 ULTI-MAG TURKEY THUG, LPA TRIGGER   REDBOOK CODE: RB-MS-S-835TTH

Overbored and vented rib barrel in Mossy Oak Break-Up Infinity finish, X-Factor ported choke tube, LPA (Lightning Pump Action) adjustable trigger, 14" length of pull, chambers 3.5" shells.

Production: *current* **Gauge/Bore:** *12 ga.*
Action: *pump-action*
Barrel Length: 20" **Wt.:** *7.25 lbs.*
Sights: *adjustable fiber optic, TRUGLO red dot*
Capacity: *6*
Stock: *black synthetic*

D2C:	NIB $526	Ex $400	VG+ $290	Good $265	**LMP:** $708
C2C:	Mint $510	Ex $375	VG+ $270	Good $240	Fair $125
Trade-In:	Mint $380	Ex $300	VG+ $210	Good $185	Poor $60

835 ULTI-MAG DUCK COMMANDER   REDBOOK CODE: RB-MS-S-835DCX

Ported, overbored, and vented rib barrel in Realtree Max-5 finish, Accu-Mag choke set, drilled and tapped receiver, stock engraved with Duck Commander logo, ambidextrous top safety, anti-jam elevator, chambers 3.5" shells.

Production: *current* **Gauge/Bore:** *12 ga.*
Action: *pump-action*
Barrel Length: 28" **Wt.:** *7.75 lbs.*
Sights: *TruGlo Tru-Bead*
Capacity: *6*
Stock: *synthetic with Realtree Max-5*

D2C:	NIB $528	Ex $425	VG+ $295	Good $265	**LMP:** $693
C2C:	Mint $510	Ex $375	VG+ $270	Good $240	Fair $125
Trade-In:	Mint $380	Ex $300	VG+ $210	Good $185	Poor $60

835 ULTI-MAG WATERFOWL   REDBOOK CODE: RB-MS-S-835WFL

Ported, overbored, and vented rib barrel in blue or matte blue finish, modified choke tube, 14.5" length of pull, chambers 3.5" shells. Add $84 for Mossy Oak Shadow Grass Blades model with Accu-Mag choke set. Add $149 for Realtree Max-4 model with non-ported barrel and X-Factor ported choke tube.

Production: *current* **Gauge/Bore:** *12 ga.*
Action: *pump-action*
Barrel Length: 28" **Wt.:** *7.75 lbs.*
Sights: *dual bead or fiber optic front*
Capacity: *6*
Stock: *wood or synthetic*

D2C:	NIB $420	Ex $325	VG+ $235	Good $210	**LMP:** $513
C2C:	Mint $410	Ex $300	VG+ $210	Good $190	Fair $100
Trade-In:	Mint $300	Ex $250	VG+ $170	Good $150	Poor $60

835 ULTI-MAG SLUGSTER   REDBOOK CODE: RB-MS-S-835SLG

Fluted and fully-rifled Slugster barrel in Realtree Xtra finish, LPA (Lightning Pump Action) adjustable trigger, 14" length of pull, chambers 3.5" shells.

Production: *current* **Gauge/Bore:** *12 ga.*
Action: *pump-action*
Barrel Length: 24" **Wt.:** *7.5 lbs.*
Sights: *rifle-type sights 6*
Capacity: *6*
Stock: *synthetic*

D2C:	NIB $486	Ex $375	VG+ $270	Good $245	**LMP:** $638
C2C:	Mint $470	Ex $350	VG+ $250	Good $220	Fair $115
Trade-In:	Mint $350	Ex $275	VG+ $190	Good $175	Poor $60

MOSSBERG

835 ULTI-MAG COMBO REDBOOK CODE: RB-MS-S-835CMB
Overbored, ported, and vented rib barrel in Mossy Oak Break-Up Infinity finish, Ulti-Full choke tube, 14"/14.5" length of pull, chambers 3.5" shells. Add $45 for model with LPA (Lightning Pump Action) adjustable trigger.

Production: *current* **Gauge/Bore:** *12 ga.*
Action: *pump-action*
Barrel Length: 24", 28" **Wt.:** *7.5 lbs.*
Sights: *adjustable fiber optic*
Capacity: 6
Stock: *synthetic with Dual Comb option*

D2C:	NIB $482	Ex $375	VG+ $270	Good $245	**LMP: $655**
C2C:	Mint $470	Ex $350	VG+ $250	Good $220	Fair $115
Trade-In:	Mint $350	Ex $275	VG+ $190	Good $170	Poor $60

MAVERICK 88 ALL-PURPOSE REDBOOK CODE: RB-MS-S-MA88AP
Vented rib barrel in blue finish, modified choke tube, 14" length of pull, fires 3" shells. Youth model available in 20 ga. only, with 22" barrel and 13" length of pull.

Production: *current* **Gauge/Bore:** *12 ga., 20 ga.*
Action: *pump-action*
Barrel Length: 26", 28" **Wt.:** *7 lbs.*
Sights: *bead*
Capacity: 6
Stock: *black synthetic*

D2C:	NIB $218	Ex $175	VG+ $120	Good $110	**LMP: $298**
C2C:	Mint $210	Ex $175	VG+ $110	Good $100	Fair $55
Trade-In:	Mint $160	Ex $125	VG+ $90	Good $80	Poor $30

MAVERICK 88 SLUG REDBOOK CODE: RB-MS-S-MA88SL
Barrel in blue finish, 14.5" length of pull, fires 3" shells. Add $21 for fully-rifled barrel option.

Production: *current* **Gauge/Bore:** *12 ga.*
Action: *pump-action*
Barrel Length: 24" **Wt.:** *7 lbs.*
Sights: *adjustable rifle-type sights*
Capacity: 6
Stock: *black synthetic*

D2C:	NIB $228	Ex $175	VG+ $130	Good $115	**LMP: $298**
C2C:	Mint $220	Ex $175	VG+ $120	Good $105	Fair $55
Trade-In:	Mint $170	Ex $150	VG+ $90	Good $80	Poor $30

SA-20 ALL-PURPOSE REDBOOK CODE: RB-MS-S-SA20AP
Vented rib barrel in matte blue finish, includes sport set choke tubes, fires 3" shells, 14" length of pull.

Production: *current* **Gauge/Bore:** *20 ga.*
Action: *semi-auto*
Barrel Length: 26", 28" **Wt.:** *6 lbs.*
Sights: *bead*
Capacity: 5
Stock: *black synthetic*

D2C:	NIB $426	Ex $325	VG+ $235	Good $215	**LMP: $543**
C2C:	Mint $410	Ex $300	VG+ $220	Good $195	Fair $100
Trade-In:	Mint $310	Ex $250	VG+ $170	Good $150	Poor $60

SA-20 RAILED REDBOOK CODE: RB-MS-S-SA20RL

Barrel in matte blue finish, 14" length of pull, fires 3" shells. Add $5 for model with pistol grip, top rail, mag cap tri-rail.

Production: *current* **Gauge/Bore:** *20 ga.*
Action: *semi-auto*
Barrel Length: *20"* **Wt.:** *6 lbs.*
Sights: *Ghost Ring, fiber optic front*
Capacity: *5*
Stock: *black synthetic with optional pistol grip*

D2C:	NIB $428	Ex $350	VG+ $240	Good $215	LMP: $542
C2C:	Mint $420	Ex $300	VG+ $220	Good $195	Fair $100
Trade-In:	Mint $310	Ex $250	VG+ $170	Good $150	Poor $60

930 JM PRO REDBOOK CODE: RB-MS-S-930JMP

Vented rib barrel in matte blue finish, Accu-Set choke tubes, engraved receiver, fires 3" shells. Signature Jerry Miculek model includes 8-round extended magazine tube, beveled loading gate, oversized bolt handle/bolt release, and dual gas system for lighter recoil. Also available in a 10-shot model. Add $28 for Kryptek Typhon finish (10-shot model only).

Production: *current* **Gauge/Bore:** *12 ga.*
Action: *semi-auto*
Barrel Length: *22", 24"* **Wt.:** *7.75 lbs.*
Sights: *fiber optic front*
Capacity: *8, 9*
Stock: *black synthetic, Kryptek Typhon*

D2C:	NIB $581	Ex $450	VG+ $320	Good $295	LMP: $752
C2C:	Mint $560	Ex $425	VG+ $300	Good $265	Fair $135
Trade-In:	Mint $420	Ex $350	VG+ $230	Good $205	Poor $60

930 WATERFOWL REDBOOK CODE: RB-MS-S-930WFL

Ported and vented rib barrel in matte blue finish, Accu-Set choke tubes, dual gas vent system, 14" length of pull, fires 3" shells. Add $26 for walnut stock. Add $133 for Mossy Oak Shadow Grass Blades or Realtree Max-4 finish.

Production: *current* **Gauge/Bore:** *12 ga.*
Action: *semi-auto*
Barrel Length: *28"* **Wt.:** *7.75 lbs.*
Sights: *fiber optic front*
Capacity: *5*
Stock: *black synthetic or walnut*

D2C:	NIB $536	Ex $425	VG+ $295	Good $270	LMP: $626
C2C:	Mint $520	Ex $375	VG+ $270	Good $245	Fair $125
Trade-In:	Mint $390	Ex $325	VG+ $210	Good $190	Poor $60

930 TURKEY REDBOOK CODE: RB-MS-S-930TKY

Ported and vented rib barrel in matte blue finish, XX-Full chokes, dual gas vent system, fires 3" shells. Add $133 for adjustable fiber optic sights and choice of Mossy Oak Obsession or Mossy Oak Break-Up Infinity finish. Add $96 for model with pistol grip. Add $228 for pistol grip model in Mossy Oak Break-Up Infinity finish.

Production: *current* **Gauge/Bore:** *12 ga.*
Action: *semi-auto*
Barrel Length: *24"* **Wt.:** *7.5 lbs.*
Sights: *fiber optic front or adjustable fiber optic*
Capacity: *5*
Stock: *synthetic*

D2C:	NIB $512	Ex $400	VG+ $285	Good $260	LMP: $626
C2C:	Mint $500	Ex $375	VG+ $260	Good $235	Fair $120
Trade-In:	Mint $370	Ex $300	VG+ $200	Good $180	Poor $60

MOSSBERG

930 SLUGSTER REDBOOK CODE: RB-MS-S-930SLG

Ported and fully-rifled Slugster barrel in matte blue finish, dual gas vent system, scope base, 14" length of pull, fires 3" shells.

Production: *current* **Gauge/Bore:** *12 ga.*
Action: *semi-auto*
Barrel Length: 24" **Wt.:** *7.5 lbs.*
Sights: *adjustable rifle-type sights*
Capacity: *5*
Stock: *synthetic Monte Carlo or walnut*

D2C:	NIB $484	Ex $375	VG+ $270	Good $245	LMP: $626
C2C:	Mint $470	Ex $350	VG+ $250	Good $220	Fair $115
Trade-In:	Mint $350	Ex $275	VG+ $190	Good $170	Poor $60

930 ALL-PURPOSE REDBOOK CODE: RB-MS-S-930APX

Ported and vented rib barrel in blue finish, Accu-Set choke tubes, dual gas vent system, 14" length of pull, fires 3" shells.

Production: *current* **Gauge/Bore:** *12 ga.*
Action: *semi-auto*
Barrel Length: 26", 28" **Wt.:** *7.75 lbs.*
Sights: *bead*
Capacity: *5*
Stock: *walnut*

D2C:	NIB $512	Ex $400	VG+ $285	Good $260	LMP: $652
C2C:	Mint $500	Ex $375	VG+ $260	Good $235	Fair $120
Trade-In:	Mint $370	Ex $300	VG+ $200	Good $180	Poor $60

930 SPX REDBOOK CODE: RB-MS-S-930SPX

Barrel in matte finish, Picatinny Rail, fires 3" shells. Add $99 for model with pistol grip. Add $153 for pistol grip model in Kryptek Typhon finish. Add $155 for pistol grip model in tan finish.

Production: *current* **Gauge/Bore:** *12 ga.*
Action: *semi-auto*
Barrel Length: 18.5" **Wt.:** *7.75 lbs.*
Sights: *Ghost Ring, M16-style*
Capacity: *8*
Stock: *black synthetic or Kryptek Typhon*

D2C:	NIB $670	Ex $525	VG+ $370	Good $335	LMP: $811
C2C:	Mint $650	Ex $475	VG+ $340	Good $305	Fair $155
Trade-In:	Mint $480	Ex $400	VG+ $270	Good $235	Poor $90

930 TACTICAL REDBOOK CODE: RB-MS-S-930TCT

Breacher barrel in matte finish, heat shield, dual gas vent system, fires 3" shells, 14" length of pull.

Production: *current* **Gauge/Bore:** *12 ga.*
Action: *semi-auto*
Barrel Length: 18.5" **Wt.:** *7.75 lbs.*
Sights: *white dot*
Capacity: *5*
Stock: *black synthetic*

D2C:	NIB $564	Ex $450	VG+ $315	Good $285	LMP: $704
C2C:	Mint $550	Ex $400	VG+ $290	Good $255	Fair $130
Trade-In:	Mint $410	Ex $325	VG+ $220	Good $200	Poor $60

930 SPX BLACKWATER, PISTOL GRIP   REDBOOK CODE: RB-MS-S-930BKW
Barrel in matte finish, engraved receiver, dual gas vent system, 13" length of pull, fires 3" shells.

Production: *current* **Gauge/Bore:** *12 ga.*
Action: *semi-auto*
Barrel Length: *18.5"* **Wt.:** *7.75 lbs.*
Sights: *XS Ghost Ring, front sight post*
Capacity: *8*
Stock: *black synthetic with pistol grip*

D2C:	NIB $620	Ex $475	VG+ $345	Good $310	**LMP:** $891
C2C:	Mint $600	Ex $450	VG+ $310	Good $280	Fair $145
Trade-In:	Mint $450	Ex $350	VG+ $250	Good $220	Poor $90

930 HOME SECURITY   REDBOOK CODE: RB-MS-S-930HSC
Barrel in blue finish, dual gas vent system, 14" length of pull, fires 3" shells.

Production: *current* **Gauge/Bore:** *12 ga.*
Action: *semi-auto*
Barrel Length: *18.5"* **Wt.:** *7.5 lbs.*
Sights: *bead*
Capacity: *5*
Stock: *black synthetic*

D2C:	NIB $536	Ex $425	VG+ $295	Good $270	**LMP:** $631
C2C:	Mint $520	Ex $375	VG+ $270	Good $245	Fair $125
Trade-In:	Mint $390	Ex $325	VG+ $210	Good $190	Poor $60

935 TURKEY   REDBOOK CODE: RB-MS-S-935TKY
Overbored barrel in Mossy Oak Break-Up Infinity or Realtree Xtra Green finish, Ulti-Full choke tubes, dual gas vent system, 14" length of pull, chambers 3.5" shells.

Production: *current* **Gauge/Bore:** *12 ga.*
Action: *semi-auto*
Barrel Length: *22", 24"* **Wt.:** *7.5 lbs.*
Sights: *adjustable fiber optic*
Capacity: *5*
Stock: *synthetic with Mossy Oak Break-Up Infinity or Realtree Xtra Green*

D2C:	NIB $628	Ex $500	VG+ $350	Good $315	**LMP:** $840
C2C:	Mint $610	Ex $450	VG+ $320	Good $285	Fair $145
Trade-In:	Mint $450	Ex $375	VG+ $250	Good $220	Poor $90

935 WATERFOWL   REDBOOK CODE: RB-MS-S-935WFL
Overbored and vented rib barrel in matte black, Accu-Mag choke set, dual gas vent system, sling, chambers 3.5" shells. Add $137 for model with Mossy Oak Shadow Grass Blades or Realtree Max-4 finish.

Production: *current* **Gauge/Bore:** *12 ga.*
Action: *semi-auto*
Barrel Length: *26", 28"* **Wt.:** *7.75 lbs.*
Sights: *fiber optic front*
Capacity: *5*
Stock: *black synthetic, Mossy Oak Shadow Grass Blades, Realtree Max-4*

D2C:	NIB $614	Ex $475	VG+ $340	Good $310	**LMP:** $703
C2C:	Mint $590	Ex $425	VG+ $310	Good $280	Fair $145
Trade-In:	Mint $440	Ex $350	VG+ $240	Good $215	Poor $90

MOSSBERG

SILVER RESERVE II FIELD   REDBOOK CODE: RB-MS-S-SRS2FL
Vented rib barrel in blue finish, shell ejectors, field choke tube set, silver receiver with scroll engraving, fires 3" shells, 14" length of pull. Subtract $88 for extractor model, available in bantam version (20 ga., 13" length of pull). Extractor model available with fixed-full/fixed modified choke option.

Production: *current* **Gauge/Bore:** *12 ga., 20 ga., 28 ga., .410*
Action: *O/U*
Barrel Length: 26", 28" **Wt.:** *7.5 lbs.*
Sights: *front bead*
Capacity: 2
Stock: *satin select black walnut*

D2C:	NIB $609	Ex $475	VG+ $335	Good $305	LMP: $824
C2C:	Mint $590	Ex $425	VG+ $310	Good $275	Fair $145
Trade-In:	Mint $440	Ex $350	VG+ $240	Good $215	Poor $90

SILVER RESERVE II SPORTING   REDBOOK CODE: RB-MS-S-SRS2SP
Ported and vented rib barrel in blue finish, sport set of choke tubes, shell extractors, silver receiver with scroll engraving, stock with raised comb, fires 3" shells, 14" length of pull.

Production: *current* **Gauge/Bore:** *12 ga.*
Action: *O/U*
Barrel Length: 28" **Wt.:** *7.5 lbs.*
Sights: *dual bead*
Capacity: 2
Stock: *satin select black walnut*

D2C:	NIB $680	Ex $525	VG+ $375	Good $340	LMP: $905
C2C:	Mint $660	Ex $475	VG+ $340	Good $310	Fair $160
Trade-In:	Mint $490	Ex $400	VG+ $270	Good $240	Poor $90

SILVER RESERVE II SUPER SPORT   REDBOOK CODE: RB-MS-S-SRS2SU
High-profile extra-wide vent rib, ported barrel in blue finish, shell ejectors, sport set of choke tubes, silver receiver with scroll engraving, stock with adjustable raised comb, fires 3" shells. Add $108 for stock with adjustable comb.

Production: *current* **Gauge/Bore:** *12 ga.*
Action: *O/U*
Barrel Length: 30", 32" **Wt.:** *8.5 lbs.*
Sights: *dual bead fiber optic*
Capacity: 2
Stock: *satin select black walnut with fixed raised or adjustable comb*

D2C:	NIB $981	Ex $750	VG+ $540	Good $495	LMP: $1,108
C2C:	Mint $950	Ex $700	VG+ $500	Good $445	Fair $230
Trade-In:	Mint $700	Ex $550	VG+ $390	Good $345	Poor $120

SILVER RESERVE II SIDE-X-SIDE   REDBOOK CODE: RB-MS-S-SRS2SS
Barrel in blue finish, silver receiver with scroll engraving, field set of choke tubes, shell extractors, fires 3" shells, 14.25 length of pull.

Production: *current* **Gauge/Bore:** *12 ga., 20 ga., 28 ga.*
Action: *SxS*
Barrel Length: 26", 28" **Wt.:** *7.5 lbs.*
Sights: *front bead*
Capacity: 2
Stock: *satin select black walnut*

D2C:	NIB $898	Ex $700	VG+ $495	Good $450	LMP: $1,067
C2C:	Mint $870	Ex $625	VG+ $450	Good $405	Fair $210
Trade-In:	Mint $640	Ex $525	VG+ $360	Good $315	Poor $90

MAVERICK HS12 REDBOOK CODE: RB-MS-S-MVHS12

Barrel in matte blue finish, modified and improved cylinder choke tubes, Picatinny rails (on top of receiver and below bottom barrel), embellished receiver, fires 3" shells.

Production: *current* **Gauge/Bore:** *12 ga.*
Action: *O/U*
Barrel Length: *18.5"* **Wt.:** *6.25 lbs.*
Sights: *fiber optic front, rear slot*
Capacity: *2*
Stock: *black synthetic*

D2C:	NIB $449	Ex $350	VG+ $250	Good $225	**LMP: $564**
C2C:	Mint $440	Ex $325	VG+ $230	Good $205	Fair $105
Trade-In:	Mint $320	Ex $275	VG+ $180	Good $160	Poor $60

MAVERICK HUNTER REDBOOK CODE: RB-MS-S-MVHNTR

Matte blue barrel, modified and improved cylinder choke tubes, embellished receiver, 14.25" length of pull, fires 3" shells.

Production: *current* **Gauge/Bore:** *12 ga.*
Action: *O/U*
Barrel Length: *18.5", 28"* **Wt.:** *7 lbs.*
Sights: *front bead*
Capacity: *2*
Stock: *black synthetic*

D2C:	NIB $402	Ex $325	VG+ $225	Good $205	**LMP: $503**
C2C:	Mint $390	Ex $300	VG+ $210	Good $185	Fair $95
Trade-In:	Mint $290	Ex $250	VG+ $160	Good $145	Poor $60

New England Firearms

New England Firearms began producing firearms in 1987 and the company was purchased by Marlin in 2000. Later, Remington Arms Company bought Marlin. Today, all of these companies are owned by Cerberus Capital Management.

PARDNER REDBOOK CODE: RB-NF-S-PARDNE

2.75" or 3" chambers depending on gauge, break-open action, safety transfer bar mechanism on hammer, color case-hardened receiver, fixed or modified choke tube, blue finish, add $15 for 32" barrel.

Production: *1987–2008* **Gauge/Bore:** *12 ga., 16 ga., 20 ga., 28 ga., .410*
Action: *single-shot*
Barrel Length: *24", 26", 28", 32"* **Wt.:** *5–6 lbs.*
Sights: *bead front*
Capacity: *1*
Stock: *walnut stained hardwood or black synthetic*

D2C:	NIB $145	Ex $125	VG+ $80	Good $75	
C2C:	Mint $140	Ex $125	VG+ $80	Good $70	Fair $35
Trade-In:	Mint $110	Ex $100	VG+ $60	Good $55	Poor $30

NEW ENGLAND FIREARMS

PARDNER SPECIAL PURPOSE 10-GAUGE   REDBOOK CODE: RB-NF-S-PARSPE

Blue barrel and receiver, Mossy Oak brand camouflage finish on synthetic offering, recoil pad, full or fixed choke, transfer bar safety system.

Production: *discontinued 2008* **Gauge/Bore:** *10 ga., 12 ga.*

Action: *single-shot*

Barrel Length: 28", 32" **Wt.:** *9.5 lbs.*

Sights: *bead front*

Capacity: *1*

Stock: *hardwood, black synthetic, or camouflage synthetic*

D2C:	NIB $165	Ex $150	VG+ $95	Good $85	
C2C:	Mint $160	Ex $125	VG+ $90	Good $75	Fair $40
Trade-In:	Mint $120	Ex $100	VG+ $70	Good $60	Poor $30

PARDNER TURKEY GUN   REDBOOK CODE: RB-NF-S-TURGUN

Fixed or full choke tube, transfer bar safety system, 3 or 3.5" chamber.

Production: *1999–2008* **Gauge/Bore:** *10 ga., 12 ga.*

Action: *single-shot*

Barrel Length: 24" **Wt.:** *6–9 lbs.*

Sights: *bead front*

Capacity: *1*

Stock: *hardwood with camouflage or matte black finish*

D2C:	NIB $125	Ex $100	VG+ $70	Good $65	
C2C:	Mint $120	Ex $100	VG+ $70	Good $60	Fair $30
Trade-In:	Mint $90	Ex $75	VG+ $50	Good $45	Poor $30

SURVIVOR SERIES   REDBOOK CODE: RB-NF-S-SURVIV

Removable forend and hollow stock hold additional ammo, 3" chamber, blue or electroless nickel finish, sling swivels, transfer bar safety.

Production: *1992–2006* **Gauge/Bore:** *12 ga., 20 ga., .410/.45 LC*

Action: *single-shot*

Barrel Length: 20", 22" **Wt.:** *~6 lbs.*

Sights: *bead front*

Capacity: *1*

Stock: *synthetic thumbhole*

D2C:	NIB $187	Ex $150	VG+ $105	Good $95	
C2C:	Mint $180	Ex $150	VG+ $100	Good $85	Fair $45
Trade-In:	Mint $140	Ex $125	VG+ $80	Good $70	Poor $30

TRACKER SLUG GUN   REDBOOK CODE: RB-NF-S-TRACSG

Cylinder bore barrel, transfer bar safety, walnut or camouflage finish, recoil pad.

Production: *1992–discontinued* **Gauge/Bore:** *10 ga., 12 ga., 20 ga.*

Action: *single-shot*

Barrel Length: 24" **Wt.:** *6 lbs.*

Sights: *adjustable*

Capacity: *1*

Stock: *American hardwood*

D2C:	NIB $135	Ex $125	VG+ $75	Good $70	
C2C:	Mint $130	Ex $100	VG+ $70	Good $65	Fair $35
Trade-In:	Mint $100	Ex $100	VG+ $60	Good $50	Poor $30

Noble Manufacturing Company

In 1948, Nobles Worldwide was founded when Warren Nobles, the lead engineer for the B-36 bomber ammunition chute, began making ammunition chutes for military aircraft and naval vessels. The Noble Manufacturing Company operated within that corporate structure in Haydenville, Massachusetts, from the early 1950s to about 1971 and manufactured reasonably priced, utilitarian semi-automatic, lever-action, and pump action shotguns and pump action rifles. The company also imported Spanish side-by-side shotguns from 1953-1971 and manufactured guns for other private labels.

MODEL 40 HAMMERLESS SLIDE-ACTION REPEATING REDBOOK CODE: RB-NB-S-M40HAM

Multi-choke, grooved slide handle, no checkering on hardwood, tubular magazine, buttplate.

Production: *1952–1956* **Gauge/Bore:** *12 ga.*

Action: *pump-action*

Barrel Length: 28" **Wt.:** *~7.5 lbs.*

Sights: *bead front*

Capacity: *5*

Stock: *pistol-grip hardwood*

D2C:	NIB $180	Ex $155	VG+ $100	Good $90	
C2C:	Mint $180	Ex $125	VG+ $90	Good $85	Fair $45
Trade-In:	Mint $130	Ex $125	VG+ $80	Good $65	Poor $30

MODEL 50 SLIDE-ACTION REDBOOK CODE: RB-NB-S-M50SLA

Modified or full choke, tubular magazine, no checkering on stock, grooved forend.

Production: *1953–1955* **Gauge/Bore:** *12 ga.*

Action: *pump-action*

Barrel Length: 28" **Wt.:** *N/A*

Sights: *bead front*

Capacity: *5*

Stock: *pistol-grip hardwood*

D2C:	NIB $150	Ex $120	VG+ $85	Good $75	
C2C:	Mint $150	Ex $125	VG+ $80	Good $70	Fair $35
Trade-In:	Mint $110	Ex $100	VG+ $60	Good $55	Poor $30

MODEL 60 HAMMERLESS SLIDE-ACTION REPEATING REDBOOK CODE: RB-NB-S-M60HSA

Solid frame, adjustable choke, recoil pad, grooved slide hammer.

Production: *1955–1966* **Gauge/Bore:** *12 ga., 16 ga.*

Action: *pump-action*

Barrel Length: 28" **Wt.:** *~7.5 lbs.*

Sights: *bead front*

Capacity: *5*

Stock: *pistol-grip hardwood*

D2C:	NIB $200	Ex $180	VG+ $110	Good $100	
C2C:	Mint $200	Ex $150	VG+ $100	Good $90	Fair $50
Trade-In:	Mint $150	Ex $125	VG+ $80	Good $70	Poor $30

MODEL 65 REDBOOK CODE: RB-NB-S-M65XXX

Modified or Full chokes, tubular magazine, no recoil pad, plain stock, grooved slide handle.

Production: 1955–1966 **Gauge/Bore:** 12 ga., 16 ga.

Action: pump-action

Barrel Length: 28" **Wt.:** ~7.5 lbs.

Sights: bead front

Capacity: 5

Stock: pistol-grip hardwood

D2C:	NIB $180	Ex $155	VG+ $100	Good $90	
C2C:	Mint $180	Ex $125	VG+ $90	Good $85	Fair $45
Trade-In:	Mint $130	Ex $125	VG+ $80	Good $65	Poor $30

MODEL 66CLP REDBOOK CODE: RB-NB-S-M66CLP

Solid frame, 3" chamber, ventilated rib, adjustable choke, plain stock and slide handle, recoil pad, plain barrel, key lock fire-control mechanism.

Production: 1967–discontinued **Gauge/Bore:** 12 ga., 16 ga.

Action: pump-action

Barrel Length: 28" **Wt.:** 7.5 lbs.

Sights: bead front

Capacity: 5

Stock: pistol grip hardwood

D2C:	NIB $190	Ex $160	VG+ $105	Good $95	
C2C:	Mint $190	Ex $150	VG+ $100	Good $90	Fair $45
Trade-In:	Mint $140	Ex $125	VG+ $80	Good $70	Poor $30

MODEL 66RCLP HAMMERLESS SLIDE-ACTION REPEATING REDBOOK CODE: RB-NB-S-M66RCL

Solid frame, 3" chamber, key lock fire-control mechanism, ventilated rib, adjustable choke, checkering on slide handle, recoil pad.

Production: 1967–discontinued **Gauge/Bore:** 12 ga., 16 ga.

Action: pump-action

Barrel Length: 28" **Wt.:** 7.5 lbs.

Sights: bead front

Capacity: 5

Stock: checkered pistol-grip hardwood

D2C:	NIB $240	Ex $195	VG+ $135	Good $120	
C2C:	Mint $240	Ex $175	VG+ $120	Good $110	Fair $60
Trade-In:	Mint $180	Ex $150	VG+ $100	Good $85	Poor $30

MODEL 66RLP REDBOOK CODE: RB-NB-S-M66RLP

Solid frame, key lock fire-control mechanism, 3" chamber, ventilated rib, checkering on slide handle, recoil pad, comes with Full or Modified choke.

Production: 1967–discontinued **Gauge/Bore:** 12 ga., 16 ga.

Action: pump-action

Barrel Length: 28" **Wt.:** 7.5 lbs.

Sights: bead front

Capacity: 5

Stock: checkered pistol-grip hardwood

D2C:	NIB $240	Ex $195	VG+ $135	Good $120	
C2C:	Mint $240	Ex $175	VG+ $120	Good $110	Fair $60
Trade-In:	Mint $180	Ex $150	VG+ $100	Good $85	Poor $30

MODEL 66XL   REDBOOK CODE: RB-NB-S-M66XLX

Solid frame, 3" chamber, key lock fire-control mechanism, ventilated rib, adjustable choke, checkering on slide grip only, plain barrel, full or modified chokes included.

Production: *1967–discontinued* **Gauge/Bore:** *12 ga., 16 ga.*
Action: *pump-action*
Barrel Length: 28" **Wt.:** *7.5 lbs.*
Sights: *bead front*
Capacity: *5*
Stock: *plain pistol-grip hardwood*

D2C:	NIB $190	Ex $160	VG+ $105	Good $95	
C2C:	Mint $190	Ex $150	VG+ $100	Good $90	Fair $45
Trade-In:	Mint $140	Ex $125	VG+ $80	Good $70	Poor $30

MODEL 70CLP HAMMERLESS SLIDE-ACTION REPEATING   REDBOOK CODE: RB-NB-S-M70CLP

Solid frame, adjustable choke, checkering on forearm, recoil pad.

Production: *1958–discontinued* **Gauge/Bore:** *.410*
Action: *pump-action*
Barrel Length: 26" **Wt.:** *6 lbs.*
Sights: *bead front*
Capacity: *5*
Stock: *checkered hardwood*

D2C:	NIB $200	Ex $180	VG+ $110	Good $100	
C2C:	Mint $200	Ex $150	VG+ $100	Good $90	Fair $50
Trade-In:	Mint $150	Ex $125	VG+ $80	Good $70	Poor $30

MODEL 70RCLP   REDBOOK CODE: RB-NB-S-M70RCL

Solid frame, ventilated rib, adjustable choke, checkering on forearm, recoil pad.

Production: *1967–discontinued* **Gauge/Bore:** *.410*
Action: *pump-action*
Barrel Length: 26" **Wt.:** *6 lbs.*
Sights: *bead front*
Capacity: *5*
Stock: *checkered hardwood*

D2C:	NIB $240	Ex $195	VG+ $135	Good $120	
C2C:	Mint $240	Ex $175	VG+ $120	Good $110	Fair $60
Trade-In:	Mint $180	Ex $150	VG+ $100	Good $85	Poor $30

MODEL 70RLP   REDBOOK CODE: RB-NB-S-M70RLP

Solid frame, ventilated rib, no adjustable choke, checkering on forearm, recoil pad.

Production: *1967–discontinued* **Gauge/Bore:** *.410*
Action: *pump-action*
Barrel Length: 26" **Wt.:** *6 lbs.*
Sights: *bead front*
Capacity: *5*
Stock: *checkered hardwood*

D2C:	NIB $200	Ex $180	VG+ $110	Good $100	
C2C:	Mint $200	Ex $150	VG+ $100	Good $90	Fair $50
Trade-In:	Mint $150	Ex $125	VG+ $80	Good $70	Poor $30

NOBLE MANUFACTURING

MODEL 70XL REDBOOK CODE: RB-NB-S-M70XLX
Solid frame, no checkering on forearm, no adjustable choke, checkering on forearm, recoil pad.

Production: *1958–discontinued* **Gauge/Bore:** *.410*
Action: *pump-action*
Barrel Length: 26" **Wt.:** *6 lbs.*
Sights: *bead front*
Capacity: *5*
Stock: *hardwood*

D2C:	NIB $150	Ex $120	VG+ $85	Good $75	
C2C:	Mint $150	Ex $125	VG+ $80	Good $70	Fair $35
Trade-In:	Mint $110	Ex $100	VG+ $60	Good $55	Poor $30

MODEL 80 AUTO-LOADING REDBOOK CODE: RB-NB-S-M80AUT
Recoil-operated, full choke, fluted and slotted forearm.

Production: *1964–discontinued* **Gauge/Bore:** *.410*
Action: *semi-auto*
Barrel Length: 26" **Wt.:** *6 lbs.*
Sights: *bead front*
Capacity: *3*
Stock: *plain pistol-grip hardwood*

D2C:	NIB $300	Ex $255	VG+ $165	Good $150	
C2C:	Mint $290	Ex $225	VG+ $150	Good $135	Fair $70
Trade-In:	Mint $220	Ex $175	VG+ $120	Good $105	Poor $30

MODEL 166L DEER GUN REDBOOK CODE: RB-NB-S-M166LD
Solid frame, key lock fire-control mechanism, 2.75" chamber, plain barrel, dovetailed receiver, checkering on slide handle, sling swivels, carry strap included.

Production: *1967–discontinued* **Gauge/Bore:** *12 ga.*
Action: *pump-action*
Barrel Length: 24" **Wt.:** *7.3 lbs.*
Sights: *Lyman peep rear sight, post ramp front*
Capacity: *5*
Stock: *checkered pistol-grip hardwood*

D2C:	NIB $300	Ex $255	VG+ $165	Good $150	
C2C:	Mint $290	Ex $225	VG+ $150	Good $135	Fair $70
Trade-In:	Mint $220	Ex $175	VG+ $120	Good $105	Poor $30

MODEL 420 HAMMERLESS DOUBLE REDBOOK CODE: RB-NB-S-M420HD
Boxlock, plain extractors, double trigger, 3" magnum chamber, modified and full chokes included, engraved frame, checkering on forearm.

Production: *1958–discontinued* **Gauge/Bore:** *12 ga., 16 ga., 20 ga., .410*
Action: *SxS*
Barrel Length: 26", 28" **Wt.:** *6.8 lbs.*
Sights: *bead front*
Capacity: *2*
Stock: *checkered walnut*

D2C:	NIB $375	Ex $295	VG+ $210	Good $190	
C2C:	Mint $360	Ex $275	VG+ $190	Good $170	Fair $90
Trade-In:	Mint $270	Ex $225	VG+ $150	Good $135	Poor $60

MODEL 450E HAMMERLESS DOUBLE   REDBOOK CODE: RB-NB-S-M450EH
Boxlock, engraved frame, selective auto ejectors, double trigger, 3" chamber, M and F chokes included, checkering on beavertailed forearm, recoil pad.

Production: *1967–discontinued* **Gauge/Bore:** *12 ga., 16 ga., 20 ga.*

Action: *SxS*

Barrel Length: 28" **Wt.:** *~6 lbs.*

Sights: *bead front*

Capacity: *2*

Stock: *checkered pistol-grip hardwood*

D2C:	NIB $450	Ex $360	VG+ $250	Good $225	
C2C:	Mint $440	Ex $325	VG+ $230	Good $205	Fair $105
Trade-In:	Mint $320	Ex $275	VG+ $180	Good $160	Poor $60

MODEL 602CLP   REDBOOK CODE: RB-NB-S-M602CL
Solid frame, key lock fire control, 3" chamber, ventilated rib, adjustable choke, checkering on slide handle, recoil pad, plain barrel.

Production: *1958–discontinued* **Gauge/Bore:** *20 ga.*

Action: *pump-action*

Barrel Length: 28" **Wt.:** *6.5 lbs.*

Sights: *bead front*

Capacity: *5*

Stock: *checkered pistol-grip hardwood*

D2C:	NIB $200	Ex $180	VG+ $110	Good $100	
C2C:	Mint $200	Ex $150	VG+ $100	Good $90	Fair $50
Trade-In:	Mint $150	Ex $125	VG+ $80	Good $70	Poor $30

MODEL 602RCLP HAMMERLESS SLIDE-ACTION REPEATING   REDBOOK CODE: RB-NB-S-M602LP
Solid frame, key lock fire control mechanism, 3" chamber, tubular magazine, ventilated rib, adjustable choke, checkering on slide handle, recoil pad.

Production: *1967–discontinued* **Gauge/Bore:** *20 ga.*

Action: *pump-action*

Barrel Length: 28" **Wt.:** *6.5 lbs.*

Sights: *bead front*

Capacity: *5*

Stock: *checkered pistol-grip hardwood*

D2C:	NIB $275	Ex $230	VG+ $155	Good $140	
C2C:	Mint $270	Ex $200	VG+ $140	Good $125	Fair $65
Trade-In:	Mint $200	Ex $175	VG+ $110	Good $100	Poor $30

MODEL 602RLP   REDBOOK CODE: RB-NB-S-M602RL
Non-adjustable choke, F or M chokes included, solid frame, key lock fire-control mechanism, 3" chamber, tubular magazine, ventilated rib, recoil pad.

Production: *1967–discontinued* **Gauge/Bore:** *20 ga.*

Action: *pump-action*

Barrel Length: 28" **Wt.:** *6.5 lbs.*

Sights: *bead front*

Capacity: *5*

Stock: *checkered pistol-grip hardwood*

D2C:	NIB $240	Ex $195	VG+ $135	Good $120	
C2C:	Mint $240	Ex $175	VG+ $120	Good $110	Fair $60
Trade-In:	Mint $180	Ex $150	VG+ $100	Good $85	Poor $30

NOBLE MANUFACTURING

MODEL 602XL   REDBOOK CODE: RB-NB-S-M602XL
Solid frame, plain barrel, F or M chokes included, checkering on slide handle, no recoil pad, 3" chamber, ventilated rib.

Production: *1958–discontinued* **Gauge/Bore:** *20 ga.*

Action: *pump-action*

Barrel Length: 28" **Wt.:** *6.5 lbs.*

Sights: *bead front*

Capacity: *5*

Stock: *plain pistol-grip hardwood*

D2C:	NIB $180	Ex $155	VG+ $100	Good $90	
C2C:	Mint $180	Ex $125	VG+ $90	Good $85	Fair $45
Trade-In:	Mint $130	Ex $125	VG+ $80	Good $65	Poor $30

MODEL 662   REDBOOK CODE: RB-NB-S-MOD662
Aluminum receiver, solid frame, key lock fire-control mechanism, 3" chamber, tubular magazine, ventilated rib, adjustable choke, checkering on stock and slide handle, recoil pad.

Production: *1966–discontinued* **Gauge/Bore:** *20 ga.*

Action: *pump-action*

Barrel Length: 28" **Wt.:** *4.5 lbs.*

Sights: *bead front*

Capacity: *5*

Stock: *checkered hardwood*

D2C:	NIB $240	Ex $195	VG+ $135	Good $120	
C2C:	Mint $240	Ex $175	VG+ $120	Good $110	Fair $60
Trade-In:	Mint $180	Ex $150	VG+ $100	Good $85	Poor $30

OMEGA SHOTGUNS

Omega Shotguns

These shotguns were imported by Kassnar Imports in Harrisburg, Pennsylvania.

STANDARD OVER-UNDER   REDBOOK CODE: RB-OS-S-OVUNST
Boxlock action, ventilated rib, single trigger, blue metal, hammerless, 2.75" or 3" chamber, fixed chokes, automatic safety, checkering on stock and forearm.

Production: *1984–1994* **Gauge/Bore:** *12 ga., 28 ga., .410*

Action: *O/U*

Barrel Length: 26", 28" **Wt.:** *5.5–7.5 lbs.*

Sights: *bead front*

Capacity: *2*

Stock: *European walnut*

D2C:	NIB $355	Ex $275	VG+ $200	Good $180	
C2C:	Mint $350	Ex $250	VG+ $180	Good $160	Fair $85
Trade-In:	Mint $260	Ex $200	VG+ $140	Good $125	Poor $60

DELUXE OVER-UNDER REDBOOK CODE: RB-OS-S-OVUNDE
Ventilated rib, IC/M, M/F or F/F chokes. Single trigger, automatic safety, checkering on pistol-grip, tulip forend.

Production: *1984–1990* **Gauge/Bore:** *20 ga, 28 ga., .410*

Action: *O/U*

Barrel Length: *26", 28"* **Wt.:** *5.5–6 lbs.*

Sights: *bead front*

Capacity: *2*

Stock: *European walnut*

D2C:	NIB $415	Ex $325	VG+ $230	Good $210	
C2C:	Mint $400	Ex $300	VG+ $210	Good $190	Fair $100
Trade-In:	Mint $300	Ex $250	VG+ $170	Good $150	Poor $60

STANDARD SIDE-BY-SIDE REDBOOK CODE: RB-OS-S-STASBS
F/F choke, double trigger, manual safety, boxlock action.

Production: *1984–1989* **Gauge/Bore:** *20 ga., 28 ga., .410*

Action: *SxS*

Barrel Length: *26"* **Wt.:** *5.5 lbs.*

Sights: *N/A*

Capacity: *2*

Stock: *checkered beech wood*

D2C:	NIB $215	Ex $175	VG+ $120	Good $110	
C2C:	Mint $210	Ex $150	VG+ $110	Good $100	Fair $50
Trade-In:	Mint $160	Ex $125	VG+ $90	Good $80	Poor $30

DELUXE SIDE-BY-SIDE REDBOOK CODE: RB-OS-S-DELSBS
Checkering on stock and forearm, low ribbed barrel, F/F choke, double trigger, manual safety, semi-pistol grip.

Production: *1984–1989* **Gauge/Bore:** *.410*

Action: *SxS*

Barrel Length: *26"* **Wt.:** *5.5 lbs.*

Sights: *N/A*

Capacity: *2*

Stock: *checkered European walnut*

D2C:	NIB $250	Ex $200	VG+ $140	Good $125	
C2C:	Mint $240	Ex $175	VG+ $130	Good $115	Fair $60
Trade-In:	Mint $180	Ex $150	VG+ $100	Good $90	Poor $30

STANDARD SINGLE-SHOT REDBOOK CODE: RB-OS-S-STDSIN
Matte-chromed receiver, top lever break, was originally imported from Korea.

Production: *1984–1987* **Gauge/Bore:** *12 ga., 16 ga., 20 ga., 28 ga., .410*

Action: *single-shot*

Barrel Length: *26", 28", 30"* **Wt.:** *~5.5 lbs.*

Sights: *N/A*

Capacity: *1*

Stock: *Indonesian walnut*

D2C:	NIB $150	Ex $125	VG+ $85	Good $75	
C2C:	Mint $150	Ex $125	VG+ $80	Good $70	Fair $35
Trade-In:	Mint $110	Ex $100	VG+ $60	Good $55	Poor $30

DELUXE SINGLE-SHOT REDBOOK CODE: RB-OS-S-DELSIN
Fully blue receiver, ventilated rib, top lever break, was originally imported from Korea, checkering on walnut.

Production: *1984–1987* **Gauge/Bore:** *12 ga., 16 ga., 20 ga., 28 ga., .410*					
Action: *single-shot*					
Barrel Length: 26", 28", 30" **Wt.:** *~5.5 lbs.*	D2C:	NIB $200	Ex $175	VG+ $110	Good $100
Sights: *N/A*	C2C:	Mint $200	Ex $150	VG+ $100	Good $90	Fair $50
Capacity: *1*	Trade-In:	Mint $150	Ex $125	VG+ $80	Good $70	Poor $30
Stock: *Indonesian walnut*					

Parker Brothers

After spending a few years in the business of manufacturing other products, Charles Parker founded Parker Brothers with his sons to manufacture firearms. The company was bought in 1934 by the Remington Arms Company, and Remington continued to produce firearms under the brand until 1942. Including the models manufactured after the Remington purchase of the company, the brand produced over 242,000 shotguns. Parker Brothers made 10 grades of side-by-side and 5 grades of single barrel trap shotguns. The brand was revived in 1999 when Parker Bros. Makers opened its doors to reproduce the models that had made the brand so famous. It is difficult for collectors to differentiate between the early firearms and the later reproductions, but early models can usually be identified in three ways. First, the frame size and serial number can always be found on the rear barrel lug. Second, the flat of the action is always marked with the grade of the gun, and that grade will be expressed in numerals for earlier guns and letters for later models. Lastly, the barrel rib of the gun will be marked with a "Parker Brothers, Meridian CT" stamp, along with the grade of steel that was used in its manufacture. Early Parker Brothers shotguns are highly collectible and revered for their quality and for their durability, as most early models are still shootable.

HAMMERLESS DOUBLE-BARREL VH GRADE REDBOOK CODE: RB-PK-S-VHVHVH
Boxlock action, double trigger, blue case-hardened receiver. Only 2,297 guns had single triggers and command a high premium. Straight stocks are also rare and have higher value. More than double the value for VHE model with automatic ejectors. .410 bore and 28 gauge models may bring up to 5x standard value.

Production: *discontinued* **Gauge/Bore:** *12 ga., 16 ga., 20 ga., 28 ga.*					
Action: *SxS*					
Barrel Length: 26"–32" **Wt.:** *6.8–8.5 lbs.*	D2C:	NIB - -	Ex $1,925	VG+ $1,385	Good $1,255
Sights: *bead front*	C2C:	Mint $2,800	Ex $1,750	VG+ $1,260	Good $1,130	Fair $580
Capacity: *2*	Trade-In:	Mint $2,070	Ex $1,425	VG+ $980	Good $880	Poor $270
Stock: *pistol-grip walnut*					

Photo Courtesy of
Rock Island Auction Company

HAMMERLESS DOUBLE-BARREL PH GRADE REDBOOK CODE: RB-PK-S-PHPHPH
Boxlock action, most have twist barrels, fluid steel barrel. 10 gauge With fluid steel barrel is very rare. More than double the value for PHE model with automatic ejectors. Very few .410 bore models were made and would bring many times standard value.

Production: *discontinued* **Gauge/Bore:** *12 ga., 16 ga., 20 ga., 28 ga.*					
Action: *SxS*					
Barrel Length: 26"–32" **Wt.:** *6.8–8.5 lbs.*	D2C:	NIB $1,500	Ex $1,150	VG+ $825	Good $750
Sights: *bead front*	C2C:	Mint $1,400	Ex $1,050	VG+ $750	Good $675	Fair $345
Capacity: *2*	Trade-In:	Mint $1,070	Ex $850	VG+ $590	Good $525	Poor $150
Stock: *pistol-grip walnut*					

HAMMERLESS DOUBLE-BARREL GH GRADE REDBOOK CODE: RB-PK-S-GHGHGH
Popular model, "Parker Special Steel" marked on barrels, moderate engraving, 10 ga. model very rare.

Photo Courtesy of
Rock Island Auction Company

Production: *discontinued* **Gauge/Bore:** *12 ga., 16 ga., 20 ga., 28 ga.*
Action: *SxS*
Barrel Length: *26"–32"* **Wt.:** *6.8–8.5 lbs.*
Sights: *bead front*
Capacity: *2*
Stock: *pistol-grip walnut*

D2C:	NIB $6,600	Ex $5,025	VG+ $3,630	Good $3,300	
C2C:	Mint $6,340	Ex $4,575	VG+ $3,300	Good $2,970	Fair $1,520
Trade-In:	Mint $4,690	Ex $3,700	VG+ $2,580	Good $2,310	Poor $660

HAMMERLESS DOUBLE-BARREL DH GRADE REDBOOK CODE: RB-PK-S-DHDHDH
Boxlock action, more engraving than the GH model, fine finishing on walnut, Titanic barrels on most. Very few with Parker single triggers. Very few with ventilated ribs. 8 and 10 ga. are extremely rare. Add 35% with automatic ejectors.

Photo Courtesy of
Rock Island Auction Company

Production: *discontinued* **Gauge/Bore:** *12 ga., 16 ga., 20 ga., 28 ga.*
Action: *SxS*
Barrel Length: *26"–32"* **Wt.:** *6.8–8.5 lbs.*
Sights: *bead front*
Capacity: *2*
Stock: *pistol-grip walnut*

D2C:	NIB $7,600	Ex $5,800	VG+ $4,180	Good $3,800	
C2C:	Mint $7,300	Ex $5,250	VG+ $3,800	Good $3,420	Fair $1,750
Trade-In:	Mint $5,400	Ex $4,275	VG+ $2,970	Good $2,660	Poor $780

HAMMERLESS DOUBLE-BARREL CH GRADE REDBOOK CODE: RB-PK-S-CHCHCH
Boxlock action, blue case-hardened receiver, more scroll and game-scene engraving than DH model, Acme steel barrels, very few have straight-grip stocks, 8 and and 10 gauge are very rare. Add 35% for automatic ejectors. Add 700% for .410 model.

Photo Courtesy of
Rock Island Auction Company

Production: *discontinued* **Gauge/Bore:** *12 ga., 16 ga., 20 ga., 28 ga.*
Action: *SxS*
Barrel Length: *26"–32"* **Wt.:** *6.8–8.5 lbs.*
Sights: *bead front*
Capacity: *2*
Stock: *pistol-grip walnut*

D2C:	NIB $15,400	Ex $11,725	VG+ $8,470	Good $7,700	
C2C:	Mint $14,790	Ex $10,650	VG+ $7,700	Good $6,930	Fair $3,545
Trade-In:	Mint $10,940	Ex $8,625	VG+ $6,010	Good $5,390	Poor $1,560

HAMMERLESS DOUBLE-BARREL BH GRADE REDBOOK CODE: RB-PK-S-BHBHBH
Boxlock action, blue case-hardened receiver, available with a variety of styles of engraving, rare to find straight-grip stock, rare to find beavertail forend. Add 35% for automatic ejector. Add 450% for 28 gauge.

Photo Courtesy of
Rock Island Auction Company

Production: *discontinued* **Gauge/Bore:** *12 ga., 16 ga., 20 ga., 28 ga.*
Action: *SxS*
Barrel Length: *26"–32"* **Wt.:** *6.8–8.5 lbs.*
Sights: *bead front*
Capacity: *2*
Stock: *pistol-grip walnut*

D2C:	NIB $18,000	Ex $13,700	VG+ $9,900	Good $9,000	
C2C:	Mint $17,280	Ex $12,425	VG+ $9,000	Good $8,100	Fair $4,140
Trade-In:	Mint $12,780	Ex $10,100	VG+ $7,020	Good $6,300	Poor $1,800

PARKER REPRODUCTIONS

Photo Courtesy of
Rock Island Auction Company

HAMMERLESS DOUBLE-BARREL AH GRADE REDBOOK CODE: RB-PK-S-AHAHAH

Boxlock action, blue case-hardened receiver, highly engraved, fine walnut, Acme steel barrel, straight grip
stock is rare. Automatic ejectors add 30%. Add 75% for 20 gauge. Add 250% for 28 gauge.

Production: *discontinued* **Gauge/Bore:** *12 ga., 16 ga., 20 ga., 28 ga.*
Action: *SxS*
Barrel Length: 26"–32" **Wt.:** *6.8–8.5 lbs.*
Sights: *bead front*
Capacity: 2
Stock: *pistol-grip walnut*

D2C:	NIB $31,500	Ex $23,950	VG+ $17,325	Good $15,750	
C2C:	Mint $30,240	Ex $21,750	VG+ $15,750	Good $14,175	Fair $7,245
Trade-In:	Mint $22,370	Ex $17,650	VG+ $12,290	Good $11,025	Poor $3,150

HAMMERLESS DOUBLE-BARREL AAH GRADE REDBOOK CODE: RB-PK-S-AAHAAH

Boxlock action, blue case-hardened receiver, Whitworth or Peerless barrels, high-quality extensive engraving, ventilated rib very rare,
single trigger very rare, straight grip stock is rare. Add 30% for automatic ejectors. Add 35% for 16 gauge. Add 250% for 28 gauge. Add 75% for 20 gauge.

Production: *discontinued* **Gauge/Bore:** *12 ga., 16 ga., 20 ga., 28 ga.*
Action: *SxS*
Barrel Length: 26"–32" **Wt.:** *6.8–8.5 lbs.*
Sights: *bead front*
Capacity: 2
Stock: *pistol-grip walnut*

D2C:	NIB $49,500	Ex $37,625	VG+ $27,225	Good $24,750	
C2C:	Mint $47,520	Ex $34,175	VG+ $24,750	Good $22,275	Fair $11,385
Trade-In:	Mint $35,150	Ex $27,725	VG+ $19,310	Good $17,325	Poor $4,950

Photo Courtesy of
Rock Island Auction Company

SINGLE-SHOT TRAP SC GRADE REDBOOK CODE: RB-PK-S-SSTSCG

Automatic ejector, variety of grades available with varying engraving and finishing.

Production: *discontinued* **Gauge/Bore:** *12 ga.*
Action: *single-shot*
Barrel Length: 30", 32", 34" **Wt.:** *7.5–8.5 lbs.*
Sights: *bead front*
Capacity: 1
Stock: *pistol-grip walnut*

D2C:	NIB $7,650	Ex $5,825	VG+ $4,210	Good $3,825	
C2C:	Mint $7,350	Ex $5,300	VG+ $3,830	Good $3,445	Fair $1,760
Trade-In:	Mint $5,440	Ex $4,300	VG+ $2,990	Good $2,680	Poor $780

Photo Courtesy of
Rock Island Auction Company

TROJAN HAMMERLESS DOUBLE-BARREL, 12 GAUGE REDBOOK CODE: RB-PK-S-TROJAN

Boxlock action, double trigger, extractors, blue case-hardened receiver, add 40% for 20 gauge.

Production: *discontinued* **Gauge/Bore:** *12 ga., 16 ga., 20 ga.*
Action: *SxS*
Barrel Length: 26", 28", 30" **Wt.:** *6.3–7.8 lbs.*
Sights: *bead front*
Capacity: 2
Stock: *pistol-grip walnut*

D2C:	NIB $3,500	Ex $2,675	VG+ $1,925	Good $1,750	
C2C:	Mint $3,360	Ex $2,425	VG+ $1,750	Good $1,575	Fair $805
Trade-In:	Mint $2,490	Ex $1,975	VG+ $1,370	Good $1,225	Poor $360

Parker-Hale Ltd.

Located in Birmingham, England, Parker-Hale Ltd. was founded by Alfred Gray Parker and Arthur Hale in 1880. The company introduced Parkerifling, a process by which military service rifles could be converted to .22 caliber for recruit training just before World War I broke out. The Ministry of Munitions had an overwhelming need for Parkerifling, such that Mr. Hale was excused from active military service so that he could contribute to the war effort by running the company and helping to meet those demands. The company continued to thrive for decades after, but in the aftermath of the Dunblane massacre in 1996, bans on handguns and societal pressures led to dwindling sales, and the company was sold to Modular Industries. In November 2000, John Rothery Co. Ltd purchased the brand and continues to manufacture accessories only.

MODEL 640A   REDBOOK CODE: RB-PH-S-MO640A
Beavertail forend, single non-selective trigger, case-hardened receiver, automatic safety, hand-checkered walnut, raised matted rib, English scroll design on receiver. Pricing research for this model proves inconclusive at this time. There have not been any recent sales on the secondary market to suggest a price range.

Production: *1986–discontinued* **Gauge/Bore:** *12 ga., 16 ga., 20 ga.*

Action: *SxS*

Barrel Length: 26", 28" **Wt.:** *N/A*

Sights: *bead front*

Capacity: *2*

Stock: *pistol-grip walnut*

MODEL 640E   REDBOOK CODE: RB-PH-S-MO640E
Boxlock action, double trigger, extractor, blued receiver, case-hardened finish. Pricing research for this model proves inconclusive at this time. There have not been any recent sales on the secondary market to suggest a price range.

Production: *1986–discontinued* **Gauge/Bore:** *12 ga., 16 ga., 20 ga.*

Action: *SxS*

Barrel Length: 26", 28" **Wt.:** *N/A*

Sights: *bead front*

Capacity: *2*

Stock: *straight-grip walnut*

MODEL 645A   REDBOOK CODE: RB-PH-S-MO645A
Boxlock action, IC/M and M/F chokes included, single non-selective trigger, automatic safety, hand-checkering on stock and forend, beavertail forend, English scroll design on receiver. Pricing research for this model proves inconclusive at this time. There have not been any recent sales on the secondary market to suggest a price range.

Production: *1986–1993* **Gauge/Bore:** *12 ga., 16 ga., 20 ga.*

Action: *SxS*

Barrel Length: 26", 28" **Wt.:** *~6 lbs.*

Sights: *bead front*

Capacity: *2*

Stock: *pistol-grip walnut*

MODEL 645E REDBOOK CODE: RB-PH-S-MO645E

IC/M and M/F chokes included, double trigger, straight grip, splinter forend, checkered stock and forend. Pricing research for this model proves inconclusive at this time. There have not been any recent sales on the secondary market to suggest a price range.

Production: *1986–1990* **Gauge/Bore:** *12 ga., 16 ga., 20 ga.*

Action: *SxS*

Barrel Length: 26", 28" **Wt.:** *~6 lbs.*

Sights: *bead front*

Capacity: *2*

Stock: *straight-grip walnut*

Parker Reproductions

Parker Reproductions formed in order to clone exactly the shotguns that had previously been made by a company called "Parker Brothers," only using modern steels and dimensions. All reproductions manufactured are high grade and were produced in Tochigi, Japan, under the direction of the Parker Reproduction Division of Reagent Chemical & Research, Inc. of New Jersey until January 1989 when the Japanese manufacturer opted to pursue production of automobile parts over firearms. The company's stock was sold, but no other models have been produced since. A flood destroyed much of the remaining inventory in 1999, making the guns even more scarce. Available models are highly collectible and pricing is largely a function of the customization of each specific shotgun.

Photo Courtesy of
Rock Island Auction Company

HAMMERLESS DOUBLE-BARREL DHE GRADE, 12 GAUGE REDBOOK CODE: RB-PD-S-DHEXXX

Choice of splinter or beavertail forearm, single or double trigger, case-colored and scroll engraved receiver.

Production: *discontinued* **Gauge/Bore:** *12 ga., 20 ga., 28 ga.*

Action: *SxS*

Barrel Length: 26", 28" **Wt.:** *5.3–6.8 lbs.*

Sights: *bead front*

Capacity: *2*

Stock: *select walnut pistol-grip or straight*

D2C:	NIB $5,311	Ex $4,050	VG+ $2,925	Good $2,660	
C2C:	Mint $5,100	Ex $3,675	VG+ $2,660	Good $2,390	Fair $1,225
Trade-In:	Mint $3,780	Ex $2,975	VG+ $2,080	Good $1,860	Poor $540

HAMMERLESS DOUBLE-BARREL BHE GRADE LIMITED EDITION, 12 GAUGE REDBOOK CODE: RB-PD-S-BHELEX

Fine-line checkering, engraving, straight or pistol-grip stock, single-selective or double triggers, Japanese bank note scroll engraving around game scenes. Only about 100 made.

Photo Courtesy of
Rock Island Auction Company

Production: *discontinued* **Gauge/Bore:** *12 ga., 20 ga., 28 ga., .410*

Action: *SxS*

Barrel Length: 26", 28" **Wt.:** *5–5.7 lbs.*

Sights: *bead front*

Capacity: *2*

Stock: *American walnut*

D2C:	NIB $10,481	Ex $7,975	VG+ $5,765	Good $5,245	
C2C:	Mint $10,070	Ex $7,250	VG+ $5,250	Good $4,720	Fair $2,415
Trade-In:	Mint $7,450	Ex $5,875	VG+ $4,090	Good $3,670	Poor $1,050

HAMMERLESS DOUBLE-BARREL A-1 SPECIAL GRADE, 12 GAUGE REDBOOK CODE: RB-PD-S-A1SPEC

Single-selective or double triggers, Japanese fine-scroll engraving with game scenes, 32 LPI checkering, case included, rosewood grip cap, serial numbers in gold, barrel flats and frame water table are jeweled.

Production: *1988–discontinued* **Gauge/Bore:** *12 ga., 20 ga., 28 ga.*

Action: *SxS*

Barrel Length: *26", 28"* **Wt.:** *5–5.7 lbs.*

Sights: *bead front*

Capacity: *2*

Stock: *French walnut*

D2C:	NIB $17,481	Ex $13,300	VG+ $9,615	Good $8,745	
C2C:	Mint $16,790	Ex $12,075	VG+ $8,750	Good $7,870	Fair $4,025
Trade-In:	Mint $12,420	Ex $9,800	VG+ $6,820	Good $6,120	Poor $1,770

Pedersen Custom Guns

Pedersen Custom Guns was a division of O.F. Mossberg in North Haven, Connecticut, and guns carrying the Pedersen name were manufactured in O.F. Mossberg's facilities from 1973 to 1975. The company is best known for two double barrel models, the Model 200 and the Model 2500. The Model 200 was a higher-end shotgun that was offered in two grades with prices that average somewhere between four and five times as much as the more affordable Model 2500.

MODEL 1000 HUNTING REDBOOK CODE: RB-PC-S-1000HU

Various chokes included, boxlock action, automatic ejectors, single-selective trigger, silver inlays on receiver, engraved receiver. Pricing here reflects Grade I models. Grade II models are less valuable.

Production: *1973–1975* **Gauge/Bore:** *12 ga., 20 ga.*

Action: *O/U*

Barrel Length: *26", 28", 30"* **Wt.:** *N/A*

Sights: *bead front*

Capacity: *2*

Stock: *select walnut*

D2C:	NIB $2,250	Ex $1,725	VG+ $1,240	Good $1,125	
C2C:	Mint $2,160	Ex $1,575	VG+ $1,130	Good $1,015	Fair $520
Trade-In:	Mint $1,600	Ex $1,275	VG+ $880	Good $790	Poor $240

MODEL 1000 MAGNUM REDBOOK CODE: RB-PC-S-1000MA

3" magnum chamber, IM/F choke included, ventilated rib, checkering on stock and forearm. Pricing here reflects Grade I models. Grade II models are less valuable.

Production: *1973–1975* **Gauge/Bore:** *12 ga.*

Action: *O/U*

Barrel Length: *30"* **Wt.:** *N/A*

Sights: *bead front*

Capacity: *2*

Stock: *select walnut*

D2C:	NIB $1,800	Ex $1,375	VG+ $990	Good $900	
C2C:	Mint $1,730	Ex $1,250	VG+ $900	Good $810	Fair $415
Trade-In:	Mint $1,280	Ex $1,025	VG+ $710	Good $630	Poor $180

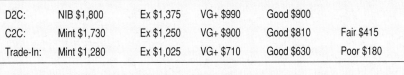

MODEL 1000 SKEET REDBOOK CODE: RB-PC-S-1000SK

3" chamber, SK choke included, selective single trigger, boxlock, ventilated rib, checkering on stock
and grip, available in Grade I and II with differing grades of wood. Pricing here reflects Grade I models. Grade II models are less valuable.

Production: *1973–1975* **Gauge/Bore:** *12 ga.*

Action: *O/U*

Barrel Length: 26", 28" **Wt.:** *N/A*

Sights: *bead front*

Capacity: *2*

Stock: *skeet-style walnut*

D2C:	NIB $2,250	Ex $1,725	VG+ $1,240	Good $1,125	
C2C:	Mint $2,160	Ex $1,575	VG+ $1,130	Good $1,015	Fair $520
Trade-In:	Mint $1,600	Ex $1,275	VG+ $880	Good $790	Poor $240

MODEL 1000 TRAP REDBOOK CODE: RB-PC-S-1000TR

3" chamber, M/F or IM/F chokes included, boxlock action, automatic ejectors, selective-single trigger,
ventilated rib, checkering on stock and forend, available in Grade I and II with varying walnut qualities.
Pricing here reflects Grade I models. Grade II models are less valuable.

Production: *1973–1975* **Gauge/Bore:** *12 ga.*

Action: *O/U*

Barrel Length: 30", 32" **Wt.:** *N/A*

Sights: *bead front*

Capacity: *2*

Stock: *trap-style Monte Carlo hardwood*

D2C:	NIB $2,125	Ex $1,625	VG+ $1,170	Good $1,065	
C2C:	Mint $2,040	Ex $1,475	VG+ $1,070	Good $960	Fair $490
Trade-In:	Mint $1,510	Ex $1,200	VG+ $830	Good $745	Poor $240

*Photo Courtesy of
Rock Island Auction Company*

MODEL 1500 HUNTING REDBOOK CODE: RB-PC-S-1500HU

Boxlock action, automatic ejectors, single-selective trigger, 3" chamber, ventilated rib, IM/F choke, checkering on pistol grip and forearm.

Production: *1973–1975* **Gauge/Bore:** *12 ga.*

Action: *O/U*

Barrel Length: 26", 28", 30" **Wt.:** *7–7.5 lbs.*

Sights: *bead front*

Capacity: *2*

Stock: *pistol-grip walnut*

D2C:	NIB $950	Ex $725	VG+ $525	Good $475	
C2C:	Mint $920	Ex $675	VG+ $480	Good $430	Fair $220
Trade-In:	Mint $680	Ex $550	VG+ $380	Good $335	Poor $120

MODEL 1500 SKEET REDBOOK CODE: RB-PC-S-1500SK

SK choke included, boxlock action, automatic ejector, selective-single trigger, 3" chamber, ventilated rib, checkering on pistol-grip and forearm.

Production: *1973–1975* **Gauge/Bore:** *12 ga.*

Action: *O/U*

Barrel Length: 27" **Wt.:** *7–7.5 lbs.*

Sights: *bead front*

Capacity: *2*

Stock: *skeet-style walnut*

D2C:	NIB $1,000	Ex $775	VG+ $550	Good $500	
C2C:	Mint $960	Ex $700	VG+ $500	Good $450	Fair $230
Trade-In:	Mint $710	Ex $575	VG+ $390	Good $350	Poor $120

MODEL 1500 TRAP REDBOOK CODE: RB-PC-S-1500TR

M/F and IM/F chokes included, boxlock action, automatic ejectors, selective-single trigger, 3" chamber, ventilated rib, checkering on pistol-grip and forend.

Production: *1973–1975* **Gauge/Bore:** *12 ga.*
Action: *O/U*
Barrel Length: 30", 32" **Wt.:** *7–7.5 lbs.*
Sights: *bead front*
Capacity: *2*
Stock: *trap-style Monte Carlo*

D2C:	NIB $1,000	Ex $775	VG+ $550	Good $500	
C2C:	Mint $960	Ex $700	VG+ $500	Good $450	Fair $230
Trade-In:	Mint $710	Ex $575	VG+ $390	Good $350	Poor $120

MODEL 2000 HAMMERLESS DOUBLE REDBOOK CODE: RB-PC-S-2000HD

M/F and IC/M chokes included, boxlock action, automatic ejectors, selective-single trigger, checkering on pistol grip and forearm, elaborate engraving. Pricing here reflects Grade I models. Grade II models are less valuable.

Production: *1973–1974* **Gauge/Bore:** *12 ga., 20 ga.*
Action: *SxS*
Barrel Length: 26", 28", 30" **Wt.:** *N/A*
Sights: *bead front*
Capacity: *2*
Stock: *fancy walnut*

D2C:	NIB $2,250	Ex $1,725	VG+ $1,240	Good $1,125	
C2C:	Mint $2,160	Ex $1,575	VG+ $1,130	Good $1,015	Fair $520
Trade-In:	Mint $1,600	Ex $1,275	VG+ $880	Good $790	Poor $240

MODEL 2500 HAMMERLESS DOUBLE REDBOOK CODE: RB-PC-S-2500HD

IC/M and M/F chokes included, boxlock action, automatic ejectors, selective-single triggers, checkering on stock and slide handle, ventilated rib.

Production: *1973–1974* **Gauge/Bore:** *12 ga., 20 ga.*
Action: *SxS*
Barrel Length: 26", 28", 30" **Wt.:** *N/A*
Sights: *bead front*
Capacity: *2*
Stock: *pistol-grip hardwood*

D2C:	NIB $650	Ex $500	VG+ $360	Good $325	
C2C:	Mint $630	Ex $450	VG+ $330	Good $295	Fair $150
Trade-In:	Mint $470	Ex $375	VG+ $260	Good $230	Poor $90

MODEL 4000 HAMMERLESS SLIDE-ACTION REPEATING REDBOOK CODE: RB-PC-S-4000SA

Full-coverage floral engraving on receiver, 3" chamber, ventilated rib, checkering on stock and slide handle, custom version of Mossberg Model 500.

Production: *1975–discontinued* **Gauge/Bore:** *12 ga., 20 ga., .410*
Action: *pump-action*
Barrel Length: 26", 28", 30" **Wt.:** *6–8 lbs.*
Sights: *bead front*
Capacity: *3*
Stock: *select hardwood*

D2C:	NIB $430	Ex $350	VG+ $240	Good $215	
C2C:	Mint $420	Ex $300	VG+ $220	Good $195	Fair $100
Trade-In:	Mint $310	Ex $250	VG+ $170	Good $155	Poor $60

MODEL 4000 TRAP REDBOOK CODE: RB-PC-S-4000TR

F choke, recoil pad, full-coverage floral engraving on receiver, ventilated rib, checkering on stock and slide handle.

Production: *1975–discontinued* **Gauge/Bore:** *12 ga.*
Action: *pump-action*
Barrel Length: 30" **Wt.:** *N/A*
Sights: *bead front*
Capacity: *3*
Stock: *Monte Carlo trap-style*

D2C:	NIB $550	Ex $425	VG+ $305	Good $275	
C2C:	Mint $530	Ex $400	VG+ $280	Good $250	Fair $130
Trade-In:	Mint $400	Ex $325	VG+ $220	Good $195	Poor $60

MODEL 4500 REDBOOK CODE: RB-PC-S-MO4500

Simpler engraving than 4000 model, 3" chamber, ventilated rib, checkering on stock and slide handle, custom version of Mossberg Model 500.

Production: *1975–discontinued* **Gauge/Bore:** *12 ga.*
Action: *pump-action*
Barrel Length: 26", 28", 30" **Wt.:** *6–8 lbs.*
Sights: *bead front*
Capacity: *3*
Stock: *select hardwood*

D2C:	NIB $440	Ex $350	VG+ $245	Good $220	
C2C:	Mint $430	Ex $325	VG+ $220	Good $200	Fair $105
Trade-In:	Mint $320	Ex $250	VG+ $180	Good $155	Poor $60

Perazzi USA

In 1957, Daniele Perazzi patented his first firearm design at the tender age of 16, and at 25, he founded his own firearms company, Armi Perazzi, in Botticino Mattina, Italy. He spent the rest of his life working in that company, and his son and daughter now carry on his legacy. The company imported products into the U.S. through Ithaca and Winchester in the 1970s but subsequently opened an American subsidiary, Perazzi USA, just outside of Los Angeles in Azusa, California. The company is known for using only the highest quality materials and methods, including using centuries-old walnut root for stocks and forends and engraving all gun components completely by hand. Perazzi is also known for creating shotguns completely to customers' specifications, allowing shooters to customize orders in any number of ways and by using any of several grades of materials. Since most Perazzi shotguns in existence were custom built, pricing for specific guns varies widely, even within each major model group. Note that our pricing for the models below reflects guns produced with the most basic materials and at the lowest grades Perazzi offers. Because of the exemplary care with which Perazzi produces firearms, the company is esteemed as one of the greatest shotgun manufacturers in the world.

DB81 SPECIAL REDBOOK CODE: RB-PZ-S-DB81SP

2.75" chamber, wide vent rib, M/F chokes, detachable trigger with flat springs, beavertail forend, adjustable comb.

Production: *discontinued* **Gauge/Bore:** *12 ga.*
Action: *O/U*
Barrel Length: 29.5", 31.5" **Wt.:** *N/A*
Sights: *bead front*
Capacity: *2*
Stock: *customizable walnut*

D2C:	NIB $10,000	Ex $7,600	VG+ $5,500	Good $5,000	
C2C:	Mint $9,600	Ex $6,900	VG+ $5,000	Good $4,500	Fair $2,300
Trade-In:	Mint $7,100	Ex $5,600	VG+ $3,900	Good $3,500	Poor $1,020

DC12 REDBOOK CODE: RB-PZ-S-DC12XX
Flat tapered rib, removable trigger with flat or coil springs, game or beavertail forend, gold plated trigger, blue receiver.

Production: *current* **Gauge/Bore:** *12 ga.*
Action: *SxS*
Barrel Length: *26.7"–31.5"* **Wt.:** *N/A*
Sights: *bead front*
Capacity: *2*
Stock: *English style or pistol-grip hardwood*

D2C:	NIB $16,515	Ex $12,575	VG+ $9,085	Good $8,260	
C2C:	Mint $15,860	Ex $11,400	VG+ $8,260	Good $7,435	Fair $3,800
Trade-In:	Mint $11,730	Ex $9,250	VG+ $6,450	Good $5,785	Poor $1,680

MX1 REDBOOK CODE: RB-PZ-S-MX1XXX
Interchangeable chokes, flat tapered rib, half-ventilated side rib, removable trigger with flat or coil springs, Schnabel forend, blue or nickel plated frame.

Production: *current* **Gauge/Bore:** *12 ga.*
Action: *O/U*
Barrel Length: *27.5"–29.5"* **Wt.:** *N/A*
Sights: *fiber-optic*
Capacity: *2*
Stock: *customizable hardwood*

D2C:	NIB $6,000	Ex $4,575	VG+ $3,300	Good $3,000	
C2C:	Mint $5,760	Ex $4,150	VG+ $3,000	Good $2,700	Fair $1,380
Trade-In:	Mint $4,260	Ex $3,375	VG+ $2,340	Good $2,100	Poor $600

MX3 REDBOOK CODE: RB-PZ-S-MX3XXX
Ramped tapered rib, modified stock, 2.75" chamber, fixed or interchangeable choke, checkering on stock, beavertail forend, detachable trigger.

Production: *discontinued* **Gauge/Bore:** *12 ga.*
Action: *O/U*
Barrel Length: *29.5"–31.5"* **Wt.:** *7–8.5"*
Sights: *bead front*
Capacity: *2*
Stock: *customizable hardwood*

D2C:	NIB $6,600	Ex $5,025	VG+ $3,630	Good $3,300	
C2C:	Mint $6,340	Ex $4,575	VG+ $3,300	Good $2,970	Fair $1,520
Trade-In:	Mint $4,690	Ex $3,700	VG+ $2,580	Good $2,310	Poor $660

MX7 REDBOOK CODE: RB-PZ-S-MX7XXX
Non-removable trigger group, fixed coil spring trigger, ventilated rib, available in single-shot configuration as well, adjustable cheekpiece.

Production: *1992–discontinued* **Gauge/Bore:** *12 ga.*
Action: *O/U*
Barrel Length: *29.5", 31.5"* **Wt.:** *N/A*
Sights: *bead front*
Capacity: *2*
Stock: *customizable walnut*

D2C:	NIB $5,900	Ex $4,500	VG+ $3,245	Good $2,950	
C2C:	Mint $5,670	Ex $4,075	VG+ $2,950	Good $2,655	Fair $1,360
Trade-In:	Mint $4,190	Ex $3,325	VG+ $2,310	Good $2,065	Poor $600

PERAZZI USA

MX8 OVER-UNDER REDBOOK CODE: RB-PZ-S-MX8OUX

Interchangeable chokes, flat or tapered rib, half ventilated side ribs, removable trigger with flat or coil springs, beavertail forend, blue or nickel plated receiver.

Production: *current* **Gauge/Bore:** *12 ga., 20 ga.*

Action: *O/U*

Barrel Length: 29.5"–31.5" **Wt.:** *N/A*

Sights: *fiber-optic*

Capacity: 2

Stock: *customizable hardwood*

D2C:	NIB $13,000	Ex $9,900	VG+ $7,150	Good $6,500	
C2C:	Mint $12,480	Ex $8,975	VG+ $6,500	Good $5,850	Fair $2,990
Trade-In:	Mint $9,230	Ex $7,300	VG+ $5,070	Good $4,550	Poor $1,320

MX8 SINGLE-SHOT REDBOOK CODE: RB-PZ-S-MX8SSX

Full choke or interchangeable on request, ramped tapered rib, removable with flat or coil springs, beavertail forend, top single, blue or nickel-plated frame. Market research provides no conclusive pricing suggestion(s) for this particular model. The model is either too rare or contains too many custom options, which drastically affects pricing.

Production: *current* **Gauge/Bore:** *12 ga.*

Action: *single-shot*

Barrel Length: 32", 34", 35" **Wt.:** *N/A*

Sights: *bead front*

Capacity: 1

Stock: *customizable hardwood*

MX8 COMBO REDBOOK CODE: RB-PZ-S-MX8COM

Full choke or interchangeable choke on request with both barrel styles, ramped tapered rib on single barrel, IM Full choke or interchangeable chokes on request with over-under barrel, ramped tapered rib for over-under barrel, removable trigger with flat or coil springs, beavertail forend, blue or nickel plated frame. Research suggests pricing for this model is inconclusive at this time.

Production: *current* **Gauge/Bore:** *12 ga.*

Action: *single-shot, O/U*

Barrel Length: 32", 34", 35" (single-shot barrel) 29.5, 31.5", 34" (over-under barrel) **Wt.:** *N/A*

Sights: *bead front*

Capacity: 1, 2

Stock: *customizable hardwood*

MX8/20 REDBOOK CODE: RB-PZ-S-MX8X20

Ventilated rib, removable trigger group, round forend, fixed chokes, interchangeable chokes on request.

Production: *1993–discontinued* **Gauge/Bore:** *20 ga.*

Action: *O/U*

Barrel Length: 26", 28" **Wt.:** *N/A*

Sights: *bead front*

Capacity: 2

Stock: *customizable walnut*

D2C:	NIB $9,015	Ex $6,875	VG+ $4,960	Good $4,510	
C2C:	Mint $8,660	Ex $6,225	VG+ $4,510	Good $4,060	Fair $2,075
Trade-In:	Mint $6,410	Ex $5,050	VG+ $3,520	Good $3,160	Poor $930

PERAZZI USA

MX9 REDBOOK CODE: RB-PZ-S-MX9XXX
Adjustable point of impact, adjustable comb, screw in chokes or fixed chokes, ventilated rib inserts, removable trigger group, available in several grades.

Production: *1993–discontinued* **Gauge/Bore:** *12 ga.*
Action: *O/U*
Barrel Length: 29.5", 30.5", 32", 34" **Wt.:** *N/A*
Sights: *bead front*
Capacity: *2*
Stock: *customizable hardwood*

D2C:	NIB $6,750	Ex $5,150	VG+ $3,715	Good $3,375	
C2C:	Mint $6,480	Ex $4,675	VG+ $3,380	Good $3,040	Fair $1,555
Trade-In:	Mint $4,800	Ex $3,800	VG+ $2,640	Good $2,365	Poor $690

MX10 REDBOOK CODE: RB-PZ-S-MX10XX
Full choke or interchangeable choke on request, adjustable tapered rib, adjustable comb, beavertail forend, adjustable point of impact, top single rib, blue or nickel-plated frame.

Production: *current* **Gauge/Bore:** *12 ga.*
Action: *single-shot*
Barrel Length: 32", 34", 35" **Wt.:** *N/A*
Sights: *bead front*
Capacity: *1*
Stock: *hardwood or silicon*

D2C:	NIB $11,500	Ex $8,750	VG+ $6,325	Good $5,750	
C2C:	Mint $11,040	Ex $7,950	VG+ $5,750	Good $5,175	Fair $2,645
Trade-In:	Mint $8,170	Ex $6,450	VG+ $4,490	Good $4,025	Poor $1,170

MX10 COMBO REDBOOK CODE: RB-PZ-S-MX10CO
Full choke or interchangeable choke on request with both barrel styles, adjustable rib with four notches on single barrel, adjustable tapered rib with ventilated side ribs or half ventilated side ribs on over-under barrel, adjustable point of impact, blue or nickel plated frame.

Production: *current* **Gauge/Bore:** *12 ga.*
Action: *single-shot, O/U*
Barrel Length: 32", 34", 35" **Wt.:** *N/A*
Sights: *bead front*
Capacity: *1, 2*
Stock: *hardwood or silicon*

D2C:	NIB $17,120	Ex $13,025	VG+ $9,420	Good $8,560	
C2C:	Mint $16,440	Ex $11,825	VG+ $8,560	Good $7,705	Fair $3,940
Trade-In:	Mint $12,160	Ex $9,600	VG+ $6,680	Good $5,995	Poor $1,740

MX10RS UNSINGLE REDBOOK CODE: RB-PZ-S-MX10RS
Full choke or interchangeable on request, adjustable tapered rib, removable trigger with flat or coil springs, adjustable comb, beavertail forend, adjustable point of impact, blue or nickel frame.

Production: *current* **Gauge/Bore:** *12 ga.*
Action: *unsingle*
Barrel Length: 32", 34", 35" **Wt.:** *N/A*
Sights: *bead front*
Capacity: *1*
Stock: *hardwood or silicon*

D2C:	NIB $8,950	Ex $6,825	VG+ $4,925	Good $4,475	
C2C:	Mint $8,600	Ex $6,200	VG+ $4,480	Good $4,030	Fair $2,060
Trade-In:	Mint $6,360	Ex $5,025	VG+ $3,500	Good $3,135	Poor $900

PERAZZI USA

MX10RS COMBO REDBOOK CODE: RB-PZ-S-10RSCO

Full choke or interchangeable choke on request with both barrel styles, adjustable tapered rib with four notches on single barrel, adjustable tapered rib with ventilated side ribs or half ventilated side ribs on over-under barrel, adjustable point of impact, blue or nickel plated frame, removable trigger with flat or coil springs.

Production: *current* **Gauge/Bore:** *12 ga.*
Action: *unsingle, O/U*
Barrel Length: *32", 34", 35" (unsingle barrel)*
29.5", 31.5", 34" (over-under barrel) **Wt.:** *N/A*
Sights: *bead front*
Capacity: *1, 2*
Stock: *hardwood or silicon*

D2C:	NIB $16,860	Ex $12,825	VG+ $9,275	Good $8,430	
C2C:	Mint $16,190	Ex $11,650	VG+ $8,430	Good $7,590	Fair $3,880
Trade-In:	Mint $11,980	Ex $9,450	VG+ $6,580	Good $5,905	Poor $1,710

MX12 REDBOOK CODE: RB-PZ-S-MX12XX

Interchangeable chokes, flat tapered rib, half ventilated side rib, non-removable single-selective trigger with coil springs, beavertail forend, blue or nickel plated.

Production: *current* **Gauge/Bore:** *12 ga.*
Action: *O/U*
Barrel Length: *27.5"–34"* **Wt.:** *N/A*
Sights: *bead front*
Capacity: *2*
Stock: *customizable hardwood*

D2C:	NIB $11,000	Ex $8,375	VG+ $6,050	Good $5,500	
C2C:	Mint $10,560	Ex $7,600	VG+ $5,500	Good $4,950	Fair $2,530
Trade-In:	Mint $7,810	Ex $6,175	VG+ $4,290	Good $3,850	Poor $1,110

MX12/3 REDBOOK CODE: RB-PZ-S-MX12X3

Fixed or interchangeable chokes on request, adjustable rib with 3 notches, ventilated side ribs, non-removable single-selective trigger with coil spring, adjustable comb, beavertail forend.

Production: *current* **Gauge/Bore:** *12 ga.*
Action: *O/U*
Barrel Length: *27.5", 28.4", 29.5", 31.5", 34"* **Wt.:** *N/A*
Sights: *fiber-optic*
Capacity: *2*
Stock: *hardwood or silicon*

D2C:	NIB $9,000	Ex $6,850	VG+ $4,950	Good $4,500	
C2C:	Mint $8,640	Ex $6,225	VG+ $4,500	Good $4,050	Fair $2,070
Trade-In:	Mint $6,390	Ex $5,050	VG+ $3,510	Good $3,150	Poor $900

MX12 SC2 REDBOOK CODE: RB-PZ-S-12SC2X

Fixed or interchangeable chokes, flat parallel ribs, half solid side ribs, non-removable single-selective trigger with coil springs, game-style forend, gold-plated trigger, nickel plated receiver.

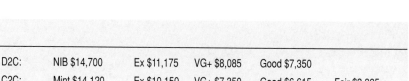

Production: *current* **Gauge/Bore:** *12 ga.*
Action: *O/U*
Barrel Length: *26.7"–31.5"* **Wt.:** *N/A*
Sights: *bead front*
Capacity: *2*
Stock: *English style or pistol-grip hardwood*

D2C:	NIB $14,700	Ex $11,175	VG+ $8,085	Good $7,350	
C2C:	Mint $14,120	Ex $10,150	VG+ $7,350	Good $6,615	Fair $3,385
Trade-In:	Mint $10,440	Ex $8,250	VG+ $5,740	Good $5,145	Poor $1,470

MX12 SC3 REDBOOK CODE: RB-PZ-S-12SC3X

Fixed or interchangeable chokes on request, flat parallel rib, half-solid side ribs, non-removable single-selective trigger with coil springs, game-style forend.

Production: *current* **Gauge/Bore:** *12 ga.*

Action: *O/U*

Barrel Length: *26.7"–31.5"* **Wt.:** *N/A*

Sights: *bead front*

Capacity: *2*

Stock: *English style or pistol-grip hardwood*

D2C:	NIB $14,400	Ex $10,950	VG+ $7,920	Good $7,200	
C2C:	Mint $13,830	Ex $9,950	VG+ $7,200	Good $6,480	Fair $3,315
Trade-In:	Mint $10,230	Ex $8,075	VG+ $5,620	Good $5,040	Poor $1,440

MX12 EXTRA REDBOOK CODE: RB-PZ-S-M12EXT

Fixed or interchangeable chokes on request, flat parallel rib, half solid side ribs, non-removable single-selective trigger with coil springs, game-style forend, engraving on receiver, gold-plated trigger. Research reveals pricing for this model is inconclusive at this time.

Production: *current* **Gauge/Bore:** *12 ga.*

Action: *O/U*

Barrel Length: *26.7"–31.5"* **Wt.:** *N/A*

Sights: *bead front*

Capacity: *2*

Stock: *English style or pistol-grip hardwood*

MX14L COMBO REDBOOK CODE: RB-PZ-S-MX14LC

Full choke or interchangeable choke on request with unsingle barrel, ramped tapered rib on unsingle barrel, IM Full choke or interchangeable choke on request for over-under barrel, ramped tapered rib and side ribs or half-ventilated side ribs on over-under barrel, removable trigger with flat or coil springs, adjustable trigger, adjustable comb, beavertail forend, engraved frame, nickel-plated receiver.

Production: *current* **Gauge/Bore:** *12 ga.*

Action: *unsingle, O/U*

Barrel Length: *32", 34" (unsingle barrel) 29.5", 31.5"* (over-under barrel) **Wt.:** *N/A*

Sights: *bead front*

Capacity: *1, 2*

Stock: *hardwood or silicon*

D2C:	NIB $13,150	Ex $10,000	VG+ $7,235	Good $6,575	
C2C:	Mint $12,630	Ex $9,075	VG+ $6,580	Good $5,920	Fair $3,025
Trade-In:	Mint $9,340	Ex $7,375	VG+ $5,130	Good $4,605	Poor $1,320

MX14 COMBO REDBOOK CODE: RB-PZ-S-MX14CO

Full choke or interchangeable choke on request with single-shot barrel, ramped tapered rib on single-shot barrel, IM Full choke or interchangeable choke on request with over-under barrel, ramped tapered rib and side ribs on over-under barrel, removable trigger with flat or coil springs, adjustable comb, beavertail forend, blue or nickel plated frame.

Production: *current* **Gauge/Bore:** *12 ga.*

Action: *unsingle, O/U*

Barrel Length: *32", 34" (single-shot barrel) 29.5", 31.5" (over-under barrel)* **Wt.:** *N/A*

Sights: *bead front*

Capacity: *1, 2*

Stock: *hardwood or silicon*

D2C:	NIB $8,500	Ex $6,475	VG+ $4,675	Good $4,250	
C2C:	Mint $8,160	Ex $5,875	VG+ $4,250	Good $3,825	Fair $1,955
Trade-In:	Mint $6,040	Ex $4,775	VG+ $3,320	Good $2,975	Poor $870

MX15 REDBOOK CODE: RB-PZ-S-MX15XXX
Adjustable comb, beavertail forend, adjustable point of impact, full choke or interchangeable.

Production: *current* **Gauge/Bore:** *12 ga.*
Action: *unsingle*
Barrel Length: 32", 34", 35" **Wt.:** *N/A*
Sights: *bead front*
Capacity: *1*
Stock: *hardwood or silicon*

D2C:	NIB $6,900	Ex $5,250	VG+ $3,795	Good $3,450	
C2C:	Mint $6,630	Ex $4,775	VG+ $3,450	Good $3,105	Fair $1,590
Trade-In:	Mint $4,900	Ex $3,875	VG+ $2,700	Good $2,415	Poor $690

MX15L REDBOOK CODE: RB-PZ-S-MX15LX
Full or interchangeable choke, adjustable tapered rib, removable trigger with flat or
coil springs, adjustable comb, beavertail forend, adjustable point of impact, engraved frame, nickel plated receiver.

Production: *current* **Gauge/Bore:** *12 ga.*
Action: *unsingle*
Barrel Length: 32", 34", 35" **Wt.:** *N/A*
Sights: *bead front*
Capacity: *1*
Stock: *hardwood or silicon*

D2C:	NIB $7,500	Ex $5,700	VG+ $4,125	Good $3,750	
C2C:	Mint $7,200	Ex $5,175	VG+ $3,750	Good $3,375	Fair $1,725
Trade-In:	Mint $5,330	Ex $4,200	VG+ $2,930	Good $2,625	Poor $750

MX20 STANDARD REDBOOK CODE: RB-PZ-S-MX20ST
Fixed or interchangeable chokes, flat parallel rib, half-solid side ribs, non-removable single-selective trigger with coil springs, game-style forend.

Production: *current* **Gauge/Bore:** *20 ga.*
Action: *O/U*
Barrel Length: 26.7"–29.5" **Wt.:** *N/A*
Sights: *bead front*
Capacity: *2*
Stock: *English style or pistol-grip hardwood*

D2C:	NIB $9,950	Ex $7,575	VG+ $5,475	Good $4,975	
C2C:	Mint $9,560	Ex $6,875	VG+ $4,980	Good $4,480	Fair $2,290
Trade-In:	Mint $7,070	Ex $5,575	VG+ $3,890	Good $3,485	Poor $1,020

MX2000 REDBOOK CODE: RB-PZ-S-MX2000
Full choke or interchangeable on request, adjustable tapered rib, removable trigger
with flat or coil springs, adjustable comb, beavertail forend, adjustable point of impact,
engraved frame, blue frame with gold inlay or nickel plated frame without gold inlay.

Production: *current* **Gauge/Bore:** *12 ga.*
Action: *unsingle*
Barrel Length: 32", 34", 35 **Wt.:** *N/A*
Sights: *bead front*
Capacity: *1*
Stock: *hardwood or silicon*

D2C:	NIB $12,310	Ex $9,375	VG+ $6,775	Good $6,155	
C2C:	Mint $11,820	Ex $8,500	VG+ $6,160	Good $5,540	Fair $2,835
Trade-In:	Mint $8,750	Ex $6,900	VG+ $4,810	Good $4,310	Poor $1,260

MX2000S   REDBOOK CODE: RB-PZ-S-MX200S

Flat rib, half solid side ribs, none removable trigger, single-selective trigger with coil springs, game style forend, engraved blue frame with gold inlay or nickel plated without gold inlay.

Production: *current* **Gauge/Bore:** *12 ga., 20 ga.*

Action: *O/U*

Barrel Length: *26"–29"* **Wt.:** *N/A*

Sights: *bead front*

Capacity: *2*

Stock: *English style or pistol-grip hardwood*

D2C:	NIB $12,790	Ex $9,725	VG+ $7,035	Good $6,395	
C2C:	Mint $12,280	Ex $8,850	VG+ $6,400	Good $5,760	Fair $2,945
Trade-In:	Mint $9,090	Ex $7,175	VG+ $4,990	Good $4,480	Poor $1,290

MX2000S/3   REDBOOK CODE: RB-PZ-S-2000S3

Fixed or interchangeable chokes on request, adjustable rib with 3 notches, ventilated side ribs, adjustable comb, beavertail forend.

Production: *current* **Gauge/Bore:** *12 ga.*

Action: *O/U*

Barrel Length: *27.5", 28.4", 29.5", 31.5", 34"* **Wt.:** *N/A*

Sights: *bead front*

Capacity: *2*

Stock: *hardwood or silicon*

D2C:	NIB $14,500	Ex $11,025	VG+ $7,975	Good $7,250	
C2C:	Mint $13,920	Ex $10,025	VG+ $7,250	Good $6,525	Fair $3,335
Trade-In:	Mint $10,300	Ex $8,125	VG+ $5,660	Good $5,075	Poor $1,470

MX200RS COMBO   REDBOOK CODE: RB-PZ-S-200RSC

Full choke or interchangeable choke on request with both barrels, adjustable tapered rib with four notches on unsingle barrel, adjustable tapered rib with four notches and ventilated side ribs or half-ventilated side ribs on over-under barrel, removable trigger with flat or coil springs, adjustable comb, beavertail forend, adjustable point of impact, engraved frame, blue frame with gold inlay or nickel plated frame without gold inlays.

Production: *current* **Gauge/Bore:** *12 ga.*

Action: *unsingle, O/U*

Barrel Length: 32", 34", 35" (unsingle barrel)
29.5", 31.5", 34" (over-under barrel) **Wt.:** *N/A*

Sights: *bead front*

Capacity: *1, 2*

Stock: *hardwood or silicon*

D2C:	NIB $17,500	Ex $13,300	VG+ $9,625	Good $8,750	
C2C:	Mint $16,800	Ex $12,075	VG+ $8,750	Good $7,875	Fair $4,025
Trade-In:	Mint $12,430	Ex $9,800	VG+ $6,830	Good $6,125	Poor $1,770

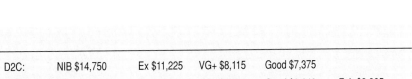

MX2000/3   REDBOOK CODE: RB-PZ-S-20003X

Interchangeable chokes, adjustable rib, paralleled or tapered rib, half-ventilated side ribs, removable trigger with flat or coil springs, beavertail forend, adjustable point of impact, engraved frame, blue frame with gold inlay or nickel plated frame without inlays.

Production: *current* **Gauge/Bore:** *12 ga., 20 ga.*

Action: *O/U*

Barrel Length: *29.5"–31.5"* **Wt.:** *N/A*

Sights: *fiber-optic*

Capacity: *2*

Stock: *hardwood or synthetic both with adjustable comb*

D2C:	NIB $14,750	Ex $11,225	VG+ $8,115	Good $7,375	
C2C:	Mint $14,160	Ex $10,200	VG+ $7,380	Good $6,640	Fair $3,395
Trade-In:	Mint $10,480	Ex $8,275	VG+ $5,760	Good $5,165	Poor $1,500

PERAZZI USA

MX2000/8 OVER-UNDER REDBOOK CODE: RB-PZ-S-2000X8

Interchangeable chokes, flat parallel or tapered rib, half-ventilated side ribs, removable trigger
with flat or coil springs, beavertail forend, engraved frame, blue frame with gold inlays or nickel frame without gold inlays.

Production: *current* **Gauge/Bore:** *12 ga., 20 ga.*
Action: *O/U*
Barrel Length: 29.5"–31.5" **Wt.:** *N/A*
Sights: *fiber-optic*
Capacity: 2
Stock: *customizable hardwood*

D2C:	NIB $13,900	Ex $10,575	VG+ $7,645	Good $6,950	
C2C:	Mint $13,350	Ex $9,600	VG+ $6,950	Good $6,255	Fair $3,200
Trade-In:	Mint $9,870	Ex $7,800	VG+ $5,430	Good $4,865	Poor $1,410

MX2000/8 SINGLE-SHOT REDBOOK CODE: RB-PZ-S-20008S

Full choke or interchangeable choke on request for single-shot barrel, ramped tapered rib on single-shot and
over-under barrel, IM full chokes or interchangeable chokes on request for over-under barrels, removable trigger with flat or coil
springs, beavertail forend, engraved frame, blue frame with gold inlay or nickel plated frame without gold inlay. Research reveals pricing for
this model is inconclusive at this time.

Production: *current* **Gauge/Bore:** *12 ga.*
Action: *single-shot, O/U*
Barrel Length: 32", 34", 35" (single-shot barrel) 29.5, 31.5", 34" (over-under barrel) **Wt.:** *N/A*
Sights: *bead front*
Capacity: *1, 2*
Stock: *customizable hardwood*

MX2000/8 COMBO REDBOOK CODE: RB-PZ-S-20008C

Full or interchangeable choke on request for single-shot barrel, IM Full
choke or interchangeable choke on over-under barrels, ramped tapered rib on
single-shot barrel, ramped tapered rib with ventilated side ribs or ventilated side ribs on
over-under barrel, removable trigger with flat or coil springs, engraved frame, blue receiver with gold inlays or nickel
plated frame without gold inlays, beavertail forend. Research reveals pricing for this model is inconclusive at this time.

Production: *current* **Gauge/Bore:** *12 ga.*
Action: *single-shot, O/U*
Barrel Length: 32", 34", 35" (single-shot barrel) 29.5, 31.5", 34" (over-under barrel) **Wt.:** *N/A*
Sights: *bead front*
Capacity: 2
Stock: *customizable hardwood*

MX2000/10 COMBO REDBOOK CODE: RB-PZ-S-200010

Full choke or interchangeable choke on request, single barrel has adjustable
rib with four notches, over and under barrel has adjustable rib and ventilated
side ribs or half ventilated side ribs, removable trigger with flat or coil springs, adjustable stock comb, beavertail forend,
adjustable point of impact, engraved frame blue frame with gold inlays or nickel plate frame without gold inlays.

Production: *current* **Gauge/Bore:** *12 ga.*
Action: *single-shot, O/U*
Barrel Length: 29.5", 31.5", 34" (over-under barrel)
32", 34", 35" (single-shot barrel) **Wt.:** *N/A*
Sights: *bead front*
Capacity: *1, 2*
Stock: *hardwood or silicon*

D2C:	NIB $14,750	Ex $11,225	VG+ $8,115	Good $7,375	
C2C:	Mint $14,160	Ex $10,200	VG+ $7,380	Good $6,640	Fair $3,395
Trade-In:	Mint $10,480	Ex $8,275	VG+ $5,760	Good $5,165	Poor $1,500

MX2005 OVER-UNDER REDBOOK CODE: RB-PZ-S-2005OU

Interchangeable chokes, adjustable rib, parallel or tapered rib, half-ventilated side ribs, removable trigger with flat or coil springs, adjustable comb on stock, beavertail forend, adjustable point of impact, engraved frame, nickel plated or blue frame.

Production: *current* **Gauge/Bore:** *12 ga.*
Action: *O/U*
Barrel Length: 29.5"–31.5" **Wt.:** *N/A*
Sights: *fiber-optic*
Capacity: 2
Stock: *hardwood or synthetic both with adjustable comb*

D2C:	NIB $10,200	Ex $7,775	VG+ $5,610	Good $5,100	
C2C:	Mint $9,800	Ex $7,050	VG+ $5,100	Good $4,590	Fair $2,350
Trade-In:	Mint $7,250	Ex $5,725	VG+ $3,980	Good $3,570	Poor $1,020

MX2005 UNSINGLE REDBOOK CODE: RB-PZ-S-2005UN

Full choke or interchangeable choke, adjustable rib, removable trigger with flat or coil springs, adjustable comb, beavertail forend, adjustable point of impact, engraved frame, nickel plated or blue receiver.

Production: *current* **Gauge/Bore:** *12 ga.*
Action: *unsingle*
Barrel Length: 34" **Wt.:** *N/A*
Sights: *bead front*
Capacity: 1
Stock: *hardwood or silicon*

D2C:	NIB $10,060	Ex $7,650	VG+ $5,535	Good $5,030	
C2C:	Mint $9,660	Ex $6,950	VG+ $5,030	Good $4,530	Fair $2,315
Trade-In:	Mint $7,150	Ex $5,650	VG+ $3,930	Good $3,525	Poor $1,020

MX2005 COMBO REDBOOK CODE: RB-PZ-S-2005CO

Full choke or interchangeable choke on request with both barrel styles, adjustable rib with five notches on single barrel, IM full choke or interchangeable on request, removable trigger with flat or coil springs, beavertail forend, adjustable point of impact, engraved frame, nickel plated or blue frame.

Production: *current* **Gauge/Bore:** *12 ga.*
Action: *unsingle, O/U*
Barrel Length: 34" (unsingle barrel) 31.5" (over-under barrel) **Wt.:** *N/A*
Sights: *bead front*
Capacity: 1, 2
Stock: *hardwood or silicon*

D2C:	NIB $12,000	Ex $9,125	VG+ $6,600	Good $6,000	
C2C:	Mint $11,520	Ex $8,300	VG+ $6,000	Good $5,400	Fair $2,760
Trade-In:	Mint $8,520	Ex $6,725	VG+ $4,680	Good $4,200	Poor $1,200

MX2008 REDBOOK CODE: RB-PZ-S-2008OU

Interchangeable chokes, adjustable rib, parallel or tapered rib, half-ventilated side ribs, removable trigger with flat or coil springs, adjustable comb, beavertail forend, adjustable point of impact, engraved frame, nickel plated or blue finished receiver.

Production: *current* **Gauge/Bore:** *12 ga.*
Action: *O/U*
Barrel Length: 29.5"–31.5" **Wt.:** *N/A*
Sights: *fiber-optic*
Capacity: 2
Stock: *hardwood or synthetic both with adjustable comb*

D2C:	NIB $13,000	Ex $9,900	VG+ $7,150	Good $6,500	
C2C:	Mint $12,480	Ex $8,975	VG+ $6,500	Good $5,850	Fair $2,990
Trade-In:	Mint $9,230	Ex $7,300	VG+ $5,070	Good $4,550	Poor $1,320

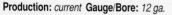

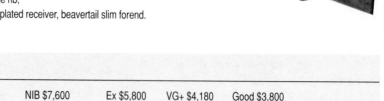

MXS REDBOOK CODE: RB-PZ-S-MSXXXX

Fixed or 4 interchangeable chokes, flat tapered rib, half-ventilated side rib,
non-removable single-selective trigger with coil spring, blue or nickel-plated receiver, beavertail slim forend.

Production: *current* **Gauge/Bore:** *12 ga.*
Action: *O/U*
Barrel Length: 28.7", 30", 32" **Wt.:** *N/A*
Sights: *fiber-optic*
Capacity: *2*
Stock: *standard hardwood*

D2C:	NIB $7,600	Ex $5,800	VG+ $4,180	Good $3,800	
C2C:	Mint $7,300	Ex $5,250	VG+ $3,800	Good $3,420	Fair $1,750
Trade-In:	Mint $5,400	Ex $4,275	VG+ $2,970	Good $2,660	Poor $780

TM-1 REDBOOK CODE: RB-PZ-S-TM1XXX

Full choke or interchangeable chokes, ramped tapered rib, removable trigger with coil springs, beavertail forend, blue or nickel-plated frame.

Production: *current* **Gauge/Bore:** *12 ga.*
Action: *single-shot*
Barrel Length: 32", 34", 35 **Wt.:** *N/A*
Sights: *bead front*
Capacity: *1*
Stock: *customizable hardwood*

D2C:	NIB $3,000	Ex $2,300	VG+ $1,650	Good $1,500	
C2C:	Mint $2,880	Ex $2,075	VG+ $1,500	Good $1,350	Fair $690
Trade-In:	Mint $2,130	Ex $1,700	VG+ $1,170	Good $1,050	Poor $300

*Photo Courtesy of
Rock Island Auction Company*

TMX SPECIAL REDBOOK CODE: RB-PZ-S-TMXSPE

Ultra-high rib, interchangeable choke tubes are optional, adjustable trigger.

Production: *current* **Gauge/Bore:** *12 ga.*
Action: *single-shot*
Barrel Length: 32", 34" **Wt.:** *~8 lbs.*
Sights: *bead front*
Capacity: *1*
Stock: *select walnut*

D2C:	NIB $3,400	Ex $2,600	VG+ $1,870	Good $1,700	
C2C:	Mint $3,270	Ex $2,350	VG+ $1,700	Good $1,530	Fair $785
Trade-In:	Mint $2,420	Ex $1,925	VG+ $1,330	Good $1,190	Poor $360

TM9 REDBOOK CODE: RB-PZ-S-TM9STD

Full choke or interchangeable choke on request, ramped tapered rib, removable trigger group with coil springs, blue or nickel plated frame, beavertail forend.

Production: *current* **Gauge/Bore:** *12 ga.*
Action: *single-shot*
Barrel Length: 32", 34", 35" **Wt.:** *N/A*
Sights: *bead front*
Capacity: *1*
Stock: *customizable hardwood*

D2C:	NIB $8,000	Ex $6,100	VG+ $4,400	Good $4,000	
C2C:	Mint $7,680	Ex $5,525	VG+ $4,000	Good $3,600	Fair $1,840
Trade-In:	Mint $5,680	Ex $4,500	VG+ $3,120	Good $2,800	Poor $810

PERAZZI USA

TM9X REDBOOK CODE: RB-PZ-S-TM9XXX
Adjustable comb, full choke or interchangeable chokes, removable trigger with coil springs, beavertail forend, adjustable point of impact, blue or nickel-plated frame.

Production: *current* **Gauge/Bore:** *12 ga.*
Action: *single-shot*
Barrel Length: *32", 34", 35* **Wt.:** *N/A*
Sights: *bead front*
Capacity: *1*
Stock: *hardwood or silicon*

D2C:	NIB $8,700	Ex $6,625	VG+ $4,785	Good $4,350	
C2C:	Mint $8,360	Ex $6,025	VG+ $4,350	Good $3,915	Fair $2,005
Trade-In:	Mint $6,180	Ex $4,875	VG+ $3,400	Good $3,045	Poor $870

MIRAGE OVER/UNDER REDBOOK CODE: RB-PZ-S-MIRAGE
Ventilated rib or interchangeable choke on request, single-selective trigger, adjustable comb, checkered forend and buttstock.

Production: *discontinued 1998* **Gauge/Bore:** *12 ga.*
Action: *O/U*
Barrel Length: *27.6", 29.5", 31.5"* **Wt.:** *7–8 lbs.*
Sights: *bead front*
Capacity: *2*
Stock: *customizable hardwood*

D2C:	NIB $7,000	Ex $5,325	VG+ $3,850	Good $3,500	
C2C:	Mint $6,720	Ex $4,850	VG+ $3,500	Good $3,150	Fair $1,610
Trade-In:	Mint $4,970	Ex $3,925	VG+ $2,730	Good $2,450	Poor $720

Remington Arms Company

REMINGTON

In 1816, Eliphalet Remington II founded E. Remington and Sons—what has become the largest U.S. manufacturer of shotguns and rifles—in Ilion, New York. After some restructuring and acquisitions, the company changed its name to Remington Arms Company and relocated to Huntsville, Alabama. In 2007, Remington was purchased by the Freedom Group, a firearms manufacturer holding company owned by Cerberus Capital Management. With its nearly 200 years in existence, Remington is the oldest continuously operating manufacturer in North America and the only U.S. company which produces both firearms and ammunition domestically. Remington has produced nearly every type of firearm over the years, many of which are the best known and best-selling firearms in history. The highly esteemed company continues to produce a staggering array of weapons, and one of their most popular models is the Model 870 shotgun, which is available in a number of variations for clay, hunting, law enforcement, and military uses.

870 AMERICAN CLASSIC REDBOOK CODE: RB-RE-S-870AMC
Vent rib barrel in high-polish blue finish, engraved receiver with gold fill, white diamond grip cap, ventilated recoil pad, and white line spacer.

Production: *current* **Gauge/Bore:** *12 ga., 20 ga., 28 ga.*
Action: *pump-action*
Barrel Length: *25", 26", 28"* **Wt.:** *6 lbs., 6.1 lbs., 7 lbs.*
Sights: *front bead*
Capacity: *5*
Stock: *American walnut*

D2C:	NIB $1,050	Ex $800	VG+ $580	Good $525	LMP: $1,249
C2C:	Mint $1,010	Ex $725	VG+ $530	Good $475	Fair $245
Trade-In:	Mint $750	Ex $600	VG+ $410	Good $370	Poor $120

REMINGTON

870 WINGMASTER REDBOOK CODE: RB-RE-S-870WMX

Vent rib barrel, receiver machined from solid billet of steel, Rem choke, twin-action bars. Barrel options include vent rib modified and light contour with vent rib. Add $56 for .410 bore model. Add $112 for 28 ga. models.

Production: *current* **Gauge/Bore:** *12 ga., 20 ga., 28 ga., .410*
Action: *pump-action*
Barrel Length: 25", 26", 28", 30" **Wt.:** *6 lbs.–7.2 lbs.*
Sights: *front bead*
Capacity: *5*
Stock: *American walnut*

D2C:	NIB $780	Ex $600	VG+ $430	Good $390	LMP: $830
C2C:	Mint $750	Ex $550	VG+ $390	Good $355	Fair $180
Trade-In:	Mint $560	Ex $450	VG+ $310	Good $275	Poor $90

870 WINGMASTER CLASSIC TRAP REDBOOK CODE: RB-RE-S-870WMT

Light vent rib barrel in high-gloss blue finish, Rem choke, specialized trap choke tubes (single, mid-handicap, and long handicap), scroll-engraved receiver machined from solid billet of steel, twin action bars.

Production: *current* **Gauge/Bore:** *12 ga.*
Action: *pump-action*
Barrel Length: 30" **Wt.:** *8.2 lbs.*
Sights: *ivory front sight, steel mid bead*
Capacity: *5*
Stock: *Monte Carlo with American Walnut*

D2C:	NIB $960	Ex $750	VG+ $530	Good $480	LMP: $1,098
C2C:	Mint $930	Ex $675	VG+ $480	Good $435	Fair $225
Trade-In:	Mint $690	Ex $550	VG+ $380	Good $340	Poor $120

870 ADL WINGMASTER DELUXE REDBOOK CODE: RB-RE-S-ADLDEL

Extension beavertail forend, fine checkering, blue steel receiver, models with a matted top barrel or a vent rib barrel will command slightly higher premiums.

Production: *1950–1963* **Gauge/Bore:** *12 ga., 16 ga., 20 ga.*
Action: *pump-action*
Barrel Length: 26", 28", 30" **Wt.:** *6.5–7 lbs.*
Sights: *bead front*
Capacity: *5*
Stock: *hardwood pistol grip*

D2C:	NIB $330	Ex $275	VG+ $185	Good $165	
C2C:	Mint $320	Ex $250	VG+ $170	Good $150	Fair $80
Trade-In:	Mint $240	Ex $200	VG+ $130	Good $120	Poor $60

870 AP WINGMASTER STANDARD REDBOOK CODE: RB-RE-S-APWING

Takedown style, hammerless, chokes included, 3-shot wooden magazine plug, 2 3/4" chamber, crossbolt safety, matted receiver top, grooved forend, walnut buttplate, steel barrel. Model with vent rib barrel commands a slightly higher premium.

Production: *1950–1980* **Gauge/Bore:** *12 ga., 16 ga., 20 ga.*
Action: *pump-action*
Barrel Length: 28" **Wt.:** *7.3 lbs.*
Sights: *bead front*
Capacity: *5*
Stock: *American walnut pistol grip*

D2C:	NIB $230	Ex $175	VG+ $130	Good $115	
C2C:	Mint $230	Ex $175	VG+ $120	Good $105	Fair $55
Trade-In:	Mint $170	Ex $150	VG+ $90	Good $85	Poor $30

870 TB WINGMASTER TRAP REDBOOK CODE: RB-RE-S-TBWING

Checkering on stock and foregrip, recoil pad, 2 3/4" chamber, Remington proof-steel matte finished barrel.

Production: *1950–discontinued* **Gauge/Bore:** *12 ga.*
Action: *pump-action*
Barrel Length: 28", 30" **Wt.:** *8 lbs.*
Sights: *bead front*
Capacity: 5
Stock: *American walnut*

D2C:	NIB $690	Ex $525	VG+ $380	Good $345	
C2C:	Mint $670	Ex $500	VG+ $350	Good $315	Fair $160
Trade-In:	Mint $490	Ex $400	VG+ $270	Good $245	Poor $90

870 R WINGMASTER RIOT REDBOOK CODE: RB-RE-S-RWRIOT

Blue or parkerized metal, IC choke, no checkering on pistol grip stock.

Production: *1950–1991* **Gauge/Bore:** *12 ga., 16 ga.*
Action: *pump-action*
Barrel Length: 18", 20" **Wt.:** *6.7 lbs.*
Sights: *bead front*
Capacity: 5
Stock: *plain hardwood pistol-grip*

D2C:	NIB $375	Ex $300	VG+ $210	Good $190	
C2C:	Mint $360	Ex $275	VG+ $190	Good $170	Fair $90
Trade-In:	Mint $270	Ex $225	VG+ $150	Good $135	Poor $60

870 SA WINGMASTER SKEET REDBOOK CODE: RB-RE-S-WSKEET

Vent rib barrel, SK choke, extension beavertail forend.

Production: *1950–1982* **Gauge/Bore:** *12 ga., 16 ga., 20 ga., 28 ga., .410*
Action: *pump-action*
Barrel Length: 26" **Wt.:** *6.8–7.5 lbs.*
Sights: *ivory bead front, metal bead rear*
Capacity: 5
Stock: *pistol-grip walnut*

D2C:	NIB $410	Ex $325	VG+ $230	Good $205	
C2C:	Mint $400	Ex $300	VG+ $210	Good $185	Fair $95
Trade-In:	Mint $300	Ex $250	VG+ $160	Good $145	Poor $60

870 DEER GUN BRUSHMASTER DELUXE REDBOOK CODE: RB-RE-S-BRUSHD

Choke plain barrel, satin finished walnut forend and stock, recoil pad.

Production: *discontinued* **Gauge/Bore:** *12 ga.*
Action: *pump-action*
Barrel Length: 20" **Wt.:** *N/A*
Sights: *none*
Capacity: 5
Stock: *Monte Carlo*

D2C:	NIB $330	Ex $275	VG+ $185	Good $165	
C2C:	Mint $320	Ex $250	VG+ $170	Good $150	Fair $80
Trade-In:	Mint $240	Ex $200	VG+ $130	Good $120	Poor $60

870 FIELD WINGMASTER   REDBOOK CODE: RB-RE-S-FIELDW

Checkering on stock and forearm, screw in choke tubes, hammerless, plain or ventilated rib.

Production: *1964–discontinued* **Gauge/Bore:** *12 ga., 16 ga., 20 ga., 28 ga., .410*
Action: *pump-action*
Barrel Length: 26", 28", 30" **Wt.:** *6.5–7 lbs.*
Sights: *bead front*
Capacity: 5
Stock: *walnut*

D2C:	NIB $430	Ex $350	VG+ $240	Good $215	
C2C:	Mint $420	Ex $300	VG+ $220	Good $195	Fair $100
Trade-In:	Mint $310	Ex $250	VG+ $170	Good $155	Poor $60

870 WINGMASTER NRA EDITION   REDBOOK CODE: RB-RE-S-870NRA

3" chamber, vent rib barrel, 3 choke tubes included, NRA logo on both sides of blue barrel, glossy finish on walnut, checkering on stock and forend, gold-plated trigger.

Production: *2006–discontinued* **Gauge/Bore:** *12 ga.*
Action: *pump-action*
Barrel Length: 28" **Wt.:** *7.5 lbs.*
Sights: *ivory bead front, metal bead rear*
Capacity: 5
Stock: *American walnut*

D2C:	NIB $390	Ex $300	VG+ $215	Good $195	
C2C:	Mint $380	Ex $275	VG+ $200	Good $180	Fair $90
Trade-In:	Mint $280	Ex $225	VG+ $160	Good $140	Poor $60

870 POLICE   REDBOOK CODE: RB-RE-S-870PXX

3" chamber, Parkerized finish, blue metal finish, non-binding twin action, receiver milled from solid block of steel, steel-lined grooved forend, inertia firing pin, Flexitab feeding system, cross-bolt safety, sling swivel studs.

Production: *current* **Gauge/Bore:** *12 ga.*
Action: *pump-action*
Barrel Length: 18", 20" **Wt.:** *N/A*
Sights: *rifle sights, bead sights, ghost ring sights, or tritium night sights*
Capacity: 7, 8
Stock: *wood, folding, Speedfeed, or synthetic*

D2C:	NIB $610	Ex $475	VG+ $340	Good $305	
C2C:	Mint $590	Ex $425	VG+ $310	Good $275	Fair $145
Trade-In:	Mint $440	Ex $350	VG+ $240	Good $215	Poor $90

870 MISSISSIPPI MAGNUM DUCK   REDBOOK CODE: RB-RE-S-MISSMD

3" magnum chamber, decorated receiver, full-choke barrel, gloss polished blue barrel, full choke.

Production: *1983–discontinued* **Gauge/Bore:** *12 ga.*
Action: *pump-action*
Barrel Length: 30", 32" **Wt.:** *7.8 lbs.*
Sights: *front bead*
Capacity: 4
Stock: *American walnut*

D2C:	NIB $1,040	Ex $800	VG+ $575	Good $520	
C2C:	Mint $1,000	Ex $725	VG+ $520	Good $470	Fair $240
Trade-In:	Mint $740	Ex $600	VG+ $410	Good $365	Poor $120

870 EXPRESS REDBOOK CODE: RB-RE-S-870EXX

Vent rib barrel in matte black finish, modified Rem choke, receiver machined from a solid billet of steel, twin-action bars, fires 2.75" and 3" shells.

Production: *current* **Gauge/Bore:** *12 ga., 20 ga.*
Action: *pump-action*
Barrel Length: *26", 28"* **Wt.:** *7.5 lbs.*
Sights: *front bead*
Capacity: *4*
Stock: *laminated hardwood*

D2C:	NIB $360	Ex $275	VG+ $200	Good $180	**LMP:** $417
C2C:	Mint $350	Ex $250	VG+ $180	Good $165	Fair $85
Trade-In:	Mint $260	Ex $225	VG+ $150	Good $130	Poor $60

870 EXPRESS PISTOL GRIP REDBOOK CODE: RB-RE-S-870EXP

Barrel in matte blue finish, extended and ported tactical Rem choke, tactical-style forend, cross bolt safety, fires 3" shells.

Production: *current* **Gauge/Bore:** *12 ga.*
Action: *pump-action*
Barrel Length: *18.5"* **Wt.:** *N/A*
Sights: *bead*
Capacity: *7*
Stock: *Pachmayr synthetic pistol grip*

D2C:	NIB $410	Ex $325	VG+ $230	Good $205	**LMP:** $497
C2C:	Mint $400	Ex $300	VG+ $210	Good $185	Fair $95
Trade-In:	Mint $300	Ex $250	VG+ $160	Good $145	Poor $60

870 EXPRESS SLUG REDBOOK CODE: RB-RE-S-870EXS

Heavy contour, fully-rifled barrel in matte finish, contour barrels, cantilever system providing scope mount platform, receiver machined from solid billet of steel, twin action bars

Production: *current* **Gauge/Bore:** *12 ga., 20 ga.*
Action: *pump-action*
Barrel Length: *18.5", 23"* **Wt.:** *7.2 lbs., 8 lbs.*
Sights: *none*
Capacity: *5*
Stock: *synthetic*

D2C:	NIB $480	Ex $375	VG+ $265	Good $240	**LMP:** $545
C2C:	Mint $470	Ex $350	VG+ $240	Good $220	Fair $115
Trade-In:	Mint $350	Ex $275	VG+ $190	Good $170	Poor $60

870 EXPRESS TURKEY REDBOOK CODE: RB-RE-S-870EXT

Vent rib turkey barrel, extra-full Rem choke tube, receiver machined from a solid billet of steel, twin action bars.

Production: *discontinued* **Gauge/Bore:** *12 ga., 16 ga., 20 ga.*
Action: *pump-action*
Barrel Length: *21"* **Wt.:** *7.2 lbs.*
Sights: *bead*
Capacity: *5*
Stock: *Express wood*

D2C:	NIB $380	Ex $300	VG+ $210	Good $190	
C2C:	Mint $370	Ex $275	VG+ $190	Good $175	Fair $90
Trade-In:	Mint $270	Ex $225	VG+ $150	Good $135	Poor $60

870 EXPRESS TURKEY CAMO REDBOOK CODE: RB-RE-S-870XTC

Vent rib barrel in standard Express finish, Turkey extra-full Rem choke, stock with integrated sling swivel attachment, drilled and tapped receiver for use with Weaver rail (not included), fires 2.75" and 3" shells.

Production: *current* **Gauge/Bore:** *12 ga.*
Action: *pump-action*
Barrel Length: 21" **Wt.:** *7.2 lbs.*
Sights: *bead*
Capacity: *5*
Stock: *synthetic in Mossy Oak Break-Up Infinity*

D2C:	NIB $460	Ex $350	VG+ $255	Good $230	**LMP:** $492
C2C:	Mint $450	Ex $325	VG+ $230	Good $210	Fair $110
Trade-In:	Mint $330	Ex $275	VG+ $180	Good $165	Poor $60

870 EXPRESS COMBO REDBOOK CODE: RB-RE-S-870XCM

Vent rib barrel plus fully-rifled deer barrel in matte finish, modified Rem choke tube, twin action bars, receiver machined from solid billet of steel, fires 3" shells.

Production: *current (28" barrel discontinued)* **Gauge/Bore:** *12 ga., 20 ga.*
Action: *pump-action*
Barrel Length: 20", 26", 28" **Wt.:** *7.5 lbs.*
Sights: *front bead, rifle-type sights*
Capacity: *5*
Stock: *hardwood*

D2C:	NIB $570	Ex $450	VG+ $315	Good $285	**LMP:** $606
C2C:	Mint $550	Ex $400	VG+ $290	Good $260	Fair $135
Trade-In:	Mint $410	Ex $325	VG+ $230	Good $200	Poor $60

870 EXPRESS SHURSHOT SYNTHETIC CANTILEVER REDBOOK CODE: RB-RE-S-870XSC

Fully rifled barrel in standard Express finish, cantilever scope mount, ambidextrous ShurShot stock with sling swivel.

Production: *current* **Gauge/Bore:** *20 ga.*
Action: *pump-action*
Barrel Length: 18.5" **Wt.:** *N/A*
Sights: *none*
Capacity: *5*
Stock: *synthetic with thumbhole*

D2C:	NIB $570	Ex $450	VG+ $315	Good $285	**LMP:** $571
C2C:	Mint $550	Ex $400	VG+ $290	Good $260	Fair $135
Trade-In:	Mint $410	Ex $325	VG+ $230	Good $200	Poor $60

870 EXPRESS SHURSHOT SYNTHETIC TURKEY REDBOOK CODE: RB-RE-S-870XST

Vent rib barrel, ambidextrous ShurShot stock with sling swivel, standard Express finish on barrel and receiver, shoots 2.75" and 3" shells, Turkey extra-full Rem choke.

Production: *current* **Gauge/Bore:** *12 ga.*
Action: *pump-action*
Barrel Length: 21", 23" **Wt.:** *7.4 lbs., 7.8 lbs.*
Sights: *front bead*
Capacity: *5*
Stock: *synthetic in Mossy Oak Obsession with thumbhole*

D2C:	NIB $510	Ex $400	VG+ $285	Good $255	**LMP:** $536
C2C:	Mint $490	Ex $375	VG+ $260	Good $230	Fair $120
Trade-In:	Mint $370	Ex $300	VG+ $200	Good $180	Poor $60

REMINGTON

870 EXPRESS SUPER MAGNUM REDBOOK CODE: RB-RE-S-870XSM

Vent rib barrel in matte or walnut finish, Rem choke tube, receiver machined from a solid billet of steel, twin action bars, fires 2.75", 3" or 3.5" shells.

Production: *current* **Gauge/Bore:** *12 ga.*
Action: *pump-action*
Barrel Length: *28"* **Wt.:** *7.5 lbs.*
Sights: *front bead*
Capacity: *3, 4*
Stock: *walnut or synthetic*

D2C:	NIB $400	Ex $325	VG+ $220	Good $200	**LMP:** $469
C2C:	Mint $390	Ex $300	VG+ $200	Good $180	Fair $95
Trade-In:	Mint $290	Ex $225	VG+ $160	Good $140	Poor $60

870 EXPRESS SUPER MAGNUM COMBO REDBOOK CODE: RB-RE-S-870XMC

Vent rib barrel plus fully rifled deer barrel in matte finish, Rem choke tube, receiver machined from a solid billet of steel, twin action bars.

Production: *current* **Gauge/Bore:** *12 ga.*
Action: *pump-action*
Barrel Length: *20", 26"* **Wt.:** *7.3 lbs.*
Sights: *front bead, rifle-type sights*
Capacity: *3, 4*
Stock: *walnut*

D2C:	NIB $540	Ex $425	VG+ $300	Good $270	**LMP:** $629
C2C:	Mint $520	Ex $375	VG+ $270	Good $245	Fair $125
Trade-In:	Mint $390	Ex $325	VG+ $220	Good $190	Poor $60

870 EXPRESS SUPER MAGNUM TURKEY CAMO REDBOOK CODE: RB-RE-S-870XMT

Vent rib barrel in Mossy Oak Break-Up Infinity finish, Turkey extra-full Rem choke, receiver machined from a solid billet of steel, twin action bars, fires 2.75", 3" or 3.5" shells.

Production: *discontinued* **Gauge/Bore:** *12 ga.*
Action: *pump-action*
Barrel Length: *23"* **Wt.:** *7.3 lbs.*
Sights: *twin bead*
Capacity: *3, 4*
Stock: *synthetic with Mossy Oak Break-Up Infinity*

D2C:	NIB $480	Ex $375	VG+ $265	Good $240	
C2C:	Mint $470	Ex $350	VG+ $240	Good $220	Fair $115
Trade-In:	Mint $350	Ex $275	VG+ $190	Good $170	Poor $60

870 EXPRESS SUPER MAGNUM TURKEY/WATERFOWL REDBOOK CODE: RB-RE-S-870XTW

Vent rib barrel, Wingmaster HD Waterfowl and Turkey extra-full Rem chokes, Mossy Oak Bottomland camo finish, drilled and tapped receiver, SuperCell recoil pad, fires 2.75", 3" or 3.5" shells.

Production: *current* **Gauge/Bore:** *12 ga.*
Action: *pump-action*
Barrel Length: *20", 26"* **Wt.:** *7.25 lbs.*
Sights: *HiViz fiber optic*
Capacity: *3, 4*
Stock: *synthetic with Mossy Oak Bottomland*

D2C:	NIB $530	Ex $425	VG+ $295	Good $265	**LMP:** $629
C2C:	Mint $510	Ex $375	VG+ $270	Good $240	Fair $125
Trade-In:	Mint $380	Ex $300	VG+ $210	Good $190	Poor $60

REMINGTON

870 EXPRESS SUPER MAGNUM WATERFOWL CAMO REDBOOK CODE: RB-RE-S-870XMW

Vent rib barrel in Mossy Oak Deer Blind camo finish, Turkey extra-full Rem "Over-Decoys" choke, bolt design keeps cycle stroke equal for all shell lengths, supplied with sling.

Production: *28" current, 30" discontinued* **Gauge/Bore:** *12 ga.*
Action: *pump-action*
Barrel Length: *28", 30"* **Wt.:** *7.5 lbs., 7.6 lbs.*
Sights: *HiViz front bead*
Capacity: *3, 4*
Stock: *synthetic with Mossy Oak Duck Blind camo finish*

D2C:	NIB $600	Ex $475	VG+ $330	Good $300	**LMP: $629**
C2C:	Mint $580	Ex $425	VG+ $300	Good $270	Fair $140
Trade-In:	Mint $430	Ex $350	VG+ $240	Good $210	Poor $60

870 EXPRESS SYNTHETIC REDBOOK CODE: RB-RE-S-870XSN

Barrel in standard Express finish, improved cylinder choke, twin action bars, fires 2.75" and 3" shells.

Production: *current* **Gauge/Bore:** *12 ga.*
Action: *pump-action*
Barrel Length: *18"* **Wt.:** *7.3 lbs.*
Sights: *front bead*
Capacity: *5, 7*
Stock: *black synthetic*

D2C:	NIB $385	Ex $300	VG+ $215	Good $195	**LMP: $420**
C2C:	Mint $370	Ex $275	VG+ $200	Good $175	Fair $90
Trade-In:	Mint $280	Ex $225	VG+ $160	Good $135	Poor $60

870 EXPRESS SYNTHETIC DEER REDBOOK CODE: RB-RE-S-870XSD

Fully rifled barrel in Express black matte finish, receiver machined from a solid billet of steel, twin action bars, rubber recoil pad. Also available in model with hardwood finish.

Production: *current* **Gauge/Bore:** *12 ga.*
Action: *pump-action*
Barrel Length: *20"* **Wt.:** *7 lbs.*
Sights: *rifle-type sights*
Capacity: *5*
Stock: *hardwood or synthetic with Monte Carlo comb*

D2C:	NIB $410	Ex $325	VG+ $230	Good $205	**LMP: $463**
C2C:	Mint $400	Ex $300	VG+ $210	Good $185	Fair $95
Trade-In:	Mint $300	Ex $250	VG+ $160	Good $145	Poor $60

870 EXPRESS SYNTHETIC 7-ROUND REDBOOK CODE: RB-RE-S-870XS7

Fully rifled barrel in Express black matte finish, improved cylinder choke, one-piece magazine tube chambers six 2.75" or 3" shells.

Production: *current* **Gauge/Bore:** *12 ga., 20 ga.*
Action: *pump-action*
Barrel Length: *18.5"* **Wt.:** *6 lbs., 7.5 lbs.*
Sights: *front bead*
Capacity: *6*
Stock: *black synthetic*

D2C:	NIB $380	Ex $300	VG+ $210	Good $190	**LMP: $443**
C2C:	Mint $370	Ex $275	VG+ $190	Good $175	Fair $90
Trade-In:	Mint $270	Ex $225	VG+ $150	Good $135	Poor $60

870 EXPRESS TACTICAL   REDBOOK CODE: RB-RE-S-870TCT

Ported barrel, tactical Rem choke tube, Picatinny rail with XS Ghost Ring sight, drilled and tapped receiver, sling swivel studs, fires 2.75" or 3" shells.

Production: *current* **Gauge/Bore:** *12 ga.*
Action: *pump-action*
Barrel Length: *18.5"* **Wt.:** *7.5 lbs.*
Sights: *XS Ghost Ring Sight Rail with XS front blade*
Capacity: *7*
Stock: *black synthetic*

D2C:	NIB $550	Ex $425	VG+ $305	Good $275	LMP: $601
C2C:	Mint $530	Ex $400	VG+ $280	Good $250	Fair $130
Trade-In:	Mint $400	Ex $325	VG+ $220	Good $195	Poor $60

870 EXPRESS TACTICAL MAGPUL   REDBOOK CODE: RB-RE-S-870XTM

Barrel in weather-resistant Cerakote Flat Dark Earth finish, ported and extended choke, receiver machined from solid steel, one-piece magazine tube, spacer system, cheek risers for use with optics, MOE forend, SuperCell recoil pad.

Production: *current* **Gauge/Bore:** *12 ga.*
Action: *pump-action*
Barrel Length: *18.5"* **Wt.:** *7.5 lbs.*
Sights: *XS Ghost Ring, front XS white dot*
Capacity: *7*
Stock: *synthetic with Flat Dark Earth, adjustable Magpul SGA*

D2C:	NIB $770	Ex $600	VG+ $425	Good $385	LMP: $898
C2C:	Mint $740	Ex $550	VG+ $390	Good $350	Fair $180
Trade-In:	Mint $550	Ex $450	VG+ $310	Good $270	Poor $90

870 EXPRESS TACTICAL A-TACS CAMO   REDBOOK CODE: RB-RE-S-870TCC

Barrel in A-TACS camo finish, breaching choke, Picatinny rail with integral XS Ghost Ring sight, SpeedFeed IV pistol grip stock, drilled and tapped receiver, SuperCell recoil pad.

Production: *current* **Gauge/Bore:** *12 ga.*
Action: *pump-action*
Barrel Length: *18.5"* **Wt.:** *7.5 lbs.*
Sights: *XS Ghost Ring, front XS white dot*
Capacity: *7*
Stock: *SpeedFeed IV pistol grip with A-TACS camo*

D2C:	NIB $640	Ex $500	VG+ $355	Good $320	LMP: $720
C2C:	Mint $620	Ex $450	VG+ $320	Good $290	Fair $150
Trade-In:	Mint $460	Ex $375	VG+ $250	Good $225	Poor $90

870 EXPRESS TACTICAL GREY   REDBOOK CODE: RB-RE-S-870TCG

Barrel in gunmetal grey powder-coat finish, extended and ported tactical Rem choke, drilled and tapped receiver, sling swivels.

Production: *discontinued* **Gauge/Bore:** *12 ga.*
Action: *pump-action*
Barrel Length: *18.5"* **Wt.:** *7.5 lbs.*
Sights: *front bead*
Capacity: *7*
Stock: *black synthetic*

D2C:	NIB $515	Ex $400	VG+ $285	Good $260	
C2C:	Mint $500	Ex $375	VG+ $260	Good $235	Fair $120
Trade-In:	Mint $370	Ex $300	VG+ $210	Good $185	Poor $60

REMINGTON

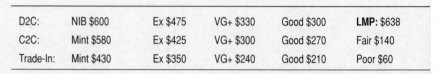

870 EXPRESS TACTICAL BLACKHAWK REDBOOK CODE: RB-RE-S-870XBH
Barrel in black oxide finish, 7-position adjustable stock, recoil reduction system, enhanced pistol grip, right or left-handed sling mount, drilled and tapped receiver, SuperCell recoil pad, fires 3" shells.

Production: *current* **Gauge/Bore:** *12 ga.*
Action: *pump-action*
Barrel Length: 18" **Wt.:** *7 lbs.*
Sights: *front bead*
Capacity: *7*
Stock: *adjustable synthetic with pistol grip*

D2C:	NIB $600	Ex $475	VG+ $330	Good $300	LMP: $638
C2C:	Mint $580	Ex $425	VG+ $300	Good $270	Fair $140
Trade-In:	Mint $430	Ex $350	VG+ $240	Good $210	Poor $60

870 TAC DESERT RECON REDBOOK CODE: RB-RE-S-870TDR
Barrel in olive drab powder-coat finish, extended and ported tactical Rem choke, 2-or 3-shot magazine extension, fires 2.75" or 3" shells.

Production: *discontinued* **Gauge/Bore:** *12 ga.*
Action: *pump-action*
Barrel Length: 18", 20" **Wt.:** *7.5 lbs., 7.6 lbs.*
Sights: *front bead*
Capacity: *7*
Stock: *synthetic with Tiger Stripe Products Digital Tiger Desert camo*

D2C:	NIB $650	Ex $500	VG+ $360	Good $325	
C2C:	Mint $630	Ex $450	VG+ $330	Good $295	Fair $150
Trade-In:	Mint $470	Ex $375	VG+ $260	Good $230	Poor $90

870 SPECIAL PURPOSE MARINE MAGNUM REDBOOK CODE: RB-RE-S-870MMG
Barrel in electroless nickel-plated finish, receiver machined from a solid billet of steel, twin action bars, includes padded Cordura and sling swivel studs.

Production: *current* **Gauge/Bore:** *12 ga.*
Action: *pump-action*
Barrel Length: 18" **Wt.:** *7.5 lbs.*
Sights: *front bead*
Capacity: *6*
Stock: *cut-checkered synthetic*

D2C:	NIB $760	Ex $600	VG+ $420	Good $380	LMP: $841
C2C:	Mint $730	Ex $525	VG+ $380	Good $345	Fair $175
Trade-In:	Mint $540	Ex $450	VG+ $300	Good $270	Poor $90

870 SPS SHURSHOT SYNTHETIC TURKEY REDBOOK CODE: RB-RE-S-870SST
Wingmaster HD extended Rem choke, receiver drilled and tapped for scope mounts, Realtree APG HD camo finish, sling swivel studs, 3 lb. competition-style trigger, fires 3.5" shells.

Production: *current* **Gauge/Bore:** *12 ga.*
Action: *pump-action*
Barrel Length: 23" **Wt.:** *7.5 lbs.*
Sights: *TruGlo fiber optic, rifle-type front sight*
Capacity: *5*
Stock: *synthetic thumbhole with pistol grip and Realtree APG HD camo*

D2C:	NIB $580	Ex $450	VG+ $320	Good $290	LMP: $681
C2C:	Mint $560	Ex $425	VG+ $290	Good $265	Fair $135
Trade-In:	Mint $420	Ex $325	VG+ $230	Good $205	Poor $60

870 SPS SUPER MAGNUM TURKEY/PREDATOR REDBOOK CODE: RB-RE-S-870SMT

Mossy Oak Obsession finish, ShurShot pistol grip stock, Wingmaster HD Turkey/Predator Rem Choke, TruGlo 30mm red/green dot scope, drilled and tapped receiver with Weaver rail, 1:35" Parabolic Ultragon rifling, accepts 2.75" and 3" 1 slugs. Includes padded quick-attach sling.

Production: *current* **Gauge/Bore:** *12 ga.*
Action: *pump-action*
Barrel Length: 20" **Wt.:** *7.25 lbs.*
Sights: *none*
Capacity: *5*
Stock: *synthetic thumbhole with Mossy Oak Obsession camo*

D2C:	NIB $660	Ex $525	VG+ $365	Good $330	LMP: $710
C2C:	Mint $640	Ex $475	VG+ $330	Good $300	Fair $155
Trade-In:	Mint $470	Ex $375	VG+ $260	Good $235	Poor $90

870 SPS SHURSHOT SYNTHETIC SUPER SLUG REDBOOK CODE: RB-RE-S-870SUS

Fully-rifled and extra-heavy 1" diameter barrel with longitudinal flutes, ShurShot pistol grip stock, Wingmaster HD Turkey/Predator Rem Choke, SuperCell recoil pad, drilled and tapped receiver with Weaver rail included, Parabolic Ultragon rifling grooves with 1:35" twist rate, accepts 2.75" or 3" slugs.

Production: *current* **Gauge/Bore:** *12 ga.*
Action: *pump-action*
Barrel Length: 25.5" **Wt.:** *7.9 lbs.*
Sights: *none*
Capacity: *5*
Stock: *synthetic thumbhole*

D2C:	NIB $680	Ex $525	VG+ $375	Good $340	LMP: $829
C2C:	Mint $660	Ex $475	VG+ $340	Good $310	Fair $160
Trade-In:	Mint $490	Ex $400	VG+ $270	Good $240	Poor $90

Photo Courtesy of Rock Island Auction Company

870 TC TRAP REDBOOK CODE: RB-RE-S-870TCT

Satin finish on walnut forend, vent rib barrel, Rem-Choke tubes included, screw in choke tubes.

Production: *1951–discontinued* **Gauge/Bore:** *12 ga.*
Action: *pump-action*
Barrel Length: 28", 30" **Wt.:** *N/A*
Sights: *bead front*
Capacity: *5*
Stock: *walnut*

D2C:	NIB $600	Ex $475	VG+ $330	Good $300	
C2C:	Mint $580	Ex $425	VG+ $300	Good $270	Fair $140
Trade-In:	Mint $430	Ex $350	VG+ $240	Good $210	Poor $60

878 "AUTOMASTER" REDBOOK CODE: RB-RE-S-878AUT

Gas piston operated, quick-change barrels, takedown style, hammerless, solid-breech barrel, cross-bolt safety, checkering on pistol grip and forend, 14" length of pull.

Production: *1959–1963* **Gauge/Bore:** *12 ga.*
Action: *semi-auto*
Barrel Length: 26", 28", 30" **Wt.:** *~7 lbs.*
Sights: *none*
Capacity: *3*
Stock: *walnut*

D2C:	NIB $290	Ex $225	VG+ $160	Good $145	
C2C:	Mint $280	Ex $225	VG+ $150	Good $135	Fair $70
Trade-In:	Mint $210	Ex $175	VG+ $120	Good $105	Poor $30

REMINGTON

887 NITRO MAG REDBOOK CODE: RB-RE-S-887NMX

Cold hammer-forged barrel with solid, ArmorLokt rustproof finish (on barrel and receiver), modified Rem choke, built-in sling swivel studs, receiver machined from solid steel, stock with specially contoured grip panels, fires 2.75", 3", or 3.5" shells. Available with 28" solid stepped rib barrel and Rem choke.

Production: *2009–current* **Gauge/Bore:** *12 ga.*
Action: *pump-action*
Barrel Length: 26", 28" **Wt.:** *7.4 lbs.*
Sights: *HiViz fiber optic*
Capacity: *5*
Stock: *synthetic*

D2C:	NIB $410	Ex $325	VG+ $230	Good $205	**LMP:** $445
C2C:	Mint $400	Ex $300	VG+ $210	Good $185	Fair $95
Trade-In:	Mint $300	Ex $250	VG+ $160	Good $145	Poor $60

887 NITRO MAG WATERFOWL CAMO REDBOOK CODE: RB-RE-S-887NMW

Cold hammer-forged, solid rib barrel, ArmorLokt rustproof finish (on barrel and receiver), Waterfowl modified Rem choke, built-in sling swivel studs, receiver machined from solid steel, twin steel action bars, stock with specially contoured grip panels, fires 2.75", 3", or 3.5" shells.

Production: *2009–current* **Gauge/Bore:** *12 ga.*
Action: *pump-action*
Barrel Length: 28" **Wt.:** *7.5 lbs.*
Sights: *HiViz fiber optic*
Capacity: *5*
Stock: *synthetic with Advantage Max-4 HD camo*

D2C:	NIB $510	Ex $400	VG+ $285	Good $255	**LMP:** $598
C2C:	Mint $490	Ex $375	VG+ $260	Good $230	Fair $120
Trade-In:	Mint $370	Ex $300	VG+ $200	Good $180	Poor $60

887 NITRO MAG CAMO COMBO REDBOOK CODE: RB-RE-S-887NMC

Cold hammer-forged, solid rib Waterfowl barrel, ArmorLokt rustproof finish, built-in sling swivel studs, receiver machined from solid steel, twin steel action bars, stock with specially contoured grip panels, fires 2.75", 3", or 3.5" shells. Also included is a Turkey barrel with HiViz fiber optic sight, Waterfowl extended and Turkey super-full Rem choke.

Production: *2009–current* **Gauge/Bore:** *12 ga.*
Action: *pump-action*
Barrel Length: 22", 28" **Wt.:** *7.5 lbs.*
Sights: *HiViz front, HiViz fiber optic*
Capacity: *5*
Stock: *synthetic with Mossy Oak Break-Up Infinity*

D2C:	NIB $680	Ex $525	VG+ $375	Good $340	**LMP:** $728
C2C:	Mint $660	Ex $475	VG+ $340	Good $310	Fair $160
Trade-In:	Mint $490	Ex $400	VG+ $270	Good $240	Poor $90

887 NITRO MAG TACTICAL REDBOOK CODE: RB-RE-S-887NMT

Cold hammer-forged, solid stepped rib barrel in matte black, ArmorLokt rustproof finish, ported and extended tactical Rem choke, built-in sling swivel studs, solid-steel-machined receiver, barrel clamp with integral Picatinny rails, twin steel action bars, stock with specially contoured grip panels, fires 2.75", 3", or 3.5" shells.

Production: *2010–current* **Gauge/Bore:** *12 ga.*
Action: *pump-action*
Barrel Length: 18.5" **Wt.:** *6.875 lbs.*
Sights: *HiViz front*
Capacity: *7*
Stock: *synthetic*

D2C:	NIB $490	Ex $375	VG+ $270	Good $245	**LMP:** $534
C2C:	Mint $480	Ex $350	VG+ $250	Good $225	Fair $115
Trade-In:	Mint $350	Ex $275	VG+ $200	Good $175	Poor $60

REMINGTON

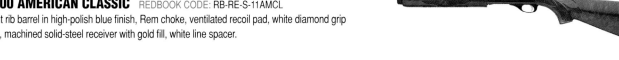

1100 AMERICAN CLASSIC REDBOOK CODE: RB-RE-S-11AMCL

Vent rib barrel in high-polish blue finish, Rem choke, ventilated recoil pad, white diamond grip cap, machined solid-steel receiver with gold fill, white line spacer.

Production: *current* **Gauge/Bore:** *12 ga., 20 ga., 28 ga.*
Action: *semi-auto*
Barrel Length: 25", 26", 28" **Wt.:** *6.5 lbs., 7 lbs., 8 lbs.*
Sights: *front bead*
Capacity: *5*
Stock: *American walnut*

D2C:	NIB $1,480	Ex $1,125	VG+ $815	Good $740	LMP: $1,649
C2C:	Mint $1,430	Ex $1,025	VG+ $740	Good $670	Fair $345
Trade-In:	Mint $1,060	Ex $850	VG+ $580	Good $520	Poor $150

1100 CLASSIC TRAP REDBOOK CODE: RB-RE-S-11CLST

Light contour vent rib barrel in high-polish blue finish, Rem choke, gold-embellished receiver, competition-style stock with 2" drop at heel, 14.5" length of pull, 2 3/4" chamber.

Production: *current* **Gauge/Bore:** *12 ga.*
Action: *semi-auto*
Barrel Length: 30" **Wt.:** *8.25 lbs.*
Sights: *ivory front sight, steel mid bead*
Capacity: *5*
Stock: *cut-checkered American walnut*

D2C:	NIB $1,120	Ex $875	VG+ $620	Good $560	LMP: $1,308
C2C:	Mint $1,080	Ex $775	VG+ $560	Good $505	Fair $260
Trade-In:	Mint $800	Ex $650	VG+ $440	Good $395	Poor $120

1100 COMPETITION REDBOOK CODE: RB-RE-S-11CMPX

Overbored vent rib barrel in blue finish, ProBore choke, receiver and internal parts in nickel Teflon finish, fires 2.75" shells.

Production: *discontinued* **Gauge/Bore:** *12 ga.*
Action: *semi-auto*
Barrel Length: 30" **Wt.:** *8.1 lbs.*
Sights: *ivory front sight, steel mid bead*
Capacity: *5*
Stock: *American walnut*

D2C:	NIB $1,060	Ex $825	VG+ $585	Good $530	
C2C:	Mint $1,020	Ex $750	VG+ $530	Good $480	Fair $245
Trade-In:	Mint $760	Ex $600	VG+ $420	Good $375	Poor $120

1100 COMPETITION SYNTHETIC REDBOOK CODE: RB-RE-S-11CMPS

Vent rib barrel in high-gloss blue finish, ProBore choke, receiver & internal parts in nickel Teflon finish, SuperCell recoil pad, stock and forend with carbon fiber appearance, fires 2.75" shells.

Production: *current* **Gauge/Bore:** *12 ga.*
Action: *semi-auto*
Barrel Length: 30" **Wt.:** *8 lbs.*
Sights: *ivory front sight, steel mid bead*
Capacity: *5*
Stock: *synthetic with adjustable comb*

D2C:	NIB $1,150	Ex $875	VG+ $635	Good $575	LMP: $1,279
C2C:	Mint $1,110	Ex $800	VG+ $580	Good $520	Fair $265
Trade-In:	Mint $820	Ex $650	VG+ $450	Good $405	Poor $120

REMINGTON

1100 SPORTING SERIES REDBOOK CODE: RB-RE-S-11SPTG

Vent rib barrel in high-gloss blue finish, set of 4 Rem interchangeable choke tubes. 12 ga. and 20 ga. models have contoured light target barrels. Add $59 for 28 ga. and .410 models with 27" barrels.

Production: *current* **Gauge/Bore:** *12 ga., 20 ga., 28 ga., .410*
Action: *semi-auto*
Barrel Length: 27," 28" **Wt.:** *6.5 lbs., 7 lbs., 8 lbs.*
Sights: *bead*
Capacity: *5*
Stock: *American walnut*

D2C:	NIB $1,110	Ex $850	VG+ $615	Good $555	**LMP:** $1,230
C2C:	Mint $1,070	Ex $775	VG+ $560	Good $500	Fair $260
Trade-In:	Mint $790	Ex $625	VG+ $440	Good $390	Poor $120

1100 PREMIER SPORTING SERIES REDBOOK CODE: RB-RE-S-11PRSP

Vent rib barrel in blue finish, set of Rem interchangeable choke tubes, embellished nickel receiver, 12 ga. and 20 ga. models have contoured light target barrels. Hard case is also included.

Production: *discontinued* **Gauge/Bore:** *12 ga., 20 ga., 28 ga., .410*
Action: *semi-auto*
Barrel Length: 27," 28" **Wt.:** *6.25 lbs., 7 lbs., 8 lbs.*
Sights: *front bead*
Capacity: *5*
Stock: *American walnut*

D2C:	NIB $1,370	Ex $1,050	VG+ $755	Good $685	
C2C:	Mint $1,320	Ex $950	VG+ $690	Good $620	Fair $320
Trade-In:	Mint $980	Ex $775	VG+ $540	Good $480	Poor $150

1100 TAC 4 REDBOOK CODE: RB-RE-S-11TAC4

Vent rib barrel in matte black, Rem choke, sling swivel studs, 4-shot tube extension, fully adjustable sight, receiver drilled and tapped for scope mounts, fires 2.75" shells.

Production: *current* **Gauge/Bore:** *12 ga.*
Action: *semi-auto*
Barrel Length: 22" **Wt.:** *7.75 lbs.*
Sights: *front bead*
Capacity: *9*
Stock: *synthetic*

D2C:	NIB $820	Ex $625	VG+ $455	Good $410	**LMP:** $1,015
C2C:	Mint $790	Ex $575	VG+ $410	Good $370	Fair $190
Trade-In:	Mint $590	Ex $475	VG+ $320	Good $290	Poor $90

1100 G3 REDBOOK CODE: RB-RE-S-1100G3

3" magnum chamber, Teflon coated internal parts, PVD coated receiver, checkering on pistol grip and forearm, 5 ProBore choke tubes, R3 recoil pad.

Production: *2006–discontinued* **Gauge/Bore:** *12 ga., 20 ga.*
Action: *semi-auto*
Barrel Length: 26", 28" **Wt.:** *N/A*
Sights: *front bead*
Capacity: *5*
Stock: *American walnut w/ carbon reinforcements*

D2C:	NIB $930	Ex $725	VG+ $515	Good $465	
C2C:	Mint $900	Ex $650	VG+ $470	Good $420	Fair $215
Trade-In:	Mint $670	Ex $525	VG+ $370	Good $330	Poor $120

11-87 SPORTSMAN FIELD   REDBOOK CODE: RB-RE-S-1187SF

Vent rib barrel in blue finish, modified Rem choke, solid-steel-machined receiver, nickel-plated bolt, gold trigger.

Production: *current* **Gauge/Bore:** *12 ga., 20 ga.*
Action: *semi-auto*
Barrel Length: 26", 28" **Wt.:** *7.25 lbs., 8.25 lbs.*
Sights: *dual bead*
Capacity: *5*
Stock: *fleur-di-lis-checkered walnut*

D2C:	NIB $720	Ex $550	VG+ $400	Good $360	LMP: $845
C2C:	Mint $700	Ex $500	VG+ $360	Good $325	Fair $170
Trade-In:	Mint $520	Ex $425	VG+ $290	Good $255	Poor $90

11-87 SPORTSMAN CAMO   REDBOOK CODE: RB-RE-S-1187SC

Vent rib barrel, Mossy Oak New Break-Up camo finish, modified Rem choke, receiver machined from solid steel, sling swivel studs.
Subtract $111 for matte black finish.

Production: *current* **Gauge/Bore:** *12 ga., 20 ga.*
Action: *semi-auto*
Barrel Length: 26", 28" **Wt.:** *7.5 lbs., 7.75 lbs., 8.25 lbs.*
Sights: *bead*
Capacity: *5*
Stock: *synthetic, Mossy Oak New Break-Up*

D2C:	NIB $720	Ex $550	VG+ $400	Good $360	LMP: $905
C2C:	Mint $700	Ex $500	VG+ $360	Good $325	Fair $170
Trade-In:	Mint $520	Ex $425	VG+ $290	Good $255	Poor $90

11-87 SPORTSMAN SYNTHETIC DEER   REDBOOK CODE: RB-RE-S-1187SD

Fully rifled barrel in blue finish, receiver machined from solid steel, cantilever for scope mounting, sling swivels on stock and forend cap.

Production: *current* **Gauge/Bore:** *12 ga., 20 ga.*
Action: *semi-auto*
Barrel Length: 21" **Wt.:** *7.5 lbs., 8.5 lbs.*
Sights: *none*
Capacity: *5*
Stock: *synthetic*

D2C:	NIB $810	Ex $625	VG+ $450	Good $405	LMP: $929
C2C:	Mint $780	Ex $575	VG+ $410	Good $365	Fair $190
Trade-In:	Mint $580	Ex $475	VG+ $320	Good $285	Poor $90

11-87 SPORTSMAN SHURSHOT CAMO CANTILEVER   REDBOOK CODE: RB-RE-S-1187SS

Fully-rifled barrel in matte black metal finish, ShurShot pistol grip stock, Realtree Hardwoods HD camo, drilled and
tapped receiver machined from solid steel, Weaver rail scope mount, SuperCell recoil pad, front and rear sling swivels.

Production: *current* **Gauge/Bore:** *12 ga.*
Action: *semi-auto*
Barrel Length: 23" **Wt.:** *8 lbs.*
Sights: *none*
Capacity: *5*
Stock: *synthetic with Realtree Hardwoods HD camo*

D2C:	NIB $930	Ex $725	VG+ $515	Good $465	LMP: $1,012
C2C:	Mint $900	Ex $650	VG+ $470	Good $420	Fair $215
Trade-In:	Mint $670	Ex $525	VG+ $370	Good $330	Poor $120

REMINGTON

REMINGTON

11-87 PREMIER 20-GAUGE   REDBOOK CODE: RB-RE-S-PRE20G
Small frame receiver, vent rib barrel, barrels built to receive Rem-Chokes, gloss finish on walnut, checkering on pistol grip and forearm.

Production: *1999–2006* **Gauge/Bore:** *20 ga.*
Action: *semi-auto*
Barrel Length: *26", 28"* **Wt.:** *~7 lbs.*
Sights: *twin bead*
Capacity: *5*
Stock: *walnut*

D2C:	NIB $930	Ex $725	VG+ $515	Good $465	
C2C:	Mint $900	Ex $650	VG+ $470	Good $420	Fair $215
Trade-In:	Mint $670	Ex $525	VG+ $370	Good $330	Poor $120

11-87 UPLAND SPECIAL   REDBOOK CODE: RB-RE-S-UPLAND
3" chamber, straight grip, standard choke tubes, satin finish on walnut.

Production: *2000–2006* **Gauge/Bore:** *12 ga., 20 ga.*
Action: *semi-auto*
Barrel Length: *23"* **Wt.:** *6.5–7.3 lbs.*
Sights: *twin bead*
Capacity: *5*
Stock: *walnut*

D2C:	NIB $790	Ex $625	VG+ $435	Good $395	
C2C:	Mint $760	Ex $550	VG+ $400	Good $360	Fair $185
Trade-In:	Mint $570	Ex $450	VG+ $310	Good $280	Poor $90

11-87 PREMIER SPORTING CLAYS   REDBOOK CODE: RB-RE-S-PRESPC
Rubber buttpad, matte blue finish on receiver top, barrel, and rib. Vent rib, 5 included RemChoke tubes.

Production: *1992–1999* **Gauge/Bore:** *12 ga.*
Action: *semi-auto*
Barrel Length: *26", 28"* **Wt.:** *N/A*
Sights: *stainless steel mid bead*
Capacity: *5*
Stock: *target style walnut*

D2C:	NIB $780	Ex $600	VG+ $430	Good $390	
C2C:	Mint $750	Ex $550	VG+ $390	Good $355	Fair $180
Trade-In:	Mint $560	Ex $450	VG+ $310	Good $275	Poor $90

11-87 PREMIER TRAP   REDBOOK CODE: RB-RE-S-PRTRAP
Right or left-handed models, 2.75" chamber, vent rib overbored barrel, RemTrap choke tubes, only takes 12 ga. target loads.

Production: *1987–1998* **Gauge/Bore:** *12 ga.*
Action: *semi-auto*
Barrel Length: *30"* **Wt.:** *8.3 lbs.*
Sights: *bead front*
Capacity: *5*
Stock: *deluxe walnut or Monte Carlo*

D2C:	NIB $820	Ex $625	VG+ $455	Good $410	
C2C:	Mint $790	Ex $575	VG+ $410	Good $370	Fair $190
Trade-In:	Mint $590	Ex $475	VG+ $320	Good $290	Poor $90

11-87 SPS BIG GAME CAMO REDBOOK CODE: RB-RE-S-SPSBGC
Plain barrel, straight stock, camo finish.

Production: *1992–1996* **Gauge/Bore:** *12 ga.*
Action: *semi-auto*
Barrel Length: 21" **Wt.:** *N/A*
Sights: *rifle sight*
Capacity: *5*
Stock: *brown camo synthetic*

D2C:	NIB $560	Ex $450	VG+ $310	Good $280	
C2C:	Mint $540	Ex $400	VG+ $280	Good $255	Fair $130
Trade-In:	Mint $400	Ex $325	VG+ $220	Good $200	Poor $60

11-87 SPS-T CAMO REDBOOK CODE: RB-RE-S-SPSTCA
Vent rib barrel, IC and Turkey Super Full RemChoke tubes.

Production: *1993–2000* **Gauge/Bore:** *12 ga.*
Action: *semi-auto*
Barrel Length: 21" **Wt.:** *N/A*
Sights: *HiViz fiber optic*
Capacity: *5*
Stock: *synthetic camo*

D2C:	NIB $610	Ex $475	VG+ $340	Good $305	
C2C:	Mint $590	Ex $425	VG+ $310	Good $275	Fair $145
Trade-In:	Mint $440	Ex $350	VG+ $240	Good $215	Poor $90

11-87 SPECIAL PURPOSE SYNTHETIC REDBOOK CODE: RB-RE-S-SPSSYN
Vent rib barrel, comes with IC, Modified, and Full RemChoke tubes. Black matte metal finishing, camouflage version available.

Production: *1991–2007* **Gauge/Bore:** *12 ga.*
Action: *semi-auto*
Barrel Length: 26", 28" **Wt.:** *N/A*
Sights: *bead front*
Capacity: *5*
Stock: *black synthetic*

D2C:	NIB $643	Ex $500	VG+ $355	Good $325	
C2C:	Mint $620	Ex $450	VG+ $330	Good $290	Fair $150
Trade-In:	Mint $460	Ex $375	VG+ $260	Good $230	Poor $90

11-87 SPS SUPER MAG REDBOOK CODE: RB-RE-S-SPSMAG
Available in camo as well, 3.5" magnum chamber.

Production: *2000–2007* **Gauge/Bore:** *12 ga.*
Action: *semi-auto*
Barrel Length: 26", 28" **Wt.:** *8.3 lbs.*
Sights: *bead front*
Capacity: *5*
Stock: *black synthetic*

D2C:	NIB $675	Ex $525	VG+ $375	Good $340	
C2C:	Mint $650	Ex $475	VG+ $340	Good $305	Fair $160
Trade-In:	Mint $480	Ex $400	VG+ $270	Good $240	Poor $90

REMINGTON

11-87 SPS-T SUPER MAGNUM REDBOOK CODE: RB-RE-S-SUPMAG
Monte Carlo comb, 3.5" chamber, choke tubes included.

Production: *2002–2007* **Gauge/Bore:** *12 ga.*
Action: *semi-auto*
Barrel Length: 23" **Wt.:** ~8 lbs.
Sights: *iron*
Capacity: 5
Stock: *Mossy Oak Obsession camouflage*

D2C:	NIB $931	Ex $725	VG+ $515	Good $470	
C2C:	Mint $900	Ex $650	VG+ $470	Good $420	Fair $215
Trade-In:	Mint $670	Ex $525	VG+ $370	Good $330	Poor $120

VERSA MAX SYNTHETIC REDBOOK CODE: RB-RE-S-VSMXSN
Cold hammer-forged vent rib barrel in TriNyte finish, internal components plated in nickel Teflon, ProBore flush-mount set (5), drilled and tapped anodized aluminum receiver, SuperCell recoil pad, fires 2.75", 3" or 3.5" shells. Also included are stock adjustment plates and Versaport gas system to regulate cycling pressure. Available in left-hand model.

Production: *current* **Gauge/Bore:** *12 ga.*
Action: *semi-auto*
Barrel Length: 26", 28" **Wt.:** 7.7 lbs.
Sights: *HiViz fiber optic*
Capacity: 3, 4
Stock: *synthetic*

D2C:	NIB $1,150	Ex $875	VG+ $635	Good $575	LMP: $1,427
C2C:	Mint $1,110	Ex $800	VG+ $580	Good $520	Fair $265
Trade-In:	Mint $820	Ex $650	VG+ $450	Good $405	Poor $120

VERSA MAX SPORTSMAN REDBOOK CODE: RB-RE-S-VSMXSP
Cold hammer-forged vent rib barrel in black oxide finish, ProBore extended full choke, anodized aluminum receiver, self-cleaning pistons, SuperCell recoil pad, fires 2.75", 3" or 3.5" shells. Versaport gas system regulates cycling pressure. Also available in 22" barrel option with ProBore Wingmaster Turkey extended full choke. Available with Mossy Oak Obsession camo upgrade.

Production: *current* **Gauge/Bore:** *12 ga.*
Action: *semi-auto*
Barrel Length: 22", 26", 28" **Wt.:** N/A
Sights: *ivory front sight, steel mid bead*
Capacity: 3, 4
Stock: *synthetic, Mossy Oak Obsession*

D2C:	NIB $940	Ex $725	VG+ $520	Good $470	LMP: $1,045
C2C:	Mint $910	Ex $650	VG+ $470	Good $425	Fair $220
Trade-In:	Mint $670	Ex $550	VG+ $370	Good $330	Poor $120

VERSA MAX WOOD TECH REDBOOK CODE: RB-RE-S-VSMXWT
Vent rib barrel in TriNyte finish, ProBore flush-mount choke set (4), drilled and tapped aluminum receiver in matte black, enlarged trigger guard opening, SuperCell recoil pad, fires 2.75", 3" or 3.5" shells. Also included are three comb inserts and Versaport gas system to regulate cycling pressure.

Production: *2014–current* **Gauge/Bore:** *12 ga.*
Action: *semi-auto*
Barrel Length: 28" **Wt.:** 7.75 lbs.
Sights: *HiViz fiber optic*
Capacity: 3, 4
Stock: *Wood Tech synthetic*

D2C:	NIB $1,320	Ex $1,025	VG+ $730	Good $660	LMP: $1,630
C2C:	Mint $1,270	Ex $925	VG+ $660	Good $595	Fair $305
Trade-In:	Mint $940	Ex $750	VG+ $520	Good $465	Poor $150

REMINGTON

VERSA MAX WATERFOWL, MOSSY OAK DUCK BLIND CAMO   REDBOOK CODE: RB-RE-S-VSMXWF

Cold hammer-forged vent rib barrel, nickel Teflon-plated internal components, Mossy Oak Duck Blind camo finish, ProBore extended choke set (4), drilled and tapped aluminum receiver, enlarged trigger guard opening, SuperCell recoil pad, fires 2.75", 3" or 3.5" shells. Also included are three comb inserts and Versaport gas system to regulate cycling pressure. Also available in left-handed model.

Production: *current* **Gauge/Bore:** *12 ga.*

Action: *semi-auto*

Barrel Length: *28"* **Wt.:** *7.7 lbs.*

Sights: *HiViz fiber optic*

Capacity: *3, 4*

Stock: *synthetic*

D2C:	NIB $1,360	Ex $1,050	VG+ $750	Good $680	**LMP:** $1,630
C2C:	Mint $1,310	Ex $950	VG+ $680	Good $615	Fair $315
Trade-In:	Mint $970	Ex $775	VG+ $540	Good $480	Poor $150

VERSA MAX WATERFOWL PRO   REDBOOK CODE: RB-RE-S-VSMXWP

Vent rib barrel, nickel Teflon-plated internal components, Mossy Oak Blades camo finish, ProBore extended choke set (4), drilled and tapped aluminum receiver, SuperCell recoil pad, sling swivel studs, enlarged bolt release button and bolt handle, fires 2.75", 3" or 3.5" shells.

Production: *2014–current* **Gauge/Bore:** *12 ga.*

Action: *semi-auto*

Barrel Length: *28"* **Wt.:** *7.75 lbs.*

Sights: *HiViz fiber optic*

Capacity: *3, 4*

Stock: *Realtree synthetic*

D2C:	NIB $1,470	Ex $1,125	VG+ $810	Good $735	**LMP:** $1,730
C2C:	Mint $1,420	Ex $1,025	VG+ $740	Good $665	Fair $340
Trade-In:	Mint $1,050	Ex $825	VG+ $580	Good $515	Poor $150

VERSA MAX AP HD CAMO   REDBOOK CODE: RB-RE-S-VSMXAP

Vent rib barrel, nickel Teflon-plated internal components, Realtree AP HD camo finish, ProBore extended choke set (4), drilled and tapped aluminum receiver, SuperCell recoil pad, stock adjustment plates, fires 2.75", 3" or 3.5" shells.

Production: *current* **Gauge/Bore:** *12 ga.*

Action: *semi-auto*

Barrel Length: *26"* **Wt.:** *7.7 lbs.*

Sights: *HiViz fiber optic*

Capacity: *3, 4*

Stock: *synthetic with Realtree AP HD camo finish*

D2C:	NIB $1,210	Ex $925	VG+ $670	Good $605	**LMP:** $1,630
C2C:	Mint $1,170	Ex $850	VG+ $610	Good $545	Fair $280
Trade-In:	Mint $860	Ex $700	VG+ $480	Good $425	Poor $150

VERSA MAX TACTICAL   REDBOOK CODE: RB-RE-S-VSMXTX

Vent rib barrel in matte black finish, ProBore choke system with IC and tactical extended choke tubes, matte black anodized aluminum receiver, Picatinny rail and barrel clamp, SuperCell recoil pad, extended bolt handle and bolt release button, fires 3" shells.

Production: *2014–current* **Gauge/Bore:** *12 ga.*

Action: *semi-auto*

Barrel Length: *22"* **Wt.:** *7.75 lbs.*

Sights: *HiViz front*

Capacity: *9*

Stock: *synthetic*

D2C:	NIB $1,130	Ex $875	VG+ $625	Good $565	**LMP:** $1,427
C2C:	Mint $1,090	Ex $800	VG+ $570	Good $510	Fair $260
Trade-In:	Mint $810	Ex $650	VG+ $450	Good $400	Poor $120

VERSA MAX COMPETITION TACTICAL   REDBOOK CODE: RB-RE-S-VSMXCT

Vent rib barrel in matte black finish, ProBore choke set (5), aluminum receiver in green Cerakote finish, Picatinny rail and barrel clamp, carbon fibertwo-shot extension, SuperCell recoil pad, oversized controls, enlarged loading port, fires 2.75" or 3" shells. Also includes Versaport gas system to regulate cycling pressure.

Production: *2014–current* **Gauge/Bore:** *12 ga.*
Action: *semi-auto*
Barrel Length: 22" **Wt.:** *8 lbs.*
Sights: *fiber optic front, XS Express rear*
Capacity: *9, 11*
Stock: *synthetic*

D2C:	NIB $1,550	Ex $1,200	VG+ $855	Good $775	**LMP:** $1,699
C2C:	Mint $1,490	Ex $1,075	VG+ $780	Good $700	Fair $360
Trade-In:	Mint $1,110	Ex $875	VG+ $610	Good $545	Poor $180

Photo Courtesy of Rock Island Auction Company

MODEL 1882   REDBOOK CODE: RB-RE-S-1882XX

Damascus or steel barrel, blue case-hardened barrel, checkered pistol-grip, hard rubber buttplate, optional engraving. Models with higher grading can command higher premiums. Pricing here reflects the Model 1882 Grade I.

Production: *1882–1889* **Gauge/Bore:** *10 ga., 12 ga.*
Action: *SxS*
Barrel Length: 28", 30" **Wt.:** *N/A*
Sights: *none*
Capacity: *2*
Stock: *hardwood*

D2C:	NIB $1,850	Ex $1,425	VG+ $1,020	Good $925	
C2C:	Mint $1,780	Ex $1,300	VG+ $930	Good $835	Fair $430
Trade-In:	Mint $1,320	Ex $1,050	VG+ $730	Good $650	Poor $210

MODEL 1894 HAMMERLESS   REDBOOK CODE: RB-RE-S-1894HA

Fluid steel or Damascus barrel, blue case-hardened barrel, checkered pistol-grip. Fluid steel barrels add 25%. 10 ga. and 16 ga. bring higher premium due to scarcity. Engraved models should be priced individually due to their variations. Standard AE model pictured here, no engraving.

Photo Courtesy of Rock Island Auction Company

Production: *1894–1910* **Gauge/Bore:** *10 ga., 12 ga., 16 ga.*
Action: *SxS*
Barrel Length: 26"–30" **Wt.:** *N/A*
Sights: *none*
Capacity: *2*
Stock: *hardwood*

D2C:	NIB $1,395	Ex $1,075	VG+ $770	Good $700	
C2C:	Mint $1,340	Ex $975	VG+ $700	Good $630	Fair $325
Trade-In:	Mint $1,000	Ex $800	VG+ $550	Good $490	Poor $150

Photo Courtesy of Rock Island Auction Company

MODEL 1900   REDBOOK CODE: RB-RE-S-1900HA

Steel or Damascus barrel, snap forearm, pistol grip stock, case-hardened receiver, no engraving originally offered with this model. Model was made a step below the 1894 version to compete with lower priced firearms on the market.

Production: *1900–1910* **Gauge/Bore:** *12 ga., 16 ga.*
Action: *SxS*
Barrel Length: 26"–32" **Wt.:** *N/A*
Sights: *none*
Capacity: *2*
Stock: *hardwood*

D2C:	NIB $1,350	Ex $1,050	VG+ $745	Good $675	
C2C:	Mint $1,300	Ex $950	VG+ $680	Good $610	Fair $315
Trade-In:	Mint $960	Ex $775	VG+ $530	Good $475	Poor $150

*Photo Courtesy of
Rock Island Auction Company*

10A STANDARD   REDBOOK CODE: RB-RE-S-10ASTD

Takedown style, no checkering, various chokes, blue metal finishing. Pricing is for the standard/field grade model. Pricing will vary for models 10B-10F which have varying levels of engraving and wood quality.

Production: *1907–1929* **Gauge/Bore:** *12 ga., 16 ga., 20 ga.*

Action: *pump-action*

Barrel Length: 26"–32" **Wt.:** *N/A*

Sights: *bead front*

Capacity: *6*

Stock: *walnut*

D2C:	NIB $420	Ex $325	VG+ $235	Good $210	
C2C:	Mint $410	Ex $300	VG+ $210	Good $190	Fair $100
Trade-In:	Mint $300	Ex $250	VG+ $170	Good $150	Poor $60

*Photo Courtesy of
Rock Island Auction Company*

MODEL 11   REDBOOK CODE: RB-RE-S-MODE11

Blue barrel, checkering on walnut, for solid or vented rib add additional cost. Available in 11B Special with engraving, 11D Tournament, 11E Expert (pictured here), 11F premier with heavy engraving, and 11R riot with a 20" barrel. Variations of this model will command different premiums. Pricing is shown for Model 11A Standard grade.

Production: *1905–1947* **Gauge/Bore:** *12 ga., 16 ga., 20 ga.*

Action: *semi-auto*

Barrel Length: 26"–32" **Wt.:** *N/A*

Sights: *bead front*

Capacity: *5*

Stock: *walnut*

D2C:	NIB $800	Ex $625	VG+ $440	Good $400	
C2C:	Mint $770	Ex $575	VG+ $400	Good $360	Fair $185
Trade-In:	Mint $570	Ex $450	VG+ $320	Good $280	Poor $90

MODEL 17   REDBOOK CODE: RB-RE-S-MODE17

Takedown style, hammerless, tubular magazine, bottom ejecting, blue barrel, no checkering on stock. Pricing shown for 17A standard model. Pricing will vary for models 17B-17P due to the variations in finishes and materials.

Production: *1921–1933* **Gauge/Bore:** *20 ga.*

Action: *pump-action*

Barrel Length: 26"–32" **Wt.:** *N/A*

Sights: *bead front*

Capacity: *5*

Stock: *walnut*

D2C:	NIB $499	Ex $400	VG+ $275	Good $250	
C2C:	Mint $480	Ex $350	VG+ $250	Good $225	Fair $115
Trade-In:	Mint $360	Ex $300	VG+ $200	Good $175	Poor $60

*Photo Courtesy of
Rock Island Auction Company*

MODEL 29   REDBOOK CODE: RB-RE-S-MODE29

Hammerless, tubular magazine, bottom ejecting, takedown style, guns with 32" barrels command a higher premium. Available in other grades: Special, Trap, Tournament, Expert (pictured here), Premier, and Riot. These variants will all bring different premiums. Add 40% for 32" barrels. Add 25% for ventilated rib barrels.

Production: *1930–1933* **Gauge/Bore:** *12 ga.*

Action: *pump-action*

Barrel Length: 26"–32" **Wt.:** *N/A*

Sights: *bead front*

Capacity: *5*

Stock: *hardwood*

D2C:	NIB $475	Ex $375	VG+ $265	Good $240	
C2C:	Mint $460	Ex $350	VG+ $240	Good $215	Fair $110
Trade-In:	Mint $340	Ex $275	VG+ $190	Good $170	Poor $60

REMINGTON

*Photo Courtesy of
Rock Island Auction Company*

MODEL 31   REDBOOK CODE: RB-RE-S-MODE31

Takedown style, blue barrel, add 50% for guns with 32" barrel, add 40% for stocks with checkering, for early banded barrels add 25%. Model 31 TC pictured here. Available in many grades with variations in wood, metal, and finishes. Pricing here is for the Model 31A standard.

Production: *1931–1949* **Gauge/Bore:** *12 ga., 16 ga., 20 ga.*

Action: *pump-action*

Barrel Length: 26"–32" **Wt.:** *N/A*

Sights: *none*

Capacity: *2, 4*

Stock: *walnut*

D2C:	NIB $530	Ex $425	VG+ $295	Good $265	
C2C:	Mint $510	Ex $375	VG+ $270	Good $240	Fair $125
Trade-In:	Mint $380	Ex $300	VG+ $210	Good $190	Poor $60

*Photo Courtesy of
Rock Island Auction Company*

MODEL 32   REDBOOK CODE: RB-RE-S-MODE32

Automatic ejectors, either two triggers or single-selective trigger(after 1938), solid or ventilated rib add 10%. Grades available: Standard, Skeet, Target Grade (pictured here), Tournament, Expert, and Premier. Pricing available here for standard model.

Production: *1932–1944* **Gauge/Bore:** *12 ga.*

Action: *O/U*

Barrel Length: 26", 28", 30" **Wt.:** *N/A*

Sights: *bead front*

Capacity: *2*

Stock: *walnut*

D2C:	NIB $2,330	Ex $1,775	VG+ $1,285	Good $1,165	
C2C:	Mint $2,240	Ex $1,625	VG+ $1,170	Good $1,050	Fair $540
Trade-In:	Mint $1,660	Ex $1,325	VG+ $910	Good $820	Poor $240

*Photo Courtesy of
Rock Island Auction Company*

MODEL 105CTI   REDBOOK CODE: RB-RE-S-105CTI

3" chamber, ProBore chokes included, TriNyte black metal finishing, 14.3" length of pull, satin finish on walnut, bottom feed and ejection, carbon-fiber titanium receiver for reduced weight, checkering on pistol-grip stock. CTI model available until 2008, CTII model offered until 2009.

Production: *2006–2009* **Gauge/Bore:** *12 ga.*

Action: *semi-auto*

Barrel Length: 26", 28" **Wt.:** *~7 lbs.*

Sights: *twin bead*

Capacity: *4*

Stock: *American walnut*

D2C:	NIB $1,220	Ex $950	VG+ $675	Good $610	
C2C:	Mint $1,180	Ex $850	VG+ $610	Good $550	Fair $285
Trade-In:	Mint $870	Ex $700	VG+ $480	Good $430	Poor $150

*Photo Courtesy of
Rock Island Auction Company*

MODEL 11-48   REDBOOK CODE: RB-RE-S-1148XX

A lighter, more streamlined version of the Model 11, checkering on stock and forearm, blue metal finishing. Grades available: A standard, R riot, B special, D tournament, F premier, RSS rifled slug special. The various grades command different premiums. Pricing reflects standard model.

Production: *1949–1968* **Gauge/Bore:** *12 ga., 16 ga., 20 ga., 28 ga., .410*

Action: *semi-auto*

Barrel Length: 26" **Wt.:** *N/A*

Sights: *twin bead*

Capacity: *5*

Stock: *American walnut*

D2C:	NIB $290	Ex $225	VG+ $160	Good $145	
C2C:	Mint $280	Ex $225	VG+ $150	Good $135	Fair $70
Trade-In:	Mint $210	Ex $175	VG+ $120	Good $105	Poor $30

REMINGTON

*Photo Courtesy of
Rock Island Auction Company*

MODEL 48 SPORTSMAN   REDBOOK CODE: RB-RE-S-48SPOR

Blued metal, checkering on walnut, add 20% for vent rib barrel. Pricing shown for standard model. Offered in Special, Tournament, and Premier grades which bring very different premiums due to their grade of wood, checkering, and engraving.

Production: *1948–1968* **Gauge/Bore:** *12 ga., 16 ga., 20 ga.*
Action: *semi-auto*
Barrel Length: 26", 28", 32" **Wt.:** *N/A*
Sights: *bead front*
Capacity: *3*
Stock: *walnut*

D2C:	NIB $360	Ex $275	VG+ $200	Good $180	
C2C:	Mint $350	Ex $250	VG+ $180	Good $165	Fair $85
Trade-In:	Mint $260	Ex $225	VG+ $150	Good $130	Poor $60

11-96 EURO LIGHTWEIGHT   REDBOOK CODE: RB-RE-S-96EURO

Vent rib barrel, 3 RemChokes included, blue finished barrel, fine-line engraving on receiver, checkering on stock.

Production: *1996–1999* **Gauge/Bore:** *12 ga.*
Action: *semi-auto*
Barrel Length: 26", 28" **Wt.:** *~7 lbs.*
Sights: *bead front*
Capacity: *4*
Stock: *Claro walnut*

D2C:	NIB $780	Ex $600	VG+ $430	Good $390	
C2C:	Mint $750	Ex $550	VG+ $390	Good $355	Fair $180
Trade-In:	Mint $560	Ex $450	VG+ $310	Good $275	Poor $90

*Photo Courtesy of
Rock Island Auction Company*

MODEL 58 SPORTSMAN   REDBOOK CODE: RB-RE-S-58SPOR

Tubular magazine, scroll-engraved blue receiver, checkering on walnut stock, was Remington's first gas-operated shotgun.

Production: *1956–1963* **Gauge/Bore:** *12 ga., 16 ga., 20 ga.*
Action: *semi-auto*
Barrel Length: 26", 28", 30" **Wt.:** *N/A*
Sights: *bead front*
Capacity: *3*
Stock: *walnut pistol grip*

D2C:	NIB $360	Ex $275	VG+ $200	Good $180	
C2C:	Mint $350	Ex $250	VG+ $180	Good $165	Fair $85
Trade-In:	Mint $260	Ex $225	VG+ $150	Good $130	Poor $60

MODEL 300 IDEAL   REDBOOK CODE: RB-RE-S-MOD300

Single-selective trigger, automatic ejectors, blue metal finish, semi-gloss walnut finish, black recoil pad.

Production: *2000–2001* **Gauge/Bore:** *12 ga.*
Action: *O/U*
Barrel Length: 26", 28", 30" **Wt.:** *7.6 lbs.*
Sights: *twin bead*
Capacity: *2*
Stock: *walnut*

D2C:	NIB $1,200	Ex $925	VG+ $660	Good $600	
C2C:	Mint $1,160	Ex $850	VG+ $600	Good $540	Fair $280
Trade-In:	Mint $860	Ex $675	VG+ $470	Good $420	Poor $120

REMINGTON

Photo Courtesy of
Rock Island Auction Company

MODEL 3200   REDBOOK CODE: RB-RE-S-MO3200

Ventilated rib barrels, single-selective trigger, automatic ejector, blue finish on metal, checkering on walnut stock.

Production: *1973–1984*   **Gauge/Bore:** *12 ga.*
Action: *O/U*
Barrel Length: 26", 28", 30"   **Wt.:** *N/A*
Sights: *bead front*
Capacity: *2*
Stock: *walnut*

D2C:	NIB $1,190	Ex $925	VG+ $655	Good $595	
C2C:	Mint $1,150	Ex $825	VG+ $600	Good $540	Fair $275
Trade-In:	Mint $850	Ex $675	VG+ $470	Good $420	Poor $120

MODEL 396   REDBOOK CODE: RB-RE-S-MOD396

Interchangeable RemChoke system, satin finish on walnut stock, blue finished metal, scroll engraving on receiver. Several variations were made including, skeet, sporting, and custom grade models. Different models command different premiums. Pricing here reflects the Model 396 Sporting.

Production: *1996–1999*   **Gauge/Bore:** *12 ga.*
Action: *O/U*
Barrel Length: 30"   **Wt.:** *~8 lbs.*
Sights: *bead front*
Capacity: *2*
Stock: *fancy American walnut*

D2C:	NIB $1,650	Ex $1,275	VG+ $910	Good $825	
C2C:	Mint $1,590	Ex $1,150	VG+ $830	Good $745	Fair $380
Trade-In:	Mint $1,180	Ex $925	VG+ $650	Good $580	Poor $180

PEERLESS (MODEL 320)   REDBOOK CODE: RB-RE-S-PEERLE

Vent rib barrel, comes with 3 Remington choke tubes (IC, M, F), removable sideplates.

Production: *1993–1999*   **Gauge/Bore:** *12 ga.*
Action: *O/U*
Barrel Length: 26", 28", 30"   **Wt.:** *N/A*
Sights: *bead front*
Capacity: *2*
Stock: *American walnut*

D2C:	NIB $900	Ex $700	VG+ $495	Good $450	
C2C:	Mint $870	Ex $625	VG+ $450	Good $405	Fair $210
Trade-In:	Mint $640	Ex $525	VG+ $360	Good $315	Poor $90

Photo Courtesy of
Rock Island Auction Company

90-T   REDBOOK CODE: RB-RE-S-90TXXX

Checkering on stock and forearm, full choke barrel, matte black receiver, elongated forcing cone.

Production: *1991–1997*   **Gauge/Bore:** *12 ga.*
Action: *single-shot*
Barrel Length: 32", 34"   **Wt.:** *8.3 lbs.*
Sights: *bead front*
Capacity: *1*
Stock: *walnut*

D2C:	NIB $1,650	Ex $1,275	VG+ $910	Good $825	
C2C:	Mint $1,590	Ex $1,150	VG+ $830	Good $745	Fair $380
Trade-In:	Mint $1,180	Ex $925	VG+ $650	Good $580	Poor $180

PREMIER STS COMPETITION REDBOOK CODE: RB-RE-S-PRESTS

Overbored barrels, engraved nickel-plated receiver, high-gloss finished stock. Add 15% for adjustable stock, checkering on pistol-grip and forend, Schnabel forend, ProBore chokes included, 3" chamber. Available in field grade, upland grade, and Ruffed Grouse Society edition.

Production: 2006–discontinued **Gauge/Bore:** 12 ga.
Action: O/U
Barrel Length: 28", 30", 32" **Wt.:** 7.8 lbs.
Sights: bead front
Capacity: 2
Stock: walnut

D2C:	NIB $1,960	Ex $1,500	VG+ $1,080	Good $980	
C2C:	Mint $1,890	Ex $1,375	VG+ $980	Good $885	Fair $455
Trade-In:	Mint $1,400	Ex $1,100	VG+ $770	Good $690	Poor $210

SPR 100 SPORTING REDBOOK CODE: RB-RE-S-SPR100

Originally manufactured in Baikal, Russia, single trigger, ejectors, checkering on stock and forearm, black recoil pad.

Production: 2005–2008 **Gauge/Bore:** 12 ga., .20 ga., .410
Action: single-shot
Barrel Length: 29.5", 28.5", 26" **Wt.:** 6.3 lbs.
Sights: bead front
Capacity: 1
Stock: walnut

D2C:	NIB $150	Ex $125	VG+ $85	Good $75	
C2C:	Mint $150	Ex $125	VG+ $80	Good $70	Fair $35
Trade-In:	Mint $110	Ex $100	VG+ $60	Good $55	Poor $30

SPR 210 REDBOOK CODE: RB-RE-S-SPR210

Single-selective trigger, box lock receiver, nickel plated receiver, choke tubes in 12 and 20 gauge, fixed chokes in 28 ga. and .410, blue receiver offered with 20" barrel, checkering on walnut stock, black recoil pad. Add $30 for 28 ga. and .410 models.

Production: 2005–2008 **Gauge/Bore:** 12 ga., 16 ga., 20 ga., 28 ga., .410
Action: SxS
Barrel Length: 26", 28" **Wt.:** 6.8 lbs.
Sights: bead front
Capacity: 2
Stock: walnut

D2C:	NIB $390	Ex $300	VG+ $215	Good $195	
C2C:	Mint $380	Ex $275	VG+ $200	Good $180	Fair $90
Trade-In:	Mint $280	Ex $225	VG+ $160	Good $140	Poor $60

SPR 220 REDBOOK CODE: RB-RE-S-SPR220

Double trigger, chokes tubes included, extractor, nickel or blue receiver, recoil pad, no checkering.

Production: 2005–2008 **Gauge/Bore:** 12 ga., 20 ga.
Action: SxS
Barrel Length: 20" **Wt.:** 6.3 lbs.
Sights: bead front
Capacity: 2
Stock: walnut

D2C:	NIB $360	Ex $275	VG+ $200	Good $180	
C2C:	Mint $350	Ex $250	VG+ $180	Good $165	Fair $85
Trade-In:	Mint $260	Ex $225	VG+ $150	Good $130	Poor $60

REMINGTON

SPR 310   REDBOOK CODE: RB-RE-S-SPR310
Vent rib barrel, choke tubes included, single-selective trigger, auto ejector, checkering on walnut, recoil pad.

Production: *2005–2008* Gauge/Bore: *12 ga., 16 ga., 20 ga., 28 ga., .410*
Action: *O/U*
Barrel Length: 26", 28" Wt.: *7.5 lbs.*
Sights: *bead front*
Capacity: *2*
Stock: *walnut*

D2C:	NIB $620	Ex $475	VG+ $345	Good $310	
C2C:	Mint $600	Ex $450	VG+ $310	Good $280	Fair $145
Trade-In:	Mint $450	Ex $350	VG+ $250	Good $220	Poor $90

RIZZINI

Rizzini SRL

Battista Rizzini founded the Rizzini Company in 1966 in Brescia, Italy. His three children are now involved in the business that he grew to worldwide recognition. The company makes both over/under and side-by-side shotguns and rifles. All products are 100% made in Italy, and the manufacturing building includes a space where the company's founder himself works to design new products. Just a few years ago, Battista Rizzini contracted with Ivano Tanfoglio of Fratelli Tanfoglio S.R.L. to combine the traditional craftsmanship and the modern technology of the respective companies in the creation of a new line of shotguns known as Rizzini & Tanfoglio. Rizzini firearms designed for hunting and competition and custom models made to order are distributed in the U.S. by Rizzini USA in Gunnison, Utah. The distributorship is owned and operated by Fierce Products, under the oversight of CEO John Mogle.

ARTEMIS   REDBOOK CODE: RB-RZ-S-ARTEMI
Coin-finished or case-hardened action, scroll engraving, box lock, automatic ejectors, single-selective trigger, chrome-lined bores, round-knob Prince of Wales grip, Schnabel forend, 3" chamber, 5 interchangeable chokes.

Production: *current* Gauge/Bore: *12 ga., 16 ga., 20 ga.*
Action: *O/U*
Barrel Length: 26"-30" Wt.: *5.9–6.8 lbs.*
Sights: *none*
Capacity: *2*
Stock: *Turkish walnut*

D2C:	NIB $4,000	Ex $3,050	VG+ $2,200	Good $2,000	**LMP:** $4,196
C2C:	Mint $3,840	Ex $2,775	VG+ $2,000	Good $1,800	Fair $920
Trade-In:	Mint $2,840	Ex $2,250	VG+ $1,560	Good $1,400	Poor $420

ARTEMIS DELUXE   REDBOOK CODE: RB-RZ-S-ARTDEL
Hand finished engraving, automatic ejector, single-selective trigger, chrome-lined barrel, glossy blue finish, vent or solid full side ribs, Prince of Wales or English pistol grip, Schnabel or round forend.

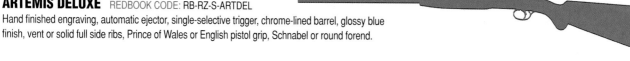

Production: *current* Gauge/Bore: *12 ga., 16 ga., 20 ga., 28 ga., .410*
Action: *O/U*
Barrel Length: 26", 28", 29", 30" Wt.: *6.3–6.8 lbs.*
Sights: *none*
Capacity: *2*
Stock: *Grade III Turkish walnut*

D2C:	NIB $5,830	Ex $4,450	VG+ $3,210	Good $2,915	**LMP:** $6,995
C2C:	Mint $5,600	Ex $4,025	VG+ $2,920	Good $2,625	Fair $1,345
Trade-In:	Mint $4,140	Ex $3,275	VG+ $2,280	Good $2,045	Poor $600

ARTEMIS LIGHT   REDBOOK CODE: RB-RZ-S-ARTLIG
26 LPI checkering, side plates with coin finish, scroll engraving, chrome-lined barrel, vented top rib, round knob Prince of Wales grip, Schnabel forend, 5 interchangeable chokes.

Production: *current* **Gauge/Bore:** *12 ga., 16 ga., 20 ga., 28 ga., .410*

Action: *O/U*

Barrel Length: *26"-30"* **Wt.:** *5.2–6.4 lbs.*

Sights: *none*

Capacity: *2*

Stock: *Turkish walnut*

D2C:	NIB $4,030	Ex $3,075	VG+ $2,220	Good $2,015	**LMP:** $4,295
C2C:	Mint $3,870	Ex $2,800	VG+ $2,020	Good $1,815	Fair $930
Trade-In:	Mint $2,870	Ex $2,275	VG+ $1,580	Good $1,415	Poor $420

AURUM   REDBOOK CODE: RB-RZ-S-AURUMX
Nickel-chrome steel barrel, gloss barrel finish, brazed rib on barrel, automatic shell ejectors, single-selective trigger, low profile box lock action, chrome-lined barrel, Prince of Wales pistol grip, Schnabel forend, polished oil wood finish.

Production: *current* **Gauge/Bore:** *12 ga., 16 ga., 20 ga., 28 ga., .410*

Action: *O/U*

Barrel Length: *26", 28", 29", 30"* **Wt.:** *6.3–6.8 lbs.*

Sights: *bead front*

Capacity: *2*

Stock: *Turkish walnut*

D2C:	NIB $3,360	Ex $2,575	VG+ $1,850	Good $1,680	**LMP:** $3,599
C2C:	Mint $3,230	Ex $2,325	VG+ $1,680	Good $1,515	Fair $775
Trade-In:	Mint $2,390	Ex $1,900	VG+ $1,320	Good $1,180	Poor $360

BR 440   REDBOOK CODE: RB-RZ-S-BR440X
Battery fully removable, interchangeable with coil springs, ventilated rib.

Production: *current* **Gauge/Bore:** *12 ga.*

Action: *SxS*

Barrel Length: *28"–30"* **Wt.:** *N/A*

Sights: *rectangular front*

Capacity: *2*

Stock: *hardwood*

D2C:	NIB $7,010	Ex $5,350	VG+ $3,860	Good $3,505	**LMP:** $7,495
C2C:	Mint $6,730	Ex $4,850	VG+ $3,510	Good $3,155	Fair $1,615
Trade-In:	Mint $4,980	Ex $3,950	VG+ $2,740	Good $2,455	Poor $720

BR320   REDBOOK CODE: RB-RZ-S-BR320X
Minimal scroll engraving, boxlock, single-selective trigger, chrome-lined bores, glossy blue barrel finish, ventilated top rib, pistol grip stock, palm swell, adjustable comb.

Production: *current* **Gauge/Bore:** *12 ga., 20 ga., 28 ga.*

Action: *O/U*

Barrel Length: *28"–30"* **Wt.:** *N/A*

Sights: *red rectangular front*

Capacity: *2*

Stock: *Turkish walnut*

D2C:	NIB $3,400	Ex $2,600	VG+ $1,870	Good $1,700	**LMP:** $3,995
C2C:	Mint $3,270	Ex $2,350	VG+ $1,700	Good $1,530	Fair $785
Trade-In:	Mint $2,420	Ex $1,925	VG+ $1,330	Good $1,190	Poor $360

RIZZINI

BR550 REDBOOK CODE: RB-RZ-S-BR550X

Minimal scroll engraving, boxlock, automatic ejectors, single-selective trigger, chrome-lined bores, glossy blue barrel, pistol grip stock, palm swell.

Production: *current* **Gauge/Bore:** *12 ga., 20 ga., 28 ga.*
Action: *O/U*
Barrel Length: 28"–30" **Wt.:** *N/A*
Sights: *red rectangular front*
Capacity: *2*
Stock: *hardwood*

D2C:	NIB $3,650	Ex $2,775	VG+ $2,010	Good $1,825	**LMP:** $3,995
C2C:	Mint $3,510	Ex $2,525	VG+ $1,830	Good $1,645	Fair $840
Trade-In:	Mint $2,600	Ex $2,050	VG+ $1,430	Good $1,280	Poor $390

FIERCE 1 REDBOOK CODE: RB-RZ-S-FIERCE1

Light scroll engraving, back-bored barrel, extended forcing cone, interchangeable chokes, ventilated rib.

Production: *current* **Gauge/Bore:** *12 ga., 20 ga., 28 ga.*
Action: *O/U*
Barrel Length: 28"–32" **Wt.:** *N/A*
Sights: *bead front*
Capacity: *2*
Stock: *hardwood*

D2C:	NIB $4,120	Ex $3,150	VG+ $2,270	Good $2,060	**LMP:** $4,260
C2C:	Mint $3,960	Ex $2,850	VG+ $2,060	Good $1,855	Fair $950
Trade-In:	Mint $2,930	Ex $2,325	VG+ $1,610	Good $1,445	Poor $420

OMNIUM REDBOOK CODE: RB-RZ-S-OMNIUM

Flat, blue, or coin finish, minimal scroll engraving, single-selective trigger, automatic ejector, full side rib, ventilated top rib, pistol-grip stock, Schnabel forend, interchangeable chokes.

Production: *current* **Gauge/Bore:** *12 ga., 20 ga.*
Action: *O/U*
Barrel Length: 26.5", 28", 30", 32" **Wt.:** *6.3–6.8 lbs.*
Sights: *bead front*
Capacity: *2*
Stock: *walnut*

D2C:	NIB $2,400	Ex $1,825	VG+ $1,320	Good $1,200	**LMP:** $2,632
C2C:	Mint $2,310	Ex $1,675	VG+ $1,200	Good $1,080	Fair $555
Trade-In:	Mint $1,710	Ex $1,350	VG+ $940	Good $840	Poor $240

ROUND BODY REDBOOK CODE: RB-RZ-S-ROUNDB

Hand finished in oil, long tang trigger guard, chrome-moly lined ventilated rib barrels, screw chokes, single-selective trigger, ventilated rib, coin or color case-hardened frame, Prince of Wales pistol grip stock, straight forend.

Production: *current* **Gauge/Bore:** *12 ga., 16 ga., 20 ga., 28 ga., .410*
Action: *SxS*
Barrel Length: 26"–30" **Wt.:** *6.2–7 lbs.*
Sights: *bead front*
Capacity: *2*
Stock: *Turkish walnut*

D2C:	NIB $4,360	Ex $3,325	VG+ $2,400	Good $2,180	**LMP:** $4,687
C2C:	Mint $4,190	Ex $3,025	VG+ $2,180	Good $1,965	Fair $1,005
Trade-In:	Mint $3,100	Ex $2,450	VG+ $1,710	Good $1,530	Poor $450

ROUND BODY EL   REDBOOK CODE: RB-RZ-S-ROUNEL
Single-selective trigger, fixed or interchangeable chokes, full rib, full hand engraving.

Production: *current* **Gauge/Bore:** *12 ga., 16 ga., 20 ga.*
Action: *O/U*
Barrel Length: 26"–30" **Wt.:** *N/A*
Sights: *none*
Capacity: *2*
Stock: *walnut*

D2C:	NIB $6,200	Ex $4,725	VG+ $3,410	Good $3,100	LMP: $6,695
C2C:	Mint $5,960	Ex $4,300	VG+ $3,100	Good $2,790	Fair $1,430
Trade-In:	Mint $4,410	Ex $3,475	VG+ $2,420	Good $2,170	Poor $630

S 790 EL   REDBOOK CODE: RB-RZ-S-S790EL
Low-profile action, chrome-plated action, names in gold engraving, ventilated side and top ribs, chrome-lined glossy-blue barrel, 5" forcing cones, pistol grip stock, palm swell, 3" chamber.

Production: *current* **Gauge/Bore:** *12 ga., 20 ga., 28 ga.*
Action: *O/U*
Barrel Length: 28"–32" **Wt.:** *7.8 lbs.*
Sights: *bead front*
Capacity: *2*
Stock: *walnut*

D2C:	NIB $8,900	Ex $6,775	VG+ $4,895	Good $4,450	LMP: $9,395
C2C:	Mint $8,550	Ex $6,150	VG+ $4,450	Good $4,005	Fair $2,050
Trade-In:	Mint $6,320	Ex $5,000	VG+ $3,480	Good $3,115	Poor $900

S1000   REDBOOK CODE: RB-RZ-S-S1000X
Scroll engraved side plates, fixed or interchangeable chokes, ventilated rib, single-selective trigger, long forcing cones.

Production: *current* **Gauge/Bore:** *12 ga., 20 ga., 28 ga.*
Action: *O/U*
Barrel Length: 28"–32" **Wt.:** *N/A*
Sights: *bead front*
Capacity: *2*
Stock: *Turkish walnut*

D2C:	NIB $4,200	Ex $3,200	VG+ $2,310	Good $2,100	LMP: $4,685
C2C:	Mint $4,040	Ex $2,900	VG+ $2,100	Good $1,890	Fair $970
Trade-In:	Mint $2,990	Ex $2,375	VG+ $1,640	Good $1,470	Poor $420

S2000   REDBOOK CODE: RB-RZ-S-S2000X
Engraved side place, fixed or interchangeable chokes, ventilated rib, single-selective trigger.

Production: *current* **Gauge/Bore:** *12 ga., 20 ga., 28 ga.*
Action: *O/U*
Barrel Length: 28"–32" **Wt.:** *N/A*
Sights: *bead front*
Capacity: *2*
Stock: *walnut*

D2C:	NIB $5,330	Ex $4,075	VG+ $2,935	Good $2,665	LMP: $5,595
C2C:	Mint $5,120	Ex $3,700	VG+ $2,670	Good $2,400	Fair $1,230
Trade-In:	Mint $3,790	Ex $3,000	VG+ $2,080	Good $1,870	Poor $540

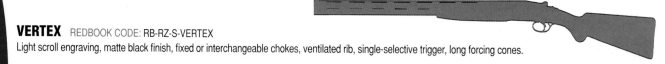

VERTEX REDBOOK CODE: RB-RZ-S-VERTEX

Light scroll engraving, matte black finish, fixed or interchangeable chokes, ventilated rib, single-selective trigger, long forcing cones.

Production: *current* **Gauge/Bore:** *12 ga., 20 ga., 28 ga.*
Action: *O/U*
Barrel Length: *28"–32"* **Wt.:** *N/A*
Sights: *bead front*
Capacity: *2*
Stock: *walnut*

D2C:	NIB $2,510	Ex $1,925	VG+ $1,385	Good $1,255	LMP: $2,980
C2C:	Mint $2,410	Ex $1,750	VG+ $1,260	Good $1,130	Fair $580
Trade-In:	Mint $1,790	Ex $1,425	VG+ $980	Good $880	Poor $270

Rock Island Armory

The Rock Island Armory trademark was acquired in 1985 by Pahrump, Nevada-based Armscor USA, an American subsidiary of Arms Corporation of the Philippines headquartered in Marikina, Philippines. Rock Island firearms have been manufactured in the Philippines since Armscor's acquisition of the brand, but plans are being made to begin manufacturing at the U.S. facility in Nevada soon. Firearms bearing the Rock Island trademark are distributed internationally, with most going to the U.S.

M5 SHOTGUN REDBOOK CODE: RB-RI-S-M5SHOT

Steel barrel in parkerized or matte nickel finish, heat shield, cross bolt safety, jeweled bolt,
twin slide action bars, chambered for 2.75" and 3" shells, approximately 13.75" length of pull. Add $12 for matte nickel finish.

Production: *current* **Gauge/Bore:** *12 ga.*
Action: *pump-action*
Barrel Length: *20"* **Wt.:** *7 lbs.*
Sights: *bead front*
Capacity: *5, 6*
Stock: *synthetic with shell storage*

D2C:	NIB $210	Ex $175	VG+ $120	Good $105	LMP: $219
C2C:	Mint $210	Ex $150	VG+ $110	Good $95	Fair $50
Trade-In:	Mint $150	Ex $125	VG+ $90	Good $75	Poor $30

Rossi

Amadeo Rossi founded the company that is his namesake in 1889. Most of the products are manufactured in San Leopoldo, Brazil, but they are widely distributed internationally. The company formed BrazTech International L.D. in 1997 to be the exclusive importer of Rossi firearms in North America after importing through Interarms of Alexandria, Virginia, for several years. The company has contracted with Forjas Taurus, S.A. for Taurus to have the rights and the equipment to manufacture the company's handguns, but other product lines are manufactured in-house. Rossi currently manufactures several lines of single-shot shotguns, and members of the original family still run the company today.

S411280BS   REDBOOK CODE: RB-RO-S-S41128
Modified choke, steel barrel, blue finish on metal, spur hammer, transfer bar safety action, 3" chamber.

Production: *current* **Gauge/Bore:** *.410*
Action: *single-shot*
Barrel Length: 28" **Wt.:** *4 lbs.*
Sights: *bead front*
Capacity: *1*
Stock: *black synthetic*

D2C:	NIB $140	Ex $125	VG+ $80	Good $70	LMP: $170
C2C:	Mint $140	Ex $100	VG+ $70	Good $65	Fair $35
Trade-In:	Mint $100	Ex $100	VG+ $60	Good $50	Poor $30

S411220YS   REDBOOK CODE: RB-RO-S-S41122
Shortened stock for youth, modified choke, steel barrel, spur hammer, sling swivel studs.

Production: *current* **Gauge/Bore:** *.410*
Action: *single-shot*
Barrel Length: 22" **Wt.:** *3.8 lbs.*
Sights: *ramp front fiber-optic*
Capacity: *1*
Stock: *black synthetic*

D2C:	NIB $150	Ex $125	VG+ $85	Good $75	LMP: $170
C2C:	Mint $150	Ex $125	VG+ $80	Good $70	Fair $35
Trade-In:	Mint $110	Ex $100	VG+ $60	Good $55	Poor $30

S201280BS   REDBOOK CODE: RB-RO-S-S20128
Modified choke, steel barrel, blue metal finish, spur hammer, transfer bar safety action.

Production: *current* **Gauge/Bore:** *20 ga.*
Action: *single-shot*
Barrel Length: 28" **Wt.:** *5.3 lbs.*
Sights: *bead front*
Capacity: *1*
Stock: *black synthetic*

D2C:	NIB $160	Ex $125	VG+ $90	Good $80	LMP: $170
C2C:	Mint $160	Ex $125	VG+ $80	Good $75	Fair $40
Trade-In:	Mint $120	Ex $100	VG+ $70	Good $60	Poor $30

S201230BS   REDBOOK CODE: RB-RO-S-S20123
Rifled barrel, drilled and tapped for scope mounting, matte blue finish, steel barrel.

Production: *current* **Gauge/Bore:** *20 ga.*
Action: *single-shot*
Barrel Length: 23" **Wt.:** *6.3 lbs.*
Sights: *ramp front fiber-optic*
Capacity: *1*
Stock: *Brazilian hardwood*

D2C:	NIB $290	Ex $225	VG+ $160	Good $145	LMP: $322
C2C:	Mint $280	Ex $225	VG+ $150	Good $135	Fair $70
Trade-In:	Mint $210	Ex $175	VG+ $120	Good $105	Poor $30

S201220YS REDBOOK CODE: RB-RO-S-S20122

Modified choke, blue metal finishing, steel barrel, spur hammer, transfer bar safety action, 3" chamber.

Production: *current* Gauge/Bore: *12 ga.*					
Action: *single-shot*					
Barrel Length: 22" Wt.: *5 lbs.*	D2C:	NIB $150	Ex $125	VG+ $85	Good $75	LMP: $170
Sights: *bead front*	C2C:	Mint $150	Ex $125	VG+ $80	Good $70	Fair $35
Capacity: *1*	Trade-In:	Mint $110	Ex $100	VG+ $60	Good $55	Poor $30
Stock: *black synthetic*					

S121280BS REDBOOK CODE: RB-RO-S-S12128

Modified choke, steel barrel, blue finished metal, spur hammer, transfer bar safety action, 3" chamber.

Production: *current* Gauge/Bore: *12 ga.*					
Action: *single-shot*					
Barrel Length: 28" Wt.: *5.3 lbs.*	D2C:	NIB $160	Ex $125	VG+ $90	Good $80	LMP: $170
Sights: *bead front*	C2C:	Mint $160	Ex $125	VG+ $80	Good $75	Fair $40
Capacity: *1*	Trade-In:	Mint $120	Ex $100	VG+ $70	Good $60	Poor $30
Stock: *black synthetic*					

S121230BS REDBOOK CODE: RB-RO-S-S12123

Matte blue finish, steel barrel, rifled barrel for slug shots.

Production: *current* Gauge/Bore: *12 ga., 20 ga.*					
Action: *single-shot*					
Barrel Length: 23" Wt.: *6.3 lbs.*	D2C:	NIB $220	Ex $175	VG+ $125	Good $110	LMP: $322
Sights: *ramp front fiber-optic*	C2C:	Mint $220	Ex $175	VG+ $110	Good $100	Fair $55
Capacity: *1*	Trade-In:	Mint $160	Ex $125	VG+ $90	Good $80	Poor $30
Stock: *black synthetic*					

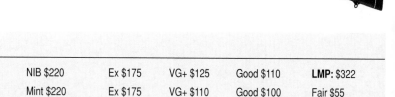

J.P. Sauer & Sohn (Sauer & Sohn)

The original permutation of the Sauer Company was located in Suhl, Germany, in 1751 by Lorenz Sauer. It holds rank as the oldest firearms manufacturer in Germany. In 1840, after the company had changed hands within the family, John Paul Sauer and his son, Lorenz changed the name of the company to J.P. Sauer and Sohn. The company was the first firearms manufacturer in Suhl to be contracted to make weapons for the German Military. J.P. Sauer and Sohn produced everything from pistols to shotguns, and their products were lauded as the best in the world. When Germany was divided, the original company was thrust behind the Iron Curtain. However, in 1951, a new incarnation of the original Sauer Company opened in Western Germany. This new company had exclusive rights to everything that belonged to the original company. In the 1970s, Sauer and Sohn joined forces with Swiss Arms AG (SIG Arms AG) to produce the ever popular brand of "SIG-Sauer" pistols. These guns, which are currently produced, are hot commodities on the market today.

Photo Courtesy of
Rock Island Auction Company

ROYAL DOUBLE-BARREL REDBOOK CODE: RB-SH-S-ROYALD

Boxlock action, single-selective trigger, automatic ejector, scalloped frame, blue metal, checkering on stock, side clips, cocking indicators, steel barrel, cheek piece.

SAUER & SOHN

Production: *1955–1977* **Gauge/Bore:** *12 ga., 20 ga.*

Action: *SxS*

Barrel Length: *26", 28", 30"* **Wt.:** *N/A*

Sights: *bead front*

Capacity: *2*

Stock: *European walnut*

D2C:	NIB $1,833	Ex $1,400	VG+ $1,010	Good $920	
C2C:	Mint $1,760	Ex $1,275	VG+ $920	Good $825	Fair $425
Trade-In:	Mint $1,310	Ex $1,050	VG+ $720	Good $645	Poor $210

ARTEMIS DOUBLE-BARREL REDBOOK CODE: RB-SH-S-ARTEMI

Holland & Holland type sidelock, Greener crossbolt double underlugs, double-sear safeties, single-selective trigger, selective auto-ejectors, Grade I has fine-line engraving, Grade II has full English arabesque engraving, Krupp-Special steel barrels, M/F choke, beavertail forend, recoil pad.

Production: *1966–1977* **Gauge/Bore:** *12 ga.*

Action: *SxS*

Barrel Length: *28"* **Wt.:** *6.5 lbs.*

Sights: *bead front*

Capacity: *2*

Stock: *pistol-grip walnut*

D2C:	NIB $4,200	Ex $3,200	VG+ $2,310	Good $2,100	
C2C:	Mint $4,040	Ex $2,900	VG+ $2,100	Good $1,890	Fair $970
Trade-In:	Mint $2,990	Ex $2,375	VG+ $1,640	Good $1,470	Poor $420

BBF 54 OVER-UNDER COMBO REDBOOK CODE: RB-SH-S-BBH54X

Blitz action, front set trigger, slide-operated rear safety, F choke, Monte Carlo comb and cheek piece, checkering on stock and forend, sling swivels, engraving on receiver.

Production: *discontinued 1986* **Gauge/Bore:** *16 ga./.222 Rem., .243 Win., 6.5x57R, 7x57R, 7x65R, .30-06 Spfld*

Action: *O/U*

Barrel Length: *28"* **Wt.:** *~6 lbs.*

Sights: *folding leaf rear*

Capacity: *2*

Stock: *Monte Carlo style walnut*

D2C:	NIB $3,020	Ex $2,300	VG+ $1,665	Good $1,510	
C2C:	Mint $2,900	Ex $2,100	VG+ $1,510	Good $1,360	Fair $695
Trade-In:	Mint $2,150	Ex $1,700	VG+ $1,180	Good $1,060	Poor $330

MODEL 66 OVER/UNDER TRAP REDBOOK CODE: RB-SH-S-66TRAP

F/F or M/F chokes, trap style stock, sidelock action, selective-single trigger, selective auto-ejectors, automatic safety, steel barrel, ventilated rib, checkering on stock and forend, recoil pad. Pricing research for this model proves inconclusive at this time. There have not been any recent sales on the secondary market to suggest a price range.

Production: *1966–1975* **Gauge/Bore:** *12 ga.*

Action: *O/U*

Barrel Length: *30"* **Wt.:** *7.5 lbs.*

Sights: *bead front*

Capacity: *2*

Stock: *walnut*

SAUER & SOHN

MODEL 66 OVER/UNDER SKEET REDBOOK CODE: RB-SH-S-6SKEET
Wide ventilated rib, SK chokes, skeet-style stock, ventilated beavertail forearm, non-automatic safety. Pricing research for this model proves inconclusive at this time. There have not been any recent sales on the secondary market to suggest a price range.

Production: *1966–1975* **Gauge/Bore:** *12 ga.*
Action: *O/U*
Barrel Length: 26" **Wt.:** *N/A*
Sights: *bead front*
Capacity: *2*
Stock: *walnut*

MODEL 66 OVER/UNDER FIELD REDBOOK CODE: RB-SH-S-6FIELD
Purdey-system action, Holland & Holland sidelocks, selective-single trigger, selective-auto ejectors, automatic safety, 3 grades of engraving available, ventilated rib, M/F choke included, checkering on stock and forend, recoil pad. Pricing research for this model proves inconclusive at this time. There have not been any recent sales on the secondary market to suggest a price range.

Production: *1966–1975* **Gauge/Bore:** *12 ga.*
Action: *O/U*
Barrel Length: 28" **Wt.:** *7.3 lbs.*
Sights: *bead front*
Capacity: *2*
Stock: *walnut*

Savage Arms

SAVAGE ARMS

Arthur Savage founded Savage Arms in 1894 in Westfield, Massachusetts, and the company quickly began producing rifles, handguns, and ammunition. Savage Arms introduced the first hammerless lever-action rifle, which developed into the renowned Model 1899, best known as the Model 99. By World War I, the company acquired and merged with several others to form the world's largest firearm manufacturer at the time. Savage is well known for the .300 Savage sporting cartridge and, in recent years, for AccuTrigger and AccuStock rifle accessories. The company also ventured into the shotgun market with a few offerings in 20 and 12 gauges and by acquiring Stevens Arms in 1920, the maker of the well-known Model 87 which was later marketed as the Savage Model 6. Through the years, the company has changed hands several times, and it is now a part of ATK Sporting Group.

STEVENS 555 REDBOOK CODE: RB-SV-S-STV555
Black-carbon steel barrel, single selective trigger, manual safety, 5 interchangeable choke tubes, lightweight alloy receiver, matte oil finish.

Production: *current* **Gauge/Bore:** *12 ga., 20 ga.*
Action: *O/U*
Barrel Length: 26", 28" **Wt.:** *5.5 lbs., 6 lbs.*
Sights: *bead*
Capacity: *2*
Stock: *Turkish walnut*

D2C:	NIB $610	Ex $475	VG+ $340	Good $305	LMP: $692
C2C:	Mint $590	Ex $425	VG+ $310	Good $275	Fair $145
Trade-In:	Mint $440	Ex $350	VG+ $240	Good $215	Poor $90

STEVENS 320 PUMP FIELD GRADE REDBOOK CODE: RB-SV-S-STV32F

Bottom loading, right ejection, dual slide-bars, rotary bolt, vent rib sporting barrel, 3" chamber, removable choke tubes, 14.5" length of pull. Optional field/security combo model includes 18.5" security barrel with cylinder choke. Add $33 for combo.

Production: *current* **Gauge/Bore:** *12 ga.*
Action: *pump-action*
Barrel Length: 18.5", 28" **Wt.:** *6.8 lbs–7.45 lbs.*
Sights: *bead*
Capacity: 5
Stock: *synthetic*

D2C:	NIB $260	Ex $200	VG+ $145	Good $130	**LMP:** $251
C2C:	Mint $250	Ex $200	VG+ $130	Good $120	Fair $60
Trade-In:	Mint $190	Ex $150	VG+ $110	Good $95	Poor $30

STEVENS 320 PUMP SECURITY REDBOOK CODE: RB-SV-S-STV32S

Bottom loading, right ejection, dual slide-bars, rotary bolt, 3" chamber, cylinder choke. Add $26 for ghost ring sights or $40 for pistol grip with heat shield.

Production: *current* **Gauge/Bore:** *12 ga.*
Action: *pump-action*
Barrel Length: 18.5" **Wt.:** *6.8 lbs.*
Sights: *bead, ghost ring*
Capacity: 5
Stock: *synthetic*

D2C:	NIB $195	Ex $150	VG+ $110	Good $100	**LMP:** $234
C2C:	Mint $190	Ex $150	VG+ $100	Good $90	Fair $45
Trade-In:	Mint $140	Ex $125	VG+ $80	Good $70	Poor $30

STEVENS 350 PUMP REDBOOK CODE: RB-SV-S-STV350

Bottom loading, right ejection with dual slide-bars, and vent rib, 14.5" length of pull and 2.375" drop at comb.

Production: *current* **Gauge/Bore:** *12 ga.*
Action: *pump-action*
Barrel Length: 18.5" **Wt.:** *7.6 lbs.*
Sights: *ghost ring*
Capacity: 5
Stock: *synthetic*

D2C:	NIB $250	Ex $200	VG+ $140	Good $125	**LMP:** $276
C2C:	Mint $240	Ex $175	VG+ $130	Good $115	Fair $60
Trade-In:	Mint $180	Ex $150	VG+ $100	Good $90	Poor $30

212 SLUG REDBOOK CODE: RB-SV-S-212SLG

Single adjustment AccuTrigger, drilled and tapped for scope mounts, oversized bolt handle. Also available in camouflage, add $57.

Production: *current* **Gauge/Bore:** *12 ga.*
Action: *bolt-action*
Barrel Length: 22" **Wt.:** *7.45 lbs.*
Sights: *none*
Capacity: 2
Stock: *synthetic*

D2C:	NIB $565	Ex $450	VG+ $315	Good $285	**LMP:** $664
C2C:	Mint $550	Ex $400	VG+ $290	Good $255	Fair $130
Trade-In:	Mint $410	Ex $325	VG+ $230	Good $200	Poor $60

220 SLUG REDBOOK CODE: RB-SV-S-220SLG
Single adjustment AccuTrigger, drilled and tapped for scope mounts, oversized bolt handle. Also available in camouflage (add $64) and camouflage/stainless (add $164). Left handed available in black.

Production: *current* **Gauge/Bore:** *20 ga.*
Action: *bolt-action*
Barrel Length: *22"* **Wt.:** *7 lbs., 7.75 lbs.*
Sights: *none*
Capacity: *2*
Stock: *synthetic*

D2C:	NIB $495	Ex $400	VG+ $275	Good $250	**LMP:** $582
C2C:	Mint $480	Ex $350	VG+ $250	Good $225	Fair $115
Trade-In:	Mint $360	Ex $300	VG+ $200	Good $175	Poor $60

SAVAGE ARMS

SKB Arms Company

SKB ARMS COMPANY

Considered to be founded by Mr. Shigyo SaKaBa, a gunsmith appointed by a feudal lord to oversee his clan's firearm manufacturing operation, SKB Arms Company was established in Tokyo, Japan, in 1855. The shotguns produced by the company quickly became known for their superior quality of construction. Today, SKB claims to marry the craftsmanship of the old world with the ever-changing, superior technology of the new world in shotgun construction. SKB's guns are imported all over the world and have been imported to the United States since 1968. The company produces several Trap, Field, and Clay models of over/under type shotguns. SKB markets that their shotguns are constructed conservatively, focusing on performance as opposed to popular aesthetics.

*Photo Courtesy of
Rock Island Auction Company*

IS300 FIELD REDBOOK CODE: RB-SK-S-IS300F
Inertia System with compression spring to dampen recoil and provide kinetic energy to cycle action. Chrome-lined, back-bored barrels with rotating bolt that locks directly into barrel collar. F, M, and IC choke tubes. 14.5" length of pull and shim assortment for variable cast and drop. Add $90 for camouflage or walnut stock.

Production: *current* **Gauge/Bore:** *12 ga.*
Action: *semi-auto*
Barrel Length: *26", 28", 30"* **Wt.:** *6.69–6.94 lbs.*
Sights: *none*
Capacity: *5*
Stock: *synthetic, walnut*

D2C:	NIB $590	Ex $450	VG+ $325	Good $295	**LMP:** $625
C2C:	Mint $570	Ex $425	VG+ $300	Good $270	Fair $140
Trade-In:	Mint $420	Ex $350	VG+ $240	Good $210	Poor $60

IS300 TARGET REDBOOK CODE: RB-SK-S-IS300T
Inertia System with compression spring to dampen recoil and provide kinetic energy to cycle action. Chrome-lined, back-bored barrels with rotating bolt that locks directly into barrel collar. Features adjustable comb stock with left-right and up-down positioning and shim assortment for variable cast and drop. 14.5" length of pull. F, IM, and M choke tubes.

Production: *current* **Gauge/Bore:** *12 ga.*
Action: *semi-auto*
Barrel Length: *26", 28", 30"* **Wt.:** *7.19 lbs., 7.31 lbs.*
Sights: *bead front*
Capacity: *5*
Stock: *walnut*

D2C:	NIB $820	Ex $625	VG+ $455	Good $410	**LMP:** $870
C2C:	Mint $790	Ex $575	VG+ $410	Good $370	Fair $190
Trade-In:	Mint $590	Ex $475	VG+ $320	Good $290	Poor $90

90TSS TRAP   REDBOOK CODE: RB-SK-S-90TSST

Features adjustable comb and buttplate, Pachmayr buttpad, and choice of right and left-hand cast.
Includes mechanical trigger system with coil springs and manual top tang safety integral barrel
selector. Ventilated rib barrel with 2 3/4" chamber. Length of pull approximately 14.25-15.5". F, IM, and M choke tubes.

Production: *current* **Gauge/Bore:** *12 ga.*

Action: *O/U*

Barrel Length: 30", 32" **Wt.:** *N/A*

Sights: *target*

Capacity: *2*

Stock: *Grade II walnut*

D2C:	NIB $1,670	Ex $1,275	VG+ $920	Good $835	**LMP:** $1,750
C2C:	Mint $1,610	Ex $1,175	VG+ $840	Good $755	Fair $385
Trade-In:	Mint $1,190	Ex $950	VG+ $660	Good $585	Poor $180

90TSS SPORTING   REDBOOK CODE: RB-SK-S-90TSSP

Features adjustable comb and buttplate, Pachmayr buttpad, and choice of right and left-hand cast.
Includes mechanical trigger system with coil springs and manual top tang safety integral barrel selector.
Ventilated rib barrel with 2 3/4" chamber. Length of pull approximately 14.25-15.5". M, IC, and SK choke tubes.

Production: *current* **Gauge/Bore:** *12 ga., 20 ga.*

Action: *O/U*

Barrel Length: 28", 30", 32" **Wt.:** *N/A*

Sights: *target*

Capacity: *2*

Stock: *Grade II walnut*

D2C:	NIB $1,670	Ex $1,275	VG+ $920	Good $835	**LMP:** $1,750
C2C:	Mint $1,610	Ex $1,175	VG+ $840	Good $755	Fair $385
Trade-In:	Mint $1,190	Ex $950	VG+ $660	Good $585	Poor $180

90TSS SKEET   REDBOOK CODE: RB-SK-S-90TSSK

Features fixed comb and buttplate, Pachmayr buttpad, and choice of right and left-hand cast. Includes
mechanical trigger system with coil springs and manual top tang safety integral barrel selector. Ventilated
rib barrel with 2 3/4" chamber. 14.5" length of pull. M, IC, and SK choke tubes.

Production: *current* **Gauge/Bore:** *12 ga., 20 ga.*

Action: *O/U*

Barrel Length: 28", 30", 32" **Wt.:** *N/A*

Sights: *target*

Capacity: *2*

Stock: *Grade II walnut*

D2C:	NIB $1,350	Ex $1,050	VG+ $745	Good $675	**LMP:** $1,470
C2C:	Mint $1,300	Ex $950	VG+ $680	Good $610	Fair $315
Trade-In:	Mint $960	Ex $775	VG+ $530	Good $475	Poor $150

MODEL 200   REDBOOK CODE: RB-SK-S-MOD200

Features platform lump barrel design with chrome lined AISI 4140 steel barrels, single trigger, V
spring power action, manual safety, and automatic ejectors. Sculpted and hand engraved with bright
blue finish, fine line hand checkering, and beavertail forend.
14.5" length of pull. Thin wall choke tube system with
F, IM, M, IC, and SK chokes. Add $150 for 28 and .410 models.

Production: *current* **Gauge/Bore:** *12 ga., 20 ga., 28 ga., .410*

Action: *SxS*

Barrel Length: 26", 28", 30" **Wt.:** *N/A*

Sights: *bead front*

Capacity: *2*

Stock: *Prince of Wales walnut*

D2C:	NIB $1,430	Ex $1,100	VG+ $790	Good $715	**LMP:** $2,100
C2C:	Mint $1,380	Ex $1,000	VG+ $720	Good $645	Fair $330
Trade-In:	Mint $1,020	Ex $825	VG+ $560	Good $505	Poor $150

SKB ARMS COMPANY

MODEL 200HR REDBOOK CODE: RB-SK-S-M200HR

Chrome lined target barrels with raised vent rib and bright blue finish. Thin wall choke tube system with F, IM, M, IC, and SK chokes. Single trigger, V spring power action, manual safety, and automatic ejectors. Accented with sculpted and hand engraved receiver, fine line hand checkering, and Schnabel forend. 14.5" length of pull. Add $125 for 28 and .410 models.

Production: *current* **Gauge/Bore:** *12 ga., 20 ga., 28 ga., .410*					
Action: *SxS*					
Barrel Length: 28", 30" **Wt.:** *N/A*	D2C:	NIB $2,315	Ex $1,775	VG+ $1,275	Good $1,160	LMP: $2,500
Sights: *bead front*	C2C:	Mint $2,230	Ex $1,600	VG+ $1,160	Good $1,045	Fair $535
Capacity: 2	Trade-In:	Mint $1,650	Ex $1,300	VG+ $910	Good $815	Poor $240
Stock: *pistol grip*					

MODEL 250 REDBOOK CODE: RB-SK-S-MOD250

Bison bone charcoal case hardening and chrome lined barrels with bright blue finish. Single trigger, and thin wall choke tube system with F, IM, M, IC, and SK chokes. Accented with sculpted and hand engraved side plate receiver, fine line hand checkering, and beavertail forend. 14.5" length of pull. Add $125 for 28 and .410 models.

Production: *current* **Gauge/Bore:** *12 ga., 20 ga., 28 ga., .410*					
Action: *SxS*					
Barrel Length: 26", 28", 30" **Wt.:** *N/A*	D2C:	NIB $2,700	Ex $2,075	VG+ $1,485	Good $1,350	LMP: $2,600
Sights: *none*	C2C:	Mint $2,600	Ex $1,875	VG+ $1,350	Good $1,215	Fair $625
Capacity: 2	Trade-In:	Mint $1,920	Ex $1,525	VG+ $1,060	Good $945	Poor $270
Stock: *Prince of Wales walnut*					

590 FIELD REDBOOK CODE: RB-SK-S-MOD590

Chrome lined 3" chambers and bores with jeweled monobloc and automatic ejectors. SKB competition choke tube system includes F, M, and IC chokes. Features 14.5" length of pull, Pachmayr pad, mechanical trigger system with coil springs, and manual top tang safety integral barrel selector. Laser engraved receiver with bright blue highlights.

Production: *current* **Gauge/Bore:** *12 ga., 20 ga.*					
Action: *SxS*					
Barrel Length: 26", 28", 30" **Wt.:** *7.12 lbs.–7.87 lbs.*	D2C:	NIB $1,250	Ex $950	VG+ $690	Good $625	LMP: $1,300
Sights: *none*	C2C:	Mint $1,200	Ex $875	VG+ $630	Good $565	Fair $290
Capacity: 2	Trade-In:	Mint $890	Ex $700	VG+ $490	Good $440	Poor $150
Stock: *walnut*					

M 7000SL REDBOOK CODE: RB-SK-S-7000SL

Holland & Holland style 7 pin removable sidelocks with safety sears. Single trigger and thin wall choke tube system with F, IM, M, IC, and SK chokes. 14.5" length of pull. Bison-bone charcoal case hardening, chrome line barrels with bright blue finish, sculpted and hand engraved side lock receiver, and fine line hand checkering. Special orders starting at $6,700.

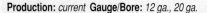

Production: *current* **Gauge/Bore:** *12 ga., 20 ga.*					
Action: *SxS*					
Barrel Length: 28", 30" **Wt.:** *N/A*	D2C:	NIB $6,260	Ex $4,775	VG+ $3,445	Good $3,130	LMP: $6,500
Sights: *none*	C2C:	Mint $6,010	Ex $4,325	VG+ $3,130	Good $2,820	Fair $1,440
Capacity: 2	Trade-In:	Mint $4,450	Ex $3,525	VG+ $2,450	Good $2,195	Poor $630
Stock: *Prince of Wales walnut*					

CENTURY III FIXED COMB   REDBOOK CODE: RB-SK-S-CENT3F

Vent rib, 2 3/4" chrome lined chamber and bore, jeweled monobloc, and shell extractor. F, IM, and M competition chokes. 14.375" length of pull, gold plated trigger, and manual top tang safety. Fixed comb and Pachmayr XLT buttpad. Steel receiver with laser engraving and bright blue finish. Walnut stock available in standard or Monte Carlo.

Production: *current* **Gauge/Bore:** *12 ga.*

Action: *single-shot*

Barrel Length: 30", 32" **Wt.:** *N/A*

Sights: *target*

Capacity: *1*

Stock: *Grade II walnut*

D2C:	NIB $1,150	Ex $875	VG+ $635	Good $575	LMP: $1,150
C2C:	Mint $1,110	Ex $800	VG+ $580	Good $520	Fair $265
Trade-In:	Mint $820	Ex $650	VG+ $450	Good $405	Poor $120

CENTURY III ADJUSTABLE COMB   REDBOOK CODE: RB-SK-S-CENT3A

Vent rib, chambered for 2 3/4". F, IM, and M competition chokes. 14.37" length of pull, gold-plated trigger, and manual top tang safety. Adjustable comb. Right-left cast. Fixed Pachmayr XLT buttpad. Laser engraved receiver with bright blue finish. Standard or Monte Carlo stock. Standard stock also available with adjustable buttplate system and 14-15.25" length of pull; add $130.

Production: *current* **Gauge/Bore:** *12 ga.*

Action: *single-shot*

Barrel Length: 30", 32" **Wt.:** *N/A*

Sights: *target*

Capacity: *1*

Stock: *Grade II walnut*

D2C:	NIB $1,300	Ex $1,000	VG+ $715	Good $650	LMP: $1,300
C2C:	Mint $1,250	Ex $900	VG+ $650	Good $585	Fair $300
Trade-In:	Mint $930	Ex $750	VG+ $510	Good $455	Poor $150

L.C. Smith

Lyman Cornelius (L.C.) Smith partnered with W.H. Baker in the manufacture of the Baker Three-Barrel Gun in Syracuse, New York, in 1879 but then took over their business entirely in 1880. In 1884, he began manufacturing double barrel hammer shotguns in varying grades, designated at first by letters but then by numbers starting in 1886. In 1888, he sold the company to John Hunter, Sr. in Fulton, New York. In 1889, Hunter Arms Company built a factory in Fulton, New York, to continue production of L.C. Smith guns and multiple "trade name" guns for others, such as Montgomery Ward & Co., Sears, Roebuck and Co, etc. In 1945, Marlin Firearms Company of New Haven, Connecticut, bought the Hunter Arms Company and continued to produce quality L.C. Smith shotguns, all stamped "LC SMITH GUN COMPANY," as a subsidiary of Marlin until 1951 when the factory was closed. The Marlin Firearms Company reintroduced the brand in 1969 and produced limited quantities of Field Grade and De Luxe Model shotguns until production ceased in 1971. Then, Marlin Firearms Company imported guns from Italy and distributed them under the L.C. Smith brand from 2004-2010. Though the history of the brand is sporadic and varied, L.C. Smith shotguns continue to be some of the most collectible long guns in early American gun history.

Photo Courtesy of
Rock Island Auction Company

NO. 00   REDBOOK CODE: RB-SM-S-HLCS00

Plain Armour steel barrels, engraving absent on lock plates, stamped "LC Smith," right barrel marked "HUNTER ARMS CO. MAKERS-FULTON, NY," checkered forend and grip, 16 gauge added in 1906, 20 gauge added in 1908, option of automatic ejectors and/or Hunter One-Trigger available for additional cost.

Production: *1898–1914* **Gauge/Bore:** *10 ga., 12 ga., 16 ga., 20 ga.*

Action: *SxS*

Barrel Length: 26"–32" **Wt.:** *8 lbs.*

Sights: *bead front*

Capacity: *2*

Stock: *English walnut, checkered half pistol grip*

D2C:	NIB $769	Ex $600	VG+ $425	Good $385	
C2C:	Mint $740	Ex $550	VG+ $390	Good $350	Fair $180
Trade-In:	Mint $550	Ex $450	VG+ $300	Good $270	Poor $90

NO. 0   REDBOOK CODE: RB-SM-S-HLCS0X
Introduced with Twist steel barrels, but changed to Damascus steel in 1899,
London Steel barrel offered as an option in 1907, choke-bored, lock plates stamped with "L.C. SMITH,"
border engraving around perimeter, available in lightweight after 1907, automatic ejectors were optional beginning in 1898 for added cost.

Photo Courtesy of Rock Island Auction Company

Production: *1894–1914* **Gauge/Bore:** *10 ga., 12 ga., 16 ga., 20 ga.*
Action: *SxS*
Barrel Length: 26"–32" **Wt.:** *N/A*
Sights: *bead front*
Capacity: *2*
Stock: *English walnut, half pistol grip, checkered*

D2C:	NIB $1,161	Ex $900	VG+ $640	Good $585	
C2C:	Mint $1,120	Ex $825	VG+ $590	Good $525	Fair $270
Trade-In:	Mint $830	Ex $675	VG+ $460	Good $410	Poor $120

Photo Courtesy of Rock Island Auction Company

NO. 1   REDBOOK CODE: RB-SM-S-HLCS1X
Damascus steel barrels, choke-bored with line engravings, "L.C. Smith" engraved on the locks, minimal line and scroll pattern engravings, minimal engraving on frame, trigger guard and forend metal, more ornate in later production, early models had laminated steel barrels, "HUNTER ARMS CO" stamped on rib extension, "FULTON, NY"— stamped below, option of full pistol grip, automatic ejectors and Hunter One-Trigger for added cost.

Production: *1890–1914* **Gauge/Bore:** *10 ga., 12 ga., 16 ga., 20 ga.*
Action: *SxS*
Barrel Length: 26"–32" **Wt.:** *N/A*
Sights: *bead front*
Capacity: *2*
Stock: *English walnut, half pistol grip, checkered*

D2C:	NIB $637	Ex $500	VG+ $355	Good $320	
C2C:	Mint $620	Ex $450	VG+ $320	Good $290	Fair $150
Trade-In:	Mint $460	Ex $375	VG+ $250	Good $225	Poor $90

NO. 2   REDBOOK CODE: RB-SM-S-HLCS2X
Early barrels were of Chain Damascus, later in Crown Steel, 20 gauge available in 1907, "HUNTER ARMS CO, MAKERS, FULTON, NY" stamped on barrel extension, ducks were commonly engraved on right lock plate, usually a quail engraved in a circle on the left, lightweight model was available for added cost, automatic ejectors were optional.

Photo Courtesy of Rock Island Auction Company

Production: *1890–1914* **Gauge/Bore:** *8 ga., 10 ga., 12 ga., 16 ga., 20 ga.*
Action: *SxS*
Barrel Length: 28", 30", 32" **Wt.:** *N/A*
Sights: *bead front*
Capacity: *2*
Stock: *English walnut, full or half pistol grip, standard or Monte Carlo*

D2C:	NIB $2,112	Ex $1,625	VG+ $1,165	Good $1,060	
C2C:	Mint $2,030	Ex $1,475	VG+ $1,060	Good $955	Fair $490
Trade-In:	Mint $1,500	Ex $1,200	VG+ $830	Good $740	Poor $240

NO. 3   REDBOOK CODE: RB-SM-S-HLCS3X
Nitro Steel or Chain Damascus steel barrels, "finest medium-grade on the market", ducks were usually engraved in an oval on the right side lock with quail in an oval on the left, 20 gauge was introduced in 1907, "HUNTER ARMS CO, FULTON, NY" stamped on barrel extension, lightweights were available in 12 and 16 gauge, automatic ejectors available for added cost.

Photo Courtesy of Rock Island Auction Company

Production: *1894–1912* **Gauge/Bore:** *8 ga., 10 ga., 12 ga., 16 ga., 20 ga.*
Action: *SxS*
Barrel Length: 28", 30", 32" **Wt.:** *6.5 lbs–6.8 lbs.*
Sights: *bead front*
Capacity: *2*
Stock: *English walnut, straight or pistol grip*

D2C:	NIB $3,062	Ex $2,350	VG+ $1,685	Good $1,535	
C2C:	Mint $2,940	Ex $2,125	VG+ $1,540	Good $1,380	Fair $705
Trade-In:	Mint $2,180	Ex $1,725	VG+ $1,200	Good $1,075	Poor $330

SMITH, L.C.

NO. 4   REDBOOK CODE: RB-SM-S-HLCS4X

"Medium high-priced gun" with Nitro Steel barrels, rib extension engraved with "HUNTER ARMS CO, FULTON, NY," forend with delicate checkering, 20 gauge offered in 1907, lightweights offered in 12, 16 and 20 gauges, automatic ejectors were available for added cost, low production numbers affect value.

Production: *1894–1914* **Gauge/Bore:** *8 ga., 10 ga., 12 ga., 16 ga., 20 ga.*

Action: *SxS*

Barrel Length: 26"–32" **Wt.:** *N/A*

Sights: *bead front*

Capacity: *2*

D2C:	NIB $4,115	Ex $3,150	VG+ $2,265	Good $2,060	
C2C:	Mint $3,960	Ex $2,850	VG+ $2,060	Good $1,855	Fair $950
Trade-In:	Mint $2,930	Ex $2,325	VG+ $1,610	Good $1,445	Poor $420

Stock: *French or English walnut, finely figured, standard or Monte Carlo, straight or pistol grip*

NO. 5   REDBOOK CODE: RB-SM-S-HLCS5X

Nitro Steel or Damascus Steel barrels, elaborate engraving with many variations due to custom orders, inside of lock plate was damascened with polished parts, usual engravings were flowers and scroll designs on the frame and trigger guard, barrels were engraved near the frame or muzzle, 20 gauge model introduced in 1907, top rib engraved "MADE TO ORDER BY THE HUNTER ARMS CO, FULTON, NY," lightweight models were available in 12, 16 and 20 gauges, available with automatic ejectors as an option, low production numbers affects value. No pricing available at this time.

Production: *1894–1912* **Gauge/Bore:** *8 ga., 10 ga., 12 ga., 16 ga., 20 ga.*

Action: *SxS*

Barrel Length: 26", 32" **Wt.:** *N/A*

Sights: *bead front*

Capacity: *2*

Stock: *French or English walnut, straight or pistol grip, standard or Monte Carlo*

PIGEON   REDBOOK CODE: RB-SM-S-HLCSPG

Nitro Steel or Chainette Damascus Steel barrels, 20 gauge models were not initially available but were introduced in 1907 and only offered in Nitro Steel, one side lock engraved with pigeon in flight with a blue rock on the other side lock, another pigeon is engraved on the rib extension, inlaid across the rib is a precious metal bar, "HUNTER ARMS CO, MAKERS, FULTON, NY" engraved forward of the bar, lightweight models were available in 12, 16, and 20 gauges, optional Hunter One-Trigger for added cost, automatic ejectors available for additional cost.

Production: *1893–1913* **Gauge/Bore:** *10 ga., 12 ga., 16 ga., 20 ga.*

Action: *SxS*

Barrel Length: 26", 28", 30", 32" **Wt.:** *N/A*

Sights: *bead front*

Capacity: *2*

D2C:	NIB $6,339	Ex $4,825	VG+ $3,490	Good $3,170	
C2C:	Mint $6,090	Ex $4,375	VG+ $3,170	Good $2,855	Fair $1,460
Trade-In:	Mint $4,510	Ex $3,550	VG+ $2,480	Good $2,220	Poor $660

Stock: *choice French figured walnut, straight or pistol grip, standard or Monte Carlo*

MONOGRAM   REDBOOK CODE: RB-SM-S-HLCSMO

Name and style did not change in 1912-1913, Sir Joseph Whitworth Fluid Compressed Steel barrels, muzzle and breech ends engraved, lock plates had scroll work, birds with scroll work and flowers covering the frame and trigger guard, two-triggers and ejectors, right barrel was hand-engraved "SIR JOSEPH WHITWORTH FLUID COMPRESSED STEEL," left barrel engraved "MADE TO ORDER BY THE HUNTER ARMS CO, FULTON, NY," the rib extension engraved "L.C. SMITH MONOGRAM GRADE." Hunter One-Trigger was optional for added cost.

Photo Courtesy of Rock Island Auction Company

Production: *1892–1945* **Gauge/Bore:** *10 ga., 12 ga., 16 ga., 20 ga.*

Action: *SxS*

Barrel Length: 26", 28", 30", 32" **Wt.:** *N/A*

Sights: *bead front*

Capacity: *2*

D2C:	NIB $12,723	Ex $9,675	VG+ $7,000	Good $6,365	
C2C:	Mint $12,220	Ex $8,800	VG+ $6,370	Good $5,730	Fair $2,930
Trade-In:	Mint $9,040	Ex $7,125	VG+ $4,970	Good $4,455	Poor $1,290

Stock: *imported walnut, highly figured*

SMITH, L.C.

A1 REDBOOK CODE: RB-SM-S-HLCSA1

Damascus Steel barrels with chain pattern, lock plates were engraved with dog scenes and scroll work, with automatic ejectors, low production numbers.

Production: *1891–1902* Gauge/Bore: *10 ga., 12 ga., 16 ga.*					
Action: *SxS*					
Barrel Length: 28", 30", 32" **Wt.:** *N/A*	D2C:	NIB $5,735	Ex $4,375	VG+ $3,155	Good $2,870	
Sights: *bead front*	C2C:	Mint $5,510	Ex $3,975	VG+ $2,870	Good $2,585	Fair $1,320
Capacity: *2*	Trade-In:	Mint $4,080	Ex $3,225	VG+ $2,240	Good $2,010	Poor $600

Stock: *English walnut, fine checkering, full, three-quarter, or half pistol grip*

A2 REDBOOK CODE: RB-SM-S-HLCSA2

Damascus Steel or Sir Joseph Whitworth Fluid Compressed Steel barrels, inside of the side locks damascened and polished, four common elaborate engraving patterns and scroll work such as hunting scene or birds and dogs in bas-relief, right barrel engraved with "MADE TO ORDER BY THE HUNTER ARMS CO, FULTON, NY," left barrel engraved "SIR JOSEPH WHITWORTH FLUID COMPRESSED STEEL", the rib engraved with "HUNTER ARMS CO, FULTON, NY," lightweight model available with Krupp Steel barrels.

Production: *1891–1916* Gauge/Bore: *10 ga., 12 ga., 16 ga., 20 ga.*					
Action: *SxS*					
Barrel Length: 26", 28", 30", 32" **Wt.:** *N/A*	D2C:	NIB $8,950	Ex $6,825	VG+ $4,925	Good $4,475	
Sights: *bead front*	C2C:	Mint $8,600	Ex $6,200	VG+ $4,480	Good $4,030	Fair $2,060
Capacity: *2*	Trade-In:	Mint $6,360	Ex $5,025	VG+ $3,500	Good $3,135	Poor $900

Stock: *select French, English or Circassian walnut*

A3 REDBOOK CODE: RB-SM-S-HLCSA3

Sir Joseph Whitworth Fluid Compressed Steel barrels, "finest gun in the world for the price", with streaks of lightning inlaid in gold on side of the barrels with additional scroll engraving, engraving includes setter in the left lock plate and a pointer on the right, top of frame elaborately ornamented with oak leaf, serial number hand engraved on the water table of the frame, barrels, trigger guard and forend metal, locks are damascened, 20 gauge added in 1907, only 19 guns produced. No pricing available at this time.

Production: *1894–discontinued* Gauge/Bore: *10 ga., 12 ga., 16 ga., 20 ga.*

Action: *SxS*

Barrel Length: 26", 28", 30", 32" **Wt.:** *N/A*

Sights: *bead front*

Capacity: *2*

Stock: *select Circassian walnut, configuration at customer request*

FIELD REDBOOK CODE: RB-SM-S-HLCSFD

Armour Steel barrels, chokes bored from cylinder to full at customer request, L.C. SMITH stamped on lock plates, plain with no engraving, right barrel stamped "L.C. SMITH FIELD GRADE", and the left barrel marked "THE HUNTER ARMS CO, FULTON, NY," available with ivory sights and recoil pad for additional cost, Hunter One-Trigger optional for added cost, automatic ejectors were available for additional cost, .410 gauge added to production in later.

Photo Courtesy of Rock Island Auction Company

Production: *1912–1950* Gauge/Bore: *12 ga., 16 ga., 20 ga., .410*					
Action: *SxS*					
Barrel Length: 26", 28", 30", 32" **Wt.:** *N/A*	D2C:	NIB $1,596	Ex $1,225	VG+ $880	Good $800	
Sights: *bead front*	C2C:	Mint $1,540	Ex $1,125	VG+ $800	Good $720	Fair $370
Capacity: *2*	Trade-In:	Mint $1,140	Ex $900	VG+ $630	Good $560	Poor $180

Stock: *American walnut, half pistol, full pistol or straight grip, checkered*

IDEAL REDBOOK CODE: RB-SM-S-HLCSID

London Steel barrels, bored from cylinder to full choke, locks engraved with simple oak leaf design, trigger guard and frame with minimal engraving, "L.C. SMITH" roll stamped on lock plates, right barrel roll-stamped "L.C. SMITH IDEAL GRADE", the left barrel marked, "THE HUNTER ARMS CO, FULTON, NY," with two-triggers, Hunter One-Trigger available for added cost, automatic ejectors optional, .410 gauge available later, available in Damascus Steel for additional cost.

Photo Courtesy of
Rock Island Auction Company

Production: *1912–1950* **Gauge/Bore:** *12 ga., 16 ga., 20 ga., .410*

Action: *SxS*

Barrel Length: 26", 28", 30", 32" **Wt.:** *N/A*

Sights: *bead front*

Capacity: *2*

Stock: *American walnut*

D2C:	NIB $2,575	Ex $1,975	VG+ $1,420	Good $1,290	
C2C:	Mint $2,480	Ex $1,800	VG+ $1,290	Good $1,160	Fair $595
Trade-In:	Mint $1,830	Ex $1,450	VG+ $1,010	Good $905	Poor $270

SKEET SPECIAL REDBOOK CODE: RB-SM-S-HLCSSS

London Steel barrels, custom-built to order, available with selective or non-selective Hunter One-Trigger, beaver tail forend and automatic ejectors, custom stock for no additional charge, clay pigeon superimposed on a flying partridge engraved on left lock plate, right lock plate engraved with flying partridge, no engraving on frame, other barrel lengths available.

Photo Courtesy of
Rock Island Auction Company

Production: *1926–1948* **Gauge/Bore:** *12 ga., 16 ga., 20 ga., .410*

Action: *SxS*

Barrel Length: 26", 27", 28" **Wt.:** *N/A*

Sights: *bead front*

Capacity: *2*

Stock: *walnut, straight grip, checkered*

D2C:	NIB $4,635	Ex $3,525	VG+ $2,550	Good $2,320	
C2C:	Mint $4,450	Ex $3,200	VG+ $2,320	Good $2,090	Fair $1,070
Trade-In:	Mint $3,300	Ex $2,600	VG+ $1,810	Good $1,625	Poor $480

PREMIER SKEET REDBOOK CODE: RB-SM-S-HLCSPS

Selective single trigger, automatic ejectors, streamline beavertail forend, checkered butt, hand-checkered and engraved on one side with clay-bird and a quail in flight on the other, right barrel engraved "L.C. SMITH-12 GA-PREMIER SKEET, FULTON, NY, USA," limited quantity produced.

Photo Courtesy of
Rock Island Auction Company

Production: *1949–1950* **Gauge/Bore:** *12 ga., 20 ga.*

Action: *SxS*

Barrel Length: 26", 27", 28" **Wt.:** *N/A*

Sights: *bead front*

Capacity: *2*

Stock: *walnut, straight grip*

D2C:	NIB $5,349	Ex $4,075	VG+ $2,945	Good $2,675	
C2C:	Mint $5,140	Ex $3,700	VG+ $2,680	Good $2,410	Fair $1,235
Trade-In:	Mint $3,800	Ex $3,000	VG+ $2,090	Good $1,875	Poor $540

TRAP REDBOOK CODE: RB-SM-S-HLCSTP

Crown Steel barrels, lock plate engraved with trap shooting scene showing trap house and five shooters, two triggers, automatic ejector, right barrel roll-stamped "L.C. SMITH TRAP GRADE", left barrel stamped "HUNTER ARMS CO, INC, MFRS FULTON, NY," Hunter One-Trigger available for added cost, Damascus Steel barrels| were optional until 1917.

Photo Courtesy of
Rock Island Auction Company

Production: *1912–1940* **Gauge/Bore:** *12 ga., 16 ga., 20 ga., .410*

Action: *SxS*

Barrel Length: 26", 28", 30", 32" **Wt.:** *N/A*

Sights: *bead front*

Capacity: *2*

Stock: *American walnut, full, half pistol or straight grip*

D2C:	NIB $3,600	Ex $2,750	VG+ $1,980	Good $1,800	
C2C:	Mint $3,460	Ex $2,500	VG+ $1,800	Good $1,620	Fair $830
Trade-In:	Mint $2,560	Ex $2,025	VG+ $1,410	Good $1,260	Poor $360

SPECIALTY REDBOOK CODE: RB-SM-S-HLCSSP

Nitro Steel or Damascus Steel barrels, bored as ordered, "L.C. SMITH" engraved on lock plates, quail engraved on left lock plate, waterfowl scene engraved on right, serial number engraved on trigger guard extension, regular rib with precious metal bar inlaid at junction of rib and extension, left barrel with "HUNTER ARMS CO, INC, MFRS FULTON, NY, USA," and right barrel stamped "L.C. SMITH SPECIALTY GRADE", .410 gauge available later, Hunter One-Trigger for added cost, automatic ejectors available for added cost.

Photo Courtesy of
Rock Island Auction Company

Production: 1912–1950 **Gauge/Bore:** 12 ga., 16 ga., 20 ga., .410
Action: SxS
Barrel Length: 26", 28", 30", 32" **Wt.:** N/A
Sights: bead front
Capacity: 2
Stock: figured walnut, full, half pistol, or straight grip

D2C:	NIB $5,815	Ex $4,425	VG+ $3,200	Good $2,910	
C2C:	Mint $5,590	Ex $4,025	VG+ $2,910	Good $2,620	Fair $1,340
Trade-In:	Mint $4,130	Ex $3,275	VG+ $2,270	Good $2,040	Poor $600

FIELD GRADE MODEL (MARLIN) REDBOOK CODE: RB-SM-S-MLCSFG

No engraving or markings on lock plates, "L.C. SMITH FIELD GRADE" stamped on water table of receiver, modified and full choke, full length ventilated rib serrated on top, double triggers, extractors, splinter forend hand-checkered, frame is case-hardened, auto top tang safety, rib stamped "L.C. SMITH 12 GA" in script and letters filled with gold color, trigger plate stamped "THE MARLIN FIREARMS CO, NORTH HAVEN, CONN", serial number begins with FWM.

Photo Courtesy of
Rock Island Auction Company

Production: 1968–1971 **Gauge/Bore:** 12 ga.
Action: SxS
Barrel Length: 28" **Wt.:** 6.8 lbs.
Sights: front and mid bead
Capacity: 2
Stock: American walnut, full pistol grip with cap, checkered

D2C:	NIB $1,128	Ex $875	VG+ $625	Good $565	
C2C:	Mint $1,090	Ex $800	VG+ $570	Good $510	Fair $260
Trade-In:	Mint $810	Ex $650	VG+ $440	Good $395	Poor $120

DELUXE MODEL (MARLIN) REDBOOK CODE: RB-SM-S-MLCSDM

No engraving or markings on lock plates, "L.C. SMITH DELUXE MODEL" stamped on water table of receiver, modified and full choke, full length aluminum ventilated rib serrated on top made by Simmons, double triggers, extractors, beavertail forend, frame is case-hardened, auto top tang safety, rib stamped "L.C. SMITH 12 GA" in script and letters filled with gold color, trigger plate stamped "THE MARLIN FIREARMS CO, NORTH HAVEN, CONN", only 189 guns were manufactured.

Production: 1968–1971 **Gauge/Bore:** 12 ga.
Action: SxS
Barrel Length: 28" **Wt.:** 6.8 lbs.
Sights: one white bullet shaped, one white bead
Capacity: 2
Stock: American walnut, full pistol grip with cap, checkered

D2C:	NIB $1,587	Ex $1,225	VG+ $875	Good $795	
C2C:	Mint $1,530	Ex $1,100	VG+ $800	Good $715	Fair $370
Trade-In:	Mint $1,130	Ex $900	VG+ $620	Good $560	Poor $180

Squires Bingham International, Inc.

Roy Squires and William Bingham, two Englishmen, opened a photo print shop and merchandising firm in the Philippines in 1905 called Squires, Bingham & Co. The business expanded to include many varied products, including firearms and ammunition, and by the 1930s, the company was well known for retail sales of sporting arms. In 1941, under the new ownership of Celso Tuason, the company began to manufacture its own line of firearms. In 1952, manufacturing that had previously been headquartered elsewhere was brought to the Philippines under the name Squires Bingham Manufacturing Company., Inc. By the 1960s, Tuason passed management of the company down to his three sons, with the firearms portion of the business going to Demetrio "Bolo" Tuason. At that time, the name given to the company and the firearms it produced became Arms Corporation of the Philippines, or Armscor. In 2001, Squires Bingham International, Inc. was formed in Quezon City as a dealership to distribute Armscor guns and ammunition through its storefront and its dealership network.

M30 DI/C REDBOOK CODE: RB-SQ-S-M30DIC
3" chamber, interchangeable choke, serration on receiver, contoured barrel, damascened bolt.

Production: *current* **Gauge/Bore:** *12 ga.*

Action: *pump-action*

Barrel Length: *26", 28"* **Wt.:** *7.7–7.9 lbs.*

Sights: *bead front*

Capacity: *5*

Stock: *hardwood*

D2C:	NIB $421	Ex $325	VG+ $235	Good $215	LMP: $421
C2C:	Mint $410	Ex $300	VG+ $220	Good $190	Fair $100
Trade-In:	Mint $300	Ex $250	VG+ $170	Good $150	Poor $60

M30 FS REDBOOK CODE: RB-SQ-S-M30FSB
3" chamber, interchangeable choke, serration on receiver, parkerized finish, contoured barrel, damascened bolt, cross-bolt safety.

Production: *current* **Gauge/Bore:** *12 ga.*

Action: *pump-action*

Barrel Length: *20"* **Wt.:** *7.5 lbs.*

Sights: *bead front*

Capacity: *5*

Stock: *black polymer*

D2C:	NIB $398	Ex $325	VG+ $220	Good $200	LMP: $398
C2C:	Mint $390	Ex $275	VG+ $200	Good $180	Fair $95
Trade-In:	Mint $290	Ex $225	VG+ $160	Good $140	Poor $60

M30 R6 REDBOOK CODE: RB-SQ-S-M30R6B
3" chamber, serration on receiver, parkerized finish, contoured barrel, damascened bolt, polymer forearm.

Production: *current* **Gauge/Bore:** *12 ga.*

Action: *pump-action*

Barrel Length: *20"* **Wt.:** *7.5 lbs.*

Sights: *bead front*

Capacity: *5*

Stock: *black polymer*

D2C:	NIB $371	Ex $300	VG+ $205	Good $190	LMP: $371
C2C:	Mint $360	Ex $275	VG+ $190	Good $170	Fair $90
Trade-In:	Mint $270	Ex $225	VG+ $150	Good $130	Poor $60

M30 R8 REDBOOK CODE: RB-SQ-S-M30R8B
3" chamber, interchangeable choke, serration on receiver, parkerized finish, contoured barrel, damascened bolt, cross bolt safety.

Production: *current* **Gauge/Bore:** *12 ga.*

Action: *pump-action*

Barrel Length: *20"* **Wt.:** *7.5 lbs.*

Sights: *bead front*

Capacity: *7*

Stock: *black polymer*

D2C:	NIB $384	Ex $300	VG+ $215	Good $195	LMP: $384
C2C:	Mint $370	Ex $275	VG+ $200	Good $175	Fair $90
Trade-In:	Mint $280	Ex $225	VG+ $150	Good $135	Poor $60

M30 SAS   REDBOOK CODE: RB-SQ-S-M30SAS
3" chamber, interchangeable choke, serration on receiver, parkerized finish, contoured barrel, damascened bolt, cross-bolt safety.

Production: *current* **Gauge/Bore:** *12 ga.*
Action: *pump-action*
Barrel Length: 20" **Wt.:** *7.9 lbs.*
Sights: *bead front*
Capacity: *7*
Stock: *black polymer*

D2C:	NIB $422	Ex $325	VG+ $235	Good $215	**LMP:** $422
C2C:	Mint $410	Ex $300	VG+ $220	Good $190	Fair $100
Trade-In:	Mint $300	Ex $250	VG+ $170	Good $150	Poor $60

Stevens Arms Co., J.

J. Stevens Arms Company was founded by Joshua Stevens in 1864. Originally located in Chicopee Falls, Massachusetts, the company was called J. Stevens & Co. and after a few changes in structure, it became J. Stevens Arms & Tool Co. The company originally focused on single-shot pistols and rifles. In 1887, the company developed the popular .22 LR cartridge, which took the company to new heights. By the turn of the 20th century, Stevens was one of the largest and most popular firearms manufacturers in the world. By 1920, the Savage Arms Company purchased Stevens and merged the two companies, making them the largest firearms manufacturer in the world at that time. Today, Savage continues to produce several shotguns under the Stevens name.

*Photo Courtesy of
Rock Island Auction Company*

MODEL 67 PUMP   REDBOOK CODE: RB-SJ-S-67PUMP
3" chamber, steel receiver, various choke options, blue steel, side-ejection, plain or ventilated rib, corn-cob style forend.

Production: *discontinued 1989* **Gauge/Bore:** *12 ga., 20 ga., .410*
Action: *pump-action*
Barrel Length: 21", 26", 28", 30" **Wt.:** *6.3–7.5 lbs.*
Sights: *optional rifle*
Capacity: *5*
Stock: *walnut*

D2C:	NIB $226	Ex $175	VG+ $125	Good $115	
C2C:	Mint $220	Ex $175	VG+ $120	Good $105	Fair $55
Trade-In:	Mint $170	Ex $150	VG+ $90	Good $80	Poor $30

*Photo Courtesy of
Rock Island Auction Company*

MODEL 77 SLIDE-ACTION REPEATER   REDBOOK CODE: RB-SJ-S-77SARE
M or F choke, no checkering, recoil pad, grooved slide handle.

Production: *discontinued* **Gauge/Bore:** *12 ga., 16 ga., 20 ga., .410*
Action: *pump-action*
Barrel Length: 26", 28" **Wt.:** *7.5 lbs.*
Sights: *bead front*
Capacity: *5*
Stock: *pistol-grip walnut*

D2C:	NIB $181	Ex $150	VG+ $100	Good $95	
C2C:	Mint $180	Ex $125	VG+ $100	Good $85	Fair $45
Trade-In:	Mint $130	Ex $125	VG+ $80	Good $65	Poor $30

*Photo Courtesy of
Rock Island Auction Company*

MODEL 94 SINGLE-SHOT   REDBOOK CODE: RB-SJ-S-94SING
Takedown style, automatic ejector, F choke included, no checkering on stock or forend, visible hammer.

Production: *discontinued* **Gauge/Bore:** *12 ga., 16 ga., 28 ga., .410*
Action: *single-shot*
Barrel Length: 26" 28", 30", 32" **Wt.:** *~6 lbs.*
Sights: *bead front*
Capacity: *1*
Stock: *pistol-grip walnut*

D2C:	NIB $135	Ex $125	VG+ $75	Good $70	
C2C:	Mint $130	Ex $100	VG+ $70	Good $65	Fair $35
Trade-In:	Mint $100	Ex $100	VG+ $60	Good $50	Poor $30

MODEL 95 SINGLE-SHOT   REDBOOK CODE: RB-SJ-S-95SING
Solid frame, visible hammer, plain extractor, 3" chamber, M or F choke, no checkering on walnut, grooved forearm.

Production: *discontinued* **Gauge/Bore:** *12 ga.*
Action: *single-shot*
Barrel Length: 28", 30" **Wt.:** *~7.3 lbs.*
Sights: *bead front*
Capacity: *1*
Stock: *pistol-grip walnut*

D2C:	NIB $103	Ex $100	VG+ $60	Good $55	
C2C:	Mint $100	Ex $75	VG+ $60	Good $50	Fair $25
Trade-In:	Mint $80	Ex $75	VG+ $50	Good $40	Poor $30

MODEL 107 SINGLE-SHOT HAMMER   REDBOOK CODE: RB-SJ-S-107SSH
Takedown style, automatic ejectors, F choke only, no checkering on stock or forearm.

Production: *discontinued* **Gauge/Bore:** *12 ga., 16 ga., 20 ga., .410*
Action: *single-shot*
Barrel Length: 28", 30" **Wt.:** *~6 lbs.*
Sights: *bead front*
Capacity: *1*
Stock: *pistol-grip walnut*

D2C:	NIB $130	Ex $100	VG+ $75	Good $65	
C2C:	Mint $130	Ex $100	VG+ $70	Good $60	Fair $30
Trade-In:	Mint $100	Ex $75	VG+ $60	Good $50	Poor $30

MODEL 124 CROSS BOLT REPEATER   REDBOOK CODE: RB-SJ-S-124CBR
Straight pull action, tenet forearm, IC/M/F chokes, hammerless, solid frame.

Production: *discontinued 1952* **Gauge/Bore:** *12 ga.*
Action: *bolt-action*
Barrel Length: 28" **Wt.:** *~7 lbs.*
Sights: *bead front*
Capacity: *3*
Stock: *plastic*

D2C:	NIB $187	Ex $150	VG+ $105	Good $95	
C2C:	Mint $180	Ex $150	VG+ $100	Good $85	Fair $45
Trade-In:	Mint $140	Ex $125	VG+ $80	Good $70	Poor $30

STEVENS ARMS

MODEL 240 OVER/UNDER REDBOOK CODE: RB-SJ-S-240XXX
Visible hammer, takedown style, pistol-grip and forend are plastic, double trigger, boxlock frame.

Production: 1940–1949 **Gauge/Bore:** 0.41

Action: O/U

Barrel Length: 26" **Wt.:** 6 lbs.

Sights: bead front

Capacity: 2

Stock: plastic

D2C:	NIB $480	Ex $375	VG+ $265	Good $240	
C2C:	Mint $470	Ex $350	VG+ $240	Good $220	Fair $115
Trade-In:	Mint $350	Ex $275	VG+ $190	Good $170	Poor $60

Photo Courtesy of
Rock Island Auction Company

MODEL 620 HAMMERLESS SLIDE ACTION REPEATING REDBOOK CODE: RB-SJ-S-620HSR
Takedown style, F/M/IC/C chokes included, checkering on pistol-grip and slide handle.

Production: discontinued **Gauge/Bore:** 12 ga., 16 ga., 20 ga.

Action: pump-action

Barrel Length: 26"–32" **Wt.:** 6–7.8 lbs.

Sights: bead front

Capacity: 5

Stock: pistol-grip walnut

D2C:	NIB $280	Ex $225	VG+ $155	Good $140	
C2C:	Mint $270	Ex $200	VG+ $140	Good $130	Fair $65
Trade-In:	Mint $200	Ex $175	VG+ $110	Good $100	Poor $30

Photo Courtesy of
Rock Island Auction Company

MODEL 530 HAMMERLESS DOUBLE REDBOOK CODE: RB-SJ-S-530HDX
Boxlock action, double trigger, M/F C/M F/F chokes, checkering on pistol-grip and forend, some models have recoil pad.

Production: discontinued **Gauge/Bore:** 12 ga., 16 ga., 20 ga., .410

Action: SxS

Barrel Length: 26"–32" **Wt.:** 6–7.5 lbs.

Sights: bead front

Capacity: 2

Stock: walnut

D2C:	NIB $364	Ex $300	VG+ $205	Good $185	
C2C:	Mint $350	Ex $275	VG+ $190	Good $165	Fair $85
Trade-In:	Mint $260	Ex $225	VG+ $150	Good $130	Poor $60

MODEL 820 HAMMERLESS SLIDE-ACTION REPEATING REDBOOK CODE: RB-SJ-S-820HSA
Solid frame, IC/M/F chokes, no checkering on pistol-grip, grooved slide handle, early models had plastic stocks.

Production: discontinued 1954 **Gauge/Bore:** 12 ga.

Action: pump-action

Barrel Length: 28" **Wt.:** 7.5 lbs.

Sights: bead front

Capacity: 5

Stock: pistol grip walnut

D2C:	NIB $147	Ex $125	VG+ $85	Good $75	
C2C:	Mint $150	Ex $125	VG+ $80	Good $70	Fair $35
Trade-In:	Mint $110	Ex $100	VG+ $60	Good $55	Poor $30

Stoeger Industries

Stoeger Industries was established in 1924 and first operated as a gun store in New York City. The company later moved to New Jersey, but when it was acquired by Beretta Holdings as part of the Benelli USA division, the company was relocated to Accokeek, Maryland. Stoeger manufactures pistols and a complete line of shotguns of the pump, side-by-side, and over/under varieties, along with shotgun gauges. Tactical handguns and shotguns are also offered.

MODEL 2000   REDBOOK CODE: RB-SR-S-MO2000
3" chamber, inertia recoil operating system, ventilated rib barrel, 5 choke tubes included, checkering on walnut stock, synthetic available in camouflage, matte metal.

Production: *2001–2013* **Gauge/Bore:** *12 ga.*

Action: *semi-auto*
Barrel Length: *18.5", 24", 26", 28", 30"* **Wt.:** *6.7–7.5 lbs.*
Sights: *red bar front*
Capacity: *5*
Stock: *walnut or synthetic*

D2C:	NIB $500	Ex $400	VG+ $275	Good $250	
C2C:	Mint $480	Ex $350	VG+ $250	Good $225	Fair $115
Trade-In:	Mint $360	Ex $300	VG+ $200	Good $175	Poor $60

MODEL 2000 DELUXE   REDBOOK CODE: RB-SR-S-M2000D
Engraved receiver, gold trigger, 3" chamber, inertia drive system, recoil reducer, Weaver scope base, checkering on walnut.

Production: *discontinued* **Gauge/Bore:** *12 ga.*

Action: *semi-auto*
Barrel Length: *18.5", 24", 26", 28", 30"* **Wt.:** *6.7–7.5 lbs.*
Sights: *red bar front*
Capacity: *5*
Stock: *high-grade walnut*

D2C:	NIB $645	Ex $500	VG+ $355	Good $325	
C2C:	Mint $620	Ex $450	VG+ $330	Good $295	Fair $150
Trade-In:	Mint $460	Ex $375	VG+ $260	Good $230	Poor $90

MODEL 2000 SLUG   REDBOOK CODE: RB-SR-S-M2000S
3" chamber, smooth bore barrel, other barrel lengths offered for additional cost.

Production: *2003–discontinued* **Gauge/Bore:** *12 ga.*

Action: *semi-auto*
Barrel Length: *24"* **Wt.:** *6.7 lbs.*
Sights: *rifle sights*
Capacity: *5*
Stock: *black synthetic*

D2C:	NIB $500	Ex $400	VG+ $275	Good $250	
C2C:	Mint $480	Ex $350	VG+ $250	Good $225	Fair $115
Trade-In:	Mint $360	Ex $300	VG+ $200	Good $175	Poor $60

STOEGER

M3500 REDBOOK CODE: RB-SR-S-MO3500

Inertia driven barrels fitted with a ventilated, stepped rib. Receiver drilled and tapped for scope mounting. Chambered for 2 3/4", 3", and 3 1/2" shells. Includes IC, M, F, and XFT chokes. User-adjustable stock drop, 14.375" length of pull, 2 1/2" drop at heel, and 1.5" drop at comb. Includes recoil reducer. Black; add $100 for Realtree Max-5 and Realtree APG; add $120 for Realtree APG with steady grip.

Production: *current* **Gauge/Bore:** *12 ga.*
Action: *semi-auto*
Barrel Length: 24", 26", 28" **Wt.:** *7.45 lbs–7.65 lbs.*
Sights: *red-bar front*
Capacity: *4*
Stock: *synthetic*

D2C:	NIB $646	Ex $500	VG+ $360	Good $325	LMP: $679
C2C:	Mint $630	Ex $450	VG+ $330	Good $295	Fair $150
Trade-In:	Mint $460	Ex $375	VG+ $260	Good $230	Poor $90

M3000 REDBOOK CODE: RB-SR-S-MO3000

Receiver drilled and tapped for scope mounting. Chambered for 2 3/4" and 3". IC, M, and XFT chokes. 14.375" length of pull, 2 1/2" drop at heel, and 1.5" drop at comb. Overall length 45.75–49.75". Optional recoil reducer. Black; add $50 for 26"or 28" Realtree Max-5 and Realtree APG; add $80 for 24" Realtree APG with steady grip.

Production: *current* **Gauge/Bore:** *12 ga.*
Action: *semi-auto*
Barrel Length: 24", 26", 28" **Wt.:** *7.3–7.5 lbs.*
Sights: *red-bar*
Capacity: *4*
Stock: *synthetic*

D2C:	NIB $530	Ex $425	VG+ $295	Good $265	LMP: $599
C2C:	Mint $510	Ex $375	VG+ $270	Good $240	Fair $125
Trade-In:	Mint $380	Ex $300	VG+ $210	Good $190	Poor $60

M3020 REDBOOK CODE: RB-SR-S-MO3020

Inertia driven. Receiver drilled and tapped for scope mounting. Chambered for 2 3/4" and 3". IC, M, and XFT chokes. User-adjustable stock drop and changing shims with 14.25" length of pull, 2" drop at heel, and 1.25" drop at comb. Overall length 49.75". Black; add $50 for 26" Realtree APG or 28" Realtree Max-5.

Production: *current* **Gauge/Bore:** *20 ga.*
Action: *semi-auto*
Barrel Length: 26", 28" **Wt.:** *5.6 lbs., 5.7 lbs.*
Sights: *red-bar front*
Capacity: *4*
Stock: *synthetic*

D2C:	NIB $570	Ex $450	VG+ $315	Good $285	LMP: $599
C2C:	Mint $550	Ex $400	VG+ $290	Good $260	Fair $135
Trade-In:	Mint $410	Ex $325	VG+ $230	Good $200	Poor $60

P-350 PUMP REDBOOK CODE: RB-SR-S-P350PS

Chambered for 2 3/4", 3" and 3 1/2". C, IC, M, F, and XFT choke tubes, including extra-full extended turkey choke. Includes non-turkey configurations only. Optional turkey configuration only stocks and recoil reducer. 14.375" length of pull, 2" drop at heel, and 1.375" drop at comb. Black; add $100 for Realtree Max-5 or Realtree APG; add $130 for Realtree APG with SteadyGrip.

Production: *current* **Gauge/Bore:** *12 ga.*
Action: *pump-action*
Barrel Length: 18.5", 24", 26", 28" **Wt.:** *6.6–6.9 lbs.*
Sights: *red-bar front*
Capacity: *4*
Stock: *synthetic*

D2C:	NIB $355	Ex $275	VG+ $200	Good $180	LMP: $349
C2C:	Mint $350	Ex $250	VG+ $180	Good $160	Fair $85
Trade-In:	Mint $260	Ex $200	VG+ $140	Good $125	Poor $60

P-350 DEFENSE PUMP   REDBOOK CODE: RB-SR-S-P350DS
Chambered for 2 3/4", 3" and 3 1/2". Cylinder fixed choke. 14.5" length of pull, 2.25" drop at heel, and 1.5" drop at comb. Overall length 40.25". Add $30 for pistol grip.

Production: *current* **Gauge/Bore:** *12 ga.*
Action: *pump-action*
Barrel Length: *18.5"* **Wt.:** *7.1 lbs.*
Sights: *blade front*
Capacity: *4*
Stock: *synthetic*

D2C:	NIB $380	Ex $300	VG+ $210	Good $190	LMP: $349
C2C:	Mint $370	Ex $275	VG+ $190	Good $175	Fair $90
Trade-In:	Mint $270	Ex $225	VG+ $150	Good $135	Poor $60

THE GRAND   REDBOOK CODE: RB-SR-S-TGRAND
Includes automatic safety and fully adjustable comb. Barrel extractor lifts shell from chamber. Chambered for 2 3/4" and 3". Overall length 46" with 14.5" length of pull and 2.25" drop at heel. Extended M, Extended F, and Extended IM chokes.

Production: *current* **Gauge/Bore:** *12 ga.*
Action: *single-shot*
Barrel Length: *30"* **Wt.:** *9.1 lbs.*
Sights: *red fiber-optic front*
Capacity: *1*
Stock: *A-Grade satin walnut*

D2C:	NIB $600	Ex $475	VG+ $330	Good $300	LMP: $679
C2C:	Mint $580	Ex $425	VG+ $300	Good $270	Fair $140
Trade-In:	Mint $430	Ex $350	VG+ $240	Good $210	Poor $60

CONDOR FIELD   REDBOOK CODE: RB-SR-S-CONDOR
Single trigger with shell extractor. Chambered for 2 1/2", 2 3/4", and 3". Overall length 40-44" with 14.5" length of pull, 2 1/2" drop at heel, and 1.5" drop at comb. 12, 20, and 28 gauge have IC and M chokes. .410 has fixed chokes.

Production: *current* **Gauge/Bore:** *12 ga., 20 ga., 28 ga., .410*
Action: *O/U*
Barrel Length: *24", 26", 28"* **Wt.:** *6 lbs.–7.4 lbs.*
Sights: *brass bead*
Capacity: *2*
Stock: *A-Grade satin walnut*

D2C:	NIB $490	Ex $375	VG+ $270	Good $245	LMP: $499
C2C:	Mint $480	Ex $350	VG+ $250	Good $225	Fair $115
Trade-In:	Mint $350	Ex $275	VG+ $200	Good $175	Poor $60

CONDOR COMPETITION   REDBOOK CODE: RB-SR-S-CONCOM
Single-selective trigger with ported barrel and automatic ejector. Chambered for 2 3/4" and 3". Overall length 47" with 14.5" length of pull, 2 1/2" drop at heel, and adjustable drop at comb. Extended IC, M, and F chokes (2 each). 12 gauge also available left-handed.

Production: *current* **Gauge/Bore:** *12 ga., 20 ga.*
Action: *O/U*
Barrel Length: *30"* **Wt.:** *7.3 lbs., 7.8 lbs.*
Sights: *brass bead, silver mid-bead*
Capacity: *2*
Stock: *AA-Grade gloss walnut*

D2C:	NIB $650	Ex $500	VG+ $360	Good $325	LMP: $679
C2C:	Mint $630	Ex $450	VG+ $330	Good $295	Fair $150
Trade-In:	Mint $470	Ex $375	VG+ $260	Good $230	Poor $90

STOEGER

CONDOR SUMPREME REDBOOK CODE: RB-SR-S-CONSUP

Single-selective trigger with automatic ejector. Features screw-in IC and M chokes, ventilated rib, and machine-turned, monobloc sides. Chambered for 2 3/4" and 3". 42" or 44" overall length with 14.5" length of pull, 2 1/2" drop at heel, and 1.5" drop at comb.

Production: *current* **Gauge/Bore:** *12 ga., 20 ga.*
Action: *O/U*
Barrel Length: 26", 28" **Wt.:** *6.8 lbs.–7.4 lbs.*
Sights: *brass bead, silver mid-bead*
Capacity: 2
Stock: *AA-Grade gloss walnut*

D2C:	NIB $660	Ex $525	VG+ $365	Good $330	LMP: $649
C2C:	Mint $640	Ex $475	VG+ $330	Good $300	Fair $155
Trade-In:	Mint $470	Ex $375	VG+ $260	Good $235	Poor $90

CONDOR OUTBACK REDBOOK CODE: RB-SR-S-CONOUT

Boxlock type action with single trigger and shell extractor shoots a variety of ammo. Features jeweled monobloc sides and machine-turned receiver. Chambered for 2 3/4" and 3". Screw-in IC and M chokes. 36" overall length with 14.5" length of pull, 2 1/2" drop at heel, and 1.5" drop at comb. Add $50 for polished nickel with black-finished walnut forend.

Production: *current* **Gauge/Bore:** *12 ga., 20 ga.*
Action: *O/U*
Barrel Length: 20" **Wt.:** *6.5 lbs., 7 lbs.*
Sights: *notched rear, fixed blade front*
Capacity: 2
Stock: *A-Grade satin walnut, black finished walnut*

D2C:	NIB $390	Ex $300	VG+ $215	Good $195	LMP: $499
C2C:	Mint $380	Ex $275	VG+ $200	Good $180	Fair $90
Trade-In:	Mint $280	Ex $225	VG+ $160	Good $140	Poor $60

CONDOR LONGFOWLER OVER AND UNDER REDBOOK CODE: RB-SR-S-CONLOU

Chambered for 2 3/4" and 3" with single trigger and shell extractor. Extended IC and extended M chokes. 46" overall length reaches out to the edge of the decoys. 14.5" length of pull, 2 1/2" drop at heel, and 1.5" drop at comb.

Production: *current* **Gauge/Bore:** *12 ga., 20 ga.*
Action: *O/U*
Barrel Length: 30" **Wt.:** *7 lbs., 7.5 lbs.*
Sights: *brass bead*
Capacity: 2
Stock: *A-Grade satin walnut*

D2C:	NIB $435	Ex $350	VG+ $240	Good $220	LMP: $499
C2C:	Mint $420	Ex $325	VG+ $220	Good $200	Fair $105
Trade-In:	Mint $310	Ex $250	VG+ $170	Good $155	Poor $60

UPLANDER LONGFOWLER SIDE BY SIDE REDBOOK CODE: RB-SR-S-UPLNDL

Chambered for 2 3/4" and 3" with single trigger and shell extractor. Extended IC and Extended M chokes. 46" overall length reaches out to the edge of the decoys. 14.5" length of pull, 2 1/2" drop at heel, and 1.5" drop at comb.

Production: *current* **Gauge/Bore:** *12 ga., 20 ga.*
Action: *SxS*
Barrel Length: 30" **Wt.:** *7.5 lbs., 7.6 lbs.*
Sights: *brass bead*
Capacity: 2
Stock: *A-Grade satin walnut*

D2C:	NIB $410	Ex $325	VG+ $230	Good $205	LMP: $499
C2C:	Mint $400	Ex $300	VG+ $210	Good $185	Fair $95
Trade-In:	Mint $300	Ex $250	VG+ $160	Good $145	Poor $60

STOEGER

UPLANDER FIELD REDBOOK CODE: RB-SR-S-UPLNDR

English design with double triggers. 12, 20, and 28 gauge models chambered for 2 3/4" and 3" with IC and M chokes. .410 chambered for 2 1/2" and 3" with fixed F&F choke. Tang-mounted safety automatically engages when gun is broken open. 14.5" length of pull, 2 1/2" drop at heel, and 1.5" drop at comb. Add $50 for 12, 20, and 28 gauge models.

Production: *current* **Gauge/Bore:** *12 ga., 20 ga., 28 ga., .410*

Action: *SxS*

Barrel Length: 26", 28" **Wt.:** *7 lbs.–7.5 lbs.*

Sights: *brass bead*

Capacity: *2*

Stock: *A-Grade satin walnut*

D2C:	NIB $399	Ex $325	VG+ $220	Good $200	**LMP:** $499
C2C:	Mint $390	Ex $300	VG+ $200	Good $180	Fair $95
Trade-In:	Mint $290	Ex $225	VG+ $160	Good $140	Poor $60

UPLANDER SUPREME REDBOOK CODE: RB-SR-S-UPLNDS

Single, gold-plated trigger, shell extractor, and IC and M chokes. Chambered for 2 3/4" and 3". Tang-mounted safety automatically engages when gun is broken open. 14.5" length of pull, 2 1/2" drop at heel, and 1.5" drop at comb.

Production: *current* **Gauge/Bore:** *12 ga., 20 ga.*

Action: *SxS*

Barrel Length: 26", 28" **Wt.:** *7.3–7.5 lbs.*

Sights: *brass bead, silver mid-bead*

Capacity: *2*

Stock: *AA-Grade gloss walnut*

D2C:	NIB $460	Ex $350	VG+ $255	Good $230	**LMP:** $549
C2C:	Mint $450	Ex $325	VG+ $230	Good $210	Fair $110
Trade-In:	Mint $330	Ex $275	VG+ $180	Good $165	Poor $60

UPLANDER SPECIAL REDBOOK CODE: RB-SR-S-UPLNDP

3" chamber, fixed chokes, straight grip, checkering on forearm, double trigger.

Production: *discontinued* **Gauge/Bore:** *12 ga., 20 ga., 28 ga.*

Action: *SxS*

Barrel Length: 24", 26" **Wt.:** *7.3 lbs.*

Sights: *brass bead front*

Capacity: *2*

Stock: *Brazilian hardwood*

D2C:	NIB $380	Ex $300	VG+ $210	Good $190	
C2C:	Mint $370	Ex $275	VG+ $190	Good $175	Fair $90
Trade-In:	Mint $270	Ex $225	VG+ $150	Good $135	Poor $60

UPLANDER ENGLISH REDBOOK CODE: RB-SR-S-UPLNDE

3" chamber, no checkering, available with short stock as well, fixed chokes.

Production: *discontinued* **Gauge/Bore:** *20 ga., .410*

Action: *SxS*

Barrel Length: 24" **Wt.:** *7 lbs.*

Sights: *bead front*

Capacity: *2*

Stock: *straight grip walnut*

D2C:	NIB $415	Ex $325	VG+ $230	Good $210	
C2C:	Mint $400	Ex $300	VG+ $210	Good $190	Fair $100
Trade-In:	Mint $300	Ex $250	VG+ $170	Good $150	Poor $60

STOEGER

DOUBLE DEFENSE OVER AND UNDER
REDBOOK CODE: RB-SR-S-DBLDOU

Tactical length with two Picatinny rail accessory mounts and shell extractor. 14.5" length of pull, 2 1/2" drop at heel, and 1.5" drop at comb. Chambered for 2 3/4" and 3" with IC and Fixed IC chokes. Burris sight/scope and flashlight not included.

Production: current **Gauge/Bore:** 12 ga., 20 ga.
Action: O/U
Barrel Length: 20" **Wt.:** 6.6 lbs., 7.1 lbs.
Sights: green fiber-optic front
Capacity: 2
Stock: black finished walnut

D2C:	NIB $460	Ex $350	VG+ $255	Good $230	**LMP: $479**
C2C:	Mint $450	Ex $325	VG+ $230	Good $210	Fair $110
Trade-In:	Mint $330	Ex $275	VG+ $180	Good $165	Poor $60

DOUBLE DEFENSE SIDE BY SIDE
REDBOOK CODE: RB-SR-S-DBLDSS

Tactical length with two Picatinny rail accessory mounts and shell extractor. 14.5" length of pull, 2 1/2" drop at heel, and 1.5" drop at comb. Chambered for 2 3/4" and 3" with IC and Fixed IC chokes. Burris sight/scope and flashlight not included. Black-finished walnut. 12 gauge also available in black synthetic.

Production: current **Gauge/Bore:** 12 ga., 20 ga.
Action: SxS
Barrel Length: 20" **Wt.:** 6.4 lbs.
Sights: green fiber-optic front
Capacity: 2
Stock: synthetic, black finished walnut

D2C:	NIB $450	Ex $350	VG+ $250	Good $225	**LMP: $499**
C2C:	Mint $440	Ex $325	VG+ $230	Good $205	Fair $105
Trade-In:	Mint $320	Ex $275	VG+ $180	Good $160	Poor $60

COACH GUN SUPREME
REDBOOK CODE: RB-SR-S-CCHSUP

Single or double trigger features pre-fitted soft rubber recoil, beavertail forend, and shell extractor. Chambered for 2 3/4" and 3" with IC and M chokes. 36.5" overall length with 14.5" length of pull, 2 1/2" drop at heel, and 1.5" drop at comb. Finish choices include polished nickel, blue, or blue with stainless receiver.

Production: current **Gauge/Bore:** 12 ga., 20 ga.
Action: SxS
Barrel Length: 20" **Wt.:** 6.4 lbs., 6.5 lbs.
Sights: brass bead
Capacity: 2
Stock: AA-Grade gloss walnut

D2C:	NIB $450	Ex $350	VG+ $250	Good $225	**LMP: $549**
C2C:	Mint $440	Ex $325	VG+ $230	Good $205	Fair $105
Trade-In:	Mint $320	Ex $275	VG+ $180	Good $160	Poor $60

COACH SINGLE AND DOUBLE TRIGGER
REDBOOK CODE: RB-SR-S-CCHSDT

Classic stagecoach defense design with single or double triggers. 12 and 20 gauge models chambered for 2 3/4" and 3" with fixed IC and fixed M chokes. .410 chambered for 2 1/2" and 3" with fixed F&F choke. 36.5" overall with 14.5" length of pull, 2 1/2" drop at heel, and 1.5" drop at comb. Blue or polished nickel-plated finishes. Add $50 for black-finished hardwood/polished nickel.

Production: current **Gauge/Bore:** 12 ga., 20 ga., .410
Action: SxS
Barrel Length: 20" **Wt.:** 6.5 lbs.–7 lbs.
Sights: brass bead
Capacity: 2
Stock: A-Grade satin walnut

D2C:	NIB $415	Ex $325	VG+ $230	Good $210	**LMP: $449**
C2C:	Mint $400	Ex $300	VG+ $210	Good $190	Fair $100
Trade-In:	Mint $300	Ex $250	VG+ $170	Good $150	Poor $60

Sturm Ruger & Co., Inc.

William B. Ruger and Alexander M. Sturm founded Sturm, Ruger & Co., Inc. in 1949 in their Southport, Connecticut, machine shop. Their first firearm, the Ruger Standard, was a .22 caliber pistol that drew qualities from both the German 9mm Luger and the Colt Woodsman and was popular enough to launch the company successfully. The Standard ultimately became the most successful .22 semi-automatic in history. This success fueled the company's manufacturing of other firearms, most of which found great commercial success. The company's foray into the shotgun market came with the Ruger Red Label shotgun, a high-end 12 gauge over/under shotgun. The company, most commonly known as Ruger, has won countless awards and been repeatedly recognized as one of the best U.S. firearms manufacturers. To date, Ruger has produced over 20 million firearms. Although its founders have both passed away, Sturm in 1951 and Ruger in 2002, the company continues to manufacture an extensive line of pistols, revolvers, rifles, and shotguns from its casting facilities in Newport, New Hampshire and Prescott, Arizona.

RED LABEL SHOTGUN   REDBOOK CODE: RB-RU-S-REDLAB

Pachmayr buttpad, 14.5" length of pull, 1.5" drop at comb, and 2.5" drop at heel. Ventilated rib and blue alloy steel barrel chambered for 3" shells. Includes five steel-shot compatible, screw-in Briley chokes, (two skeet, one full, one modified, and one improved cylinder).

Production: *current* **Gauge/Bore:** *12 ga.*

Action: *O/U*

Barrel Length: *26", 28", 30"* **Wt.:** *7.5–7.9 lbs.*

Sights: *brass bead front, and mid-bead*

Capacity: *2*

Stock: *American walnut*

D2C:	NIB $1,210	Ex $925	VG+ $670	Good $605	**LMP:** $1,399
C2C:	Mint $1,170	Ex $850	VG+ $610	Good $545	Fair $280
Trade-In:	Mint $860	Ex $700	VG+ $480	Good $425	Poor $150

Thompson/Center Arms

Thompson/Center Arms began in 1967 when Warren Center developed a break-action, single-shot pistol and joined forces with the K.W. Thompson Tool Company for production. Together they produced Warren Center's Contender pistol, which had a unique design to allow interchangeable barrels. This allowed a shooter to change out a barrel with another caliber by removing a single pin with a screwdriver. Due to the design's popularity the company still produces firearms with a wide range of interchangeable barrels including rimfire, centerfire, muzzleloading, and shotgun options.

ENCORE PRO HUNTER SHOTGUN SLUG   REDBOOK CODE: RB-TC-S-EPSLUG

3" chamber with fully-rifled fluted barrel. Features FlexTech stock, LimbSaver recoil pad, ambidextrous Swing Hammer, and is compatible with any other Encore Pro Hunter or Encore barrel. Drilled and tapped for a scope mount, 42.5" overall with 14" length of pull. Add $20 for 12 gauge.

Production: *current* **Gauge/Bore:** *12 ga., 20 ga.*

Action: *single-shot*

Barrel Length: *28"* **Wt.:** *7.5 lbs.*

Sights: *none*

Capacity: *1*

Stock: *synthetic*

D2C:	NIB $763	Ex $600	VG+ $420	Good $385	**LMP:** $892
C2C:	Mint $740	Ex $550	VG+ $390	Good $345	Fair $180
Trade-In:	Mint $550	Ex $450	VG+ $300	Good $270	Poor $90

THOMPSON/CENTER ARMS

ENCORE PRO HUNTER TURKEY REDBOOK CODE: RB-TC-S-EPTRKY

3" chamber with T/C Extra Full Turkey Choke, Realtree AP HD Camo stock with FlexTech recoil management and ambidextrous Swing Hammer, 14" length of pull, can be switched to a rifle or muzzleloader barrel.

Production: *current* Gauge/Bore: *12 ga., 20 ga.*
Action: *single-shot*
Barrel Length: 24", 26" Wt.: *6.3 lbs., 6.8 lbs.*
Sights: *adjustable fiber optic*
Capacity: *1*
Stock: *synthetic*

D2C:	NIB $777	Ex $600	VG+ $430	Good $390	**LMP: $892**
C2C:	Mint $750	Ex $550	VG+ $390	Good $350	Fair $180
Trade-In:	Mint $560	Ex $450	VG+ $310	Good $275	Poor $90

TRISTAR SPORTING ARMS

TriStar Sporting Arms, Ltd.

TriStar Sporting Arms, Ltd. was established in 1994 and is located in North Kansas City, Missouri. The company imports and distributes semi-automatic handguns and shotguns of the semi-automatic, over/under, sporting clay, pump action, and tactical varieties.

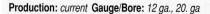

VIPER G2 SYNTHETIC REDBOOK CODE: RB-TS-S-VPG2SN

Chrome-lined vent rib barrel in matte blue finish, shot plug, cross bolt safety, easy-loading magazine, buttplate, multi-choke set (full, modified, improved cylinder), 14.25" length of pull, fires 3" shells. Add $60 for left-handed model, available in 20 gauge. Add $15 for 12 gauge youth model; add $60 for 20 gauge youth model (24" barrel, 13" length of pull).

Production: *current* Gauge/Bore: *12 ga., 20. ga*
Action: *semi-auto*
Barrel Length: 26", 28" Wt.: *6.1–6.9 lbs.*
Sights: *red fiber optic front*
Capacity: *6*
Stock: *black synthetic*

D2C:	NIB $494	Ex $400	VG+ $275	Good $250	**LMP: $519**
C2C:	Mint $480	Ex $350	VG+ $250	Good $225	Fair $115
Trade-In:	Mint $360	Ex $300	VG+ $200	Good $175	Poor $60

VIPER G2 WOOD REDBOOK CODE: RB-TS-S-VPG2WD

Chrome-lined vent rib barrel in blue finish, shot plug, cross bolt safety, easy-loading magazine, buttplate, multi-choke set (full, modified, improved cylinder), 14.25" length of pull, fires 3" shells. Add $30 for 20 gauge youth model (24" barrel, 13" length of pull).

Production: *current* Gauge/Bore: *12 ga., 20 ga.*
Action: *semi-auto*
Barrel Length: 26", 28" Wt.: *5.8–6.9 lbs.*
Sights: *red fiber optic front*
Capacity: *6*
Stock: *walnut*

D2C:	NIB $437	Ex $350	VG+ $245	Good $220	**LMP: $579**
C2C:	Mint $420	Ex $325	VG+ $220	Good $200	Fair $105
Trade-In:	Mint $320	Ex $250	VG+ $180	Good $155	Poor $60

VIPER G2 SILVER   REDBOOK CODE: RB-TS-S-VPG2SL

Chrome-lined vent rib barrel in blue finish, shot plug, silver receiver, cross bolt safety, easy-loading magazine, buttplate, multi-choke set (full, modified, improved cylinder), 14.25" length of pull, fires 3" shells. Add $50 for 28 gauge model with 2 3/4" chamber and Beretta choke tube set (full, modified, improved cylinder, extended skeet).

Production: *current* **Gauge/Bore:** *12 ga., 20 ga., 28 ga.*
Action: *semi-auto*
Barrel Length: 26", 28" **Wt.:** *5.2–6.9 lbs.*
Sights: *red fiber optic front*
Capacity: *5, 6*
Stock: *select walnut*

D2C:	NIB $623	Ex $475	VG+ $345	Good $315	**LMP: $639**
C2C:	Mint $600	Ex $450	VG+ $320	Good $285	Fair $145
Trade-In:	Mint $450	Ex $350	VG+ $250	Good $220	Poor $90

VIPER G2 SPORTING   REDBOOK CODE: RB-TS-S-VG2S12

Chrome-lined ported vent rib barrel in blue finish, multi-choke set (full, modified, improved cylinder), shot plug, cross bolt safety, easy-loading magazine, adjustable comb, buttplate, 14.25" length of pull, fires 3" shells.

Production: *current* **Gauge/Bore:** *12 ga., 28 ga.*
Action: *semi-auto*
Barrel Length: 30" **Wt.:** *7.4 lbs.*
Sights: *red fiber optic front*
Capacity: *6*
Stock: *select walnut*

D2C:	NIB $568	Ex $450	VG+ $315	Good $285	**LMP: $789**
C2C:	Mint $550	Ex $400	VG+ $290	Good $260	Fair $135
Trade-In:	Mint $410	Ex $325	VG+ $230	Good $200	Poor $60

VIPER G2 SR SPORT   REDBOOK CODE: RB-TS-S-VPG2SR

Chrome-lined vent rib barrel in blue finish, shot plug, red anodized receiver, cross bolt safety, easy-loading magazine, buttplate, multi-choke set (full, modified, improved cylinder), 14.25" length of pull, fires 3" shells.

Production: *2014–current* **Gauge/Bore:** *12 ga.*
Action: *semi-auto*
Barrel Length: 30" **Wt.:** *7.2 lbs.*
Sights: *fiber optic front*
Capacity: *6*
Stock: *black synthetic*

D2C:	NIB $496	Ex $400	VG+ $275	Good $250	**LMP: $609**
C2C:	Mint $480	Ex $350	VG+ $250	Good $225	Fair $115
Trade-In:	Mint $360	Ex $300	VG+ $200	Good $175	Poor $60

VIPER G2 CAMO   REDBOOK CODE: RB-TS-S-VPG2CM

Chrome-lined vent rib barrel in Realtree Advantage Timber camo finish, shot plug, cross bolt safety, easy-loading magazine, buttplate, multi-choke set (full, modified, improved cylinder), 14.25" length of pull, fires 3" shells. 28 gauge model available in Realtree Max-4 camo finish only. Also available in 20 gauge youth model (24" barrel, 13" length of pull). Add $60 for left-handed full-size model, available in 20 gauge.

Production: *current* **Gauge/Bore:** *12 ga., 20 ga.*
Action: *semi-auto*
Barrel Length: 24", 26", 28" **Wt.:** *6.2–6.9 lbs.*
Sights: *green fiber optic front*
Capacity: *6*
Stock: *synthetic with Realtree Advantage Timber or Realtree Max-4*

D2C:	NIB $450	Ex $350	VG+ $250	Good $225	**LMP: $609**
C2C:	Mint $440	Ex $325	VG+ $230	Good $205	Fair $105
Trade-In:	Mint $320	Ex $275	VG+ $180	Good $160	Poor $60

TRISTAR SPORTING ARMS

VIPER G2 TURKEY REDBOOK CODE: RB-TS-S-VPG2TK

Chrome-lined vent rib barrel in Realtree Advantage Timber camo finish, extended turkey choke, pistol grip, Picatinny rail (not installed), shot plug, cross bolt safety, easy-loading magazine, buttplate, multi-choke set (full, modified, improved cylinder), 14.25" length of pull, fires 3" shells.

Production: *current* **Gauge/Bore:** *12 ga.*
Action: *semi-auto*
Barrel Length: 24" **Wt.:** *6.8 lbs.*
Sights: *green fiber optic front*
Capacity: *6*

D2C:	NIB $497	Ex $400	VG+ $275	Good $250	**LMP:** $639
C2C:	Mint $480	Ex $350	VG+ $250	Good $225	Fair $115
Trade-In:	Mint $360	Ex $300	VG+ $200	Good $175	Poor $60

Stock: *synthetic with pistol grip and Realtree Advantage Timber camo*

RAPTOR SYNTHETIC REDBOOK CODE: RB-TS-S-RPTRSN

Chrome-lined barrel in matte blue finish, Beretta/Benelli choke set (full, modified, improved cylinder), matte blue receiver, gas-operated, cross bolt safety, zero-plane stock, ventilated buttplate, 14.25" length of pull, fires 3" shells.

Production: *current* **Gauge/Bore:** *12 ga., 20 ga.*
Action: *semi-auto*
Barrel Length: 26", 28" **Wt.:** *6.8 lbs., 6.9 lbs.*
Sights: *red fiber optic front*
Capacity: *6*

D2C:	NIB $409	Ex $325	VG+ $225	Good $205	**LMP:** $409
C2C:	Mint $400	Ex $300	VG+ $210	Good $185	Fair $95
Trade-In:	Mint $300	Ex $250	VG+ $160	Good $145	Poor $60

Stock: *black synthetic*

RAPTOR ATAC TURKEY REDBOOK CODE: RB-TS-S-RPTRTK

Chrome-lined barrel in black finish, Mossy Oak Break-Up Infinity camo, extended choke set plus extended tactical choke, Picatinny rail with mounted Ghost Ring sight, gas-operated, cross bolt safety, zero-plane stock, ventilated buttplate, sling swivel studs, 14.25" length of pull, fires 3" shells.

Production: *current* **Gauge/Bore:** *12 ga.*
Action: *semi-auto*
Barrel Length: 24" **Wt.:** *7 lbs.*
Sights: *fiber optic front, ghost ring rear*
Capacity: *6*

D2C:	NIB $352	Ex $275	VG+ $195	Good $180	**LMP:** $489
C2C:	Mint $340	Ex $250	VG+ $180	Good $160	Fair $85
Trade-In:	Mint $250	Ex $200	VG+ $140	Good $125	Poor $60

Stock: *synthetic with pistol grip and Mossy Oak Break-Up Infinity camo*

RAPTOR ATAC HOME DEFENSE REDBOOK CODE: RB-TS-S-RPTRHD

Chrome-lined barrel in black finish, extended choke set plus extended tactical choke, Picatinny rail with mounted Ghost Ring sight, gas-operated, cross bolt safety, zero-plane stock, ventilated buttplate, sling swivel studs, 14.25" length of pull, fires 3" shells. Add $50 for Kryptek Typhon finish. Add $80 for Digital Camo finish.

Production: *current* **Gauge/Bore:** *12 ga.*
Action: *semi-auto*
Barrel Length: 20" **Wt.:** *7 lbs.*
Sights: *fiber optic front, ghost ring rear*
Capacity: *6*

D2C:	NIB $384	Ex $300	VG+ $215	Good $195	**LMP:** $439
C2C:	Mint $370	Ex $275	VG+ $200	Good $175	Fair $90
Trade-In:	Mint $280	Ex $225	VG+ $150	Good $135	Poor $60

Stock: *black synthetic with pistol grip; available in Kryptek Typhon or Digital Camo finish*

RAPTOR YOUTH REDBOOK CODE: RB-TS-S-RPTRYO

Chrome-lined barrel in matte blue finish, cross bolt safety, buttplate, multi-choke set (full, modified, improved cylinder), 13" length of pull, fires 3" shells. Add $50 for Muddy Girl camo finish. Add $80 for Vista camo finish.

Production: *current* **Gauge/Bore:** *20 ga.*
Action: *semi-auto*
Barrel Length: 24" **Wt.:** 6.5 lbs.
Sights: *red fiber optic front*
Capacity: 6
Stock: *black synthetic, Muddy Girl or Vista camo finish*

D2C:	NIB $365	Ex $300	VG+ $205	Good $185	LMP: $409
C2C:	Mint $360	Ex $275	VG+ $190	Good $165	Fair $85
Trade-In:	Mint $260	Ex $225	VG+ $150	Good $130	Poor $60

TSA MAG REDBOOK CODE: RB-TS-S-TSMGBK

Chrome-lined barrel in matte black finish, multi-choke set (full, modified, improved cylinder), two-piston system, cross bolt safety, buttplate, sling swivel studs, made from durable injection molding, chambers 2 3/4", 3" or 3 1/2" shells.

Production: *current* **Gauge/Bore:** *12 ga.*
Action: *semi-auto*
Barrel Length: 26", 28" **Wt.:** 7.3 lbs.
Sights: *red fiber optic front*
Capacity: 6
Stock: *black synthetic*

D2C:	NIB $418	Ex $325	VG+ $230	Good $210	LMP: $639
C2C:	Mint $410	Ex $300	VG+ $210	Good $190	Fair $100
Trade-In:	Mint $300	Ex $250	VG+ $170	Good $150	Poor $60

TSA MAG CAMO REDBOOK CODE: RB-TS-S-TSMGCM

Chrome-lined barrel in Realtree Max-4 camo finish, multi-choke set (full, modified, improved cylinder), two-piston system, cross bolt safety, buttplate, sling swivel studs, made from durable injection molding, chambers 2 3/4", 3" or 3 1/2" shells. . Model with 24" barrel comes in Realtree Advantage Timber camo finish.

Production: *current* **Gauge/Bore:** *12 ga.*
Action: *semi-auto*
Barrel Length: 24", 26", 28" **Wt.:** 7.2–7.4 lbs.
Sights: *green fiber optic front*
Capacity: 6
Stock: *synthetic with Realtree Max-4 or Realtree Advantage Timber camo*

D2C:	NIB $521	Ex $400	VG+ $290	Good $265	LMP: $729
C2C:	Mint $510	Ex $375	VG+ $270	Good $235	Fair $120
Trade-In:	Mint $370	Ex $300	VG+ $210	Good $185	Poor $60

HUNTER MAG REDBOOK CODE: RB-TS-S-HNMGBK

Chrome-lined barrel in matte black finish, multi-choke set (full, modified, improved modified, improved cylinder, skeet), top tang safety, single selective trigger, extractor, buttplate, sling swivel studs, chambers 2 3/4", 3"or 3 1/2" shells.

Production: *current* **Gauge/Bore:** *12 ga.*
Action: *O/U*
Barrel Length: 28" **Wt.:** 7.6 lbs.
Sights: *red fiber optic front*
Capacity: 2
Stock: *black synthetic*

D2C:	NIB $523	Ex $400	VG+ $290	Good $265	LMP: $639
C2C:	Mint $510	Ex $375	VG+ $270	Good $240	Fair $125
Trade-In:	Mint $380	Ex $300	VG+ $210	Good $185	Poor $60

TRISTAR SPORTING ARMS

HUNTER MAG CAMO REDBOOK CODE: RB-TS-S-HNMGCM

Chrome-lined barrel in camo finish, multi-choke set (full, modified, improved modified, improved cylinder, skeet), top tang safety, single selective trigger, extractor, buttplate, sling swivel studs, chambers 2 3/4", 3" or 3 1/2" shells. Model with 26" barrel comes in Mossy Oak Break-Up Infinity camo finish; model with 28" barrel comes in Mossy Oak Duck Blind camo finish.

Production: *current* **Gauge/Bore:** *12 ga.*
Action: *O/U*
Barrel Length: *26", 28"* **Wt.:** *7.4 lbs., 7.6 lbs.*
Sights: *green fiber optic front*
Capacity: *2*
Stock: *synthetic with Mossy Oak Break-Up Infinity or Mossy Oak Duck Blind*

D2C:	NIB $576	Ex $450	VG+ $320	Good $290	LMP: $729
C2C:	Mint $560	Ex $400	VG+ $290	Good $260	Fair $135
Trade-In:	Mint $410	Ex $325	VG+ $230	Good $205	Poor $60

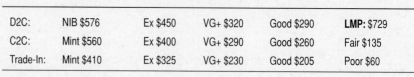

SETTER S/T REDBOOK CODE: RB-TS-S-STTRST

Chrome-lined vent rib barrel in high-polished blue finish, multi-choke set (full, modified, improved modified, improved cylinder, skeet), silver receiver, top tang safety, single selective trigger, extractors, buttplate, sling swivel studs, chambers 3" shells.

Production: *current* **Gauge/Bore:** *12 ga., 20 ga.*
Action: *O/U*
Barrel Length: *26", 28"* **Wt.:** *6.3 lbs., 7.2 lbs.*
Sights: *brass bead front*
Capacity: *2*
Stock: *high-gloss walnut*

D2C:	NIB $421	Ex $325	VG+ $235	Good $215	LMP: $559
C2C:	Mint $410	Ex $300	VG+ $220	Good $190	Fair $100
Trade-In:	Mint $300	Ex $250	VG+ $170	Good $150	Poor $60

HUNTER EX SERIES REDBOOK CODE: RB-TS-S-HNTREX

Chrome-lined barrel in blue finish, multi-choke set (full, modified, improved modified, improved cylinder, skeet), silver receiver, top tang safety, single selective trigger, extractor, buttplate, 14.25" length of pull, chambers 3" shells (28 gauge and .410 bore models chamber 2 3/4" shells). Add $30 for .410 model. Add $30 for 28 gauge model with aluminum alloy frame (4.8 lbs.).

Production: *current* **Gauge/Bore:** *12 ga., 20 ga., 28 ga., .410*
Action: *O/U*
Barrel Length: *26", 28"* **Wt.:** *5.7–7.2 lbs.*
Sights: *red fiber optic front*
Capacity: *2*
Stock: *walnut*

D2C:	NIB $520	Ex $400	VG+ $290	Good $260	LMP: $639
C2C:	Mint $500	Ex $375	VG+ $260	Good $235	Fair $120
Trade-In:	Mint $370	Ex $300	VG+ $210	Good $185	Poor $60

HUNTER EX LT REDBOOK CODE: RB-TS-S-HNEXLT

Chrome-lined barrel in blue finish, multi-choke set (full, modified, improved modified, improved cylinder, skeet), solid aluminum alloy frame, sealed action reinforced with steel hinge pin & steel firing pin, top tang safety & barrel selector, single selective trigger, extractor, buttplate, 14.25" length of pull, chambers 3" shells.

Production: *current* **Gauge/Bore:** *12 ga., 20 ga.*
Action: *O/U*
Barrel Length: *26", 28"* **Wt.:** *5.4–6.8 lbs.*
Sights: *red fiber optic front*
Capacity: *2*
Stock: *cut-checkered walnut*

D2C:	NIB $558	Ex $425	VG+ $310	Good $280	LMP: $669
C2C:	Mint $540	Ex $400	VG+ $280	Good $255	Fair $130
Trade-In:	Mint $400	Ex $325	VG+ $220	Good $200	Poor $60

SPORTING OVER/UNDER   REDBOOK CODE: RB-TS-S-SPTGOU

Chrome-lined barrel in blue finish, 10mm target rib, multi-choke set (full, modified, improved modified, improved cylinder, skeet), silver receiver, top tang safety, single selective trigger, extractor, buttplate, 14.25" length of pull, fires 3" shells.

Production: *current* **Gauge/Bore:** *12 ga.*
Action: *O/U*
Barrel Length: *30"* **Wt.:** *7.5 lbs.*
Sights: *red fiber optic front*
Capacity: *2*
Stock: *walnut pistol grip*

D2C:	NIB $675	Ex $525	VG+ $375	Good $340	LMP: $819
C2C:	Mint $650	Ex $475	VG+ $340	Good $305	Fair $160
Trade-In:	Mint $480	Ex $400	VG+ $270	Good $240	Poor $90

COBRA FIELD PUMP   REDBOOK CODE: RB-TS-S-COBFDP

Chrome-lined barrel in matte blue finish, multi-choke set (full, modified, improved cylinder), extended forearm, cross bolt safety, Turkish sling swivel studs, buttplate, fires 3" shells. Add $50 for Turkey model with fixed pistol grip, drilled & tapped receiver, and extended turkey choke.

Production: *current* **Gauge/Bore:** *12 ga.*
Action: *pump-action*
Barrel Length: *24", 26", 28"* **Wt.:** *6.5–6.9 lbs.*
Sights: *green fiber optic front*
Capacity: *6*
Stock: *black synthetic, pistol grip option*

D2C:	NIB $277	Ex $225	VG+ $155	Good $140	LMP: $349
C2C:	Mint $270	Ex $200	VG+ $140	Good $125	Fair $65
Trade-In:	Mint $200	Ex $175	VG+ $110	Good $100	Poor $30

COBRA FIELD CAMO PUMP   REDBOOK CODE: RB-TS-S-COBCMP

Chrome-lined barrel in matte blue finish, camo finish, multi-choke set (full, modified, improved cylinder), extended forearm, cross bolt safety, Turkish sling swivel studs, buttplate, fires 3" shells. Add $60 for Turkey model with fixed pistol grip, drilled & tapped receiver, and extended turkey choke.

Production: *current* **Gauge/Bore:** *12 ga.*
Action: *pump-action*
Barrel Length: *24", 26", 28"* **Wt.:** *6.5–6.9 lbs.*
Sights: *green fiber optic front*
Capacity: *6*
Stock: *synthetic with camo finish, pistol grip option*

D2C:	NIB $345	Ex $275	VG+ $190	Good $175	LMP: $429
C2C:	Mint $340	Ex $250	VG+ $180	Good $160	Fair $80
Trade-In:	Mint $250	Ex $200	VG+ $140	Good $125	Poor $60

COBRA TACTICAL PUMP   REDBOOK CODE: RB-TS-S-COTCTP

Spring-loaded forearm, faux extended mag tube, matte black finish, matte black anodized aluminum receiver with dovetailing for scope rings, 14.25" length of pull.

Production: *current* **Gauge/Bore:** *12 ga.*
Action: *pump-action*
Barrel Length: *20"* **Wt.:** *6.3 lbs.*
Sights: *raised blade front*
Capacity: *6*
Stock: *black synthetic*

D2C:	NIB $253	Ex $200	VG+ $140	Good $130	LMP: $304
C2C:	Mint $250	Ex $175	VG+ $130	Good $115	Fair $60
Trade-In:	Mint $180	Ex $150	VG+ $100	Good $90	Poor $30

COBRA MARINE TACTICAL PUMP REDBOOK CODE: RB-TS-S-COTCPM

Spring-loaded forearm, mounted Picatinny rail, chrome-lined barrel and chamber, brushed nickel finish, shot plug, choke tube, extended railed forend, sling swivels, 14.25" length of pull, fires 3" shells.

Production: *2014–current* **Gauge/Bore:** *12 ga.*
Action: *pump-action*
Barrel Length: *18.5"* **Wt.:** *6.2–6.9 lbs.*
Sights: *raised blade front*
Capacity: *6*
Stock: *black synthetic*

D2C:	NIB $302	Ex $250	VG+ $170	Good $155	**LMP:** $369
C2C:	Mint $290	Ex $225	VG+ $160	Good $140	Fair $70
Trade-In:	Mint $220	Ex $175	VG+ $120	Good $110	Poor $60

COBRA FORCE PUMP REDBOOK CODE: RB-TS-S-COFRPU

Spring-loaded forearm, mounted Picatinny rail, matte black finish, single unit receiver, fixed pistol grip stock with soft rubber grip, faux extended mag tube, removable muzzle brake choke, shot plug, sling swivel studs, fires 3" shells.

Production: *current* **Gauge/Bore:** *12 ga.*
Action: *pump-action*
Barrel Length: *20"* **Wt.:** *6.5 lbs.*
Sights: *bridge front, ghost ring rear*
Capacity: *6*
Stock: *black synthetic with pistol grip; available in Kryptek Typhon or Digital Camo finish*

D2C:	NIB $290	Ex $225	VG+ $160	Good $145	**LMP:** $399
C2C:	Mint $280	Ex $225	VG+ $150	Good $135	Fair $70
Trade-In:	Mint $210	Ex $175	VG+ $120	Good $105	Poor $30

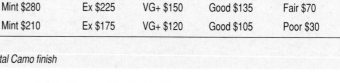

TEC 12 TACTICAL PUMP/AUTO REDBOOK CODE: RB-TS-S-TEC12T

Chrome-lined barrel in matte black finish, semi-automatic with selectable pump-action option, inertia rotary bolt (for enhanced action response in semi-auto mode), mounted Picatinny rail, ported cylinder choke, cross bolt safety, swivel studs (installed) plus military sling swivel set, vertical pistol grip, fires 3" shells.

Production: *current* **Gauge/Bore:** *12 ga.*
Action: *pump-action/semi-auto*
Barrel Length: *20"* **Wt.:** *7.45 lbs.*
Sights: *red fiber optic bead front, adjustable ghost ring rear*
Capacity: *6*
Stock: *black synthetic with pistol grip*

D2C:	NIB $537	Ex $425	VG+ $300	Good $270	**LMP:** $689
C2C:	Mint $520	Ex $375	VG+ $270	Good $245	Fair $125
Trade-In:	Mint $390	Ex $325	VG+ $210	Good $190	Poor $60

Ugartechea Armas

Headquartered in Eibar, Spain, Armas Ugartechea was founded in 1922 by Ignacio Ugartecheas. The company has remained within the family, being run by its founder, his son, and currently his grandson (all of whom bear the same name). The company has changed shape over the years, moving from mass production of shotguns to more of a custom shop outfit with only a handful of workers. Though most well known for their quality side by side, double-barreled shotguns, the company one manufactures pistols and rifles. It also produced over-under double-barreled shotguns, but production of those models has ceased. The shotguns produces by Armas Ugartechea are modeled from patents used in the construction of some of the most famous English shotgun manufacturers. However, Armas Ugartechea guns are more affordable than those offered by English competition.

TRISTAR SPORTING ARMS

UGARTECHEA ARMAS

UPLAND CLASSIC GRADE I BOXLOCK (MODEL 30)   REDBOOK CODE: RB-UG-S-GRADEI

Anson and Deeley boxlock action, chopper-lump forged steel barrel and frame, concave rib, double triggers, dual shell extractors, case colored receiver with no engraving, hand-checkered stock, splinter forend, automatic safety, 2 3/4" chamber except 20 guage and .410 with 3" chamber, IC/M chokes. Add $200 for 28 gauge. and add $300 for .410.

Production: *current* **Gauge/Bore:** *12 ga., 16 ga., 20 ga., 28 ga., .410*

Action: *SxS*

Barrel Length: 28" **Wt.:** *5.3–7 lbs.*

Sights: *bead front*

Capacity: *2*

Stock: *straight walnut*

D2C:	NIB $1,102	Ex $850	VG+ $610	Good $555	**LMP:** $1,695
C2C:	Mint $1,060	Ex $775	VG+ $560	Good $500	Fair $255
Trade-In:	Mint $790	Ex $625	VG+ $430	Good $390	Poor $120

UPLAND CLASSIC GRADE II BOXLOCK (MODEL 40)   REDBOOK CODE: RB-UG-S-GRADII

Coin finish receiver with moderate engraving, Anson and Deeley boxlock action, chopper-lump forged steel barrel and frame, double triggers, concave rib, dual shell extractors, splinter forend, checkered butt, IC/M chokes. Add $300 for 28 gauge and add $400 for .410.

Production: *current* **Gauge/Bore:** *12 ga., 16 ga., 20 ga., 28 ga., .410*

Action: *SxS*

Barrel Length: 28" **Wt.:** *5.3–7 lbs.*

Sights: *bead front*

Capacity: *2*

Stock: *straight walnut*

D2C:	NIB $1,424	Ex $1,100	VG+ $785	Good $715	**LMP:** $1,995
C2C:	Mint $1,370	Ex $1,000	VG+ $720	Good $645	Fair $330
Trade-In:	Mint $1,020	Ex $800	VG+ $560	Good $500	Poor $150

UPLAND CLASSIC GRADE III BOXLOCK (MODEL 40 EX)   REDBOOK CODE: RB-UG-S-GRAIII

Automatic southgate shell ejectors, case colored receiver with moderate engraving, Anson and Deeley boxlock action, chopper-lump forged steel barrels and frame, double triggers, concave rib, splinter forend, checkered butt, IC/M chokes. Custom options may increase value. Add $300 for 28 gauge.

Production: *current* **Gauge/Bore:** *12 ga., 16 ga., 20 ga., 28 ga.*

Action: *SxS*

Barrel Length: 28" **Wt.:** *5.3–7 lbs.*

Sights: *bead front*

Capacity: *2*

Stock: *straight walnut*

D2C:	NIB $2,500	Ex $1,900	VG+ $1,375	Good $1,250	**LMP:** $2,395
C2C:	Mint $2,400	Ex $1,725	VG+ $1,250	Good $1,125	Fair $575
Trade-In:	Mint $1,780	Ex $1,400	VG+ $980	Good $875	Poor $270

UPLAND CLASSIC GRADE IV SIDELOCK (MODEL 75 EX)   REDBOOK CODE: RB-UG-S-GRADIV

Sidelock action with double intercepting sears, front yielding trigger, gas escape valves, chopper-lump forged steel barrel and frame, concave rib, automatic southgate shell ejectors, IC/M chokes, case colored receiver with English-style scroll hand engraving, splinter forend, checkered butt. Custom options may increase value. Add $300 for 28 gauge.

Production: *current* **Gauge/Bore:** *12 ga., 16 ga., 20 ga., 28 ga.*

Action: *SxS*

Barrel Length: 28" **Wt.:** *5.3–7 lbs.*

Sights: *bead front*

Capacity: *2*

Stock: *straight walnut*

D2C:	NIB $2,515	Ex $1,925	VG+ $1,385	Good $1,260	**LMP:** $3,195
C2C:	Mint $2,420	Ex $1,750	VG+ $1,260	Good $1,135	Fair $580
Trade-In:	Mint $1,790	Ex $1,425	VG+ $990	Good $885	Poor $270

UGARTECHEA ARMAS

UPLAND CLASSIC GRADE V SIDELOCK (MODEL 110) REDBOOK CODE: RB-UG-S-GRADEV

Round body sidelock action with double intercepting sears, front yielding trigger, gas escape valves, chopper-lump forged steel barrel and frame, concave rib, IC/M chokes, automatic southgate shell ejectors, case colored receiver with English-style scroll hand engraving, splinter forend, hand rubbed oil finish. Custom options may bring higher values. Add $300 for 28 gauge and add $400 for .410.

Photo Courtesy of
Rock Island Auction Company

Production: *current* Gauge/Bore: *12 ga., 16 ga., 20 ga., 28 ga., .410*					
Action: *SxS*					
Barrel Length: 28" Wt.: *5.3–7 lbs.*	D2C:	NIB $3,122	Ex $2,375	VG+ $1,720	Good $1,565	**LMP: $4,195**
Sights: *bead front*	C2C:	Mint $3,000	Ex $2,175	VG+ $1,570	Good $1,405	Fair $720
Capacity: *2*	Trade-In:	Mint $2,220	Ex $1,750	VG+ $1,220	Good $1,095	Poor $330
Stock: *straight walnut*					

CUSTOM GRADE 257 SIDELOCK REDBOOK CODE: RB-UG-S-GRA257

Sidelock with intercepting sears, double triggers, hinged front trigger, case colored or coin finished receiver with deep relief floral hand engraving, concave rib, automatic southgate ejectors, gas escape valves, chopper-lump barrels, IC/M chokes, 2 3/4" chamber. Custom options may increase value.

Production: *current* Gauge/Bore: *16 ga., 20 ga.*					
Action: *SxS*					
Barrel Length: 28" Wt.: *6.3–6.5 lbs.*	D2C:	NIB $3,845	Ex $2,925	VG+ $2,115	Good $1,925	**LMP: $4,295**
Sights: *bead front*	C2C:	Mint $3,700	Ex $2,675	VG+ $1,930	Good $1,735	Fair $885
Capacity: *2*	Trade-In:	Mint $2,730	Ex $2,175	VG+ $1,500	Good $1,350	Poor $390
Stock: *straight walnut*					

CUSTOM GRADE 357 SIDELOCK REDBOOK CODE: RB-UG-S-GRA357

Sidelock with intercepting sears, double triggers, hinged front trigger, case colored or coin finished receiver with fine scroll engraving, concave rib, automatic southgate ejectors, IC/M chokes, gas escape valves, chopper-lump barrel, splinter forend. This is a special order only firearm and prices may vary with custom options.

Production: *current* Gauge/Bore: *16 ga., 20 ga.*					
Action: *SxS*					
Barrel Length: 26"–30" Wt.: *5.8–6 lbs.*	D2C:	NIB $4,195	Ex $3,200	VG+ $2,310	Good $2,100	**LMP: $4,595**
Sights: *bead front*	C2C:	Mint $4,030	Ex $2,900	VG+ $2,100	Good $1,890	Fair $965
Capacity: *2*	Trade-In:	Mint $2,980	Ex $2,350	VG+ $1,640	Good $1,470	Poor $420
Stock: *straight walnut*					

CUSTOM GRADE 2000 SIDELOCK REDBOOK CODE: RB-UG-S-GR2000

Case colored or coin finished receiver with very fine wildlife hand engraving, sidelock with intercepting sears, double triggers, hinged front trigger, concave rib, automatic southgate ejectors, gas escape valves, chopper-lump barrel, upgraded walnut stock with hand-rubbed oil finish. This is a special order only firearm and prices may vary with custom options.

Production: *current* Gauge/Bore: *16 ga., 20 ga.*					
Action: *SxS*					
Barrel Length: 26"–30" Wt.: *5.8–6 lbs.*	D2C:	NIB $5,095	Ex $3,875	VG+ $2,805	Good $2,550	**LMP: $5,295**
Sights: *bead front*	C2C:	Mint $4,900	Ex $3,525	VG+ $2,550	Good $2,295	Fair $1,175
Capacity: *2*	Trade-In:	Mint $3,620	Ex $2,875	VG+ $1,990	Good $1,785	Poor $510
Stock: *straight walnut*					

MODEL AOC/SG REDBOOK CODE: RB-UG-S-AOCSGX

Anson and Deeley boxlock action, scalloped action shaping, automatic safety, chopper lump barrels, game concave rib, southgate-style auto ejectors, border scroll engraved receiver and guard, splinter forend, double triggers with articulating front trigger, case hardened receiver, slight premium for coin finish. Add $220 for 28 gauge. and add $475 for .410 model.

Production: *current* **Gauge/Bore:** *12 ga., 16 ga., 20 ga., 28 ga., .410*

Action: *SxS*

Barrel Length: 28", 29", 30" **Wt.:** *N/A*

Sights: *bead front*

Capacity: *2*

Stock: *straight walnut*

D2C:	NIB $2,697	Ex $2,050	VG+ $1,485	Good $1,350	**LMP: $3,775**
C2C:	Mint $2,590	Ex $1,875	VG+ $1,350	Good $1,215	Fair $625
Trade-In:	Mint $1,920	Ex $1,525	VG+ $1,060	Good $945	Poor $270

Weatherby, Inc.

Roy Weatherby began experimenting with wildcat cartridges in the 1940s and later developed the famous Weatherby Magnum cartridges that are still popular today. Weatherby also worked to rechamber existing rifles and develop new ones to accommodate his high speed, lightweight cartridges. Early attempts were built on Mauser actions, but in 1957, Weatherby introduced his own proprietary action in the Mark V, which has come to be a landmark bolt-action rifle. Over the years, Weatherby added to his product lines, and the company now offers semi-automatic and pump action shotguns in addition to apparel and accessories. In 1983, Roy's son, Ed Weatherby, took charge of the company, and the Weatherby name is still associated with extreme accuracy and quality. The company is currently located in Paso Robles, California.

PA-08 SYNTHETIC REDBOOK CODE: RB-WE-S-PA08SY

Includes IC, M, and F chokes. Injection-molded stock, matte black metalwork, vented top, 3" chamber, chrome-lined barrel, swivel studs included.

Production: *current* **Gauge/Bore:** *12 ga., 20 ga.*

Action: *pump-action*

Barrel Length: 26", 28" **Wt.:** *6.5–7.3 lbs.*

Sights: *brass bead front*

Capacity: *6*

Stock: *black synthetic*

D2C:	NIB $350	Ex $275	VG+ $195	Good $175	**LMP: $399**
C2C:	Mint $340	Ex $250	VG+ $180	Good $160	Fair $85
Trade-In:	Mint $250	Ex $200	VG+ $140	Good $125	Poor $60

PA-08 SYNTHETIC SLUG GUN COMBO REDBOOK CODE: RB-WE-S-SYNSGC

14" length of pull, 3" chamber, injection-molded stock, swivel studs included, comes with 28" field barrel and 24" rifled barrel with cantilever scope mount base.

Production: *current* **Gauge/Bore:** *12 ga.*

Action: *pump-action*

Barrel Length: 24", 28" **Wt.:** *7 lbs.*

Sights: *brass bead front*

Capacity: *6*

Stock: *black synthetic*

D2C:	NIB $460	Ex $350	VG+ $255	Good $230	**LMP: $549**
C2C:	Mint $450	Ex $325	VG+ $230	Good $210	Fair $110
Trade-In:	Mint $330	Ex $275	VG+ $180	Good $165	Poor $60

PA-08 SYNTHETIC WATERFOWLER 3.0 REDBOOK CODE: RB-WE-S-SYNWAT

Includes IC, M, and F chokes. 3" chamber, 14" length of pull, injection-molded synthetic stock, Mothwing Marsh Mimicry camouflage pattern, swivel studs included.

Production: *current* **Gauge/Bore:** *12 ga.*
Action: *pump-action*
Barrel Length: 26", 28" **Wt.:** *7–7.2 lbs.*
Sights: *brass bead front*
Capacity: 6
Stock: *camouflage synthetic*

D2C:	NIB $340	Ex $275	VG+ $190	Good $170	**LMP:** $399
C2C:	Mint $330	Ex $250	VG+ $170	Good $155	Fair $80
Trade-In:	Mint $250	Ex $200	VG+ $140	Good $120	Poor $60

PA-08 TURKEY REDBOOK CODE: RB-WE-S-TURKEY

Includes F choke, 3" chamber, 14" length of pull, dual-action bar system, removable choke tube, Mothwing Spring Mimicry camouflage pattern, swivel studs included.

Production: *current* **Gauge/Bore:** *12 ga.*
Action: *pump-action*
Barrel Length: 22" **Wt.:** *7 lbs.*
Sights: *brass bead front*
Capacity: 6
Stock: *camouflage synthetic*

D2C:	NIB $355	Ex $275	VG+ $200	Good $180	**LMP:** $399
C2C:	Mint $350	Ex $250	VG+ $180	Good $160	Fair $85
Trade-In:	Mint $260	Ex $200	VG+ $140	Good $125	Poor $60

PA-08 UPLAND REDBOOK CODE: RB-WE-S-08UPLA

Includes IC, M, and F chokes. 3" chamber, 14" length of pull, gloss finish on walnut stock, vented top rib, chrome lined barrel.

Production: *current* **Gauge/Bore:** *12 ga., 20 ga.*
Action: *pump-action*
Barrel Length: 26", 28" **Wt.:** *6.5–7.3 lbs.*
Sights: *brass bead front*
Capacity: 6
Stock: *walnut*

D2C:	NIB $340	Ex $275	VG+ $190	Good $170	**LMP:** $449
C2C:	Mint $330	Ex $250	VG+ $170	Good $155	Fair $80
Trade-In:	Mint $250	Ex $200	VG+ $140	Good $120	Poor $60

PA-08 UPLAND SLUG COMBO REDBOOK CODE: RB-WE-S-UPSLUG

Includes IC, M, and F chokes. 14" length of pull, 3" chamber, gloss finish on walnut stock, 28" field barrel has gloss black finish, 24" rifled barrel with cantilever scope mount is in matte black, swivel studs.

Production: *current* **Gauge/Bore:** *12 ga.*
Action: *pump-action*
Barrel Length: 24", 28" **Wt.:** *7.3 lbs.*
Sights: *brass bead front*
Capacity: 6
Stock: *walnut*

D2C:	NIB $580	Ex $450	VG+ $320	Good $290	**LMP:** $649
C2C:	Mint $560	Ex $425	VG+ $290	Good $265	Fair $135
Trade-In:	Mint $420	Ex $325	VG+ $230	Good $205	Poor $60

PA-08 TR REDBOOK CODE: RB-WE-S-PA08TR

Fixed cylinder, 14" length of pull, 3" chamber, Kryptec Typhon pattern, injection-molded synthetic stock, chrome-lined barrel, matte black metalwork, swivel studs.

Production: *current* **Gauge/Bore:** *12 ga., 20 ga.*
Action: *pump-action*
Barrel Length: 18.5" **Wt.:** *5.7–6.5 lbs.*
Sights: *blade white-dot front*
Capacity: *5, 6*
Stock: *synthetic*

D2C:	NIB $330	Ex $275	VG+ $185	Good $165	**LMP:** $399
C2C:	Mint $320	Ex $250	VG+ $170	Good $150	Fair $80
Trade-In:	Mint $240	Ex $200	VG+ $130	Good $120	Poor $60

PA-08 KNOXX HD REDBOOK CODE: RB-WE-S-KNOXHD

Non-ventilated rib, IC and cylinder choke, adjustable stock, black pistol grip.

Production: *discontinued* **Gauge/Bore:** *12 ga.*
Action: *pump-action*
Barrel Length: 18" **Wt.:** *7 lbs.*
Sights: *bead front*
Capacity: *5*
Stock: *black synthetic*

D2C:	NIB $440	Ex $350	VG+ $245	Good $220	
C2C:	Mint $430	Ex $325	VG+ $220	Good $200	Fair $105
Trade-In:	Mint $320	Ex $250	VG+ $180	Good $155	Poor $60

PA-08 KNOXX STRUTTER X REDBOOK CODE: RB-WE-S-KNSTRU

Ventilated rib, choke tubes, Knoxx recoil reduction system, pistol grip in camouflage or black.

Production: *discontinued* **Gauge/Bore:** *12 ga.*
Action: *pump-action*
Barrel Length: 24" **Wt.:** *7 lbs.*
Sights: *bead front*
Capacity: *5*
Stock: *camouflage or black synthetic*

D2C:	NIB $440	Ex $350	VG+ $245	Good $220	
C2C:	Mint $430	Ex $325	VG+ $220	Good $200	Fair $105
Trade-In:	Mint $320	Ex $250	VG+ $180	Good $155	Poor $60

PA-459 TURKEY REDBOOK CODE: RB-WE-S-PA459T

Includes X-F chokes, 13.5" length of pull, 3" chamber, rubber texturized grip, removable extended ported choke tube, Mothwing Spring Mimicry camouflage pattern, Picatinny accessory rail.

Production: *current* **Gauge/Bore:** *12 ga.*
Action: *pump-action*
Barrel Length: 21.3" **Wt.:** *6.7 lbs.*
Sights: *fixed front LPA-style ghost ring rear*
Capacity: *5, 6*
Stock: *camouflage synthetic*

D2C:	NIB $470	Ex $375	VG+ $260	Good $235	**LMP:** $549
C2C:	Mint $460	Ex $325	VG+ $240	Good $215	Fair $110
Trade-In:	Mint $340	Ex $275	VG+ $190	Good $165	Poor $60

WEATHERBY

SA-08 DELUXE   REDBOOK CODE: RB-WE-S-SA08DE

Includes IC, M, and F chokes. 14" length of pull, 3" chamber, high gloss finish on walnut, high luster finish on metal, vented top rib, dual-valve system.

Production: *current* **Gauge/Bore:** *12 ga., 20 ga.*
Action: *semi-auto*
Barrel Length: 26", 28" **Wt.:** *6–6.7 lbs.*
Sights: *brass bead front*
Capacity: *6*
Stock: *walnut*

D2C:	NIB $650	Ex $500	VG+ $360	Good $325	**LMP:** $799
C2C:	Mint $630	Ex $450	VG+ $330	Good $295	Fair $150
Trade-In:	Mint $470	Ex $375	VG+ $260	Good $230	Poor $90

SA-08 DELUXE- 28 GAUGE   REDBOOK CODE: RB-WE-S-DELU28

Includes IC, M, and F chokes. High gloss finish on the select grade walnut stock, 22 LPI checkering on pistol grip and forend, alloy receiver, chrome-lined vented top rib barrel.

Production: *current* **Gauge/Bore:** *28 ga.*
Action: *semi-auto*
Barrel Length: 26", 28" **Wt.:** *5.5 lbs.*
Sights: *brass bead front*
Capacity: *6*
Stock: *walnut*

D2C:	NIB $800	Ex $625	VG+ $440	Good $400	**LMP:** $849
C2C:	Mint $770	Ex $575	VG+ $400	Good $360	Fair $185
Trade-In:	Mint $570	Ex $450	VG+ $320	Good $280	Poor $90

SA-08 SYNTHETIC   REDBOOK CODE: RB-WE-S-SA08SY

Includes IC, M and F chokes. 14" length of pull, 3" chamber, injection-molded synthetic stock, matte black metalwork vented top rib.

Production: *current* **Gauge/Bore:** *12 ga., 20 ga.*
Action: *semi-auto*
Barrel Length: 26", 28" **Wt.:** *6–6.5 lbs.*
Sights: *brass bead front*
Capacity: *6*
Stock: *black synthetic*

D2C:	NIB $540	Ex $425	VG+ $300	Good $270	**LMP:** $599
C2C:	Mint $520	Ex $375	VG+ $270	Good $245	Fair $125
Trade-In:	Mint $390	Ex $325	VG+ $220	Good $190	Poor $60

SA-08 SYNTHETIC WATERFOWLER 3.0   REDBOOK CODE: RB-WE-S-WATER3

Includes IC, M, and F chokes. 14" length of pull, 3" chamber, injection-molded stock, Mothwing Marsh Mimicry camouflage pattern.

Production: *current* **Gauge/Bore:** *12 ga.*
Action: *semi-auto*
Barrel Length: 26", 28" **Wt.:** *6.5 lbs.*
Sights: *brass bead front*
Capacity: *6*
Stock: *camouflage synthetic*

D2C:	NIB $660	Ex $525	VG+ $365	Good $330	**LMP:** $749
C2C:	Mint $640	Ex $475	VG+ $330	Good $300	Fair $155
Trade-In:	Mint $470	Ex $375	VG+ $260	Good $235	Poor $90

SA-08 UPLAND   REDBOOK CODE: RB-WE-S-SA08UP
Includes IC, M, and F chokes. 3" chamber, 14" length of pull, satin finish on walnut stock, matte black metalwork, vented top rib, dual-valve system.

Production: *current* **Gauge/Bore:** *12 ga., 20 ga.*
Action: *semi-auto*
Barrel Length: 26", 28" **Wt.:** *6–6.7 lbs.*
Sights: *brass bead front*
Capacity: *6*
Stock: *walnut*

D2C:	NIB $650	Ex $500	VG+ $360	Good $325	**LMP:** $799
C2C:	Mint $630	Ex $450	VG+ $330	Good $295	Fair $150
Trade-In:	Mint $470	Ex $375	VG+ $260	Good $230	Poor $90

SA-459 TURKEY   REDBOOK CODE: RB-WE-S-SA459T
Includes X-F chokes, 13.5" length of pull, 3" chamber, rubber texturized grip, removable extended ported choke tube, Mothwing Spring Mimicry camouflage pattern, Picatinny accessory rail.

Production: *current* **Gauge/Bore:** *12 ga., 20 ga.*
Action: *semi-auto*
Barrel Length: 22" **Wt.:** *6–7 lbs.*
Sights: *fixed front, adjustable rear LPA ghost ring*
Capacity: *5*
Stock: *camouflage composite*

D2C:	NIB $630	Ex $500	VG+ $350	Good $315	**LMP:** $699
C2C:	Mint $610	Ex $450	VG+ $320	Good $285	Fair $145
Trade-In:	Mint $450	Ex $375	VG+ $250	Good $225	Poor $90

PA-459 DIGITAL TR   REDBOOK CODE: RB-WE-S-459DIG
13.5" length of pull, 3" chamber, universal digital camouflage pattern, rubber textured grip areas, removable extended and ported cylinder choke tube, matte black metalwork, swivel studs included.

Production: *current* **Gauge/Bore:** *12 ga.*
Action: *pump-action*
Barrel Length: 18.5" **Wt.:** *6.5 lbs.*
Sights: *fixed front, adjustable rear LPA style ghost-ring rear*
Capacity: *5, 6*
Stock: *camouflage synthetic*

D2C:	NIB $470	Ex $375	VG+ $260	Good $235	**LMP:** $549
C2C:	Mint $460	Ex $325	VG+ $240	Good $215	Fair $110
Trade-In:	Mint $340	Ex $275	VG+ $190	Good $165	Poor $60

PA-459 TR   REDBOOK CODE: RB-WE-S-PA45TR
Extended and ported cylinder choke tube, 13.5" length of pull, 3" chamber, rubber textured-grip areas, chrome-lined barrel, matte black metalwork, swivel studs included.

Production: *current* **Gauge/Bore:** *12 ga., 20 ga.*
Action: *pump-action*
Barrel Length: 18.5" **Wt.:** *5.7–6.5 lbs.*
Sights: *fixed front, adjustable rear LPA style ghost-ring rear*
Capacity: *5, 6*
Stock: *black synthetic*

D2C:	NIB $470	Ex $375	VG+ $260	Good $235	**LMP:** $499
C2C:	Mint $460	Ex $325	VG+ $240	Good $215	Fair $110
Trade-In:	Mint $340	Ex $275	VG+ $190	Good $165	Poor $60

WEATHERBY

WBY-X PA-08 BLACK REAPER TR   REDBOOK CODE: RB-WE-S-BLAREA

Fixed cylinder choke, 14" length of pull, 3" chamber, Proveil Reaper black pattern, injection-molded synthetic stock, chrome-lined barrel, matte black metalwork, swivel studs included.

Production: *current* **Gauge/Bore:** *12 ga., 20 ga.*
Action: *pump-action*
Barrel Length: 18.5" **Wt.:** *6–6.5 lbs.*
Sights: *blade white dot front*
Capacity: *5, 6*
Stock: *synthetic*

D2C:	NIB $270	Ex $225	VG+ $150	Good $135	**LMP:** $399
C2C:	Mint $260	Ex $200	VG+ $140	Good $125	Fair $65
Trade-In:	Mint $200	Ex $175	VG+ $110	Good $95	Poor $30

WBY-X PA-08 TYPHON TR   REDBOOK CODE: RB-WE-S-TYPHON

Fixed cylinder choke, 14" length of pull, 3" chamber, Kryptec Typhon pattern, injection-molded stock, chrome-lined barrel, matte black metalwork, swivel studs included.

Production: *current* **Gauge/Bore:** *12 ga., 20 ga.*
Action: *pump-action*
Barrel Length: 18.5" **Wt.:** *5.7–6.5 lbs.*
Sights: *blade white dot front*
Capacity: *5, 6*
Stock: *synthetic*

D2C:	NIB $370	Ex $300	VG+ $205	Good $185	**LMP:** $399
C2C:	Mint $360	Ex $275	VG+ $190	Good $170	Fair $90
Trade-In:	Mint $270	Ex $225	VG+ $150	Good $130	Poor $60

WBY-X PA-459 TYPHON TR   REDBOOK CODE: RB-WE-S-459TYP

13.5" length of pull, 3" chamber, Kryptec Typhon pattern, ergo buttstock with textured grip, 13.5" length of pull, chrome-lined barrel, extended and ported cylinder choke tube, swivel studs included.

Production: *current* **Gauge/Bore:** *12 ga., 20 ga.*
Action: *pump-action*
Barrel Length: 18.5" **Wt.:** *5.7–6.5 lbs.*
Sights: *fixed front, adjustable rear LPA style ghost-ring rear*
Capacity: *5, 6*
Stock: *synthetic*

D2C:	NIB $540	Ex $425	VG+ $300	Good $270	**LMP:** $549
C2C:	Mint $520	Ex $375	VG+ $270	Good $245	Fair $125
Trade-In:	Mint $390	Ex $325	VG+ $220	Good $190	Poor $60

WBY-X SA-459 BLACK REAPER TR   REDBOOK CODE: RB-WE-S-BLACTR

Extended and ported cylinder choke tube, 13.5" length of pull, 3" chamber, Proveil Reaper black patter, gas-operated, oversized hourglass bolt handle, chrome-lined barrel, swivel studs included.

Production: *current* **Gauge/Bore:** *12 ga., 20 ga.*
Action: *semi-auto*
Barrel Length: 18.5" **Wt.:** *6–6.5 lbs.*
Sights: *fixed front, adjustable rear LPA style ghost-ring rear*
Capacity: *5, 6*
Stock: *synthetic*

D2C:	NIB $680	Ex $525	VG+ $375	Good $340	**LMP:** $749
C2C:	Mint $660	Ex $475	VG+ $340	Good $310	Fair $160
Trade-In:	Mint $490	Ex $400	VG+ $270	Good $240	Poor $90

WEATHERBY

WBY-X SA-08 GH2 REDBOOK CODE: RB-WE-S-WBYGH2
Includes IC, M, and F chokes. 12.5" length of pull, 3" chamber, injection-molded stock with pink spider web accent pattern, dual-valve system, vented top-rib, swivel studs included.

Production: *current* **Gauge/Bore:** *20 ga.*
Action: *semi-auto*
Barrel Length: 24" **Wt.:** *5.7 lbs.*
Sights: *bead front*
Capacity: *5, 6*
Stock: *synthetic*

D2C:	NIB $670	Ex $525	VG+ $370	Good $335	LMP: $699
C2C:	Mint $650	Ex $475	VG+ $340	Good $305	Fair $155
Trade-In:	Mint $480	Ex $400	VG+ $270	Good $235	Poor $90

WBY-X SA-08 KRYPTEK COMPACT REDBOOK CODE: RB-WE-S-KRYCOM
Includes IC, M, and F chokes. 3" chamber, 12.5" length of pull, Kryptec Highlander camouflage pattern, dual-valve system, vented top rib, swivel studs included.

Production: *current* **Gauge/Bore:** *20 ga.*
Action: *semi-auto*
Barrel Length: 24" **Wt.:** *5.7 lbs.*
Sights: *bead front*
Capacity: *5, 6*
Stock: *synthetic*

D2C:	NIB $575	Ex $450	VG+ $320	Good $290	LMP: $699
C2C:	Mint $560	Ex $400	VG+ $290	Good $260	Fair $135
Trade-In:	Mint $410	Ex $325	VG+ $230	Good $205	Poor $60

SA-459 TR REDBOOK CODE: RB-WE-S-SA459R
3" chamber, 13.5" length of pull, gas operated, removable extended and ported cylinder choke tube, oversized hourglass bolt handle, swivel studs included.

Production: *current* **Gauge/Bore:** *12 ga., 20 ga.*
Action: *semi-auto*
Barrel Length: 18.5" **Wt.:** *6–6.5 lbs.*
Sights: *fixed front, adjustable ghost-ring rear*
Capacity: *5, 6*
Stock: *synthetic*

D2C:	NIB $620	Ex $475	VG+ $345	Good $310	LMP: $699
C2C:	Mint $600	Ex $450	VG+ $310	Good $280	Fair $145
Trade-In:	Mint $450	Ex $350	VG+ $250	Good $220	Poor $90

Photo Courtesy of Rock Island Auction Company

ATHENA D'ITALIA III REDBOOK CODE: RB-WE-S-ATHIII
3" chamber, choke tubes included, ejectors, four-lock boxlock action, chrome-plated side plates, gold gamebird scene engraved on chrome-plated receiver, tang-operated, checkered oil-finished walnut, pierced top lever.

Production: *discontinued* **Gauge/Bore:** *12 ga., 20 ga.*
Action: *O/U*
Barrel Length: 26", 28" **Wt.:** *6.5–8 lbs.*
Sights: *bead front*
Capacity: *2*
Stock: *walnut*

D2C:	NIB $2,120	Ex $1,625	VG+ $1,170	Good $1,060	
C2C:	Mint $2,040	Ex $1,475	VG+ $1,060	Good $955	Fair $490
Trade-In:	Mint $1,510	Ex $1,200	VG+ $830	Good $745	Poor $240

WEATHERBY

ATHENA D'ITALIA IV   REDBOOK CODE: RB-WE-S-ATHEIV

3" chamber, boxlock action, high-luster finish on walnut stock, hand checkering on stock and forearm, recoil pad, engraved side plates, nickel-finished engraved receiver, ventilated rib.

Photo Courtesy of Rock Island Auction Company

Production: *1989–2002* **Gauge/Bore:** *12 ga., 20 ga., 28 ga.*
Action: *O/U*
Barrel Length: *26", 28"* **Wt.:** *6.5–8 lbs.*
Sights: *bead front*
Capacity: *2*
Stock: *walnut*

D2C:	NIB $2,290	Ex $1,750	VG+ $1,260	Good $1,145	
C2C:	Mint $2,200	Ex $1,600	VG+ $1,150	Good $1,035	Fair $530
Trade-In:	Mint $1,630	Ex $1,300	VG+ $900	Good $805	Poor $240

CENTURION DELUXE   REDBOOK CODE: RB-WE-S-CENDEL

Gas operated, checkering on pistol grip, engraving on receiver, vent-ribbed barrel, higher quality walnut than Centurion standard model.

Production: *1972–1981* **Gauge/Bore:** *12 ga.*
Action: *semi-auto*
Barrel Length: *various barrel lengths* **Wt.:** *7–8 lbs.*
Sights: *bead front*
Capacity: *3*
Stock: *walnut*

D2C:	NIB $450	Ex $350	VG+ $250	Good $225	
C2C:	Mint $440	Ex $325	VG+ $230	Good $205	Fair $105
Trade-In:	Mint $320	Ex $275	VG+ $180	Good $160	Poor $60

CENTURION FIELD GRADE   REDBOOK CODE: RB-WE-S-CENFGR

Checkering on pistol grip and forearm, 3" barrel, recoil pad, gas operated, ventilated rib.

Production: *1972–1981* **Gauge/Bore:** *12 ga.*
Action: *semi-auto*
Barrel Length: *various barrel lengths* **Wt.:** *7–8 lbs.*
Sights: *bead front*
Capacity: *3*
Stock: *walnut*

D2C:	NIB $370	Ex $300	VG+ $205	Good $185	
C2C:	Mint $360	Ex $275	VG+ $190	Good $170	Fair $90
Trade-In:	Mint $270	Ex $225	VG+ $150	Good $130	Poor $60

CENTURION TRAP GUN   REDBOOK CODE: RB-WE-S-CENTRA

Full choke barrel, checkering on stock, ventilated rib, pistol grip.

Production: *discontinued* **Gauge/Bore:** *12 ga.*
Action: *semi-auto*
Barrel Length: *30"* **Wt.:** *7–8 lbs.*
Sights: *bead front*
Capacity: *3*
Stock: *walnut*

D2C:	NIB $400	Ex $325	VG+ $220	Good $200	
C2C:	Mint $390	Ex $300	VG+ $200	Good $180	Fair $95
Trade-In:	Mint $290	Ex $225	VG+ $160	Good $140	Poor $60

MODEL 82 REDBOOK CODE: RB-WE-S-MODE82
2.75" or 3" chamber, gas operated, alloy receiver, checkering on stock and foregrip, ventilated rib, screw in choke tubes.

Production: *1982–1989* **Gauge/Bore:** *12 ga.*
Action: *semi-auto*
Barrel Length: 22"–30" **Wt.:** *7.5 lbs.*
Sights: *bead front*
Capacity: *3*
Stock: *deluxe walnut*

D2C:	NIB $550	Ex $425	VG+ $305	Good $275	
C2C:	Mint $530	Ex $400	VG+ $280	Good $250	Fair $130
Trade-In:	Mint $400	Ex $325	VG+ $220	Good $195	Poor $60

MODEL 92 REDBOOK CODE: RB-WE-S-MODE92
2.75" or 3" chamber, gas operated, ultra-short slide action, twin rails, ventilated rib barrels, engraved black alloy receiver, checkered pistol grip and forearm, blue metal finishing.

Production: *1982–1989* **Gauge/Bore:** *12 ga.*
Action: *semi-auto*
Barrel Length: 26"–30" **Wt.:** *7.5 lbs.*
Sights: *bead front*
Capacity: *3*
Stock: *deluxe walnut*

D2C:	NIB $530	Ex $425	VG+ $295	Good $265	
C2C:	Mint $510	Ex $375	VG+ $270	Good $240	Fair $125
Trade-In:	Mint $380	Ex $300	VG+ $210	Good $190	Poor $60

MODEL SAS FIELD CAMO REDBOOK CODE: RB-WE-S-SASCAM
Ventilated rib barrel, inlcudes five Briley choke tubes, HiViz front sight. Also available in Field Synthetic model with black stock.

Production: *2000–discontinued* **Gauge/Bore:** *12 ga.*
Action: *semi-auto*
Barrel Length: 24", 26", 28" **Wt.:** *7.5–7.8 lbs.*
Sights: *bead front*
Capacity: *3*
Stock: *synthetic camouflage*

D2C:	NIB $815	Ex $625	VG+ $450	Good $410	
C2C:	Mint $790	Ex $575	VG+ $410	Good $370	Fair $190
Trade-In:	Mint $580	Ex $475	VG+ $320	Good $290	Poor $90

MODEL SAS FIELD SLUG REDBOOK CODE: RB-WE-S-SASFIE
3" chamber, rifled barrel, cantilever base, Monte Carlo style stock, forearm with sling swivel.

Production: *2003–2007* **Gauge/Bore:** *12 ga.*
Action: *semi-auto*
Barrel Length: 22" **Wt.:** *7.5 lbs.*
Sights: *bead front*
Capacity: *3*
Stock: *checkered walnut*

D2C:	NIB $830	Ex $650	VG+ $460	Good $415	
C2C:	Mint $800	Ex $575	VG+ $420	Good $375	Fair $195
Trade-In:	Mint $590	Ex $475	VG+ $330	Good $295	Poor $90

WEATHERBY

MODEL SAS FIELD SPORTING CLAYS REDBOOK CODE: RB-WE-S-SASFSC
Ventilated rib barrel, extended choke tubes, 3" chamber.

Production: *2002–2005* **Gauge/Bore:** *12 ga.*
Action: *semi-auto*
Barrel Length: 26", 28", 30" **Wt.:** *7–7.8 lbs.*
Sights: *bead front*
Capacity: *3*
Stock: *pistol-grip walnut*

D2C:	NIB $860	Ex $675	VG+ $475	Good $430	
C2C:	Mint $830	Ex $600	VG+ $430	Good $390	Fair $200
Trade-In:	Mint $620	Ex $500	VG+ $340	Good $305	Poor $90

*Photo Courtesy of
Rock Island Auction Company*

OLYMPIAN STANDARD/SKEET/TRAP REDBOOK CODE: RB-WE-S-OLYSST
Engraving on receiver, all models command similar premiums, 3" chamber, single-selective trigger, automatic ejectors.

Production: *discontinued 1980* **Gauge/Bore:** *12 ga., 20 ga.*
Action: *O/U*
Barrel Length: 26", 28", 30", 32" **Wt.:** *6.8–8.8 lbs.*
Sights: *bead front*
Capacity: *2*
Stock: *pistol-grip walnut*

D2C:	NIB $950	Ex $725	VG+ $525	Good $475	
C2C:	Mint $920	Ex $675	VG+ $480	Good $430	Fair $220
Trade-In:	Mint $680	Ex $550	VG+ $380	Good $335	Poor $120

*Photo Courtesy of
Rock Island Auction Company*

ORION REDBOOK CODE: RB-WE-S-ORIONX
Automatic ejectors, case-colored boxlock action, gold single-selective trigger, half-round pistol grip, semi-beavertail forearm. Orion offered in Field Grade, Classic, Sporting Clays, English Field, Upland, and Skeet models.

Production: *discontinued* **Gauge/Bore:** *12 ga., 20 ga., 28 ga., .410*
Action: *O/U*
Barrel Length: 26"–34" **Wt.:** *6–7 lbs.*
Sights: *bead front*
Capacity: *2*
Stock: *pistol-grip walnut*

D2C:	NIB $1,210	Ex $925	VG+ $670	Good $605	
C2C:	Mint $1,170	Ex $850	VG+ $610	Good $545	Fair $280
Trade-In:	Mint $860	Ex $700	VG+ $480	Good $425	Poor $150

*Photo Courtesy of
Rock Island Auction Company*

PATRICIAN REDBOOK CODE: RB-WE-S-PATRIC
Various choke combinations in early models, ventilated rib barrel, blue metal finishing, checkering on stock and forend, recoil pad.

Production: *1972–1982* **Gauge/Bore:** *12 ga.*
Action: *pump-action*
Barrel Length: 26", 28", 30" **Wt.:** *7.6 lbs.*
Sights: *bead front*
Capacity: *4*
Stock: *pistol-grip walnut*

D2C:	NIB $420	Ex $325	VG+ $235	Good $210	
C2C:	Mint $410	Ex $300	VG+ $210	Good $190	Fair $100
Trade-In:	Mint $300	Ex $250	VG+ $170	Good $150	Poor $60

REGENCY FIELD GRADE REDBOOK CODE: RB-WE-S-REGENC

Ventilated rib barrel, boxlock action, engraved false sideplates, single-selective trigger, automatic ejectors, blue finish, checkering on walnut. Trap grade commands the same premium.

Photo Courtesy of Rock Island Auction Company

Production: *1972–1980* **Gauge/Bore:** *12 ga., 20 ga.*
Action: *O/U*
Barrel Length: *26", 28", 30"* **Wt.:** *6–7.5 lbs.*
Sights: *bead front*
Capacity: *2*
Stock: *walnut*

D2C:	NIB $1,510	Ex $1,150	VG+ $835	Good $755	
C2C:	Mint $1,450	Ex $1,050	VG+ $760	Good $680	Fair $350
Trade-In:	Mint $1,080	Ex $850	VG+ $590	Good $530	Poor $180

Webley & Scott

Located in Birmingham, England—a firearms manufacturing center of the world, Webley & Scott has a two hundred-year history of gunmaking. The company was founded by William Davies when he began making bullet molds in the late 18th century, and it was later taken over by his descendants. The firearms upon which the company built its initial success were handguns, but the company branched out and produced air rifles and shotguns later. Major shotgun product lines were the 700 Series of side-by-side shotguns released in 1949 and the 900 Series of over/under shotguns released in 2010. Webley & Scott shotguns are manufactured today in Turkey, and they were imported to the U.S. by several different companies before distribution was taken over exclusively by Centurion International of Reno, Nevada in 2013.

2000 PREMIUM REDBOOK CODE: RB-WS-S-2000PR

Boxlock action, heavy-duty hammer springs, moly-chrome receiver, charcoal case-color hardening, jeweled monobloc walls, manual safety, chrome-lined barrels, V-spring action, automatic ejectors, oil-finished walnut, 3" chamber, five thin-walled English Teague style chokes.

Production: *current* **Gauge/Bore:** *12 ga.*
Action: *O/U*
Barrel Length: *28", 30"* **Wt.:** *7.1 lbs.*
Sights: *brass bead front*
Capacity: *2*
Stock: *select-grade Turkish walnut*

D2C:	NIB $2,030	Ex $1,550	VG+ $1,120	Good $1,015	**LMP:** $2,499
C2C:	Mint $1,950	Ex $1,425	VG+ $1,020	Good $915	Fair $470
Trade-In:	Mint $1,450	Ex $1,150	VG+ $800	Good $715	Poor $210

3000 SIDELOCK REDBOOK CODE: RB-WS-S-3000SL

7-pin side lock, heavy-duty hammer springs, moly-chrome steel receiver, case color hardening, jeweled mono-lock walls, manual safety, chrome-line barrels, V-spring action, automatic ejectors, oil-finished walnut, 3" chamber, five English Teague style chokes included.

Production: *current* **Gauge/Bore:** *12 ga., 20 ga.*
Action: *O/U*
Barrel Length: *28"* **Wt.:** *7 lbs.*
Sights: *brass bead front*
Capacity: *2*
Stock: *Turkish walnut*

D2C:	NIB $5,680	Ex $4,325	VG+ $3,125	Good $2,840	**LMP:** $5,999
C2C:	Mint $5,460	Ex $3,925	VG+ $2,840	Good $2,560	Fair $1,310
Trade-In:	Mint $4,040	Ex $3,200	VG+ $2,220	Good $1,990	Poor $570

WS912D SPORTER DELUXE REDBOOK CODE: RB-WS-S-WS912D

Included chokes are: C, IC, M, IM, F. Manual safety, 3" chamber, rubber recoil pad, Schnabel forend, single trigger, silver chrome receiver finish, black chrome barrel finish, boxlock action, heavy-duty hammer springs, moly-chrome steel receiver, jeweled monobloc walls, chrome-lined barrels, automatic ejectors, engraving covers the majority of the action.

Production: *current* Gauge/Bore: *12 ga.*					
Action: *O/U*					
Barrel Length: 28" Wt.: *7.4 lbs.*	D2C:	NIB $1,148	Ex $875	VG+ $635	Good $575	LMP: $1,299
Sights: *fiber-optic*	C2C:	Mint $1,110	Ex $800	VG+ $580	Good $520	Fair $265
Capacity: *2*	Trade-In:	Mint $820	Ex $650	VG+ $450	Good $405	Poor $120
Stock: *pistol grip walnut*					

WS912K SPORTER REDBOOK CODE: RB-WS-S-WS912K

Included chokes are: C, IC, M, IM, F. Manual safety, 3" chamber, rubber recoil pad, Schnabel forend, single trigger, black chrome finish on receiver and barrel, solid middle rib, heavy-duty hammer springs, moly-chrome steel CNC receiver, jeweled monobloc walls, manual safety, chrome-lined barrels, automatic ejectors, oil-finished walnut.

Production: *current* Gauge/Bore: *12 ga.*					
Action: *O/U*					
Barrel Length: 28" Wt.: *7.4 lbs.*	D2C:	NIB $1,121	Ex $875	VG+ $620	Good $565	LMP: $1,249
Sights: *fiber-optic front*	C2C:	Mint $1,080	Ex $775	VG+ $570	Good $505	Fair $260
Capacity: *2*	Trade-In:	Mint $800	Ex $650	VG+ $440	Good $395	Poor $120
Stock: *pistol grip walnut*					

WS920J JUNIOR REDBOOK CODE: RB-WS-S-WS920J

Included chokes: C, IC, M, IM, F. Manual safety, 3" chamber, rubber recoil pad, Schnabel forend, single trigger, black chrome finish on receiver and barrel, gated barrel selectors, heavy-duty hammer springs, moly-chrome steel receiver, jeweled monobloc walls, manual safety, chrome-lined barrels, automatic ejectors, oil-finished walnut.

Production: *current* Gauge/Bore: *20 ga.*					
Action: *O/U*					
Barrel Length: 28" Wt.: *6.3 lbs.*	D2C:	NIB $1,263	Ex $975	VG+ $695	Good $635	LMP: $1,299
Sights: *fiber-optic*	C2C:	Mint $1,220	Ex $875	VG+ $640	Good $570	Fair $295
Capacity: *2*	Trade-In:	Mint $900	Ex $725	VG+ $500	Good $445	Poor $150
Stock: *pistol grip walnut*					

WS920K SPORTER REDBOOK CODE: RB-WS-S-WS920K

Included chokes are: C, IC, M, IM, F. Manual safety, 3" chamber, rubber recoil pad, Schnabel forend, single-trigger, barrel selector, black chrome finish on receiver and barrel, solid middle rib, boxlock action, heavy-duty hammer springs, moly-chrome steel receiver, jeweled monobloc walls, manual safety, chrome-lined barrels, automatic ejectors, oil-finished walnut.

Production: *current* Gauge/Bore: *20 ga.*					
Action: *O/U*					
Barrel Length: 26" Wt.: *6.3 lbs.*	D2C:	NIB $1,035	Ex $800	VG+ $570	Good $520	LMP: $1,249
Sights: *fiber-optic*	C2C:	Mint $1,000	Ex $725	VG+ $520	Good $470	Fair $240
Capacity: *2*	Trade-In:	Mint $740	Ex $600	VG+ $410	Good $365	Poor $120
Stock: *pistol grip walnut*					

WS928 SPORTER REDBOOK CODE: RB-WS-S-WS928S

Included chokes: C, IC, M, IM, F. Manual safety, 3" chamber, rubber recoil pad, Schnabel forend, single trigger, matte black receiver finish, black chrome barrel finish, solid middle rib, boxlock design, heavy-duty hammer springs, aluminum anodized receiver, jeweled monobloc walls, manual safety, chrome-lined barrels, automatic ejectors, oil-finished walnut, 2.75" chamber.

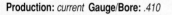

Production: *current* **Gauge/Bore:** *28 ga.*

Action: *O/U*

Barrel Length: 28" **Wt.:** *5.9 lbs.*

Sights: *fiber-optic front*

Capacity: *2*

Stock: *pistol grip walnut*

D2C:	NIB $1,035	Ex $800	VG+ $570	Good $520	**LMP:** $1,249
C2C:	Mint $1,000	Ex $725	VG+ $520	Good $470	Fair $240
Trade-In:	Mint $740	Ex $600	VG+ $410	Good $365	Poor $120

WS941 SPORTER REDBOOK CODE: RB-WS-S-WS941S

Included chokes are: C, IC, M, IM, F. Manual safety, 3" chamber, rubber recoil pad, Schnabel forend, single trigger, barrel selector, matte black receiver finish, black chrome barrel finish, solid middle rib, boxlock action, heavy-duty hammer springs, aluminum anodized receiver, jeweled monobloc walls, manual safety, chrome-lined barrels, automatic ejectors, oil-finished walnut.

Production: *current* **Gauge/Bore:** *.410*

Action: *O/U*

Barrel Length: 26" **Wt.:** *5.5 lbs.*

Sights: *fiber-optic front*

Capacity: *2*

Stock: *pistol grip walnut*

D2C:	NIB $1,035	Ex $800	VG+ $570	Good $520	**LMP:** $1,249
C2C:	Mint $1,000	Ex $725	VG+ $520	Good $470	Fair $240
Trade-In:	Mint $740	Ex $600	VG+ $410	Good $365	Poor $120

SIDE-BY-SIDE 3000 REDBOOK CODE: RB-WS-S-SIDE30

Automatic safety, oil-finished select walnut, five interchangeable chokes, single trigger, manual safety, ventilated middle rib, ventilated top rib, automatic ejectors, hand-oiled walnut, English scroll engraving and checkering.

Production: *current* **Gauge/Bore:** *12 ga., 20 ga.*

Action: *SxS*

Barrel Length: 28", 30" **Wt.:** *6.4 lbs.*

Sights: *fiber-optic front*

Capacity: *2*

Stock: *walnut*

D2C:	NIB $5,480	Ex $4,175	VG+ $3,015	Good $2,740	**LMP:** $5,999
C2C:	Mint $5,270	Ex $3,800	VG+ $2,740	Good $2,470	Fair $1,265
Trade-In:	Mint $3,900	Ex $3,075	VG+ $2,140	Good $1,920	Poor $570

SIDE-BY-SIDE 2000 REDBOOK CODE: RB-WS-S-SIDE20

Oil-finished walnut, automatic ejectors, fixed or five interchangeable chokes, double front-articulated trigger, automatic safety, flat top rib, 3" chamber, English scroll engraving and checkering, thin-walled English style chokes.

Production: *current* **Gauge/Bore:** *12 ga., 20 ga.*

Action: *SxS*

Barrel Length: 28", 30" **Wt.:** *6.4 lbs.*

Sights: *bead front*

Capacity: *2*

Stock: *half-pistol style Turkish walnut*

D2C:	NIB $2,312	Ex $1,775	VG+ $1,275	Good $1,160	**LMP:** $2,499
C2C:	Mint $2,220	Ex $1,600	VG+ $1,160	Good $1,045	Fair $535
Trade-In:	Mint $1,650	Ex $1,300	VG+ $910	Good $810	Poor $240

WS 800 REDBOOK CODE: RB-WS-S-WS800X

High-density rubber recoil pad, 5 chokes included, 3" chamber, optional sling mounts, textured foregrip and palm swell, matte blue metal finish, chrome-lined barrels, ventilated rib.

Production: *current* **Gauge/Bore:** *12 ga.*

Action: *semi-auto*

Barrel Length: 28" **Wt.:** *6.4 lbs.*

Sights: *bead front*

Capacity: *2*

Stock: *composite stock or synthetic walnut finish*

D2C:	NIB $692	Ex $550	VG+ $385	Good $350	**LMP:** $749
C2C:	Mint $670	Ex $500	VG+ $350	Good $315	Fair $160
Trade-In:	Mint $500	Ex $400	VG+ $270	Good $245	Poor $90

Winchester Repeating Arms Company

Oliver Winchester founded the Winchester Repeating Arms Company in 1866 after buying control of the New Haven Arms Company—formerly the Volcanic Repeating Arms Company that was founded by Horace Smith and Daniel Wesson of the famed Smith & Wesson. Winchester went on to produce some of the most famous and collectible firearms in history. In 1931, Olin bought the Winchester Repeating Arms Company and combined it with the Western Cartridge Company. In 1981, Winchester employees formed the U.S. Repeating Arms Company and manufactured Winchester brand firearms under licenses from Olin. After a bankruptcy in 1989, the company was sold to the Belgian firearms maker, the Herstal Group, who continued production in the original New Haven, Connecticut, location until 2006 when the factory was closed after over 140 years. The Olin Corporation then decided to produce the Winchester brand by contracting with Browning for manufacturing. Miroku in Japan also licensed some models for production. In 2008, Herstal Group's Fabrique Nationale began producing Winchester models in its Columbia, South Carolina, plant. Under these and other licenses and contractual agreements, Winchester-branded rifles and shotguns continue to be produced today.

SUPER X2 COMPOSITE REDBOOK CODE: RB-WN-S-SPX2CP

Vented rib barrel in matte finish, choke set (full, modified, improved cylinder), gas-operated, sling swivel studs, 14.25" length of pull, 1.75" drop at comb, 2" drop at heel, fires 3" shells.

Production: *discontinued 2004* **Gauge/Bore:** *12 ga.*

Action: *semi-auto*

Barrel Length: 26", 28" **Wt.:** *7.75 lbs., 8 lbs.*

Sights: *bead front*

Capacity: *5*

Stock: *synthetic*

D2C:	NIB $730	Ex $575	VG+ $405	Good $365	**LMP:** $835
C2C:	Mint $710	Ex $525	VG+ $370	Good $330	Fair $170
Trade-In:	Mint $520	Ex $425	VG+ $290	Good $260	Poor $90

SUPER X2 FIELD REDBOOK CODE: RB-WN-S-SPX2FD

Back-bored vent rib barrel in anodized finish, Invector-Plus choke tube system (full, modified, improved cylinder), gas-operated, drilled and tapped receiver, 14.25" length of pull, 1.75" drop at comb, 2" drop at heel, fires 3" shells.

Production: *discontinued 2005* **Gauge/Bore:** *12 ga.*

Action: *semi-auto*

Barrel Length: 26", 28" **Wt.:** *7.25 lbs., 7.5 lbs.*

Sights: *bead front*

Capacity: *5*

Stock: *walnut*

D2C:	NIB $742	Ex $575	VG+ $410	Good $375	**LMP:** $934
C2C:	Mint $720	Ex $525	VG+ $380	Good $335	Fair $175
Trade-In:	Mint $530	Ex $425	VG+ $290	Good $260	Poor $90

SUPER X2 SPECIAL FIELD REDBOOK CODE: RB-WN-S-SPX2SF

Gloss-finished barrel with light-style vented rib, Invector-Plus choke set (full, modified, improved cylinder), TruGlo fiber optic sight includes set of five extra fibers and colors, sporting style buttpad with hard heel, 14.25" length of pull, 1.75" drop at comb, 2" drop at heel, fires 3" shells.

Production: *discontinued 2007* **Gauge/Bore:** *12 ga.*
Action: *semi-auto*
Barrel Length: 26", 28" **Wt.:** *6.75 lbs.*
Sights: *TruGlo front fiber optic*
Capacity: *5*
Stock: *standard-grade walnut with cut-checkered grip*

D2C:	NIB $700	Ex $550	VG+ $385	Good $350	LMP: $910
C2C:	Mint $680	Ex $500	VG+ $350	Good $315	Fair $165
Trade-In:	Mint $500	Ex $400	VG+ $280	Good $245	Poor $90

SUPER X2 NWTF TURKEY REDBOOK CODE: RB-WN-S-SPX2TK

Vented rib barrel, Invector-Plus extra-full extended turkey choke set, gas-operated, receiver drilled and tapped for red-dot-type sight, sling swivel studs, brass NWTF medallion, 14.25" length of pull, 1.75" drop at comb, 2" drop at heel, fires 3 1/2" shells. Available in Mossy Oak Obsession or Mossy Oak New Break-Up and Dura-Touch Armor Coating.

Production: *discontinued 2008* **Gauge/Bore:** *12 ga.*
Action: *semi-auto*
Barrel Length: 24" **Wt.:** *7.5 lbs.*
Sights: *TruGlo removable three-dot*
Capacity: *5*
Stock: *synthetic with Dura-Touch Armor Coating*

D2C:	NIB $1,236	Ex $950	VG+ $680	Good $620	LMP: $1,236
C2C:	Mint $1,190	Ex $875	VG+ $620	Good $560	Fair $285
Trade-In:	Mint $880	Ex $700	VG+ $490	Good $435	Poor $150

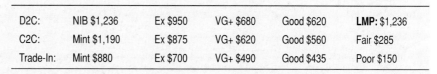

SUPER X2 UNIVERSAL HUNTER FIELD REDBOOK CODE: RB-WN-S-SPX2UH

Vented rib barrel with Invector-Plus choke tube system (full, modified, improved cylinder), gas-operated, stock and forearm coated with Dura-Touch Armor Coating, sling swivel studs, 14.25" length of pull, 1.75" drop at comb, 2" drop at heel, fires 2 3/4", 3", and 3 1/2" shells.

Production: *discontinued 2006* **Gauge/Bore:** *12 ga.*
Action: *semi-auto*
Barrel Length: 26" **Wt.:** *7.75 lbs.*
Sights: *bead front*
Capacity: *5*
Stock: *synthetic with Dura-Touch Armor Coating*

D2C:	NIB $1,050	Ex $800	VG+ $580	Good $525	LMP: $1,185
C2C:	Mint $1,010	Ex $725	VG+ $530	Good $475	Fair $245
Trade-In:	Mint $750	Ex $600	VG+ $410	Good $370	Poor $120

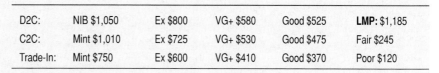

SUPER X2 UNIVERSAL HUNTER T REDBOOK CODE: RB-WN-S-SPX2HT

Back-bored vent rib barrel with Invector-Plus choke tube system (full, modified, improved cylinder, extra-full extended turkey), gas-operated, drilled and tapped receiver, Active Valve system, stock and forearm coated with Dura-Touch Armor Coating, sling swivel studs, 14.25" length of pull, fires 2 3/4", 3", and 3 1/2" shells. Model can be configured for turkey, pheasant and waterfowl.

Production: *discontinued 2008* **Gauge/Bore:** *12 ga.*
Action: *semi-auto*
Barrel Length: 26" **Wt.:** *7.75 lbs.*
Sights: *TruGlo fiber optic front & rear*
Capacity: *5*
Stock: *synthetic with Dura-Touch Armor Coating*

D2C:	NIB $950	Ex $725	VG+ $525	Good $475	LMP: $1,252
C2C:	Mint $920	Ex $675	VG+ $480	Good $430	Fair $220
Trade-In:	Mint $680	Ex $550	VG+ $380	Good $335	Poor $120

WINCHESTER

SUPER X2 MAGNUM GREENHEAD   REDBOOK CODE: RB-WN-S-SPX2MG

Invector-Plus vented rib barrel and choke set (full, modified, improved cylinder), Dura-Touch Greenhead finish, aluminum alloy receiver, sling swivel studs, 14.25" length of pull, 1.75" drop at comb, 2" drop at heel, fires 3 1/2" shells.

Production: *discontinued 2006* **Gauge/Bore:** *12 ga.*
Action: *semi-auto*
Barrel Length: 28" **Wt.:** *8 lbs.*
Sights: *bead front*
Capacity: *5*
Stock: *synthetic with Dura-Touch Greenhead*

D2C:	NIB $1,000	Ex $775	VG+ $550	Good $500	LMP: $1,036
C2C:	Mint $960	Ex $700	VG+ $500	Good $450	Fair $230
Trade-In:	Mint $710	Ex $575	VG+ $390	Good $350	Poor $120

SUPER X2 CANTILEVER DEER   REDBOOK CODE: RB-WN-S-SPX2CD

Barrel in matte finish, fold-down rear sight, scope mount (scope not included), 14.25" length of pull, 1.75" drop at comb, 2" drop at heel, fires 3" slugs or sabots.

Production: *discontinued 2004* **Gauge/Bore:** *12 ga.*
Action: *semi-auto*
Barrel Length: 22" **Wt.:** *7.25 lbs.*
Sights: *TruGlo fiber optic front*
Capacity: *5*
Stock: *synthetic with Dura-Touch Armor Coating*

D2C:	NIB $875	Ex $675	VG+ $485	Good $440	LMP: $880
C2C:	Mint $840	Ex $625	VG+ $440	Good $395	Fair $205
Trade-In:	Mint $630	Ex $500	VG+ $350	Good $310	Poor $90

SUPER X2 CAMO WATERFOWL   REDBOOK CODE: RB-WN-S-SPX2CW

Back-bored vented rib barrel, Mossy Oak New Shadow Grass finish, Invector-Plus choke system, 14.25" length of pull, 1.75" drop at comb, 2" drop at heel, fires 3 1/2" shells.

Production: *discontinued 2006* **Gauge/Bore:** *12 ga.*
Action: *semi-auto*
Barrel Length: 28" **Wt.:** *8 lbs.*
Sights: *bead front*
Capacity: *5*
Stock: *synthetic with Dura-Touch Armor Coating and Mossy Oak New Shadow Grass camo*

D2C:	NIB $1,000	Ex $775	VG+ $550	Good $500	LMP: $1,185
C2C:	Mint $960	Ex $700	VG+ $500	Good $450	Fair $230
Trade-In:	Mint $710	Ex $575	VG+ $390	Good $350	Poor $120

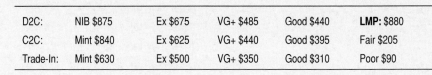

SUPER X2 PRACTICAL MK I   REDBOOK CODE: RB-WN-S-SPX2P1

Matte finish, Dura-Touch Armor-coated stock, Standard Invector choke system, improved cylinder choke tube, sling swivel studs, 14.25" length of pull, 1.75" drop at comb, 2" drop at heel, fires 2 3/4" shells

Production: *discontinued 2008* **Gauge/Bore:** *12 ga.*
Action: *semi-auto*
Barrel Length: 22" **Wt.:** *8 lbs.*
Sights: *TruGlo front fiber optic*
Capacity: *8*
Stock: *synthetic with Dura-Touch Armor Coating*

D2C:	NIB $880	Ex $675	VG+ $485	Good $440	LMP: $908
C2C:	Mint $850	Ex $625	VG+ $440	Good $400	Fair $205
Trade-In:	Mint $630	Ex $500	VG+ $350	Good $310	Poor $90

SUPER X2 PRACTICAL MK II   REDBOOK CODE: RB-WN-S-SPX2P2

Matte finish, Dura-Touch Armor-coated stock, Standard Invector choke system, Active Valve gas system, Weaver-style cantilever rail, sling swivel studs, 14.25" length of pull, 1.75" drop at comb, 2" drop at heel, fires 2 3/4" shells.

Production: *discontinued 2007* **Gauge/Bore:** *12 ga.*

Action: *semi-auto*

Barrel Length: 22" **Wt.:** *8 lbs.*

Sights: *TruGlo fiber optic, Ghost Ring rear*

Capacity: *8*

Stock: *synthetic with Dura-Touch Armor Coating*

D2C:	NIB $1,000	Ex $775	VG+ $550	Good $500	LMP: $1,287
C2C:	Mint $960	Ex $700	VG+ $500	Good $450	Fair $230
Trade-In:	Mint $710	Ex $575	VG+ $390	Good $350	Poor $120

SUPER X2 SPORTING CLAYS   REDBOOK CODE: RB-WN-S-SPX2SC

Vented rib barrel in matte finish, Invector-Plus choke set (full, modified, improved modified, improved cylinder, skeet), Active Valve gas system, two gas pistons, 14.375" length of pull, 1.5" drop at comb, 2.375" drop at heel (drop and cast adjustment spacers included), fires 3" shells.

Production: *discontinued 2008* **Gauge/Bore:** *12 ga.*

Action: *semi-auto*

Barrel Length: 28", 30" **Wt.:** *7.75 lbs., 8 lbs.*

Sights: *bead front*

Capacity: *5*

Stock: *Grade I walnut with adjustable spacers*

D2C:	NIB $800	Ex $625	VG+ $440	Good $400	LMP: $839
C2C:	Mint $770	Ex $575	VG+ $400	Good $360	Fair $185
Trade-In:	Mint $570	Ex $450	VG+ $320	Good $280	Poor $90

SUPER X2 SIGNATURE II   REDBOOK CODE: RB-WN-S-SPX2S2

Back-bored and vented rib barrel in high-gloss finish, Invector-Plus choke set (full, modified, improved modified, improved cylinder, skeet), red anodized aluminum alloy receiver, Dura-Touch Armor Coating, Active Valve gas system, two gas pistons, 14.375" length of pull, 1.5" drop at comb, 2.375" drop at heel (drop and cast adjustment spacers included), fires 3" shells.

Production: *discontinued 2007* **Gauge/Bore:** *12 ga.*

Action: *semi-auto*

Barrel Length: 28", 30" **Wt.:** *8 lbs., 8.25 lbs.*

Sights: *bead front*

Capacity: *5*

Stock: *hardwood with black metallic fleck paint, Dura-Touch Armor Coating and adjustable spacers*

D2C:	NIB $1,015	Ex $775	VG+ $560	Good $510	LMP: $1,015
C2C:	Mint $980	Ex $725	VG+ $510	Good $460	Fair $235
Trade-In:	Mint $730	Ex $575	VG+ $400	Good $360	Poor $120

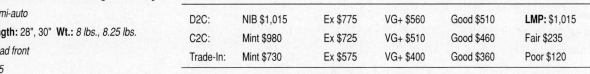

SUPER X2 SIGNATURE RED SPORTING   REDBOOK CODE: RB-WN-S-SPX2SR

Back-bored and vented rib barrel in red anodized finish, Invector-Plus choke set (full, modified, improved/modified, improved cylinder, skeet), red anodized aluminum alloy receiver, adjustable hardwood stock with black metallic fleck paint, Dura-Touch Armor Coating, Active Valve gas system, two gas pistons, 14.375" length of pull, fires 3" shells.

Production: *discontinued 2008* **Gauge/Bore:** *12 ga.*

Action: *semi-auto*

Barrel Length: 28", 30" **Wt.:** *8 lbs., 8.25 lbs.*

Sights: *bead front*

Capacity: *5*

Stock: *hardwood with anodized red finish, Dura-Touch Armor Coating and adjustable spacers*

D2C:	NIB $800	Ex $625	VG+ $440	Good $400	LMP: $852
C2C:	Mint $770	Ex $575	VG+ $400	Good $360	Fair $185
Trade-In:	Mint $570	Ex $450	VG+ $320	Good $280	Poor $90

WINCHESTER

SUPER X3 EXHIBITION/SPORTING REDBOOK CODE: RB-WN-S-SPX3ES

Vented rib barrel in matte black, Invector-Plus choke tube set (modified, improved modified, improved cylinder), red anodized alloy receiver, adjustable hardwood stock with black metallic fleck paint, Dura-Touch coating, .742 Back-bored Technology, Active Valve gas system, two gas pistons, Inflex Technology recoil pad with hard heel insert, 14.25" length of pull, fires 3" shells.

Production: *discontinued 2011* **Gauge/Bore:** *12 ga.*

Action: *semi-auto*

Barrel Length: *28", 30"* **Wt.:** *7.25 lbs., 7.5 lbs.*

Sights: *fiber optic front*

Capacity: *5*

Stock: *Dura-Touch Armor Coating*

D2C:	NIB $1,360	Ex $1,050	VG+ $750	Good $680	LMP: $1,479
C2C:	Mint $1,310	Ex $950	VG+ $680	Good $615	Fair $315
Trade-In:	Mint $970	Ex $775	VG+ $540	Good $480	Poor $150

SUPER X3 ALL-PURPOSE FIELD REDBOOK CODE: RB-WN-S-SPX3AP

Vented rib barrel in matte black, Invector-Plus choke tube set (full, modified, improved cylinder), Mossy Oak New Break-Up camouflage finish, Dura-Touch Armor Coating, .742 Back-bored Technology, Active Valve gas system, sling swivel studs, 14.25" length of pull, fires 3 1/2" shells.

Production: *discontinued 2010* **Gauge/Bore:** *12 ga.*

Action: *semi-auto*

Barrel Length: *26", 28"* **Wt.:** *7 lbs., 7.25 lbs.*

Sights: *bead front*

Capacity: *5*

Stock: *Mossy Oak New Break-Up camo finish and Dura-Touch Armor Coating*

D2C:	NIB $1,240	Ex $950	VG+ $685	Good $620	LMP: $1,469
C2C:	Mint $1,200	Ex $875	VG+ $620	Good $560	Fair $290
Trade-In:	Mint $890	Ex $700	VG+ $490	Good $435	Poor $150

SUPER X3 COMPOSITE REDBOOK CODE: RB-WN-S-SPX3CP

Vented rib barrel in gunmetal gray Perma-Cote finish, Invector-Plus choke tube set (full, modified, improved cylinder), Mossy Oak New Break-Up camouflage finish, adjustable stock (spacer set included) with Dura-Touch Armor Coating stock, .742 Back-bored Technology, Active Valve gas system, sling swivel studs, 14.25" length of pull, fires 3" shells. Add $140 for model with 3 1/2" chamber.

Production: *discontinued 2012* **Gauge/Bore:** *12 ga., 20 ga.*

Action: *semi-auto*

Barrel Length: *26", 28"* **Wt.:** *6.75 lbs., 7.25 lbs.*

Sights: *bead front*

Capacity: *5*

Stock: *synthetic with Dura-Touch Armor Coating*

D2C:	NIB $1,199	Ex $925	VG+ $660	Good $600	LMP: $1,199
C2C:	Mint $1,160	Ex $850	VG+ $600	Good $540	Fair $280
Trade-In:	Mint $860	Ex $675	VG+ $470	Good $420	Poor $120

SUPER X3 FIELD REDBOOK CODE: RB-WN-S-SX3FLD

Matte black aluminum alloy receiver, .742" Back-bored Technology, vent rib, 3" chrome plated chamber and bore, Invector-Plus choke tubes, Active Valve system, Pachmayr Decelerator recoil pad, ambidextrous crossbolt safety, drop-out trigger group. Add $70 for 20 gauge.

Production: *current* **Gauge/Bore:** *12 ga., 20 ga.*

Action: *semi-auto*

Barrel Length: *26", 28"* **Wt.:** *6.4-6.9 lbs.*

Sights: *brass bead front*

Capacity: *5*

Stock: *satin oil finish walnut*

D2C:	NIB $1,069	Ex $825	VG+ $590	Good $535	LMP: $1,069
C2C:	Mint $1,030	Ex $750	VG+ $540	Good $485	Fair $250
Trade-In:	Mint $760	Ex $600	VG+ $420	Good $375	Poor $120

SUPER X3 FIELD COMPACT REDBOOK CODE: RB-WN-S-SX3FDC

Shorter length of pull than full-sized Field model, matte black aluminum alloy receiver, .742"
Back-bored Technology, vent rib, 3" chrome plated chamber and bore, Invector-Plus choke tubes,
Active Valve system, Pachmayr Decelerator recoil pad, ambidextrous crossbolt safety, drop-out trigger group.

Production: *current* **Gauge/Bore:** *12 ga., 20 ga.*
Action: *semi-auto*
Barrel Length: 24", 26", 28" **Wt.:** *6.3–6.9 lbs.*
Sights: *brass bead front*
Capacity: *5*
Stock: *satin oil finish walnut*

D2C:	NIB $980	Ex $750	VG+ $540	Good $490	**LMP:** $1,069
C2C:	Mint $950	Ex $700	VG+ $490	Good $445	Fair $230
Trade-In:	Mint $700	Ex $550	VG+ $390	Good $345	Poor $120

SUPER X3 NWTF CANTILEVER TURKEY REDBOOK CODE: RB-WN-S-SX3NCT

Invector-Plus extra-full turkey choke tube, .742" Back-bored technology, Weaver-style cantilever rail, Quadra-Vent
ports, drop-out trigger, ambidextrous crossbolt safety, Inflex Technology recoil pad, Mossy Oak Break-Up Infinity finish.

Production: *current* **Gauge/Bore:** *12 ga., 20 ga.*
Action: *semi-auto*
Barrel Length: 24" **Wt.:** *7.1 lbs., 7.5 lbs.*
Sights: *fiber optic front, adjustable rear*
Capacity: *5*
Stock: *synthetic Mossy Oak camo*

D2C:	NIB $1,080	Ex $825	VG+ $595	Good $540	**LMP:** $1,199
C2C:	Mint $1,040	Ex $750	VG+ $540	Good $490	Fair $250
Trade-In:	Mint $770	Ex $625	VG+ $430	Good $380	Poor $120

SUPER X3 SPORTING (ADJUSTABLE COMB) REDBOOK CODE: RB-WN-S-SX3SPA

Nickel plated bolt, carrier, slide, and cocking handle. Chrome plated chamber and bore, .742" Back-bored technology,
ported barrel, Pachmayr Decelerator recoil pad, custom Active Valve system, extended Invector-Plus choke tube,
ambidextrous crossbolt safety, drop-out trigger.

Production: *current* **Gauge/Bore:** *12 ga.*
Action: *semi-auto*
Barrel Length: 28", 30", 32" **Wt.:** *~6.5 lbs.*
Sights: *fiber optic front*
Capacity: *5*
Stock: *Grade II/III walnut with adjustable comb*

D2C:	NIB $1,490	Ex $1,150	VG+ $820	Good $745	**LMP:** $1,699
C2C:	Mint $1,440	Ex $1,050	VG+ $750	Good $675	Fair $345
Trade-In:	Mint $1,060	Ex $850	VG+ $590	Good $525	Poor $150

SUPER X3 UNIVERSAL HUNTER REDBOOK CODE: RB-WN-S-SX3UNH

Textured grip surfaces on stock, Mossy Oak Break-Up Infinity finish, .742" Back-bored technology, hard
chrome chamber and bore, vent rib, Active Valve gas system, Quadra-Vent ports, drop-out trigger,
ambidextrous crossbolt safety, drilled and tapped receiver, cast/drop shims and spacers. Subtract $70 for 20 gauge.

Production: *current* **Gauge/Bore:** *12 ga., 20 ga.*
Action: *semi-auto*
Barrel Length: 26", 28" **Wt.:** *6.6–7 lbs.*
Sights: *fiber optic front*
Capacity: *5*
Stock: *synthetic with Mossy Oak finish*

D2C:	NIB $1,050	Ex $800	VG+ $580	Good $525	**LMP:** $1,229
C2C:	Mint $1,010	Ex $725	VG+ $530	Good $475	Fair $245
Trade-In:	Mint $750	Ex $600	VG+ $410	Good $370	Poor $120

SUPER X3 WATERFOWL HUNTER REDBOOK CODE: RB-WN-S-SX3WFH

Mossy Oak Shadow Grass Blades finish, .742" Back-bored technology, Invector-Plus choke system, hard chrome chamber and bore, vent rib, Active Valve gas system, Quadra-Vent ports, drop-out trigger group, ambidextrous crossbolt safety, cast/drop shims and spacers. Add $60 for 3 1/2" chamber. Add $60 for 20 gauge model.

Production: *current* **Gauge/Bore:** *12 ga., 20 ga.*
Action: *semi-auto*
Barrel Length: 26", 28" **Wt.:** *6.6–7.1 lbs.*
Sights: *fiber optic front*
Capacity: *5*
Stock: *synthetic with Mossy Oak finish*

D2C:	NIB $1,040	Ex $800	VG+ $575	Good $520	LMP: $1,139
C2C:	Mint $1,000	Ex $725	VG+ $520	Good $470	Fair $240
Trade-In:	Mint $740	Ex $600	VG+ $410	Good $365	Poor $120

SUPER X3 WATERFOWL REALTREE MAX-5 REDBOOK CODE: RB-WN-S-SX3WFR

Limited production, aluminum alloy receiver, Realtree Max-5 finish, chrome plated chamber and bore, vent rib, Active Valve gas system, includes three Invector-Plus choke tubes, Inflex Technology recoil pad. Add $60 for 3 1/2" chamber.

Production: *current* **Gauge/Bore:** *12 ga., 20 ga.*
Action: *semi-auto*
Barrel Length: 26", 28" **Wt.:** *6.6–7.1 lbs.*
Sights: *fiber optic front*
Capacity: *5*
Stock: *synthetic Realtree Max-5 finish*

D2C:	NIB $1,050	Ex $800	VG+ $580	Good $525	LMP: $1,139
C2C:	Mint $1,010	Ex $725	VG+ $530	Good $475	Fair $245
Trade-In:	Mint $750	Ex $600	VG+ $410	Good $370	Poor $120

SUPER X3 BLACK SHADOW REDBOOK CODE: RB-WN-S-SX3BLS

Blue finish, .742" Back-bored technology, Invector-Plus choke tube system, hard chrome chamber and bore, self-adjusting Active Valve system, Quadra-Vent ports, drop-out trigger group, ambidextrous crossbolt safety, Inflex Technology recoil pad. Add $70 for 3 1/2" chamber. Add $70 for 20 gauge model.

Production: *current* **Gauge/Bore:** *12 ga., 20 ga.*
Action: *semi-auto*
Barrel Length: 26", 28" **Wt.:** *6.6–7.1 lbs.*
Sights: *brass bead front*
Capacity: *5*
Stock: *black synthetic*

D2C:	NIB $910	Ex $700	VG+ $505	Good $455	LMP: $999
C2C:	Mint $880	Ex $650	VG+ $460	Good $410	Fair $210
Trade-In:	Mint $650	Ex $525	VG+ $360	Good $320	Poor $120

SUPER X3 CANTILEVER BUCK REDBOOK CODE: RB-WN-S-SX3CLB

Rifled barrel, matte black aluminum alloy receiver, Weaver-style cantilever rail, self-adjusting Active Valve system, drop-out trigger group, ambidextrous crossbolt safety, Inflex Technology recoil pad. Add $40 for 20 gauge model.

Production: *current* **Gauge/Bore:** *12 ga., 20 ga.*
Action: *semi-auto*
Barrel Length: 22" **Wt.:** *7.5–7.8 lbs.*
Sights: *fiber optic front*
Capacity: *5*
Stock: *black synthetic*

D2C:	NIB $1,060	Ex $825	VG+ $585	Good $530	LMP: $1,149
C2C:	Mint $1,020	Ex $750	VG+ $530	Good $480	Fair $245
Trade-In:	Mint $760	Ex $600	VG+ $420	Good $375	Poor $120

SUPER X3 COYOTE REDBOOK CODE: RB-WN-S-SX3COY

Aluminum alloy receiver, matte black finish, drilled and tapped for scope, chrome plated barrel, matte black barrel finish, active valve system, pistol grip stock, interchangeable recoil pads, interchangeable comb pieces, 2 3/4" shells.

Production: *current* **Gauge/Bore:** *12 ga., 20 ga.*
Action: *semi-auto*
Barrel Length: 24" **Wt.:** *7.4 lbs.*
Sights: *TruGlo fiber optic front and rear*
Capacity: *4*
Stock: *composite with textured panels*

D2C:	NIB $980	Ex $750	VG+ $540	Good $490	**LMP:** $1,199
C2C:	Mint $950	Ex $700	VG+ $490	Good $445	Fair $230
Trade-In:	Mint $700	Ex $550	VG+ $390	Good $345	Poor $120

MODEL 101 FIELD REDBOOK CODE: RB-WN-S-101FLD

20 LPI checkering, low-profile receiver, steel grip cap, back-bored barrel, chrome-plated chamber and bore, Invector-Plus choke tubes, White Line Spacer Pachmayr Decelerator recoil pad, deep relief receiver engraving.

Production: *current* **Gauge/Bore:** *12 ga.*
Action: *O/U*
Barrel Length: 26", 28" **Wt.:** *6.7–7 lbs.*
Sights: *brass bead front*
Capacity: *2*
Stock: *Grade II/III walnut*

D2C:	NIB $1,644	Ex $1,250	VG+ $905	Good $825	**LMP:** $1,899
C2C:	Mint $1,580	Ex $1,150	VG+ $830	Good $740	Fair $380
Trade-In:	Mint $1,170	Ex $925	VG+ $650	Good $580	Poor $180

MODEL 101 PIGEON GRADE TRAP (ADJUSTABLE COMB) REDBOOK CODE: RB-WN-S-101PGT

20 LPI checkering, adjustable comb, nickel plated receiver, classic pigeon engraving, Invector-Plus choke tubes, ported barrels, adjustable trigger, hard chrome-plated chamber and bore, White Line Spacer Pachmayr Decelerator recoil pad, 10mm runway rib.

Production: *current* **Gauge/Bore:** *12 ga.*
Action: *O/U*
Barrel Length: 30", 32" **Wt.:** *7.5–7.8 lbs.*
Sights: *TruGlo Tru-Bead interchangeable fiber-optic front sight*
Capacity: *2*
Stock: *Grade II/III walnut*

D2C:	NIB $2,293	Ex $1,750	VG+ $1,265	Good $1,150	**LMP:** $2,679
C2C:	Mint $2,210	Ex $1,600	VG+ $1,150	Good $1,035	Fair $530
Trade-In:	Mint $1,630	Ex $1,300	VG+ $900	Good $805	Poor $240

MODEL 101 PIGEON TRAP REDBOOK CODE: RB-WN-S-101PTP

20 LPI checkering, adjustable comb, low-profile nickel plated receiver, classic pigeon engraving, Invector-Plus choke tubes, back-bored barrels, ported barrels, adjustable trigger, hard chrome-plated chambers and bores, White Line Spacer Pachmayr Decelerator recoil pad.

Production: *current* **Gauge/Bore:** *12 ga.*
Action: *O/U*
Barrel Length: 30", 32" **Wt.:** *7.5–7.8 lbs.*
Sights: *TruGlo Tru-Bead interchangeable fiber-optic front sight*
Capacity: *2*
Stock: *Grade II/III walnut*

D2C:	NIB $2,200	Ex $1,675	VG+ $1,210	Good $1,100	**LMP:** $2,519
C2C:	Mint $2,120	Ex $1,525	VG+ $1,100	Good $990	Fair $510
Trade-In:	Mint $1,570	Ex $1,250	VG+ $860	Good $770	Poor $240

WINCHESTER

MODEL 101 SPORTING REDBOOK CODE: RB-WN-S-101SPT

20 LPI checkering, low-profile receiver, back-bored technology, steel grip cap, Invector-Plus choke tubes, adjustable trigger shoe, hard chrome-plated chamber and bores.

Production: current **Gauge/Bore:** 12 ga.
Action: O/U
Barrel Length: 28", 30", 32" **Wt.:** 7.1 lbs.
Sights: TruGlo Tru-Bead interchangeable fiber-optic front sight
Capacity: 2
Stock: Grade II/III walnut

D2C:	NIB $2,135	Ex $1,625	VG+ $1,175	Good $1,070	**LMP:** $2,379
C2C:	Mint $2,050	Ex $1,475	VG+ $1,070	Good $965	Fair $495
Trade-In:	Mint $1,520	Ex $1,200	VG+ $840	Good $750	Poor $240

MODEL 101 DELUXE FIELD REDBOOK CODE: RB-WN-S-101DFD

Vented rib, Invector-Plus choke system (full, modified, improved cylinder), engraved low-profile receiver with silver nitride finish, Pachmayr Decelerator recoil pad with no-snag heel, 1.375" drop at comb, 2.375" drop at heel, 13.625" length of pull, fires 3" shells.

Production: discontinued 2011 **Gauge/Bore:** 12 ga.
Action: O/U
Barrel Length: 26", 28", 30" **Wt.:** 7.25–7.5 lbs.
Sights: bead front
Capacity: 2
Stock: Grade II walnut

D2C:	NIB $1,679	Ex $1,300	VG+ $925	Good $840	**LMP:** $1,679
C2C:	Mint $1,620	Ex $1,175	VG+ $840	Good $760	Fair $390
Trade-In:	Mint $1,200	Ex $950	VG+ $660	Good $590	Poor $180

MODEL 101 LIGHT REDBOOK CODE: RB-WN-S-101LGT

Vented rib, Invector-Plus choke system (full, modified, improved cylinder), .742 Back-bored Technology, aluminum alloy receiver with engraved hunting scene, Pachmayr Decelerator recoil pad with white-line spacer, 13.625" length of pull, fires 3" shells.

Production: discontinued 2011 **Gauge/Bore:** 12 ga.
Action: O/U
Barrel Length: 26", 28" **Wt.:** 6 lbs., 6.25 lbs.
Sights: bead front
Capacity: 2
Stock: Grade II select walnut

D2C:	NIB $2,039	Ex $1,550	VG+ $1,125	Good $1,020	**LMP:** $2,039
C2C:	Mint $1,960	Ex $1,425	VG+ $1,020	Good $920	Fair $470
Trade-In:	Mint $1,450	Ex $1,150	VG+ $800	Good $715	Poor $210

MODEL 101 PIGEON SPORTING REDBOOK CODE: RB-WN-S-101PSP

High-gloss ported barrels, vent rib, Invector-Plus choke system and five Signature extended tubes (light-full, improved modified, modified, improved cylinder, skeet), 10mm runway rib, receiver with silver nitride finish, 13.625" length of pull (includes adjustable trigger shoe for fine-tuning LOP), fires 3" shells.

Production: discontinued **Gauge/Bore:** 12 ga.
Action: O/U
Wt.: 7 lbs., 7.25 lbs.
Sights: ...etition front, mid-bead
Stock: ...walnut with oiled finish

D2C:	NIB $2,580	Ex $1,975	VG+ $1,420	Good $1,290	**LMP:** $2,619
C2C:	Mint $2,480	Ex $1,800	VG+ $1,290	Good $1,165	Fair $595
Trade-In:	Mint $1,840	Ex $1,450	VG+ $1,010	Good $905	Poor $270

MODEL 101 MOSSY OAK DUCK BLIND REDBOOK CODE: RB-WN-S-101DKB

Mossy Oak Duck Blind camouflage finish, Invector-Plus choke system with three tubes (full, modified, improved cylinder), grooved forearm, vented Pachmayr Decelerator recoil pad with white line spacer, 1.375" drop at comb, fires 3" shells.

Production: *discontinued 2008* **Gauge/Bore:** *12 ga.*

Action: *O/U*

Barrel Length: 28" **Wt.:** *7.25 lbs.*

Sights: *brass bead front*

Capacity: *2*

Stock: *synthetic with Mossy Oak Duck Blind*

D2C:	NIB $1,950	Ex $1,500	VG+ $1,075	Good $975	**LMP:** $2,239
C2C:	Mint $1,880	Ex $1,350	VG+ $980	Good $880	Fair $450
Trade-In:	Mint $1,390	Ex $1,100	VG+ $770	Good $685	Poor $210

MODEL 1300 BLACK SHADOW REDBOOK CODE: RB-WN-S-13BKSH

Non-glare matte finish on barrel and receiver, vented rib, modified choke tube, 13.75" length of pull, fires 2 3/4" and 3" magnum shells. Add $25 for Deer model with rifled slug barrel and drilled & tapped receiver. Add $69 for 12 gauge slug model with rifled and non-vented rib 22" barrel and low-profile Weaver-style cantilever scope mount, magnum shells. Also available in a 12 gauge slug model with rifled and non-vented rib 22" barrel and low-profile Weaver-style cantilever scope mount.

Production: *discontinued 2007* **Gauge/Bore:** *12 ga., 20 ga.*

Action: *pump-action*

Barrel Length: 26", 28" **Wt.:** *6.75–7.25 lbs.*

Sights: *bead front*

Capacity: *5*

Stock: *synthetic*

D2C:	NIB $300	Ex $250	VG+ $165	Good $150	**LMP:** $357
C2C:	Mint $290	Ex $225	VG+ $150	Good $135	Fair $70
Trade-In:	Mint $220	Ex $175	VG+ $120	Good $105	Poor $30

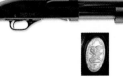

MODEL 1300 DEFENDER, 8-SHOT REDBOOK CODE: RB-WN-S-13DEF8

Cylinder bore barrel in non-glare matte finish, removable TruGlo fiber optic sight, 1.5" drop at comb, 2.5" drop at heel, 14" length of pull, fires 3" buckshot loads or rifled slugs. Also available in 12 gauge model with pistol grip option.

Production: *discontinued 2007* **Gauge/Bore:** *12 ga., 20 ga.*

Action: *pump-action*

Barrel Length: 18" **Wt.:** *6.25 lbs., 6.5 lbs.*

Sights: *TruGlo removable fiber optic*

Capacity: *8*

Stock: *synthetic*

D2C:	NIB $300	Ex $250	VG+ $165	Good $150	**LMP:** $364
C2C:	Mint $290	Ex $225	VG+ $150	Good $135	Fair $70
Trade-In:	Mint $220	Ex $175	VG+ $120	Good $105	Poor $30

MODEL 1300 CAMP DEFENDER REDBOOK CODE: RB-WN-S-13CDEF

WinChoke system, buttpad, 1.5" drop at comb, 2.5" drop at heel, 14" length of pull, fires 3" shells. With optional WinChoke rifled choke tube (available separately), this model can accurately fire Foster slugs or sabots.

Production: *discontinued 2007* **Gauge/Bore:** *12 ga.*

Action: *pump-action*

Barrel Length: 22" **Wt.:** *6.75 lbs.*

Sights: *adjustable open sights*

Capacity: *8*

Stock: *satin finish hardwood*

D2C:	NIB $400	Ex $325	VG+ $220	Good $200	**LMP:** $392
C2C:	Mint $390	Ex $300	VG+ $200	Good $180	Fair $95
Trade-In:	Mint $290	Ex $225	VG+ $160	Good $140	Poor $60

WINCHESTER

MODEL 1300 PRACTICAL DEFENDER, 8-SHOT REDBOOK CODE: RB-WN-S-13PDEF

WinChoke system, buttpad, NRA logo grip cap, 1.5" drop at comb, 2.5" drop at heel, 14" length of pull, fires 3" shells. With optional WinChoke rifled choke tube (available separately), this model can double as a deer gun, firing Foster slugs or sabots.

Production: *discontinued 2006* **Gauge/Bore:** *12 ga.*
Action: *pump-action*
Barrel Length: 22" **Wt.:** *6.5 lbs.*
Sights: *TruGlo adjustable open*
Capacity: *8*
Stock: *synthetic*

D2C:	NIB $400	Ex $325	VG+ $220	Good $200	**LMP:** $392
C2C:	Mint $390	Ex $300	VG+ $200	Good $180	Fair $95
Trade-In:	Mint $290	Ex $225	VG+ $160	Good $140	Poor $60

MODEL 1300 WALNUT FIELD REDBOOK CODE: RB-WN-S-13WAFD

WinChoke system (full, modified, improved cylinder), vent rib, Speed Pump, buttpad, 1.5" drop at comb, 2.5" drop at heel, 14" length of pull, fires 3" shells.

Production: *discontinued 2007* **Gauge/Bore:** *12 ga.*
Action: *pump-action*
Barrel Length: 26", 28" **Wt.:** *7.25 lbs.*
Sights: *bead front*
Capacity: *5*
Stock: *gloss-finish walnut*

D2C:	NIB $412	Ex $325	VG+ $230	Good $210	**LMP:** $444
C2C:	Mint $400	Ex $300	VG+ $210	Good $190	Fair $95
Trade-In:	Mint $300	Ex $250	VG+ $170	Good $145	Poor $60

MODEL 1300 UPLAND SPECIAL FIELD REDBOOK CODE: RB-WN-S-13USFD

WinChoke system (full, modified, improved cylinder), vent rib, Speed Pump, compact forearm, straight-grip stock, buttpad, 1.5" drop at comb, 2.5" drop at heel, 14" length of pull, fires 3" shells.

Production: *discontinued 2007* **Gauge/Bore:** *12 ga., 20 ga.*
Action: *pump-action*
Barrel Length: 24" **Wt.:** *6.75 lbs.*
Sights: *bead front*
Capacity: *5*
Stock: *gloss-finish walnut*

D2C:	NIB $407	Ex $325	VG+ $225	Good $205	**LMP:** $444
C2C:	Mint $400	Ex $300	VG+ $210	Good $185	Fair $95
Trade-In:	Mint $290	Ex $250	VG+ $160	Good $145	Poor $60

MODEL 1300 SPORTING FIELD REDBOOK CODE: RB-WN-S-13SPFD

WinChoke system (set of 5), vent rib, TruGlo Tru-Bead sight includes four additional fiber optic elements in a variety of colors, Pachmayr Decelerator recoil pad, 1.5" drop at comb, 2.5" drop at heel, 14" length of pull, fires 3" shells. Also available in compact model with shorter stock (13" length of pull) and rear-positioned forearm.

Production: *discontinued 2007* **Gauge/Bore:** *12 ga.*
Action: *pump-action*
Barrel Length: 28" **Wt.:** *7.5 lbs.*
Sights: *TruGlo Tru-Bead front, mid-bead*
Capacity: *5*
Stock: *cut-checkered satin finish walnut*

D2C:	NIB $460	Ex $350	VG+ $255	Good $230	**LMP:** $444
C2C:	Mint $450	Ex $325	VG+ $230	Good $210	Fair $110
Trade-In:	Mint $330	Ex $275	VG+ $180	Good $165	Poor $60

MODEL 1300 COASTAL MARINE   REDBOOK CODE: RB-WN-S-13CSMN

Nickel-plated stainless steel barrel, anodized aluminum alloy receiver, sling swivel studs 1.5" drop at comb, 2.5" drop at heel, 14" length of pull, fires 3" shells.

Production: *discontinued 2006* **Gauge/Bore:** *12 ga.*
Action: *pump-action*
Barrel Length: 18" **Wt.:** *6.5 lbs.*
Sights: *TruGlo removable fiber optic front*
Capacity: *7*
Stock: *synthetic with Dura-Touch Armor Coating*

D2C:	NIB $529	Ex $425	VG+ $295	Good $265	**LMP: $575**
C2C:	Mint $510	Ex $375	VG+ $270	Good $240	Fair $125
Trade-In:	Mint $380	Ex $300	VG+ $210	Good $190	Poor $60

MODEL 1300 UNIVERSAL HUNTER   REDBOOK CODE: RB-WN-S-13UHTR

WinChoke system (full, modified, improved cylinder, extra-long, extra-full extended turkey), vent rib, Mossy Oak New Break-Up camouflage finish, drilled & tapped receiver, 1.5" drop at comb, 2.5" drop at heel, 13.75" length of pull, fires 3" shells.

Production: *discontinued 2007* **Gauge/Bore:** *12 ga.*
Action: *pump-action*
Barrel Length: 26" **Wt.:** *7 lbs.*
Sights: *TruGlo removable three-dot*
Capacity: *5*
Stock: *synthetic with Mossy Oak New Break-Up*

D2C:	NIB $446	Ex $350	VG+ $250	Good $225	**LMP: $517**
C2C:	Mint $430	Ex $325	VG+ $230	Good $205	Fair $105
Trade-In:	Mint $320	Ex $250	VG+ $180	Good $160	Poor $60

MODEL 1300 UNIVERSAL HUNTER FIELD   REDBOOK CODE: RB-WN-S-13UHTF

WinChoke system (full, modified, improved cylinder, extra-long, extra-full extended turkey), vent rib, Speed Pump action, Mossy Oak New Break-Up camouflage finish, aluminum alloy receiver drilled and tapped for scope or red-dot-type sight, 13.75" length of pull, fires 3" shells.

Production: *discontinued 2006* **Gauge/Bore:** *12 ga.*
Action: *pump-action*
Barrel Length: 26" **Wt.:** *7 lbs.*
Sights: *none*
Capacity: *5*
Stock: *synthetic with Mossy Oak New Break-Up*

D2C:	NIB $450	Ex $350	VG+ $250	Good $225	**LMP: $472**
C2C:	Mint $440	Ex $325	VG+ $230	Good $205	Fair $105
Trade-In:	Mint $320	Ex $275	VG+ $180	Good $160	Poor $60

MODEL 1300 RANGER   REDBOOK CODE: RB-WN-S-13RNGX

WinChoke system, vent rib, Speed Pump action, 1.5" drop at comb, 2.5" drop at heel, 14" length of pull, fires 2 3/4" and 3" magnum shells. Add $25 for compact model with shorter stock (13" length of pull) and rear-positioned forearm.

Production: *discontinued 2005* **Gauge/Bore:** *12 ga., 20 ga.*
Action: *pump-action*
Barrel Length: 28" **Wt.:** *7.25 lbs., 7.5 lbs.*
Sights: *bead front*
Capacity: *5*
Stock: *satin-finished hardwood*

D2C:	NIB $310	Ex $250	VG+ $175	Good $155	**LMP: $367**
C2C:	Mint $300	Ex $225	VG+ $160	Good $140	Fair $75
Trade-In:	Mint $230	Ex $175	VG+ $130	Good $110	Poor $60

MODEL 1300 RANGER GLOSS REDBOOK CODE: RB-WN-S-13RNGG

WinChoke system, vent rib, 1.5" drop at comb, 2.5" drop at heel, 14" length of pull, fires 2 3/4" and 3" magnum shells. Also available is a compact model with shorter stock (13" length of pull) and rear-positioned forearm.

Production: *discontinued 2007* **Gauge/Bore:** *12 ga., 20 ga.*
Action: *pump-action*
Barrel Length: 26", 28" **Wt.:** *7 lbs., 7.5 lbs.*
Sights: *bead front*
Capacity: 5
Stock: *high-gloss hardwood*

D2C:	NIB $342	Ex $275	VG+ $190	Good $175	LMP: $391
C2C:	Mint $330	Ex $250	VG+ $180	Good $155	Fair $80
Trade-In:	Mint $250	Ex $200	VG+ $140	Good $120	Poor $60

MODEL 1300 RANGER DEER REDBOOK CODE: RB-WN-S-13RNGD

Rifled barrel with vented rib, receiver drilled and tapped for add-on scope mounts, 1.5" drop at comb, 2.5" drop at heel, 14" length of pull, fires 3" shells. Also available is a compact model with shorter stock (13" length of pull) and rear-positioned forearm.

Production: *discontinued 2007* **Gauge/Bore:** *12 ga., 20 ga.*
Action: *pump-action*
Barrel Length: 26", 28" **Wt.:** *6.75 lbs.*
Sights: *TruGlo adjustable metal rifle-type sights*
Capacity: 5
Stock: *satin finish hardwood with cut-checkering*

D2C:	NIB $310	Ex $250	VG+ $175	Good $155	LMP: $396
C2C:	Mint $300	Ex $225	VG+ $160	Good $140	Fair $75
Trade-In:	Mint $230	Ex $175	VG+ $130	Good $110	Poor $60

MODEL 1300 NWTF SHORT TURKEY REDBOOK CODE: RB-WN-S-13TFST

Mossy Oak New Break-Up or Mossy Oak Obsession camouflage, extra-long extra-full extended turkey tube choke, receiver drilled and tapped for scope or red-dot-type sight, National Wild Turkey Federation medallion on grip cap, 1.5" drop at comb, 2.5" drop at heel, 14" length of pull, fires 3" shells.

Production: *discontinued 2006* **Gauge/Bore:** *12 ga.*
Action: *pump-action*
Barrel Length: 18" **Wt.:** *6.5 lbs.*
Sights: *TruGlo adjustable metal fiber optic*
Capacity: 5
Stock: *synthetic with Mossy Oak Obsession or Mossy Oak New Break-Up camo*

D2C:	NIB $494	Ex $400	VG+ $275	Good $250	LMP: $507
C2C:	Mint $480	Ex $350	VG+ $250	Good $225	Fair $115
Trade-In:	Mint $360	Ex $300	VG+ $200	Good $175	Poor $60

MODEL 1300 NWTF BUCK & TOM REDBOOK CODE: RB-WN-S-13TFBT

Mossy Oak New Break-Up camouflage, extra-long extra-full extended turkey choke plus extended rifledchoke for deer, smooth-bore barrel, receiver drilled and tapped for scope or electronic sight, National Wild Turkey Federation medallion on grip cap, 1.5" drop at comb, 2.5" drop at heel, 14" length of pull, fires 3" shells.

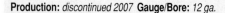

Production: *discontinued 2007* **Gauge/Bore:** *12 ga.*
Action: *pump-action*
Barrel Length: 22" **Wt.:** *6.75 lbs.*
Sights: *TruGlo fiber optic front and rear*
Capacity: 5
Stock: *synthetic with Mossy Oak New Break-Up camo*

D2C:	NIB $520	Ex $400	VG+ $290	Good $260	LMP: $556
C2C:	Mint $500	Ex $375	VG+ $260	Good $235	Fair $120
Trade-In:	Mint $370	Ex $300	VG+ $210	Good $185	Poor $60

WINCHESTER

MODEL 1300 NEW SHADOW GRASS REDBOOK CODE: RB-WN-S-13NSHG

Mossy Oak New Shadow Grass camouflage finish, vent rib, WinChoke system (full, modified, improved cylinder), Speed Pump action, 1.5" drop at comb, 2.5" drop at heel, 13.75" length of pull, fires 2 3/4" and 3" magnum shells.

Production: *discontinued 2006* **Gauge/Bore:** *12 ga.*
Action: *pump-action*
Barrel Length: 26", 28" **Wt.:** *7 lbs., 7.25 lbs.*
Sights: *bead front*
Capacity: *5*
Stock: *synthetic with Mossy Oak New Shadow Grass camo*

D2C:	NIB $450	Ex $350	VG+ $250	Good $225	LMP: $472
C2C:	Mint $440	Ex $325	VG+ $230	Good $205	Fair $105
Trade-In:	Mint $320	Ex $275	VG+ $180	Good $160	Poor $60

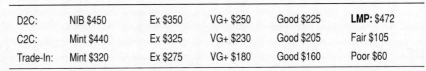

SPEED PUMP WALNUT FIELD REDBOOK CODE: RB-WN-S-SPPWFD

.742 back-bored chrome-plated barrels in matte finish, set of three choke tubes (full, modified, improved cylinder), 1.625" drop at comb, 2" drop at heel, 13.75" length of pull, fires 3" shells.

Production: *discontinued 2009* **Gauge/Bore:** *12 ga.*
Action: *pump-action*
Barrel Length: 26", 28" **Wt.:** *7 lbs., 7.25 lbs.*
Sights: *bead front*
Capacity: *5*
Stock: *Grade I walnut with satin finish*

D2C:	NIB $385	Ex $300	VG+ $215	Good $195	LMP: $419
C2C:	Mint $370	Ex $275	VG+ $200	Good $175	Fair $90
Trade-In:	Mint $280	Ex $225	VG+ $160	Good $135	Poor $60

SELECT FIELD REDBOOK CODE: RB-WN-S-SLCFLD

Invector-Plus choke system with three tubes (full, modified, improved cylinder), vent rib, engraved low-profile receiver, oval-style checkering, 1.5" drop at comb, 2" drop at heel, 14.25" length of pull, fires 3" shells.

Production: *discontinued 2006* **Gauge/Bore:** *12 ga.*
Action: *O/U*
Barrel Length: 26", 28" **Wt.:** *7 lbs., 7.25 lbs.*
Sights: *bead front*
Capacity: *2*
Stock: *high-gloss walnut*

D2C:	NIB $1,350	Ex $1,050	VG+ $745	Good $675	LMP: $1,498
C2C:	Mint $1,300	Ex $950	VG+ $680	Good $610	Fair $315
Trade-In:	Mint $960	Ex $775	VG+ $530	Good $475	Poor $150

SELECT WHITE FIELD, TRADITIONAL REDBOOK CODE: RB-WN-S-SLCWFT

Invector-Plus choke system with three tubes (full, modified, improved cylinder), vent rib, engraved silver nitride receiver, traditional checkering, 1.5" drop at comb, 2" drop at heel, 14.25" length of pull, fires 3" shells. Also available in Extreme model with grooved forearm and grip and oval-style checkering.

Production: *discontinued 2007* **Gauge/Bore:** *12 ga.*
Action: *O/U*
Barrel Length: 26", 28" **Wt.:** *7 lbs., 7.25 lbs.*
Sights: *bead front*
Capacity: *2*
Stock: *walnut*

D2C:	NIB $1,250	Ex $950	VG+ $690	Good $625	LMP: $1,533
C2C:	Mint $1,200	Ex $875	VG+ $630	Good $565	Fair $290
Trade-In:	Mint $890	Ex $700	VG+ $490	Good $440	Poor $150

WINCHESTER

SELECT PLATINUM FIELD REDBOOK CODE: RB-WN-S-SLCPFD

Lightweight back-bored barrels, Invector-Plus choke system with three Signature extended tubes (full, modified, improved cylinder), vent rib, engraved silver nitride receiver, oiled walnut stock with Schnabel forearm, includes molded ABS hard case, 14.25" length of pull, fires 3" shells.

Production: *discontinued 2008* **Gauge/Bore:** *12 ga.*
Action: *O/U*
Barrel Length: *26", 28", 30"* **Wt.:** *7.25 lbs., 7.5 lbs.*
Sights: *bead front*
Capacity: *2*
Stock: *Grade II/III walnut with oiled finish*

D2C:	NIB $2,015	Ex $1,550	VG+ $1,110	Good $1,010	**LMP:** $2,359
C2C:	Mint $1,940	Ex $1,400	VG+ $1,010	Good $910	Fair $465
Trade-In:	Mint $1,440	Ex $1,150	VG+ $790	Good $710	Poor $210

SELECT FIELD II REDBOOK CODE: RB-WN-S-SLCFD2

Vented rib barrels in blue finish, Invector-Plus choke system with three tubes (modified, improved cylinder, improved modified), engraved gray nitride receiver with waterfowl motif in cattail scrollwork, solid buttpad, 14.5" length of pull, fires 3" shells.

Production: *discontinued 2007* **Gauge/Bore:** *12 ga.*
Action: *O/U*
Barrel Length: *26", 28"* **Wt.:** *7 lbs., 7.25 lbs.*
Sights: *bead front*
Capacity: *2*
Stock: *Grade II satin-finish walnut*

D2C:	NIB $1,350	Ex $1,050	VG+ $745	Good $675	**LMP:** $1,533
C2C:	Mint $1,300	Ex $950	VG+ $680	Good $610	Fair $315
Trade-In:	Mint $960	Ex $775	VG+ $530	Good $475	Poor $150

SELECT MIDNIGHT REDBOOK CODE: RB-WN-S-SLCMDN

Vented rib barrels in high-gloss blue finish, Invector-Plus choke system with three tubes (full, modified, improved cylinder), engraved high-gloss blue receiver with gold-accented waterfowl motif, grip-enhancing oval checkering pattern, buttpad, 14.5" length of pull, fires 3" shells.

Production: *discontinued 2007* **Gauge/Bore:** *12 ga.*
Action: *O/U*
Barrel Length: *26", 28"* **Wt.:** *7 lbs., 7.25 lbs.*
Sights: *bead front*
Capacity: *2*
Stock: *Grade II/III satin-finish walnut*

D2C:	NIB $1,630	Ex $1,250	VG+ $900	Good $815	**LMP:** $2,380
C2C:	Mint $1,570	Ex $1,125	VG+ $820	Good $735	Fair $375
Trade-In:	Mint $1,160	Ex $925	VG+ $640	Good $575	Poor $180

SELECT TRADITIONAL ELEGANCE REDBOOK CODE: RB-WN-S-SLCELG

Vented rib barrels, Invector-Plus choke system with three tubes (full, modified, improved cylinder), engraved trigger guard and receiver with waterfowl motif, traditional checkering, deluxe buttpad, 14.5" length of pull, fires 3" shells. Also available in Extreme model with grip-enhancing oval cut-checkering and dual tapered locking lugs.

Production: *discontinued 2007* **Gauge/Bore:** *12 ga.*
Action: *O/U*
Barrel Length: *26", 28"* **Wt.:** *7 lbs., 7.25 lbs.*
Sights: *bead front*
Capacity: *2*
Stock: *walnut*

D2C:	NIB $1,600	Ex $1,225	VG+ $880	Good $800	**LMP:** $2,320
C2C:	Mint $1,540	Ex $1,125	VG+ $800	Good $720	Fair $370
Trade-In:	Mint $1,140	Ex $900	VG+ $630	Good $560	Poor $180

SELECT ENERGY SPORTING REDBOOK CODE: RB-WN-S-SLCENS

Ported and vented rib barrels in high-polish finish, Invector-Plus choke system with three tubes (full, modified, improved cylinder), .742" Back-bored Technology, set of five colored fiber optic inserts, grip-enhancing oval cut-checkering, 14.625" length of pull, fires 2 3/4" shells. Add $165 for model with adjustable comb.

Production: *discontinued 2007* **Gauge/Bore:** *12 ga.*
Action: *O/U*
Barrel Length: 28", 30", 32" **Wt.:** *7.25_7.75 lbs.*
Sights: *TruGlo Tru-Bead competition front*
Capacity: *2*
Stock: *walnut*

D2C:	NIB $1,510	Ex $1,150	VG+ $835	Good $755	**LMP: $1,950**
C2C:	Mint $1,450	Ex $1,050	VG+ $760	Good $680	Fair $350
Trade-In:	Mint $1,080	Ex $850	VG+ $590	Good $530	Poor $180

SELECT ENERGY TRAP, ADJUSTABLE COMB REDBOOK CODE: RB-WN-S-SLCENT

Ported and vented rib barrels, Invector-Plus choke system with three tubes (full, modified, improved cylinder), wide runway rib, adjustable comb, 14.625" length of pull, adjustable trigger shoe for fine-tuning length of pull, fires 2 3/4" shells.

Production: *discontinued 2005* **Gauge/Bore:** *12 ga.*
Action: *O/U*
Barrel Length: 30", 32" **Wt.:** *7.75 lbs.*
Sights: *TruGlo Tru-Bead fiber optic front, mid-bead*
Capacity: *2*
Stock: *walnut*

D2C:	NIB $1,600	Ex $1,225	VG+ $880	Good $800	**LMP: $2,172**
C2C:	Mint $1,540	Ex $1,125	VG+ $800	Good $720	Fair $370
Trade-In:	Mint $1,140	Ex $900	VG+ $630	Good $560	Poor $180

SUPREME SELECT FIELD REDBOOK CODE: RB-WN-S-SUPSLF

Light-contour barrels in blue finish, engraved receiver, Invector-Plus choke system with three tubes (full, modified, improved cylinder), low-profile receiver with heavy-duty ejectors and dual tapered locking lugs, tapered forearm, chrome-plated 3" chambers, 14.25" length of pull.

Production: *discontinued 2004* **Gauge/Bore:** *12 ga.*
Action: *O/U*
Barrel Length: 26" 28" **Wt.:** *7 lbs., 7.25 lbs.*
Sights: *bead front*
Capacity: *2*
Stock: *walnut*

D2C:	NIB $1,050	Ex $800	VG+ $580	Good $525	**LMP: $1,239**
C2C:	Mint $1,010	Ex $725	VG+ $530	Good $475	Fair $245
Trade-In:	Mint $750	Ex $600	VG+ $410	Good $370	Poor $120

SUPREME SELECT SPORTING REDBOOK CODE: RB-WN-S-SUPSLS

Light-contour barrels in blue finish, Invector-Plus choke system with three tubes (full, modified, improved cylinder), low-profile two-tone receiver with heavy-duty ejectors and dual tapered locking lugs, cut-checkered stock and forearm, rounded recoil pad heel, adjustable trigger shoe, chrome-plated 2 3/4" chambers, 14.25" length of pull.

Production: *discontinued 2004* **Gauge/Bore:** *12 ga.*
Action: *O/U*
Barrel Length: 28", 30" **Wt.:** *7.25 lbs., 7.5 lbs.*
Sights: *bead front*
Capacity: *2*
Stock: *walnut*

D2C:	NIB $1,075	Ex $825	VG+ $595	Good $540	**LMP: $1,406**
C2C:	Mint $1,040	Ex $750	VG+ $540	Good $485	Fair $250
Trade-In:	Mint $770	Ex $625	VG+ $420	Good $380	Poor $120

WINCHESTER

WINCHESTER

SUPREME SELECT, ELEGANCE REDBOOK CODE: RB-WN-S-SUPSLE

Back-bored light-profile barrels in deep blue finish, Invector-Plus choke system with three tubes (full, modified, improved cylinder), low-profile grayed receiver with dual locking pin design, hard buttplate, chrome-plated 3" chambers, 14.25" length of pull.

Production: *discontinued 2004* Gauge/Bore: *12 ga.*
Action: *O/U*
Barrel Length: *26", 28"* Wt.: *7 lbs., 7.25 lbs.*
Sights: *bead front*
Capacity: *2*
Stock: *Grade III cut-checkered walnut*

D2C:	NIB $1,875	Ex $1,425	VG+ $1,035	Good $940	LMP: $1,987
C2C:	Mint $1,800	Ex $1,300	VG+ $940	Good $845	Fair $435
Trade-In:	Mint $1,340	Ex $1,050	VG+ $740	Good $660	Poor $210

SXP BLACK SHADOW REDBOOK CODE: RB-WN-S-SXPBLS

3 1/2" chamber, textured gripping surfaces, Invector-Plus choke tube system, hard chrome chamber and bore, black-chrome protection on bolt, 3-shot adapter with speed-plug system, rotary bolt, drop-out trigger group, crossbolt safety, Inflex Technology recoil pad, chrome-plated barrel.

Production: *current* Gauge/Bore: *12 ga., 20 ga.*
Action: *pump-action*
Barrel Length: *26", 28"* Wt.: *6.8–7 lbs.*
Sights: *brass front bead*
Capacity: *4*
Stock: *synthetic black*

D2C:	NIB $350	Ex $275	VG+ $195	Good $175	LMP: $379
C2C:	Mint $340	Ex $250	VG+ $180	Good $160	Fair $85
Trade-In:	Mint $250	Ex $200	VG+ $140	Good $125	Poor $60

SXP FIELD REDBOOK CODE: RB-WN-S-SXPFLD

Traditional checkering, back-bored barrel, 3" chamber, Invector-Plus choke tube system, hard-chrome chamber and bore, black-chrome protection on bolt, speed-plug system, drop-out trigger group, crossbolt safety, premium recoil pad.

Production: *current* Gauge/Bore: *12 ga.*
Action: *pump-action*
Barrel Length: *26", 28"* Wt.: *6.8 lbs.*
Sights: *brass front bead*
Capacity: *4*
Stock: *satin finished walnut*

D2C:	NIB $340	Ex $275	VG+ $190	Good $170	LMP: $399
C2C:	Mint $330	Ex $250	VG+ $170	Good $155	Fair $80
Trade-In:	Mint $250	Ex $200	VG+ $140	Good $120	Poor $60

SXP DEFENDER REDBOOK CODE: RB-WN-S-SXPDEF

Non-slip grip on stock and forearm, tactical ribbed forearm, hard-chromed chamber and bore, alloy receiver, rotary bolt, drop-out trigger group, crossbolt safety, black-chrome protection, Inflex-Technology recoil pad, 13 3/4" length of pull.

Production: *current* Gauge/Bore: *12 ga.*
Action: *pump-action*
Barrel Length: *18"* Wt.: *6.5 lbs.*
Sights: *brass bead front*
Capacity: *5*
Stock: *black polymer*

D2C:	NIB $290	Ex $225	VG+ $160	Good $145	LMP: $349
C2C:	Mint $280	Ex $225	VG+ $150	Good $135	Fair $70
Trade-In:	Mint $210	Ex $175	VG+ $120	Good $105	Poor $30

SXP ULTIMATE DEFENDER REDBOOK CODE: RB-WN-S-SXPULD

Aluminum alloy receiver, matte black finish, drilled and tapped for scope base, matte chrome barrel, hard-chrome chamber and bore, 3" chamber, sling swivel studs, Picatinny scope base, hard-chrome plating on magazine tube, 13 3/4" length of pull.

Production: *current* **Gauge/Bore:** *12 ga.*
Action: *pump-action*
Barrel Length: 18" **Wt.:** *7.5 lbs.*
Sights: *rear ghost ring, ramp front*
Capacity: *5*
Stock: *composite matte-black*

D2C:	NIB $440	Ex $350	VG+ $245	Good $220	**LMP:** $539
C2C:	Mint $430	Ex $325	VG+ $220	Good $200	Fair $105
Trade-In:	Mint $320	Ex $250	VG+ $180	Good $155	Poor $60

SXP MARINE DEFENDER REDBOOK CODE: RB-WN-S-SXPMDR

Matte-chrome barrel plating, alloy receiver, drilled and tapped for scope mounting, textured gipping surface on stock, tactical ribbed forearm, hard-chromed chamber and bore, Invector-Plus choke tube system, rotary bolt, drop-out trigger group, crossbolt safety, Inflex-Technology recoil pad, 13 3/4" length of pull.

Production: *current* **Gauge/Bore:** *12 ga.*
Action: *pump-action*
Barrel Length: 18" **Wt.:** *6.3 lbs.*
Sights: *brass bead front*
Capacity: *5*
Stock: *synthetic black*

D2C:	NIB $360	Ex $275	VG+ $200	Good $180	**LMP:** $399
C2C:	Mint $350	Ex $250	VG+ $180	Good $165	Fair $85
Trade-In:	Mint $260	Ex $225	VG+ $150	Good $130	Poor $60

SXP ULTIMATE MARINE DEFENDER REDBOOK CODE: RB-WN-S-SXPUMD

Aluminum alloy receiver, drilled and tapped for scope mounts, matte black receiver finish, matte chrome barrel, hard-chrome chamber and bore, 3" chamber, sling swivel studs, Picatinny scope base, Door-Breacher choke tube.

Production: *current* **Gauge/Bore:** *12 ga.*
Action: *pump-action*
Barrel Length: 18" **Wt.:** *7.5 lbs.*
Sights: *rear ghost ring, ramp front*
Capacity: *5*
Stock: *synthetic black*

D2C:	NIB $490	Ex $375	VG+ $270	Good $245	**LMP:** $539
C2C:	Mint $480	Ex $350	VG+ $250	Good $225	Fair $115
Trade-In:	Mint $350	Ex $275	VG+ $200	Good $175	Poor $60

SXP TURKEY HUNTER REDBOOK CODE: RB-WN-S-SXPTKH

Textured gripping surfaces on stock, non-glare finish, back-bored barrel, 3 1/2" chamber, Invector-Plus extra-full turkey choke tube, hard-chromed chamber and bore, alloy receiver, drilled and tapped for scope mounting, rotary bolt, drop-out trigger group, crossbolt safety, Inflex Technology recoil pad, black chrome protection on bolt, 13 3/4" length of pull.

Production: *current* **Gauge/Bore:** *12 ga.*
Action: *pump-action*
Barrel Length: 24" **Wt.:** *6.6 lbs.*
Sights: *TruGlo fiber optic adjustable front and rear*
Capacity: *4*
Stock: *synthetic Mossy Oak camo*

D2C:	NIB $480	Ex $375	VG+ $265	Good $240	**LMP:** $519
C2C:	Mint $470	Ex $350	VG+ $240	Good $220	Fair $115
Trade-In:	Mint $350	Ex $275	VG+ $190	Good $170	Poor $60

WINCHESTER

SXP BLACK SHADOW DEER REDBOOK CODE: RB-WN-S-SXPBSD
Textured gripping surfaces on stock, non-glare matte-black finish, fully-rifled barrel, 3" chamber, black-chrome protection on bolt, Picatinny rail, 3-shot adapter, speed-plug system, rotary bolt, drop-out trigger group, crossbolt safety, Inflex-Technology recoil pad, 13 3/4" length of pull.

Production: current **Gauge/Bore:** 12 ga.
Action: pump-action
Barrel Length: 22" **Wt.:** 6.9 lbs.
Sights: TruGlo fiber-optic front, adjustable rear
Capacity: 4
Stock: synthetic black

D2C:	NIB $460	Ex $350	VG+ $255	Good $230	LMP: $519
C2C:	Mint $450	Ex $325	VG+ $230	Good $210	Fair $110
Trade-In:	Mint $330	Ex $275	VG+ $180	Good $165	Poor $60

SXP CAMP/FIELD COMBO REDBOOK CODE: RB-WN-S-SXPCFC
Aluminum alloy receiver, anodized black receiver finish, non-glare matte finish barrel, chrome-plated chamber and bore, 3 Invector-Plus choke tubes, sling swivel studs, Inflex Technology recoil pad, Defender barrel.

Production: current **Gauge/Bore:** 12 ga.
Action: pump-action
Barrel Length: 26", 28" **Wt.:** 6.8 lbs.
Sights: ivory bead front
Capacity: 5
Stock: synthetic black

D2C:	NIB $450	Ex $350	VG+ $250	Good $225	LMP: $479
C2C:	Mint $440	Ex $325	VG+ $230	Good $205	Fair $105
Trade-In:	Mint $320	Ex $275	VG+ $180	Good $160	Poor $60

SXP COMPACT FIELD REDBOOK CODE: RB-WN-S-SXPCPF
Aluminum alloy receiver, matte black receiver finish, hard-chrome plated chamber and bore, matte finished barrel, 3" chamber, speed-plug system, checkering on stock, 13" length of pull, 3 Invector-Plus choke tubes, Inflex Technology recoil pad.

Production: current **Gauge/Bore:** 12 ga.
Action: pump-action
Barrel Length: 26", 28" **Wt.:** 6.6–6.8 lbs.
Sights: brass bead front
Capacity: 4
Stock: satin finished hardwood

D2C:	NIB $360	Ex $275	VG+ $200	Good $180	LMP: $399
C2C:	Mint $350	Ex $250	VG+ $180	Good $165	Fair $85
Trade-In:	Mint $260	Ex $225	VG+ $150	Good $130	Poor $60

SXP EXTREME DEFENDER REDBOOK CODE: RB-WN-S-SXPEXD
Aluminum alloy receiver with matte black finish, drilled and tapped for scope mount, black-chrome barrel, 3" chamber, adjustable cheek piece, non-adjustable length of pull, sling swivel studs, Picatinny scope mount, Door-Breecher choke.

Production: current **Gauge/Bore:** 12 ga.
Action: pump-action
Barrel Length: 18" **Wt.:** 7.5 lbs.
Sights: ghost ring rear, ramp front
Capacity: 5
Stock: ATI pistol grip synthetic black

D2C:	NIB $450	Ex $350	VG+ $250	Good $225	LMP: $559
C2C:	Mint $440	Ex $325	VG+ $230	Good $205	Fair $105
Trade-In:	Mint $320	Ex $275	VG+ $180	Good $160	Poor $60

SXP EXTREME MARINE DEFENDER   REDBOOK CODE: RB-WN-S-SXPEMD

Aluminum alloy receiver, matte black finish on receiver, drilled and tapped for scope mount, matte-chrome barrel, 3" chamber, non-adjustable length of pull, adjustable cheek piece, sling swivel studs, Door-Breecher choke rube, Picatinny rails, 13 3/4" length of pull.

Production: *current* **Gauge/Bore:** *12 ga.*

Action: *pump-action*

Barrel Length: *18"* **Wt.:** *7.5 lbs.*

Sights: *ghost ring rear, ramp front*

Capacity: *5*

Stock: *ATI pistol grip synthetic black*

D2C:	NIB $460	Ex $350	VG+ $255	Good $230	**LMP:** $619
C2C:	Mint $450	Ex $325	VG+ $230	Good $210	Fair $110
Trade-In:	Mint $330	Ex $275	VG+ $180	Good $165	Poor $60

SXP TRAP   REDBOOK CODE: RB-WN-S-SXPTRP

Aluminum alloy receiver, matte-black receiver finish, hard-chrome plated chamber and bore, 3" chamber, speed-plug system, Invector-Plus choke tubes, Inflex Technology recoil pad, 14.3" length of pull.

Production: *current* **Gauge/Bore:** *12 ga.*

Action: *pump-action*

Barrel Length: *30", 32"* **Wt.:** *6.5 lbs.*

Sights: *TruGlo fiber-optic front*

Capacity: *5*

Stock: *hardwood*

D2C:	NIB $430	Ex $350	VG+ $240	Good $215	**LMP:** $479
C2C:	Mint $420	Ex $300	VG+ $220	Good $195	Fair $100
Trade-In:	Mint $310	Ex $250	VG+ $170	Good $155	Poor $60

SXP BUCK/BIRD COMBO   REDBOOK CODE: RB-WN-S-SXPBBC

Chrome-plated chamber and bore, vented rib, matte black chrome finish, aluminum alloy receiver, Invector-Plus choke tube set (full, modified, improved cylinder), Influx Technology recoil pad, fires 3" shells. Also included is a fully rifled 22" deer barrel with TruGlo sights.

Production: *discontinued 2013* **Gauge/Bore:** *12 ga.*

Action: *pump-action*

Barrel Length: *26", 28"* **Wt.:** *6.75 lbs.*

Sights: *brass bead front, TruGlo sights*

Capacity: *5*

Stock: *satin*

D2C:	NIB $590	Ex $450	VG+ $325	Good $295	**LMP:** $630
C2C:	Mint $570	Ex $425	VG+ $300	Good $270	Fair $140
Trade-In:	Mint $420	Ex $350	VG+ $240	Good $210	Poor $60

Zbrojovka BRNO

Opened in 1918, Ceskoslavensko Zbrojovka began as a state-owned firearms company in Brno, Czechoslovakia. The company dissolved in 1924 but reopened the same year in Prague, and in its present form, the company is a subsidiary of Ceska zbrojovka Uhersky Brod, better known as CZ or CZ-USA domestically, the firearms manufacturing conglomerate that purchased BRNO in 2006. The BRNO brand now produces sporting arms under the name Zbrojovka BRNO with Augustin Necas acting as chief designer. The company's initial government ties ensured that early models were designed for military use, including some models manufactured during World War II for Nazi Germany. Early models also included Mannlicher and Mauser rifles and the British BREN light machine gun. At present, the company is known for high end, fixed breech firearms like over/under rifles and shotguns and combination guns.

ZBROJOVKA

BRNO COMBO
REDBOOK CODE: RB-BO-S-COMBOX

Non-adjustable trigger, cold hammer-forged barrel, multi-cylinder, pistol grip-style stock.

Production: *current* **Gauge/Bore:** *12 ga./.308 Win or .30-06 Spfld.*
Action: *O/U*
Barrel Length: 23.6" **Wt.:** *6.5 lbs.*
Sights: *height-adjustable fiber-optic front*
Capacity: *2*
Stock: *walnut*

D2C:	NIB $1,675	Ex $1,275	VG+ $925	Good $840	
C2C:	Mint $1,610	Ex $1,175	VG+ $840	Good $755	Fair $390
Trade-In:	Mint $1,190	Ex $950	VG+ $660	Good $590	Poor $180

BRNO COMPETITION (TRAP/SKEET)
REDBOOK CODE: RB-BO-S-COMPTN

3-position trigger system, sliding border on buttplate, manual safety, extra set of interchangeable choke tubes, gilded trigger blade, plasma nitride surface coating.

Production: *current* **Gauge/Bore:** *12 ga.*
Action: *O/U*
Barrel Length: 28", 30" **Wt.:** *7.2-7.4 lbs.*
Sights: *fiber-optic front*
Capacity: *2*
Stock: *walnut*

D2C:	NIB $2,184	Ex $1,675	VG+ $1,205	Good $1,095	
C2C:	Mint $2,100	Ex $1,525	VG+ $1,100	Good $985	Fair $505
Trade-In:	Mint $1,560	Ex $1,225	VG+ $860	Good $765	Poor $240

ZOLI INTERNATIONAL

Zoli International, LLC

Based in Bulverde, Texas, Zoli International, LLC is the exclusive importation and distribution arm for the Italian shotgun manufacturer, ZOLI. The company was started by Antonio Zoli in 2013, and it handles all of the Italian-based manufacturer's business affairs within the United States. In years prior to 2013, ZOLI shotguns were imported and distributed in the United States through a number of other companies. In addition to shotguns, ZOLI produces bolt-action rifles. The company continues to operate with true artisanship, and most of its components are made in-house.

KRONOS BLACK
REDBOOK CODE: RB-ZI-S-KRONOB

Solid steel forged action, detachable trigger group, Boss-type locking system, interchangeable Flush-ZoliChokes or Extended-ZoliChokes.

Production: *current* **Gauge/Bore:** *12 ga., 20 ga., 28 ga.*
Action: *O/U*
Barrel Length: 28"–34" **Wt.:** *N/A*
Sights: *bead front*
Capacity: *2*
Stock: *hardwood*

D2C:	NIB $4,273	Ex $3,250	VG+ $2,355	Good $2,140	**LMP:** $5,200
C2C:	Mint $4,110	Ex $2,950	VG+ $2,140	Good $1,925	Fair $985
Trade-In:	Mint $3,040	Ex $2,400	VG+ $1,670	Good $1,500	Poor $450

KRONOS SILVER   REDBOOK CODE: RB-ZI-S-KRONOS
Solid steel forged action, detachable trigger group, Boss-type locking system, interchangeable Flush-ZoliChokes or Extended-ZoliChokes.

Production: *current* **Gauge/Bore:** *12 ga., 20 ga., 28 ga.*
Action: *O/U*
Barrel Length: 28"–34" **Wt.:** *N/A*
Sights: *bead front*
Capacity: *2*
Stock: *hardwood*

D2C:	NIB $4,890	Ex $3,725	VG+ $2,690	Good $2,445	**LMP: $5,200**
C2C:	Mint $4,700	Ex $3,375	VG+ $2,450	Good $2,205	Fair $1,125
Trade-In:	Mint $3,480	Ex $2,750	VG+ $1,910	Good $1,715	Poor $510

Z-SPORT   REDBOOK CODE: RB-ZI-S-ZSPORT
Gold relief on action, non-glare stippled top, corrosion resistant silver finish, finely checkered, oil finished walnut.

Production: *current* **Gauge/Bore:** *12 ga., 20 ga., 28 ga.*
Action: *O/U*
Barrel Length: 29.5"–34" **Wt.:** *N/A*
Sights: *bead front*
Capacity: *2*
Stock: *Turkish walnut*

D2C:	NIB $6,017	Ex $4,575	VG+ $3,310	Good $3,010	**LMP: $6,140**
C2C:	Mint $5,780	Ex $4,175	VG+ $3,010	Good $2,710	Fair $1,385
Trade-In:	Mint $4,280	Ex $3,375	VG+ $2,350	Good $2,110	Poor $630

Z-EXTRA   REDBOOK CODE: RB-ZI-S-ZEXTRA
Full-coverage deep scroll engraving, Z logo in gold, French gray finish, rejuvinated oil finish, silver-color combination lock case included.

Production: *current* **Gauge/Bore:** *12 ga., 20 ga., 28 ga.*
Action: *O/U*
Barrel Length: 28"–32" **Wt.:** *N/A*
Sights: *bead front*
Capacity: *2*
Stock: *extra-fancy Turkish walnut*

D2C:	NIB $4,733	Ex $3,600	VG+ $2,605	Good $2,370	**LMP: $7,660**
C2C:	Mint $4,550	Ex $3,275	VG+ $2,370	Good $2,130	Fair $1,090
Trade-In:	Mint $3,370	Ex $2,675	VG+ $1,850	Good $1,660	Poor $480

Z-AMBASSADOR EL   REDBOOK CODE: RB-ZI-S-AMBAEL
Hand-shaped frame, deep-scroll hand-engraving, hand-rubbed oil finish, ventilated rib.

Production: *current* **Gauge/Bore:** *12 ga., 20 ga., 28 ga.*
Action: *O/U*
Barrel Length: 28"–32" **Wt.:** *N/A*
Sights: *fiber-optic front*
Capacity: *2*
Stock: *Turkish walnut*

D2C:	NIB $11,720	Ex $8,925	VG+ $6,450	Good $5,860	**LMP: $11,720**
C2C:	Mint $11,260	Ex $8,100	VG+ $5,860	Good $5,275	Fair $2,700
Trade-In:	Mint $8,330	Ex $6,575	VG+ $4,580	Good $4,105	Poor $1,200

ZOLI INTERNATIONAL

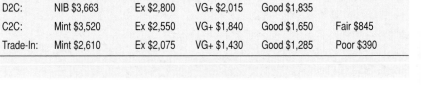

Z-AMBASSADOR SL   REDBOOK CODE: RB-ZI-S-AMBASL

Hand-shaped frame, fully hand engraved, gold inlays of game scenes, hand-rubbed oil finish, ventilated top rib.

Production: *current* **Gauge/Bore:** *12 ga., 20 ga., 28 ga.*					
Action: *O/U*					
Barrel Length: 28"–32" **Wt.:** *N/A*	D2C:	NIB $14,445	Ex $11,000	VG+ $7,945	Good $7,225	**LMP:** $14,445
Sights: *bead front*	C2C:	Mint $13,870	Ex $9,975	VG+ $7,230	Good $6,505	Fair $3,325
Capacity: *2*	Trade-In:	Mint $10,260	Ex $8,100	VG+ $5,640	Good $5,060	Poor $1,470
Stock: *Turkish walnut*					

COLUMBUS   REDBOOK CODE: RB-ZI-S-COLUMB

Detachable trigger group, Boss-type locking system, silver-soldered barrels, fine checkering, wooden buttplate, game scene engraving.

Production: *discontinued* **Gauge/Bore:** *12 ga., 20 ga., 28 ga.*					
Action: *O/U*					
Barrel Length: 28"–34" **Wt.:** *N/A*	D2C:	NIB $3,663	Ex $2,800	VG+ $2,015	Good $1,835	
Sights: *bead front*	C2C:	Mint $3,520	Ex $2,550	VG+ $1,840	Good $1,650	Fair $845
Capacity: *2*	Trade-In:	Mint $2,610	Ex $2,075	VG+ $1,430	Good $1,285	Poor $390
Stock: *Turkish walnut*					

Z-EXPEDITION   REDBOOK CODE: RB-ZI-S-EXPEDI

Deep scroll engraving, gold game scene, French gray finish on receiver, fine-cut checkering, hand-rubbed oil finish, titanium nitride treated choke and trigger mechanism.

Production: *current* **Gauge/Bore:** *12 ga., 20 ga., 28 ga.*					
Action: *O/U*					
Barrel Length: 28"–32" **Wt.:** *N/A*	D2C:	NIB $4,275	Ex $3,250	VG+ $2,355	Good $2,140	**LMP:** $4,275
Sights: *bead front*	C2C:	Mint $4,110	Ex $2,950	VG+ $2,140	Good $1,925	Fair $985
Capacity: *2*	Trade-In:	Mint $3,040	Ex $2,400	VG+ $1,670	Good $1,500	Poor $450
Stock: *Turkish walnut*					

APPENDIX A: MANUFACTURERS

Arrieta & Cía
arrietashotguns.com

AYA, Aquirre y Aranzabal, S.A.
aya-fineguns.com

Baikal
eaacorp.com/baikal

Benelli USA
benelliusa.com

Beretta USA
berettausa.com

Bernardelli, Vincenzo
bernardelli.com

Breda Meccanica Bresciana
bredafucili.com

Browning Arms Co.
browning.com

Century International Arms, Inc.
centuryarms.com

Charles Daly
charlesdaly-us.com

Chiappa Firearms
chiappafirearms.com

Churchill, E.J.
ejchurchill.com

Connecticut Shotgun Manufacturing Company
connecticutshotgun.com

CZ-USA
cz-usa.com

David McKay Brown Ltd.
mckaybrown.com

Escort Shotguns
legacysports.com

Fabarm USA
fabarmusa.com

Fausti USA, Inc.
faustiusa.com

FNH USA
fnhusa.com

Franchi
franchiusa.com

Gamba, Renato
renatogamba.it

Garbi, Armas
armasgarbi.com

Grulla Armas, S.L.
grullaarmas.com

Guerini, Caesar
gueriniusa.com

H&R 1871, LLC
hr1871.com

Holland & Holland
hollandandholland.com

Huglu
huglu.com

Ithaca Gun Company
ithacagun.com

Iver Johnson Arms, Inc.
iverjohnsonarms.com

Kel-Tec CNC Industries, Inc.
keltecweapons.com

Krieghoff International, Inc.
krieghoff.com

Lebeau-Courally
lebeau-courally.com/hunting

Marocchi
www.marocchiarmi.it

Mossberg, O.F. & Sons, Inc.
mossberg.com

Perazzi
perazzi.com

Remington Arms Company, LLC
remington.com

Rizzini USA
rizziniusa.com

Rock Island Armory (Armscor USA)
us.armscor.com

Savage Arms
savagearms.com

SKB Arms Company
skbshotguns.com

Squires Bingham Co., Inc.
squiresbinghamph.com

Stoeger Industries
stoegerindustries.com

Sturm, Ruger & Co., Inc.
ruger.com

Thompson/Center Arms
tcarms.com

TriStar Sporting Arms, Ltd. *tristararms.com*

Ugartechea, Armas
ugartecheashotguns.com

Weatherby, Inc.
weatherby.com

Webley & Scott, USA
webleyandscott.com

Winchester Repeating Arms
winchesterguns.com

Zbrojovka Brno
zbrojovka-brno.cz

Zoli International, LLC
zoli.it

APPENDIX A

APPENDIX B: ORGANIZATIONS

A Girl and A Gun

A ladies only organization established by women shooters for women shooters with a passion for pistol, rifle, and shotgun sports. The organization's mission is "to educate and encourage women about firearms usage and safety and to promote women's shooting interest and participation in the competitive shooting sports."
agirlandagunclub.com

America's 1st Freedom

An official journal of the National Rifle Association that is focused on the constitutional right to bear arms. America's 1st Freedom features the latest news concerning Second Amendment freedoms.
nranews.com/americas1stfreedom

American Handgunner

A magazine devoted to handguns, hunting, competition shooting, tactical knives, and shooting-related activities that features reviews on guns, knives, ammunition, shooting gear, historical articles, self-defense, and gun rights information.
americanhandgunner.com

American Rifleman

A firearms publication owned by the National Rifle Association. The publication includes information on guns, newsletters, reviews, guides, galleries, videos, blogs, training tips, and top stories on guns.
americanrifleman.org

Collectors Firearms

A gun auction website with one of the largest collections of militaria, uniforms, weapons, and memorabilia. Collectors Firearms features all kinds of antique and modern vintage firearms.
collectorsfirearms.com

Civilian Marksmanship Program (CMP)

"The Civilian Marksmanship Program is a national organization dedicated to training and educating U.S. citizens in responsible uses of firearms and air guns through gun safety training, marksmanship training, and competitions." With an emphasis on youth, the CMP Mission promotes firearm safety and marksmanship training.
odcmp.com

Combat Focus Shooting

A program that features handgun courses and instruction with a focus on real world defense scenarios. This shooting program is "designed to help the student become a more efficient shooter in the context of a dynamic critical incident."
combatfocusshooting.com

Gun Broker

"The World's Largest Online Auction of Firearms and Accessories," Gun Broker provides a secure and safe way to purchase guns and hunting and shooting accessories while promoting responsible gun ownership.
gunbroker.com

International Defensive Pistol Association (IDPA)

"The International Defensive Pistol Association is the governing body of a shooting sport that simulates self-defense scenarios and real life encounters." Founded in 1996, the IDPA was formed to appeal to shooters worldwide. The organization has more than 22,000 members, representing 50 countries.
idpa.com

International Practical Shooting Confederation (IPSC)

– "The IPSC was established to promote, maintain, improve, and advance the sport of IPSC shooting, to safeguard its principles, and to regulate its conduct worldwide in order to cultivate safe, recreational use."
ipsc.org

National Rifle Association of America (NRA)

An influential American lobbying group and large supporter of the Second Amendment. Known as "America's longest standing civil rights organization." Formed in 1871 by Union veterans Col. William C. Church and Gen. George Wingate. The NRA sponsors marksmanship events and publishes firearm-based magazines such as American Rifleman, American Hunter, America's 1st Freedom, Shooting Illustrated, Shooting Sports USA and NRA Insights.
nra.org

APPENDIX B: ORGANIZATIONS

National Shooting Sports Foundation (NSSF)

Known as "the trade association for the firearms industry." The NSSF promotes, protects, and preserves hunting and shooting sports.
nssf.org

NRA Insights

An NRA publication geared towards young shooters. The publication includes stories, gun safety, games, videos, tips, and pointers.
nrainsights.org

Rock Island Auction Company

One of the largest and most important firearm auction houses, specializing in antique and collectible models from all eras.
rockislandauction.com

Second Amendment Foundation (SAF)

Strong supporter of Second Amendment rights. Promotes firearm rights through educational and legal action programs designed to inform the public about the gun control debate.
saf.org

Shooting Illustrated

An NRA publication that highlights firearm news, weekly polls, tips, feature stories, blogs, videos, galleries, and firearm-related gear.
shootingillustrated.com

Shooting Sports USA

An NRA publication that focuses on competition shooting news.
nrapublications.org/index.php/shooting-sports-usa

Sniper's Hide

snipershide.scout.com

Shooting for Women Alliance (SFWA)

A nonprofit organization dedicated to educate women and youth worldwide about personal defense, firearms safety, conservation, and enjoyment of the shooting sports.
shootingforwomenalliance.com

Sporting Classics

Formed 1981, Sporting Classics is a bi-monthly magazine that consistently publishes some of the best hunting, fishing, and outdoor writing and photography.
sportingclassics.com

Springfield Armory Museum

From 1777 to 1968, the Springfield Armory Museum was the primary manufacturing center for U.S. Military-issued firearms. Courtesy of Wikipedia. com: "The Springfield Armory National Historic Site commemorates the critical role of the nation's first armory by preserving and interpreting the world's largest historic U.S. military small arms collection, along with historic archives, buildings, and landscapes." *nps.gov/spar/index.htm*

Tactical-Life

Owned by Harris Publications, Tactical-Life is an umbrella website for the following publications: Tactical Weapons, Guns & Weapons for Law Enforcement, Special Weapons for Military & Police, Rifle Firepower, Combat Handguns, Tactical Knives, Guns of the Old West, and The New Pioneer.
tactical-life.com

The Sportsman Channel

A television channel designed for outdoor enthusiasts with a focus on hunting, shooting, and fishing for entertainment and educational purposes. Known as "the leader in outdoor TV for the American sportsman."
thesportsmanchannel.com

United States Practical Shooting Association (USPSA)

– "The premier competitive shooting organization in the world." The USPSA site offers a club finder, articles for competitors, a rule book, match announcements, and top news about the organization.
uspsa.org

USA Carry

A leading concealed carry online resource featuring concealed carry articles, news, and training. USA Carry also features a directory where users can discover firearm instructors, gun shops, ranges, and gunsmiths.
usacarry.com

Women & Guns

A firearms publication for women that provides information on firearms, self-defense, articles, events seminars, and training information for women.
womenshooters.com

BIBLIOGRAPHY & WORKS REFERENCED

Berettausa.com

Bluebookofgunvalues.com

Budsgunshop.com

Browning.com

Carpenteri, Stephen D. *Shooter's Bible.* 104th ed. New York, NY: Skyhorse Pub., 2012.

Cheaperthandirt.com

Collectorsfirearms.com

Cornell, Joseph Madden., and Dan Shideler. *Standard Catalog of Browning Firearms.* Iola, WI: Gun Digest, 2008.

Cz-usa.com

Ezell, Edward C. *Small Arms of the World.* 12th ed. New York: Stackpole, 1993.

Firearmspriceguide.com

Fjestad, S. P. *Blue Book of Gun Values.* 34th ed. Minneapolis, MN: Blue Book Publications, 2013.

Flayderman, Norm. *Flayderman's Guide to Antique American Firearms.* 9th ed. Iola, WI: Gun Digest.

Fnhusa.com

GalleryofGuns.com

Genitron.com

Gunbroker.com

Gunsamerica.com

Hr1871.com

Icollector.com

Kimberamerica.com

Lee, Jerry. *2014 Standard Catalog of Firearms: The Collector's Price and Reference Guide.* 24th ed. Iola, WI: Gun Digest, 2014.

Lee, Jerry. *Gun Digest.* 68th ed. Chicago: Gun Digest, 2014.

Remington.com

Rock Island Auction Company

Ruger.com

Slickguns.com

Thefirearmblog.com

Thefiringline.com

Whichgun.com

Wikipedia.com

PHOTOGRAPHY CREDITS

The following companies and individuals have contributed photography for this book. We greatly appreciate their assistance.

Armas Garbi

Arrieta & Cia

AyA Aguirre y Aranzabal

Baikal

Benelli

Beretta

Bernardelli

Breda

Browning

Caesar Guerini USA

Chiappa

CZ-USA

E.J. Churchill

Escort Shotguns

Fabarm USA

Fausti USA

FNH USA

Franchi USA

Grulla Armas

H&R 1871

Holland & Holland

Huglu

Ithaca Guns

Iver Johnson Arms

Krieghoff International

Marocchi

O.F. Mossberg & Sons, Inc.

Perazzi USA

Remington Arms Company

Renato Gamba

Rock Island Auction Company

Rossi

Savage Arms

SKB Arms Company

Squires Bingham International, Inc.

Stoeger Industries

Sturm, Ruger & Co., Inc.

Thompson Center Arms

TriStar Sporting Arms, Ltd.

Ugartachea Armas

Weatherby

Winchester Repeating Arms

OTHER GREAT BOOKS BY

Making Ammo

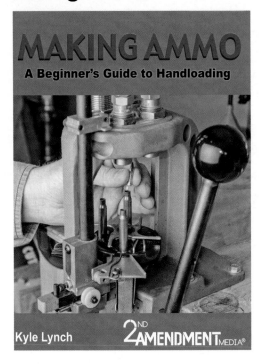

Through the direction of an experienced reloader, you will learn:

- Everything you need to know about bullets, primers, cases, and powder
- What materials and equipment you will need to produce accurate cartridges without breaking the bank
- How to inspect, record, test, and track the results of your efforts

ISBN:0794842577   Retail Price: $23.95

Book of the Long Range Rifle

Guided by the knowledge of an expert long-range shooter, you will learn how to:

- Choose a rifle based upon your shooting goals

- Utilize techniques that will allow you to adjust for wind, distance, and elevation in order to hit your target

- Manage your data and keep it accessible in the field and at the range

- Choose the best ammunition and explore the pros and cons of various shooting positions

ISBN: 0794842585   Retail Price: $23.95

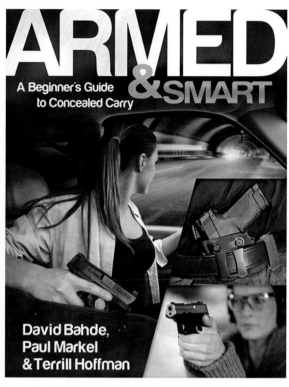
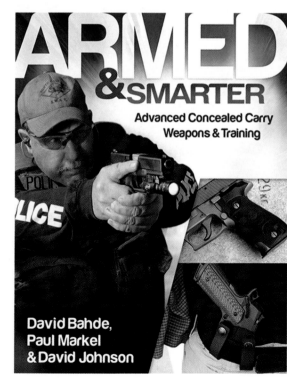

OTHER GREAT BOOKS BY 2ND AMENDMENT MEDIA®

In a grid-down situation, the world may look much different than the one we now know. Natural disasters, economic crises, terrorist attacks, or any other situation causing a societal breakdown may occur at any time. In today's unstable world climate, it is important to be prepared for any and all possible disaster or grid-down situations. Our Grid-Down Survival Guide series will help you understand what you need to know and how to be prepared when society breaks down. We offer guides focused on topics such as:

• First Aid	ISBN: 0794842674	Retail Price: $9.95
• Small Arms	ISBN: 079484264X	Retail Price: $9.95
• Home Defense	ISBN: 0794842666	Retail Price: $9.95
• Urban Defense	ISBN: 0794842658	Retail Price: $9.95
• Bug-Out Bags	ISBN: 0794843476	Retail Price: $9.95
• Survival Foods	ISBN: 0794843484	Retail Price: $9.95
• Alternative Power and Fuel	ISBN: 0794843492	Retail Price: $9.95
• Communications	ISBN: 0794843506	Retail Price: $9.95

GRID DOWN SURVIVAL GUIDE 1 — FIRST AID — AARON IWANCIW

GRID DOWN SURVIVAL GUIDE 2 — SMALL ARMS — PAUL MARKEL

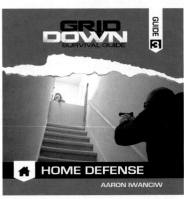

GRID DOWN SURVIVAL GUIDE 3 — HOME DEFENSE — AARON IWANCIW

GRID DOWN SURVIVAL GUIDE 4 — URBAN DEFENSE — AARON IWANCIW

GRID DOWN SURVIVAL GUIDE 5 — BUG-OUT BAGS

GRID DOWN SURVIVAL GUIDE 6 — SURVIVAL FOODS

GRID DOWN SURVIVAL GUIDE 7 — ALTERNATIVE POWER & FUEL

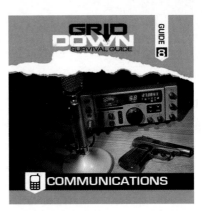

GRID DOWN SURVIVAL GUIDE 8 — COMMUNICATIONS

ANOTHER GREAT BOOK BY 2ND AMENDMENT MEDIA®

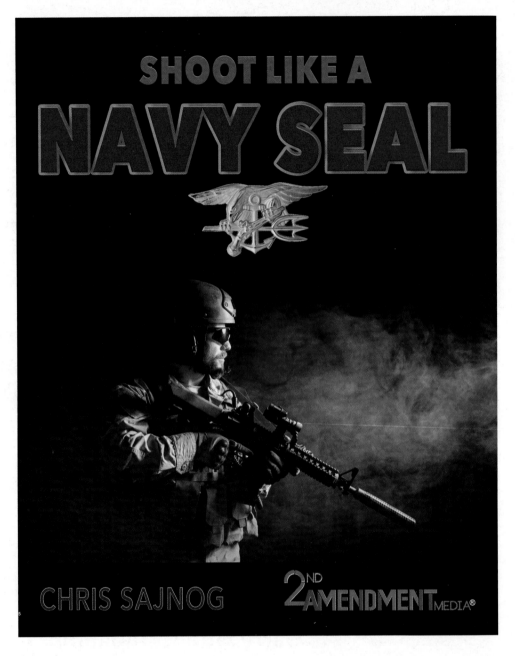

ISBN: 0794843514   Retail Price: $19.95

2nd Amendment Media is proud to publish the work of Chris Sajnog, a former Navy SEAL and the Master Training Specialist who wrote the curriculum for the Navy SEAL Sniper Course. Sajnog has captured his training techniques in 2nd Amendment Media's *Shoot Like A Navy SEAL*. He gives no-nonense, step-by-step instructions, clearly communicating methods that have been proven to create sharpshooters in one of the most elite forces in our country. Any shooter will benefit from the body of knowledge this renowned expert offers in this upcoming book.